Handbook of Religious Experience

RALPH W. HOOD JR. EDITOR

Religious Education Press
Birmingham, Alabama

Library of Congress Cataloging-in-Publication Data
Handbook of religious experience / Ralph W. Hood, Jr., editor.
Includes bibliographical references and indexes.
ISBN 0-89135-094-2
1. Experience (Religion) 2. Religions. I. Hood, Ralph W..
BL53.H286 1994
291.4'2—dc20 94-38150
CIP

Religious Education Press
5316 Meadow Brook Road
Birmingham, Alabama 35242
10 9 8 7 6 5 4 3 2

Religious Education Press publishes books exclusively in religious education and in areas closely related to religious education. It is committed to enhancing and professionalizing religious education through the publication of serious, significant, and scholarly works.

PUBLISHER TO THE PROFESSION

Contents

Foreword 1
Ralph W. Hood Jr.

PART I

Faith Traditions and Religious Experience

1. Judaism and Religious Experience 13
Janet L. Jacobs
2. Catholicism and Religious Experience 30
Michael J. Donahue
3. Protestantism and Religious Experience 49
Ronald E. Hopson and Kurt Openlander
4. Islam and Religious Experience 72
Fouad Moughrabi
5. Buddhism and Religious Experience 87
Gui-Young Hong
6. Hinduism and Religious Experience 122
Kaisa Puhakka

PART II

The Broader Context of Religious Experience

7. Philosophy and Religious Experience 144
Herbert Burhenn
8. The Sociological Context of Religious Experience 161
Margaret M. Poloma

9. Phenomenological Psychology and Religious Experience . . 183
David M. Wulff

PART III

Depth Psychologies and Religious Experience

10. Freudian Theory and Religious Experience 200
Edward P. Shafranske
11. Jungian Theory and Religious Experience 231
Fredrica R. Halligan
12. Object Relations Theory and Religious Experience 254
Benjamin Beit-Hallahmi

PART IV

Major Psychological Orientations and Religious Experience

13. Developmental Theory and Religious Experience 269
Kalevi Tamminen and Kari E. Nurmi
14. Cognitive Theory and Religious Experience 312
Beverly J. (Macy) McCallister
15. Affective Theory and Religious Experience 353
Peter C. Hill
16. Behavioral Theory and Religious Experience 378
H. Newton Malony

PART V

Specific Psychological Perspectives and Religious Experience

17. Role Theory and Religious Experience 397
Nils G. Holm
18. Attribution Theory and Religious Experience 421
Bernard Spilka and Daniel N. McIntosh
19. Attachment Theory and Religious Experience 446
Lee A. Kirkpatrick

PART VI

Specialty Concerns and Religious Experience

20. The Body and Religious Experience 476
Carole A. Rayburn

21. Transpersonal Theory and Religious Experience 495
Susan F. Greenwood
22. Feminist Theory and Religious Experience 520
Mary Jo Neitz

PART VII

Education and Facilitation of Religious Experience

23. Religious Instruction and Religious Experience 535
James Michael Lee
24. The Facilitation of Religious Experience 568
Ralph W. Hood Jr.
Contributors 598
Index of Names 603
Index of Subjects 621

FOREWORD

It has been several years since James Michael Lee approached me with the idea of editing a book on religious experience. It took a few years for the shape of this handbook to become clear to me. One goal was to place religious experience within the context of major faith traditions. This contextualizing of religious experience within major faith traditions required scholars both knowledgeable in the scientific study of religion and intimate with a particular faith tradition. The identification of such persons for six major faith traditions (Judaism, Catholicism, Protestantism, Islam, Buddhism, and Hinduism) was a first sure step. Besides contextualizing religious experience within major faith traditions, it was clear that the broadest possible treatment of religious experience would require the full range of modern psychology to be applied. From depth psychologies to transpersonal and feminist perspectives; from behavioral to cognitive theories; from attribution to attachment theory. The goal was to provide an authoritative summary of what contemporary psychology understands about religious experience. In addition, authorities in sister disciplines such as sociology and philosophy would provide an additional contextualization for the psychological study of religious experience.

It quickly became apparent that various theories and areas in psychology differed in their concern with religious experience. In some cases, such as classical Freudian theory or in object relations theories there is an established tradition of the psychological exploration of religious experience. In others, such as attachment theory and cognitive theory, the study of religious experience is just beginning. In some areas, such as developmental theory, there is a diverse body of knowledge yet to be integrated. In other areas, such as role theory, there is a firm body of knowledge likely to be unfamiliar to American psychologists. In select areas such as affective theory, a psychology of religious experience awaits its birth. Yet whatever the psychological theory, however general or specific, whether classical or modern, whatever its data base, our knowledge of religious experience is enhanced when considered from so many perspectives. And if our knowledge of religious experience is enhanced, so too can religious experience be facilitated and taught.

The authorities who have authored these chapters are diverse. Some are accomplished younger scholars; others are senior researchers. Many are nationally and internationally recognized authorities in their fields. As a group they represent male and female; a diversity of ethnic membership; a range of nationalities. Some are ordained within their faith traditions; others are lay members of a faith tradition; some stand outside any faith tradition. However, all are scholars of stature whose interest in religious experience is matched by truly authoritative knowledge. They have made the editing of this text less onerous than it might otherwise have been.

Religious Experience

The subject of religious experience courts controversy. Neither the term religion nor the term experience has an untroubled history. W.C. Smith (1963) has carefully traced the various connotations of religion and specific nouns identifying religions long thought by social scientists to be merely descriptive, such as Christianity or Buddhism. Wulff (1991:3) relies upon Smith's analysis to summarize the term religion under the heading, "A Reified Object." Religion, perhaps derived from the Latin *religio*, in Smith's analysis is not a term designating only family resemblances. Rather, whether in reference to feeling or to action, religion necessitates a response in the face of a power that is more than merely human. It is a response necessarily implying an awareness of the transcendent. The variety of responses possible give the family resemblances that otherwise characterize what have come to be called religions.

In the face of religious pluralism, the term religion came to have a pejorative connotation, referring to beliefs and practices felt to be erroneous and a proper focus of condemnation. Such condemnation assumed a standard by which error could be readily identified. By the time of the Enlightenment, religion was a generic term for a system of belief in need of adequate explanation. As Preus (1987) has noted, social scientists heavily influenced by Enlightenment thought took it as nonproblematic that explanations of religion were required that both defined the social sciences and rejected the language of religions as in any sense descriptively true in their own right. A modern scholar of religion, La Barre (1970:1) echoes this sentiment when he notes, "There is no mystery about religion. The genuine mysteries lie in what religion *purports to be about;* the mystery of life and the mystery of the universe (emphasis in the original)." It is in this sense that Smith reminds us how recent an invention the term religion is and how it has come to have a pejorative connotation, necessarily implying an outsider's perspective of what insiders merely purport to know. Likewise, Preus has masterfully demonstrated that initially the social-scientific study of religion was explanatory in the sense of necessarily attempting to refute what those within faith traditions purported to know but in fact were in error about.

Social-scientific explanations of religion must be tempered by postmodern considerations of the social sciences (Rosenau, 1992). One need not accept postmodern critiques uncritically to be mindful of the tremendous influence of largely literary-based critiques such as deconstructionism on the uncritical use of criteria by which religions, either as belief systems or forms of life, can be denigrated by social scientists, especially social psychologists seeking "explanations" (Parker, 1989; Parker and Shotter, 1990). Likewise, appeals to methodologically based criteria have themselves come under attack insofar as the case for methodological pluralism has been persuasively argued (Roth, 1987). In every possible domain social-scientific explanations are unmasked as another form of description. As with all descriptions, explanations must stop somewhere. In a postmodern view the term religion is less pejorative than Smith's analysis implies. All explanations are descriptions outside that which they claim to be in need of explanation; all descriptions are explanations insofar as they stay within that which is felt to be adequately described. Even within depth psychologies, explanations rooted in Oedipal analyses, to cite but one example, become themselves suspect as masking scientific orthodoxies as suspect as any religious orthodoxies (Deleuze and Guitarri, 1983). Despite more than a century of social-scientific analysis of religion, Bowker (1973) reminds us that it is still not unreasonable to suggest that part of our sense of God comes from God. In postmodern terms, religion once again gains a mystery beyond those who would have what are only purported mysteries finally explained. Religions, as Wittgenstein stated more than once of language games, are played. Thus, the necessity of considering religion as a form of life within which descriptions themselves are adequate explanations (Sherry, 1977).

If the term religion has a curious and difficult history, only partly alluded to above, how much more the term *experience*. While etymological analysis is forever problematic, it is worthy of note that one derivative of experience is from the Latin, *experientia*, meaning "to go through" (Weekley, 1967:538). In this sense, to experience is have a first person subjective appreciation that is neither merely affect or cognition, but a more totalization of what it is that has happened or occurred. Not irrelevant is the linkage of experience to such terms as *expert* and *experiment* both of which imply authoritative knowledge either by one who has been in the position to have known firsthand or in terms of the conditions under which firsthand knowledge can be acquired. The appeal to experience in this sense is absolute and fundamental. An appeal to experience is a claim that what is the case is what is actually found or encountered (J. E. Smith, 1968: 21-45).

It was William James who perhaps first introduced the linkage of religion and experience in what has since become the study of *religious experience* (J. E. Smith, 1985). In his Gifford lectures, James's focus was upon varieties of religious experience. Religion for James entailed an awareness of that power articulated as crucial to the initial use of the term religion noted by W.C. Smith above. This is James's sense of the divine, taken seriously and not trivialized. It is the divine encountered in experience. As such, religious experience entered the social-science literature as a form of apologetics, Protestant at that. Neither the doctrines nor the dogmas of religion interested James. It was to the actual experience of religion that James turned his interests in defining what has become the study of a heretofore nonexistent field, that of religious experience. From this beginning, issues as to the evidential basis of religious experience; their proximate origins; the possibility of their explanation, and indeed, their proper description has been a major concern of the social-scientific study of religion.

This *Handbook of Religious Experience* is in response to the need for a detailed summary of what social scientists understand about religious experience. In an initial contact letter I sought authorities who were willing to confront from within their own expertise what is known about religious experience. Religion was defined in Jamesean fashion as some sense of the transcendent, whatever its ontological status is assumed to be. Experience was suggested to be an encompassing phenomenon, broader than merely behavior, affect, or cognition. A sense of totalization or of having gone through something worthy of recognition. The task admirably confronted by some twenty-four authors has resulted in this handbook that should be of use to authorities in a wide variety of fields, from the social sciences to religious education.

Faith Traditions and Religious Experience

It is no easy task to undertake a critical summary of religious experience within the context of a particular faith tradition. Yet each authority, skilled in the social sciences and intimately familiar with the tradition upon which they write, has provided more than useful insights.

Janet Jacobs reminds us that Judaism encompasses both rabbinical and mystical traditions as well as contemporary reconstruction of this faith tradition. Her account of Jewish religious experience covers prayer, ritual, study, and mysticism. The varieties of religious experience in Judaism are protected under a broad canopy ranging from forms of religious fundamentalism to creative innovations associated with lesbian and gay reconstructions. Jacob's analysis reveals the dynamic process of continual transformation and maintenance within contemporary Judaism.

Michael Donahue focuses upon American Catholicism. He finds surprisingly little social-scientific literature to help in accounting for the persistence of identity among American Catholics. He explores the "deep structures" of American Catholicism as revealed from historical, sociological, and theoretical perspectives. Donahue finds the persistence of Catholic identity to be rooted in its sacraments and community as well as in its cosmic stories and cultivation of an analogical imagination.

Ronald Hopson and Kurt Openlander focus upon the Protestant tradition, tracing its historical roots in the great personage of Luther, as well as documenting its varieties of accommodation to various cultures. Their analyses of such mainstream figures in the psychology of religion as Gordon Allport and William James, as well as their discussion of conversion experiences, remind us just how heavily influenced by Protestantism the scientific study of religion is (especially in America). Their critical use of both depth and object relations psychology on issues of central concern to Protestantism is both critical of reductionistic tendencies within Protestantism and hopeful of the power of this tradition to protest against all limiting conditions.

Fouad Moughrabi confronts the Islamic tradition and appropriately reminds us that familiar distinctions commonly accepted in other traditions do not hold for Islam. At its core, Islam makes no distinction between the sacred and the temporal. Thus, Islamic religious experience is necessarily analyzed in social and political contexts in a manner likely to be disturbing to those familiar with traditions separating the sacred and the secular and for whom the acceptance of modernity has been an accomplished historical fact.

Gui-Young Hong confronts the long tradition of Buddhism in light of the difficult task of understanding a tradition that is of immense diversity rooted in different sociocultural contexts. In this tradition of immense diversity in doctrine and forms of life there is a normative unity in fundamental morality and a shared commonality in the goal of salvation. Gui-Young Hong explores varieties of Buddhist experience in a manner sensitive to historical and sociocultural contexts noting how psychology must not strip Buddhism of contextual factors if one is to gain a proper understanding of it.

Kaisa Puhakka undertakes the immensely difficult task of a tradition perhaps as old as any, Hinduism. Despite the immense diversity of beliefs and practices within Hinduism, Puhakka emphasizes that all Hindu faithful believe in a reality that transcends the mundane, empirical, or phenomenal world. Puhakka's analysis of the differences between the yogin's process of self-transformation and the mystic's quest for union or oneness emphasizes the pragmatic value of devotional practices in Hinduism, whatever their goal or aim. In particular, she emphasizes that the very nature of transcendence in Hinduism permits the methods of yoga to be incorporated into a myriad of contexts of religious quest that both illuminate and account for the richness of the Hindu tradition.

The Broader Context of Religious Experience

Philosophical and sociological considerations allow the placing of religious experience in a broader context, outside of any specific faith tradition. While other disciplines are relevant, particularly anthropology, it is mainly in philosophy and sociology that direct linkages to the contemporary psychology of religion are found.

Herbert Burhenn surveys recent philosophical discussions of religious experience, particularly the literature relevant to the evidential basis of religious experience. The tradition of both Schleiermacher and James is found to still be central to contemporary philosophical discussion of religious experience, most often made, as Burhenn notes, from a very narrow empirical base. Still, the value of social scientists taking philosophical discussion of religious experience seriously cannot be questioned, even if, as Burhenn notes, the concept itself can be.

Margaret Poloma discusses religious experience in terms of what others have seen, with but limited sight, as incompatible sociologies: those of Emile Durkheim and Max Weber. She notes that Durkheim's "social facts" paradigm and Weber's "social definition" paradigm can be combined into an interdisciplinary model for a more complete understanding of religious experience in postmodern society.

David Wulff reminds us that psychologists of religion at the turn of the century took it for granted that religious experience was their proper object of study. However, with the rise of depth psychologies and behaviorism, the introspective study of experience was deemed to be radically insufficient. Contemporary phenomenology is largely a reaction against the theoretical and methodological constraints that denigrate reflection upon human experience. He distinguishes between the phenomenology of religion, with its emphasis upon historical and cross cultural perspectives, and phenomenology of religion, with its tendency to focus upon experience occurring within the context of a single tradition, often familiar to the investigator. Wulff reviews both classic and contemporary phenomenological research and provides a cogent and critical assessment of contemporary efforts to develop phenomenological methodologies.

Depth Psychologies and Religious Experience

Among modern psychologies, it is the depth psychologies that have most consistently discussed, explored, and in some cases offered explanations for religious experience. Freudian, Jungian, and object relations theories remain among the most culturally influential psychologies of religion, both in America and abroad.

Edward Shafranske provides a summary of what is now classical Freudian psychology. He correctly notes the concern of Freud with the immense value culture places upon religion. As Shafranske argues, Freud's critique of religion was fundamentally political, aimed at generating a paradigm shift in which science would usurp the cultural authority of religion. Sensitive to both ontogenetic and phylogenetic considerations of the development of religion, Freud's plea for the authority of science over religion ultimately required him to shift his analysis of religion as illusion to delusion. Freudian concepts, especially unconscious psychic determinism and the Oedipus complex, have become so central to Freudian critiques of religion as to themselves be identified as orthodoxies. Not surprisingly, Shafranske ends his analysis of Freudian theory and religious experience with a critique of one of these concepts, the Oedipus complex.

Fredrica Halligan begins her analysis of Jungian theory and religious experience with an appropriate quote from Jung noting the necessity of the psychologist to focus upon the human side of religious experience independent of its contextual solidification in orthodox creeds. Halligan makes use of the rich data base of dreams as one meaningful way in which felt experience of the divine is manifested. She presents a brief history of Jungian thought and an analysis of a four-stage model of levels of consciousness to distinguish Jungian analytic from Freudian psychoanalytic thought. She then writes with poetic passion on Jungian theory and techniques and their relevance for the contemporary study of religious experience.

Benjamin Beit-Hallahmi begins his discussion of object relations theory by noting its roots in classical Freudian theory. Noting how the term "object relations" has come to mean for two generations of psychoanalytic writers the internal representations of relations with significant others, he articulates how modern object relations theory focuses upon the representational world as the basis for an essentially developmental theory in which internal representations are the basis of future psychic structures and for the person's character. He then goes on to document the long history of object relations interpretations of religious experience that are among the few psychological theories that take the specific content and form of religious experience seriously. For Beit-Hallahmi, such theories are most impressive when they purport to offer genuine scientific explanations of religious experience. In this sense, and others, object relations theory is never quite outside the shadow of Freud.

Major Psychological Orientations and Religious Experience

While the depth psychologies have long occupied themselves with religious experience, modern schools of psychology vary in the attention they pay to religious experience. Yet no school or area of psychology seems irrelevant to religious experience. One function of this section is to provide authoritative summaries of the relevance of specific psychological orientation to religious experience.

Kalevi Tamminen and Kari Nurmi focus upon developmental theory and empirically based studies of religious experience. Within the empirical psychology of religion, developmental studies of religious experience, especially in childhood and adolescence, have not been ignored. They note problems in the conceptualization of religious development, especially in theories that would demand a sequential pattern of religious development presumed normative for all. They describe religious development in terms of a variety of theories and paradigms. Such diversity assures that no unified grand theory of religious development is possible at this stage, if indeed it is a reasonable goal at all. While much of the empirical research is limited, both in scope and methodology, Tamminen and Nurmi note that nevertheless the gradual accumulation of findings in developmental psychology of religion in general, and religious experience in particular, is one of the firmer foundations of the contemporary empirical psychology of religion.

Beverly McCallister identifies cognitive psychology with the investigation of how people think, learn, perceive, remember, and present knowledge. Such a broad approach to psychology cannot help but be relevant to religious experience. She notes, that as with any experience, religious experience should be described in terms of structured representation obtained from prior experiences, an event, the interaction between these two, and whatever motivates these processes. Relating these tenets to religious experience, McCallister applies the insights of modern cognitive psychology to conversion, ritualistic behavior, altered states, and denominational differences in cognitive style.

Peter Hill notes that it is ironic that religious experience, often equated with emotion or feeling, is so absent from the empirical literature on affect. He also notes that there is little consensus on how to conceptualize the terms affect or feeling, and really no established theory of affect, much less an established affective theory of religious experience. Thus, without a broader theoretical framework, he links emotions to religious experience in isolated studies. Still, Hill does an authoritative job of discussing modern theories and research on affect and recommends that we return to William James insofar as we begin to both research and theorize meaningfully about the affective component of religious experience.

H. Newton Malony broadens the definition of both behavior and experience to present an analysis of behavioral theory and religious experience. Building upon his earlier developed S-O-R model, he conceptualizes religious experience as an "event" that encompasses the three behavioral experiences of perception, thought, and action. This basic model permits a grounding of behavioral theory in basic learning processes. Theoretical discussions of religious experience in associationist, operant, and social learning theories provides understanding of behavioral data, devoid of the metaphysical claims so often seen as antithetical to religious experience. As such, Malony demonstrates how a methodological behaviorism can aid in not only understanding, but facilitating religious experience.

Specific Psychological Perspectives and Religious Experience

That the major psychological orientations offer insights into religious experience is perhaps not surprising given the breadth of their concerns. However, with specific psychological orientations, often associated with more limited scope, there is interest in the study of religious experience, especially within role theory, attribution theory, and attachment theory. No small part of this interest has been generated by researchers identified with these specific orientations who continue to make contributions in the psychology of religion.

Nils Holm discusses the rich variety of role theory relevant to religious experience. Structural-analytical, interactionist, and perceptual models are discussed. Of particular relevance to American readers is the predominance of Sundén's role theory which has been of prominent use in Nordic countries among folklorists and psychologists of religion. Sundén's theory addresses itself to how a world of religious experience is possible. Of particular importance is Sundén's analysis of religious experience as involving both preparation and a process of learning that is similar in principle to what occurs in the natural sciences. Thus, Sundén's role theory is scientific in both form and structure and yet can favorably contribute to an understanding of distinctively religious experiences.

Bernard Spilka and Daniel McIntosh remind us that after more than a century of research on religious experience, questions exceed answers. Citing the lack of theory as perhaps the major reason, they offer insights into religious experience from the perspective of attribution theory. They note that not only is attribution theory a major perspective in contemporary social psychology, but it should appeal to the scholar interested in religious experience insofar as it deals directly with subjective interpretations of experience. After exploring a variety of classifications of religious experience, Spilka and McIntosh demonstrate the fruitfulness of attributional explanations in understanding religious experience in light of three basic elements: characteristics of the experiencer, the experience, and the context.

Lee Kirkpatrick approaches religious experience from another mainstream social psychological theory, attachment. He is careful to distinguish ecological attachment theory as developed by John Bowlby and extended by numerous empirical researchers, from less empirically based but more theory-driven psychodynamic perspectives, especially object relations theory. Attachment theory is precise in its predictions and capable of modification in light of empirical research. The theory postulates the existence of behavioral systems in humans (and other primates as well) that have been naturally selected to maintain proximity between infants and their caregivers. Extensive empirical research has identified three basic attachment patterns: secure, avoidant, and anxious/ambivalent. Successful measurement of these attachment patterns in adults has resulted in an emerging body of empirical research in the psychology of religion in which new light is shed upon the experience of God and other religious experiences such as conversion, glossolalia, and prayer. In an area dominated by discussion of largely Protestant forms of religion, Kirkpatrick's speculations on attachment theory and Eastern religious traditions is most welcome.

Specialty Concerns and Religious Experience

Within the contemporary psychology of religion specialty concerns have emerged that sufficiently define areas of scholarly interest that are not neatly contained either within depth psychologies, major psychological orientation or specific psychological perspectives. These include the study of the body in religious experience as well as transpersonal and feminist theory.

Carole Rayburn has undertaken the difficult task of reconsidering the body in religious experience. While restricted to the Judeo-Christian tradition, her analysis of embodiment both in reference to God and to the believer suggests the beginnings of a field of inquiry outside the common treatment of embodiment in terms of physiological processes. Rayburn's treatment of the body is nonreductionistic and as such can confront such controversial issues as the embodiment of God as well as the human body in various religious experiences and practices. The rich conceptualizations in this area should serve as a call to formulate more empirical research in this newly emerging area of concern.

Susan Greenwood explores the contributions of transpersonal theory to religious experience. Reminding us that transpersonal theory involves assumptions not part of traditional scientific methodology, she suggests how those interested in the evidential value of religious experience might be attracted to their theory. Her treatment of transpersonal theory includes such well-known transpersonal models as Wilber's hierarchical structuralism and Wasburn's dynamic-dialectical model. However, relying upon the possibilities of a transpersonal social psychology, Greenwood suggests the value of using a Durkheimian-Jungian foundation for transpersonal theory. Here a social psychology of religious experience is suggested in which the reconciliation of opposites stands as the key theoretical construct and the essential defining characteristic of religious experience.

Mary Jo Neitz notes that as yet feminist theory and religious experience constitutes small literature. Feminist research assumes that experience is gendered and that any analysis of experience must be contextualized, including considerations of both race and class. She documents differences in the meaning of religious experience for males and females reflecting both personality structure and gender based differences in opportunity. She finds the dominant male narratives of religious experience of little use for females. Nietz advances a more relational model of autonomy based upon the nurturing power in mothering. Unlike male models of autonomy demanding surrender, the reconceptualization of autonomy nurtured through relationships provides a more adequate model of autonomy relevant to female narratives of religious experience.

Education and Facilitation of Religious Experience

The majority of chapters in this handbook focus upon religious experience either in its traditional contexts or as illuminated by diverse perspectives. In the final two chapters the facilitation of religious experience, either by education or by quasi-experimental methods, is explored.

James Michael Lee employs his own considerable research background in religious instruction to explore how religious experience can be taught. He contends that from both a humanistic and a religious perspective, religious experience should be taught if at all possible. He notes that it is possible to teach religious experience and thus educational theory is relevant to religious experience. In terms of instructional theory, teaching for religious experience consists in substantive and a structural content. The former consists of holistic existential religious experience while the latter consists of instructional procedures which are in harmony with religious experience and productive of its outcomes. While Lee's chapter is rich in both instructional theory and pedagogical procedures, it does not contain specific empirically demonstrated procedures for teaching religious experience itself. This is no fault of his, but rather is due to the lack of a much needed body of research in this important area.

Ralph Hood reviews a variety of conceptual issues in the study of religious experience in order to provide a context for quasi-experimental studies on the facilitation of religious experience. His discussion of Schleiermacher suggests that this theologian can be cited as an exemplar for models in which the possibility of experiencing foundational realities is inductively acknowledged. Distinguishing between deliberate and spontaneous conditions known to facilitate religious experience, Hood reviews the quasi-experimental literature on psychedelics, solitude, and on set and setting contrasts. This literature suggests that whether numinous or mystical in nature, religious experiences can be facilitated either in deliberate fashion or by unwittingly creating conditions in which such experiences are likely to occur with apparent spontaneity.

REFERENCES

Bowker, J.
1973 *The sense of God.* London: Oxford University Press.

Deleuze, G., and F. Guattari
1983 *Anti-Oedipus,* Minneapolis, MN: University of Minnesota Press.

La Barre, W.
1972 *The ghost dance.* New York: Dell.

Parker, I.
1989 *The crisis in modern social psychology—and how to end it.* New York: Routledge.

Parker, I., and J. Shotter (Eds.)
1990 *Deconstructing social psychology.* New York: Routledge.

Preus, J.S.
1987 *Explaining religion.* New Haven, CT: Yale University Press.

Rosenau, P.
1992 *Post-modernism and the social sciences.* Princeton, NJ: Princeton University Press.

Roth, P.A.
1987 *Meaning and method in the social sciences: The case for methodological pluralism.* Ithaca, NY: Cornell University Press.

Sherry, P.
1977 *Religion, truth and language games.* New York: Harper & Row.
Smith, J.E.
1968 *Experience and God.* New York: Oxford University Press.
1985 Introduction. *In The varieties of religious experience.* Cambridge, MA: Harvard University Press.
Smith, W.C.
1963 *The meaning and end of religion.* New York: Macmillan.
Weekley, E.
[1921]
1967 *An etymological dictionary of modern English*, 2 vols. New York: Dover.
Wulff, D.M.
1991 *Psychology of religion: Classic and contemporary views.* New York: Wiley.

1

Judaism and Religious Experience

JANET L. JACOBS

INTRODUCTION

The concept of religious experience embraces a wide range of phenomena that within the Jewish culture is expressed through prayer, ritual, study, and mystical revelation. The diversity of the Jewish community in contemporary society has resulted in a growing discourse on what it means to be Jewish and to experience the spiritual aspects of the Jewish faith. Within this discourse, traditional orthodox, conservative, and reform Jews are engaged in a dialogue on religious experience that is informed by the modern Hasidic movement as well as women's spirituality and lesbian and gay reconstructionism. Any discussion of Jewish religious experience therefore must take into account the numerous ways in which cultural heritage, spiritual longing, and the desire for community lay the foundation for spirituality in a diversified culture.

While it is not possible to provide an in-depth analysis of the multitude of experiences that are defined as religious by the Jewish community, this chapter will focus on three areas of study: rabbinic Judaism, mysticism, and contemporary reconstructions of Judaic tradition. Within this framework, varied interpretations of religious experience will be explored as Jewish women and men have sought to define their relationship to God through their connection to a deeply rooted culture that has been both idealized and marginalized in Western society.

Religious Experience and Rabbinic Judaism

The literature on Jewish spirituality tends to separate Jewish religious experience into two distinct categories, rabbinic Judaism and mystical traditions (Katz, 1985). While the former is associated with prayer, religious practice, and the laws inscribed in the Torah (Jewish scripture), the latter is concerned with the study of Kabbalistic and Hasidic disciplines. For the most part, Jewish culture and religious studies have emphasized the importance of the rabbinic approach to spirituality, to the exclusion of the more mystical orientation. At least since the second century C.E., Jewish religious experience has been defined by an adherence to the revealed word of God as codified in the Torah and interpreted by the rabbis. According to Richard Saranson, "Torah is the bridgehead between the Jew and ultimate reality, because it is the divinely revealed blueprint of reality" (1983:50-51). The power of Torah to define Jewish experience is thus found in its symbolic representation of the divine and the laws and norms contained within scripture.

According to the rabbinic tradition, the experience of the divine is found in an adherence to the social order prescribed by God's commandments in the Torah. Following the commandments thus becomes a form of spiritual connection, as obedience and obligation define one's relationship to the transcendent (Katz, 1983). This perspective maintains that the essence of religious experience is found in the observance of *halacha,* a Hebrew term for the religious codes that govern spiritual practice and the observance of rules as interpreted by the rabbis (Gresser, 1987).

While *halacha* has many varied and diverse applications, including the governance of domestic law in Israel today, contemporary scholars such as Moshe Gresser take a more spiritual view of the commandments, suggesting that for the modern Jew *halacha* simply means "a path lived in the presence of God" (1987:19). Gresser maintains that one way in which this spiritual path may be expressed is in the performance of good deeds according to God's commandments. These deeds, known as *mitzvot*, provide a means to sanctify that which is holy and therefore contribute to the spiritual development of the Jewish adherent. An example of a spiritual act may be found in keeping the sabbath or in the commandment to honor one's parents, simple laws that when observed have specific spiritual outcomes:

> The *mitzvot* are then seen to be the cutting edge of this Torah, this instruction, instruments of access and the locus of sanctification. . . . To honor our parents in obedience to God is not just to be ethical; it is to be holy. It is not simply to protect ourselves or fulfill ourselves; it is to transcend ourselves. To obey in this context is to serve the Wholly Other, to provide access for God to

enter the world, and, in bringing oneself close to God, to engage the sanctity or holiness that reflects God's presence (Gresser, 1987:20-24).

This interpretation of *halachic* Judaism suggests that each time a commandment is followed, no matter how small or insignificant, the spiritual consciousness of the individual becomes manifest and the experience of God is known. Saranson explains this aspect of observance as the "ultimate form of worship in Judaism" (1983:54). Here he describes the importance of *mitzvot* for the individual's relationship to God:

> A series of benedictions is prescribed by the rabbis to be recited before performing God's commandments (*mitzvot*). . . . These benedictions both express and guarantee the Jew's perpetual awareness that everything experienced or enjoyed comes from God, and that all actions are performed before God. Traditional Judaic piety is God-intoxicated; nothing a Jew does is unrelated to divine service (1983:54).

The work of both Saranson and Gresser are in keeping with the philosophy of the well known Jewish scholar, Abraham Heschel, who maintains that every act of *halachic* observance has transcendent meaning:

> All *mitzvot* are means of evoking in us the awareness of living in the neighborhood of God, of living in the holy dimension. They call to mind the inconspicuous mystery of things and acts, and are reminders of our being the stewards rather than the landlords of the universe; reminders of the fact that man does not live in a spiritual wilderness, that every act of man is an encounter of the human and the holy (1959: 356).

The importance of *halacha* for Jewish religious experience has led to a feminist discourse on the meaning and value of commandments which are gender specific. In particular, family purity laws have been the focus of much controversy within the Jewish feminist community. These laws, originally found in Leviticus, specify the conditions under which individuals are made impure by the emission of bodily fluids. Although, historically, the notion of ritual impurity applies to both males and females, Rachel Adler (1993) points out that within contemporary practice, the commandments of purification focus primarily on married women who, in following *halacha*, are required to attend the *mikvah* (ritual bath) each month at the end of their menstrual cycle.

The research on the *mikvah* ritual reveals that for some women this specifically female commandment provides a spiritual connection to the divine. The most informative data on this aspect of *mitzvot* derives from the study of two populations of Jewish women: those who have converted to orthodoxy in adult life and are thus experiencing the *mikvah* for the first time; and those women who, while not orthodox in orientation, have nonetheless chosen the *mikvah* as a specifically Jewish path to God and spirituality. Two examples from the literature will help to illustrate this point. The first example is a religious experience reported by Lis Harris, a Jewish journalist who attended the *mikvah* while doing research on the Lubavitcher Hasidic sect in Brooklyn. Here she describes her response to her initiation into the rite of purification:

> Most of the people who come to the *mikvah* already know everything there is to know about preparing for it. As a precaution, however, a lengthy checklist has been taped to the wall. . . . The last words on the checklist are "now you are ready for the great *mitzvah* of *Tevilah* [immersion]. . . . " I take off the robe and stand expectantly in the chest-deep warm green water. Brachah [the attendant] tells me to keep my eyes and lips closed but not too tightly and to keep my feet apart so that the water will touch my whole body. When I go under water, I instantly curl into the fetal position because of the position of my body. When I come up, Brachah places the linen cloth over my head and I repeat the *mikvah* blessing after her. Then, the cloth removed, I go down two more times. The second time down, I see a little speed-up movie of all the religious people I know performing the ritual. . . . My grandmother floats by, curled up like me. . . . The third time down, I think of my boys suspended inside me, waiting to join the world (Harris, 1985:146-148).

For Harris, the religious experience is one of connection to her Jewish heritage and to the creation of life as symbolized first by the image of her grandmother and then by the vision of her two sons. The theme of connection also characterizes the *mikvah* experience of Shira Dicker who provides this account of her visit to the ritual bath:

> The room is small and boxy and very surreal. I am filled with a sudden powerful emotion. I endeavor to name it. . .it must be awe. Or maybe just fear. In any case, I am seized with a sense of magnitude, of serious business about to happen.
>
> I open my robe with my back to Esther [the attendant]. She holds it open as I walk down the stairs into the water. It feels thick and warm, a bit unpleasant. I descend the steps until I am standing neck-deep in the water. I look up at Esther standing at the top of the railing.
>
> "I don't know what to say," I confess. Esther nods and she leads me in reciting the *bracha*, slowly, never taking our gaze off one another. I am so naked, so open to whatever force is in this room—Esther's benevolence, the thickness of the water, the chain of the Jewish tradition, the presence of God. I stand in the tepid water, letting the force wash over and through me. Cleanse me, I think. Make me believe (1992:64).

For both Dicker and Harris, neither of whom consider themselves to be religious, the experience of the *mikvah* is extraordinary in part because of its uniqueness. For the majority of orthodox women, however, the *mikvah* is a mandatory rite of purification that must be practiced each month before resuming sexual relations. Adler (1993) thus questions the value of this specifically female ritual. In a discussion of her own wavering belief in this *halachic* tradition, Adler writes of the contradictions that the *mikvah* poses for the Jewish woman in search of the sacred:

> Existing theological justification of menstrual impurity did not help me to make sense of myself as a God-created creature. They treated me, to use Kantian terminology, as a means to someone else's end, rather than as an end in myself. To have the observance of *niddah* [ritual impurity] and *mikvah* justified to me as the instrumentality whereby my husband was entitled to lawfully cohabitate was both inadequate and insulting.
>
> Indeed, the otherness and the instrumentality of women were foundational presumptions of the men who wrote about these laws. What was significant about menstruation for them was that it made woman uniquely capable of causing men to sin by transmitting pollution to them. They never asked themselves how it would feel to be someone whom such a capacity has been assigned, or whether menstruation might have other meanings to those who menstruated (1993:39-40).

Adler's perspective offers an important insight into the contradictions that the *mikvah* poses for Jewish women who, in their observance of family purity laws, experience God through their identification with the profane. Yet, as the cases of Dicker and Harris illustrate, the *mikvah* may also be experienced as a connection to generations of other Jewish women who have found an essence of the divine in the waters of the ritual bath. Indeed, this interpretation of the *mikvah* suggests that Jewish religious experience cannot be understood apart from the experience of connection and community that *halachic* observance engenders.

THE SIGNIFICANCE OF SPIRITUAL COMMUNITY

According to Jewish law, ten people must be present to perform a religious service, the number ten signifying the Jewish community in its entirety (Saranson, 1983).[1] It is thus through the collective that the experience of God is most profound. As such, prayer becomes most meaningful in the shared context of communal worship, as the following account illustrates:

> I love to *daven* [pray], I love to *daven.* Right away the first thing I love to do is *daven.* Say *brachas* [blessings], I love to do that. It makes me feel Jewish. It makes me feel a special Jewish connection with God. *Davening* is also a social experience as well as a religious experience. It makes me feel very connected, very close toward Jews, and gives me a very warm feeling (Davidman and Greil, 1993:92).

In addition to daily and sabbath worship, the relational aspects of Jewish spirituality can also be found in rituals and practices that bring the Jewish community together in observance of holidays. For example, the Jewish Day of Atonement, the most sacred day of the Jewish year, is observed with a communal fast and a day of worship, during which the community as a whole asks God to forgive the sins and transgressions of the Jewish people (Jacobs, 1992). On this day of fasting and reflection, the congregation collectively lists the wrongdoings of humankind, asking God for forgiveness in the following way:

> We have sinned against You by being heartless,
> And we have sinned against you by speaking recklessly
> We have sinned against you openly and in secret. . . .
> For this and other sins we ask for your forgiveness (Harlow, 1978:407).

Similarly, the celebration of Passover, the holiday that commemorates the liberation from Egypt, represents yet another dimension of Jewish religious experience, as it is defined by connection and the self-in-relation. This annual ritual, the most observed of all the Jewish holidays in the United States, has been embraced by both religious and secular Jews alike who find in the ritual of liberation an identification with the suffering of the past and a renewal of hope for the future. During the *seder*, the Passover feast which recounts the Jews' departure from Egypt, participants are reminded of their connection to the ancient Jews who had been enslaved:

> In each and every generation, Jews should experience the Exodus as if we ourselves had just been liberated from Egypt along with the Jews of that time. For it is written: "And you shall tell your child on that day, 'This is what God did to liberate me from Egypt.' For God did not only liberate our ancestors, but us, their descendants, as well. . . . " It was the unshakable solidarity of the Jewish people, our unity with each other and our culture, that kept us alive during two thousand years of persecution. For how many times have we faced annihilation? How many times has despair threatened to overwhelm us? But this unbreakable bond stood between us and destruction (Cantor, 1982:14-15).

As the Passover service indicates, God is experienced through the individual's relationship to the community and to the cultural roots of the Jewish people. This shared spiritual consciousness is also evident in one other important aspect of rabbinic tradition, the study of Torah which, like prayer and ritual, has a communal orientation, as scholars dialogue with one another in their search for the revealed word of God.

THE RELIGIOUS EXPERIENCE OF TORAH

The study of Torah and its Talmudic interpretations has been considered the intellectual path through which Jewish religious experience is attained.

As such, Saranson writes:

> There is both a cognitive and normative element of the Torah: it is both studied and practiced. Torah study puts the Jew in touch with the revealed mind of God and hence with "the way things really are," affording a series of explanations for the vicissitudes of individual and group life (1983:51).

In comparison with other religious practices, the study of Torah has traditionally been the domain of rabbis and scholars, privileged men who were permitted access to the knowledge of God through disciplined schooling and an all-embracing commitment to Jewish studies. Thus, as Vanessa Ochs concludes, Torah scholars are an elite group who hold a special status in Jewish culture:

> Those who are well-versed in the study of Talmud are considered among the elite of the Jewish community. . . . If you know Talmud, you are, as Rabbi Brovender said, taken seriously. You are linked in conversation to all previous rabbis, to Moses, and to God. The respect due Talmudists goes beyond admiration for their absolute recall of over five thousand pages of Talmud and their ability to weave lucidly through debates. The Talmudist is revered for being pure of spirit, a master of right and virtuous living (1990:78-79).

Given the value placed on Torah scholarship it is therefore not surprising that both women and men have in recent years looked toward Talmudic studies as a path to God. Because orthodox practice has historically barred women from those institutions of learning where knowledge of the Talmud is obtained, the study of Torah has been especially meaningful for contemporary women who have found their connection to the divine in a scholarly arena previously dominated by men. Thus, the Talmudic scholar, Dvora Weisberg, offers this perspective on the relationship between the study of Torah and the experience of God:

> Torah is sometimes referred to in Jewish textual tradition as a path. Study of Torah is for me an attempt to follow that path, which I believe leads toward God. . . . God's voice echoes through the texts I study, but I don't see study as a one-way street. Studying Torah leads me into a dialogue with God; if God is offering questions and answers, then I too am countering with my own concerns. . . . When I study, I feel that I am an active participant in a process that began with the Jewish people, an ongoing search for God's will and our place in the universe (1992:276-277).

The rabbinic tradition, as it has thus far been described through *halacha, mitzvot,* spiritual community, and the study of Torah, is the primary means through which Jewish religious experience is categorized and researched. The emphasis on traditional observance and study, however, has tended to obscure the less well-known mystical traditions that also characterize Jewish spirituality. Beginning with the twelfth century, mystical religious practice assumed an increasingly significant role in Jewish culture. During this time period, the study of Torah became intertwined with the mystical aspirations of a group of scholars who, in their search for God, hoped to escape the suffering of the mundane world.

Jewish Mysticism and Contemporary Religious Experience

For the most part, the writings on Jewish mysticism assume a historical perspective that focuses on three periods of spiritual development within Jewish culture. The first period, which began in Spain in the twelfth century, led to the development of the Kabbalah, a series of esoteric writings on the nature of God. The Kabbalah then became the basis for the Safed mystical tradition of the sixteenth century and later for the Hasidic movement of the eighteenth century. These three spiritual traditions, like other mystical belief systems, focus on an inner experience of God and the possibility of spiritual unification with the creative life force.

As the foundation for Jewish mysticism, the Kabbalah developed a doctrine of emanation which conceptualized the existence of a godhead, Ein Sof, an unlimited, unqualified, and unchangeable divine principle. According to the mystical beliefs, this godhead created the world out of its own infinite being through a process of divine emanations (Green, 1983). From an original spark of light, ten emanations (the mystical numbers known as *sefirot*) broke away, resulting in the succeeding creation of the higher and lower orders of the world. The task of the mystic was to contemplate the various emanations of the godhead and thus to transcend ordinary consciousness by contemplating the mysteries of creation (Green, 1983).

Expanding on the doctrine of emanation, the Safed mystics of the sixteenth century understood religious experience as the reunification of two aspects of the godhead which had been separated during the creation of the lower-order world. The Safed mystics believed that Shekinah, the tenth mystical number and the feminine principle of God, was separated from the source of creation because of Adam's sin. Within this movement, the separation of Shekinah came to symbolize the diaspora, as the Safed mystics, many of whom were descendants of the Jews who had been expelled from Spain, attributed their suffering to the suffering that God experienced at the loss of Shekinah. The quest for spiritual unification therefore became identified with Shekinah, the wandering emanation which signified the dislocation and alienation of the exiled Jew (Fine, 1984).

Isaac Luria, perhaps the best known of the Safed mystics, described the mystical goal as that of repair and restoration of the godhead. According to Luria, such a restoration could be achieved through contemplation of the divine name which, if done properly and by individuals whose souls were pure, would bring about the reuniting of the male and female principles within the divine being (Fine, 1984). Among the meditative techniques that Luria espoused was that of spiritual merging with the deceased. Lawrence Fine offers this fascinating description of Luria's meditative practice:

> The adept was instructed to begin by stretching himself out on the grave of a departed sage—one with whom he shared spiritual kinship—and concentrate on "arousing" the soul of that *saddiq* [sage]. After successfully achieving this, the mystic was directed to focus attention on cleaving with his soul to that of the sage. This was followed by meditation on various letter combinations constituting esoteric names of God; . . . These exercises resulted in an experience of automatic speech in which the sage on whose grave one was lying revealed mysteries of the Torah (1984:23).

An example of this type of mystical experience is found in the life of Hiyyam Vital, a student of Luria. Vital carefully recorded the visions that he experienced throughout his life. Here he describes what transpired in the year 1571 when he was sent to meditate at the graves of two sages:

> There I prostrated myself at the grave of Abbaye of blessed memory and first performed the unification of the Mouth and the Nose of the Holy Ancient One. Sleep fell upon me and then I awoke but I saw nothing. Then I again prostrated myself on Abbaye's actual grave and I performed the unification recorded in my master's own handwriting but as I was engaged in combining, as is well known, the letters of the Tetragrammaton with those of *Adonai* [the representation of God], my thoughts became confused and I was unable to combine them, so I ceased from reflecting on that combination of letters. It then seemed to me in my thought as if a voice was saying to me: "Retract! Retract!" many times. . . . So I tried to combine the letters and this time I was successful. . . . Behold, all this passed through my mind. Then a great dread and trembling seized hold of all my limbs and my hands trembled. My lips, too, were trembling in a highly exaggerated manner, moving quickly and concurrently and with great speed as if a voice was perched on my tongue between my lips. It said with great speed more than a hundred times: "What can I say? What can I say." I tried to steady myself and prevent my lips from moving but was unable to still them at all. . . . Then it repeated: "Wisdom and knowledge will be given to you from heaven like the knowledge attained by Rabbi Akiva" (Jacobs, 1976: 131-132).

Because the Safed spiritual renaissance linked the experience of suffering and alienation with a mystical path that held the promise of salvation, the Safed mystics appealed to later generations of Jews who found solace in the spiritual healing that mysticism offered. In particular, the Hasidic movements of the eighteenth and nineteenth centuries embraced the principles of the Kabbalah. In a departure from the asceticism of the Safed mystics, however, the Hasidic philosophy stressed the presence of god in all living things, teaching that divine revelation was possible for all those who followed the Hasidic way of life (Green, 1983).

Among the Jews in Eastern Europe, Hasidism flourished during a time of political oppression and despair. Thus Martin Buber, in his work on the origins and meanings of Hasidic Judaism, discusses the impact of social factors on the emergence of mysticism within the Jewish culture:

> If we ask now about the character of the historical situation in which the spark of mystical existence leaps over into the people, then we find for the most part that it is a time of a more or less public inner crisis of the religion. If the validity and reality of faith of the traditional contents and structures of religion are shaken, whether because of an increasing degeneration or because of an extraordinary event, if, therefore, the response of this religion to the problematic of human existence, the existence of the individual and the existence of the people, becomes questionable, then mysticism not infrequently rises up against the spreading doubt, against the breaking out of despair. . . . The fact that the people accept mysticism to such an extent is conditioned by social motives, by social changes, by social strivings . . . the life-force that it presents to religion has its source in the inner religious dynamic itself (1960: 63-4).

As Buber suggests, Hasidism had great appeal to the Jews of Russia and Poland, who hoped to transcend personal suffering through a connection to the sacred. With the guidance of enlightened teachers, the followers of Hasidism sought to discover the spark of God within themselves. Through observance, prayer, and study, the men of the Hasidic communities embarked on a mystical path that was imbued with religious piety, while the women were taught that God could be found in the service of their husbands and families.

Today, Hasidism remains a strong force in contemporary Jewish culture, providing support for the Jewish fundamentalist movement that has proliferated in the latter part of the twentieth century. Among the most prolific of the contemporary Hasidic sects is the Lubavitcher movement, a charismatic tradition that originated in Poland and has successfully gained converts in the United States. The research on the Lubavitcher offers some of the most valuable insights into the survival of mystical Judaism. Here a male student describes the relationship among prayer, the study of Torah, and the discovery of God:

> I think in terms of having a genuine way to understand the writings of the sages, the prophets—writings of men whose connection to the divine was a very, very close one. I think in studying Judaism from its inner sources, as Chassidism is, the inside aspect of Torah, to study and understand the revealed aspect of Torah from the inside . . . gives us a very special connection with

> those who have closeness with God. This closeness becomes mystical too. . . . I tend to experience more of this state of timelessness in the states of *davening* [praying]. Above time, transtemporal. . .and the unlimitedness of God if it can be experienced at all by ourselves is certainly attained in the act of prayer. It is a very powerful service. The act of praying certainly brings us closest to God (Sklar, 1991: 75-76).

While prayer and study are the means through which male followers discover the essence of the divine, Lubavitcher women must find their spiritual path in the performance of domestic responsibilities (Davidman, 1991; Harris, 1985). In the following account, a woman who recently converted to Hasidism offers this perspective on religious experience:

> Despite what everybody believes, the synagogue is not the center of Jewish life. The home is, and I don't think you'll find many women in this community hiding in the shadows in their homes. I never think, "Ah, now I am going to the synagogue where I will focus all my religious feeling." There's a place for religious feeling in everything I do. The rituals I perform and the prayers I say as I go about my daily life keep me from becoming blase about it. They force me to think about the sanctity of the ordinary facts of my existence (Harris, 1985:125).

In addition to the practice of traditional Hasidism, there are still other ways in which Jewish spirituality has been reaffirmed and reconstructed in modern society. One interesting phenomenon has been the development of what might appropriately be termed "new age" Judaism, a type of spiritual renewal that frequently involves the study of the Kabbalah and Jewish mysticism. Rabbi Yonassen Gershon, for example, views the Hasidic legacy as a shamanic tradition, drawing a parallel between the shaman's initiation into divine knowledge and the Hasidic leader's initiation into the spiritual realm:

> Often the spirit messenger sent to initiate the seeker was Elijah the Prophet, who because he was taken up alive into heaven. . . . was believed to live eternally.
>
> Early descriptions of Israel Baal Shem Tov, the eighteenth-century founder of Hasidism, portray him in this mode. There exists a letter attributed to him which describes how he first met his spirit teacher while immersing in the *mikveh* (ritual purification pool) at the age of eighteen. He was then instructed to go to a local cave between two mountains, where this angelic messenger taught him from a secret book. Later the spirit revealed that he was Ahiyah the Shilonite, the teacher of Elijah the Prophet (Gershon, 1987:186-187).

Gershon believes that the continuation of this spiritual heritage can be found in a merging of Hasidic teachings with new age consciousness, a blend of mystical tradition and shamanic practice which has become a source for spiritual healing in modern culture. Somewhat less esoteric are the spiritual innovations that have developed in response to the changing nature of contemporary Judaism. These innovations, while less mystical in character, nevertheless retain the spiritual values of the Jewish mystics who understood their relationship to God through the historical realities of social oppression and persecution.

Judaism and the Reconstruction of Religious Experience

Over the last three decades in the United States, mainstream religion has undergone a number of significant changes in response to feminist and heterosexist critiques of traditional religious practice and interpretation of scripture. Within Judaism, the search for religious experience among heterosexual women and lesbian and gay adherents has been particularly problematic as the accepted paths to God have historically excluded women and homosexuals. As pointed out earlier in the chapter, it has only been in the latter half of the twentieth century that women have been permitted to study Torah, a change that has come slowly to the more liberal sectors of the Jewish community. In spite of the marginalized position that both women and homosexuals have held in traditional Jewish culture, members of both of these groups have sought to remain connected to their Jewish heritage and to seek the experience of God through observance of the commandments. The result has been the development of new forms of Jewish liturgy and ritual which affirm the value of diversity for the Jewish community.

For Rabbi Laura Geller the process of innovation is itself a religious experience that brings those who seek change closer to God. In this regard, she writes:

> There are no important moments in the life of a Jew for which there are no blessings. God is present at all times; it is up to us to notice God, to feel God's presence, to celebrate that which is holy in our own experience. Sometimes we are remembering, uncovering, discovering—exploring Torah with new eyes, different questions. But failing that, we invent. . . . I learn something different about God through my connection to my mother, my husband, my son, my teachers, my students, my friends. God is the Thou I discover through my encounter with the human thous in my life, people of whom I can say, "For seeing your face is like seeing the face of God." I ache to find prayers that speak toward the totality of divinity, words I can use that bind me to other Jews as they connect me with God (1992:246).

Similarly, the feminist scholar Ellen Umansky discusses the need for innovation within a tradition that has been exclusionary. She concludes, as does Geller, that the spiritual quest is ongoing and is linked to the possibilities of change that Judaism holds:

> Those who argue that liturgy cannot be changed have lost sight of Judaism as a living religion. How meaningful today are images of God as King, Lord, and Shepherd? And why, if both men and women have been created in God's image, should we not address the Divine as Father *and* Mother, Master and Mistress of Heaven? . . . Three thousand years ago, Moses stood at Mt. Sinai and received the Ten Commandments from God. When he came down the mountain and saw the Israelites worshiping a golden calf, he broke the tablets in anger. Perhaps he did so not only to warn us against idolatry but also to make clear that not even God's words are irrevocably carved in stone (1992:234).

The creativity and innovation envisioned by Geller and Umansky has taken form in the construction of prayers, rituals, and blessings that embody an ethic of tolerance that has been at the core of Jewish thought, if not always Jewish practice. This spirit of innovation is exemplified, for example, by the establishment of synagogues that welcome gay and lesbian Jews. One congregation created the following invocation for the Jewish High Holy days:

> How good it is to gather, in a rainbow of affections and sexual preferences, in the house of a God who loves each of us as we are created, who loves without limit and forever. How sweet it is to gather, women and men together, in the house of a God who transcends human limits and categories (Kahn, 1989: 182).

Yoel Kahn points out the significance of this liturgy from a theological standpoint:

> This passage is also a theological statement: God loves each one of us, not despite our sexuality but because of it. This prayer celebrates the diversity of human sexuality as part of creation itself. If religious language and symbols have been used historically as tools of oppression against lesbian and gay Jews, then we use liturgy today to express an affirmative message of God's acceptance and love. Liturgy, like other religious symbols, tells us who we are and conveys a vision of what we and the world might be (Kahn, 1989:182).

As Kahn suggests, the prayers of the lesbian and gay congregants provides a means to experience divine affirmation and thus to discover the spiritual self that might otherwise be denied in traditional observance. So too, the feminist adaptation of *Rosh Hodash*, the ritual for the new moon, has given new spiritual meaning to a ceremony that has traditionally been associated with women and domestic culture. Vicki Hollander has written a poetic liturgy for *Rosh Hodash* which captures the spiritual essence of Jewish women who, through the cycles of the moon, seek an ancient connection to godliness and the divine. Here is an excerpt from the opening ceremony:

Like the moon,
we shed our layers.
Leave them at the door.
We who caretake life.
We who are healers.
We are doers.
We who mother
  the world.
It's time for us.
This time for us.
We step inside the sacred circle.
We make space for ourselves
to be. (Hollander, 1992:314-315)

The diversity within the Jewish community has also led to a greater emphasis on spiritual healing for those who have been victimized by violence and illness. A lesbian rabbi offers this insight on the meaning of religious experience for people who suffer from AIDS:

> Two years ago, I gave an impassioned sermon about AIDS to my congregation on the High Holy Days. . . . I will always be grateful that I gave that sermon. After services were over, a thin woman stood apart from the crowd and waited to speak to me. After almost everyone else had left, she approached me and asked to speak with me alone. Once we had gone into another room, the woman told me that *she* was the person about whom I had just spoken. . . . Taking my hands in hers, she said to me: "I haven't been in a synogogue in years. When I got AIDS, I was sure that God had abandoned me. But now that my life may soon be over, I felt the need to come back to my Jewish roots. I have never heard a rabbi speak the way you did today. Thank you. I want you to know that it means a great deal to me. I think you've helped me come home" (La Escondida, 1989:222-226).

This AIDS victim interpreted her illness as an abandonment by God. The recognition she received from the rabbi renewed her faith in Judaism, a reconnection that would provide a source of comfort and hope as her illness progressed. When the rabbi spoke of God, her words became the vehicle through which the spirit of the sufferer was restored.

Others have turned to ritual as a source of healing and spiritual empowerment. Research in this area suggests that ritual healing is an important dimension of the women's spirituality movement (Jacobs, 1989). Among Jewish women who have been victimized, the *mikvah* provides a ritual context in which to heal the spiritual violation of sexual abuse. Drawing on the cleansing aspects of the ritual bath, Rabbi Sue Ann Wasserman created a rite of purification for a friend who had been raped.

> When Laura was raped, I wanted to find a way to support her as a friend. As a rabbi, I needed to find a way for Judaism to respond to her. The *mikvah* seemed the most appropriate ritual for several reasons. (1) It was predominantly our foremothers' ritual. (2) It requires the whole body. (3) Its waters flow in and out—representing continuity and process. (4) Its waters symbolically flow from Eden, a place of wholeness. (5) The natural waters remind us of the constant intermingling presence of the Creator in our own lives. (6) Finally, water itself is cleansing, supportive, and life sustaining (Levitt and Wasserman, 1992:322).

In this rite of healing, the rape victim immerses herself three times in the *mikvah* and then recites a liturgy that asks God to help all those who have suffered:

> God give us the strength
> to transcend setbacks and pain
> to put our difficulties into perspective
> God give us the strength
> to fight against all forms of injustice
> whether they be subtle or easily apparent.
> (Levitt and Wasserman, 1992:325)

This innovative use of tradition and ritual illustrates the creativity that victimized women and others have brought to the practice of Jewish spirituality. This form of religious experience, while vastly different from those which focus on observance and *halacha,* speaks to the need for spiritual meaning in the lives of contemporary Jews who have sought out alternative paths to God and to their identification with the Jewish community. The adaptation of the *mikvah* ceremony is a reminder that within Jewish culture, religious experience remains linked to the social realities of victimization and political oppression.

CONCLUSION

This chapter has attempted to provide an overview of the variety of religious experiences that are found within Judaism. While there are undoubtedly many Jewish religious experiences that have not been described here, the analysis of data represents the most significant trends within Jewish studies. As a diverse and changing culture, the Jewish community embraces principles of religious fundamentalism as well as the values of innovation and creativity. Within this broad spectrum of religious identification, rabbinic tradition exists alongside the mystical and more contemporary movements. Each of these aspects of Jewish culture has a unique relationship to the divine, which sustains a connection to Jewish heritage and to a faith that carries with it the memory of struggle and salvation.

NOTES AND REFERENCES

1. While orthodox practice does not recognize women as part of the *minyan* [quorum], conservative and reform Judaism counts women among the number needed to perform a service.

Adler, R.
1993 In your blood, live; re-visions of a theology of purity. *Tikkun* 8:38-41.

Buber, M.
1960 *The origin and meaning of Hasidism.* New York: Horizon Press.

Cantor, A.
1982 An egalitarian hagada. *Lilith* 9:9-24.

Davidman, L.
1991 *Tradition in a rootless world,* Berkeley, CA: University of California Press.

Davidman, L. and A. L. Griel
1993 Gender and the experience of conversion: The case of "returnees" to modern orthodox Judaism. *Sociological Analysis* 54:83-100.

Dicker, S.
1992 Mikveh. *Tikkun* 7:62-64.

Fine, L.
1984 *Safed spirituality; Rules of mystical piety, the beginning of wisdom.* New York: Paulist Press.
1986 The contemplative practice of Yihudim in Lurianic Kabbalah. In *Jewish spirituality II,* edited by A. Green. New York: Crossroad.

Geller, L.
1992 Encountering the divine presence. In *Four centuries of Jewish women's spirituality,* edited by E.M. Umansky and D. Ashton. Boston: Beacon Press.

Gershom, Y.
1987 Shamanism in the Jewish tradition. In *Shamanism: An expanded view of reality,* compiled by Shirley Nicholson. Wheaton, IL: Theosophical Publishing House.

Green, A.
1983 Religion and Mysticism: The case of Judaism. In *Take Judaism, for example: Studies toward the comparison of religions,* edited by J. Neusner. Chicago: University of Chicago Press.

Gresser, M.
1987 Spiritual formation in *halachic* Judaism: The role of *mitzvah. Studies in Formative Spirituality* 8:17-32.

Harlow, J.
1978 *Mahzor for Rosh Hashanah and Yom Kippur.* New York: The Rabbinical Assembly.

Harris, L.
1985 *Holy days: The world of a Hasidic family.* New York: Summit Books.

Hollander, V.
1992 A Rosh Hodesh ceremony. In *Four centuries of Jewish women's spirituality,* edited by E. M. Umansky and D. Ashton. Boston: Beacon Press.

Jacobs, J. L.
1989 The effect of ritual healing on female victims of abuse: A study of empowerment and transformation. *Sociological Analysis* 50:265-279.
1992 Religious ritual and mental health. In *Religion and mental health,* edited by J.F. Schumaker. New York: Oxford University Press.

Jacobs, L.
1976 *Jewish mystical testimonies.* New York: Schocken Books.

Kahn, Y. H.
1989 The liturgy of gay and lesbian Jews. In *Twice blessed,* edited by C. Balka and A. Rose. Boston: Beacon Press.

Katz, Jacob
1986 Halakhah and Kabbalah as competing disciplines of study. In *Jewish spirituality II,* edited by A. Green. New York: Crossroad.
La Escondida
1989 Journey toward wholeness: Reflections of a lesbian rabbi. In *Twice blessed,* edited by C. Balka and A. Rose. Boston: Beacon Press.
Levitt, L. and S. A. Wasserman
1992 *Mikvah:* Ceremony for Laura. In *Four centuries of Jewish women's spirituality,* edited by E. M. Umansky and D. Ashton. Boston: Beacon Press.
Ochs, V. L.
1990 *Words on fire: One woman's journey into the sacred.* New York: Harcourt Brace Jovanovich.
Saranson, R. S.
1983 Religion and worship. In *Take Judaism, for example: Studies toward the comparison of religions,* edited by J. Neusner. Chicago: University of Chicago Press.
Sklar, D.
1991 A phenomenological investigation of the Hasidic experience: An analysis of philosophic, religious, and psychological dimensions. Doctoral dissertation, Union Institute.
Webber, J.
1983 Between law and custom: Women's experience of Judaism. *In Women's religious experience: Cross cultural perspectives,* edited by P. Holden. Totowa, NJ: Barnes & Noble.
Weisberg, D.
1992 The study of Torah as a religious act. In *Four centuries of Jewish women's spirituality,* edited by E.M. Umansky and D. Ashton. Boston: Beacon Press.
Umansky, E.M.
1992 Reclaiming the covenant: A Jewish feminist's search for meaning. In *Four centuries of Jewish women's spirituality,* edited by E. M. Umansky and D. Ashton. Boston: Beacon Press.

2

Catholicism and Religious Experience

MICHAEL J. DONAHUE

To discuss what is unique and defining about the Catholic religious experience, to make some definitive statement about "what it means to be Catholic" and ultimately why one might choose to become or remain Catholic at a time of increasing disaffection from many forms of formal or institutional religion is surely a daunting task. Some small comfort can be taken by delimiting the range of Catholicism to be considered. For the present discussion, "religious experience" will mean "religion as experienced" by the average believer; not the unusual or mystical or peak experiences (which, however are reported by some 35 percent of United States citizens; Greeley, 1975), but the daily religion of the believer in the pew. For sake of space and competence, consideration is limited to Catholicism as practiced in the United States, primarily within the last twenty-five or so years, after the dissemination of the reforms of the Second Vatican Council. In addition, as my academic credentials are those of a social psychologist of religion, rather than historian, theologian, or clinician, the present discussion will for the most part take the form of a literature review, examining what perspectives on the uniqueness of Catholicism are present in the social-science literature, and which seem most useful.

Taking such an approach, one is surprised at the relative lack of literature on the topic. The usual journals of religious research, including *Sociology of Religion* (formerly *Sociological Analysis*, and before that the *American Catholic Sociological Review*), the *Journal for the Scientific Study of Religion,* the *Review of Religious Research*, and the newly established *International Journal for the Psychology of Religion* have amazingly little to offer. The various psychology of religion texts and anthologies, offered little additional help. Recently published books in the social-scientific study of religion (as reviewed in the research journals) include a fair number of books on the history of Catholicism in various cultures, and a fair amount on the Catholic church and what are sometimes referred to as "the pelvic issues" (abortion, homosexuality, contraception, celibacy, the ordination of women), but not much on what makes Catholic religious experience unique.

As I reviewed the available literature, a second question also occurred to me, aside from the issue of uniqueness. Many unique objects are museum pieces; many unique organizations wither and die. Aside from what makes Catholics different there is, in the present context, an even more compelling question: Why do Catholics stay Catholic?

Consider the circumstances. Survey data indicate that in the late sixties and early seventies, there was a decline in church attendance at Catholic churches, a decline in financial support for parishes (Greeley, 1990), and a decline in the acceptance of the authority of the church hierarchy to address moral questions, as reflected in the precipitous change in the number of Catholics who agreed with the church's traditional condemnation of premarital sex and artificial birth control (see D'Antonio, Davidson, Hoge, and Wallace, 1989; Greeley, McCready, and McCourt, 1976). It is true that while Catholic church attendance in the United States declined, attendance also declined slightly for other churches in the period 1967-1969 (from 42 to 40 percent), part of continuing decline that had begun in 1958 at 49 percent). But while other "mainline" Christian churches saw a decline in membership, and the percent of the population stating that they had no religious preference increased, Catholic church membership did not decline. (For documentation of trend data, see *Religion in America,* 1985.) Why? Why had there been this curious continuity of identification with Catholicism while measures of commitment to the church had declined?

In recent years, the division in the Catholic house has grown louder, frequently spilling on to the front pages of newspapers (see, for example, Briggs, 1992). And yet there have been no mass defections (no pun intended). Surely this must mean that there is a great number of people who refer to themselves as Catholics while they profoundly disagree with "official church teaching" on important issues. Hunter Lewis reports in his book, *A Question of Values* (a book not without anti-Catholic overtones) the case of "a pseudonymous member of a Catholic order [who] describes herself as a 'practicing Zen, Catholic, lesbian, feminist nun'" (p.4). Why would a person continue identification with a tradition which would seem to be at odds with many of her other self-identifications? And yet one can be sure that this person consciously identified herself as "Catholic" before she made the other self-identifications she listed.

Similarly, much has been made lately of what is variously known as "cafeteria Catholicism," "a shopper's mentality," "selective" or "pick-and-choose" Catholicism, frequently by members of the church hierarchy (McBrien, 1992:53). Members of the church hierarchy complain that Catholics cannot simply decide what portions of the doctrine please them and adhere to that; they need to make themselves responsible to the entire doctrine of the church. But do those who rail against such selectivity really want the churches filled only with those who are completely "on the program"? Is a "loyal opposition" an oxymoron for Catholics?

There is also some interesting empirical data relating to this issue of the wide range of belief present within the Catholic community. For example, when researchers classify denominations according to their perceived theological orientation, the Catholic church is frequently characterized as "conservative" or "traditional." But when the strength of various religious beliefs such as the divinity of Christ, or the reality of biblical miracles are measured across denominations, Catholics are most frequently in the mid-range, between the most liberal and the most conservative. When examining religious belief data among adults in several different denominations (from the study described in Benson, Williams, and Johnson, 1987) I have found that Catholics sometimes attain their "mid-range" status due to a somewhat higher standard deviation on the particular measure involved. In other words, Catholics are "average," not because they agree on common moderate opinions, but because the range of belief that Catholics express is wider than that of others, and the average rating is in the middle. This in turn confirms my subjective impression of life in the Catholic community. When Protestants have disputes over belief or practice, their tendency is to schism; Catholics, apparently, prefer to stay together and fight.

Why should this be the case? Why is identifying oneself as Catholic so important? Why is the label so tenacious? Is it the case, "as the writer John Powers remarked, 'It's almost as hard to stop being a Catholic as it is to stop being a black'" (Greeley and Durkin, 1984:8; see also Occhiogrosso, 1987). Arguments from ethnicity would have some relevance here; the identity of Irish, Polish, Italian, or Hispanic heritage with Catholicism, at least in a social or folk-religion sense, is strong. But identification with European ethnic backgrounds in the general population has declined as individuals move further and further from immigrant roots; membership in the Catholic church has not shown a corollary decline. (Identification of Hispanics with the Catholic church has shown a decline, but that is outside the scope of the present discussion.) So again the question: what is it about a Catholic identity that is attractive? Why are membership figures stable why other measures of support decline? What is there that is unique about the Catholic experience that might make identification with Catholicism continue to be attractive while other mainline Christian denominations have experienced membership declines?

Examining books used for the training of those converting to Catholicism might seem helpful in identifying this unique Catholic character (e.g., Duffy, 1984; RCIA, 1988; Shreck, 1984). But, perhaps not surprisingly, such sources tend to dwell on ritual, practices, theology, and "culture" of Catholicism; it is not their purpose to examine more closely what might be called the "deep structure" of Catholicism.

Several recent works have, however, examined that "deep structure." Four such approaches will be examined here, in varying degrees of depth: a historian, two theologians, and a sociologist. In each case we will consider what the author presents as the defining characteristic of the Catholic religious experience. Each will be examined in turn to see what they consider to be the defining characteristics of Catholicism, and what light they can shed on the issue of why Catholics stay Catholic. But first, there will be a consideration of the *sine qua non* of Catholic religious experience: the Eucharist.

THE EUCHARIST

No discussion of the religious experience of Catholics can be meaningful without treatment, *a priori*, of the place of the Eucharist in the spiritual life of the Catholic. The documents of the Second Vatican Council speak in the most exalted terms of the centrality of the Eucharist in the life of the church:

> The other sacraments, as well as every ministry of the church and every work of the apostolate, are linked with the Holy Eucharist and are directed toward it. . . .
>
> The Eucharist shows itself to be the source and the apex of the whole work of preaching the gospel. . .
>
> The Eucharistic action is the very heartbeat of the congregation of the faithful over which the priest presides (Decree on Priests, art.5).
>
> [The Eucharist is] a sacrament of love, a sign of unity, a bond of charity, a paschal banquet in which Christ is consumed, the mind is filled with grace, and a pledge of future glory is given to us (Decree on Liturgy, art.47). (Translations taken from Abbott and Gallagher, 1966)

Similarly, both theological treatises on the sacraments and the texts written for instruction in the faith invariably refer to the Eucharist as the "central" sacrament of the Catholic faith. Throughout the faith life of the Catholic, the celebration of the Eucharist will play a prominent role. It will be the framework within which Confirmation and most often marriage is celebrated. A retreat which may mark the spiritual awakening of a young man or women will often be characterized by the celebration of the Eucharist in a particularly intimate or community-creating setting. (Many young people report that such experiences have been very influential in their spiritual development; see Kelley, Benson, and Donahue, 1986). Funerals of parents and other loved ones will occur during Masses, and before death, Catholics often receive *viaticum*, a final reception of the sacrament in order that they may bring the unique presence of Christ "on the way with you," e.g., on the way to heaven. Thus the religious experience of the Catholic is punctuated throughout by the experience of Eucharist.

The centrality of the Eucharist may be at least one reason why the defection of Catholics to other faiths has historically been low and relatively stable, one reason why even those who do not endorse the entire doctrinal or moral framework nevertheless remain affiliated with the church. Greeley (1990) notes that "since 1960 the proportion of those who are born Catholic yet no longer consider themselves Catholic has been constant (age distribution taken into account) at one out of seven" (p.5). One reason may be that, while some Protestant services may seem more or less similar to each other, there isn't any other place for a Catholic to "go to Mass." No other tradition places such central stress on this particular expression of the Christian experience.

Attention now turns to four recent treatments of other characteristics of the Catholic religious experience.

THE HISTORIAN: DOLAN

In a widely quoted history of *The American Catholic Experience*, Jay Dolan listed what he considered to be the defining characteristics of what he referred to as "devotional Catholicism." These four were authority, sin, ritual, and the miraculous. These were characteristics which "set Catholics apart from other people in the United States" before the Second Vatican Council.

The *authority* to which he refers was the unquestioned authority of the hierarchy of the church, in the model most frequent presented as the rejected "pre-Vatican II understanding"; that authority flows from God, to the pope, to his representative the bishops, to their representative, the priest. During the periods of greatest migration to the United States, this authority was further reinforced by the social realities of the support and community found in the church settings for Catholic immigrants. Recently arrived in a new country, ostracized as the "drunken Irish" or the "huddled masses" and "wretched refuse" of the "teeming shores" of southern Europe, Catholic immigrants found natural support in their churches. The priest, better educated and able to help guide the immigrants through the difficult processes of acculturation was admired, respected—and obeyed.

The *sense of sin* was that of an Augustinian understanding of a human nature tainted by original sin and thus always a source of temptation. This, Dolan says, was most strongly reflected in the institution of the parish mission, Catholic revival meetings in which sermons on the consequences of sin and the tortures of the damned sent people flocking to confession.

The concept of *ritual* was present not only in the Mass, performed with strictly regimented gestures and in a quasi-magical language, but most especially in the devotion to the saints, each with its own "cult" (then a technical theological term designating only a particular set of rituals and beliefs). Each nationality strongly identified with not only a particular patron saint or saints, but with particular manifestations of Mary, the mother of Jesus and Mother of God. (For those unfamiliar with such devotions, Carroll's [1992] recent treatment of popular devotions among Italians may be enlightening.)

The culture of ritual in turn fostered two other characteristics of devotional Catholicism. The first was individualism; the reliance on one's own efforts to save one's soul through ritual observances, novenas, and the like. This individualism was fostered in several ways. The fact that the liturgy was conducted in Latin, by a priest who had his back to the congregation encouraged various private devotions (prayer books, rosaries, and the like) by the faithful who were said to be "attending" or even "hearing" as opposed to "participating in" Mass. In addition, the various cults or appearances of Jesus and Mary (e.g., the Sacred Heart, the Miraculous Medal, Our Lady of Fatima) each with its own assurances of salvation if certain practices were observed (medals or scapulars worn, Masses attended on First Fridays or consecutive Saturdays) further encouraged private, noncommunal effort.

The second characteristic encouraged by Catholic ritual was, to quote Dolan (p. 231) "its emphasis on certain key values which in the nineteenth century were identified with the feminine personality": emotionalism and sentimentality, varieties of religious imagery which were derided as "lacrimose [sic], sentimental, and effeminate." In addition to this, of course, was the widespread role of women in all areas of church life with the exception of sacerdotal ministry.

The fourth trait of devotional Catholicism was its openness to the *miraculous*, in devotion not only to officially sanctioned miracle-sites such as Lourdes and Fatima, but with scapulars and private and folk religious practices for the curing of illness, the findings of lost objects, and the like.

Every observer will recognize these characteristics as descriptive of much of the Catholic church before the Second Vatican Council, and the more conservative church members since the Council. But it is clear that these particular characteristics are much less in evidence than they once were. The point in discussing them is that, while they may have been *descriptive* of Catholic practice, I would argue that, at some level, they were not, they could not have been *definitive* of Catholicism for the believers. If they had been definitive, if they had been at the root of what it meant to be Catholic, then large numbers of members would have left the church when these emphases began to change in the church in the late 1950s, and during the post-Conciliar period. In much of church life since the Vatican II, these same practices are criticized as being "pre-Vatican II" at best, if not simply wrong and the sort of excesses and abuses which the Council had been convened to correct.

The point is, if these characteristics of authority, sin, ritual, and the miraculous had defined large numbers of people's relationship with the divine, and Catholicism de-emphasized and in some cases eliminated them, those who found them defining would have left the church, perhaps falling away from religious faith in general.

In this context, it is interesting to note the results of one study concerning what happens when members of the Church of Jesus Christ of Latter-day Saints leave their church (Albrecht and Bahr, 1983). The Mormon church places strong emphasis on its unique authority as the locus of the divinely restored authority. Members are told that this issue of authority is central to the Mormon self-understanding and that there are essentially only two alternatives: either the restored authority of the Mormon church, or the continuing (and, as Mormons believe, apostate) authority of the Catholic church, all other Christian churches being offshoots and derivative from that (see Richards, 1976). Not surprising, Albrecht and Bahr found that when Mormons left their church they were most likely either to lose all interest in religion, or to become Catholic. The issue of authority was definitive for them.

In a similar way, if authority, sin, ritual, and the miraculous had in fact been definitive for Catholics in the United States in the 1940s and 1950s, there would have been massive membership declines, and perhaps even schism after the Second Vatican Council, given the declining emphasis in each of these areas. In fact, neither occurred. Therefore, while these four characteristics may have been descriptive, they were not in fact definitive, but reflective of some more basic reality; some underlying characteristics which were still reflected in the Catholic church for the vast majority of its members. This, in fact, was exactly the tack taken by those who presented the reforms of the Council to the laity: yes, everything looks different, but in fact, at base, everything is the same; this is the same church in new clothing. On what then, is that sameness based? What could these characteristics have been?

THE THEOLOGIANS: MCBRIEN AND ROHR

McBrien

Richard McBrien, chair (at the time) of the theology department of the University of Notre Dame, and considered a voice for the "progressive" wing of the Catholic church in the United States, published a two-volume work entitled *Catholicism* in 1980. In this work, his purpose was to present a systematic, scholarly, and historical overview of the doctrine and morality in Catholicism. At the end of the work, McBrien turns to "the question of Catholicism's distinctiveness" and offers the following suggestions as to what sets Catholicism off from other traditions. The first he says, and most obvious, is the papacy. But he suggests that a "more fruitful, and. . . nuanced" understanding of Catholicism's uniqueness might be found in "identifying and describing various *characteristics* of Catholicism. . . each of which. . . Catholicism shares with one or another church or tradition" but which are unique "in the precise *configuration* in which they are found within Catholicism" (p.1172).

For McBrien, one important characteristics is catholicity with a small "c"; the ability of the tradition to adapt to a wide variety of cultures and settings, theologies, spiritualities. Indeed, some have argued that the reason that Catholicism avoided schism over theological issues for so long was that, as each new theological insight arose, it would be embodied within some movement or order within the church, changed just enough to include it within the broad umbrella of, if not orthodoxy, then non-heresy. Consider, for example, the differences between Franciscan, Dominican, and Jesuit spiritualities. McBrien contends that what makes Catholicism unique is this "both/and" rather than "either/or" characteristic to Catholicism; "not nature *or* grace, . . . not reason *or* faith, . . . not law *or* Gospel, . . . not Scripture *or* tradition, . . . not faith *or* works, . . . not freedom *or* authority, . . . not unity *or* diversity" (p.1174) but creative syntheses of these, in a constantly shifting and counterbalancing dance.

McBrien also suggests three "theological foci" of Catholicism: sacramentality, mediation, and communion. The first two are closely related: sacramentality holds that God is encountered through visible realities; God through Christ, Christ through the church, the church through the sacraments. Mediation states that the encounter with God, while mediated, is real and not simply symbolic. Lastly, communion indicates that the transcendent reality is best understood, not in individuality, but in communion, or community with others.

Rohr

Another more recent attempt to examine the issue of Catholic uniqueness is presented by Richard Rohr in a book whose title was instantly attractive in the present context: *Why Be Catholic?* (Rohr and Martos, 1989) Rohr, a Franciscan priest and popular speaker in Catholic circles, collaborated with Martos to produce a printed version of Rohr's reflections on what is unique, both good and bad, in American Catholicism.

As positive aspects of American Catholicism, he lists the following:

-An appreciation of creation, as a forum for an encounter with God.

-An approach to spirituality that is catholic, holistic, and an invitation to personal holiness.

-An experience of community. This is similar to the "communion" concept that McBrien presents, but he makes a point of noting that he considers this aspect of American Catholicism woefully undeveloped. He considers that there is too little "faith sharing" in the sense of individuals expressing their faith by discussing with others how God has acted in their lives; there is too much of the individualism of which Dolan spoke. "Even when moved to step in the direction of community, Catholics often are motivated by the idea of 'what's in it for me'" (p.21).

- A call to social transformation, self-criticism, and self-renewal, each as part of the renewal of the social order which Catholics see as part of the incarnation of the divine plan.
- A profound sense of history; a sort of "Catholic patience" as it were, which is the simultaneous advantage and disadvantage of refusing to move quickly on most issues of importance; constantly taking the long view with the faith that in the long run (albeit sometimes the very long run) things will be ordered as they should.
- An optimistic attitude toward human nature and human behavior. "Catholic morality has tended to be lax except in the area of sexuality, where for cultural reasons it has been scrupulously rigorous" (p.32). This "laxity" is not the laxity of uncaring, but rather one in which excommunications and public disciplining is less frequent than in some other traditions. Pope John XXIII is quoted as follows: "See all things, ignore most things, correct some things" (Greeley and Durkin, 1984: 94).

Summing up, Rohr states that "the Catholic church is where you have to look to find Christians who are larger than life" (p.33): the saints, living and dead who are offered as models of the Christian life. But, consistent with the standard Protestant and sociological critiques (e.g., Durkheim, 1951/1897), Rohr laments that this has produced a tendency to assign holiness to a particular class of "holy people"; the vast majority of Catholics sit back and point at these others. He quotes an aphorism to the effect that Catholicism produces a few spiritual giants; Protestantism, many spiritual midgets.

Like so many modern American Catholic writers, Rohr's perspective has been influenced by the writings of Carl Jung and the insights of depth psychology. Consistent with this, he also offers observations on what he refers to as the "shadow side" of Catholicism. This includes, as we have seen, an over-emphasis on individuality rather than community, and an "uncatholic Catholicism": too great an emphasis on the immediate and the practical rather than the historical and the wise. Over-emphasis on such areas as ethnic tradition, institutional concerns, or Catholic traditions and practices in place of scriptural teachings are also areas of possible shortcomings.

Rohr sums much of this up in a critique of what he calls "consumer Catholicism." This he defines as an undemanding Catholicism, far too willing to be integrated into society rather than challenge it. Too much is being made of the practical, too little of wisdom. "We are losing touch with the language of symbolism, [with] our ability to be sacramental. . . .Catholic prayer life. . . has collapsed into talk about prayer" (pp.63-65). He perceives a very real threat in all this.

> Consumer Catholicism could very well be the end of the Catholic tradition. . . . It is the pretense of Catholicism, but without its soul. It would perpetuate the masculine structures of the church at the expense of losing the femininity of its openness to God. It would deceive us into thinking that as long as we have parishes . . . schools, . . . educational and social programs, . . . religious goods and bookstores, then the Catholic tradition must be alive and well. . . . It is activity without purpose, words without meaning, a shell without substance (p.67).

Note first that "feminine" aspects of religiousness derided in the account presented by Dolan are here considered a corrective and counterpoint to the masculine. Note also that, for Rohr, the "problem," the difficulty facing American Catholicism lies, not exclusively but largely, in its members; they are not realizing the tradition of their church (although to some degree because it has not been well presented to them). Rohr suggests that the primary corrective for much of this is a reinvigorating of the centrality of the Eucharist in Catholic life (about which more later) and the centrality of "connectedness," of the "community of faith." He notes that there are a number of movements and programs which seek to address these problems, but says that they "have thus far reached only a fraction of American Catholics. Religious experience for most Catholics is still a problem area, still an unexplored territory" (p.80).

Thus, Rohr seems concerned about a large body of Catholic laity who are essentially "getting bored," who are wandering away from the challenge of their faith into intellectualism, formalism, and ossified tradition. He sees religious experience as a "problem," as a core experience which fewer and fewer have contact with, and himself as a prophetic voice calling the church to reorient itself toward its true roots.

McBrien and Rohr share much in their assessment of what is uniquely Catholic. Neither Rohr nor McBrien, however, are social scientists, and neither has addressed the issues they present empirically. McBrien's analysis (not surprisingly) is essentially theological, to which Rohr adds his reflections about certain excesses in the religious orientation of the general body of believers. The Catholic tradition, however, has also always acknowledged the concept of the *sensus fidelium,* the idea that the believers themselves, and not just the teachers and theologians, are also "sacraments" and "revelations" of the will of God, and that issues of faith and practice must be responsive to what is believed and experienced by the individual members. Such an understanding would seem to indicate that the research methods of social science—survey, data analysis, content analysis, the summation of the experience and beliefs of the great body of members—would be enlightening in this area. We next turn to an analysis employing that approach.

THE SOCIOLOGIST: GREELEY

Why do Catholics remain committed and involved in their church in spite of disagreement on what would seem to be fundamental issues of doctrine and practice? The body of research that most directly addresses these questions as I have framed them here (so directly, in fact, that I hasten to note that I had framed the questions before I was familiar with his work) is that of Andrew Greeley. Greeley's research is based strongly on theologian David Tracy's (1982) book *The Analogical Imagination* and also integrates the writings of theologians such as McBrien. It is presented here because it also differs in several important ways from the treatments we have discussed thus far.

First, it is presented as a rigorously social-scientific approach. It is based on a formal theory of religion which has been developed in propositional form with testable hypotheses (Greeley, 1982). Second, Greeley has tested the components of his theory utilizing unusually high-quality data bases. Using profits from his best-selling fiction works (e.g., Greeley, 1981a), he has paid to have religiousness measures included as part of the General Social Survey (GSS). The GSS is a personal-interview survey of 1500 U.S. households conducted by the National Opinion Research Center. The average GSS survey is over 500 items in length, requiring some 90 minutes to complete, covering a wide variety of political, social, and personal issues, with a response rate of 74 to 79 percent (see Davis and Smith, 1992).

He has also tested the theory's predictions using the International Study of Values, the International Social Survey Project, and other nationally representative data sets. And he has taken his analysis the additional step of analyzing the relationship between the uniquely Catholic images of God and the world and such topics as attitudes toward women, the labor movement, and sexual fulfillment in marriage.

Lastly, his work deserves notice here because of the lack of attention it has generally received in the social-scientific study of religion. None of the recent psychology of religion texts (Byrnes, 1984; Meadow and Kahoe, 1984; Spilka, Hood, and Gorsuch, 1985) presents a treatment of his findings. Indeed, even Wulff's (1991) otherwise encyclopedic *magnum opus* fails to examine his research, in spite of its scientific quality. Greeley also complains that his work has been ignored or discounted by the hierarchy of the Catholic church in the United States (Greeley, 1989a). It may be hoped that this presentation will bring his writings to the attention of a wider audience.

The Conceptual Framework

Greeley has presented his approach and findings in several settings, both technical and popular; indeed he sometimes uses scenes in his fiction works to present findings from his research (see Greeley, 1990:203). In this presentation, we will use his framework as he presents it in his book *The Catholic Myth*:

> Catholics differ from other Americans in that their imaginations tend be more "sacramental" (or to use David Tracy's [1982] term, "analogical"). . . . Catholics are more likely to imagine God as present in the world and the world as revelatory instead of bleak. Much that is thought to be distinctively Catholic results from this distinctive style of imagining (p. 4).

For Greeley, the essential distinction between Catholicism and Protestantism (and indeed between Catholicism and most other religions) is the distinction between an analogical or sacramental image of God, in which God is made present in and through the world and interpersonal relationships, and a dialectical image of God, one in which God is "radically other than" the world. The difference between the two is fundamental. In the former view, God is made manifest in the world, and disorders in the world and society are ultimately "correctable"; they can be made to be more congruent with the divine order which underlies them. In the latter, the world is "god-forsaken," fallen, and by its nature beyond saving; Christians are called to be "in the world but not of it."

In the analogical or sacramental understanding, God is present to the believer in the world. That which is divine can be caught up in images which are concrete and real without the divine being trapped in or limited to those objects and thereby become idolatrous. This is in contrast to Protestant sensibilities that so quickly balk at the use of realistic and concrete images (e.g., statues). For Greeley, this is the explanation for the Catholic tradition of appropriating local cultural and religious symbolism into Catholicism. Theologically, God is already present in the ways in which the native cultures have experienced God; such practices can justly be turned to the "right" worship of God, since the missionaries do not come to bring an absent God to heathens, but a right understanding of the God they were attempting to worship.

A Case in Point: Sexuality

It is in this context that Greeley discusses what he would consider to be a right understanding of sexuality. Like Saint Paul's matrimonial imagery in the Epistles, or the famous theological treatises on the Song of Solomon as a hymn on the relation between the soul and God, sexuality becomes sacramental. If God is present in each of the lovers, then the love itself manifests God to each of the partners, and God is present in the very act of love itself. Greeley takes this insight to its local conclusion: "All love affairs in the Catholic tradition of sacramentality are *menage à trois*" (1990:43). However clearly this understanding may be derived from the analogical imagination (and it shall be shown in later sections that there are empirical relations between an analogical understanding of God and sexual satisfaction), Greeley calls the unwillingness to integrate such an understanding of sexuality into official Catholic teachings as "the most grievous failure in the history of Catholic Christianity" (Greeley and Durkin, 1984:68).

Mary

For Greeley, another important reflection of this analogical imagination is in the Catholic imagery of Mary, the mother of Jesus. One of the most notable changes in the Catholic church since the Second Vatican Council has been the decline in the emphasis on Marian practices and devotions in much of the Catholic church. As Hans Küng (1976), a prominent and controversial theologian, has put it, "during the time after the council this exaggerated Marian cult has completely lost its force. . . in theology and the life of the church (p. 462)." But more recently there has been some growing interest in Mary as a phenomenon in the psychology and sociology of religious belief (e.g., Carroll, 1983, 1985, 1992; Greeley, 1977; Hood, Morris, and Watson, 1991; Zimdars-Swartz, 1991) as well as in other, more nontraditional circles (e.g., Stanford, 1988; the cover subtitles Stanford's book, "A psychic channels the controversial prophecy of Fatima for a New Age").

Greeley sees Marian imagery and devotion as having a continuing impact on the Catholic imagination. It is here, he contends, in the Mother of God, that the feminine in God resides for Catholics. The fact that she is hailed as "Mother of God" makes it easy to see in her aspects of God's motherhood of creation. And he finds empirical evidence that this imagery continues to operate even in the post-Conciliar church.

> In our research on young Catholics, many of whom never went to May Crownings and most of whom never heard a Marian sermon, we found that the image of Mary is even more powerful for Catholics than the image of God or Jesus. It correlates positively with political and social concern, pro-feminist orientations, warm relations with the opposite sex, and frequent prayer. There is no evidence that the image of Mary is the source of "antiwoman" sentiments as some radical feminists claim; . . . for young Catholics just the opposite is the case. There is no more convincing proof that it is the appeal of the analogical imagination which binds Catholic to their tradition than the persistence of the Mary image and its positive impact on the lives of young Catholics (1990:62; see also Fee, Greeley, McCready, and Sullivan, 1981).

Mary, then, continues to be of importance to young Catholics. But there are broader questions which must be addressed to test the model which Greeley is positing. Is there a uniquely Catholic "imagining" of God? Does it really comprise the larger mass of believers, distinguishing between Catholics and Protestants? And does it have the wide range of impact on belief and behavior that Greeley contends? Each point will be considered in turn.

Measures and Method

Greeley has used a number of different measures to examine the religious imagery. In his study of *Young Catholics* in the United States and

Canada (Fee et al., 1981) he focused on "warm" religious images: the endorsement of images of God as a lover, Mary and Jesus as "warm," and heaven as a "paradise of pleasure and delight." In his study of *The Religious Imagination* published that same year (Greeley, 1981b) he proposed a "GRACE" scale composed of ratings of various positive ratings of God, heaven, Jesus, and Mary. But for his most recent research, he has settled upon a GRACE scale consisting solely of images of God. "Respondents are asked to locate themselves on a seven-point continuum between four forced choices of how they picture God—father/mother, master/spouse, judge/lover, and king/friend. In each case, the option listed second (mother, spouse, lover, friend) is scored as more "GRACE-ful."

This latter approach has some psychometric drawbacks. First, at least as presented in his sources, the high-scoring answer is always presented on the same side of the continuum. This may lead to some tendency for "acquiescent" responding—people simply checking the same side of the continuum on each item. In addition, in other studies, (e.g., Greeley, 1993) he has reduced the scale to a four-point continuum in which the scale score consists of how many times the respondent has checked the option that they are "extremely likely" to view God in that way. This in turn subjects the measure to concerns about extremity response bias (e.g., Greenleaf, 1992). But Greeley's findings, as we shall see, hold up under a variety of analytical procedures (percent response, correlation, and regression), and are so robust that it is unlikely that these psychometric concerns explain a great deal of the variance in his findings. Attention now turns to the relevance of these images for the individual believer.

While his earlier research concentrates largely on Catholics, and therefore provides little evidence for Protestant-Catholic differences in God images, Greeley's work with the General Social Survey (GSS) supports the notion of differences in God images between Catholics and Protestants, with Catholics more likely to endorse the "grace"-oriented images (1989b; 1993). In at least one study (Greeley, 1988) using GSS data from 1984-1986, he found that the God as "mother" and "friend" images showed Catholic-Protestant differences only for Catholics under the age of forty. But more importantly, these differences in images do in fact produce differences in other attitudes and behaviors.

The Influence of GRACE

Greeley has tested this effect of image on attitudes and behaviors in two ways. One is to examine the relationship between endorsement of the GRACE scale and other attitudes and behaviors within Catholic samples to determine whether the more Catholic images lead to certain predictable outcomes. Such effects have been confirmed in a wide variety of content areas.

Perhaps the most interesting findings are those that provide evidence for the conceptual validity of the GRACE scale as uniquely Catholic. It might, for example, be presumed that such an image of God and the supernatural might be associated with a more generally liberal attitude on a variety of matters. In fact, the older, more elaborate GRACE measure (which included the belief that heaven is a "paradise of pleasure and delight") was *negatively* correlated with support for premarital cohabitation, divorce, homosexuality, birth control, and abortion under some circumstances, and no significant correlation was observed between the measure and the belief that it was important for the Catholic church to update its teachings in the area of sexual morality. He does caution however, that while the correlation is negative "even those who are high on the grace scale are scarcely likely to endorse in overwhelming numbers" (Greeley, 1981b:43).

Using the more refined GRACE scale based only on images of God, he found that:

–when both partners in a marriage score high on the scale, they are more likely to report they are "very satisfied" with their marriage, that their sexual adjustment is "excellent" and that their value consensus is "excellent" (Greeley, 1990).

–Catholics scoring high on the GRACE are more likely to display tolerance and flexibility with respect to issues of AIDS policy (Greeley, 1991) and are more likely to support expenditures on environmental issues (Greeley, 1993) (both based on 1988 GSS data).

Protestant-Catholic Differences

In addition to examining the relation of a GRACE orientation to attitudes among Catholics, Greeley has also tested a number of hypotheses by examining Protestant-Catholic differences on large numbers of social and political issues. If the Catholic sensibility assumes a world (both physical and social) which reveals God, while the Protestant sensibility is one of a dialectical separation of God and the world, then certain predictions about social, political, and interpersonal attitudes of each group would follow. Most intriguingly, he has tested this proposition using data from the International Study of Values, using thirty-six measures in six English-speaking countries. Among his basic hypotheses, consistent with the distinction between analogical and dialectical images of God were:

> Protestants will be especially likely to deplore vices which diminish personal integrity, honesty, and sense of duty. Catholics will be especially likely to be offended by actions which seem to violate relationship networks—adultery, prostitution, suicide. Catholics . . . will . . . advocate social change so that the disclosure of God will be improved. Protestants . . . will be less optimistic about and less supportive of social change (1989b:487).

Examining thirty-six comparisons based on these and similar predictions, he found that twenty-one of them were supported, but only in the English-speaking countries (including the United States); data for West Germany and the Netherlands were not supportive. He also examined predictions about interpersonal relationships: that Catholics would be more likely to visit relatives, live near relatives, and have more interrelated relationship networks (that my friends are also friends with each other). Each of these were supported. He also found that Catholic married couples under strain increase, rather than decrease, their interactions with those close to them; they rely on their relationships as a source of grace and strength.

Greeley's concept of religion "as imagination before it is anything else" thus goes a long way to answering the question of why Catholics remain Catholic even though they disagree. As Greeley puts it, they stay Catholic because they like being Catholic. Or as one person he interviewed put it:

> "Why should I leave?" a young Catholic man asked me. "I like being Catholic. I'm proud of it. I'd be out of place as anything else. So I disagree with the pope and despise the jerk that's my pastor. Is it any more their religion than mine? I'd have to give up too much if I left" (Greeley, 1990:28).

SUMMARY AND CONCLUSIONS

There clearly is broad agreement among the four perspectives on the nature of Catholicism that have been examined here. Dolan's characteristics of "ritual" and "the miraculous" clearly fit within the context of the sacramental imagination, while also displaying the drawbacks that can be associated with that form of spirituality. His comments on authority, and the decline in support for authority over time also fit within Greeley's comments on the importance of relationships in the analogical imagination. In the nineteenth and early twentieth centuries, a less-uneducated, poor, working-class Catholic laity relied on and was led by an educated clergy. As the laity became increasingly educated, the hierarchy failed to change its leadership style quickly enough to reflect this new relationship and the relationship soured. Much of Greeley's (1990) *The Catholic Myth* traces this developmental process and its ramifications.

McBrien's themes of catholicity, sacramentality, mediation, and communion are also consistent with the analogical imagination. Rohr, however, seems to be concerned that to the extent there is a threat to the Catholic tradition, it may lie in a Catholic laity that refuses to challenge itself, that refuses to be "a sign of contradiction," that is not truly living its faith. In contrast, Greeley invariably presents the hierarchy of the church as the problem, a group of men to whom he refers with phrases like "damn fools. . . in lieu of more scatological language" (Greeley, 1990:7). For Greeley, Catholics remain Catholics in spite of their institutional church; for Rohr, the drift away from a lived Catholicism among the faithful is becoming dangerous. Rohr suggests that what is needed is a reinvigoration of the faith life by the believers, a rededication to the prophetic mission. Greeley (Greeley and Durkin, 1984) suggests a) that the hierarchy should reemphasize certain traditional themes, such as better liturgy and homilies, renewed devotion to Mary and the saints, more traditional church design to reintroduce "sacramental" imagery, and b) certain new themes should be sounded: the sacramentality of sex and the femininity of God.

The increasing shortage of priests, the constancy in teachings on the ordination of women and birth control, the declining financial support of churches leading to budget deficits and the closing of parishes, the lack of trained catechists or even knowledgeable adult volunteers to pass on a living tradition to the next generation (Kelly et al., 1986) all are coming to a head. Whether it is Rohr's reinvigoration of the faithful, Greeley's new leadership from the hierarchy, or both, somebody better do something. This can't go on forever. American Catholicism must change or lose its distinctiveness.

REFERENCES

Abbott, W. M., and J. Gallagher (Eds.)
1966 *The documents of Vatican II.* Piscataway, NJ: New Century.

Albrecht, S. L., and H. M. Bahr
1983 Patterns of religious disaffiliation: A study of lifelong Mormons, Mormon converts, and former Mormons. *Journal for the Scientific Study of Religion* 22:366-379.

Benson, P. L., D. L. Williams, and A. L. Johnson
1987 *The quicksilver years: The hopes and fears of early adolescence.* New York: Harper & Row.

Briggs, K. A.
1992 *Holy siege: The year that shook Catholic America.* New York: Harper San Francisco.

Byrnes, J. F.
1984 *The psychology of religion.* New York: Free Press.

Carroll, M. P.
1983 Visions of the Virgin Mary: the effects of family structure on Marian apparitions. *Journal for the Scientific Study of Religion* 22:205-221.
1985 The Virgin Mary at La Salette and Lourdes: Whom did the children see? *Journal for the Scientific Study of Religion* 24:56-74.
1992 *Madonnas that maim: Popular Catholicism in Italy since the fifteenth century.* Baltimore, MD: John Hopkins University Press.

D'Antonio, W., J. Davidson, D. Hoge, and R. Wallace
1989 *American Catholic laity in a changing church.* Kansas City, MO: Sheed and Ward.

Davis, J. A., and T. W. Smith
1992 *The NORC General Social Survey: A user's guide.* Guides to Major Social Science Data Bases, Vol. 1. Newbury Park, CA: Sage.

Dolan, J. P.
1985 *The American Catholic experience.* Garden City, NY: Doubleday.

Duffy, R. A.
1984 *On becoming a Catholic: The challenge of Christian initiation.* San Francisco: Harper & Row.

Durkheim, E.
[1897]
1951 *Suicide.* Translated by J.A. Spaulding and G. Thompson. New York: Free Press.
Fee, J. .L., A. M. Greeley, W. C. McCready, and T. L. Sullivan
1981 *Young Catholics: A report to the Knights of Columbus.* Los Angeles: Sadlier.
Greeley, A. M.
1977 *The Mary myth: On the femininity of God.* New York: Seabury.
1981a *The Cardinal sins.* New York: Warner Books.
1981b *The religious imagination.* Los Angeles: Sadlier.
1982 *Religion: A secular theory.* New York: Free Press.
1988 Evidence that a maternal image of God correlates with liberal politics. *Sociology and Social Research* 72:150-154.
1989a Sociology and the Catholic church: Four decades of bitter memories. *Sociological Analysis* 50:393-397.
1989b Protestant and Catholic: Is the analogical imagination extinct? *American Sociological Review* 54:485-502
1990 *The Catholic myth: The behavior and beliefs of American Catholics.* New York: Scribner's.
1991 Religion and attitude toward AIDS policy. *Sociology and Social Research* 75:126-132.
1993 Religion and attitudes toward the environment. *Journal for the Scientific Study of Religion* 32:19-28.
Greeley, A. M., and M. G. Durkin
1984 *How to save the Catholic church.* New York: Viking Press.
Greeley, A. M., W. C. McCready, and K. McCourt
1976 *Catholic schools in a declining church.* Kansas City, MO: Sheed and Ward.
Greenleaf, E. A.
1992 Measuring extreme response style. *Public Opinion Quarterly* 56:328-351.
Hood, R. W., R. J. Morris, and P. J. Watson
1991 Male commitment to the cult of the Virgin Mary and the passion of Christ as a function of early maternal bonding. *The International Journal for the Psychology of Religion* 1:221-223.
Kelly, F. D., P. L. Benson, and M. J. Donahue
1986 *Toward effective parish religious education for children and young people: A national study.* Washington, DC: National Catholic Educational Association.
Küng, H.
1976 *On being a Christian.* [*Christ sein*; Edward Quinn, trans] Garden City, NY: Doubleday.
Lewis, H.
1990 *A question of values: Six ways we make the personal choices that shape our lives.* San Francisco: Harper San Francisco.
McBrien, R. P.
1980 *Catholicism* (2 vols.) Minneapolis, MN: Winston.
1992 *Report on the Church: Catholicism after Vatican II.* San Francisco: Harper San Francisco.
Meadow, M. J. and R. D. Kahoe
1984 *Psychology of religion: Religion in individual lives.* New York: Harper & Row.
Occhiogrosso, P.
1987 *Once a Catholic: Prominent Catholics and ex-Catholics reveal the influence of the church on their lives and work.* Boston: Houghton Mifflin.
RCIA: Rite of Christian initiation of adults: Study edition.
1988 New York: Catholic Book Publishing Company.
Religion in America, 50 years: 1935-1985.
1985 The Gallup Report, No.236.
Richards, L.
1976 *A marvelous work and a wonder.* Salt Lake City: Deseret Book Company.
Rohr, R., and J. Martos
1989 *Why be Catholic? Understanding our experience and tradition.* Cincinnati, OH: St. Anthony Messenger Press.

Schreck, A.
1984 *Catholic and Christian: An explanation of commonly misunderstood Catholic beliefs.* Ann Arbor, MI: Servant Books.
Spilka, B., R. W. Hood Jr., and R. L. Gorsuch
1985 *The psychology of religion: An empirical approach.* Englewood Cliffs, NJ: Prentice-Hall.
Stanford, R.
1988 *Fatima prophecy.* New York: Ballantine Books.
Tracy, D.
1982 *The Analogical Imagination.* New York: Crossroad.
Wulff, D.
1991 *Psychology of religion: Classic and contemporary views.* New York: Wiley.
Zimdars-Swartz, S.L.
1991 *Encountering MARY: From LaSalette to Medjugore.* Princeton, NJ: Princeton University Press.

3

Protestantism and Religious Experience

RONALD E. HOPSON AND KURT OPENLANDER

THE HISTORICAL CONTEXT OF THE PROTESTANT REFORMATION

Protestant religious experience may be understood as a series of events and circumstances interwoven by accidents of political and religious history, combining to form a tapestry of traditions ranging from near Roman Catholicism, Anglican, and Episcopal churches to nonaffiliated fundamentalist sects and cults on the right and Unitarianism on the left. The development of Protestantism may be understood within the context of a larger revolution, the Renaissance. During the Renaissance, human possibility was expanding rapidly as the understanding of the universe and of the nature of man underwent revolutionary shifts.

The Roman Catholic Church had been ideally suited to life in the Middle Ages, when a dominant institution was needed to provide a sense of coherence for a culture characterized by bare subsistence and illiteracy which otherwise would have been vulnerable to social breakdown. Medieval life and thought were dominated by religion, and the church was thus dominant in political matters. However, with the Renaissance and its reintroduction of classical thought, society began to undergo rapid change. Perhaps the most profound effect of the Renaissance was the emerging emphasis on the individual and the resulting deemphasis on the community. The community had been largely centered around the church, and there was interdependence between the church and the community. Theologically, human's relationship to God was understood to be mediated by the church. There was no direct connection between God and the individual. Instead, God was revealed through the sacraments administered by the priests, who had the most direct link with God; and the sacraments were generally administered in the presence of the community of believers.

With the advent of the printing press and the spread of literacy, the scriptures began to be translated from Latin into the languages of the people. A middle class based on commerce and trade arose, and no longer was there universal dependence on the land, much of which was owned by the church. Society became increasingly defined by the individual and less defined by the community, and the church's autocratic domination of sociopolitical life became less tenable.

The Christian religion was propagated around the world by such explorers as Vasco da Gama, who was under the patronage of Prince Henry the Navigator of Portugal. The specifically evangelical motives of these voyages are unclear; however, by the end of the eighteenth century, European peoples "had mastered a larger proportion of the earth's surface than had any earlier group of mankind" (Latourette, 1965:164).

Internal problems threatened to stem the growth of Christianity. Corruption was rampant among the hierarchy of the Roman Church, extending even to include the papacy. The most significant aspect of this corruption was the wholesale purchasing of religious authority by regional monarchs. Thus, the church became the vehicle for legitimization of the political authority, particularly in Europe. It is in this context that the protest which was to become Protestantism emerged.

Martin Luther and the Protestant Reformation

Martin Luther's challenge to the church hierarchy at Wittenberg is generally regarded as the beginning of Protestantism. Martin Luther was the first-born child of prosperous parents and was educated in the best German style available in that day. Though initially pursuing legal education, after a fortuitous brush with death (Luther was nearly struck by lightning), he began to study theology. Eventually he was assigned to teach theology at the University of Wittenberg, where he began his journey toward Lutheranism.

The nature of Luther's protest may be understood in the light of personal and situational factors in his life. Latourette (1953) and Atkinson (1968) note that Luther struggled with temptations (*Anfechtungen*) throughout his early years. His was a life of depression, anxiety, and guilt of the kind later captured in William James's (1961) discussion of the sick soul. He struggled greatly to secure a sense of salvation and make himself acceptable to God according to the Observant Augustinians to which he pledged allegiance.

Yet, despite his efforts, inner peace was not available to him. His vain attempts to mitigate the profound sense of guilt and sin with which he struggled finally yielded relief when he stumbled upon Paul's declaration: "The just shall live by faith." This was like a "light breaking in on the darkness" of his guilt and despair. He amplified this phrase and added the word "alone." Thus, human effort was not only ineffectual but also unwarranted because salvation came "through faith alone." Luther had finally found a way out of the torturous efforts to earn salvation.

Along with the inner turmoil which characterized Luther's life, he also observed corruption and inconsistency among the church hierarchy of his day. The conflict most troubling to him centered on the handling of indulgences. This custom, by which the pope could remit sins through the adherent's payment of an indulgence to the church, had developed over the course of several centuries. This use of indulgences had become a main source of income for the pope as well as local church officials. Disturbed by the abuses of this system for purely economic ends, Luther challenged the efficacy of indulgences and argued that the pope had no power over the disposition of the soul (Latourette, 1953). This led to Luther inviting a debate on the issue of indulgences in the usual manner of posting a challenge to the disputed practice on the door of the castle church. The date of Luther's famous nailing of his ninety-five theses to the door of the church at Wittenberg, October 31, 1517, is usually regarded as the beginning of Protestantism.

Luther's objections became widespread in part due to the recent invention of the printing press. His declarations against indulgences were quickly absorbed into the general unrest of the peasant classes and the protest spread rapidly beyond German borders. Within fifty years, the Protestant Reformation had branched into most of Western Europe including Great Britain. This advance was furthered by the work of Huldreich Zwingli and Jean (John) Calvin.

Calvin and the Spread of the Reformation

Calvin, born July 10, 1509, was an essential figure in the firm establishment of Protestantism outside of Germany and Scandinavia. Under him, Geneva became the headquarters of extensive missionary activity which he directed with decisiveness and superb organization. He corresponded with and influenced Reformed Church leaders in France, England, Scotland, the Netherlands, Germany, Denmark, Sweden, and Poland. Without Calvin, the Protestant Reformation clearly would have been much more limited in scope and historic effects.

Calvin underwent a sudden conversion around the autumn of 1533 which was marked by his anxious quest for salvation and "true religion," and which had been preceded by a protracted process of self-examination and study. As a result of his conversion experience, he found himself at philosophical odds with the Catholic church, for in the "Preface to Psalms" in his *Opera,* he provocatively describes himself as having been so obstinately addicted to papal superstition that he had great difficulty extricating himself from that quagmire!

Calvin's reaction to his conversion was to attempt to reform the church from within, to restore its status as the "true church" (Johnson, 1977). He believed that all revelation stems from the Word (the Bible) and not from tradition or the authority of the church, the Word creates and guards the church through its impact on people (Dillenberger and Welch, 1954). He maintained that the church was subordinate to the "Word of God" which was available to all believers through scripture and preaching. Thus, the church was to subordinate itself to the primacy of the preached and printed Word. This historical emphasis upon the literal understanding of scripture has experienced a renewal in present day Protestantism, despite the historical-critical tradition which has arisen in biblical scholarship.

Calvin emphasized righteous living through the moral code as prescribed in scripture (Dillenberger and Welch, 1954). He called for an authoritarian church which required an oath of allegiance of all citizens and made ready use of excommunication in order to govern morals. Calvin's doctrine of divine election necessitated that proof of election be manifest through correct doctrine, a worthy life, and faithful attendance on the sacraments which meant in practice membership in a Calvinist congregation. This was the amalgam of individualistic and institutional Protestantism which was to be imported to America by the Puritans and which would form the basis of the Protestant experience in America (Latourette, 1965).

The Church in England

The rise of Protestantism in England contrasts with the rise of Protestantism on the European continent. The break with Rome was not instituted by the religious or politically oppressed classes but rather by the infamous love affair of Henry VIII and Anne Boleyn, with whom Henry sought to produce a legitimate male heir. The religious revolt which was sparked by Henry's desire to divorce his first wife and marry Anne was accepted by the English, as they had tired of papal interference in matters of state and resented the great amounts of money which flowed out of England to Rome to support the church hierarchy.

After Henry's death, his children vacillated between close allegiance and strong opposition to the traditions of the Roman church, culminating finally in the "Elizabethan settlement" by which Elizabeth I declared herself the "supreme governor" of England in all matters both ecclesiastical and secular.

One group within England (the Puritans) was highly dissatisfied with the "Elizabethan settlement." The Puritans insisted that the Roman church was corrupt and the English church must purge itself of all remnants of Roman influence. They decried the authority of the Queen in ecclesiastical matters and insisted upon a presbyterian form of church governance (i.e., local authority in ecclesiastical matters).

Protestantism in the "New World"

Protestant attitudes toward Africans and Native Americans. The English politico-religious protest led to an emphasis upon evangelism, and the most obvious focus of such sentiment was the New World settlements in the Americas (Marty, 1987). The Puritans who sailed to North America were fervent for missionizing. Some of the natives had been evangelized by Spanish Catholics. The Catholic missionaries were somewhat tolerant of the native culture, rituals, and customs; by contrast, the settlers' attitude toward the Native Americans is perhaps best captured in a statement by the famous Boston cleric Cotton Mather, who wrote in 1702: "We may guess that probably the Devil decoyed those miserable savages hither, in hopes that the gospel of the Lord Jesus Christ would never come here to destroy or disturb his absolute empire over them" (cited in Marty, 1970:6). This sentiment was woven into the fabric of the new American society such that over one hundred years later, in 1815, Samuel Worcester, pastor of Tabernacle Church of Salem, Massachusetts, exclaimed "My brethren, the heathen do need the gospel. There is no other remedy for them" (cited in Wood, 1990:21).

The attitude toward Native Americans was paralleled in the attitude toward Africans. The Puritans could not reasonably imagine the existence of "native societies that were physically distinct from [their] own without being morally inferior" (Wood, 1990:33). However, this assumption of inferiority did not lead inexorably to the enslavement of Africans and Indians; indeed, there were ambivalent voices among the Puritans regarding slavery. Jordan (1974) cites an incident in which Massachusetts magistrates in 1646 arrested two mariners who had abducted two Africans and sold them in Massachusetts. The ambivalence over slavery was not sufficient, however, to avoid its spread, even in the North, where economic arguments were of virtually no weight.

The emphasis upon domination and conversion of the African and Native populations was a consequence of the fusion of economic and religious ideals. The Native American was criticized for not working the land to its maximum productivity. Thus, seizing the land from the Native was an act in concert with the plan of God. The African's enslavement was necessary, especially in the South, as the tobacco fields required labor which was "cheap, permanent, mobile, and tireless" (Jordan, 1974:39). The economic necessity was seamlessly woven together with the religious assumptions of inferiority and depravity of the Natives and Africans. This blending of cultural tradition with religious ideal continues to be a source of serious criticism of Protestantism, as will be seen in later discussion.

Early American church membership. The establishment of Protestantism in America was based upon the blending of seven major affiliations:

Congregationalist, Presbyterian, Episcopalian, Baptist, Quaker, Reformed, and Lutheran. In 1758, Jonathan Edwards was to call the new nation the "principal nation of the Reformation."

Though all of the major variations of Protestantism on the European continent were represented in the colonies, there was not to be a plurality of religious folk among the newly arrived Europeans for another two-hundred years. The total membership of these denominations combined comprised less than ten percent of the population of the original thirteen colonies, and the vast majority of the early European Americans were unchurched.

The Great Awakening. The small numbers of persons who were members of churches in the thirteen colonies was a cause for concern among clergy, and the Great Awakening was a consequence of this growing concern. Blending Pietist convictions with Calvinist theology, clergy of the Great Awakening maintained that religious experience was an important "evidence" of election. These clergy began preaching "with impassioned conviction the necessity of a deep inward transformation rather than the mere outward performance of religious ceremony" (Latourette, 1953). Perhaps the most famous of these clergy was Jonathan Edwards. Through his persuasive, deliberative rhetoric, hundreds professed conversion during the period 1734-1735. These revivals were accompanied by high emotionality and graphic depictions of the nature and consequences of sin. The Great Awakening brought the first great influx of members into organized religion in the thirteen colonies. It also provided the master pattern for the Protestant emphasis upon individual religious experience, conversion, and evangelism (Morrison, 1965). This revival movement was brought to an end by the Revolutionary War.

The American Revolution. The most noteworthy aspect of the American revolution was the introduction of the concept of religious freedom and the related doctrine of the separation of church and state. These views were a radical departure from Christian precedent and European custom (Marty, 1959). The doctrine of the separation of church and state served to accommodate American religious pluralism in the form of denominationalism. Each denomination had "equal opportunity" to advance its claims, as the government would take no formal role in interdenominational squabbles. Paradoxically, the doctrine of separation of church and state also secured the alliance between religion and republic by establishing a modified form of state religion . Benjamin Franklin, though little known for his role in the religious debates during the founding of the country, argued the "necessity of a publik religion" which would produce a common morality and advance the collective good of the American society, especially in regard to economic productivity and advantage. The role of religion in reinforcing the public order was definitively captured by Alexis de Tocqueville when he called religion "the first [of America's] political institutions . . . [and its] main business is to purify, control, and restrain that excessive and exclusive

[American] taste for well-being" (cited in Bellah et al., 1985:223).

The Second Great Awakening. The Great Awakening had been the watershed event for establishing the importance of religious membership for the soon-to-be-born nation, and what has come to be known as the Second Great Awakening established the expanded landscape of religious pluralism which continues to characterize North American Protestant religious experience (Marty, 1959, 1987). Begun by Presbyterian preachers, the Second Great Awakening exploded into being at Cane Ridge, Kentucky, in 1801. The majority of participants in the Cane Ridge revival were of established denominations (e.g., Episcopal, Presbyterian, and Congregationalist). The result of the Cane Ridge experience, and other events of the Second Great Awakening, was the consolidation of smaller affiliations (e.g., Baptists and Methodists), sects (e.g., Spiritualists, Millerites, Mormons), and movements which were to become denominations (e.g., the Churches of God, the Churches of Christ, and Disciples of Christ). Also, the Cane Ridge revival provided the characteristic form—camp meetings with dramatic conversion experiences—of American religious experience for several decades to follow (Johnson, 1977; Bloom, 1992).

The Second Great Awakening facilitated the westward expansion of the United States. The doctrine of Manifest Destiny, which was central to the founding of the country, was renewed with the Second Great Awakening: pioneers, moved by their enthusiastic and evangelistic religious convictions, carried and spread their religion on the westward expansion. The Second Great Awakening also brought an increase in world missionary societies and led to the founding of several colleges and theological seminaries (Latourette, 1953); thus, Protestantism had begun to establish itself as amenable to both the political and academic values of the young republic. This early accommodation would prove to be an enduring aspect of mainline Protestantism in the United States.

Marty (1970) has described several crises which the young nation was to face within one hundred years of its founding. One was industrialization and the rise of the cities; another was the institution of slavery. Industrialization required a change in the focus of revivalism in America: the roving evangelists, who were increasing in number throughout the northeast, began to turn their attention to cities rather than to rural areas. Though it was argued by some during this era that the increasing emphasis on acquisition was not in keeping with the spirit of the gospel, even such notable religious leaders as Lyman Beecher maintained that there was such abundance available in this new land that poverty was of necessity a result of sin. Thus, along with the political and academic accommodation which had become characteristic of Protestantism, the expanding economic order had found accommodation with the Protestant ethic.

Slavery and Protestantism. Slavery permanently splintered the Protestant church in America. Initially, Protestant clergy had decried the institution of slavery. The 1780 conference of the Methodist Episcopal Church declared slavery contrary to the laws of God and called for preachers holding slaves to free them (Fuller, 1876). Yet, by 1859, the southern branch of the Methodists had undergone complete change, criticizing any who would try to interfere with master-slave relations. The Preface to *Moral Philosophy* published by the Southern Methodist Publishing House of Nashville, Tennessee, stated the intention of the publication to "give a full and correct view of the slavery question. It shows to the youth of our land that slavery is not a sin; that it was established originally by the Divine Being, for wise, just, and benevolent purposes; that it was directly sanctioned by Christ and his apostles, and is not, therefore, 'the sum of all villainies'" (cited in Fuller, 1876:56). In 1818 at their General Assembly, Presbyterians called slavery "a gross violation of the most precious and sacred rights of human nature; as utterly inconsistent with the law of God"; yet, by 1838, most Presbyterians ignored this teaching. The third major group with a large southern membership, the Baptists, had early spoken against slavery, only to turn silent or become prudent apologists for slavery since the cotton-based economy of the South required cheap labor.

The divisions which arose over the issue of slavery were never healed. The major denominations of the South, Baptists and Methodists, were to experience schisms as a consequence of the slavery question. In addition to the schism between white church members of the North and South, the issue of slavery also divided African-Americans from whites. Upon reconstruction, there began a mass exodus of blacks from the white denominations of the South. However, after the Civil War the numbers of blacks who were church members multiplied rapidly: separate congregations were developed for black Episcopalians while the Methodists and Baptists formed separate denominations (e.g., African-Methodist Episcopal, African-Methodist Episcopal Zion, and the National Baptist Convention). The black person was seen as an ally of the "hated conqueror" (i.e., the North). Also, proscriptions against interracial marriage were reinforced. By the period of reconstruction, the Protestant church had become one of the major institutions contributing to the consolidation of racism in the United States. By the end of the nineteenth century mainstream American Protestantism had consolidated its comfortable relationship with the political, academic, economic, and social order of the society. Indeed, nearly one hundred years later, it could be truthfully stated that Sunday morning at 11:00 is the most segregated hour in America.

Protestant accommodation to social context. The Protestant churches of both the North and South enjoyed a period of prolific growth after the Civil War. Membership increased and the economic clout of organized churches also increased. Affluent members were heartily welcomed within the churches and leading ministers endorsed the equivalence of spiritual and material well-being. The Pauline text "I wish above all that you may prosper and be in good health, even as your soul prospers" took on material and economic connotations. The preaching of Protestant America helped inspire the rapid industrialization sweeping the country in the latter part of the nineteenth century. The doctrines of providence, elections, working out one's salvation and proving God's favor were appropriated to the new industrial context. Though sometimes cautious about making the association explicit, the Protestant ethic was at least implicitly wedded to the emerging creed known popularly as Social Darwinism, or "Survival of the Fittest," by many Protestant preachers (Marty, 1970:152).

THE PSYCHOLOGY OF PROTESTANT RELIGIOUS EXPERIENCE

The conjunction of the Protestant religious ethic with emerging sociocultural perspectives of the late nineteenth century inevitably led to the consideration of religious experience by the emerging discipline of psychology. As early as the 1880s publications appeared which brought psychological insights to bear on the phenomenon of religion. By 1899, the first book entitled *The Psychology of Religion* was published (Starbuck, 1899, cited in Beit-Hallahmi, 1974).

The emerging discipline of the psychology of religion in America focused primarily upon Protestant religious experience. G. Stanley Hall and his students are usually credited with founding the psychology of religion in America. Hall and Edwin Starbuck introduced the use of questionnaires to study religious phenomena (e.g., conversion). Assuming Protestant Christianity as normative and ideal, Hall viewed religion as advantageous for the human family and wrote extensively on the role of religious education in the normal development of the child (Hall, 1904, cited in Wulff, 1991). With the work of Hall, Starbuck, Leuba, Pratt, and others, religious experience in Protestant America began to become codified. This codification was to set the parameters for investigation of religious experience for nearly the remainder of the century. The psychology of religious experience was to be understood within the existing scientific paradigms and was to be taken as an observable, measurable, comprehensible phenomenon; the transcendent and ineffable aspects of religion were not seen as a proper or manageable subject of study in the psychology of religion. However, the most significant name in the psychology of religion, William James, would reject these parameters and pursue precisely the path of the exceptional or transrational as the proper study of the psychology of religion.

William James

William James's *Varieties of Religious Experience* continues to stand as the great classic in the field of the psychology of religion. In contrast to the work of his contemporaries (e.g., Hall, Pratt, and others) and that of subsequent researchers, James was not interested in the "ordinary religious believer, who follows the conventional observances of his country" (James, 1961:24). The religion of the masses James saw as habitual, and therefore irrelevant to the depths of religious experience; however, he viewed extraordinary individual religious experience as particularly valuable and telling.

James presents an analysis of Protestant religious experience based upon "intuitive comprehension" (Wulff, 1991:485) informed by relevant philosophical, psychological, sociological, and historical approaches. The genius of James may be seen in the fact that the broad categorization of religious experience into two types largely anticipates the understanding of religious experience derived from the past forty years of empirical research.

Types of religious experience. James's two religious types are the healthy-minded and the sick soul. The healthy-minded individual is characterized by a constitutional optimism that absorbs even apparently negative life circumstances within a prevailing view of the benevolence of life. James draws an analogy between the religious optimist and the Protestant Reformation. "To the believer in moralism and works with his anxious query, 'What shall I do to be saved?' Luther and Wesley replied: 'You are saved now, if you would but believe it'" (p.100). The initial effectiveness of the Protestant Reformation James attributes to the optimistic doctrine of Luther and Wesley. This view contrasts with that of many scholars who suggest that the genesis of Luther's protests was in part his depression. James argues that Luther's doctrine of justification by faith invites an attitude of surrender, a "dying to be truly born." The achievement of this state of surrender requires that "something must give way" in the individual, "and this event is frequently sudden and automatic, and leaves on the subject an impression that he has been wrought on by an external power" (p.101).

The second religious type is the sick soul. James characterizes this person as being incapable of simply absorbing evil within a conviction of the benevolence of life. Rather, for the sick soul, evil is of "the very essence" of life, and as such, the sick soul is inclined toward an attitude of melancholia. James cites the story of the Electress Dowager when dining one day with Martin Luther. In her admiration for Luther she declared: "Doctor, I wish you may live forty years to come." "Madam," replied Luther, "rather than live forty years more, I would give up my chance of Paradise" (cited in James, 1961:121). James suggests that the sick soul may potentially experience a more veridical view of life than the healthy-minded, because of the relentless reality of suffering in the world.

The potential of the sick soul for a fuller view of reality is in accord with Carl Jung's suggestion that the Protestant Reformation potentiates an expanded experience of life for those embracing the doctrine of justification through faith alone, as this doctrine removes the structures (e.g., confession and indulgences) which mitigate the sense of tragedy, sinfulness, and finitude (Jung, 1958). The reformed person stands alone before God; thus, the potential to either be overcome by life or to transcend life is greater.

James associates the healthy-minded religious experience with the "once-born"—those for whom a religious conversion is not necessary in order to experience the sense of being at peace with the world. The task of the sick soul is the unification of the self; thus, a conversion experience (i.e., "twice-born") is more characteristic of the sick soul type. Subsequent research associating conversion with life dissatisfaction and upheaval (Spilka, Hood, and Gorsuch, 1985) confirms this view. James suggests that the "coarser religions" which offer revivalistic fervor, intense emotionality, and miraculous possibilities, may be particularly suited for the constitution of the sick soul. This view provides insight into the present-day trend of rapid growth among fundamentalist Protestant traditions which emphasize conversion and subsequent relief from life's struggles (Hartz and Everett, 1989).

Religious conversion. James presents the best description of the phenomenology of religious conversion in the literature on the psychology of religion (Edie, 1987). James's essential categories of conversion, sudden and gradual, have been confirmed in most subsequent research on the issue. Recent research has elaborated on these categories, finding intellectual, affective, and volitional elements operating differently for sudden versus gradual converts (summarized in Spilka et al., 1985).

The theology of the Reformation as exemplified in the revivalistic awakenings of the early part of the nineteenth century laid the groundwork for conversion to become the "standard form" for the beginnings of religious experience in the Protestant tradition. Similar to the view of Freud, James understands the conversion experience as the "sometimes sudden inrushing" of previously unconscious aspects of the personality. The conditions suggested by James for a sudden conversion experience to occur, emotional sensibility and a tendency toward suggestibility or passivity, have been appended by the observation that the sudden conversion experience involves a significant interpersonal component (Paloutzian, 1981). The interpersonal component of religious conversion has been understood from a Durkheimian perspective as ritual acts by which social groups reaffirm themselves. Wimberley et al. (1975) surveyed participants in a Billy Graham crusade and found that the conversion experience was a "public performance" which provided group identity and solidarity and confirmed one's membership in the group. The role of the conversion experience in solidifying one's identity and membership within a particular community has been discussed from a Durkheimian perspective by several authors in the sociological tradition. The contextual effects discussed by Sargent (1957) are discussed by James as they reflect the Protestant emphasis upon collective religious experience (i.e., church life) yielding individual religious benefit. In accord with James's view, persons who report having undergone a sudden conversion experience were more likely to regress during projective psychological testing and present primitive, non-logical material (Allison, 1968). However, these persons were able to integrate these non-logical elements adequately, indicating that sudden conversion experiences are not by definition maladaptive.

Mysticism. James concludes his study of religious experience with a discussion of mysticism. James outlines four qualities of mysticism: 1) Ineffability. The mystical experience defies verbal expression and is "more like states of feeling than like states of intellect"; 2) Noetic. The mystical experience mediates "states of insight into depths of truth unplumbed by the discursive intellect. They are illuminations, revelations, full of significance and importance"; 3) Transiency. Mystical states do not endure though they may recur; and 4) Passivity. The person experiencing a mystical state feels "as if his own will were in abeyance, and as if he were grasped and held by a superior power" (James, 1961:300). These categories are in accord with the findings of such researchers in the area of mystical experience as Stace (1960) and Hood (1973). Stace (1960) outlines two gross categories of mystical experience: introversive and extroversive. The introversive mystical experience is characterized by the loss of a sense of time and space and union with the transcendent and a corresponding loss of sense of self. Extroversive mysticism conveys a sense of horizontal unity wherein all things are "alive" and are a part of one Whole (Spilka et al., 1985).

James maintains that mystical states can be induced by chemical agents such as nitrous oxide. Recent research on the effects of hallucinogenic agents on the experience of mystical states accords with this view, although findings suggests that the attribution of religious meaning to these experiences is both context-dependent and related to the subject's prior religious sentiment (Pahnke, 1967). The mystical experience conveys a sense of the unity of life which is pervaded by beneficent meaning and purpose (Hood, 1975), and has been found to be associated with positive affect and negatively related to poor mental health (Greeley, 1975).

Rausch and Voss (1987) suggest that due to the uniquely individualistic nature of mystical experience and the detachment from ecclesiastical authority which mystical experience makes possible, mysticism was an important precursor of the Protestant Reformation. Indeed, such mystics as Meister Eckhart, though Catholic, influenced the thought and writing of Martin Luther. It is estimated that currently 30 to 40 percent of the population report having had mystical experiences, albeit broadly defined; however, these experiences are most prevalent among Catholic and noninstitutional Protestant groups (Back and Bourque, 1970).

Gordon Allport

The tension between individualism and collectivism has been a continuing theme within Protestant religious experience (Marty, 1970). During the first quarter of the twentieth century Protestantism became divided into two camps: the social gospel movement made up of those who advocated social concern and critique of the social order; and the individualists, who emphasized personal mores such as sexual morality and support of prohibition, and individual salvation. Both camps advocated American imperialism, were anti-Catholic and anti-immigrant, and supported prohibition. Despite the fact that the social gospel movement was highly critical of the social order, there was a gaping blind spot in its concern for the situation of the black American.

Ironically, the attitude of the Protestant church toward the African-American was to lead to the revitalization of study in the psychology of religion. Gordon Allport is considered second only to William James in importance in the psychology of religion, and his seminal work on the psychology of religion may best be illustrated with his study of prejudice. He observed a finding he considered paradoxical in his study of prejudice in the South (1958): the more influential religion had been upon a person during his or her childhood, the greater the degree of prejudice, while the less important religion was during the person's upbringing, the less prejudice he or she reported. This finding puzzled Allport, as he was a devout Episcopalian and understood the Christian message to be anathema to prejudice and racial bigotry. Allport solicited the help of Catholic and Protestant clergy to explore the meaning of this peculiar finding. Two groups were culled from a Baptist Bible class, irregular attenders to a Baptist church, and Catholic parishioners identified as those for whom "their faith really meant something" or those "who seemed influenced more by political and social aspects of religious activities" (Allport, 1958:421). All persons were asked to fill out a questionnaire from which Allport derived two religious factors: institutional and interior. "Belonging to a church because it is a safe, powerful, superior in-group is likely to be the mark of an authoritarian character and to be linked with prejudice. Belonging to a church because its basic creed of brotherhood expresses the ideals one sincerely believes in is associated with tolerance. Thus, the 'institutionalized' religious outlook and the 'interiorized' religious outlook have opposite effects in the personality'" (Allport, 1958:422). With this statement Allport launched the postwar revival of the psychological study of religion.

Types of religiosity. The terms "interiorized" and "institutionalized" later were changed by Allport to "intrinsic" (to replace "interiorized") and "extrinsic" (to replace "institutionalized") (Allport, 1960). Studies of the intrinsic and extrinsic dimensions of religious faith have proliferated since Allport (e.g., Hood, 1970, 1971, 1975, 1978; Hunt and King, 1971; and Gorsuch, 1984). The scale has been employed primarily in research on Protestant religious experience. The intrinsic and extrinsic dimensions have been considered conceptually distinct in contrast to Allport's initial hypothesis. Intrinsic religious orientation correlates negatively with fear of death, depression, and narcissism and positively with such variables as empathy, responsibility, and prejudice against homosexuals. Extrinsic religious orientation correlates positively with fear of death, racial and ethnic prejudice, dogmatism, and authoritarianism.

The pattern of responses on the intrinsic and extrinsic scales has been further assessed for those persons endorsing all religious items in the positive direction (the indiscriminately pro-religious) and those persons endorsing all religious items in a negative direction (the indiscriminately anti-religious). Prejudice, dogmatism, and attitudes such as superpatriotism and ethnic bigotry were highest among the indiscriminately pro-religious, followed by extrinsics, intrinsics, and the indiscriminately anti-religious. Batson and Ventis (1982) expanded upon the intrinsic and extrinsic dimensions as they described a third dimension of religiosity: religion as the quest for meaning in the personal and social worlds. As an example of this research, Batson and Raynor-Prince (1983) found that only the "quest" dimension showed a significant positive relation to cognitive complexity in the religious domain.

FURTHER STUDIES ON PROTESTANT RELIGIOUS EXPERIENCE

Since Allport, research into the psychology of religion has proliferated. Two studies may be cited as representative of contemporary research on the essential nature of Protestant religious experience. Clayton and Gladden (1974) factor-analyzed responses of two groups of university students on several scales of religious dimensions and found only a single factor, termed "religiosity," which is primarily composed of ideological commitment. At the other extreme, in a study of twenty-seven Dallas congregations representing four mainline Protestant denominations, King and Hunt (1969, 1972a, 1972b, 1975; King, 1967) found a stable set of ten religious factors: creedal assent, devotionalism, church attendance, organizational activity, financial support, religious knowledge, orientation to growth and striving, extrinsic orientation, talking and reading about religion, and the prominence of religion in everyday thoughts and feelings. It has also been suggested that religious orientation among Protestants may be developmental in nature: Watson, Howard, Hood, and Morris (1988) found that scores on the "quest" dimension peak in late adolescence and early adulthood and then decline with age, while scores on the intrinsic dimension generally increase with age.

Rokeach (1969) found significant differences between various religious traditions on the dimension of religious values. In comparisons with Catholics, Jews, and nonreligious persons, salvation was ranked highest by Protestants. There were also differences within Protestantism: "Salvation" was ranked third by Baptists, while Episcopalians ranked "Salvation" fourteenth. Ezer (1962) found that being reared in a highly devout home resulted in similarly high rates of animistic and anthropomorphic thinking for Protestants, Catholics, and Jews.

The relationship between religious affiliation and the tendency to present oneself in a culturally favorable light was explored by Crandall and Gozali (1969). They found that children who attended Catholic parochial schools and those from a fundamentalist Lutheran tradition were more likely than other children to give socially desirable though behaviorally improbable courses of action that they might take when faced with situations involving moral choice. The children reared in more religiously conservative homes showed greater defensiveness and distortion of their actual behavior. These findings suggest that a strict religious upbringing will produce an increased sensitivity to moral reputation and a greater sense of shame in response to transgression.

Religion, mental health, and social attitudes. The most persistent question regarding religion is its effects on mental health and social attitudes. Shaw (1970) found a relationship between a devout religious upbringing and adult adjustment. He found that subjects who were reared in fundamentalist homes were significantly lower than average in their use of psychological approaches to explaining human behavior. Rokeach (1973) found that those Christians who placed a high value on salvation tended to score low on measures of social compassion and expressed negative attitudes about the poor and toward equal rights. Tate and Miller (1971) examined the relationship between both intrinsic and extrinsic religiosity and the value "equality" among United Methodists. They found that equality was ranked third out of thirty-six in personal importance for the intrinsically religious, fifth by the extrinsically religious, sixth by those who were nonreligious, and ninth by those who were indiscriminately pro-religious. Lindskoog and Kirk (1975) found that among evangelical seminary students, those who scored high on a test measuring self-actualization were more ecumenical and had more liberal political and social attitudes than those who scored lower. Exploring the commonly proposed association between Protestantism and capitalism, Ray (1979) found that a Protestant Ethic scale did not differentiate Catholics from Protestants, although it did distinguish religious from nonreligious persons.

Altemeyer (1988) studied the relationship between right-wing authoritarianism and Christian orthodoxy, finding the highest authoritarianism scores among Fundamentalists and Mennonites, followed by Catholics and Lutherans, with members of the United Church of Christ, Anglicans, and the nonreligious scoring lowest. The results of the vast majority of studies examining the relationship between religious sentiment and prejudice show a curvilinear relationship between the two variables: the somewhat religious are the more likely to be prejudiced, while the truly pious and the nonreligious are less likely to be prejudiced (Hoge and Carroll, 1973; Gorsuch and Aleshire, 1974).

ANALYSIS OF RELIGIOUS EXPERIENCE IN THE PROTESTANT TRADITION

The research on religious experience accepts James's perspective that discontent and its resolution are the essence of religious experience (James,

1961; Spilka et al., 1985). The discontent which gives rise to religious experience is ontological in nature, having to do with the "sense that there is something wrong about us as we naturally stand." The religious resolution is effective as it conveys the "sense that we are saved from the wrongness by making proper connection with the higher powers" (James, 1961:393). The proper connection occurs on an individual level, though it may be mediated by the church. Conversion is the most ordinary manner in which this connection is effected, and the results of this connection are sometimes of a mystical nature.

Protestant religious experience is rooted in the experience of one man's discontent with his inability to right his private sense of wrongness as well as his discontent with the ecclesiastical structures which claimed to facilitate the person's right relationship to God. The protests nailed to the chapel door at Wittenberg may be conceived of as a protest against an unyielding sense of personal inadequacy as well as a protest against the ecclesiastical system which claimed to set the person right. The dictum "the just shall live by faith alone" addresses both the internal dilemma and the ecclesiastical dilemma.

The definitive Protestant theologian Paul Tillich has elaborated the nature of faith in the Protestant tradition (Tillich, 1952, 1957). Tillich understands the centrality of faith in Luther's formula as a protest against evaluating one's ontological status according to the state of one's feelings or the external conditions of one's life. The just shall live by faith—despite the private doubts and anxiety which may torment one as they tormented Luther. Tillich (1952) maintains that anxiety is an inevitable and necessary aspect of human living. Rather than shrinking from confrontation with this anxiety through various forms of idolatry, the "natural anxiety of being" must be met and transcended by "absolute faith."

The insertion of the word "alone" into the formula illustrates the protest against determining one's ontological status by one's standing with the ecclesiastical or political hierarchy. Tillich (1957) states: "Luther, the young monk, stood in the depth of [his] boundary situation and dared to reject all safeguards that piety and the church wished to extend to him. He remained in it and learned in it that just this [faith alone] and only this is the situation in which the divine 'Yes' over the whole of human existence can be received; for this 'yes' is not founded on any human achievement, it is an unconditional and free sovereign judgment from above human possibilities" (1957:201).

Tillich maintains that Luther's emphasis upon faith is a radical commitment to direct confrontation with the nature of one's existence. Tillich reads Luther as demanding that all "conditioned" (i.e., finite) symbols of one's ontological status be denied. He understands the Protestant Reformation as protests against these finite symbols: "The Protestant protest has rightly destroyed the magical elements in Catholic sacramentalism. . . . It should be a permanent task of Christian theology . . . to draw the line between the spiritual and the magical use of the sacramental element" (Tillich, 1957:xxiii). The "spiritual" use of the sacramental element maintains the symbolic dimension of the sacraments and insures that the gulf between the actual and the manifest be traversed by faith alone. The "magical" Catholic use of the sacraments reduces the actual to the manifest and faith becomes a matter of signs, dogma, and ritual.

Faith may be construed as the capacity to live "as if." Winnicott (1971) has discussed in great detail the importance of fantasy and the capacity to live "as if," in the absence of any literal external referent. Winnicott understands the moment of encounter with the breech between the actual and the desired as the moment of faith. With the development of object permanence, the child must act "as if" the object exists, even though the object is not accessible to the senses. Luther's formula calls for precisely this mode of living. The individual is charged to believe by faith, in the absence of any external, or indeed internal, evidence. The capacity to live "as if" frees the person to transcend the sometimes oppressive reality of the material world. For the Protestant, the work of living is at the level of the imagination. Dogma and ritual, when overinvested with meaning, are inferior external referents which offer a defensive retreat from confrontation with the actuality of human existence.

The Catholic church maintains seven dimensions of life as sacramental: Birth and the sacrament of baptism; consolidation of identity and the sacrament of confirmation; acknowledgement of sin and the sacrament of reconciliation; acceptance of grace and the sacrament of the Holy Eucharist; decision regarding one's life work and the sacrament of Holy Orders; decision about one's life partner and the sacrament of marriage; and death and the sacrament of the sick. The sacraments, dogma, and symbols of the church serve to express and contain the crises and possibilities of each phase of life.

The use of dogma and ritual as a defense against the "unruly and arbitrary" nature of the supernatural has been discussed by Carl Jung (1958). Jung suggests that the unconscious (i.e., nature, and by extension, God) is experienced as dangerous and arbitrary. Dogma and rituals of the church provide a mediating and protective function, rendering the world predictable and relatively safe. With the Protestant Reformation, "the dogmatic fence was broken down and the ritual lost its authority; man had to face his inner experience without the protection and guidance of dogma and ritual" (Jung, 1958:21). As these rituals are overturned, the individual is left with no symbolic assistance. The overturning of the symbol is a moment of great crisis or opportunity for Protestantism. "The Protestant is left to God alone. He has to digest his sins by himself; and because the absence of a suitable ritual has put it beyond his reach, he is none too sure of divine grace" (Jung, 1958:48). Tillich and Jung converge in their assessment of the potential for religious experience of the Protestant stance: "If a Protestant survives the complete loss of his church and still remains a Protestant, that is to say a man who is defenseless against God and no longer shielded by walls or communities, he has a unique spiritual opportunity for immediate religious experience" (Jung, 1958:49). Conversely, if the Protestant tradition surrenders to the temptation to appropriate culturally conditioned signs of grace (e.g., wealth, possessions, political power), it may lose its edge of protest and become a "kept" religion.

The definitive Protestant symbol is the Bible, the "word" of God. The emphasis in early Protestantism upon creeds and doctrines (e.g., the Augsburg Confession), the finding that Protestants are more conversant with scripture than Catholics, and the continuing Protestant tradition of creedal confessions, is evidence of the importance of the "word." The consequences of this emphasis upon the "word" rather than the sacraments may be elucidated by a consideration of the symbolic function of language. Cassirer (1953) and Lacan (1968) maintain that language is co-constitutive of the self. Cassirer has proposed that language may function along a dimension from the literal-exclusivistic to the symbolic-inclusive: mimetic, analogical, and symbolic. Words, when reduced to their literal dimension (Lacan: "the empty word"), constrict and narrow life and conceal the depths of human experience. When allowed full symbolic weight (Lacan: "the full word"), the "word" may provide a "grounding" in reality which transcends the particular and concrete aspects of one's life.

The literalization of the "word" (i.e., the emphasis upon inerrancy and infallibility of scripture) may be seen as an "inability to sustain metaphor" (Bloom, 1992:244). Those who do not adhere to the concrete forms presented in scripture may be seen as lacking that which is necessary for right relationship to the Transcendent. Following Cassirer and Lacan, the literalization of scripture may prevent the "word" from becoming a sufficiently inclusive symbol to represent *all* persons, regardless of the concrete particulars of their existence. The virulent forms of evangelism which have afflicted many cultures attest to the potentially destructive aspects of the overinvestment in a particular symbol system. The consistent finding of association between fundamentalist religious perspectives and dogmatism, authoritarianism, and exclusivity supports this contention (Capps, 1992; Greven, 1991). The association between social and religious conservatism does not seem, however, to be inevitable. Intrinsic religiosity, which has been found to be correlated with religious conservatism, is also associated with less prejudice than is extrinsic religiosity (Spilka et al., 1985). The African-American church is also an example of a biblically fundamentalist tradition which has articulated a theologically based concern for social activism and the inclusion of all members of the society (Lincoln and Mamiya, 1990).

Tillich has also argued that the Protestant Reformation has "wrongly brought to the verge of disappearance the sacramental foundation of Christianity and with it the religious foundation of the protest itself. . . . [Protestantism] has replaced the great wealth of symbols [of the Christian tradition] by rational concepts, moral laws, and subjective emotions" (Tillich, 1957:xxxiii). The decline of the significance of religious symbols (desacralization) has important consequences for human functioning. The culture must be able to establish new and yet flexible symbols which contain and express the fears, aspirations, and ideals of the collective without becoming petrified and oppressive of the collective, as Luther claimed some aspects of Catholicism had become. The failure of institutional religious structures to provide such symbols may lead to the relegation of religion to the category of useless sentimentality (e.g., James's "habit"), which renders religion "incapable of giving help or of having any other moral effect" (Jung, 1958:32).

Wilson (1970) has argued that a consequence of the desacralization of society may be the rise of new movements which attempt to restore these symbols. These movements function as correctives to the particular socio-ethical/religious problem around which they arise (Nelson, 1987). The increase in noninstitutional religious affiliations within Protestantism may be seen as evidence of Wilson's thesis. Every major Protestant denomination has declined in membership over the past thirty years while there has been a corresponding increase in the number of nonaffiliated evangelical, charismatic, and pentecostal religious groups (Hoffman, 1992).

The emphasis in these movements is upon dramatic conversion experiences and concrete, specific rules for living. The increase in nonaffiliated fundamentalist groups and new religious movements may be seen as evidence of the failure of institutional Protestantism to provide adequate, flexible symbols to mitigate the stressors of late twentieth-century life. In the absence of adequate symbols, persons are resorting to tangible signs of grace. The insight of Jung, Tillich, and others suggests that symbols are vital to the health of a community: the symbol functions to stabilize life, mediate grace, and provide assurances regarding one's relationship to whatever one conceives of as transcendent.

CONCLUSION

The Protestant Reformation has spawned nearly one hundred eight denominations and 400 million adherents worldwide, while 34 percent of the U.S. population identifies themselves as Protestant (Gallup, 1991). The Protestant Reformation began as a protest against the reliance upon internal and external signs of grace. It emphasized the authority of individuals to interpret their relationship to the transcendent. Despite its intentions, Protestantism has typically been absorbed by and then expressed the social attitudes and economic realities of its surrounding community. While biblical teachings have undoubtedly mitigated such influences in many cases, societal conditions have frequently influenced the meaning Protestant believers have derived from the Bible. The varieties of religious experience in Protestantism have been traced from its historical moorings to its present-day dispersion. The emphasis upon church membership, conversion, religious knowledge, and personal morality which characterizes the growing edge of Protestantism today are certainly congruous with Protestant history. The current growth of traditions emphasizing dramatic religious experience may be seen as an attempt to restore the representational dimension of religious life in the absence of adequate symbols and ritual to express relationship to the divine. The genius of the Protestant Reformation was to open up the possibility of transcendent faith which was not rooted in the tangible dimensions of life. The Protestant tradition offers the possibility of participation in the symbolic dimension of life without being captured by the symbol. While the temptation of Protestantism is to appropriate finite signs to replace the symbols overturned in the reformation, the hope of Protestantism is that the protest against all limiting conditions on human life continue.

NOTES AND REFERENCES

1. The authors would like to thank Charles Ahern and Michael Ursiak for their contribution to the final draft of this work.

Allison, J.
1968 Adaptive regression and intense religious experience. *Journal of Nervous and Mental Disease* 145:452-463.

Allport, G. W.
1958 *The nature of prejudice.* Garden City, NY: Anchor.
1960 *Personality and social encounters: Selected essays.* Beacon Press.

Altemeyer, B.
1988 *Enemies of freedom; Understanding right-wing authoritarianism.* San Francisco: Jossey-Bass.

Atkinson, J.
1968 *Martin Luther and the birth of Protestantism.* Baltimore, MD: Penguin.

Back, K. W., and L. B. Bourque
1970 Can feelings be enumerated? *Behavioral Science* 15:487-496.

Balmer, R.
1993 *Mine eyes have seen the glory.* New York: Oxford University Press.

Batson, C. D., and L. Raynor-Prince
1983 Religious orientation and complexity of thought about existential concerns. *Journal for the Scientific Study of Religion* 22:38-50.

Batson, C. D., and W. L. Ventis
1982 *The religious experience: A social-psychological perspective.* New York: Oxford University Press.

Beit-Hallahmi, B.
1974 Psychology of religion 1880-1930: The rise and fall of a psychological movement. *Journal of the History of the Behavioral Sciences* 10:84-90.

Bellah, R., R. Madsen, W. Sullivan, A Swidler, and S. Tipton
1985 *Habits of the heart.* New York: Harper & Row.

Bloom, H.
1992 *The American religion.* New York: Simon & Schuster.

Capps, D.
1992 Religion and child abuse: Perfect together. *Journal for the Scientific Study of Religion* 31:1-14.
Cassirer, E.
1953 *The philosophy of symbolic forms: Volume one: Language.* New Haven, CT: Yale University Press.
Clayton, R. R., and J. W. Gladden
1974 The five dimensions of religiosity: Toward demythologizing a sacred artifact. *Journal for the Scientific Study of Religion* 13:135-143.
Crandall, V. C., and J. Gozali
1969 The social desirability responses of children of four religious-cultural groups. *Child Development* 40:751-762.
Dillenberger, J., and C. Welch
1954 *Protestant Christianity interpreted through its development.* New York: Scribner's.
Edie, J. M.
1987 *William James and phenomenology.* Bloomington, IN: Indiana University Press.
Ezer, M.
1962 The effect of religion upon children's responses to questions involving physical causality. In *The causes of behavior,* edited by J.F. Rosenblith and W. Allinsmith. Boston: Allyn & Bacon.
Fuller, E. Q.
1876 *An appeal to the records: A vindication of the Methodist Episcopal Church in it's policy and proceedings toward the South.* Cincinnati, OH: Hitchcock and Walden.
Gallup, J. G.
1991 *The Gallup poll: Public opinion 1990.* Wilmington, DE: Scholarly Resources.
Gorsuch, R. L.
1984 Measurement: The boon and bane of investigating religion. *American Psychologist* 39:228-236.
Gorsuch, R. L., and D. Aleshire
1974 Christian Faith and ethnic prejudice: A review and interpretation of research. *Journal for the Scientific Study of Religion* 13:281-307.
Greeley, A. M.
1975 *The sociology of the paranormal: A reconnaissance.* Sage Research papers in the Social Sciences, Vol. 3, series No. 90-023 (Studies in Religion and Ethnicity Series). Beverly Hills, CA: Sage.
Greven, P.
1991 *Spare the child: The religious roots of punishment and the psychological impact of physical abuse.* New York: Knopf.
Hall, G.
1904 *Adolescence: Its psychology and its relations to physiology, anthropology, sociology, sex, crime, religion, and education,* 2 vols. New York: Appleton.
Hartz, G., and H. C. Everett
1989 Fundamentalist religion and its effect on mental health. *Journal on Religion and Health* 28:207-217.
Hoffman, M. S. (Ed.)
1992 *World Almanac and Book of Facts,* 1993. Mahwah, NJ: Pharos Books.
Hood, D. R., and J. W. Carroll
1973 Religiosity and prejudice in northern and southern churches. *Journal for the Scientific Study of Religion* 12:181-187.
Hood Jr., R. W.
1970 Religious orientation and the report of religious experience. *Journal for the Scientific Study of Religion* 9:285-291.
1971 A comparison of the Allport and Feagin Scoring Procedures for Intrinsic/Extrinsic Religious Orientation. *Journal for the Scientific Study of Religion* 10:370-374.
1973 Religious orientation and the experience of transcendence. *Journal for the Scientific Study of Religion* 12:441-448.

1975 The construction and preliminary validation of a measure of reported mystical experience. *Journal for the Scientific Study of Religion* 14:29-41.

1978 The usefulness of the indiscriminately pro and anti categories of religious orientation. *Journal for the Scientific Study of Religion* 17:419-431.

Hunt, R. A., and M. B. King

1971 The intrinsic-extrinsic concept: A review and evaluation. *Journal for the Scientific Study of Religion* 10:339-356.

James, W.

[1902]

1961 *The varieties of religious experiences.* New York: Macmillan.

Johnson, P.

1977 *A history of Christianity.* Atheneum: New York.

Jordan, W.

1974 *The white man's burden.* London: Oxford University Press.

Jung, C.

1958 *Psychology and religion: West and East.* Translated by R. F. C. Hull. Bollingen Series XX. New York: Pantheon Books.

King, M.

1967 Measuring the religious variable: Nine proposed dimensions. *Journal for the Scientific Study of Religion* 6:173-190.

King, M. B., and R. A. Hunt

1969 Measuring the religious variable: Amended findings. *Journal for the Scientific Study of Religion* 8:321-323.

1972a Measuring the religious variable: Replication. *Journal for the Scientific Study of Religion* 1:240-251.

1972b *Measuring religious dimensions: Studies of congregational involvement.* Dallas: Southern Methodist University Press.

1975 Measuring the religious variable: National replication. *Journal for the Scientific Study of Religion* 14:13-22.

Lacan, J.

1968 *The language of the self.* Baltimore, MD: Johns Hopkins University Press.

Latourette, K. S.

1953 *History of Christianity.* New York: Harper & Bros.

Latourette, K. S.

1965 *Christianity through the ages.* New York: Harper & Row.

Lincoln, C., and L. H. Mamiya

1990 *The black church in the African-American experience.* Durham: Duke University Press.

Lindskoog, D., and R. E. Kirk

1975 Some life-history and attitudinal correlates of self-actualization among evangelical seminary students. *Journal for the Scientific Study of Religion* 14:51-55.

McDargh, J.

1983 *Psychoanalytic object relations theory and the study of religion.* Lanham, MD: University Press of America.

Marty, M.

1959 *A short history of Christianity.* New York: Meridian Books.

1970 *Righteous empire.* New York: Dial Press.

1987 *Religion and republic: The American circumstance.* Boston: Beacon Press.

Morrison, S. E.

1965 *The Oxford history of the American people.* New York: Oxford University Press.

Nelson, G. K.

1987 *Cults, new religions and religious creativity.* London: Routledge and Kegan Paul.

Pahnke, W. N.

1967 The mystical and/or religious element in the psychedelic experience. In *Do psychedelics have religious implications?,* edited by D. H. Salman and R. H. Prince, Montreal: R. M. Bucke Memorial Society.

Paloutzian, R.
1981 Purpose in life and value changes after conversion. *Journal of Personality and Social Psychology* 4:1153-1160.
Rausch, D., and C. H. Voss
1987 *Protestantism—Its modern meaning.* Philadelphia: Fortress.
Ray, J. J.
1979 Does authoritarianism of personality go with conservation? *Australian Journal of Psychology* 31:9-14.
Rokeach, M.
1969 Religious values and social compassion. *Review of Religious Research* 11:24-39.
1973 *The nature of human values.* New York: Free Press.
Sargent, W.
1957 *Battle for the mind.* London: Heineman.
Shaw, B. W.
1970 Religion and conceptual models of behaviour. *British Journal of Social and Clinical Psychology* 9:320-327.
Spilka, B., R. W. Hood Jr., and R. Gorsuch
1985 *The psychology of religion: An empirical approach.* Englewood Cliffs, NJ: Prentice-Hall.
Stace, W. T.
1960 *Mysticism and philosophy.* Philadelphia: Lippincott.
Starbuck, E. D.
1899 *The psychology of religion: An empirical study of the growth of religious consciousness.* New York: Scribner's.
Tate, E. D., and G. R. Miller
1971 Differences in values systems of persons with varying religious orientations. *Journal for the Scientific Study of Religion* 10:357-365.
Tillich, P.
1952 *The courage to be.* New Haven, CT: Yale University Press.
1957 *The Protestant era,* Translated by J. Adams. Chicago: University of Chicago Press.
Watson, P. J., R. Howard, R. W. Hood Jr., and R. J. Morris
1988 Age and religious orientation. *Review of Religious Research* 29:271-280.
Wilson, B.
1970 *Religious sects.* London: Weidenfeld and Nicholson.
Wimberly, R. C., T. C. Hood, C. M. Lipsey, D. Chelland, and M. Hay.
1975 Conversion in a Billy Graham Crusade: Spontaneous event or ritual performance. *The Sociological Quarterly* 16:162-170.
Winnicott, D. W.
1971 *Playing and reality.* London: Tavistock Publications.
Wood, F. G.
1990 *The arrogance of faith.* New York: Knopf.
Wulff, D. M.
1991 *Psychology of religion: Classic and contemporary views.* New York: Wiley.

4

Islam and Religious Experience

FOUAD MOUGHRABI

The Islamic experience in the modern world reconstitutes the relation between man and God on the basis of the fundamental authority of the Holy Quran. This is fundamentally a process of redefinition which involves a religious reformulation with far-reaching political implications. Unlike other monotheistic religions, Islam, at its core, makes no distinction between the spiritual and the temporal. It is at one and the same time a set of religious beliefs and dogmas as well as a pattern of behavior designed to order the relations between man and man and between man and the state. The original position in Islam consisted of the creation in Medina (the city of the Prophet) of a just order predicated on the word of God. One cannot therefore examine the Islamic religious experience without discussing it in its political and social context.

At the same time, the Islamic religious experience is a response to prevailing interpretations of the world. In the original position, Islam was in part a response to the polytheism of the tribes in the Arabian Peninsula and in part to Christianity and Judaism as they were practiced in the Near East. In the modern age, it is a response to modernism and its various manifestations in the West. From the beginnings of the nineteenth century, Islam has in fact been especially preoccupied with fashioning a response to the hegemonic power of the modernizing West and the intrusion into Muslim societies of Western and therefore alien modes of thinking and behavior.

This chapter will examine the Islamic experience in its attempts to confront modernism both as a *weltanschauung* and as a set of institutions represented by the apparatus of the modern state. The key argument here is that the modern Islamic revivalist movement in all of its parts in various Arab and Muslim countries constitutes primarily a process of rethinking and reorganization which is indigenous and in the process of evolution. For this reason, it is unlikely that we will find in the corpus of writings by Muslim activists in the current period a coherent and systematic critique of modernism or a highly developed new theory of public morality and justice. The question to be considered here is whether there is nevertheless enough there to give us an idea as to whether the current critique is serious enough to generate such theories in the future or whether it is simply all an ephemeral reaction to powerful influences from the outside.

Throughout the Muslim world there are sectarian differences as, for instance, in the case of Sunnis versus Shi'a. But the most important difference is between official Islam and the Islam of the new reformers. The former benefits from government approval—there are religious appointments and there is official government assistance. The news media propagate a version of official Islam. Friday sermons by religious authorities often endorse the ruling authorities and sing their praises. And then there is a more popular kind of Islam practiced by the masses of people who respond more enthusiastically to the sermons of charismatic religious authorities who advocate an oppositional kind of Islam. The following story illustrates the difference between the two and underscores the contradictions between them.

A picture of a new mosque, along with a story, appears in the *New York Times*: "'A new beacon of Islam,' reads the official description of the gargantuan new seafront mosque in Casablanca, Morocco, which dwarfed a solitary visitor who leaned against an enormous pillar."[1] The minaret, the highest in the world, rises more than 650 feet. At the top is a green laser beam which points the way to Mecca. The mosque sits on a promontory that juts into the Atlantic Ocean and contains fifty-four acres of traditional Moroccan marbles and mosaics as well as an eleven-hundred-ton roof that slides open to reveal the sky.

The mosque was designed by the French architect Michel Pinseau in close collaboration with the Moroccan monarch King Hassan II and took five years to complete. Work is still underway on the library, a vast underground garage, and an elaborate project designed to shift the flow of the city's sewage several miles down the coast in order to make sure that the waters washing against the mosque are pure. A national fund-raising drive has been mounted. Every morning the French language daily newspaper *Le Matin* carries the following headline on its front page: "Citizens, respond to the appeal of King Hassan II, the commander of the Faithful, the unifier, the savior, the assembler, and if you have not already done so, subscribe for the maintenance, upkeep, and management of the Hassan II Mosque."[2]

Official Moroccan government spokesmen say that the mosque is intended to present "an image of a Muslim country that is open, that is tolerant, that is cosmopolitan and that is modern." To underscore his modernizing intent, the King invited the Moroccan woman poet Amina Mrili to recite her verses at the inauguration ceremony, to the consternation of a predominantly conservative Muslim society. By most accounts, it appears that the inauguration ceremony, planned as an elaborate event, was in fact a colossal failure. Critics see the mosque as the work of a "supreme megalomaniac."[3]

As a symbol, this monument to political power contains some of the most basic contradictions that characterize Muslim societies in the modern world. The Hassan II mosque rises against the sky in the midst of a decaying and dilapidated urban sprawl in a way that detaches it from and sets it at odds with its immediate surroundings. By contrast, the great mosques in Cairo, Jerusalem, and Damascus emerge, almost logically, from the immediate social and architectural landscape. It is a natural thing for an individual, passing by, to want to go into one of these mosques for a brief moment of shelter and respite (Joseph, 1981:286). It is difficult to imagine anyone doing the same here.

A similar distinction applies to the meaning officially attributed to the mosque. It may be "open," "tolerant," "cosmopolitan," and "modern," but only in a specific and very limited way and in a particular direction. It is not open and tolerant as far as its citizens are concerned—in Morocco as elsewhere in the Arab world, Muslim opposition groups are dealt with very harshly by the state in total disregard of basic human rights and civil liberties. Openness and tolerance are directed toward the West, which the monarch, like other "modernizing" leaders in the Arab and Muslim worlds, tries to emulate. It is no accident that one of the first heads of state to be given a tour of the mosque was none other than Israeli Prime Minister Rabin, who still represents for most of Morocco's urban Muslim poor a country that is an enemy of Islam and of the Arabs.

King Hassan's version of Islam, similar to many others propagated by rulers in the Muslim world, is an "official" one, dictated more by the needs of political power than by the needs of the community of believers. This distinction is very important because it accentuates the difference between a discourse that embraces power and one that challenges it. In the great mosques throughout the Muslim world, and in the small neighborhood mosques, very few people pay much attention to the Friday sermons of preachers appointed by the state. By contrast thousands of the urban poor flock to hear the sermons of a few charismatic preachers who represent the dissident Muslim groups. Millions of cassettes of such sermons quickly circulate throughout the Muslim world and beyond.

In time, the King Hassan mosque may eventually become appropriated by common Muslims who may find in it shelter and peace. In Cairo, around the middle of the nineteenth century, Khedive Tawfiq's mother built the Rifai Mosque as a memorial to her power and celebrity. A very poor man in the area, known as Ahmad Abu Shibak, who had a saintly reputation, used to come to the mosque for prayer, meditation, and rest. In a few years, the mosque became known for the corner he occupied in it and people would go there to pray in order to be near him. In spite of the fact that five rulers of Egypt, in addition to the late Shah of Iran, are buried in that mosque, no one comes to visit their graves. In contrast, there are always candles lit where Ahmad is buried; most people come to pay their respects to him. In fact, the mosque has become known as the Rifai mosque after the name of the Sufi order to which Ahmad belonged.[4]

Throughout the Muslim world, a fierce contest is underway over the definition of society, the role of the individual, and the nature of the state. The contest pits secularists against Muslim reformers, embattled governments against increasingly militant oppositional groups which have adopted Islam as an overarching instrument of discourse and struggle.

The secularists claim that Muslim oppositional groups are attempting to seize power in order to establish theocratic tyrannies similar to the ones in place in Iran and in the Sudan. Their fear of such an eventuality has at times forced them to lend their support to governments which they have otherwise criticized as oppressive and unjust. Secularists accuse Muslim reformers of failing to provide a clear and convincing alternative to the present oppressive systems in power (Said, 1993). The reformers respond that only a return to the origins of the faith will halt the process of decay and disintegration now underway in the Muslim world. They argue that other methods such as nationalism, socialism, and capitalism have so far been unsuccessful. They maintain that a rejuvenated Islam will enable Muslim countries to gain the necessary power to become respected parts of the world community.

There is an immediacy and an urgency to the debate now underway in the Arab world which differs in a marked way from similar debates in the West between secularists and politicized religious groups. The difference derives, in part, from the weaknesses of the Arab regimes, their lack of legitimacy in the eyes of the majority of their publics, and the closeness of their alliance with and dependence upon the West. While it is far-fetched to think of religious fundamentalists seizing political power in the United States or in Europe, it is very possible that within a few years many of the key Arab governments could become Islamic republics.

Several Western "frames" of this debate have been suggested. The most common and perhaps most persistent is a media frame that places the issue under the rubric of "fundamentalism" qua terrorism and fanaticism. This negative frame relies mostly on stereotypical images of warring Muslims who engage in Holy Jihad (struggle) against the West. Occasionally, this frame is buttressed by academic interventions (Bernard Lewis, 1990, among others) that argue that a state of war exists between Islam and the West or, as in the case of Samuel Huntington (Huntington, 1993), that the contest is in reality a clash between two great civilizations.

A variant of this frame views religious fundamentalism as a kind of postmodernism in the Third World which encourages "a selective attention to the past and an eclectic reconstruction of the present" and arrives at an incoherent combination of the modern and the irrational. Pauline Rosenau (1992:152-155) quotes the following awkward, exaggerated, and erroneous caricature in Salman Rushdi's *Satanic Verses* to illustrate this point: "History the intoxicant, the creation and possession of the Devil, of the great Shaitan, the greatest of lies—progress, science, rights. . . . History is deviation from the Path, knowledge is a delusion, because the sum of knowledge was complete on the day Allah finished his revelation to Mahound. . . . Death to the Tyranny . . . of calendars, of America, of time! We seek the eternity, the timelessness of God. . . . Burn the books and trust the Book." It would be difficult to find anyone among so-called Muslim fundamentalists speaking in this manner. Muslims do not consider knowledge, even Western knowledge, a delusion; they venerate knowledge and admonish Muslims to seek it wherever it may be.

A more responsible frame has been produced by the American Academy Project which offers a more inclusive and less pejorative definition of fundamentalism. Marty and Appleby (1991) argue that "fundamentalists begin as traditionalists who perceive some challenge or threat to their core identity, both social and personal" and fight back with innovative power. They strive toward a "worldview which they have inherited or adopted and which they constantly reinforce" (pp. ix-x). Such movements reach back to "real or presumed pasts, to actual or imagined ideal original conditions and concepts" and select what they regard as fundamental. They fight against "generalized or specific enemies . . . from without or within the group" and under the banner of God.

Muslim reformers, activists, and militants nearly always say that theirs is a "movement," a "current" which is still in the process of gestation and evolution. They do not view themselves as having produced a coherent ideology with a blueprint and a set of comprehensive and concrete programs of action that govern social, economic, and political matters. Mannheim (1952) argues that a new biological generation, undergoing the impact of rapid social change, may create new collective impulses and formative principles original to itself. When this happens, says Mannheim, one will see the realization of potentialities inherent in the location and development of a new generational style or a new generation *entelechy*. In essence, what the new generation of Muslim reformers is trying to do is this: to draw from the past certain lessons or images that help them reinterpret the present and move toward the future. This is at one and the same time a restorationist and transformative view of history. It is definitely not the classic restorationist view that harks back to a golden era or a mythic ideal past and tries to reestablish this in its full glory.

What is it that modern Muslim activists wish to restore? In the first place, Muslims wish to restore the sovereignty of God in human affairs as opposed to the sovereignty of the "people" or the "state" or the "individual." Central to this objective is the belief in *tawhid*, which in mystical terms means unity with God, and in orthodox terms, proclaiming the unity of God. In the second place, Muslims wish to restore the centrality of the Quran as the Word of God. Here the charisma of the text stands opposed to the dictates of reason and tradition: "A person is not a Muslim who does not depend on the Quran and the Holy Prophet's Sunnah (sayings and deeds), but carries out the dictates of his own mind or follows the practices descending from his forefathers, or who conforms to what is happening in the world without caring to ascertain from the Quran and the Sunnah as to how to handle his affairs" (Maududi, 1980:21) In the third place, Muslim activists wish to restore patterns of behavior that are predicated on basic Islamic principles, duties, and obligations: as vice regent of God on earth, man is under obligation to learn how to take care of three crucial aspects of his being—his body, the members of his household, and members of society. To service all of these links properly a person must acquire basic knowledge of the principles of the faith. One cannot find this knowledge in one's own self (*Nafs*) which only contains corporal urges and may lead a person to drink wine, commit adultery, and be unjust to others. Neither should one rely on the advice of others who may be oppressive and use other people for selfish purposes.

The duties of every Muslim are enshrined in a set of obligations that govern every aspect of a person's life and are predicated on the following pillars: daily prayer (*Salah*) which is performed five times a day following cleaning of the body (*Wudu*-ablution); fasting during the month of Ramadan; *Zakat*, which literally means purity and cleanliness and consists of setting aside a portion of one's wealth to be given to the needy and the poor (considered a way to purify one's *Nafs*); and finally, *Hajj* or pilgrimage to Mecca at least once in one's lifetime.

These rituals are supposed to prepare the individual for a larger and more important task, namely Jihad. Here is how Maududi describes it: "It would be enough to state that the real objective of Islam is to remove the lordship of man over man and to establish the kingdom of God on Earth. To stake one's life and everything else to achieve this purpose is called *Jihad* while *Salah*, fasting, *Hajj* and *Zakat* are all meant as preparatory for this task "(Maududi, 1980:243). For most Muslim scholars, bad government—which means unjust government—is the root of all evil in the world. Here it must be noted that there are governments which do not rest upon the sovereignty of God but which are still just, and others which are Muslim and unjust. The critical difference lies in adherence to God's edicts in order to ensure justice for all. A just government is a strong one, one which will prevail over a Muslim government which is unjust. Jihad therefore becomes synonymous with the struggle for justice.

In Islam, there are four major schools of thought—Hanafite, Malikite, Shafiite, and Hanbalite—and a number of variations in the interpretation of basic texts. One approach, *Ijtihad*, which literally means individual interpretations on the basic tenets of the faith, is encouraged by the prophet himself. He showed his followers the necessity of *Ijtihad*. In one story, he ordered some of his followers to hurry to a specific town in order to carry out a particular task and ordered them not to pray the evening prayer until they got there. Because of some delays, the time for the evening prayer came while they were still on their way. Some of them decided to stop and pray at the regularly appointed hour while others, following the order of their leader, waited until they reached their destination. Upon their return, they asked the prophet for his opinion. He agreed with both sides, thereby endorsing private initiative even in such important matters (Gannoushi, 1982:34-35).

In an attempt to respond to rapid social change in their societies, Muslim reformers have tried to reaffirm the charismatic structure of the Quran and the Sunna. Despite several decades of secularizing tendencies, governments in Muslim societies have failed to partition the social and cultural space in a way that leaves a limited area for the religious sphere. The various governments tried to use the powerful instruments of modernization and its institutions as a way to counter the influence of religious rivals. They tried to coopt Islamic symbols as a way of gaining legitimacy for themselves in the eyes of their publics. When this strategy failed, they resorted to outright repression (as is the case in Egypt, Algeria, and elsewhere).

Central to the debate between secularists and Muslims is the question of how to confront modernity and how to organize the political, social, cultural, and economic space in modern Muslim societies. The key argument here is that Muslim reform activities amount to a fundamental critique of modernity and its institutions. This critique is in the process of formation and has not yet yielded major results at the levels of normative theory. It is therefore too early to make a sweeping assessment of this current. All that can be done at the moment is to take stock of what has been done so far by sketching out a basic outline of its main themes in order to see the direction in which developments appear to be heading.

Rashed Gannoushi, the leader of religious revivalism in Tunisia and one of the leading theorists of the contemporary Islamic revival, argues that we are now witnessing the end of the era of modernism in the West. He refers to it as the era of "rebellion against God" (Gannoushi, 1982:173) which brought about the "disasters of colonialism and wars, widespread famine, sexual diseases, serious economic and psychological problems, and rampant consumerism that destroyed the environment." For Gannoushi, modernism originated in Europe following a series of revolutions that began with the French (1789) and ended with the Bolshevik (1917). Modernism strangled the natural and instinctual dispositions of the individual toward God, religion, the family and public morality and glorified reason, science and progress.

In opposition to this era of *Jahiliya* (ignorance and darkness), Gannoushi suggests a new era predicated on the recognition of human instinct, the unity of the spiritual and the temporal, and the centrality of man's existence as God's vice regent on earth. Man, for him, is a religious being. He has no natural rights that he derives from himself or from others. Instead, there are rights and obligations which derive from the grace that God bestows upon the person.

Gannoushi's journey of discovery, or what he calls his journey of migration back to the self, provides an important setting for his critique of modernism and its manifestations in the Arab world. "I saw the light," he says, "in an oasis on the edge of the Sahara in the southern part of Tunisia, whose people were known as rebels and warlike" (Gannoushi, 1992:174). He was born in 1941, a period during which his hometown was caught in the middle of the Second World War that was raging between "competing Western forces." Years later, he says, this peaceful oasis became an arena of conflict between the French colonial army and the first Tunisian armed rebellion. The French army was able, after a number of atrocities and local acts of treason, to capture the soldier who had led the uprising and to execute him in the village square. The martyrdom of this soldier eventually led to another uprising in the 1950s carried out by a religious figure who became the founder of armed Islamic resistance (Jihad) against French colonialism. Here Gannoushi relates a scene that he "could never forget (as if carved in stone in my soul)" where the French soldiers dumped the bodies of dead Mujahidin (fighters) in the village square and forced the men, women, and children to walk by to look at them. The rebellion spread throughout the countryside to the point where the nationalist (secular) leadership represented by Bourguiba began to worry about its rising influence. Eventually, the nationalists won the battle and achieved independence by making their own deals with the French. The betrayal of the forces of Islamic resistance by the secular nationalist forces thus became a central point of conflict between the two groups not only in Tunisia but throughout the various countries in North Africa and elsewhere in the Arab world. Decolonization therefore meant the ascendancy of the seculars with the help of the former colonial masters and the temporary suppression of Islamic groups that formed the core of popular resistance to colonialism.

The theme of betrayal is commonly held among Muslim reformers and oppositional groups. Several historical instances illustrate its persistence throughout the Arab world. A recent example of this phenomenon is the ascendancy of the Palestine Liberation Organization as a result of the signing of the peace accords in Washington D.C. on September 13, 1993. Yasser Arafat's Fatah group has consolidated its position with the help of the Israeli government. Both the PLO and Israel have reached the conclusion that they confront the same enemy, namely, Islamic fundamentalism in the occupied territories. Muslim Palestinian dissidents are hunted down by the Israeli authorities with the assistance of the PLO.

Gannoushi's journey takes him to the Levant (Syria and Egypt) where he joins the ranks of Nasser's Arab socialist Union. He is severely disappointed as he discovers that the Arabism (nationalism) in vogue (represented by Nasserism in Egypt and the Ba'th Party in Syria) at the time is simply not "authentic" enough and fails to represent the deepest aspirations of the majority of the people.

Gannoushi departs for France in 1968 in order to pursue higher education in Paris. Here he experiences "the difficulties of life, its mad pace, its individualism, materialism, and hypocrisy" (Gannoushi, 1992:178). He finds "in this hell some peace and shelter from the tempests that pursued me in a small oasis, a tiny mosque in a humble house in a poor working class neighborhood which some North African students helped establish." It becomes the nucleus of Islamic *Da'wah* (missionary activity). He learns "humility, service to others, religious witness, and austere living." He and his friends spread out among the Muslim student community and the poor workers teaching, arguing, and spreading the message of Islam: "We went to them in their poor quarters and their rotten bars and, in the Latin Quarter, we argued with students from all over the Muslim world, especially those from North Africa." He establishes friendships that become useful in later years. His stay in Paris is described as the "most difficult part of my life."

Upon completion of his studies, he returns to Tunisia through Spain "the lost paradise of Andalus" (in reference to the golden era of Islamic rule in Spain): "I passed through Cordoba and wept in its beautiful mosque." He returns to his oasis to "renew my struggle against Westernization which, by then, had become embodied in several generations of my people, in a state and institutions, in order to rediscover the Arabism of the oasis, of Islam and its message" Gannoushi, 1992:178-179).

Gannoushi's migration (*hijra*) may be described as a journey of discovery, a Conradian "journey within" in search of authenticity and of one's place in the universe, one's roots and identity. In the contemporary Arab world, as indeed throughout the Third World, there have been many such journeys involving troublesome and transforming encounters with modernism. A 1938 novel by the Egyptian author Tawfic Al-Hakim, *A Bird From the East*, describes the sentimental journey of a young Egyptian student who goes to Paris to study literature, carrying with him tales of platonic love and ideal romance. He falls in love with a beautiful Parisian girl, becomes the prisoner of a new set of strange values and customs, is betrayed and returns to Egypt where he learns to look more realistically at the drabness and sordidness around him. Another Egyptian novelist, Yahya Hakki, describes the journey of another Egyptian student in London in his book *The Lamp of Umm Hashim* (1944). His piety and simple morality are ridiculed in the West. He falls ill and suffers a nervous breakdown. Upon his return to Cairo, the protagonist looks with horror at his childhood world and in a fit of madness breaks Umm Hashim's holy lamp, a symbol for him (a man of science and reason) of fanaticism and backwardness. The setting for Soheil Idriss's novel, *The Latin Quarter*, is the Paris of the early 1950s where a group of Arab students seek higher education and socialize with the beautiful girls of the bohemian quarter. Following a sad love affair with one of them, the hero returns to Beirut where he rebels against his mother, his friends, and their customs. Eventually, the young man returns to Paris, finishes his doctorate in literature at the Sorbonne and comes back to Beirut to become a passionate advocate of Arab nationalism (Takieddine-Amyuni, 1980:1-18).

These novels describe simple themes of unhappy encounters with Westernism, of sexual liberation and freedom. None of them, however, offers a sophisticated analysis of the encounter with the West and upon returning the difficulties of encounter with tradition. A more complex treatment of such themes is undertaken by the Sudanese novelist Tayeb Salih in his *Season of Migration to the North* (Salih, 1978). The hero of this novel is the narrator who begins as a romantic young man, spends seven happy years in London and then returns to his village in the Sudan. There he discovers Mustapha Saeed (who had also spent several years in London) engulfed in what Frantz Fanon had called a "circle of Hell" (Fanon, 1969:68-74). The narrator goes through romance, tragedy, and reconciliation and finally emerges a fully mature man who is able to rise above grudges and hatreds to become aware of the insignificance of human differences in comparison to the historical flow of events.

Tayeb Salih's narrator is the prototype of the modern Arab who comes to terms with modernity, its anxiety and its promise, by forging an identity in the midst of rapid social and political change. God is absent from the narrator's life and so are the transcendental values associated with rituals and festivals. Feelings of the absurd and of radical doubt permeate the novel. On his journey of self discovery, the narrator experiences and overcomes three major crises: upon his return to his village, he discovers an identity based on family, tribe, loving parents, brothers and sisters, and a grandfather who links him to the past. He does not reject this past completely. For him, the village represents stability and constancy in the midst of change, a place of purity because it has not been touched by foreign intruders. In the second, he is able to achieve love (and trust) by resolving what Erikson (1969) calls the crisis of intimacy. In the third, he is exposed to the germs of violence and oppression spread by Saeed, overcomes the temptation and rises above all of this to a new feeling of hope. In the end, the author depicts the following affirmation of an evolving identity:

> I must be one of those birds that exist only in one region of the world. . . . Over there is like here, neither better nor worse. But I am from here, just as the date palm standing in the courtyard of our house has grown in our house and not in anyone else's. The fact they came to our land, I know not why, does that mean that we should poison our present and our future? Sooner or later they will leave our country just as many people throughout history have left many countries. The railways, ships, factories, and schools will be ours and we'll speak their language without either a sense of guilt or a sense of gratitude. Once again we shall be as we were—ordinary people—and if we are lies we shall be lies of our own making (Salih, 1978:49-50).

Tayeb Salih's narrator discovers his ordinariness in his search for authenticity and opts for what Giddens (1991:214) calls "life politics" which ultimately concerns "political issues which flow from processes of self-actualization in post-traditional contexts, where globalizing influences intrude deeply into the reflexive project of the self." Life politics, in this case, deal with questions of how one should live in a post-traditional order and against a backdrop of existential questions. Gannoushi's journey, on the other hand, is a project of "emancipatory politics" which Giddens defines as a "generic outlook concerned above all with liberating individuals and groups from constraints which adversely affect their life chances" (Giddens, 1991: 210-211). Emancipatory politics involves two main elements: "the effort to shed shackles of the past, thereby permitting a transformative attitude toward the future; and the aim of overcoming the illegitimate domination of some individuals or groups by others" (Giddens, 1991:211). Emancipatory politics is concerned, above all, with themes of justice, equality, and participation, the very same themes that most Muslim reformers are in fact concerned with.

A recent example of scholarship which examines the Muslim phenomenon as an instance of emancipatory politics is Abrahamian's excellent analysis of Khomeinism in the Islamic Republic of Iran. "Khomeinism," he concludes, "despite its religious dimension, in many ways [it] resembles Latin American populism . . . a middle-class movement that mobilized the masses with radical sounding rhetoric against the external powers and the entrenched power-holding classes" (Abrahamian, 1993:37-38). These movements had "vague aspirations and no precise programs." They were more interested in "changing cultural and educational institutions than in overthrowing the modes of production and distribution" (Abrahamian, 1993:38).

For Giddens, modernity consists of institutions and modes of behavior which by the middle of the twentieth century have become world-historical in their impact. Its key dimensions include industrialism, capitalism, and the institutions of surveillance which are associated with the rise of the modern nation-state (Giddens, 1990).

In the contemporary Middle East, new states have emerged in the post-World War II period and gradually have become linked in varying degrees to the rise of industrialism and capitalism in the modern world. These new states were confronted with a number of crises that posed a variety of issues, among which are the question of legitimacy, decolonization, democracy, development, distribution of resources, and integration (Ahmad, 1980; 1980a; 1981). The elites which came to power in these states emerged as "modern, educated, managerial elites isolated from the productive process, alienated from their culture, and, in the face of continued dependency on external know-how and capital, unable to expand into a productive national bourgeoisie." This "power elite" in the Muslim countries concentrated its efforts on developing the mechanisms of surveillance by relying on modern bureaucratic methods of control in the context of a national-security apparatus.

The economic models implemented in these countries superimposed upon traditional societies a capitalist economy unaccompanied by capitalist culture or capitalist democracy and produced a system at odds with the cultural and political institutions of the people it exploits. This meant that large segments of the population were, for all practical purposes, excluded from the process of economic development. They were, nonetheless, subject to the rigors of the new mechanisms of surveillance, social control, and dehumanization.

How does this system of surveillance filter down to the masses and shape everyday life? New practices begin to orient social relations in the areas of modern education, organized religion, and government expertise; it is all done through elaborate bureaucracies and official ideologies. These practices produce an effect of structure, meaning and program that is far removed from the daily life of the people and has no immediate relevance to their lives. But it displaces village entertainments, small feasts, games, religious events, visits to the tombs of holy men, and other locally produced forms of imaginative life (Mitchell, 1990).

The most important effect of these official practices is that they tend to shift the locus of control over the production of symbols, so much a part of the daily life in a Muslim society, to a far away place (the national capital). The process of generating such "enframing" mechanisms and symbols is appropriated by the organs of the modern state such as the television authority, the national radio, and the Ministry of Information among many others. By and large, the new symbols appear to be alien to local people and far removed from the daily concerns and ways of life.

Yet, even though the grid of modern surveillance penetrates deep into every corner of life in the modern Middle East, society as a whole is never completely dominated by it. A variety of "miniscule," "popular" procedures serve to undermine the ubiquitous mechanisms of control. Women, for instance, wear the modest dress that covers most of the body and the head as a way of subscribing to a new pattern of Islamic behavior and as a form of resistance to dominant Western patterns of dress. Muslim attire becomes an affirmation of an identity and a rejection of Western habits. For many young men, wearing a beard becomes a similar symbol. This is part of what Kepel (1984), in his analysis of modern Egypt, calls "popular forms of resistance to oppression" that have flourished in Egypt in a "welter of forms of expression ranging from what Michel Certeau has called 'ways of getting by' to more elaborate forms of communalism like the Sufi brotherhoods" (Kepel, 1984:232).

These popular forms of resistance occur because people do have a limited margin of autonomy in areas which are immune to control by the institutions of legal political life. Mosques in poor urban neighborhoods and various religious organizations and charities often constitute the web of such resistance activities. Sometimes, more elaborate forms of resistance to oppression begin to emerge in the form of religious reform movements.

Some of them might include a militant wing that carries out para-military activities and some may simply rely on political agitation and mobilization. In nearly all cases, these forms of resistance involve a similar psychological trajectory: a process of emigration (*hijra*) from an alienated society followed by rebellion against it.

In Islamic history, the first and most important migration (*hijra*) was of course that of the prophet and his followers who escaped oppressive Mecca to Medina. Here, the prophet established the nucleus of the Muslim polity with a constitutional charter and a system of government. For Shukri Mustapha, for example, one of the leaders of Islamic fundamentalism in Egypt, *hijra* is first and foremost an act of withdrawal (spiritual and physical) from *jahiliya* society (the society that does not recognize God). In the heart of Cairo's poor suburbs, he and his followers tried to create, in tiny furnished flats, a genuinely Islamic society of their own, based on their understanding of Islam (Kepel 1984:89). For others, like the Tunisian Gannoushi, it meant *hijra* first to the Levant and then to exile in Europe. For others still, it means internal exile in the prisons of the various Arab countries. Prisons, in the Middle East, are commonly referred to as the best schools or universities of political training. This is where many Muslim activists end up receiving their basic religious education and undergo their conversion to the new Islam. If they enter prison with nothing but the rudiments of religious or political education, they will often exit as accomplished militants and effective activists.

In an attempt to defuse criticism by militant Islamic groups, the Egyptian government recently selected a poor neighborhood in which to build new low-income housing, repair sewers, pave roads, and bring in electricity and running water. The benefits of development, so long denied, have thus belatedly found their way to some of the poor. These symbolic gestures by the state are juxtaposed to self-help efforts by Islamic groups who consistently feed the poor, educate their children, provide them with basic health care, and come to their aid following a recent earthquake. In the process, Islamic groups established parallel structures which provide the kind of assistance that the modern state has given only to the privileged.

One may conclude that there is indeed an alternate Islamic religious and moral experience which differs markedly from the official experience generated by the various governments that came into being in the post-World War II period. In its broad outlines, it represents a fundamental act of rebellion against alienating experiences that result from the inclusion of the Arab world into a global system dominated by modernism and its institutions. As such, this rebellion removes large masses of people from the market of modern consumption and poses serious challenges to the modern apparatus of control and surveillance.

At its core, the new Islamic experience involves a redefinition of identity in a world which has become homogenized by the globalizing processes of modernism. It is, at the same time, an assertion of the need to respect diversity in the cultural and social spheres of life and a call for more active participation in the political sphere. The Islamic experience is therefore a call for an emancipatory politics which means justice where there is none, a more egalitarian distribution of wealth, and a more democratic system of decision making.

The theoretical work remains to be done: nowhere in the contemporary Islamic literature does one find, for example, a formulation similar to John Rawls' theory of justice or even an awareness of the rich political and philosophical critiques now being formulated in the West by major thinkers whose work represents a reformulation of the core of modernism. At the same time, major efforts need to be made to redefine social relations in a way that meets the basic criteria of democracy in an Islamic society: What are the basic guarantees of human rights and civil liberties? What guarantees are there for minorities? What is the role of women in a Muslim society?

The status of women appears to be much on the minds of the leading theoreticians of the new Islamic movement. The Sudanese scholar-political activist Hassan Turabi (1992), for example, suggests that the status of women must be redefined in a way that guarantees full equality for women in all areas of public life. He makes a distinction between "historical Islam" where certain erroneous practices have intruded into the behavior of Muslims and "real Islam" which does not sanction the oppression of women. It remains to be seen what new formulations are made and how they are implemented. Given the fact that the majority of the new activists are highly educated men and women, it is unlikely that the prevailing oppressive conditions which have characterized the status of women in Muslim societies will continue to exist. Change is much more likely to occur among the new Muslim activists and not in the more traditional societies in the Arab world (such as the more oppressive countries of the Gulf, Saudi Arabia, Kuwait, and others).

Whether the new Islamic movements eventually achieve political and cultural hegemony in the Arab world cannot be predicted. However, the social, political, economic, and cultural landscapes in the contemporary Arab world will undoubtedly be altered as a result of their emergence. So one should not be too quick to dismiss them as ephemeral ideological eruptions which are likely to be superseded or coopted by the more awesome power of the modern state.

NOTES AND REFERENCES

1. *New York Times*, 5 October 1993.
2. *New York Times*, 5 October 1993.

3. *New York Times,* 5 October 1993.
4. For this story I am indebted to Edward Said who included it in a text some of which appeared in the *Sunday New York Times Magazine*, 21 November 1993.

Abrahamian, E.
1993 *Khomeinism.* Berkeley, CA: University of California Press.

Ahmad, E.
1980 From potato sack to potato mash: The contemporary crisis of the third world. *Arab Studies Quarterly* 2:223-234.
1980a Postcolonial systems of power. *Arab Studies Quarterly* 2:350-363.
1981 The neo-fascist state: Notes on the pathology of power in the third world. *Arab Studies Quarterly* 3:170-180.

Erikson, E.
1969 *Childhood and society.* New York: Norton.

Fanon, F.
1969 *The wretched of the earth.* New York: Penguin.

Gannoushi, R.
1991 Interview. *Qira'at Siyasiyyah* (in Arabic) 1:5-40.
1992 Interview with Rashed Gannoushi. *Qira'at Siyasiyyah* (in Arabic) 2:157-184.

Giddens, A.
1991 *Modernity and self-identity.* Stanford, CA: Stanford University Press.
1990 *The consequences of modernity.* Cambridge: Polity.

Huntington, S.
1993 The clash of civilizations. *Foreign Affairs* 72:22-49.

Joseph, R.
1981 Semiotics of the Islamic mosque. *Arab Studies Quarterly* 3:275-285.

Kepel, G.
1984 *Muslim extremism in Egypt.* Berkeley, CA: University of California Press.

Lewis, B.
1990 The roots of Muslim rage. *The Atlantic Monthly.* September 47-54.

Mannheim, K.
1952 *Essays on the sociology of knowledge.* London: Routledge and Kegan Paul.

Marty, M., and S. Appleby (Eds.)
1991 *Fundamentalisms observed.* Chicago: University of Chicago Press.

Maududi, A. A'La
1980 *Fundamentals of Islam.* Lahore, Pakistan: Islamic Publications.

Mitchell, T.
1990 Everyday metaphors of power. *Theory and Society* 19:545-577.

Rosenau, P.
1992 *Post-modernism and the social sciences.* Princeton, NJ: Princeton University Press.

Said, E.
1993 The phony Islamic threat. *New York Times Magazine* November 62-65.

Salih, T.
1978 *Season of migration to the north.* London: Heinemann.

Takieddine-Amyuni, M.
1980 Tayeb Salih's "Season of migration to the north." *Arab Studies Quarterly* 2:1-18.

Turabi, H.
1992 Interview with Dr. Hassaan Turabi. *Qira'at Siyasiyyah* (in Arabic) 3:5-32.

5

Buddhism and Religious Experience

GUI-YOUNG HONG

INTRODUCTION

Understanding Buddhism and Buddhist experiences from the perspective of psychology is indeed not at all a simple task given the dearth of psychological literature on empirical studies of Buddhism, let alone Buddhism experienced by people in different cultures (see DeMartino, Fromm, and Suzuki, 1960; Govinda, 1961; Guenther, 1974; Johansson, 1969; Kalupahana, 1987 for psychologically oriented studies on Buddhism). It is particularly difficult to present a global, generalized picture of Buddhism because of the diversity of Buddhist doctrines and sects which have arisen over the past twenty-five hundred years in various regions of Asia. The lack of centralized authorities such as are institutionalized in the Roman Catholic pope or the Archbishop of Canterbury has implicitly facilitated its rooting in different sociocultural contexts and the development of divergent forms and doctrines. Buddhism in various countries has undergone transformations through interactions of the fundamental tenets of the belief system with local communities' preexisting sociocultural, historical conditions. Throughout the transformation processes, Buddhism has maintained its normative unity of fundamental morality and its ultimate goal of salvation (e.g., Conze, 1980; Spiro, 1970; Suzuki, 1959; Williams, 1989). For this reason, Buddhism is often described as a "religion" of diversity in doctrines and unity in morality (cf. Williams, 1989). The history of Buddhism is indeed a powerful demonstration of the interaction between a Buddhist normative tradition and the lives of individual Buddhists who may be understood as "context-bound" active social agents. The variability in forms of Buddhism speaks for the unlimited range of human plasticity; while its unity simultaneously proposes a boundary on its expression.

The problem of psychologically understanding Buddhism and Buddhist experiences entails at least three separate but highly interrelated problems: 1) the nature of Buddhism, 2) its relationships with individual Buddhists' experiences, and 3) methodological advances necessary to adequately explore the first two. This chapter will unfold presentations of the three problems along major themes of each problem. The first problem is addressed by presenting the history of Buddhism as well as Buddhist theoretical and practical doctrinal principles. The second problem is elaborated by positing Buddhist experiences in a specific sociocultural context. Finally, the last problem is discussed in terms of a need for a methodology which allows psychological research to examine Buddhist experiences within historical and sociocultural contexts.

For the first problem, the field needs to address an ontological question: "What is Buddhism?" By emphasizing the unique characteristics of Buddhism, the ontological problem should address symbiotic aspects of Buddhism: Buddhism as a "religion of the texts" on one hand and as a "religion of the people" on the other hand (Spiro, 1970). With a particular emphasis on the religion of the texts, the ontological question of Buddhism has put a heavy weight on normative Buddhist doctrines. Normative Buddhist doctrines have been considered as universal and therefore separate from the world in which they are embedded. The influence of Buddhist doctrines on people and societies occupying that world are seen as unidirectional *from* Buddhism *to* individual or society (e.g., Weber, 1958). The majority of social-scientific studies of Buddhism and other religions share this acontextual approach by equating the religion of the texts with the religion of the people (e.g., Durkheim, 1954; Freud, 1913/1953; Malinowski, 1948; Weber, 1963).

Emphasizing the religion of the people, on the other hand, the ontological question is examined from a reversed perspective. It is directed toward understanding how sociocultural contexts modify beliefs and practices in Buddhism. Paraphrasing Spiro (1970), individual Buddhists' experiences within their own society affect their degree of acceptance, rejection, or transformation of the normative Buddhist doctrines. In his intensive studies of Buddhism in Burmese society, Spiro demonstrated how the Burmese transformation of normative "nibbanic Buddhism (Old Buddhism)" resulted in the "kammatic Buddhism" sect which differs drastically from the normative form of Buddhism from which it arose. Since this contextual approach is still marginal in psychological and other social-scientific research on Buddhism, it will be presented in a separate section later.

Buddhism like all other religions is not solely a product of contemporary Buddhists or Buddhist communities. It is rooted in a lengthy, ongoing sequence of historical changes intermeshing the religion and its associated system of beliefs and practices in dynamic, bidirectional relationships. Thus, the ontological question requires examining the history of Buddhism and the transformation made by Buddhists in their sociocultural contexts.

The second problem of individual Buddhists' experiences needs to be approached with a question, "What and how do individual Buddhists experience in their practice of their faith?" Compared to the first problem, experiential issues have been deemed more "relevant" to the psychology of Buddhism in the past and have resulted in small line of scholarly works (e.g., Spiro, 1970). This question could be further differentiated from various angles: namely, "Whose point of view?" Knowing and understanding Buddhism and Buddhist experience from the perspectives of (academic) scholars who study Buddhism must be quite different from understanding it from the perspectives of those who actually live with Buddhist doctrines and practices. Certainly, an intellectual community's approach to Buddhist theories, doctrines, and institutions is valuable and necessary, but no less valuable are the experiences of individual followers with their everyday mental and physical practices and activities. The majority of psychological explorations of individual Buddhists' experiences have, however, been carried out from universalistic perspectives ignoring the diverse contexts in which individual Buddhists live (e.g., Faber, 1988; Fauteux, 1987; Fenner, 1987; Fontana, 1987; MacPhillamy, 1985; Page and Berkow, 1991). The psychology of Buddhism does not deny universality, but it must resist equating notions of universality with uniformity and endorsing the notion of sameness across contexts and levels of analysis. Thus, the second issue of individual experience requires sensitivity to contextual influences and the interrelation of texts and contexts (e.g., Htin Aung, 1962).

Examining the first two issues entails a methodological question, "How do psychologists understand Buddhism and Buddhist experience?" To date, the psychological understanding of religion, in general, and Buddhism, in particular, have been largely dominated by psychoanalytic and humanistic approaches operating under uniformity-universality assumptions (e.g., Cernovsky, 1988; Epstein, 1990; Suler, 1990; Welwood, 1986; see also Geertz, 1966; Shweder, 1990; Spiro, 1966 for related arguments). Accepting the validity of contemporary metatheoretical arguments on the context-dependent nature of human psychological functioning (Fiske and Shweder, 1986; Jahoda, 1993; McGuire, 1973), current "context-independent" methodologies must be reconsidered. Considering that Buddhist doctrines and institutions have undergone a continuous process of change and transformation, placing Buddhism within various historical contexts is necessary to understand its nature.

BUDDHISM IN HISTORICAL CONTEXTS

Like any other religion, Buddhism, "a religion of salvation," was born in a specific historical context.[1] When Siddhartha Gautama "rediscovered" the Four Noble Truths—the Truth of Suffering, the Truth of Cause, the Truth of Extinction, and the Truth of the Path—about twenty-five hundred years ago, the Vedic tradition was already deeply ingrained in every aspect of Indian mind and day-to-day activity through their beliefs in *samsara* and *karma.* Since the Indus civilization was conquered by Aryan invasions around 2000 B.C., the Veda civilization was developed and from the Vedas, the Caste system was created. Briefly speaking, the Vedas are literature as well as religion. The last part of the Vedas is called Upanisad or Vedanta (literally means the end of the Vedas). Within the Upanisadic philosophy, *Brahman* ("The Ultimate Reality") is posited as the highest principle of universal uniformity. The ultimate goal of life is to transform *Atman* ("the individual self") to *Brahman* ("the universal self"). As a way of achieving the ultimate goal, meditation was developed. According to the description in the *Rig-Veda*, one of the four Vedic hymns of India, the four castes were drawn from *Purusha,* an aborigine (parallel to the archetypal man in Jungian psychology). The *Brahman* caste came from his head, the *Kshatriyas* from his arms, the *Vaisyas* from his thighs, and the *Sudras* (the untouchable) from his feet. The functions and rights of each caste were strictly demarcated in a vertical hierarchy and intercaste social relationships were disallowed. It is speculated that the caste system was devised by the Aryans (Indo-Aryans) in order to differentiate themselves from the indigenous people in the Indian peninsula (Edwards, 1961).

Within these historical and sociocultural contexts, Siddhartha Gautama (c.563-c.483 B.C.), also referred as Sakyamuni, "a sage of the Sakya clan," was born as a prince to Suddhodana, a king of Sakyas, and his wife, madam Maya. The Sakyas were a Mongolian clan, a minority group of agriculturists who held the cow as their totem (Kim, 1993). Gautama born as a Kshatriyas carried out *pravrajana* (leaving home, banishment) when he was twenty-nine and became the Buddha at the age of thirty-five by attaining *bodhi* (enlightenment) after six years of meditation. As the Buddha, he preached salvation, the ultimate goal of Buddhists. Salvation refers to being free from *samsara*, the continuous cycle of the rebirth wheel. What the Buddha delivered was radically different from either teachings of the Upanisads or the Hindus. Specifically, from the beginning and throughout, the Buddha's teaching emphasized the equality of all human beings. He emphasized that a human is not "born" as a caste but "makes oneself" as a caste through one's own acts. Thus, doctrinally, the spiritual route of Buddhism was open to people from all the different social strata, even the untouchables and females. In fact, the majority of the Buddha's followers at that time were young intellectual males from high socioeconomic strata. Here, the old Buddhism faced its unintended or unconscious schism between its doctrinal principles and actual practices due to its contextual boundary even though no one from lower classes and females was rejected by the old Buddhism. After the Buddha's entering *nirvana*, the institutional hierarchy in Buddhism has not always been egalitarian, especially in terms of gender (Barnes, 1987; Cabezon, 1992).

Despite denying a predetermined caste at one's birth, the Buddha did not totally abandon the Upanisadic or the Hindu concepts of *samsara* and the *karma*. Rather, the Buddha still maintained the ideas of *samsara* and *karma*, but suggested that the chain of *karma* can be cut off only by one's own intentions and acts. The Buddha's teachings always included new concepts developed or discovered from existing Upanisadic or Hinduist concepts by transforming them.

In the past twenty-five hundred years since the Buddha's death, Buddhism has spread far beyond the borders of ancient India and the sociocultural conditions in which it originated. As Buddhism spread and developed, its doctrines and practices branched into four major sects, all of which continue through the present. These sects and the approximate times at which they arose are: Old Buddhism (the Buddha's lifetime), Hinayana Buddhism (about B.C. 280, approximately one hundred years after the Buddha entered *nirvana*), Mahayana Buddhism (circa 0 A.D.), and Ch'an Buddhism (about 500 A.D.). As Buddhism spread beyond India, its doctrines, philosophy, soteriology, and practices were locally transformed wherever it took root. The practices of Tibetan, Burmese, Chinese, Japanese, and Korean Buddhism, for example, all differ, yet they too remain quite similar (see Ch'en, 1973; Eliot, 1969; Overmyer, 1976; Gombrich and Obeyesekere, 1988; Goodman and Davidson, 1992; Kim, 1993; Spiro, 1970 for transformed Buddhism in different parts of Asia).

When a religion is imported to a society, it is inevitable that the religion settles into the local community through repeated cycles of assimilation and accommodation to already existing "local knowledge" (Geertz, 1973). Understanding Buddhist experiences must be preceded by understanding the history of Buddhism, in general, and the local history of Buddhism in a particular region in a particular country, in specific (Conze, 1980; Kalupahana, 1976). Because there exists so little consensus on how Buddhism should be divided into historical epochs, I will discuss the four major branches of Buddhism in order of their appearance. Bear in mind, however, that all four branches are actively practiced today and that no static perspective captures the full richness of diversity accompanying Buddhism's spread and development.

Old Buddhism was spread mainly within India through small groups led by the Buddha's ten disciples. Old Buddhism started with three distinct characteristics—openness, egalitarianism, and unity. Its openness overcame the tradition of the Upanisadic philosophy, its egalitarianism rejected the Brahman society's caste system, and its unity emphasized group solidarity. With these three characteristics, Old Buddhism intended to be universal in overcoming ideologies, social strata, regions, and sects. The Buddha's teachings placed an emphasis on the embodiment of doctrines while searching for the ultimate reality, rather than adherence to specified forms of commandments and action. The most distinct doctrinal foundations of the first period are salvation and the three Jewels (Treasures)—the Buddha, the Dharma (the Law, the Buddhist faith), and the Samgha (the community of believers). The Buddha also taught his followers that the Law exists both within and outside us, implying a rejection of any dichotomized distinctions. Before dying, the Buddha told Ananda, one of his ten great disciples, "make the self your light, make the Law your light" (Niwano, 1975:204). The Buddha's statement implies that people should seek salvation depending solely on themselves not through other people or any other media. Ordinary followers, however, were not ready to comprehend the depth of the Buddha's teaching. After the Buddha entered *nirvana* without appointing a successor, the Buddhist community began to lose its unity and fragmented into various sects. Each sect transformed the Old Buddhist doctrines and developed its own traditions and religious precepts. During this period, Hinayana Buddhism is recognized as the dominant descendant of old Buddhism.

The central questions in Hinayana Buddhism regard how one gains self control over one's own mind. The ideal person in Hinayana Buddhism is, therefore, an *Arhat* who is free from the illusion of attachment. However, a multitude of pointless disputes focusing on forms or styles of an event or behavior rather than its contents arose between sects and alienated many laypeople during this period. While "the True Samgha" (a small elite group of monks) of different sects were engaged in fruitful intellectual arguments with one another, laypeople were sincerely missing the Buddha's own words and visited Buddhist pagodas where the Budda's ashes were buried instead of visiting Buddhist temples and monks. These laypeople were eager to recapture the spirit of Buddhism through their own practices instead of dry theory, and through their own folk beliefs rather than philosophy. Overall, these lay movements reflected various passionate attempts to recover the Buddha's Buddhism with one's heart and body, not simply with one's head.

Mahayana Buddhism developed in northwestern and southern parts of India around A.D. 0 out of tensions between the doctrines of early Buddhism and out of the laity's demand for equal rights with the monks (Conze, 1980). Also during this period, Buddhism was introduced to East and Central Asia, Nepal, Kashmir, Ceylon, and China. As it moved beyond the borders of India, Mahayana Buddhism necessarily required transformation to fit local contexts (Kim, 1993).[2]

The central themes in Mahayana Buddhism were ontological questions: a question of existence from the point of being (*astitva*) and non-being (*nastitva)*, and a question of salvation, on how to turn to the nature of true reality (*svabhava,* "to be by itself") from the negation of being (*abhava*, "a sense of emptiness"). Soteriologically, the ideal person in Mahayana

Buddhism is a *bodhisattva-mahasattva*. A *bodhisattva* is a person who practices the teaching of Mahayana Buddhism. *Maha* means "great" and *sattva* means "person," so mahasattva is a great person who has a great goal. The *bodhisattva* has a great goal of achieving enlightenment and ultimately acquires a buddhahood by *enlightening all people*. Through Mahayana Buddhism, everyone can eventually become a Buddha and enter *nirvana* with the aid of the *bodhisattvas* who remain in the world to help save others before they attain salvation. Mahayana Buddhism emphasizes the social responsibility of the *bodhisattvas* for collective salvation. Thus, Mahayana Buddhism contrasted itself with the old Buddhism by labeling the latter as "the Lesser Vehicle" because of its focus on individual salvation exclusively through individual efforts. Refusing the term of "Lesser," the latter school named itself Theravada Buddhism, "The Buddhism of the Elders" representing teachings of old Buddhism (Spiro, 1970). Theravada Buddhism spread and flourished in many Southeast Asian countries, among which Burma, Cambodia, Ceylon, Laos, and Thailand are the most notable examples. Theravada Buddhism is best characterized by three systems that developed within it. Two of the systems—"nibbanic" (normative) Buddhism and "kammatic" (non-normative) Buddhism—are soteriological systems and one—"apotropaic" Buddhism—is nonsoteriological (see Spiro, 1970, for further details on Theravada Buddhism in Burmese context). For the purposes of this chapter, it will be sufficient to present only the first two (the soteriological) Theravada Buddhist systems.

As noted in the previous section on the Old Buddhism, nibbanic Buddhism was founded by the historical Buddha and premised suffering as an inevitable characteristic of all *samsaric* existence and the only way to reach *nirvana* by release from the rebirth cycle. The soteriological goal of nibbanic Buddhism is radical salvation—cutting the *samsaric* cycle and entering *nirvana*. Since *karma* is the cause of *samsara*, one must commit onself to the extinction of *karma* in order to achieve the goal. The nibbanic Buddhist path to *nirvana* involves adherence to Buddhist morality such as avoiding killing of all living beings and meditation. In nibbanic Buddhism, one attains salvation neither by hard work nor by faith, but by knowledge. Meditation, therefore, is considered the soteriological tool because it produces the knowledge required for salvation.

Kammatic Buddhism, on the other hand, differs from nibbanic Buddhism with respect to the degree of salvation. Thus, while nibbanic Buddhism advocates "radical salvation," kammatic Buddhism promotes "proximate salvation." That is, kammatic Buddhism views suffering as a transient state determined by one's present position in *samsara* and accepts other forms of *samsaric* existence ranging from early material richness to heavenly existence of *deva*. The soteriological aim in kammatic Buddhism is achieving a happy rebirth by improving one's position within the *samsaric* wheel. This can be accomplished by altering one's *karma* in a future life through one's good conduct in the present life. Thus, in kammatic Buddhism, one does not attain salvation by knowledge, but by merit which is considered to improve one's *karma.* With this transformation, kammatic Buddhism shifted emphasis from knowledge to works as the medium of salvation.

As Buddhism continued to expand outside of India especially to China by Bodhidharma, Ch'an Buddhism was established and developed by Huineng circa A.D. 520. The central philosophical inquiries within the Ch'an focused on cosmic questions regarding how to achieve harmony with the cosmos. Harmony, thus, was considered the proper route to enlightenment. Soteriologically, a Siddha is considered as the ideal human who can control cosmic force. The Ch'an school had flourished in two periods of Chinese history: in the T'ang and the Sung. Development of Ch'an Buddhism is a vivid example of intersection of Buddhist doctrines and local sociocultural contexts. In conjunction with Chinese practical culture, the Ch'an school was in favor of practical realization (Ch'en, 1964, 1973). They rejected Hinayana Buddhist doctrine since it offered a lot of prescribed qualifications for achieving enlightenment but did not produce many enlightened Buddhists (Conze, 1980). Ch'an Buddhists were not patient with Mahayana Buddhist tradition either since it emphasized an everlasting preparation that *bodhisattva* should make before becoming a Buddha. They reinvented a path to enlightenment in order to make it possible to be a Buddha in one's present life not using a doctrinal goal of *bodhi* but a novel aim of *wu* ("comprehension" or "awareness") which more closely corresponds to *satori* in Japanese form (Conze, 1980). With the novel way, Ch'an Buddhism produced many enlightened people. About A.D. 550, Buddhism entered Japan through Korea and was quickly integrated with traditional Japanese Shintoism, and Japan became the center of Zen Buddhism (see Suzuki, 1959).

As the brief outline above suggests, the historical development of Buddhism was not at all sudden or radically new. Buddhism grew, changed, developed, and was transformed through the rise and fall of different but interrelated doctrines and practices over the course of a long trail in historical time. As Conze (1980) expressed:

> Each new development takes place in continuity from the previous one. . . .The Buddhist capacity for metamorphosis must astound those who only see the end-products separated by long intervals of time, as different as chrysalis and butterfly. In fact they are connected by many gradations, which lead from one to the other and which only close study can detect. There is in Buddhism really no innovation, but what seems so is in fact a subtle adaptation of preexisting ideas (p.16).

Interestingly enough, Buddhist doctrinal and institutional development made through various Buddhist sects actually serve as instruments demonstrating the Buddha's teaching, "everything is impermanent." Also the subtle adaptation in specific sociocultural contexts is not at all less meaningful than radical transformation of Buddhist doctrines such as that from Hinayana Buddhism to Mahayana Buddhism if Buddhism as a religion of people is taken seriously.

In an expansive sense, the overview of Buddhism in historical context presented above highlights the potential dangers of separating a psychological understanding of religious experience from the backdrop of philosophical, soteriological, and ritual similarities/differences that arise with introduction of a religion into diverse sociocultural, historical contexts. The overview also warns us against considering Buddhism and Buddhist experiences in any uniform, normative way, since over time and over the cultures which have adopted it, Buddhism is revealed as a continuously metamorphosizing set of doctrines, practices, and emphases necessary to achieve salvation.

BUDDHIST THEORETICAL DOCTRINES AND EXPERIENCES

The Buddhist concepts selected for presentation in this chapter may, in some senses, be considered quite arbitrary. However, an attempt was made to choose Buddhist concepts which would be of most interest and illustrative value for the advancement of a psychology of Buddhism and Buddhist experience. My presentation and discussion of the concepts are based on existing literature on Buddhism, mainly from Mahayana Buddhism and my own understanding of "The Threefold Lotus Sutra," which is one of the principal Mahayana Buddhist Sutras (Williams, 1989; Yoon, 1991). Clarification of "whose point of view?"—namely, which Buddhist sect? or which sutra?—is necessary not because a specific sect or sutra itself is important, but because different contextual backdrops due to the sect or the sutra can shape Buddhists to perceive a reality differently. Mahayana Buddhism is founded on the theoretical doctrine of the Four Noble Truths—the Truth of Suffering, the Truth of Cause, the Truth of Path, and the Truth of Extinction. It also provides lay followers with practical doctrines of the Six Perfections *(paramita)* and the Eightfold Path which are elaborated guidelines made under the Truth of Path.

The Four Noble Truths

The Four Noble Truths teach Buddhists to face the reality of human suffering, to understand its real causes, to practice the *bodhisattva* way (the eightfold path and the six perfections) in daily life, and consequently to extinguish sufferings. Since the Truth of Path suggests thorough practical, daily-life guidelines for lay Buddhists, a detailed presentation will be given in a separate section.

The Truth of Suffering and the Three Principles of Reality

In order to face reality of suffering, one should start with what constitutes Buddhist reality. In Mahayana Buddhist philosophy, all phenomenal existences are understood in three dimensions: temporal, psychological, and spatial. All phenomenal existence has three distinct natures: (1) impermanent (*anitya*), (2) suffering (*dukkha*), and (3) nonsubstantial or non-self (*anatman*). The three characteristics of phenomenal existence differentiate Buddhism from other religious beliefs.

The Principle of Impermanence: The principle of impermanence addresses that there is nothing unchangeable or fixed in its form, contents, embodiment, energy, and function over temporal transitions. The existence of all things is invariably due to its interrelatedness with all other existing things. The existence of all things is possible by a joint venture of two causes of being—the primary cause and the secondary cause. The primary cause bears a potential to produce a thing, but it does not automatically produce its effect. In order to produce the effect, the primary cause needs to contact with some conditions such as a right time and/or a right place. The conditions are the secondary cause. The primary cause and the secondary cause are, therefore, also interdependent. Only when the primary cause and the secondary cause meet, due to their interconnectedness, a phenomenal reality (the effect) is produced by their conjunctive effort. It is possible for a primary cause to have a contact with different secondary causes and vice versa. However, it is not so in an entirely predetermined way but in a transforming way as a present even integrating itself with the past. Buddhists view all events in a cycle of present life as the "ripening fruit" of "the past . . . emerging out of a past that perishes and thereby lives forever" (Jacobson, 1986:50). This transformation made by individual Buddhists in addition to the principle of *samsara* and *karma* makes all things impermanent producing phenomena of multifinality. When a primary cause has a "relation" with a secondary cause through their contact, the effect of their interactions leaves behind traces as a part of *karma* and therefore *samsara*. Because of this causal relation, *samsara* is continuously rolling unless one cuts off the cycle with one's enlightenment. The enlightenment is neither some mystic perception available only to an inspired person, nor is it something given to a faith follower by an absolute authority. It is achieved through intensive "exercise of reason" (*bodhi*) (Niwano, 1975).

The Nature of Suffering: According to the principle of impermanence, one's environment including self is impermanent. Suffering is a natural sequence following the impermanent nature of the phenomenal reality. Suffering is accompanied by one's awareness of the unavoidable reality of impermanence. Suffering resulted from one's illusory attachment to a changing reality and hope for "permanence" of it. Thus, birth, aging, disease, contacting with the unpleasant, separation from the pleasant, and every wish unfulfilled are suffering. Since Buddhism views that all aspects of existence are constituted out of "five aggregates" (*pancakkhandha*): material form (*rupa*), feeling (*vedana*), perception (*sanna*), disposition (*sankhara*), and consciousness (*vinnana*), all the five aggregates are suffering.

As all translated words, *dukkha* to average Westerners is a quite problematic one. It is often understood as extreme pessimism. However, the Buddhist concept of suffering should not be described with the perspective of either optimism or pessimism. Suffering in Buddhism was not offered by the Buddha in order to make a value judgment about life—either "good or bad" or "joyful or painful" (Stambaugh, 1986). Rather, it was proposed in order to make a direct linkage between Buddhists' mind and reality. Suffering means that one is able to be in direct touch with one's reality and willing to undergo or experience it. In a contemporary psychological term, suffering is a "given reality" (Kelley and Thibaut, 1978). And unless a Buddhist actively does something about it, the given reality continuously reappears as a part of *samsara*. In this sense, truly undergoing suffering provides a secondary cause with which one transforms the given by seeing something that was not seen before experiencing suffering. Thus, the Truth of Suffering teaches Buddhists to acknowledge the real conditions of various human sufferings instead of avoiding them. Rather, they are expected to grow to understand suffering and to learn how to suffer by making an intensive and intentional commitment to suffering. That is, they seek to make all physical and psychological sufferings sufferable (or bearable) by directly encountering them.

The Principle of Non-self (Anatman): In Upanisadic tradition, it is believed that the self (*atman*) is eternal and immortal. As an unchanging entity, the self controls and governs everything in the world. Even in our contemporary daily life, people, either professionals or laypersons, often set up an ultimate entity (self) as the basis of their consciousness and they want to regard the entity as permanent and absolute. The Buddha recognized that this way of belief in self and attachment to immortal self brings further suffering, because in reality it is impermanent. Clinging to a self-propped, illusory self entails suppression of all anxieties of life and the suppression simply becomes an another added dimension of the given reality of suffering.

The principle of non-self (*anatman*) is another distinct characteristic which distinguishes Buddhism from any other major religion. Buddhadsasa (1989) summarizes the Buddha's principle of non-self as:

> Things that arise from impermanent things are themselves impermanent as are the actions connected with them. How can they be permanent? They are restless, in motion, endlessly changing. Things that do not abide create a condition that is difficult to endure. They cause dissatisfaction and sorrow. When there is change, one should not controvert nature by claiming to own one's own or another's body. These bodies are not ours; we do not possess them. They are not in our power nor did we create them. They arose from the natural power of name and form. When a person becomes attached to things within or outside oneself and believes they will always harmonize with one's desires,

> they will become an agonizing problem. A question with no solution. The Buddha, therefore, taught that one should not cling to things with one's mind even though we must by nature depend on them to exist (cited in Swearer, 1989:16).

According to the principle of non-self, anything in the world comes to be and becomes as it is. By no means does this statement imply that things exist and change by accident. Rather they exist and become what they are at a given moment ("instantaneity") through the law of causality which leads one thing to succeed another in sequence. The true nature of the becoming process is inconceivable by one's ordinary mind which has an attachment to "me," one's illusory self, and perceives the me as "mine." Rejecting the misperceived truth of me and mine due to ignorance and recognizing *anatman* is an ongoing process through which "becoming the true self" is possible. This process of rejecting the illusory self is often mistakenly labeled a "denial of self" or "negation of self" in the Western Buddhist literature (cf. Fontana, 1987). With the awareness of *anatman*, "me" and "mine" disappear because all demarcations and boundaries built up between "me" and "others" by one's own mental constructions die away (Swearer, 1989). In Zen Buddhism, the final psychological state induced by this awareness is often referred to as *satori.* In the state of *satori,* "opening the third eye," one experiences a sense of unity and harmony among all existing fragments of the universe (Suzuki, 1949). Probably the pessimistic interpretation arises due to the connotation in English (and other languages) with notions of "denial" or "negation." Instead of denying or negating self, achieving *anatman* is actually accepting the different side of a coin, namely the true self, without the false perceptions associated with one's ordinary mind and ordinary language.

The Buddhist concept of non-self is indeed very practical. Not only does it reflect the nature of existential reality, but it also serves as an instrument which breaks down the illusion of an immortal self. Nagarjuna, an Indian Buddhist philosopher who influenced further theoretical development of Mahayana Buddhist thinking, questioned that "since all existences are empty of any self-nature (*svabhava*) . . . where, by whom and in what manner could such (false) views on constancy ever arise" (cited in Ramanan, 1962:38). The intention underlying the Buddhist concept of non-self is not taking mere denial of self as the end but as the means of elevating an individual's awareness of one's false attachment to impermanence and a falsified self. Attachment to the falsified self is considered as a consequence of one's ignorance as to reality. Thus, denying illusory self also requires an active spiritual and actional commitment to finding real self.

Self and Consciousness

The Buddhist concept of self and non-self has been frequently misinterpreted in Western understandings of Buddhism as either pessimism or nihilism partially due to linguistic and philosophical differences (Stambaugh, 1986; Swearer, 1989). Even within a language, everyday language differs from the language of religion, "the language of *dhamma* (*dharma*)," to varying degrees. Everyday language is largely "physical language" used under ordinary circumstances and based on observable objects and experiences; while the language of *dharma* is "meta-physical language" based on the mental rather than the physical world (Swearer, 1989:126). The Buddha's conceptualization of self and non-self was phrased in metaphysical language but was later translated into the everyday languages of non-Indian Eastern and Western countries. Buddha developed the concept of self (*atman*) from his rejection of two Upanisadic traditions: (1) Self is eternal, and (2) self is an agent behind the five aggregates (Kalupahana, 1976). To the Buddha, none of the five constituents (form, feeling, perception, disposition, and consciousness) of self are permanent. Form, either as one's own physical body or experience of external things, is not seen as a physical entity. Rather, the form exists as a medium through which one has experiences with internal or external reality. Also, all forms eventually decay.

Feeling consists of three parts—1) the pleasant, 2) the unpleasant, 3) the neutral—as a basis for the emotion that one expresses. Furthermore, all kinds of feelings fluctuate, but a certain type of feeling is supposed to stop at some point of temporal dimension due to one's own moral as well as social regulations. Perception is a continuous process of recognizing and experiencing internal or external reality in selected terms, but ignoring the objective nature of the reality as a combined function of one's characteristics, memories, and other personal tendencies. Once one filters only certain parts of the reality, they are erroneously conceptualized (perceived) as the fixed nature of the reality. However, filtering (how and what to filter) which is central process of perception is not permanent because the combined function can change over time. To the Buddha, disposition is the foundation contributing to individual differences in feeling and perceiving a target or given reality. Disposition also refers to one's intentional activity which makes up *karma* expressed in the body, language, and consciousness.

Consciousness forms the basis of disposition. It is the mental activity that leads one to differentiate, recognize, and judge internal as well as external things. As "stream of consciousness" implies, consciousness, too, is continuously flowing and impermanent. The theory of the five aggregates emphasizes that four mental aggregates bring external stimuli into the self (through the body), feel, and differentiate them. Thus, the Buddhist concept of self as the five aggregates does not absolutely focus on only mental aspects because the theory of the five aggregates is founded on the physical body (material) which is considered no less important than the four mental aggregates. The two sides of self, material and mental, are dynamically interdependent and do not exist without each other. In their complex interrelations, the material constituents and the mental ones are seen as a source of human suffering. As Kalupahana (1976) addressed, "[The] Buddhist self is a metaphysical entity. It is a metaphysical entity solely because it is unverifiable, either through sense perception or through extrasensory perception. In short, it is not given in experience (*avisaya*)" (p.41). What the Buddha rejected was not the notion of self itself, but a misconceived individual, experiential self which was viewed as a permanent, immortal, spiritual individual self in order to feed a human craving for permanence, not to describe truth or reality. However, the Buddha did not mention any notion of the transcendental self that was rapidly developed by later Buddhist sects. A practicing Buddhist, who is taught to be ultimately responsible for cutting off the *samsara* through one's own deeds, is indeed an "active" or "passively active" creator and participant in the construction of one's own *samsara* via the *karma.*

The Truth of Cause: Causality of Reality

The Buddha did not regard the universe as God's creation, but as resulting from the causal relations by which all realities are produced. Thus, the nature of all dimensions of human reality—psychological, physical, social, or moral—as well as all existence involve two aspects: causality (*paticcasamppada*) and causally conditioned phenomena (*paticcasamuppanna dhamma).* For the Buddha, everything in the world exists only through their relations with other objects. Four characteristics of causal relations are objectivity *(tathata*), necessity (*avitathata)*, invariability (*anannathata)*, and conditionality (*idappaccayata)* (Kalupanhana, 1976). Causal relations among all the things in the world are considered to not nominally, but objectively and really, exist. With the characteristics of necessity and invariability, a certain set of conditions are associated with a certain effect with regularity. Therefore, events which look accidental are not really accidental. The occurrence of seemingly accidental phenomena are due to our "ignorance" of the causal pattern. With conditionality, the Buddha discovered a solution to disputes between the eternalist theory which advocated an "unchanging and immutable self (*atman*): and the annihilationist theory which denied continuity altogether. So the Buddha said,

> To him who perceives through proper insight the arising of the things of the world, the belief in nonexistence [=annihilation] does not occur. To him who perceives through proper insight the ceasing of the things of the world, the belief in existence [=immutability] does not arise (cited in Kalupahana, 1976:29).

To explain problems related to one's existence and experiential reality, the Buddha described "The Law of the Twelve Causes *(pariccasamuppada)"* of inner causation through active thinking processes *(bodhi).* The law of the Twelve Causes consists of "ignorance," "actions," "consciousness," "name and form (psychophysical being)," "six entrance (six gateway)," "contact," "sensation," "desire," "clinging," "existence," "birth," and "oldness and death." The famous general formulation of the law goes like this:

When this is present, that comes to be;
from the arising of this, that arises.
When this is absent, that does not come to be;
on the cessation of this, that ceases.
(cited in Kalupahana, 1976:28)

Application of the law of causation to understand one's experiential reality can be done in two methodologically different cyclic modes: *acayagami-bhaga* (roughly corresponding to John Stuart Mill's the [serial] Method of Agreement) and *apacayagmni-bhaga* (roughly parallel to Mill's the [serial] Method of Difference) (Yoon, 1991). With the first way, one continuously questions and answers in a search for the causes of the existence of "x". For example, one follows a sequence: "Why does one get old and die?" and —> "It's because one is born." —> "Why is one born?" and so on. With the second way, one questions and answers in order to find cause of nonexistence of "x". For instance, one starts with a question, "Which nonexistence produces a nonexistence of oldness and death?" —> "If one is not born, then there is no oldness and death" —> "Which nonexistence causes nonexistence of birth" —> "If one does not exist, then these is no birth," and so on.

The most fundamental question to the Buddha when he conducted *pravrajana* was why human beings get old and die. According to various Buddhist documents, the Buddha's enlightenment was possible through exercising the Law of Twelve Causes. It would go this way with the method of *acayagami-bhaga:*

> Why does one get old and die? One gets old and dies (the twelfth cause) because of one's birth (the eleventh cause). One is born to this world because of one's existence (the tenth cause) in the cycle of *samsara*. One exists because one's clinging (the ninth cause) to the five aggregates. With clinging, one easily develops a discriminating mind and struggles among people due to egocentricity. One has clinging because of desire (the eighth cause). One desires something because one wants to hold it. There are three kinds of desire, for sensual pleasure *(kama),* desire for existence (*bhava*), and desire for nonexistence (*vibhava*). When desire is intensified outward, that is clinging and the consequence of which is *bhava*. One has desire because one psychologically senses (the seventh cause) external stimulation. One senses the stimulation which exists outside of oneself because of contact (the sixth cause) with it. One can have contacts with the external stimulation because of six entrances (the fifth cause). The six entrances refers to five sense organs—eyes, ears, nose,

tongue, body, plus the mind. Through the six entrances, one perceives the existence of things. One has six entrances because of name and form, one's psychophysical being (the fourth cause). One's awareness of name and form is due to consciousness (the third cause). One exists as an organism by unifying the mind and body through consciousness. Consciousness is the fundamental power and function of one's experiences and deeds. One has consciousness because of one's actions (the second cause). Actions are expressions of consciousness and do not mean only one's "here and now" deeds but all the traces that past actions left behind (the *karma*) which determines consciousness. One acts in a certain way because of ignorance (the first cause). One does not have right view of things in the world or ignores them even though the person knows the right views. With ignorance, one repeats acts that are far away from the truth.

Attributing ignorance, not the original sin, as the first and the last cause of human suffering is a notably distinct characteristic of Buddhism. This Buddhist causality should not be misunderstood as something that is similar to Western causal analysis because the goal of Buddhist inquiry of reality is not "finding out *what it is*, but rather *how it comes about*" (Stambaugh, 1986:96, italics original). The Buddhist causality that produces a reality focuses on a process (or a path) rather than an end-product. In conjunction with the primary cause and the secondary cause, the Buddhist way of inferring causality vastly differs from Western, especially Humean, causal analysis emphasizing one-to-one correspondence between the cause and the effect.

The Truth of Path

It was, however, recognized that it is extremely difficult for most average Buddhists to understand the principle of impermanence, meaning of suffering, and the law of the twelve causes let alone to perform mental exercises with them. Thus, Mahayana Buddhism developed more practically oriented doctrines as a way of experiencing the Truth of Suffering and the Truth of Causes through day-to-day life practices and thereby understanding them. The eightfold path and the six perfections which will be discussed later were suggested as method of living daily life as the *bodhisattva* way.

The Truth of Extinction

Through the *bodhisattva* way, a Buddhist can become free from all kinds of sufferings. The state of extinction is often described as tranquil. Experiencing emptiness is a necessary prerequisite toward enlightenment and subsequently the state of extinction, *nirvana*.

Emptiness (Sunyata) and Wisdom (Prajna): The principle of *anatman* (non-self) presented by the old Buddhism is directly related to *sunyata*. *Sunyata* refers to the state of experiencing non-self, nonattachment. In the old

Buddhism, there was a tendency to treat the concept of *sunyata* in a more nihilistic way than Mahayana Buddhism. Nagarjuna (about 150-250 B.C.) elaborated the idea of emptiness with an attempt to replicate the Buddha's way of thinking and thereby to attain *prajna* (complete wisdom). Within Mahayana Buddhist doctrines, emptiness does not convey anything close to nihilism. Rather, it emphasizes affirmation of existence as a consequence of a complete cycle of the negation processes of its existence: The negation process starts with a premise of things that are in opposition to its existence and then negating them. For example, a reality that I am here can be affirmed first with a premise of a fact that I am not here and then negate the fact that I am not here. Thus, the negation processes result in an affirmation of emptiness and existence.

Through the negation processes, a Buddhist can achieve *prajna* (spontaneous, complete wisdom) which, in turn, allows one to experience an existence as a whole beyond ordinary intellectual reasoning. In this sense, Suzuki (1968:49) states that "emptiness is the result of an intuition (*prajna,* wisdom) and not the outcome of intellectual reasoning (*vijhana,* consciousness)." Attaining *prajna* means that one is free from all kinds of attachments and transcends ordinary judgmental analysis of all existences.

The Middle Path: Mahayana Buddhism was launched with its criticism of its predecessors' overemphasis on intellectual approaches with theoretical doctrines. In order to change the existing trend, Mahayana Buddhism, however, needed doctrines with which it could advocate its own standpoint. Ironically, Mahayana Buddhist monks exerted their effort in more intellectual approaches to develop its doctrines. Among them, Nagarjuna made a significant contribution to development of Mahayana Buddhist doctrines with his theory of the middle path. The central theme of the middle path is rejecting any attachment to any extremes since the attachment leads a person to have a biased perspective by differentiating things with a false classification. It also conveys practical aspects of taking the middle path by overcoming various dichotomies—me vs. others, subject vs. object, good vs. bad, East vs. West, rich vs. poor, etc.. Emptiness realized by taking the middle path should be understood as "relativity" of phenomenal existence not as a nihilistic expression. Nagarjuna stated at the beginning of his book (*Madhyamakasastra):*

"not be born and not die
not constantly present and not absolutely absent
not be same and not be different
not come and not go. . ."
(cited in Yoon, 1991:47-48, translation mine)

The only way to attain the ultimate truth of existence is continuously negating all phenomenal existence. Through the negating process, one is getting closer to the ultimate truth. Of course, it is difficult to approach to the ultimate truth with human beings' ordinary experiential, phenomenal reasoning. For that, meditation was suggested as a way of attaining transcendental reasoning and experiences which enable one to approach the ultimate truth.

Enlightenment (Bodhi) and Nirvana: The ultimate goal in Buddhism is to achieve *bodhi ("anuttara-samyak-sambodhi")* initially by emancipating oneself from attachment to self (*atman*) and gradually from all substances and to reach the state of *nirvana.* The process of freeing oneself from all objects that one clings to is emancipation in Buddhism. Once one emancipates oneself from all clingings, the person experiences a psychological state of peace or tranquility (*samadhi*). Emancipation is an essential but not the final step toward enlightenment. Enlightenment implies that understanding all existence with changed attitudes and contents of the understanding. The changed attitudes allow one to recognize changes in self and to affirm oneself in a new way. Self-affirmation is possible through changes in one's consciousness. Any habitual acceptance of self cannot guide one toward enlightenment. What insures that one has changed, is the contents of one's consciousness. However, when one's consciousness has been changed in a negative (or immoral) way, it is not considered a true change toward enlightenment. In Buddhism, changed consciousness refers to understanding the two main themes throughout the Buddha's numerous teachings: 1) causality of existence and 2) the middle path. As illustrated in the Law of the Twelve Causes, everything in the world exists based on its causal relationships with other things. The middle path (nondualism) rejects any unbalanced bias toward one extreme. The middle path exists within the coexistence of the two extremes and the two extremes exist within the middle path. Together, the two extremes are a whole and in order to understand the whole it is necessary to avoid taking only one extreme (me and mine) as the whole. One extreme (me and mine) is only a part of the whole. The whole without selfishness and self-centeredness as well as a conventional thought is the middle path. Thus, the petals falling from dying flowers already contain new blossoms and suffering already connotes joy. The middle path requires changes in one's consciousness and attitudes toward phenomenal reality by undergoing an ongoing process of self-criticism and reflection. The Buddha's teaching of the middle path is tightly interrelated with the Buddhist concept of emptiness (*sunyata*). The principle of the middle path denies an attachment even to the middle path itself. Enlightenment means reaching the other shore with the opened third eye by realization of emptiness through understanding and practicing the law of the twelve causes, the middle path. Thus, enlightenment is "not an act of the intellect, but the transforming or remodeling of one's whole being through the exercise of the most fundamental faculty innate in every one of us" (Suzuki, 1949:359-360).

Nirvana is an ideal, ultimate state that can be attained with enlightenment by realizing the impermanence and nonsubstantiality of all existence. The Sanskrit word *nirvana* literally means the extinction of one's body (death), which could be taken with negative connotations. However, the word also has a slightly different meaning that suggests the extinction of all illusions. This is an actualization of the ultimate goal of the Buddha. Once one enters *nirvana,* the individual is emancipated from all illusions and ignorance and will be never tempted by the illusions again in the future (see Johansson, 1969 for further elaboration of *nirvana*).

BUDDHIST PRACTICAL DOCTRINES AND EXPERIENCE

Early Buddhism established a marked distinction between the monastic community (monks and nuns) and the laity. In conjunction with this distinction, it allocated different sets of rules and practical doctrines for each group and applied them with different degrees of strictness. For monks and nuns, meditation was required because it was considered as a necessary tool to attain enlightenment; while the laity incurred a special duty of serving the *Sangha* (monastic orders) and attending to temples. As described earlier, the laity became gradually dissatisfied and alienated from the monastic hierarchy. They also began to object to the exclusion of laity from full participation in Buddhist principles and practices such as meditation. As Mahayana Buddhism grew and developed, the strict differentiation from practicing the Buddha's teachings became loose. Especially since Ch'an Buddhism developed in China and Zen Buddhism in Japan, meditation has become the most common tool for both the monastic community and the laity in their attempts to transfer the Buddha's teaching into actions.

The Eightfold Path

Early Mahayana Buddhism established the Eightfold Path for laity as a set of practical guidelines of executing the principle of the middle path proposed by Nagarjuna in order to attain enlightenment and eventually to reach *nirvana.* Considering the abstract nature of the theory of the middle path, the eightfold path suggests what is the right way to practice the middle path in Buddhists' daily lives in a concrete way. The eight guidelines of the Eightfold Path are right view, right thinking, right speech, right action, right living, right endeavor, right memory, and right meditation. Right view refers to not having extreme thoughts or opinions considering the three natures of reality of all existence. With right view, one eliminates "black or white" arguments initially by abandoning self-centered ways of perceiving things. Right thinking is mental preparation (attitude) when one acts according to right view. By right thinking, one is determined to try to liberate oneself from "the three evils of the mind"—greediness, resentment, and ignorance—and to understand "what is what." Right view and right thinking are essential for having correct faith in the Buddha's teaching.

Right speech is a proper attitude applied to one's daily language life. It is achieved by using right words—avoiding lying, ill and abusive speaking, and careless speaking. Right action is daily conduct performed according to the Buddha's precepts of avoiding "the three evils of body"—needless killing, stealing, and sexual misconduct. Right living means obtaining the three things necessary for life—food, clothes, and house—in a proper way through hard work and effort. These practical guidelines of right speech, right action, and right living lead people to be considerate toward other people and other things in their daily interactions (Niwano, 1975).

Right endeavor indicates one's constant engagement in exterminating already existing evils and not producing new ones. Right memory refers to remembering correct perspectives and keeping them in one's mind as the Buddha did. With right memory, one is constantly engaged in self-reflection as a way of resolving a conflict with self, other people, and all things exist in the world. Without right memory, one easily becomes self-centered by confining oneself in one's own cocoon and becoming prejudiced toward all different things through the loss of right perspective. Right meditation involves keeping consistent mental concentration (*samapatti)* in order to find the true nature of self. This does not necessarily mean mental unification only by quiet meditation. Rather, it implies contemplation even in daily life routine and is the basis of practicing the first seven guidelines on the right path (the Eightfold Path).

The Six Virtues of Perfection (Paramita)

Since the principle of the middle path and the Buddhist law of causality were reinterpreted in terms of the concept of "emptiness" proposed by Nagarjuna, Mahayana Buddhism laid more stress on the six virtues of perfection (*paramita*) as another practical guidelines for Buddhist lay followers who tried to be *boddhisattvas*. The literal meaning of *paramita* is reaching the other shore and ultimately refers to "completion." The six *paramita* consist of charity, keeping the precepts, perseverance, assiduity, meditation, and wisdom. Charity suggests three kinds of donations—the law, material goods, and fearlessness—emphasizing physical as well as mental donation without anticipating returning favors. Donating the three without thinking that one donates is a real sign of charity. Keeping the Buddha's precepts with one's own willingness indicates that one should keep trying to perfect oneself by keeping the precepts. However, this does not mean that one cannot guide other people because one is not perfect yet (Niwano, 1975). According to Mahayana Buddhism doctrines, we should not keep ourselves in an isolated physical and mental environment. Alienation from others prevents one from understanding the true nature of oneself because we do not know ourselves without knowing others (and vice versa). Perseverance refers to enduring all physical and mental sufferings by nonattachment to all worldly matters. Through perseverance, one can reach a calm and untroubled mind since it allows the person to simultaneously appreciate the two seemingly contradictory realities or worldly preferences such as sunny days and rainy days. In the calm and untroubled state, one becomes free from all the changing matters by adopting the principle of the middle path. When one reaches beyond the calm and untroubled state, the person's feeling does not fluctuate regardless of another's feedback, either good or bad. Furthermore, one becomes truly modest even though all things go smoothly as the person says or does. At the summit of perseverance, the state of being better than others becomes truly meaningless. Assiduity suggests continuous devotion to understanding the Buddha's teaching without being distracted by trivial things. With an assiduous mind, one is not affected by frequent roughness in one's practice of the Buddha's teaching because one is prepared to see the future when the roughness is gone. Meditation (*dhyana,* trance) is intended to concentrate on one's mind and having a quiet mind. This enables one to see internal and external matters from inside by reflecting on one's attitudes and deeds. This helps one find the right way of dealing with things that confuse or bother oneself. The last of the six virtues of perfection suggests development of an ability to see things in a right way and to understand the true nature of things. Wisdom in seeing things in the right way leads one to attain the law of causality, the middle path, and the concept of emptiness. All six components of *paramita* aim at perfecting oneself as well as pursuing others' welfare.

Buddhist Meditation and Mystic Experience: As a method to understand and practice all the Buddhist doctrines, meditation (*dhyana*) has been adopted as a path to the ultimate goal. Meditation simultaneously contains two meanings, its purpose and its method. It means the end state of an undistracted mind that mediation produces, as well as implies the path necessary to reach that state of mind. In Mahayana Buddhist tradition, "meditation indicates the idea of contemplation, or concentration of the mind on a single object while sitting quietly alone" (Niwano, 1975:197). However, mediation can be carried out in less orthodox forms. For example, one does not necessarily sit still in a specific position in a branch of Theravada Buddhism revitalized in Thailand in recent years (see Swearer, 1989). No matter how different, all forms of meditation share the same goal: To exert mental concentration on things and events without a self-centered idea.

To Western scholars, *nirvana* and *samsara* are often considered as opposing each other because once one enters *nirvana* then the person will never be reborn into one's *samsara.* For example, Spiro (1970:68) presents *nirvana* and *samsara* as "two parallel planes" which are "not only ontologically discontinuous . . . [but] also hedonistically dichotomous." Within the dichotomous view, *samsara* is a continuum of pleasure and suffering. Pleasure and suffering in present life is a consequence of redistribution of actions in previous life. The redistribution is governed by the law of *karma.* According to the law of *karma, samsara* and *nirvana* should be on one continuum ranging from the most unbearable suffering to the nonsuffering. The law of *karma* also suggests that good acts are rewarded in the form of an enhanced position within the wheel of life in a future life and will thus subsequently bring pleasure to the person. The law of *karma* seems to be contradictory to the doctrine of *nirvana* which regards pleasure as an illusion and thus should not be pursued. This seeming contradiction has been troublesome to some Western scholars who take it as a source of various transformed sects of Buddhism (e.g., Spiro, 1970).

However, in the principle of the middle path, the Buddha shows that the two are not necessarily opposites (see also Swearer, 1989:141-145). With conditionality, the Buddha takes the middle path, not in an eclectic sense, but in a dialectic way. Out of it, arises the concept of *nirvana.* The Upanisadic thinkers advocated mystical experiences or extrasensory perceptions attained at the highest stage of trance in yoga practices *(nirodha-samapatti)* believing those experiences and perceptions gave people knowledge on certain problems, perhaps even Ultimate Reality. On the other hand, the Materialists rejected the validity of extrasensory perception and yogic intuition and denied any kind of spirituality. Recognizing limitations of both sides, the Buddha interpreted yogic trance not as the end but as the means of knowing. To the Buddha, the highest stage of trance where perception and feeling cease is a temporary phase of quiescence (Niwano, 1975).

One of the most confusing issues of Buddhist experience to discuss in words is Buddhist mysticism and mystic experience. Even with the extreme scarcity of psychological literature on Buddhism directly addressing Buddhist mysticism (cf. Kalupahana, 1987), there is inconsistency and disagreement on the topic. It is quite understandable since any mysticism (not only Buddhist mysticism) is an awkward subject to discuss, with much depending on "whose point of view." For example, in her philosophical discussion about "the Buddhist way," Stambaugh (1986) presented the existence of Buddhist mysticism as a way leading one to "become a reality itself" not simply a way of obtaining knowledge of the reality. To Stambaugh, Buddhist mysticism is not just an end-product of spiritual union between human beings and Ultimate Reality, but a methodological path to becoming. On the other hand, when Kalupahana (1987) explained the nature and function of analytic yoga in Buddhism as a method for the "establishment of mindfulness (*satipatthana*)", he denied the global acceptance of mystical experience in Buddhism. Rather, Kalupahana stated: "[analytic] Yoga is here completely *demystified* in order to provide an epistemological means to gain an analytic view of truth" (p.75). Kalupahana credited James (1910), noting that James realized not every step of yoga involved the mystical and the spiritual, even though James did not differentiate the methods and goals of Buddhist meditation from the Brahmanical practice of yoga [see also Suzuki (1978:61-84) for his presentation of "Zen is not mysticism"].

BUDDHISM IN CULTURAL CONTEXTS

The Buddhist doctrinal world differs from the commonsense world in which individual Buddhists live. Specifically it moves beyond the everyday world in which the social scope and boundaries of individuals vary according to their position in their community. For example, the everyday world of Buddhist monks and nuns, systematically organized based on Buddhist doctrines and practices, follows few of the routines common in everyday worlds of lay followers. The daily world of laypeople, on the other hand, is arranged based on commonsense objects and practical activities. However, both the everyday worlds of monastics as well as laypeople are solidly rooted and managed using culturally available means (e.g., Bunnag, 1973).

Attaining salvation by entering *nirvana* is the ultimate goal of Buddhism; nevertheless, only a few Buddhists achieve it. This fact does not qualify only those who enter *nirvana* as "real" Buddhists. A Sanskrit scholar described ancient Indian culture by characterizing it as two radically different religious systems ("norms of conduct"): 1) the "ordinary norm" and 2) the "extraordinary norm." The ordinary norm was designed for the religious masses. Its aim was similar to that of Theravada Buddhism, enhancing one's position *within* the Wheel of Life. The extraordinary norm was intended for a religious minority whose goal was to attain salvation by achieving release *from* the Wheel. The two norms were regarded at qualitatively different levels (Edgerton, 1942 cited in Spiro, 1970). Individual Buddhists try to live with Buddhist morality either in principle or in action or in both, and living in a Buddhist context which partially overlaps with other cultural contexts is sufficient to have Buddhist experiences. This is because Buddhist contexts, like all other types of cultural contexts, provide ample opportunity for individuals to conduct themselves according to the norms of the community and engage in "appropriate" conduct.

Geertz (1966) defined culture, "[a] historically transmitted pattern of meanings embodied in symbols" (p.3). Buddhism can be considered a cultural system that possesses sacred Buddhist symbols and rituals shared among members of the cultural group. The Buddhist symbols and rituals function as a media which bring the cultural group's ethos and worldview to the same plane through Buddhist meanings (shared within the group). They also function as mediators which shape and guide the people's ethos, worldview, and even social order of their everyday world. With the extreme scarcity of literature on cultural approaches to the psychology of Buddhism, I will briefly present a review of Spiro's (1970) field work on Burmese Buddhism since his work is almost the only intensive cultural study on Buddhism and Buddhist experiences. Spiro's research is an example of contextual approaches to Buddhism and Buddhist experiences which treats Buddhism as a religion of the people rather than as a religion of texts.

Burmese Transformation of Normative Buddhism

Through his fourteen-month field work on Burmese Buddhism, Spiro

(1970) noted that certain cultural contexts actively select some normative Buddhist doctrines and actively interact with them. Starting with logical contradictions between the law of *karma* and the doctrine of *nirvana* within nibbanic (normative) Buddhism, Spiro compared nibbanic Buddhism with kammatic Buddhism, as it is expressed in Burmese society. In doing so, Spiro located Buddhism within the Burmese social, cultural, historical contexts and thoroughly examined the effect of Burmese contexts on the Burmese version of Buddhism.

When Buddhism, initially a foreign religion, was introduced to Burmese society, the Burmese already had a social milieu with existing beliefs and values. Some of them were consistent with normative Buddhist doctrines, while others clashed with normative Buddhist principles. As the Burmese encountered the foreign religion, which exerted almost no influence on Burmese society yet, they transplanted it into the Burmese context by matching Buddhist doctrines to their existing contexts. Thus, normative doctrines in Buddhism were selectively transformed and reorganized as they were imported into Burmese society.

Spiro presents a conceptual framework based upon Freudian theories, to explain the Burmese transformation of nibbanic Buddhism. The framework consists of two psychological concepts which are considered fundamental structures underlying the Burmese selection process. The first structure is congruency between the normative doctrines and the religious agents' own worldviews. It is derived from the Freudian assumption that early experience is carried throughout life with the most persistent type of "psychological residue" underlying one's cognitive and perceptual structures (p.70). However, Spiro's approach assumes that these structures are formed not only through intrapsychological processes but also through social relations in which each individual Buddhist is engaged (cf. Hong, in press; Vygotsky, 1978, 1987).

The second structure is the motivational system of religious agents. Spiro states that "belief is motivated" (p.71). Religious doctrines are accepted if they are functional in satisfying the agents' various needs to believe them. Doctrines are rejected if they frequently frustrate the agents' needs. Other doctrines are simply accepted without conviction if they are neutral to agents' needs.

The Burmese transformation of Buddhism has undergone at least three different psychological and social mechanisms—selective acceptance, selective rejection, and selective accommodation. At the very beginning, it was much easier for individual religious Burmese to accept some normative Buddhist doctrines which were consistent with their existing psychological structures. Remember that these psychological structures would have been shaped through their relationships with the world they knew, that is, existing Burmese society. Individuals' personal encounter with consonant Buddhist doctrines became a foundation that confirmed the truth of the doctrines for them. The consonant Buddhist doctrines, then, gradually gained a kind of authoritative power affecting the followers' beliefs and actions. The normative Buddhist doctrines of *karma* and impermanence acquired this characteristic and were accepted by the Burmese. When the normative doctrines were inconsistent with the existing values held by the people and the society, they were rejected. The nibbanic Buddhist concepts of *dukkha* (suffering) and *nirvana* fall into this case. The Burmese initially rejected the normative premise and meaning of suffering and interpreted them differently in a way that was consistent with their psychological and social structures. Other nibbanic Buddhist doctrines which were not dissonant, but which also did not powerfully resonated in the Burmese's minds were also accepted with weak or nonexistent intellectual or emotional conviction. The Burmese acceptance of the *arahant* is an example of this case. The discussion of these kinds of transformations will be continued in the following section.

The Doctrine of Karma and Burmese Society: Not only individually, but collectively, the doctrine of *karma* is a powerful concept allowing individual Buddhists to ease their psychological uncomfortableness and resentment of "unfair" outcomes they receive in their present life. According to procedural justice theory (Leung and Lind, 1986; Thibaut and Walker, 1975) and the relative deprivation model (Crosby, 1976), people's perceptions of fairness regarding their share does not always directly correspond to actual distribution systems. During the process of perceiving and judging justness in specific instances, people's perceptions and judgments depend on other psychological and social factors—entitlement, comparison level, need, time urgency, cultural values, and so on. When people see that their share of things is not fair and there is no systematic basis for the unfair share, the perceived unfairness can become a motivational force toward changing the status quo.

Spiro (1970) differentiated two kinds of change—"structural change" and "[*individual*] positional change" (p.439, italics added). If people believe that there is no moral authority in the distributional system whatsoever, they attempt to change the system itself (structural change). If people accept the moral authority of the system but consider the actual distribution of power and goods unfair, they are usually inclined to make the distribution system more fair without actually questioning the legitimacy of the system (positional change). The former change is usually achieved through collective action; while the latter can be made by individual actions either assisted by collective action or without it. Different societies have developed their own distributional systems designed to maintain or control the social order in their own terms, often reflecting moral authority such as religious doctrine or social, political ideologies. Thus, moral authority functions as a mental frame of reference as well as a powerful social force for the society and its individual members.

The doctrine of *karma* has been considered a powerful moral authority which provides a "moral basis" and "moral justification" of any existing social order (Spiro, 1970:439). It establishes a moral basis for a system's "*karma*-determined" distributive rules; thus, differentially allocating outcomes to individual society members is simply considered a consequence of the individual's meritorious or demeritorious acts in a previous life. By providing a moral basis for the distribution system, the doctrine of *karma* encourages individual society members to commit more meritorious actions, emphasizing the one-to-one correspondence between actions in the present life and enhanced position in a future life. The doctrine of *karma* also renders moral justification for differentially allocating power and goods among individual Buddhists because the differential outcomes result from a karmic interpretation of deservedness; "What you get is what you deserve." Thus, ostensible inequalities in the present life actually (and eventually) represent equality within the Wheel of Life. Spiro demonstrated that the "logical" consistency between *karma* and the social order in individual Buddhists' present lives, however, bore unintended and paradoxical consequences in Burmese society.

The sociohistorical backdrop of nibbanic Buddhism (from an Indian context) was quite different than the sociohistorical context of Burmese society into which nibbanic Buddhism was introduced. Nibbanic Buddhism included intellegentia who belonged to higher social strata as devotees (Weber, 1958). The political and social environments in which the historical Buddha taught his followers were relatively stable. Consequently, the devotees of Early Buddhism did not experience this social order within the Buddhist community as incongruous with the social and psychological dimensions of their daily lives. When normative Buddhism was introduced to Burma, however, Burmese marginals rather than mainstreams were the first exposed to Buddhism. Like many other social marginals, ordinary Burmese people lived in frustration and dissatisfaction with their unfair distributional system. Traditionally, this underlying, pervasive dissatisfaction with the system has made Burmese society continuously vulnerable to social change.

As a result, within historically unstable Burmese society, the doctrine of *karma* has become paradoxically intertwined with both with political stability and instability in Burma. On the one hand, the doctrine of *karma* renders the monarchical ruler, especially a king, who has accumulated a pile of merits through the cycles of his previous lives a legitimate power through "*karmic* redistribution" (Spiro, 1979:440). Thus any attempt to rebel against an existing monarchy is considered a violation of the doctrine of *karma*. As one result, then, the doctrine of *karma* plays an important role in maintaining political stability. This is the general ("decontextualized") picture that the Buddhist doctrine conveys to the "worldly" Burmese through its "otherworldly" religious texts.

On the other hand, the doctrine of *karma* also plays an equally important role as a powerful social force leading the worldly Burmese to rebel against the monarchy or the legitimate government. Accepting the legitimization of governments or monarchies does not necessarily mean that the ordinary Burmese always liked or respected them—especially in their daily ("contextualized") life experiences as the socially powerless. As noted earlier, however, the historical Buddha rejected the notion of a caste hierarchy. According to the Buddha, individual Buddhists' positions in *samsara* are determined by their efforts in the present life, even though the limits of the effort are bound to their previous *karma.* In conjunction with the notion of joint determinism, the doctrine of *karma* provided the Burmese with a driving force to change their personal position in the system. Throughout Burmese history, the attempts of individuals near the top of society to improve their social lot even more brought on the extremely disturbing, destructive political instability found in Burmese society. This occurred because significant individual positional changes within the old system simply meant having a new ruler who still enjoyed the old unbalanced distribution of power and goods (Spiro, 1970:441).

In summary, while the doctrine of *karma* proscribes structural changes, it does not discourage positional change within the structure. Unlike the most transformed function of the doctrine of *karma* as a facilitator of political stability, Burmese culture provided a different context where individual members transformed ("recontextualized") the general facilitating function into an interfering function of system stability (see Valsiner, 1994, for dynamic relations of contextualization, decontextualization, and recontextulization). Belief in *karma* also provided the Burmese with an important "ego-defensive" function protecting them from frequent failures and mishaps in their daily lives by justification and permitting external attributions to be made of the unfortunate life events (cf. Bulman and Wortman, 1977). Pains and frustrations from moral and economic failures are easily attributed to *karma* which subsequently help the Burmese restore their positive self-image.

The Concept of Dukkha and Nirvana in Burmese Society: In nibbanic Buddhism, *dukkha* (suffering) is the fundamental characteristic of all *samsaric* existence. However, the doctrinal principal in the religion of the decontextualized text does not always correspond with the beliefs of religious agents as a contextualized religion of the people. Spiro tried to demonstrate this discrepancy with his Burmese informants. His study revealed that the average Burmese Buddhist does not internalize the concept of suffering in the same way that the normative Buddhism addresses. For the Burmese, life involves suffering but it does not mean that life is equal to suffering itself (Spiro, 1970:74). According to Spiro, the Burmese frequently use a word for suffering in their daily life contexts. Thus, they experience aspects of suffering in life. However, it is difficult for the average Burmese to conclude that life is suffering when they notice other forms of life, for example, the lifestyles of rich people, or the power and privilege of authorities, etc. If lifestyles among the upper segments of Burmese society also entail suffering, then at least they differ in the degree of suffering compared to that found in the lives of average Burmese. Being exposed to different lifestyles, Burmese could make a social comparison which often leads them to believe that there are "better" alternatives within the *samsaric* world. Spiro reported that most Burmese believe that suffering is not caused by desires themselves, but by frustration due to unfulfilled desires. Thus, it is not shameful for them to have a desire to be rich or a deva, instead of cutting the desire as nibbanic Buddhism instructs. Also, if being rich or a deva brings some sort of suffering, then they are willing to bear it or willing to be "deceived" by its appearances (Spiro, 1970:75).

Entering *nirvana* is the single ultimate goal in nibbanic Buddhism and the only way to achieve the goal is by terminating suffering and freeing oneself from *samsaric* existence. In the Burmese context, however, some forms of *samsaric* existence are considered pleasurable, thus the Burmese do not see it necessary to completely cut off their attachment to the *samsaric* world. With this transformed perspective on suffering, the Burmese generally hold one of two new attitudes toward *nirvana*: "Those who conceive of it as total extinction reject it as a desirable goal, while those who accept it as a desirable goal have transformed it into a state of great pleasure, a kind of superheaven" (Spiro, 1970:76). Thus, for some Burmese Buddhists, it is more desirable to be reborn with a higher position in the *samsaric* world than to enter *nirvana.* The most distinct characteristic in the Burmese version of *samsara* and *nirvana* is that the normative Buddhist premise of the two worlds as ontologically dichotomized (two plane) entities is transformed into ontologically related ones. In order to ontologically relate the two worlds, the Burmese simply locate the two in different positions on the same plane. The qualifications of any Buddhist to enter *nirvana,* therefore, depend on their *karmic* merits or demerits instead of the extinction of all *samsaric* attachments including *karmic* merits. With this transformation of the central nibbanic Buddhist concept (prerequisites for admission to *nirvana*), *nirvana* is conceived as somewhere more or less like heaven or a superparadise by the Burmese Buddhists. A Burmese girl, one of Spiro's (1970:84) children informants, described *nirvana* as "the most enjoyable form of life" which was not very different from adult Burmese responses.

The Burmese creatively invented their own ways of resolving the conflict between the sophisticated normative Buddhist doctrine and their attachment to worldly pleasure. They transformed the religion of the text to the religion of the people in such a way that it more closely fits the Burmese context. The importance of this example for the psychology of Buddhism is that it highlights the need for understanding Buddhist experiences with not only the religion of the text, but also the religion of the people, at least in certain cultural contexts (if not all). Although they were not conducted from a psychological perspective, there are also a few other studies showing the contextualized transformation of Buddhism in China (Ch'en, 1964, 1973; Welch, 1972), Japan (Saunders, 1964; Suzuki, 1959), Sri Lanka (Gombrich and Obeyesekere, 1988), Thailand (Bunnag, 1973), and Tibet (Goodman and Davidson, 1992; Gyatso, 1975).

FUTURE PSYCHOLOGY OF BUDDHISM: A NEED FOR NEW METHODOLOGIES

If the psychology of Buddhism is (or wants to be) different from the theology, philosophy, anthropology, or sociology of Buddhism, it can be distinct by aiming its focus on the psychological functioning of individual Buddhists—their thinking, feeling, and acting—and their experiences with Buddhist contexts. The individual Buddhist's experiences are affected by their engagement with Buddhist doctrinal principles as well as ritualistic and daily life activities embedded in their historical, sociocultural contexts.

One of the most serious methodological problems that the psychology of Buddhism can make is an undifferentiated claim of universality for the goals, means, or meanings of Buddhism and Buddhist experiences. The field cannot afford either neglecting or trivializing interdependent relationships between diverse doctrines endorsed by different Buddhist sects and individual Buddhist's daily practices within their sociocultural boundaries any longer. The field of psychology of Buddhism can significantly contribute to the mainstream psychology by explicitly including the interdependent relationships as its core theme of analysis.

The distinction between traditional methodology and new methodologies should lie in their levels of analysis—a textual, ideological level and a contextual, realistic level. At the level of textual (or context-independent) analysis, Buddhist texts and doctrinal principles are examined under the assumption of universality equated with uniformity. However, even at this level the concept of universality must be scrutinized carefully for variability among the different sects or historical epochs (for example, differences between the Theravada Buddhist and Mahayana Buddhist meanings and paths to salvation). At the level of contextual (or context-dependent) analysis, the concept of universality is still viable, but it is not considered a synonym of uniformity due to diverse forms and contents of transformed Buddhist rituals and day-to-day practical activities.

If the psychology of Buddhism is interested in Buddhism as a living system into which individual Buddhists' daily lives are embedded, then its focal point should shift from studying the canonical doctrines of the religion to exploring the relationships between individual Buddhists and the religion. The latter cannot ignore the historical and sociocultural contexts of either Buddhism or individual Buddhists.

As the history of Buddhism reveals, Buddhism has continuously undergone transformation through time and place. In India, Buddhists were encouraged to pursue their Buddhist practices in a purely spiritual way. This was possible because Buddhism did not suffer from any political pressure there. Especially with King Asoka's (276-236 B.C.) patronage, Buddhist religion was considered superior to politics (Kim, 1993). Economically, Buddhist communities were nonproductive groups strictly regarding any material possessions as obstacles to enlightenment. The ultimate goal of nonpossession was to gain spiritual liberation from the slavery of materials. It was believed that one's liberation was possible only insofar as one could move away from an attachment to materials. When Buddhism was imported to China, China enjoyed its own civilization and folk religion. To the Chinese, Buddhism was not radically new, but similar to what they already knew. Even though it came from "barbarian lands," this perceived similarity facilitated translation of many Buddhist *sutras* conducted in cooperation with foreign monks who were fluent in Sanskrit. Although the Chinese attempted to preserve the original meanings of the Buddhist *sutras* through a nine stage translation process, the meanings of the translated *sutras* were unintentionally interwoven with the already existing Chinese philosophies of Lao-tzu and/or Chuan-tzu and Taoism (Conze, 1980). As presented earlier, Buddhism in China was transformed into a more practical religion than the old Buddhism but was still limited to Chinese elite groups.

Buddhism was introduced to Korea only through Chinese-translated Buddhist *sutras,* thus old Korean Buddhism was quite similar to Chinese Buddhism. Once, Buddhism in Korea was intertwined with politics especially during Koryo dynasty. Unlike sect-oriented Chinese Buddhism, Buddhism in Korea deemphasized diverse sects and facilitated unification of the sects and nation. As a consequence, Korean Buddhism has not been exclusive to elite groups. Currently, Buddhism does not have any direct linkage with any political regimes.

About 550 A.D., Chinese Buddhism was expanded to Japan through Korea. Unlike Chinese Buddhism, Buddhism in Japan became rooted in laypeople's day-to-day lives from the beginning. Consequently, it became fused with the indigenous Japanese religion, *Shintoism.* Since the Meisi revolution, Japanese Buddhism has focused on *Sukkavati* (land of Happiness, paradise) based on adherence to "The Threefold Lotus Sutra" and Zen practice.

Many Western psychological interpretations of Buddhism, especially individualistic approaches to Buddhism seem to have concentrated on individual Buddhists whose contextual backdrops are stripped from the approaches. There are a few socially and culturally oriented psychological approaches to Buddhism, but unfortunately the majority of them simply borrow the term "Buddhist" as a label for one of the many "variables" in their empirical studies (e.g., Miller, 1992). What the socially and culturally oriented study of Buddhism requires is an attempt to understand how individual Buddhists, who belong to and function as a part of a larger Buddhist community, experience self and life events (e.g., Huebner and Garrod, 1991; Muecke, 1992; Rothberg, 1992; see also Shweder, 1991). Furthermore, questions such as how Buddhist experiences of self and life events differ from non-Buddhist members in the same society; or how individual experiences within Buddhism vary among different groups of Buddhists (i.e. the laity and the monastics). This is the core of Buddhism: connectedness, causality, and transformation. Because of the multitude of temporal, social, historical, and geographical specificities laid on the foundation of its universal characteristics, the religious experiences of Buddhists must be discussed within contextual factors.

If so, it is worthwhile to note Herbrechtsmeier's (1993:15) recommendation with respect to definition of religion: "It would be better not to define religion as necessarily dealing with gods, spirits, or other suprahuman beings, but rather to consider the ways in which religious people approach and conceive of ultimate reality" (p.15).

For the future psychology of Buddhism, the field needs to recognize powerful mediating influences of Buddhist doctrinal principles, symbols, and rituals on individual Buddhist experiences considering contextual boundaries (cf. Hong, in press). If the field is not satisfied with the status quo of describing mere differences between Buddhists and non-Buddhists, then the psychology of Buddhism needs novel methodologies beyond what it has now. These novel methodologies must propose theoretical frameworks and research methods which serve to guide researchers in their explorations of the mediating processes that individual Buddhists in their cultural contexts experience.

NOTES AND REFERENCES

1. Here, I intentionally avoid starting my discussion of Buddhism with the issue of whether Buddhism is philosophy or religion (see Durkheim, 1954; Geertz, 1966; Herbrechtsmeier, 1993; Orru and Wang, 1992; Spiro, 1966). I will, however, return to this very controversial issue at the end of this chapter.
2. Since this chapter discusses Mahayana Buddhist doctrines in a separate section later, only a terse description of Mahayana Buddhism will be presented for now.

Barnes, N.S.
1987 Buddhism. In *Women in world religions,* edited by A. Sharma. Albany, NY: State University of New York Press.

Bulman, R., and C. Wortman
1977 Attribution of blame and coping in the "real world": Severe accident victims react to their lot. *Journal of Personality and Social Psychology* 35:351-363.

Bunnag, J.
1973 *Buddhist monk, Buddhist layman: A study of urban monastic organization in central Thailand.* Cambridge University Press.

Cabezon, J. I. (Ed.)
1992 *Buddhism, sexuality, and gender.* Albany, NY: State University of New York Press.
Cernovsky, Z.
1988 Psychoanalysis and Tibetan Buddhism as psychological techniques of liberation. *American Journal of Psychoanalysis* 48:56-71.
Ch'en, K. K. S.
1964 *Buddhism in China: A historical survey.* Princeton, NJ: Princeton University Press.
1973 *The Chinese transformation of Buddhism.* Princeton, NJ: Princeton University Press.
Conze, E.
1980 *A short history of Buddhism.* London: George Allen and Unwin.
Crosby, F.
1976 A model of egoistical relative deprivation. *Psychological Review* 83:85-113.
DeMartino, R., E. Fromm, and D. T. Suzuki
1960 *Zen Buddhism and psychoanalysis.* New York: Harper Colophon Books.
Durkheim, E.
1954 *The elementary forms of the religious life.* Gloncoe, IL: Free Press.
Edwards, M.
1961 *A history of India.* New York: Farrar, Straus and Cudahy.
Eliot, C.
1969 *Japanese Buddhism.* London: Routledge and Kegan Paul.
Epstein, M.
1990 Beyond the oceanic feeling: Psychoanalytic study of Buddhist meditation. *International Review of Psycho-Analysis* 17:159-166.
Faber, M. D.
1988 Back to a crossroad: Nietzsche, Freud, and the East. *New Ideas in Psychology* 6:25-45.
Fauteux, K.
1987 Seeking enlightenment in the East: Self-fulfillment or regressive longing? *Journal of the American Academy of Psychoanalysis* 15:223-246.
Fenner, P.
1987 Cognitive theories of the emotions in Buddhism and Western psychology. *Psychologia: An International Journal of Psychology in the Orient* 30:217-227.
Fiske, D. W., and R. A. Shweder
1986 *Metatheory in social science: Pluralisms and subjectivities.* Chicago: University of Chicago Press.
Fontana, D.
1987 Self-assertion and self-negation in Buddhist psychology. *Journal of Humanistic Psychology* 27:175-195.
Freud, S.
[1913]
1953 *Totem and taboo: Some points of agreement between the mental lives of savages and neurotics.* In Standard Edition, Vol.13.
Geertz, C.
1966 Religion as a cultural system. In *Anthropological approaches to the study of religion,* edited by M. Banton. New York: Praeger.
1973 *The interpretation of cultures.* New York: Basic Books.
Gombrich, R., and G. Obeyesekere
1988 *Buddhism transformed: Religious change in Sri Lanka.* Princeton, NJ: Princeton University Press.
Goodman, S. D., and R. M. Davidson (Eds.)
1992 *Tibetan Buddhism: Reason and revelation.* New York: SUNY Press.
Govinda, L. A.
1961 *The psychological attitude of early Buddhist philosophy.* London: Rider.

Guenther, H. V.
1974 *Philosophy and psychology in the Abhidharma.* Berkeley, CA: Shambala Publications.

Gyatso, T.
1975 *The Buddhism of Tibet and the key to the middle way*. London: George Allen and Unwin.
Herbrechtsmeier, W.
1993 Buddhism and the definition of religion: One more time. *Journal for the Scientific Study of Religion* 32:1-18.
Hong, G. Y.
in press Place of culture in "culture-inclusive" psychology: A comparison of cross-cultural psychology, cultural psychology, cultural-historical psychology. In *International dimension of psychology,* edited by U.P. Gielen.
Htin Aung U.
1962 *Folk elements in Burmese Buddhism*. London: Oxford University Press.
Huebner, A., and A. Garrod
1991 Moral reasoning in a karmic world. *Human Development* 34:341-352.
Jacobson, N. P.
1986 *Understanding Buddhism.* Carbondale and Edwardsville, IL: Southern Illinois University Press.
Jahoda, G.
1993 *Crossroads between a culture and mind: Continuities and change in theories of human nature.* Cambridge, MA: Harvard University Press.
James, W.
1910 *Varieties of religious experience.* New York: Longmans, Green.
Johansson, R. E. A.
1969 *The psychology of nirvana.* London: George Allen and Unwin.
Kalupahana, D. J.
1976 *Buddhist philosophy: A historical analysis.* Honolulu: University Press of Hawaii.
1987 *The principles of Buddhist psychology.* New York: SUNY Press.
Kelley, H. H., and J. W. Thibaut
1978 *Interpersonal relations: A theory of interdependence.* New York: Wiley.
Kim, J. Y.
1993 *Bulgyo Sahwoehag Weonron* [The principles of sociology of Buddhism]. Seoul: WoonJuSa.
Leung, K., and E. A. Lind
1986 Procedural justice and culture: Effects of culture, gender, and investigator status on procedural preferences. *Journal of Personality and Social Psychology* 50:1134-1140.
MacPhillamy, D. J.
1986 Some personality effects of long-term Zen monasticism and religious understanding. *Journal for the Scientific Study of Religion* 25:304-319.
Malinowski, B.
1948 *Magic, science, and religion.* Boston: Beacon Press.
Master, J. C., and W. P. Smith (Eds.)
1987 *Social comparison, social justice, and relative deprivation: Theoretical, empirical, and policy perspectives.* Hillsdale, NJ: Erlbaum.
McGuire, W. J.
1973 The yin and yang of progress in social psychology: Seven koan. *Journal of Personality and Social Psychology* 26:446-456.
Miller, A. S.
1992 Conventional religious behavior in modern Japan: A service industry perspective. *Journal for the Scientific Study of Religion* 31:207-214.
Muecke, M. A.
1992 Mother sold food, daughter sells her body: The cultural continuity of prostitution. *Social Science and Medicine* 35:891-901.

Niwano, N.
1975 *Buddhism for today: A modern interpretation of the Threefold Lotus Sutra.* New York: Weatherhill.

Orru, M., and A. Wang
1992 Durkheim, religion, and Buddhism, *Journal for the Scientific Study of Religion* 31:47-61.

Overmyer, D. C.
1976 *Dissenting sects in late traditional China.* Cambridge, MA: Harvard University Press.

Page, R. C., and D. M. Berkow
1991 Concepts of the self: Western and Eastern perspectives. *Journal of Multicultural Counseling and Development* 19:83-93.

Ramanan, K. V.
1962 *Nagarjuna's philosophy: As presented in the Maha-Prajnaparamita-Sastra.* Tokyo: Tuttle.

Rothberg, D.
1992 Buddhist responses to violence and war: Resources for a socially engaged spirituality. *Journal of Humanistic Psychology* 32:41-75.

Saunders, E. D.
1964 *Buddhism in Japan: With an outline of its origins in India.* Philadelphia: University of Pennsylvania Press.

Shweder, R. A.
1990 Cultural psychology—what is it? In *Cultural psychology: Essays on comparative human development,* edited by J. W. Stigler, R. Shweder, and G. Herdt. Cambridge: Cambridge University Press.
1991 "Moral reasoning in a karmic world": Comment. *Human Development* 34:353-362.

Spiro, M. E.
1966 Religion: Problems of definition and explanation. In *Anthropological approaches to the study of religion,* edited by M. Banton. New York: Praeger.
1970 *Buddhism and society: A great tradition and its Burmese vicissitudes.* Berkeley, CA: University of California Press.

Stambaugh, J.
1986 *The real is not the rational.* New York: SUNY Press.

Suler, J.
1990 Images of the self in Zen meditation. *Journal of Mental Imagery* 14:197-204.

Suzuki, D. T.
1949 *Essays on Zen Buddhism,* First Series. London: Rider.
1959 *Zen and Japanese culture.* New York: Bollingen Foundation.
1968 *On Indian Mahayana Buddhism.* New York: Harper & Row.
1978 *Studies in Zen.* New York: A Delta Book.

Swearer, D. K. (Ed.)
1989 *Me and mind: Selected essays of Bhikkhu Buddhadasa.* Albany: SUNY Press.

Thibaut, J. W., and L. Walker
1975 *Procedural justice: A psychological analysis.* New York: Wiley.

Valsiner, J.
1994 Epilogue: Comparative-cultural co-constructionism and its discontents. In *Child development within culturally structured environments. Vol.3: Comparative-cultural and constructivist perspectives,* edited by J. Valsiner. Norwood, NJ: Ablex.

Vygotsky, L. V.
1978 *Mind in society.* Cambridge, MA: Harvard University Press.
1987 Thinking and speech. In *The collected works of L.S. Vygotsky,* edited by R. W. Rieber and A. S. Carton and translated by N. Minick. New York: Plenum Press.

Weber, M.
1958 *The religion of India.* Glencoe, IL: Free Press.
1963 *The sociology of religion.* Boston: Beacon Press.

Welch, H.
1972 *Buddhism under Mao.* Cambridge, MA: Harvard University Press.

Welwood, J.
1986 Personality structure: Path or pathology? *Journal of Transpersonal Psychology* 18:131-142.
Williams, P.
1989 *Mahayana Buddhism: The doctrinal foundations*. London: Routledge.
Yoon, S. H.
1991 *Daeseung Bulgyoeui Haksim*. [The core of Mahayana Buddhism]. Seoul: Woori Chulpansa.

6

Hinduism and Religious Experience

KAISA PUHAKKA

OVERVIEW OF HINDUISM

A Religion of Transcendence

Hinduism consists of a rich tapestry of belief and practice spanning five millennia and myriad cultures, ethnic groups, and languages. Sacred scriptures, the *Vedas,* provide the common thread, beginning with the earliest hymns of the *Rig Veda,* composed approximately 1200 B.C., and ending with the later works known as *Upanishads* (or *Vedanta*=end of the *Vedas*) around 200 B.C. The epic literature of *Mahabharata* (Sukthankar et al, 1929-66) and *Ramayana* was composed somewhat later, between 400 B.C. and 400 A.D. Writings concerning rules of conduct and life in society also appeared during this period (Radhakrishnan and Moore, 1973). The *Vedas* and the *Upanishads* are regarded by all Hindus as sacred in the sense of containing "revealed truth." The epic literature and the writings pertaining to life in society are not regarded as sacred in this sense, even though they have had more direct impact on popular Hinduism than the *Vedas* or the *Upanishads*. The latter have greater appeal to the more serious spiritual seekers among the Hindus.

The beliefs and practices within Hinduism are remarkably diverse (Basham, 1989; Brockington, 1981; Hopkins, 1971; Knipe, 1991; Smith, 1991; Zaehner, 1962). All religious Hindus believe in a reality that transcends the mundane, empirical, or phenomenal world, but the ways of conceiving the transcendent vary greatly among the many traditions of worship and spiritual discipline. Hindus recognize both theistic and nontheistic approaches, and most are likely to agree with Radhakrishnan (1959) that "real religion can exist without a definite conception of the deity but not without a distinction between the spiritual and the profane, the sacred and the secular" (p.21).

In Hinduism the quest for transcendence takes precedence over doctrinal concerns. Religious experience and especially its transformation through spiritual discipline are held in high esteem by most Hindus, even when they are not personally questing for such transformation. On the other hand, great latitude exists regarding the interpretation of religious experience.

Not surprisingly, the transcendent quest in Hinduism begins from diverse, even contradictory, doctrinal assumptions. Yet the steps necessary for the attainment of transcendent realization are recognized to be essentially the same. In other words, the spiritual disciplines and techniques for the transformation of experience are relatively independent of theological or philosophical doctrines. Rather, they are based on observation of psychological phenomena and principles concerning the nature of mind, including conscious as well as subconscious processes.

The spiritual practices aim at modifying these processes so as to bring about the transformation necessary for transcendent realization. The foremost Hindu manual of spiritual practice is the *Yoga-Sutras* of Patanjali. Most systems of spiritual practice within Hinduism, regardless of philosophical and doctrinal differences, are substantially based on "classical yoga," as the methods and principles of the *Yoga-Sutras* have come to be known (Feuerstein, 1980). Patanjali's principles will therefore be examined in some depth. But first, a brief look at the central themes and beliefs of the Hindu view of liberation that provide the general framework for classical yoga.

The Hindu View of Liberation

Hinduism places the origin and destiny of human beings beyond the contingencies of the empirical world. The "empirical world" encompasses all phenomena that are experienced or known through the cognitive and emotional processes. This includes science, philosophy, and theology as well as religious rites. The revealed truths of the *Vedas* are beyond all these, beyond "names and forms." They concern "that which transcends the senses, which is uncaused, which is indefinable, which has neither eyes nor ears, neither hands nor feet, which is all-pervading, subtler than the subtlest—the everlasting, the source of all" (Prabhavananda and Manchester, 1975:43). The transcendent is called Brahman when viewed as the Source of all; and it is called Atman when approached within the innermost subjectivity of Self. But whether called Atman or Brahman, the ineffability of the transcendent is affirmed again and again in the *Upanishads.*

The *Vedic* sages and seers to whom the transcendent truths were revealed were ordinary people. The implication is that all human beings are capable of directly apprehending such truths. However, the methods of ordinary experience and knowledge cannot reach them; a radical transformation of consciousness is necessary. Such a transformation involves a profound alteration, or complete suspension, of the cognitive and emotional processes through which experience and knowledge are ordinarily given.

The possibility of a radical transformation of consciousness rests on the belief that within the human soul lies "an interior depth of spirit that in its essence is uncreated and deathless; and transcends the empirical world" (Radhakrishnan, 1959). According to the *Mundaka Upanishad* (Prab-havananda and Manchester, 1975:47), "The individual self, deluded by forgetfulness of his identity with the divine Self, bewildered by his ego, grieves and is sad. But when he recognizes the worshipful Lord as his own true Self, and beholds his glory, he grieves no more."

The realization of one's true identity (Self) is at the same time a letting go of the identification with the empirical ego and its physical and psychological processes. This realization signals the end of bondage to the empirical world, which is liberation or *moksha,* the highest aim of spiritual life in Hinduism. It is precisely because this Self within the human soul is itself of the essence of the transcendent that liberation is possible. The various traditions differ as to how the liberation of the transcendent Self is to be understood—whether liberation itself has "already" taken place and this fact only needs to be realized, or whether transcendent realization and liberation are a matter of gradual, progressive attainment. Also, opinions of philosophical schools differ as to whether the liberated Self achieves union or full identity with God, or whether the Self simply realizes its own nature. The Advaita or nondual Vedanta of Samkara (Deutsch, 1969; Deutsch and Van Buitenen, 1972; Murty, 1961; Rao, 1969; Roy, 1965) holds that liberation is "already attained" and only needs to be realized, and that one's true identity is not different from Brahman. The dualistic *Vedanta of Madhva* (Raghavendrachar, 1941; Rao, 1972) and the qualified nondualism of Ramanuja (Carman, 1974; Gupta, 1967; Krishanmacharya, 1971; Van Buitenen, 1968) refrain from claiming a full identity between the individual Self *(jivatman)* and Brahman. Patanjali's yoga views liberation as the attainment of complete independence of the Self, thus abiding in the Self's own nature. Yoga also views the attainment of liberation as being gradual, depending on stepwise progress in one's spiritual practice. Regardless of their differences, however, all of these schools affirm the transcendent within the innermost Self of humans, and this amounts to an affirmation of the human capacity for transcendent experience.

The Transcendent Horizon of Popular Religion

The Hindu view of the transcendent quest is at once generous and extraordinarily tough. It is generous in affirming human beings' unlimited capacity for spiritual perfection and realization of ultimate truths, which in the Judeo–Christian religions is reserved only for God. But it is tough in its denial that such perfection and realization can be attained in ordinary (untransformed) experience. The majority of Hindus indeed do not aspire to liberation from the rounds of births and deaths in the present life but are content to believe that they will reincarnate many more times before being ready for liberation. Yet, curiously, in Hinduism the transcendent horizon is not far from ordinary experience, and glimpses of it can come to those immersed in the joys and sorrows of everyday living. The transcendent horizon is reflected in the average person's understanding of the relationship between the forms of his or her experience and the reality that is beyond all forms. This understanding is illustrated in Hindu stories of the origin of the world. The theme around which many of these stories are elaborated is that Brahman dreams up the world but then forgets that he is only dreaming, and thus comes the world into existence. The existence of the world is an illusion that is maintained by forgetfulness, in just the same way as a person during sleep takes the objects and events of her dream to be really existing. The nature and origin of illusion vis-à-vis transcendent reality is a central philosophical question for Vedantic Hinduism (O'Flaherty, 1982, 1984). The best known Hindu philosopher to have addressed this question is Samkara, the eighth-century, A.D., founder of Advaita Vedanta (Thibaut, 1962; Prabhavananda and Isherwood, 1978; Mayeda, 1973). Samkara's highly sophisticated epistemological theory of illusion, and of liberation, has received considerable attention from contemporary Western and comparative philosophers (Levy, 1956; Shrivastava, 1968; Coward, 1990). Leaving aside the subtle points of Samkara's theory, the gist of it is that the diverse forms of the mundane world are illusory when viewed from the transcendent perspective. But from the mundane viewpoint, the illusoriness of phenomena does not mean they are unreal or false, for there is nothing "real" or "true" with which the illusory phenomena can be contrasted. Phenomena that are certified as extant by the methods of experience and science are thus considered "real," but less so than the transcendent reality of Brahman. This notion of degrees of reality is illustrated by his famous example of the rope and the snake. A man walking home in the dark of the night stumbles on what he takes to be a deadly snake. He breaks out in cold sweat and bolts off in panic. The next morning he discovers that what he stumbled on was not a snake but a piece of rope. Samkara's point is that the man's experience of the snake the previous night was real enough, as testified by the sweat and panic. Yet once he discovered the rope, the reality of the rope is more compelling than that of the snake. The man now sees the snake as illusory, but the experience of the snake the previous night does not thereby become unreal. Rather, the reality of the rope sublates the reality of the snake. Similarly, Brahman, once realized, sublates all of phenomenal reality.

Samkara's theory helps clarify how it is possible for a Hindu to acknowledge the ultimate illusoriness of all things of the world without falling into despair or cynicism about it. For illusoriness, understood in this profound sense, does not mean falsehood. Rather, it means creative play or *lila.* Shiva, as the four-armed, dancing Natarajan, is the Lord of the cosmos who dances the names and forms of the phenomenal world into existence and out again in intricate and ever-changing patterns. Names and forms, even those of Gods, are not weighted down by a concern with their truth or correctness; they can be taken lightly, even as the transcendent reality concealed by them is regarded with awe and worshipful respect.

The world, then, is made of the stuff of dreams and desire. But it is ultimately divine desire, divine dream, and divine forgetfulness that keeps the world going. The *Brhadaranyaka Upanishad* tells the story of Brahman who, out of unhappiness and perhaps boredom, halved himself into two, then desired to unite with the other half. But of course he could do this only by forgetting that she is his own projection or dream. How she helped him forget this is told in the *Brhadaranyaka Upanishad:*

> She thought, "How can he be united with me after producing me from himself? Well, let me hide myself." She became a cow, the other became a bull and was united with her; from that cows were born. The one became a mare, the other a stallion; the one became a she-ass, the other became a he-ass and was united with her; from that one hoofed animals were born. The one became a she-goat, the other a he-goat; the one became an ewe, the other became a ram and was united with her; from that goats and sheep were born. Thus did he project every thing that exists in pairs, down to the ants (Madhavananda, 1975:70-71).

The vast masses of the Hindu society worship God in the plethora of incarnations or "avatars" that manifest the divine. These avatars are forms of God, and the forms in turn have forms, like reflections of reflections. Thus Vishnu is one of the chief incarnations of Brahman the ultimate Godhead, and Krishna, the God of the *Bhagavad-Gita,* is an incarnation of Vishnu. Krishna, in turn takes on many forms and each of these Gods has several names. An illiterate Hindu woman of Brahmin caste was asked by this writer whether she believed that the God she worshiped at her home altar is ultimate reality. She answered, "I am a simple woman and my mind is limited, so I need to worship God in a form that I can see." This humble answer reflects the transcendent horizon beyond names and forms. The form of God, understood as form, is transparent enough to let the Divine beyond forms shine through. Such an understanding accounts for the remarkable generosity and tolerance of the Hindus in matters spiritual (Puhakka, 1976) even if not always in social or cultural identity and customs. The recognition of the illusory nature of forms allows generous and free appreciation of their play. The epic stories of the *Mahabharata* and *Ramayana* proceed much like Brahman's dream, telling stories within stories, almost endlessly, transporting the tellers and listeners into worlds within worlds. Present-day Hindus like to embellish their stories likewise, and great respect is shown to master storytellers even today.

METHODS FOR THE TRANSFORMATION OF EXPERIENCE: YOGA

Turning now to the disciplines for transformation of experience, these are undertaken by individuals who aspire to transcendent realization and liberation in this very life. The disciplines for transformation are commonly known as "yoga" and their practitioners as "yogins." They offer techniques of awareness, control, and discernment which, when practiced, transform experience from within. A review of the yoga techniques thus permits a look at transcendent experience in the making.

The *Yoga-Sutras* of Patanjali

The clearest and most detailed description of this process is found in the *Yoga-Sutras* of Patanjali, generally recognized as the authoritative manual of yogic practice in Hinduism. Yoga pervades every philosophical system and spiritual practice of Vedantic as well as Tantric Hinduism (Aranya, 1981). Patanjali is widely believed to have compiled the *Sutras* from ancient yogic principles and practices that were known and practiced in his time. By most estimates this text was written c. 200 A.D., though some scholars set the date as early as 200 B.C. There are remarkable similarities between the meditative techniques taught by the Buddha and those found in the *Yoga-Sutras.* The biographical writings about the Buddha indicate that he spent several years studying with a yogin before his enlightenment (Aranya, 1981), and it is possible that his teachings in turn influenced yogic practices of subsequent times and to some extent were incorporated in the *Yoga-Sutras.* The *Yoga-Sutras* lay down the steps for the attainment of liberation in 195 densely packed aphorisms, divided into four books. Numerous translations of this difficult work are available; all direct citations of the *Sutras* in this chapter refer to Aranya (1981), whose translation enjoys high esteem among scholars. Each *sutra* quoted is followed by the Roman numeral of the Book in which it occurs, then by the Arabic numeral of the *sutra.*

Human Bondage and Liberation in Classical Yoga

The philosophical basis of the *Yoga-Sutras* is the dualistic Samkhya system (Gupta, 1969; Larsen, 1969). According to Samkhya, pure spirit or consciousness, *Purusha,* is entangled with *Prakrti,* energy manifested as physical, biological, and mental phenomena—in short, anything that can be an object of consciousness (Feuerstein, 1980). The innermost or true Self of a person is *Purusha.* The aim of yoga is liberation of *Purusha* from its enmeshment with *Prakrti,* which is its state of bondage. Liberation in the *Yoga-*

Sutras is denoted by the Sanskrit term *kaivalya,* which has the connotation of freedom in the sense of independence. Thus liberation, in metaphysical terms, means the freedom of *Purusha* from entanglement with *Prakrti*. The emphasis of the *Yoga-Sutras,* however, is not metaphysical but practical and experiential, and it is evident that theory in this system serves pragmatic concerns (Feuerstein, 1980). The experiential emphasis will be maintained as closely as possible in the following discussion of the *Yoga-Sutras.*

In the experience of human bondage, the chief source of suffering is an identification with a sense of self or ego that appears to be the subject of one's mental, emotional, and physical states. This sense of self manifests in varying degrees of subtlety. A relatively gross manifestation, easily detectable in introspection, is a sense of ownership of impulses, emotional reactions, thoughts, images, and memories (e.g., "I am sad," "I am hungry"). Patanjali calls this "the mutable I-sense" *(asmita* or *ahamkara).* A subtler sense of self is associated with the examination or reflection upon one's own mental states. The subtlest of the ego-senses is *buddhi* or the "pure I-sense," which is also associated with the operation of discriminative intelligence. It is the "I" who knows the "I" who is sad or hungry, and also knows the "I" who reflects on and reacts to its own states. *Buddhi* is the "I" that observes and discerns with dispassion but tends to be buried under the passions, fears, and hopes of the mutable I-sense that is reactively engaged with the world.

Freedom comes about by the progressive disidentification with the manifestations of the I-sense, beginning with the relatively gross and progressing toward the subtler. Supreme liberation is attained when the last and subtlest of these identifications, the pure I-sense or *buddhi,* is dissolved. What remains then is pure spirit or Self without the I-sense, completely free and self-realized.

The foregoing is a synopsis of the aim and rationale of the discipline set forth in the *Sutras.* The essence of yoga as a way to Self-realization is given by Patanjali in the following two brief *sutras:*

> "Yoga is the suppression of the modifications of the mind.
> Then the Seer abides in Itself" (1, 2 & 3).

The "modifications of the mind" refer to mental fluctuations that occur seemingly spontaneously and constitute the stuff of ordinary mind or consciousness. "Suppression" of these fluctuations means stilling or restricting their involuntary, out of control occurrence. "Suppression" is an unfortunate term as it suggests a forcing out of conscious awareness, perhaps even "repression." However, this is not at all what is meant by Patanjali. The suppression of the mental modifications takes place in two ways: the attainment of *samadhi* and the removal of the *klesas.* These are complementary aspects of the yogic practice. *Samadhi* cuts through and moves beyond the mental fluctuations, whereas the elimination of the afflictions that create and perpetuate the mental fluctuations ensures consistency and stability of the yogic attainments.

Cultivation of *samadhi*

Samadhi refers to a state of extraordinarily intense concentration or absorption in which the mind is completely still and free of spontaneous modifications. The preparatory stages involve ethical conduct and restraint *(yama),* observances that include such things as study of yogic principles and devotional practice *(niyama).* This is followed by the cultivation of proper posture *(asana)* and control of the breathing process *(pranayama).* Yoga in its popular meaning in the West has come to be virtually identified with these last two. However, they are considered only preparatory for the practice that culminates in the attainment of *kaivalya,* and Patanjali devotes only six sutras to their description. The practice begins with *pratyahara,* or the restraining of the sense organs. This prepares the yogin for *dharana,* which Patanjali defines as "the mind's fixation on a particular point in space" (III,1). When *dhrana* becomes more concentrated, consisting of "a continuous flow of similar mental modifications [it] is called dhyana or meditation" (III,2). And when, finally, the object of meditation alone is present, without a thought of the self who is meditating, then *samadhi* is attained. The practice of *dharana, dhyana,* and *samadhi* together constitute the core of yogic discipline called *samyama* (III, 4,5).

A variety of possible objects for meditation are mentioned by Patanjali, and it is clear that the nature of the object is not essential; the control of mind or the capacity for one-pointed concentration is what is being developed. The control of mind should not be dependent on any particular object. Indeed, the power to stabilize the mind on an object of the smallest size as well as on the greatest is taken to be the mark of control (I, 40).

The depth and power of *samadhi* varies. A relatively lower level *samadhi* can be reached by a highly concentrated and subtle analysis of a fundamental yogic principle, similar to Heidegger's (1969) "meditative thinking," or the contemplative exercises in certain mystic traditions (Aranya, 1981:43; I,17). A higher, or more profound, level of *samadhi* can be attained by concentrating on the mental state in the background of subtle mental objects, such as the feeling of bliss. A still higher level of *samadhi* is attained when the recipient of the blissful feeling, the I-sense *(asmita)* is the object of one-pointed concentration.

These types of *samadhi* are called *"samadhi* with object." The yogin attains transcendent insight into the aspect of reality that is the object of *samadhi.* With the attainment of *samadhi* on any and all objects, the yogin is said to have acquired "complete knowledge of all knowable things." (Aranya, 1981:10)

But *samadhi* with object is not yet liberation, insofar as the object still holds the yogin engrossed in a mental state, however blissful or subtle this state may be. Mind itself must be transcended, for liberation is not contingent on any mental state. The transcendence of mind occurs in "objectless *samadhi*" *(nirvija samadhi)* which the yogin may undertake once he or she is proficient in the practice of *samadhi* with object. Patanjali distinguishes between objectless *samadhi* that sometimes occurs by natural causes, and objectless *samadhi* attained by yogic discipline. The former "is caused by nescience which results in objective existence" (I, 19) by which Patanjali appears to mean the various physical or psychological factors that may produce a trance-like blank mind. In such a state, thoughts and images may become blurred and dissolved into a formless "mental fog."

In contrast to such trance states, the yogic *samadhi* involves the conscious stilling of mental fluctuations and the penetration of all mental forms by awareness. The highest *samadhi* occurs when *buddhi,* the subtlemost form of the mind, is no longer the subject or center that receives awareness but is itself seen as an object. When cultivated with an attitude of supreme detachment or, rather, nonattachment *(vairagya),* this seeing eventually leads to the disappearance of the mind, and liberation is attained.

Liberation is the state of the Self-in-Itself (IV, 34), and it is the culmination of the yogic path. The *Sutras* provide techniques for stilling the incessant fluctuations of mind that prevent Self-realization. These mental fluctuations are caused by the *klesas,* to which we now turn.

Removal of Afflictions

In the literature of meditation, much has been written about *samadhi* but little about the afflictions or *klesas* (Hanna, 1993-4). *Samadhi* and liberation hold promise of soaring the clear skies of freedom, whereas the *klesas* are like the mud stuck around one's feet that pulls one back to the ground, aborting the flight. Digging up the mud and picking it off one's feet is less spectacular than spreading one's wings to fly, yet it is essential for the success of the endeavor. Similarly with the *klesas;* their removal is necessary for the attainment of stable and reliable progress on the yogic path.

Klesa is variously translated as affliction, pain, anguish, or worry (Aranya, 1981). Patanjali describes five basic categories of *klesas:* ignorance (nescience), egoism, attachment, aversion, and the craving for life or existence. The active manifestation of the *klesas* can be attenuated or even prevented by avoiding circumstances and actions that would arouse them. For this reason, the restraints *(yama)* and observances *(niyama)* are considered of utmost importance as preliminaries for the more advanced yogic practice. But removal of the active manifestations of the *klesas* by such measures is not enough; their latent basis must be eradicated as well.

Here Patanjali and his commentators go into a detailed discussion of the subconscious psychological underpinnings of the *klesas.* These are the *samskaras* and *vasanas* which, operating in conjunction with memory, create and maintain the mental clutter and changing moods that characterize ordinary consciousness.

Samskara refers to latent impression of actions, perhaps a kind of memory residual or mental image (Johnston, 1968). *Vasana* is a subtle, subconscious desire that appears to form the dynamic, motivational component (Mishra, 1963) of latent tendencies. Hanna (1993) suggests that a *samskara* is a residue of an experience, typically but not necessarily negative or traumatic, that has not been integrated with full awareness and hence is avoided or dealt with in obsessive ways. He further suggests that the interrelationships between *samskaras* and *vasanas* are highly complex: "A vasana can be both a subtle desire contained as content within a single unintegrated experience or an entire residual personality trait encompassing a matrix of samskaras. Similarly, a single samskara can contain individual vasanas or subtle desires within its own structure" (1993-4:112).

It should be evident by now that "mind" as understood in classical yoga is not a narrowly defined cognitive function or mechanism but encompasses the entire personality including subconscious, dynamic aspects as well as the body. The *klesas, samskaras,* and *vasanas* together produce mental activity and through such activity, create and maintain the human personality. It is mind in this comprehensive sense that holds human beings in bondage and suffering.

Procedures for the progressive removal of the *klesas* are provided in the *Yoga-Sutras.* The details of these procedures are beyond the scope of this chapter. Briefly summarized, they involve the preliminary restraints and observances, the application of *samyama (dharana, dhyana,* and *samadhi)* on the *klesas* themselves, the cultivation of nonattachment *(vairagya),* and a subtle technique called *pratiprasava* that results in the final dissolution and disappearance of the mind (Aranya, 1981:129-131; Hanna, 1993).

The Balance of Psychological and Spiritual Work in Yoga

Liberation requires that mind and the entire personality lose their hold on the yogin. It is clear that *samadhi* alone is not enough to bring about the disappearance of mind and its constituent *klesas, samskaras,* and *vasanas.* The one-sided emphasis on *samadhi* can lead to experiences of transcendent realization that are fleeting and often followed by a plunge into the "dark night of the soul"—a familiar phenomenon described in the mystical literature East and West (Maritain, 1980; Venkatesananda, 1984; Puhakka, 1992). For the person in the grip of the "dark night," the quest for transcendence can easily turn into a yearning for a special state of consciousness that was once experienced but now lost. An obsessional hunger for a "spiritual high" is not an uncommon affliction among persons in quest of transcendence, and it suggests that a spiritual practice, when not balanced with deep psychological purification, may have iatrogenic effects on its practitioner.

The detrimental effects of obsession with special states of consciousness or of fascination with psychic powers are clearly recognized in the *Yoga-Sutras.* They are regarded as subtle *klesas* that can become manifest in the course of yogic practice (III, 37; IV, 28) and must be removed for genuine and lasting liberation to take place. Patanjali states, "The subtle *klesas* are forsaken (i.e., destroyed) by the cessation of productivity (i.e., disappearance) of the mind" (II, 10). With the complete dissolution of the mind and all psychological states, attachment to the experience of liberation, the last fetter of human bondage, is broken and liberation attained.

YOGA AND DEVOTIONAL RELIGION

It is evident that in Hinduism devotion to God and the quest for transcendence intertwine in complex ways, yet retain their distinctness. In some cases, the quest for transcendence may not involve devotion to God at all. Some forms of devotion, on the other hand, are not concerned with transcendence at all. The latter are recognized as *pravrtti-dharma* (Aranya, 1981) or devotional practice solely concerned with attainment of worldly happiness (health, wealth, success, love, etc.) through the performance of religious worship and rites. The Heaven to which such worship is believed to secure access after death is a "worldly" heaven in which the temporary happiness and pleasures of the empirical world are long-lasting. But from the yogic viewpoint, the experiences associated with *pravrtti-dharma,* including the images of Heaven, are indistinguishable from the joys and sorrows, fears and hopes of nonreligious or secular concerns.

The devotional practices of the renunciates *(nivrtti-dharma),* however, have a genuinely transcendent goal, that of union or oneness with God or Brahman. The pursuit of this goal within Hinduism tends to take one of two forms. In one, contemplation of God with a tranquil mind purified of desires and aversions is the ideal. In the other, a fervent surrender of self to God is sought. The two approaches are by no means mutually exclusive but rather appear to reflect differences in temperament and preferred style of the devotee. The contemplative approach is exemplified in the *Bhagavad-Gita,* while self-surrender is best illustrated in the devotional practices of certain Tantric forms of Hinduism.

Contemplating God

In the contemplative approach, the devotee strives for purification and transformation, if not complete transcendence, of the empirical self or individual ego, so that union with God can be attained. The *Bhagavad-Gita* holds yogic methods in high esteem as the spiritual discipline for a devotee. Thus, the question, "When can a man be said to have achieved union with Brahman?" (Prabhavananda and Isherwood, 1972) is answered in the *Gita* as follows:

> When his mind is under perfect control and freed from all desires, so that he becomes absorbed in the Atman, and nothing else. "The light of a lamp does not flicker in a windless place": that is the metaphor which describes a yogi of one-pointed mind, who meditates upon the Atman. When, through the practice of yoga, the mind ceases its restless movements, and becomes still, he realizes the Atman (p.66).

Again, Krishna exhorts Arjuna to become a yogin:

> Great is that yogi who seeks to be with Brahman,
> Greater than those who seek to mortify the body,
> Greater than the learned,
> Greater than the doers of good works:
> Therefore, Arjuna, become a yogi (p.69).

Contemplation of God is a kind of knowing, but far more intimate than ordinary kinds of knowing. Krishna speaks of it in the following verses:

> Now I shall tell you that innermost secret:
> Knowledge of God
> Which is nearer than knowing,
> Open vision
> Direct and instant.

The devotional religion of the *Bhagavad-Gita* embraces not only the methods of yoga, but also the underlying premises that humans are capable of transcendent realization and that an effort of will is required to do so. For the devotee, yogic attainment is the means to an end, which is union with God. The God-realized yogins of the *Bhagavad-Gita* have freed themselves from ignorance, pride, and delusion, as well as worldly attachments. Having removed these *klesas* and *samskaras* and attained one-pointed concentration *(samadhi),* they "live in constant union with Atman" (Prabhavananda and Isherwood, 1972:111).

Surrendering to God

The serene and collected contemplation that is the ideal of *Bhagavad-Gita* contrasts with the passionate and exuberant devotionality found in certain forms of Tantric Hinduism. Tantrism is a highly complex tradition that by some accounts is distinct from Vedic Hinduism and may be traceable to pre-Vedic Dravidian roots (Singh, 1976). Yet much of popular Hinduism today is a blend of both Tantric and Vedic elements. A dynamic, world-affirming tradition, Tantrism embraces rather than withdraws from the forms of the senses, intellect and emotion (Avalon, 1927, 1974; Zimmer, 1964). In Tantrism, the basic dualisms of human experience are manifestations of the

Shiva-Shakti principle. The creative energy and manifestations of the world are *Shakti,* while the unmanifest, pure consciousness (the *Purusha* of Patanjali's yoga) is *Shiva.* The Tantric yogin seeks transcendence, not by separation from *Shakti,* but precisely by transcending the separation by way of awareness of, or entry into, all manifestations of *Shakti.*

In devotional Tantrism, *Shakti* is worshiped in the form of the female Goddess Kali, also known by her manifestations as Durga, Parvati, and many others (Gupta, 1977; Knipe, 1991). Transcendence of the *Shiva-Shakti* dualism is achieved by a complete self-surrender to Kali, regarded as the mother of all. Of fierce black countenance, Kali is the devourer of time *(kala).* She embodies aspects of existence that are most difficult for people to confront, such as the impermanence and inevitable death and decay of everything that lives. The devotee who surrenders himself or herself completely and with boundless love to the mother will dwell in her embrace free of fear, full of bliss. Such bliss is manifested by the God-intoxicated *sadhus* and devotees of Kali whose songs are heard in the streets of modern Calcutta.

Devotion to God is often seen by the more intellectually minded Hindus as a path that is suitable to a person of emotional temper. While this may be true, it does not capture the essence of this path, which is not emotionality but self-surrender. The surrender of one's self can effect a transformation which is not unlike the egoless states of yogic *samadhi.* This was indeed true of Sri Ramakrishna, the great saint and devotee of Kali of modern Hinduism (Nikhilananda, 1942).

The following account is given by Zimmer (1964) of a conversation with Ramakrishna on a boat sailing down the river Ganges in 1882. Ramakrishna's discourse on the boat was frequently interspersed by his entering into a *samadhi* spontaneously, or erupting into song full of devotional inspiration. His own experience appeared to be intimately connected, moment by moment, to the object of his worship, of whom he spoke as follows:

> The Divine Mother is always sportive and playful. This universe is Her play. She is self-willed and must always have her own way. She is full of bliss. . . . It is as if the Divine Mother said to the human mind in confidence, with a sign from Her eye, "Go and enjoy the world." How can one blame the mind? The mind can disentangle itself from worldliness if, through her grace, She makes it turn toward Herself" (p.567).

Tantric devotional worship contains a curious mixture of sensuous, playful permissiveness on the one hand, and ascetic self-denial on the other (see O'Flaherty, 1981). But these seemingly contradictory aspects make sense when one appreciates that self-surrender is at the heart of the worship. The devotee, denying everything to himself, permits all to God. The Mother-Goddess then becomes all-permissive, and no experience or aspect of the world needs to be denied. Further, when the self is surrendered with unwavering devotion and love, then the fierce and frightening aspects of life are experienced as the blissful play of a loving Mother.

To a devotee who has truly surrendered his or her self, there is nothing to fear and nothing to hold onto. The play has become light and transparent, with the transcendent horizon shining through the myriad forms, inspiring Ramakrishna to speak in these words:

> The Primordial Power is ever at play. She is creating, preserving, and destroying in play as it were. This Power is called Kali. Kali is verily Brahman, and Brahman is verily Kali. It is one and the same Reality. When we think of It as inactive, that is to say, not engaged in the acts of creation, preservation, and destruction, then we call it Brahman. But when It engages in these activities, then we call It Kali or Sakti. The Reality is one and the same; the difference is in name and form (Zimmer, 1964:564).

Ecstatic bliss, though a special blessing that may be bestowed to one who surrenders to God, is not the highest aim of devotional religion. The following eyewitness account, reported by Zimmer (1964), of one of Ramakrishna's spontaneous *samadhis,* suggests that an intensely blissful experience may precede, and perhaps propel the devotee into, transcendence:

> Girish [young disciple of Ramakrishna]: "You have blessed me." Ramakrishna: "How is that? I said you would succeed if you were sincere."
>
> Before Girish could respond, Sri Ramakrishna cried, with a shout of joy, "Anandamayi!" and the company saw him—as they had beheld him many times before—pass abruptly from normal consciousness to the trance state of divine absorption *(samadhi).* He remained abstracted for some time, but presently moved, and soon was back again, vivaciously participating in the conversation" (pp. 589-590).

When the ecstasy and bliss of the devotee is tempered by renunciation of even this great pleasure, then the door to transcendent realization remains open, and one may dwell, as Krishna says in the *Bhagavad-Gita,* in the "constant union with Atman." Beyond a certain point, it appears that the differences between the two paths to God, contemplation and surrender, lose their significance. Surrender, when completed, becomes contemplation; and contemplation, if it is to be more than intellectual thinking, requires surrender.

Classical Yoga and the Devotional Path

The fluctuations of the ordinary mind, however devoted, easily stray from union with the Divine. And even when focused on God, the thoughts, images, and feelings of the Divine are not the same as the Divine Itself. For the contemplative who wishes a more direct contact with God than can be effected by merely thinking about Him or Her, or by performing ritual worship, yoga offers methods for stilling the mental fluctuations and attaining *samadhi.*

The fervent self-surrender of the Tantric devotee may be powerful enough to overcome the obstacle of the straying mind. However, attachment to the experience of ecstasy and bliss is the pitfall of this path. The devotee, falling short of total surrender, becomes addicted to the immensely pleasurable sensations of this kind of experience. This danger is widely recognized in the literature of Hinduism, and, as we have seen, it is given special attention in the *Yoga-Sutras*. There the antidote to such attachment and addiction is nonattachment.

Nonattachment *(vairagya)* is not to be confused with aversion or withdrawal, which, like attachment, are types of *klesas.* Nonattachment arises from discriminative insight into the nature of phenomena, including psychological states and *klesas.* When their nature is seen with increasing depth and clarity, their effect is diminished, and thus nonattachment is cultivated. According to Patanjali, supreme nonattachment *(paravairagya)* is gained through the discriminative insight that discerns the nature of *Purusha* as not *buddhi* (i.e., free of the I-sense). The devotee may not take this last step that would wipe out all separation between the nature of God and his or her own nature. But the yoga techniques of concentration and discernment can help the devotee disentangle personal needs and attachments from the object of his or her devotion.

Yoga and devotion to God in Hinduism thus go hand in hand. But not always the entire way. For the devotee, yoga is a means to an end, which is union or oneness with God. For Patanjali, on the other hand, devotion to God may be a means while liberation and Self-realization is the end. Acknowledging that *samadhi* can be attained from devotion to God (II, 45), Patanjali's attitude toward God is one of tolerance and pragmatic appreciation. But this falls far short of assigning devotion to God an essential role in yoga (I, 23; II, 32). On the other hand, for the devotee, faith in God could not but be essential; without such faith, devotion would have no vitality.

This could become a major theological stumbling block were it not for Hinduism's great respect for the ineffability of the transcendent, on the one hand, and for the human capacity to reach the transcendent in direct experience, on the other. The Self of yoga, in its liberated state as *Purusha,* is beyond names and forms. The God of the devotee is also ultimately beyond names and forms. The Self-realized yogin and the devotee who has realized his or her union or identity with God are both beyond theological disputes. These, after all, can only be had in terms of names and forms. Later translators and commentators of the *Yoga-Sutras* tended to equate Self-realization with the realization of God (for example, Prabhavananda and Isherwood, 1953; Taimni, 1967), thus effecting a subtle shift of interpretation. However, this shift in interpretation has not necessitated altering or abandoning any of the methods for transformation provided by Patanjali.

The means-ends reversal between yogic practice and devotion to God is important when the aim is union rather than complete identity with God, as in the *Gita.* From the devotional perspective, "union" means that the self of the human being and the Self of god are in some respect distinct. From the yogic perspective, the *samadhi* in which the union is realized is incomplete insofar as it has an object (God) and a subject (the devotee, identified with *buddhi* and the mind for which God is the object).

The means-ends issue becomes less important when the devotee takes the identity of his or her Self (Atman) to be not distinct from that of God. From the yogic perspective, the realization of complete identity with God requires dissolution of the last vestiges of mind and disidentification with the I-sense *(buddhi).* Thus the yogic path is taken all the way, and its aim and that of the devotee coincide fully.

Hinduism covers the full spectrum of interpretations ranging from dualistic at one extreme, through moderate or qualified forms of nondualism, to complete nondualism at the other extreme. These provide the contours of legitimation as to what kinds of experiences are affirmed or sought after and what are denied or considered impossible and hence not pursued. As one moves toward the dualistic end of the spectrum and the separation of the human and the divine is affirmed as absolute, the impetus for transformation from within tends to diminish as does the value of Patanjali's yoga techniques. On the other hand, when one's fundamental identity with God is affirmed, as in the nondualistic end of the spectrum, the transformation of consciousness whereby this identity is realized becomes imperative.

TRANSFORMATION OF CONSCIOUSNESS THROUGH YOGA: SUMMARY AND EVALUATION

Liberation is a Transcendent, Not a Psychological State

The techniques of classical yoga aim at progressive dismantling of the psychological structures and processes and the aim is achieved with the complete dissolution of the mind. This leads to a rather startling conclusion, namely, that liberation as understood in classical yoga is not a psychological state in any of the usual meanings of the term. Psychological states are contingent on, and modifiable by, various physiological, environmental, or psychodynamic factors. Also, their content or meaning can be phenomenologically described.

None of this applies to the transcendent state of liberation. Liberation is transcendent in the precise sense that it is neither identifiable with any psychological or physiological states nor contingent on or modifiable by factors that influence such states. Alpert's (1973) experiment with his meditation teacher in India dramatically illustrates this point. Alpert gave him a high dose of LSD (over 1000 mcg; the average dose is closer to 250 mcg). The teacher, who was an accomplished yogin, reported no effects, and Alpert could detect none in his appearance or behavior. Apparently the psychological processes that would be altered in a typical LSD experience were absent or under the voluntary control of this yogin.

While psychological and in general causal analyses are an important part of yoga, such analyses pertain only to the removal of the obstacles to transcendence, not to the transcendent realization Itself. Patanjali is quite clear on this point:

> Causes do not put the nature [of Self-in-Itself] into motion, only the removal of obstacles takes place through them. This is like a farmer breaking down the barrier to let the water flow. (The hindrances being removed by the causes, the nature impenetrates by itself) (IV, 3).

The implication is that attempts to interpret or study the state of transcendence in causal or phenomenological terms are bound to be reductionistic, that is, they reduce the transcendent to the psychological, if not to the physiological. Does this mean that the quest for transcendence cannot be studied scientifically? Not at all. The suggestion from the *Yoga-Sutras* is that the best way to approach the study of transcendent realization is *via negativa:* in terms of the *klesas* and other obstacles of it, and their progressive modification and removal. The culmination of the yogic path, the state of Liberation or *kaivalya,* cannot be described, not because it is shrouded in mystery but because it is not an object of observation or experience at all. On the other hand, anything that is such an object can be studied. Indeed, ever subtler psychological phenomena become accessible to observation and description as one progresses along the yogic path (Brown and Engler, 1986). The study of these phenomena could shed new light on the deeper, constitutive aspects of human experience and personality and on the transformative process that empowers and vitalizes the transcendent quest.

Yogic Liberation and Regressed States

The tendency to think of the goal of yogic practice as being a special state of mind (or consciousness) can lead to misleading comparisons of yogic attainments with hypnotic trance and other regressed states as well as parapsychological phenomena.

Yogic *samadhi* is, indeed, sometimes described as "trance." This implies a closer relationship between *samadhi* and hypnotic or other kinds of trance states than is really the case. There are indications in the *Mahabharata* that hypnotic trance and the ability to influence a person's experience and behavior through hypnosis was recognized in Hinduism and clearly distinguished from yogic *samadhi* (Eliade, 1969). Nevertheless, *samadhi* is sometimes mistakenly believed to be a state of profound withdrawal and self-absorption, as in self-hypnosis or in deep sleep. Some of the preliminary methods in yoga indeed bear resemblance to methods of hypnotic induction; for example, the restraint of the senses to bring about one-pointed concentration. Also, there are passages in the *Upanishads* that refer to "dreamless sleep" states, such as the following: "Prajna, the Self as the universal person in dreamless sleep . . . is the origin and end of all. Whosoever knows Prajna knows all things" (Prabhavananda and Manchester, 1975:51). From this one might be tempted to conclude that falling into a deep cataleptic state is what is being recommended. As will be argued shortly, this would be a mistake.

But the larger issue here concerns whether yogic *samadhi* is regressive in the Freudian sense, or, in contemporary terms, prereflective or prepersonal. Regressed states represent a return to an earlier, presumably happier or more successful integration. Thus they signify some form of withdrawal or escape from situations that are experienced as aversive or unbearable. The interpretation of yogic liberation as a withdrawal from the world or an escape into a blissful trance reflects these meanings.

Yogic liberation, however, is most definitely not a regressed or "prepersonal" state. Let us take a closer look at the case of dreamless sleep. According to the *Yoga-Sutras,* "dreamless sleep is the mental modification produced by the condition of inertia as the state of vacuity or negation (of waking and dreaming)" (I, 10). For the yogin, this is a mental fluctuation or modification which he or she seeks to still. An extraordinarily powerful modification, it easily overwhelms the undisciplined mind and sweeps it into helpless oblivion, which is what happens to most of us every night. The yogin, however, who has successfully stilled all of his or her mental modifications, including the subconscious *klesas,* retains perfect lucidity as he or she enters the sleep state. An accurate understanding of the passage quoted earlier from the *Mandukya Upanishad* is, then, as follows. *Prajna* (=direct realization through insight) is available as the innermost essence of the Self even during a deep, dreamless sleep state when the modes of knowing that depend on the senses and the intellect are suspended. A yogin who is able to contact (know) *prajna* in dreamless sleep and not lose awareness, as ordinarily happens, "knows all things." The presence and clarity of the yogin's awareness does not waver as he or she moves in and out of various states of consciousness.

The point of the example of dreamless sleep is that freedom from being influenced by any states, rather than the attainment of some special state, is the goal of yoga. The key to understanding the yogic approach to states of consciousness, both ordinary and nonordinary, is that these are to be neither hankered after nor avoided. Patanjali goes into a lengthy discussion of parapsychological phenomena and psychic powers and their attainment through yogic methods. But he also makes it quite clear that these powers are an impediment to *samadhi* and liberation (III,37). They are not only distractions from the goal of liberation, but desire for and attachment to them constitute powerful *klesas* that, if not attended to, can derail the yogic quest.

The highest goal is not escape from or into some states of consciousness but freedom from them all. Eliade (1969) calls the attainment of this goal the "supreme reintegration." This is an appropriate description, from the psychological perspective. Before the attainment of this goal, the person's experience and actions are molded and determined by unintegrated psychic fragments—the *klesas, samskaras,* and *vasanas.* Their integration brings them under the yogin's conscious control. In more advanced stages, the yogin achieves integration of the various states of consciousness, including deep sleep and drug-induced altered states, as in the case of Alpert's teacher described earlier. Finally, even states associated with dying and death may be thus integrated.

Yoga and Mysticism

Yoga and mysticism are both concerned with transcendent realization. There are obvious similarities between yogic *samadhi* and mystical experiences. Thus the yogic *nirvija samadhi* or objectless consciousness devoid of the I-sense meets Stace's (1960) criteria for introversive mysticism. However, the ultimate goal of yoga is not *samadhi* or mystical experience but liberation. Furthermore, Patanjali's commentators (Aranya, 1981:46) recognize that *nirvija samadhi* does not necessarily lead to liberation. Mystics of various traditions are likely to agree that a mystical experience is not sufficient to guard against subsequent spiritual suffering or "sin," and that the mystic's life has a goal beyond the mystical experience.

It is in the articulation of their respective goals that the differences between mysticism and yoga become significant. Mystics disagree among themselves as to what the goal of spiritual life should be (e.g., union with God or complete identity). But regardless of these disagreements, the mystic's quest is focused on something that is, at least initially (except for the transient mystical states), experienced as outside of one's self and with which the mystic seeks enduring union or oneness (Underhill, 1961; Woods, 1980). By contrast, the original formulation of Patanjali's yoga is, from the outset, and interior journey of self-transformation. Its culmination is achieved when the yogin's innermost self, *Purusha,* "abides in Itself," not in oneness or union with God. As noted earlier, devotional practice is accorded pragmatic value in aiding the process of transformation on the yogic journey.

On the other hand, we also noted that later Vedantic commentators have interpreted the goal of yoga as being realization of God, or the identity of *Purusha* and God. That this can be done shows the neutrality of yoga with respect to theological or metaphysical interpretation. We can thus say that yoga, viewed as a method and a practice, is neither mysticism nor religion, but a psychospiritual technology for the purification and transformation of consciousness. As such, Patanjali's methods and analyses are highly relevant to mystics and religious aspirants for various traditions who wish to overcome obstacles to their transcendent quest.

The Meaning of Transcendence in Yoga

Finally, the question must be addressed: What exactly is meant by "transcendence" in yoga? Yogic liberation is not to be identified with a particular feeling such as bliss or ecstasy or feeling of unity described by mystics, nor a state of consciousness such as objectless *samadhi.* From this one might conclude that liberation for the yogin must mean extinction of all consciousness. This, however, is not at all the meaning of *kaivalya.* States of consciousness that have any content, i.e., can be described, are fluctuations of mind and subject to afflictions. They represent the interior, psychological side of human bondage from which freedom is sought. But this freedom does not mean extinction, nor even exclusion from the domain of psychological states. A person whose shackles are cut can freely roam in and out of his previous confinement. Similarly, a yogin who has attained liberation is not compelled to flee or shut out the world but can freely move in and out of psychological states. The Self who is thus liberated cannot be described or defined in either phenomenological or physiological or behavioral terms, not because this Self is shrouded in mystery, nor because It has disintegrated and dissolved into a prepersonal state, but because It has no identity in those terms. This is the meaning of transcendence in classical yoga. It is stark and uncompromising in its purity, leaving nothing to grasp and hold onto on this side of transcendence. But just for this reason, the methods of yoga can be readily incorporated and its aims interpreted in myriad contexts of religious quest.

REFERENCES

Alpert, R.
1793 *The only dance there is.* New York: Anchor.

Aranya, H.
1981 *Yoga Philosophy of Patanjali.* Albany, NY: State University of New York Press.

Avalon, A.
1927 *The great liberation (Mahanirlvana Tantra),* translated by J. Woodruffe. Madras, India. [1928]
1974 *The serpent power. The secrets of tantric an-shaktic yoga.* New York: Dover.

Basham, A.L.
1989 *The origins and development of Classical Hinduism,* edited by Kenneth R. Zysk. Boston: Beacon.

Brockington, J.L.
1981 *The sacred thread: Hinduism in its continuity and diversity.* Edinburgh: Edinburgh University Press.

Brown, D., and J. Engler
1986 The states of mindfulness meditation: A validation study, Parts I and II. In *Transformations of consciousness: Conventional and contemplative perspectives on development,* edited by K. Wilber, J. Engler, and D. Brown. Boston, MA: Shambhala.

Carman, J.B.
1974 *The theology of Ramanuja. An essay on interreligious understanding.* New York: Yale University Press.
Coward, H.
1990 *Derrida and Indian philosophy.* Albany, NY: State University of New York Press.
Deutsch, E.
1969 *Advaita Vedanta: A philosophical reconstruction.* Honolulu: East-West Center Press.
Deutsch, E., and J.A.B. Van Buitenen (Eds.)
1972 *A sourcebook of Advaita Vedanta.* Honolulu: University of Hawaii Press.
Eliade, M.
1969 *Yoga, immortality and freedom,* 2nd ed., translated by W.R. Tarsk. Princeton, NJ: Princeton University Press.
Feuerstein, G.
1980 *The philosophy of classical yoga.* New York: St. Martin's Press.
Gupta, A.S.
1967
1969 *A critical study of Ramanuja.* Banaras, India: Chowkhamba. *Classical Samkhya. A critical study.* Lucknow, India: Gour Ashram.
Gupta, S.R.S.
1977 *Mother cult.* Calcutta: Flrma KLM Private Limited. (Distr. South Asian Books).
Hanna, F.
1993-4 The confines of the mind: Patanjali and the psychology of liberation. *The Journal of the Psychology of Religion* 2-3:101-126.
Heidegger, M.
1969 *Discourse on thinking,* translated by J.M. Anderson and E.H. Freund. New York: Harper & Row.
Hopkins, T.J.
1971 *The Hindu religious tradition.* Encino, CA: Dickenson.
Johnston, C.
1968 *The Yoga-Sutras of Patanjali.* London: Stuart & Watkins.
Knipe, D.M.
1991 *Hinduism.* New York: Harper Collins.
Koller, J.M.
1970 *Oriental philosophies.* New York: Scribner.
Krishnamacharya, V. (Ed.)
1971 *Vedanta-sara of Ramanuja.* Wheaton, IL: Theosophical Publishing House.
Larsen, G.
1969 *Classical Samkhya.* Delhi, India: Motilal Banarsidass.
Levy, J.
1956 *The nature of man according to Vedanta.* London: Routledge & Kegan Paul.
Madhavananda, S.
1975 *The Brhadaranyaka Upanishad, with the Commentary of Sankaracarya,* Hollywood, CA: Vedanta Press.
Maritain, J.
1980 Natural mystical experience and the void. In *Understanding mysticism,* edited by R. Woods. Garden City, NY: Doubleday.
Mayeda, S. (Trans. & Ed.)
1973 *Samkara's Upadesasahasrika.* Tokyo: Hokuseido Press.
Mishra, R.S.
1963 *Yoga Sutras: Textbook of yoga psychology.* Garden City, NY: Anchor Books.
Murty, K.S.
1961 *Revelation and Reason in Advaita.* New York: Columbia University Press.
Nikhilananda, Swami (Trans.)
1942
1958
1980 *The gospel of Sri Ramakrishna.* New York: Ramakrishna-Vivekananda Center.

O'Flaherty, W.D.
1981 *Siva: The erotic ascetic.* New York: Oxford University Press.
1982 The dream narrative and the Indian doctrine of illusion. *Daedalus* 111:93-113.
1984 *Dreams, illusions and other realities.* Chicago: University of Chicago Press.
Prabhavananda, Swami, and F. Manchester (Trans).
1975 *The Upanishads: Breath of the eternal.* Hollywood, CA: Vedanta Press.
Prabhavananda, Swami, and C. Isherwood (Trans.)
1947 *Shankara's crest-jewel of discrimination. Vivekachudamani.* Hollywood, CA: Vedanta Press.
1972 *The Son God: Bhagavad-gita. New York: Penguin.*
1978 *How to know God.: The yoga aphorisms of Patanjali.* New York: Harper & Row.
Raghavendrachar, H.N.
1941 *Dvaita philosophy and its place in the Vedanta.* Mysore, India: University of Mysore Press.
Rao, P.N.
1972 *Epistemology of Dvaita Vedanta.* Wheaton, IL: Theosophical Publishing House.
Roy, S.S.
1965 *The heritage of Shankara.* Allahabad, India: Udayana Publications.
Shrivastava, S.N.L.
1968 *Samkara and Bradley.* Delhi, India: Motilal Banarsidass.
Singh, L.P.
1976 *Tantra: Its mystic and scientific basis.* Delhi, India: Concept Publishing Company.
Smart, N.
1968 *Doctrine and argument in Indian philosophy.* London: Allen & Unwin.
Smith, H.
1991 *The world's religions.* San Francisco: Harper San Francisco.
Staal, J.F.
1961 *Advaita and Neo-Platonism: A critical study in comparative philosophy.* Madras, India: University of Madras Press.
Stace, W.
1960 *Mysticism and philosophy.* New York: Macmillan.
Sukthankar, Vishnu S.S., et al. (Eds.)
1929-66 *The Mahabharata.* 19 Vols. Poona, India: Bhandarkar Oriental Research Institute.
Taimni, I.K.
1967 *The science of yoga: A commentary on the Yoga-Sutras in the light of modern thought.* Wheaton, IL: Theosophical Publishing House.
Thibaut, G. (Trans.)
1962 *The Vedanta-Sutras of Badarayana, with the commentary by Samkara* (vols. I & II). New York: Dover.
Underhill, E.
1961 *Mysticism.* New York: Dutton.
Van Buitenen, J.
1968 *Ramanuja on the Bhagavadgita.* Delhi, India: Motilal Banarsidass.
Venkatesananda, S.
1984 *The concise Yoga Vasistha.* Albany, NY: State University of New York Press.
Woods, J.H.
[1914]
1983 *The yoga-system of Patanjali.* Delhi, India: Motilal Banarsidass.
Woods, R. (Ed.)
1980 *Understanding mysticism.* Garden City, NY: Image.
Zaehner, R.C.
1962 *Hinduism.* New York: Oxford University Press.
Zimmer, H.
1964 *Philosophies of India.* New York: Meridian.

7

Philosophy and Religious Experience

HERBERT BURHENN

The purpose of this chapter is to survey recent philosophical discussions of religious experience as they have emerged primarily in the analytic tradition and to assess what these discussions have accomplished and where they might be headed. In the interest of even modest philosophical precision, it would seem mandatory to begin such a chapter with a definition of "religious experience." Unfortunately, the recent literature does not readily yield a helpful definition of this notion. I wish to propose instead that what is meant by "religious experience" can be understood only within the context of a particular tradition, and so I shall begin with a sort of historical rather than transcendental deduction of the concept.

THE TRADITION OF SCHLEIERMACHER AND JAMES

A number of scholars have noted that our modern Western notion of religion is a product of the eighteenth century. When Augustine wrote of "true religion," he had in mind what we might call proper piety. When Jonathan Edwards, more than a millennium later, maintained that "true religion, in great part, consists in holy affections," he meant pretty much the same thing (Edwards, 1959:95). "Religion" was sometimes used, by John Calvin, for example, to designate the relationship between human beings and God. In medieval usage, *religio* might apply specifically to the monastic life. Only in the period of the Enlightenment did "religion" commonly come to refer to a system of beliefs and practices, with several such systems to be found throughout the world (Smith, 1962: Chapter 2).

The participants in these systems of beliefs and practices presumably have many experiences. They perform sacrifices, read and copy texts, have visions, travel, bake bread, make new friends. Most of these experiences, however, have evoked remarkably little philosophical interest. "Religious experience" in the singular is clearly understood in contemporary discussion to connote something else, something more specific and perhaps more intriguing. Understanding what it connotes will require that we look briefly at two individuals without whose work the current discussion and, of course, this volume would hardly be thinkable.

The first of these is Friedrich Schleiermacher, whose *On Religion* has been called "the first book ever written on religion as such" (Smith, 1962:45). In these *Speeches to Its Cultured Despisers* Schleiermacher rejects from the outset the popular identifications of religion with morality, with doctrinal systems, or even with metaphysics. Rather, religion can be known only through experience, the very special kind of experience that he chooses to call piety:

> The contemplation of the pious is the immediate consciousness of the universal existence of all finite things, in and through the Infinite, and of all temporal things in and through the Eternal. Religion is to seek this and find it in all that lives and moves, in all growth and change, in all doing and suffering (1958:36).

Several characteristics of piety deserve particular emphasis here. Piety is an immediate consciousness which can be expressed in a wide variety of outward, and necessarily impure, forms. Indeed, Schleiermacher repeatedly proclaims his indifference to what these forms might be, especially when they are conceptual forms (1958:95). He appears to be working within a Kantian framework, seeking to establish the independence of the religious dimension of human life alongside the cognitive and the moral. In fact, his claim is much more sweeping. The immediate consciousness in which religion essentially consists is based in all our experience and is therefore foundational for both science and morality:

> True religion is sense and taste for the Infinite. To wish to have true science or true practice without religion, or to imagine it is possessed, is obstinate, arrogant delusion, and culpable error. . . . You will find every truly learned man devout and pious (1958:39).

Religious experience is accordingly not something that emerges in occasional sporadic incidents or is accessible only to the privileged or abnormal few. It is essential to any fully developed human life, even the life of its "cultured despisers," who may already be sharing in it unaware: "Were you to consider the few religious opinions and feelings that I have so slightly sketched, you would be very far from finding them all strange to you" (1958:83).

Identifying religion with a particular kind of experience has for Schleiermacher an explicitly apologetic purpose. It takes only a little historical imagination to see how attractive and powerful this move is. The claims of rational theology had been subjected to devastating criticism just a few years earlier at the hands of Hume and Kant. The developing historical criticism of the eighteenth century had defrocked the Christian past and displayed it as all too human. The new appreciation of the diversity of religions had made claims of special revelation increasingly problematic. Against this background numerous religious movements from the Puritans to the Hasidim to the Pietists, among whom Schleiermacher himself was raised, would turn inward in search of deeper religious emotion and intensity. In the *Speeches* and in a much more specifically Christian form in his *Glaubenslehre* (1963), Schleiermacher constructed a stunning apologetic by reinterpreting traditional doctrines as expressions not of mere emotion but of an immediate self-consciousness that is constitutive of the human self.

In the latter work he refined the notion of immediate self-consciousness by identifying it with the feeling of absolute dependence, in contrast to the sort of consciousness in which one feels partially free and partially dependent. In the latter form of consciousness, the sensible self-consciousness, the individual stands over against other individuals and things. In the feeling of absolute dependence, the antithesis between individuals disappears and we become conscious of ourselves not as particular individuals but as "individual finite existence in general" (1963:19). The feeling of absolute dependence, Schleiermacher insists, is simple and self-identical. It receives its temporal determination and what might be called its content from its conjunction with the sensible self-consciousness. That is, through its relationship to the sensible self-consciousness, the feeling of absolute dependence appears at a particular moment as a particular religious emotion and at another moment through a relationship to a different determination of the sensible self-consciousness as a different religious emotion. Yet the feeling of absolute dependence remains self-identical throughout the different moments of its appearance (1963:22-24).

Schleiermacher's account of the feeling of absolute dependence seems to have both a material and a formal aspect, which he did not choose to distinguish. Formally, the feeling of absolute dependence is the ultimate life-unity of the self, which is prior to the subject-object relation and which is presupposed by individual acts of knowing and doing. Materially, the feeling of absolute dependence is experienced, in that it determines the quality of a person's existence—for example, when the ready emergence of this feeling produces joy.[1] In his explication of specific Christian doctrines, Schleiermacher tends to treat the feeling of absolute dependence, which he calls more specifically the God-consciousness, in a material fashion. He is concerned, for example, with how the God-consciousness becomes dominant, and that question does not seem to make sense from a formal point of view. In his account of human self-consciousness, however, Schleiermacher incorporates a very important value-judgment: the feeling of absolute dependence is the highest level of self-consciousness. But this judgment is dependent on taking "highest" to mean primordial in the formal sense of prior to knowing and doing. Schleiermacher's blurring of these two aspects of the feeling of absolute dependence is no doubt essential to his entire project but also responsible for recurring accusations of subjectivism.

For subsequent generations Schleiermacher's understanding of religious experience would also provide a powerful hermeneutical tool, especially as his views were transmitted through his twentieth-century disciple Rudolf Otto (1923), whose account of what he calls the experience of the "numinous" likewise has both material and formal aspects. How does one make sense, for example, of a religious text which contains what appear to be patently false or silly assertions? Enlightenment rationalists, identifying religion with sets of beliefs, typically responded to such materials by dismissing them as primitive and uncivilized or, even worse, as the products of priestcraft. Treating such texts as expressions of a kind of experience made it possible to regard them positively and work with them constructively. Now they became clues to a fundamental dimension of the human self.

The other source essential for understanding contemporary philosophical discussions of religious experience is, of course, William James's *The Varieties of Religious Experience*. James brings to these lectures the attitude not of an apologist but of a searcher, one who is genuinely seeking to look at puzzling data, understand them, and draw general conclusions from them. He shares with Schleiermacher the belief "that feeling is the deeper source of religion, and that philosophic and theological formulas are secondary products" (1985:341). Beyond that point of agreement, he charts a tortuous and idiosyncratic course.

James is clearly in search of experiences which can be meaningful *for him*. He is led, first of all, toward what is intensely personal and individual. His orientation is reflected in the definition he offers of religion:

> Religion . . . shall mean for us *the feelings, acts, and experiences of individual men in their solitude, so far as they apprehend themselves to stand in relation to whatever they may consider the divine* (1985:34).

Concomitant with this focus on the intensely individual is the assumption that only a few people have religious experiences which are interesting enough to be worth studying. There is little point, James insists, in looking at the "second-hand religious life" of "your ordinary religious believer." Rather, "we must make search for the original experiences which were the pattern-setters for all this mass of suggested feeling and imitated conduct. These experiences we can only find in individuals for whom religion exists not as a dull habit, but as an acute fever rather" (1985:15).

How are we to find these stars in the religious firmament and learn about their experiences? James announces in his first lecture his intent to limit himself to literary sources: "I must confine myself to those more developed subjective phenomena recorded in literature produced by articulate and fully self-conscious men, in works of piety and autobiography" (1985:12). Despite the ambitious title of his lectures and his indefatigable love for quoting sources, he in fact limits himself, with few exceptions, to a very narrow range of writers—nineteenth-century spiritualists and mind-curers, medieval and early modern Christian saints and mystics. James lived at a time when fascinating studies of nonliterate religions were becoming available to Western scholars, studies which his contemporaries Freud, Frazer, and Durkheim found wonderfully suggestive, but James's personal attitude toward such materials was, to put it kindly, dismissive:

> In the "prayerful communion" of savages with such mumbo-jumbos of deities as they acknowledge, it is hard for us to see what genuine spiritual work—even though it were work only relative to their dark savage obligations—can possibly be done (1985:386-387).

James likewise does not hesitate to tackle the issue of evaluating religious experience. He is concerned throughout the *Varieties* to oppose those who would allow explanations of the origin of religious experience to substitute for assessing the value of the experience. The assessment should instead be carried out with reference to the quality of life religious experience yields. He often finds the yield very positive, especially in his lectures on saintliness (1985:210 ff.). On the other hand, he seems to take particular delight in finding examples of bizarre behavior on the part of the religiously experienced and even enjoys trashing a saint:

> In the main [Teresa's] idea of religion seems to have been that of an endless amatory flirtation—if one may say so without irreverence—between the devotee and the deity; and apart from helping younger nuns to go in this direction by the inspiration of her example and instruction, there is absolutely no human use in her, or sign of any general human interest (1985:278).

Though it takes him a very long while, James does finally turn his attention to what it is now fashionable to call religious epistemology—specifically, to the question of whether religious experience can provide a warrant for religious truth-claims. This issue leads him ineluctably to the examination of mysticism since mystical states seem to provide the most promising candidates for experiences that would support such claims. James's conclusion on this matter is extremely cautious: mystical states are authoritative for those who have them but not for anyone else (1985:335).[2] Those of us who do not have mystical experiences can draw only the most general of consequences from others' reports of such experiences:

> [Mystical states] break down the authority of the non-mystical or rationalistic consciousness, based upon the understanding and the senses alone. They show it to be only one kind of consciousness. They open out the possibility of other orders of truth, in which, so far as anything in us vitally responds to them, we may freely continue to have faith (1985:335).

James on several occasions speaks of a science of religions, but recognizes that such a science, however interesting its conclusions, cannot itself be a religion (1985:385). The only specifically religious conclusion that emerges from his study as *"literally and objectively true"* is the recognition *"that the conscious person is continuous with a wider self through which saving experiences come"* (1985:405). Anything else we may choose to believe—and James does not fail to tell us finally about his choices—falls into the category of overbelief.

It is now time to conclude our historical excursus and ask how it might help us to understand the contemporary philosophical discussion of religious experience. As we shall see, the work of Schleiermacher/Otto and James has dictated much of the shape of the current discussion. 1) The discussion will focus almost wholly on mystical experience and the experience of the numinous, the latter category permitting us to include individuals such as Luther who had powerful religious experiences that were certainly not mystical. Other types of experience are recognized but they do not seem to be of much philosophical interest. 2) James's epistemological conclusions may be cautious, but they are tantalizing. Some philosophers will seek to find in religious experience stronger warrants for religious beliefs. In the spirit of Schleiermacher, they will not hesitate to attempt a kind of apologetic for theism, though not for a specific historical tradition. 3) Appeals to the positive or negative "fruits" of religious experience will emerge in the discussion, and claims to explain religious experience will be embraced, rejected, or at least qualified.

EMPIRICISM AND ITS DEMISE

If one had tried to project in the early 1960s what issues would provoke intense discussion among analytic philosophers over the next three decades, religious experience would have been a very unlikely candidate to be on the list. Yet such a discussion has in fact occurred and, if current publications are any clue, shows no sign of subsiding. Just why this topic should have come to receive such attention is our next concern.

One of the best kinds of stimulus for philosophical discussion is a good foil, a position which is articulated well enough to be respectable but is also bold enough to invite attack. For the present topic such a foil was conveniently provided by the Australian philosopher C. B. Martin in his volume *Religious Belief*, published in 1959. Martin devotes a lengthy chapter of his book, with the provocative title "'Seeing' God," to a critique of the notion that religious experience is epistemologically comparable to sense experience (1959: Chapter V).

Martin asks us to consider the assertion, "I have direct experience of God." Is this, Martin wonders, an assertion about my sensations (comparable to "I seem to be looking directly at a chair") or is it an assertion that entails the existence of something apart from myself (comparable to "I am looking directly at a chair")? It appears by virtue of its linguistic form to be the latter, but on closer examination, Martin discovers, turns out to be much more like the former. We have procedures for determining whether we are looking at a chair, procedures that require reference to more than our own sensations. One of them is to find out whether others in the room also see the chair. Unfortunately, in the case of claims of experience of God, such procedures are lacking, or at least very difficult to specify. My seeing God does not entail anyone else's seeing him even if we are in the same room. It does not entail anyone else's seeing him under any conditions that I can state explicitly. Consequently, my claim to have experience of God seems very like a report only about my (private) sensation. My experience can hardly amount to a way of knowing the existence of an agency external to myself.

Martin's critique of the notion that religious experience might yield knowledge is grounded in an empirical theory of knowledge. Very similar critiques can be found in earlier empiricist philosophers. It is accordingly the severe discrediting of empiricism as a theory of knowledge that has made possible a barage of attacks on Martin and given some philosophers the courage to argue for a more positive evaluation of the epistemological value of religious experience.

Modern empiricism took shape in the seventeenth and eighteenth centuries in response to the prodigious new claims to knowledge made by the natural sciences. Empiricism is the attempt to develop a systematic theory of knowledge based on the principle that all knowledge derives from experience, for this is the principle on which the natural sciences seem to operate. The problem is to specify what is to count as experience. Empiricists have usually held that experience consists at bottom of atoms of sensation, the smallest possible units of sensation, most commonly called sense data in the twentieth century.[3] As long as I talk only about my sense data, I shall never be mistaken, just as I cannot be mistaken about my own pain. Talking about my own sense data is not likely to be satisfactory for very long, however. Yet as soon as I talk about other things the possibility of error enters in. The guiding principle for the empiricist is to be sure that all statements about more complex matters—about physical objects or causes or selves—are properly derived from statements about sense data. What is to count as proper derivation is the question on which the history of empiricism hinges (see Hempel, 1965). Fundamental to this tradition is the suspicion that certain types of statement in common use, especially some of those to be found in religious and metaphysical contexts, cannot possibly be derived from statements about sense data. But if they cannot be derived from statements about sense data, they are unconnected to experience and cannot tell us about the world. They are not false, but rather suffer the far more ignominious fate of proving to be meaningless (see Ayer, 1946: chapter VI). At best such statements might reveal their author's attitude toward life, but their mode of expression is clumsy and misleading. Rudolf Carnap (1959:80) put the point succinctly: "Metaphysicians are musicians without musical ability."

The great strength of empiricism has been its claim to embody the principle of knowledge at work in the natural sciences. Beginning in the 1950s a number of philosophers, most of them influenced by Wittgenstein's later writings, have subjected this claim to devastating attack. Empiricism, they have argued, has failed miserably as an account of scientific practice. There is no neutral, foundational kind of experience upon which more complex claims to knowledge can be erected. What we experience depends on a complex interplay between what is presented to us and the concepts we have already formed. What counts as data is a function not just of a neutral "given," but also of the concepts and hypotheses we are employing. Our scientific knowledge of the world may emerge through observation and experimentation, but it is not simply grounded in sense perception (see Brown, 1977: Chapter 6). A key element in this new understanding of scientific knowledge is the role assigned to theories. They are not, as empiricism depicted them, summaries of observations but rather shape observations and determine the kind of research that is to be done. The processes through which theories are developed, adopted, and discarded defy simple description. They may emerge through systematic observation or serendipity, and they are likely to be discarded not through straightforward falsification but only when a better theory is available. In articulating and disseminating this new view of the nature of theories, the well-known work of Thomas Kuhn on the history of science has been especially influential (Kuhn, 1970).

SWINBURNE AND THE EVIDENTIAL VALUE OF RELIGIOUS EXPERIENCE

The work of the Oxford philosopher Richard Swinburne will serve here as an example of recent optimism about the epistemological value of religious experience. Swinburne's argument is presented in a way that is reasonably compact and not excessively technical. It is part of a well-articulated and ambitious philosophical project and has received a good bit of attention from other philosophers. Several other philosophers have presented rather similar arguments.[4]

Swinburne defines a religious experience as one "which seems (epistemically) to the subject to be an experience of God (either of his just being there, or doing or bringing about something) or of some other supernatural thing" (1979:246). He thereby precludes from consideration those religious experiences which do not purport to be of anything external. Swinburne recognizes that religious experiences are normally private perceptions, ones not immediately shared by others. Since he accepts a causal theory of perception, he holds that one can have an experience of God "if and only if its seeming to him that God is present is in fact caused by God being present" (1979: 247-248).

The crucial step in Swinburne's argument is his introduction of what he calls the Principle of Credulity: "it is a principle of rationality that (in the absence of special considerations) if it seems (epistemically) to a subject that *x* is present, then probably x is present" (1979: 254). By calling this a principle of rationality, indeed an ultimate principle of rationality, he means both that anyone we should regard as rational is bound to accept it and that it neither can be nor need be justified inductively on the basis of more fundamental principles. Note that the Principle of Credulity affords no priority to sense experience over other types of experience. This formulation of the principle is plausible only because of the critique of empiricism which preceded Swinburne's work. Swinburne clearly embraces that critique, recognizing the constructive role of concepts in perception and rejecting the classic empiricist attempt to draw a clear line between what we *really* experience and our interpretations of experience (1979: 258). The immediate implication of the Principle of Credulity is obvious: "In the absence of special considerations, all religious experiences are to be taken by their subjects as genuine, and hence as substantial grounds for belief in the existence of their apparent object" (1979:254). Those who would reject the epistemic value of religious experience must now bear the burden of proof. Swinburne also makes it clear that he understands the evidential weight of religious experience to extend not only to the subject of the experience but to others as well (1979:260).

Running the Principle of Credulity up the pole may join the battle but hardly determines its outcome. The opponent has an obvious retort, a strategy we have already seen C. B. Martin employ, namely, to adduce "special considerations" which undercut the reliability of religious experience in general. Swinburne accordingly seeks to identify such considerations and assess their weight.

One important feature of ordinary perception—perception of physical objects, for example—is that I can check its reliability by comparing my own experience with that of other observers who should be in a position to have a similar experience. If I am unable to specify what sort of experience would count against my perceptual claim, Swinburne notes, "that *somewhat* lessens the apparent force of an apparent perception" (1979:263). Clearly we do find ourselves in precisely this situation in the case of most religious experiences, a consideration that Martin finds persuasive as an objection to the epistemic value of religious experience but Swinburne does not.

A second feature of ordinary perception has to do with my ability to recognize objects that I have not seen before. Clearly I can recognize such objects if they are adequately described to me. But could someone who claims to have an initial religious experience possibly be in possession of an adequate description of the object of that experience? Swinburne thinks so:

> The description of God as the one and only omnipotent, omniscient, and perfectly free person may indeed suffice for a man to recognize him—by hearing his voice, or feeling his presence, or seeing his handiwork, or by some sixth sense. Even if some of us are not very good at recognizing power, or knowledge, or freedom in the human persons whom we meet, we might well be able to recognize extreme degrees of these qualities when we cannot recognize lesser degrees (1979:268).

Swinburne acknowledges that the objection based on recognizability does indeed have some force, but again regards it as diminishing the evidential value of religious experience only slightly.

Two further and very familiar objections Swinburne dispatches in short order. 1) Suppose that we can provide a causal explanation of religious experience without reference to a religious object. Classical theism maintains that God is active in all causal processes. The only way to sustain this objection, Swinburne believes, is to demonstrate that there is no God (1979:270). 2) Claims based on religious experience often seem to conflict with one another—a favorite objection of empiricists since its classic formulation by Hume in his essay "On Miracles" (1955:29-30). Such conflicts, Swinburne acknowledges, may present a problem for specific claims, but hardly constitute a problem for the evidential value of religious experience in general. He concedes that "if there were a substantial number of religious experiences which entailed the nonexistence of a particular supernatural being, that would cast significant doubt on the credibility of claims to have perceived that being" (1979:267). In the case of God, he does not think that such a body of negative evidence exists.

Finally, Swinburne tackles the Jamesian problem: Do the religious experiences of others have evidential value for me? To deal with this issue, he introduces another fundamental principle of rationality, the Principle of Testimony: "(in the absence of special considerations) the experiences of others are (probably) as they report them" (1979:272). The value of this principle is, of course, to shift the burden of proof to those who would doubt the veracity of someone's report. Swinburne would certainly acknowledge that very good grounds might exist for questioning a report of specific religious experience, but he clearly does not believe that there are grounds for doubting the veracity of reports of religious experience in general. Nor are we totally without tests to apply to such reports. One ancient but still pertinent test is whether a religious experience brings about a practical change in the quality of life of the person who purports to have the experience (1979:273).

By this point Swinburne's argument may be looking more and more like a *tour de force*, brave but ultimately implausible. Let us conclude our discussion of Swinburne by noting two features of his position which may keep us from reaching such a conclusion prematurely.

It is essential to keep in mind, first of all, that Swinburne's approach to the issue of religious experience is possible only because of the discrediting of empiricism as a theory of knowledge. The empiricist who believes that all authentic claims to knowledge must be derived from statements about a foundational level of experience has no room for a Principle of Credulity or a Principle of Testimony. But if we reject that sort of foundationalism, then we are led to recognize that our whole picture of our world depends on our trusting many kinds of experience and also on our trusting the reports of others. Religious experience and reports about such experience are among the items to which we must grant initial credibility since there are no valid general reasons for rejecting the evidential value of this kind of experience: "Religious perceptual claims deserve to be taken as seriously as perceptual claims of any other sort" (1979:276).

We must also note very carefully just what it is that Swinburne thinks his argument has accomplished. He certainly does not want to claim that religious experience stands by itself as evidence for the existence of God. The great strength of his position is that his discussion of religious experience is part of a systematic assessment of the probability of theism.[5] Religious experience does, however, turn out to play a decisive role in this assessment. When the evidence other than religious experience is considered, theism turns out to be "neither very probable nor very improbable" (1979:289). As a hypothesis, its lack of predictive power is an unfortunate deficiency. But adducing the evidence of religious experience shifts the balance of probability: "The testimony of many witnesses to experiences apparently of God makes the existence of God probable if it is not already on other evidence very improbable" (1979:291).

PROUDFOOT AND PARTICULARISM

The implications of the decline of empiricism for our topic can be drawn in very different fashion. In his monograph *Religious Experience*, Wayne Proudfoot, working within the same philosophical perspective as Swinburne, mounts a frontal assault on Schleiermacher and his heirs, especially on his apologetic use of the appeal to religious experience. Proudfoot finds the

German theologian guilty of a gross inconsistency. Schleiermacher treats religious experience as an immediate consciousness that is not shaped by concepts and beliefs. He can then regard the language of religion as a "natural expression" of this immediate consciousness and as secondary to it (1985:24). At the same time he wants to treat the religious consciousness as intentional, that is, as having an object, namely the infinite. Without such an object, Proudfoot notes, he could not identify consciousness as religious.

Proudfoot's chief philosophic weapon is the theme that there is no raw, uninterpreted experience. All our experience is interpreted in the sense that it is shaped by our concepts and beliefs and cannot even be identified as experience without reference to them. Proudfoot is careful to differentiate his notion of interpretation from that of what he calls the hermeneutical tradition, where interpretation refers to "the decoding of texts or cultural symbols" (1985:61). He instead identifies with the pragmatic tradition and its claim that all observation is theory-laden: "We are unable to isolate and describe brute data against which to test our theories, because the data we gather is already shaped by the assumption and questions that have informed our inquiry" (1985:61).

Conveniently, Proudfoot finds that recent work in the philosophy and psychology of emotions pursues this same theme. Schleiermacher, like Hume, treats emotions as "brute" sensations. By identifying religion with emotion, he is able "to remove it from the arena in which it is dependent on particular beliefs or claims about the world" (1985:78). The work of the philosopher Errol Bedford and the psychologist Stanley Schachter suggests that this whole approach to emotions is wrong-headed. Emotions are not names for feelings. Emotions can be identified only on the basis of a cognitive appraisal which includes an explanation of what has happened to an individual. Anger, for example, is not just the name of a feeling. We can understand a feeling as anger only if we can identify a particular kind of cause for our feeling. Religious experiences, accordingly, are those experiences for which we come to believe that the best available explanation is a religious one (1985:108). James's efforts to separate the explanation and the assessment of religious experience do not escape unscathed here. James repeatedly characterizes religious experience in terms of "a sense of an unseen reality," and this characterization already embodies an explanatory hypothesis (1985:163). He is wrong to think of religious experience as a kind of incorrigible sense experience, absolutely authoritative for its recipients (1985:164).

James's purpose in distinguishing so sharply between assessment and explanation is to avoid the evil specter of reductionism, as exemplified especially by the "medical materialists" whom he attacks in the opening pages of the *Varieties*. Proudfoot's emphasis on the role of explanation in identifying religious experience forces him to confront the same bogeyman. He does so by drawing a very useful distinction between descriptive and explanatory reduction:

> An emotion, practice, or experience must be described in terms that can plausibly be attributed to the subject on the basis of available evidence. The subject's self-ascription is normative for describing the experience (1985:194).

Unless we begin by describing an experience in the subject's own terms, we do not succeed in identifying it. Once we have identified it, we are perfectly justified in engaging in explanatory reduction—"in offering an explanation of an experience in terms that are not those of the subject and that might not meet with his approval" (1985:197). Attempts, such as that of D. Z. Phillips, to condemn such explanation wholesale fail to note the difference between illegitimate descriptive reduction and perfectly normal and necessary explanatory reduction (Proudfoot, 1985:200).

Where, then, does Proudfoot's argument leave us? He has tried to do for the tradition of immediate religious experience what the critics of empiricism have done for the notion of immediate sense experience—namely, to undercut the appeal to the immediate. Just as the critics of empiricism reject the idea that our knowledge of the physical world is grounded in a foundational level of experience, so Proudfoot would have us abandon the tradition of trying to ground religious concepts and beliefs in a foundational religious experience of which the concepts and beliefs are secondary expressions. We should not conclude, of course, that there is no religious experience—only that religious experience arises through a complex interplay with concepts and beliefs. Neither experience nor belief can be regarded as somehow more fundamental than the other.

It would appear, however, that Proudfoot's argument accomplishes too much. Consider his insistence that we identify religious experience by describing it in the terms that the subject of the experience would use. The good news that accompanies this observation, as Proudfoot notes, is that we can learn about the subject's experience by studying the beliefs and concepts used to describe it (1985:219). We are not searching for an inscrutable something that can be known only by acquaintance. The bad news is that we seem to be trapped in a kind of historical particularism that makes comparative judgments and explanatory generalizations well nigh impossible. Proudfoot borrows from Arthur Danto the very important point that a phenomenon can be explained only under a description (1985:218). But how do we get from the subject's description to a description under which the experience can be explained? Only by sacrificing the particularity of the description. But Proudfoot seems reluctant to make such a sacrifice:

> If the concepts and beliefs under which the subject identifies his or her experience determine whether or not it is a religious experience, then we need to

> explain why the subject employs those particular concepts and beliefs. We must explain why the subject was confronted with this particular set of alternative ways of understanding his experience and why he employed the one he did. In general, what we want is a historical or cultural explanation (1985:223).

Proudfoot is rightly critical of the use of such vague—and essentially evocative—concepts as "the sacred" or "the numinous" because he believes that the anti-reductionist polemic associated with such terms precludes serious attempts at explanation and analysis. He is not terribly clear, however, about whether there are other less objectionable general concepts that we may use for comparative and explanatory purposes. Without such concepts we are left with an approach to religious experience which must remain idiographic rather than nomothetic and the social-scientific study of religious experience would seem out of the question.[6]

This same issue of the role of concepts in shaping experience has been central to an ongoing debate about mysticism. This debate has been occasioned by the writings of Steven Katz and several colleagues, whose work constitutes a frontal assault on the project of searching for a core of experience common to mystics in the major religious traditions.[7] Katz argues that there cannot be such a core because the experience of a mystic is essentially shaped by the concepts and beliefs of specific traditions. The following comment about Jewish mystics is intended by Katz to describe other traditions as well:

> The entire life of the Jewish mystic is permeated from childhood up by images, concepts, symbols, ideological values, and ritual behavior which there is no reason to believe he leaves behind in his experience. Rather, these images, beliefs, symbols, and rituals define, in *advance*, what the experience *he wants to have*, and which he then does have, will be like (1978a:33).

Again we find ourselves left with a radical particularism: there is no such thing as mystical experience in general, only a variety of mystical experiences shaped by diverse and apparently incommensurable traditions. Critics have attacked this position from two directions. Some have labeled Katz' epistemology a kind of "hyper-Kantianism": both Kant and Katz believe that experience is shaped by concepts, but, whereas for Kant the concepts are universally shared by human beings, for Katz the concepts are peculiar to specific cultures and religious traditions (Forgie, 1985; see also King, 1988). Other critics have searched mystical literature and their own lives for unmediated mystical experiences, experiences of "pure consciousness," a type of experience to which at least some mystical traditions clearly lay claim (Forman, 1990). The logic of Katz's particularism precludes any use of mystical experience as evidence for truth claims, as both he and his critics recognize (Katz, 1978a:22; Forgie, 1985:218).

THE IRONIC TURN

As we survey this eminently lively discussion of religious experience, we notice that its direction has taken a somewhat ironic turn. Philosophers' abandonment of empiricism and of the project of grounding knowledge in sense experience has opened up the possibility that other types of experience, even religious experience, might be considered as sources of knowledge. But the rejection of foundationalism has also made possible a critique of the tradition of seeking to ground religion in a type of experience. While some philosophers are increasingly optimistic about the evidential value of religious experience, others have used antifoundationalism to splinter religious experience into a multitude of discrete instances whose cumulative evidential value is presumably nil.

This working at cross-purposes is to be expected, I suppose, because the contemporary discussion of religious experience eventually leads us back to the pivotal issue of twentieth-century philosophy, the relationship between language and the world: Is our experience of the world shaped by our encounter with it or by the concepts we bring to that encounter? Any sober answer to this question must surely take a both/and form. As our century comes to a close, however, many philosophers are inclined to lean very heavily toward the latter half of our disjunction, for human experience seems more and more diverse to us and the old project of unifying the sciences less and less promising. But leaning too hard in either direction is likely to produce unstable positions, and it is not surprising that contemporary antifoundationalism can be used to cross-purposes.

Even in a climate of philosophical instability, however, there remain some promising possibilities for advancing the discussion of religious experience in constructive directions. One obvious limitation of the discussion we have sketched is its very narrow empirical base. These philosophers remain very much the heirs of Schleiermacher and especially James. The writings of Western theistic mystics are their principal source of accounts of religious experience, with occasional attention paid to Eastern mystical traditions.[8] Spirit possession, in contrast, a vivid and very widespread form of religious experience which many people take to have evidential value, is wholly ignored. Perhaps philosophers cannot imagine themselves sharing in this type of experience, but failure of the imagination does not justify their ignoring a phenomenon for which more than ample documentation is available.

The particularism of Katz and Proudfoot calls in doubt the very usefulness of the concept of religious experience. Even the appropriateness of "mysticism," which has an honorable if variegated history, comes into question. If religion is to be a subject for study, for scholarly description and explanation, then we cannot proceed without general concepts. We cannot proceed without using concepts which let us draw comparisons not only within but also across religious traditions. "Religious experience" is a concept with a problematic history and may very well need to be replaced or at least supplemented by concepts with a clearer and more definite content. I have found, for example, I. M. Lewis' use of the concept of religious ecstasy to yield many illuminating cross-cultural comparisons (Lewis, 1989). Philosophers can play a role in helping all scholars of religion identify what these concepts should be, rather than abandoning their colleagues to the abyss of particularism.

NOTES AND REFERENCES

1. I owe the formal/material distinction to Niebuhr (1964:123).

2. For a discussion of James's attempts, after the publication of the *Varieties,* to construe the evidential value of religious experience more generously, see Hood (1992).

3. For a comprehensive account of a twentieth-century version of empiricism, see Ayer (1955).

4. A position very similar to Swinburne's has been articulated over many years by the American philosopher William Alston. Its most complete formulation can be found in his recent book *Perceiving God.* Rather than relying on a principle of credulity, Alston introduces the notion of doxastic (belief-forming) practices, the most familiar of which is no doubt sense perception. There is an "irreducible plurality" of such practices, for neither sense perception nor other doxastic practices rest on "some deeper mode of justification" (1991:162). Furthermore, it is rational to engage in any "firmly established doxastic practice . . . provided it and its output cohere sufficiently with other firmly established doxastic practices and their output" (1991:175). The practice of especial interest to Alston is what he calls Christian Mystical Perceptual Doxastic Practice (CMP). A considerable portion of his recent volume is devoted to establishing the respectability of CMP by fending off the same sorts of objections considered by Swinburne. Alston's conclusion is also similar, though he does not opt for the language of probability: mystical experience does not provide an independent ground for belief in God, but in conjunction with other sources of justification, it furnishes a distinctive ground for such belief and the life deriving from it, distinctive because it is the only type of justification that can "tell me what God is doing vis-à-vis me at this moment" (1991:302).

5. This assessment can be found principally in Swinburne (1979 and 1987).

6. G. William Barnard has raised the further objection that Proudfoot's position would seem to rule out the possibility that religious experience could cause cultural change (1992:244).

7. This view is represented by many of the essays in the three anthologies edited by Katz (1978b, 1983, 1992). His own position is most directly stated in 1978a.

8. Yandell (1993) is notable for his attempt at a philosophical assessment of several Indian religious traditions.

Alston, W. P.
1991 *Perceiving God: The epistemology of religious experience*. Ithaca, NY: Cornell University Press.

Ayer, A. J.
1946 *Language, truth and logic*, 2nd ed. New York: Dover.
1955 *Foundations of empirical knowledge*. New York: St. Martin's Press.

Barnard, G. W.
1992 Explaining the unexplainable: Wayne Proudfoot's religious experience. *Journal of the American Academy of Religion* 60:231-256.

Brown, H. I.
1977 *Perception, theory and commitment*. Chicago: University of Chicago Press.

Carnap, R.

1959 The elimination of metaphysics through logical analysis of language. In *Logical positivism*, edited by A. J. Ayer. New York: Free Press.

Davis, C.F.
1989 *The evidential force of religious experience*. New York: Oxford University Press.

Edwards, J.
1959 *Religious affections*, edited by J. E. Smith New Haven, CT: Yale University Press.

Forgie, J.
1985 Hyper-Kantianism in recent discussions of mystical experience. *Religious Studies* 21:205-218.

Forman, R. K.
1990 *The problem of pure consciousness*. Oxford: Oxford University Press.

Hempel, C. G.
1965 Empiricist criteria of cognitive significance: Problems and changes. In *Aspects of scientific explanation*, edited by C. G. Hempel. New York: The Free Press.

Hood Jr., R. W.
1992 A Jamesean look at self and self loss in mystical experience. *Journal of the Psychology of Religion* 1:1-24.

Hume, D.
1955 *An inquiry concerning human understanding*. Indianapolis: Bobbs-Merrill.

James, W.
1985 *The varieties of religious experience*. Cambridge, MA: Harvard University Press.

Katz, S. T.
1978a Language, epistemology, and mysticism. In *Mysticism and philosophical analysis*, edited by S. T. Katz, New York: Oxford University Press.
1978b *Mysticism and philosophical analysis*. New York: Oxford University Press.
1983 *Mysticism and religious traditions*. New York: Oxford University Press.
1992 *Mysticism and language*. New York: Oxford University Press.

King, S. B.
1988 Two epistemological models for the interpretation of mysticism. *Journal of the American Academy of Religion* 56:257-280.

Kuhn, T.
1970 *The structure of scientific revolutions*, 2nd ed. Chicago: University of Chicago Press.

Lewis, I. M.
1989 *Ecstatic religion: An anthropological study of spirit possession and shamanism*, 2nd ed. New York: Routledge.

Martin, C. B.
1959 *Religious belief*. Ithaca, NY: Cornell University Press.

Niebuhr, R. R.
1964 *Schleiermacher on Christ and religion*. New York: Scribners.

Otto, R.
1923 *The idea of the holy*, translated by J.W. Harvey. Oxford: Oxford University Press.

Plantinga, A.
1983 Reason and belief in God. In *Faith and rationality*, edited by A. Plantinga and N. Wolterstorff. Notre Dame, IN: University of Notre Dame Press.

Proudfoot, W.
1985 *Religious experience*. Berkeley, CA: University of California Press.

Schleiermacher, F.
1958 *On religion: Speeches to its cultured despisers*. New York: Harper & Row.
1963 *The Christian faith*, 2 vols. New York: Harper & Row.

Smith, W.C.
1962 *The meaning and end of religion*. New York: Macmillan.

Swinburne, R.
1979 *The existence of God*. Oxford: Oxford University Press.
1987 *The coherence of theism*. Oxford: Oxford University Press.

Yandell, K.E.
1993 *The epistemology of religious experience*. Cambridge: Cambridge University Press.

8

The Sociological Context of Religious Experience

MARGARET M. POLOMA

> The Durkheimian and Weberian ways of looking at society are not logically contradictory. They are only antithetical since they focus on different aspects of social reality. It is quite correct to say that society is objective fact, coercing and even creating us. But it is also correct to say that our own meaningful acts help to support the edifice of society and may on occasion help to change it. Indeed, the two statements contain between them the paradox of social existence. That society defines us, but is in turn defined by us (Berger 1963:128-129).

Emile Durkheim and Max Weber are two of sociology's founding fathers, each of whom sowed the seeds for a dominant paradigm within the discipline (Ritzer, 1992). Durkheim (1938), insisting on the objective reality of social phenomena, provided the model for the so-called "social facts" paradigm that dominated American sociology for decades. Weber (1964), on the other hand, in stressing the importance of grasping the subjective meaning of an activity, laid the foundations for the "social definition" paradigm. These two paradigms (together with their founders) commonly have been treated as irreconcilable perspectives in sociology.

For decades the social facts paradigm had provided the principal sociological model while the social definition paradigm was reduced to the status of the "loyal opposition" (Mullins, 1973). Increasingly, however, theorists are integrating the Weberian and Durkheimian perspectives referred to by Peter Berger in the opening quotation. As noted by Ritzer (1992:457):

> Sociological theory, at least until the 1980s, was characterized by theoretical extremism of one kind or another as well as by the destructive political conflicts that often went hand in hand with such extremism. The developments that took place during the 1980s were very different from those of any previous epoch, as a wide range of theorists moved away from theoretical extremism and began to grapple with micro-macro and agency-structure integration.

Of the two paradigms, the social definitionist has been more receptive to the study of religious experience. Taking an approach that blends sociology and psychology, interrelating objective social phenomena with the study of cultural and personal interpretations of them, a social definitionist perspective may be summarized by the famous Thomas Theorem: "If [people] define a situation as real, it is real in its consequences." Psychological definitions (including experiences that are defined as "religious"), in other words, may have real institutional consequences that impact the social world. As we shall see, particularly for some sociologists working within the phenomenological tradition of the social definitionist paradigm, the focus on experience has been important for the understanding of religion. Despite the significance of religious experience for a phenomenological understanding of religion, the heavy shadow of the social facts paradigm (and its positivistic methodology) has obscured the importance of religious experience for most sociological theory and research.

In sum, a review of the history of American sociological thought reveals a discipline dominated by the social facts paradigm but haunted by the persistence of social definitionist thinking. Yet even those working within the social definitionist tradition, for the most part, have neglected the study of religious experience. It is against this backdrop that I will develop five central points relevant to the sociological context of religious experience. First, I will briefly discuss the role that theory has played in providing a frame for a sociological approach to religious experience. Second, in order to spotlight some conceptual ambiguities, I will briefly review different substantive approaches that attempt to define and describe religious experience. Then I will discuss Glock and Stark's pioneering empirical work on the multidimensionality of religion, with a focus on their discussion of the experiential dimension. Following this, I will recount the five approaches to the sociological study of religious experience identified recently by Spickard and respond to his critique of the Jamesian approach. Finally, I will close by making a case for an interdisciplinary model that includes the two major sociological paradigms for a more complete understanding of the origins, nature, and effects of religious experience in postmodern society.

RELIGIOUS EXPERIENCE IN THEORETICAL CONTEXT

Early Masters

A close reading of the major classical sociological texts that discuss religious experience reveals much less polarity between perspectives than developed in later interpretations of the works of the masters. Although Durkheim's early works, for example, represent the foundation for functionalist theory within the social facts paradigm, his later work on *The Elementary Forms of Religious Life* (Durkheim, 1947/1915) defies any simplistic categorization. Underlying Durkheim's famous definition of religion that describes religion in terms of a sacred-profane distinction is the assumption that the essence of religion has to do with collective experiences. That which is sacred, Durkheim observed, is also powerful. It attracts as well as repels individuals. This nonempirical force (which for Durkheim was nothing more than society deified) is reflected in beliefs and often experienced in religious rituals. For Durkheim, religious experience is first and foremost a collective experience: it is only the "individualized form of collective forces." As Durkheim notes (1973:198):

> Therefore, even when religion seems to be entirely within the individual conscience, it is still in society that it finds the living source from which it is nourished.

Georg Simmel, a German contemporary of Durkheim, is more likely to be placed in the social definition paradigm than in the social facts paradigm. Yet he shared with Durkheim the sociological position that general patterns of social interaction may provide the basis for religion (Johnstone, 1992). Similar feelings and impulses, including trust, compassion, a sense of justice, and the like, manifest themselves in both religious and nonreligious social interaction. In other words, according to Simmel, many emotions commonly found in everyday life, although selectively termed "religious," are in fact "social" (Wolff, 1950). As Simmel notes, "Human contact, in the purely psychological aspect of its interaction, develops that definite tendency which, heightened and differentiated to independence, is known as religion" (Simmel, 1905:361).

In Max Weber's work the sociological study of religious experience may be approached through "charisma," a concept that Eisenstadt (1968:ix) contends is "of crucial importance for understanding of the processes of institution building." Although Weber seemed to dichotomize between the charismatic aspects and the more ordinary, routine aspects of social organization, Eisenstadt insists that "the explication of the relations between charisma and institution building is perhaps the most important challenge which Weber's work poses for modern sociology." Charisma, rooted in Weberian "affective action" (as distinguished from "traditional" or "rational" forms of action) is reflected in prophetic figures and founders of major religions and serves as an important component in the development of religion.

Charismatic authority, however, is very fragile and is quick to take on either traditional or rational form. As Weber notes:

> In its pure form charismatic authority has a character specifically foreign to everyday routine structures. If this [religious movement] is not to remain a purely transitory phenomenon, but to take on the character of a permanent relationship . . . it is necessary for the character of charismatic authority to become radically changed. Indeed, in its pure form charismatic authority may be said to exist only in the process of originating (Weber, 1947:363-364).

Perhaps because of its transitory nature, the challenge of relating charisma to organizational structures made by Eisenstadt has gone largely unmet.

Durkheim, Simmel, and Weber all regarded religious experience as social phenomena out of which religious interactions, rituals, and organizations may emerge. Although a full-scale discussion of the nature of religious experience was left to social psychologist William James (1961/1902) and other scholars of religious studies, the founding fathers of sociology did provide a foundation for a complementary sociological approach. For the most part, however, the seeds planted by these early theorists failed to germinate in the works of their disciples.[1] One exception to this general observation may be seen in the works of Peter Berger. Berger has not only made religion an important part of his theoretical model, but he has also recognized the role that religious experience plays in determining the future of organized religion.

Socially Constructing Religious Reality

The tension that exists between religion and the modern world has been long noted by sociologists who have often joined other scholars of religion in writing premature obituaries for the sacred. Berger himself seemed to take that stance in his paradigmatic treatise *The Sacred Canopy* (1967). In a book written a dozen years later, Berger (1979) confesses that his earlier work on religion and modernization was "too parochial." Much of the correcting mechanism Berger used to explore "contemporary possibilities of religious affirmation" centered around religious experience. Berger (1979:ix) called for an "inductive approach"—"one that begins with ordinary human experience, explores the 'signals of transcendence' to be found in it, and moves on from there to religious affirmations about the nature of reality."

Berger's thesis rests on the assumption that "in the pluralistic situation of modernity, the authority of all religious traditions tends to be undermined" (Berger, 1979:xi). Those who would maintain a religious tradition have three options: deduction (reaffirming the authority of the tradition in defiance of the challenges to it); reduction (trying to secularize the tradition); and induction (trying to uncover and retrieve the experiences embodied in the tradition).

According to Berger, neither the deductive position taken by many religious conservatives nor the reductive position taken by many religious liberals is plausible for most modern men and women. Only the third option—that of induction—is a viable one in the face of modernity. "The inductive option is to turn to experience as the ground of all religious affirmations—one's own experience, to whatever extent this is possible, and the experience embodied in a particular range of traditions" (Berger, 1979:58).

Although Berger acknowledges the importance of religious experience in the emergence of religious aspects of culture and society, he insists that "religious experience is not universally and equally distributed among human beings" (Berger, 1979:43). Maintaining a strong sociological position that emphasizes the importance of social institutions, Berger (1979:44-45) notes:

> Religious experience breaches the reality of ordinary life, while all traditions and institutions are structures within the reality of ordinary life. . . . A religious tradition, with whatever institutions have grown up around it, exists as a fact in ordinary, everyday reality. It mediates the experience of another reality, both to those who have never had it and to those who have but who are in danger of forgetting it. Every tradition is a collective memory. . . . But the tradition not only mediates the religious experience; it also *domesticates* [italics in original] it. Whatever else it is, religious experience is dangerous. Its dangers are reduced and routinized by means of institutionalization.

Berger expresses the dialectical relationship between religious experience and religious social structures that is at the heart of his phenomenological sociology. Some people have religious experiences, and these experiences may challenge and change the social structure. Berger assumes, however, that most people do not have intense religious experiences: "Modern consciousness is not conducive to close contact with the gods" (Berger, 1979:89). But even if they do, the modern world is quick to undermine them:

> Put in phenomenological terms, there are indeed experiences of contact with the supernatural that carry within them absolute certainty, but this certainty is located only within the enclave of religious experience itself. As soon as the individual returns from this enclave into the world of everyday reality, this certainty is retained only as a memory and as such is intrinsically fragile (Berger, 1979:138).

Although Berger's unsubstantiated preconceptions about the infrequency and fragility of religious experience may be challenged through empirical research, the model he provides has been the dominant paradigm in the sociology of religion (Warner, 1993). Religious reality is socially constructed, and this emergent reality acts back upon its producers. Very intense religious experiences (those of prophets and mystics) may be discussed in terms of being catalysts in the formation of religious institutions, with some being more "gifted" in creating religious reality than are others. According to Berger, most people have not been creative mystics and prophets; most have socialized into an existing religious reality. In the modern world, however, this religious reality is very precarious and requires fresh experiences for its maintenance.

Although Berger watered some of the seeds sown by early theorists who explored religious experience, interest in the topic may be seen as an example of a discontinuity in sociology. The neglect of the topic led Rodney Stark (1965:97) to comment some thirty years ago, that since the publication of James's classic study, "virtually nothing of merit has been added to our understanding of religious experience." This neglect can be linked to the dominance of the social facts paradigm in sociology which eschewed topics that appeared too "psychological." It is only within the past decade or so, a time during which there has been an increasing acceptance of approaches that recognize the importance of both social structure and the people who shape them, that limited renewed interest in religious experience can be evidenced.

Despite increasing interest, religious experience remains a concept that suffers from poor conceptualization, operationalization, and measurement in sociology. Underlying these difficulties is the problem of satisfactorily defining *religious experience*, a problem whose solution has eluded many scholars of religion in theology, the humanities, and the social sciences alike. An overview of this literature will cast light on the problem of defining, conceptualizing, and measuring religious experience.

MYSTICISM, TRANSCENDENCE, AND RELIGIOUS EXPERIENCE

One of the ways to approach the subject of religious experience is through the writings on mysticism. A common dictionary definition of a mystic is "a person who claims to attain, or believes in the possibility of attaining insight into mysteries of transcending ordinary human knowledge, as by immediate intuition in a state of spiritual ecstasy" (*The Random House Dictionary of the English Language* [Second Edition]) This commonly accepted definition recognizes the varieties of mystical experience, experiences which range from simple intuition to visions and voices.

It is the position of this chapter that religious experience and mysticism are essentially the same phenomenon, differing only in degree.[2] As such, these two terms may be used interchangeably. As Parrinder (1976:19) notes: "The mystic . . . may be the expert, differing in degree from the ordinary believer by the intensity or frequency of his mystical visions, but he need not be different in kind, since the layman has some spiritual awareness." This fact is often obscured in scholarly writings where mysticism is described in more extreme forms, emphasizing the loss of self to Another or to Nothingness. After making a comparative study of mysticism in the world's religions,

Parrinder (1976:191) underscores the naturalness of mysticism and its similarity to what is commonly referred to as religious experience:

> The religious experience of the ordinary believer is often spoken of as "communion" with God. . . . It may be said that "communion" is not the same as "union," but it is not basically different. "Communion" means "union with," and in religious usage the difference between communion and union can be claimed as a matter of degree. Hence the religious experience of the ordinary believer is in the same class as that of the mystic; the difference is one of degree but not of kind.

Mysticism: A Substantive Approach

There are many differing approaches that seek to define and to describe the essence of mysticism. Some have dealt with mysticism chiefly as an aspect of religion, tracing the importance of mysticism in religion's development (Stall, 1975; Elwood, 1980). Others have insisted that mysticism is a "way of knowing" and that "mystical science is not dependent on the use of a religious or spiritual" vocabulary or context (Deikman, 1982:170). Theories on the essence of mysticism have differed as to whether mysticism is regarded as being "one" or "many"—"one" in that the different forms reflect a single ultimate reality or "many" in that there are several distinct and unique types (Almond, 1982). Radhakrishan (1940) has argued that all spiritual or religious experience is mystical. Zaehener (1961), on the other hand, contended that there is a clear distinction between the theistic and monistic forms of mystical experiences. Others (including Otto, 1932; Stace, 1961; and Smart, 1985) have argued that there is only one form of interior mystical experience. Those who have struggled to refine such distinctions have advanced a number of typologies, including Otto's (1932) theistic and mystical (subdivided into the "inward" and "outward" way; Zaehner's (1961) panenhenic ("eyes closed"), monistic (understanding) and theistic (love); Stace's (1961) extrovertive and introvertive mysticism; Smart's (1965) numinous and mystical and Happold's (1970) "mysticism of love and union" and "mysticism of knowledge and understanding." In sum, mysticism has been sometimes limited to "mystical union" (be it with Nothingness, with Nature or with God); at other times, it has been given a broader connotation that links mysticism with other spiritual experiences.

After reviewing these and other distinctions, Almond (1982:128) lists and describes five models that seek to interpret mystical or religious experience:

1) All mystical experience is the same. There is a unanimity about mystical utterance which points to the unanimity of mystical experience.
2) All mystical experience is the same but the various interpretations of the experience depend on the religious and/or philosophical framework of the mystic.

3) There is a small number of types of mystical experience which cut across cultural barriers.
4) There are as many different types of mystical experience as there are paradigmatic expressions of them.
5) There are as many different types of mystical experience as there are incorporated interpretations of them.

The failure of scholars to agree on the substantive nature of mystical or religious experiences has posed no little difficulty for social scientists whose task of operationalization has built upon unresolved problems in conceptualization. Given the disagreement among philosophers of religion about the nature of mysticism and religious experience, it is not surprising that both the conceptualization and measurement of religious experience has often been flawed.

RELIGIOUS EXPERIENCE AS A DIMENSION OF RELIGIOSITY

The earliest empirical works that sought to systematically explore different dimensions of religiosity during the late 1950s and early 1960s brought with them a resurgence of interest in religious experience. In an article published in 1959, Charles Glock suggested that religiosity was not a unidimensional phenomenon but that it could be divided into four separate facets: the experiential (religious feelings), the ritualistic (practices), the ideological (beliefs) and the consequential (effects). These four dimensions were empirically verified in a large-scale research project conducted by Glock and Stark (1965), and these four dimensions are widely accepted as the major components of religiosity.[3]

Glock and Stark (1965; Stark, 1965) provided the earliest sociological taxonomy of religious experience—a taxonomy that built upon those scholars who limited religious experiences to contact with a supernatural agency.[4] Glock and Stark define *religious experiences* as

> all of those feelings, perceptions, and sensations which are experienced by an actor or defined by a religious group or a society as involving some communication, however slight, with divine essence, i.e., with God, with ultimate reality, with transcendental authority (1965:42).

The typology developed by Glock and Stark reflects the assumption that what has been called *mysticism* by some religious scholars is the same as *religious experience*, differing in degree but not in essence. Such experiences range from simply noting the existence of the divine actor (feeling, sensing, etc.), to acknowledging a mutual presence, to experiencing an affective relationship, to being a fellow participant in action with the divine actor (1965:43). Glock and Stark compare religious experience to human relationships of differing intensities:

As in normal human affairs, encounters of the former types are more frequent than those of the latter—one has many more acquaintances than friends. Similarly, any more intimate relationship has likely passed through less intimate previous states.

Having made these preliminary statements, Glock and Stark proceeded to develop a taxonomy to organize and classify the "remarkedly varied phenomenon of religious experience." This configuration included four major types to correspond with the intensity of action: confirming experience, responsive experience, ecstatic experience, and revelational experience.

The confirming experience (Glock and Stark, 1965:43-46) is the most general kind of religious experience, one that provides "a sudden feeling, knowing, or intuition that the beliefs one holds are true." Its subtypes include a "generalized sense of sacredness" and a "specific awareness of the presence of divinity." Confirming experiences are relatively common, with over 40 percent of Glock and Stark's West Coast sample responding that they were certain they have experienced "a feeling that [they] were somehow in the presence of God."

Responsive experience is the next most common type of religious experience, occurring when a person feels that the awareness of presence is mutual. Responsive experiences were subdivided into three types: salvational, miraculous and sanctioning. Such experiences are highly correlated with denominational affiliation. For example, while 93 percent of the Southern Baptist sample reported being certain of salvation, only 9 percent of the Congregationalists made such a claim.

The ecstatic experience denotes an affective personal relationship between God and the person, comparable to the intimacy of friendship or even courtship. Glock and Stark, (1965:53) describe the prototype of this kind of religious encounter as "a physical and psychological upheaval of intense proportions, similar to orgasm, intoxication, seizures—an overpowering of the senses by divine 'touch.'"

Finally, the revelational experience, the fourth and least common type of religious experience, is one in which the divine "has not only taken the person to his bosom, but into his confidence" (Glock and Stark, 1965:54). This may occur through visions, voices, enlightenment and commission through which persons are sent forth to perform the bidding of the divine.[5]

Glock and Stark's elaborate discussion of the experiential dimension of religiosity has been largely ignored even by those who have pursued the measurement religious dimensions. King and Hunt (1972), for example, developed a scale which they called "personal religious experience," but most of the items had more to do with personal religious devotion (especially prayer) than religious experience. Grönblom (1984) includes cognitive items (i.e., "thinking of having grown in faith" and "thought of lying as doing something against God's will") with items that are more experiential in a single dimension. Although religious experience has come to be accepted as a bona fide component of the broader phenomenon we call "religion," few scholars, as we shall see, have done more than pay it lip service. Although research studies have employed other dimensions of religiosity, especially those tapping religious affiliation, participation, and orthodoxy, relatively few sociological theorists or researchers have utilized existent knowledge about religious experience in their scholarship.

SOCIOLOGICAL MODELS FOR STUDYING RELIGIOUS EXPERIENCE

Why is it that, although religious experience had been empirically identified as one of the dimensions of religiosity over thirty years ago, little research of either a substantive or functional nature has been conducted sociologically on the topic? Failure to make strides in identifying the essence of such experiences may be at least in part accounted for by the fuzzy conceptualization found in theological, philosophical, and religious studies literature discussed earlier. What is the relationship between religious experience and mysticism? Are all religious/mystical experiences the same or is there great diversity among them? Can religious experiences be reduced to a few different types that differ qualitatively from one another (e.g., theistic and monistic)? Although agreement on the essence of religious experiences need not have prevented sociological research, unresolved questions such as these have made it more difficult to use this dimension of religiosity as a variable in empirical investigations.

One sociologist who did explore the essence of religious experience empirically in the decade following Glock and Stark's pioneering work was Andrew Greeley. Greeley (1974, 1975) operationalized the concept as paranormal experiences, to allow both theists and nontheists alike to respond to the questions. He focused on three different measures to tap mystical experience: peak experiences, psychic (PSI) occurrences, and the occult. Using Maslow's concept of "peak experience," Greeley contended that such mountaintop experiences tend to be "religious" (although not necessarily supernatural or theistic). Being moved by a beautiful sunrise or waves pounding a beach can produce experiences that may be attributed to God or Nature. PSI experiences were measured by questions dealing with clairvoyance, extrasensory perception, and déjà-vu. Occult experiences included consulting a spiritualist, medium, or astrologer or using a horoscope to make life decisions. Based on his research, Greeley contended that mysticism is commonplace and that it has gone "mainstream," touching the lives of millions of persons (Greeley, 1987).

My own work (Poloma and Pendleton, 1991, especially Chapter 5) provides support for Greeley's treatment of religious experience as a multidimensional phenomenon. The 1985 Akron Area Survey included Greeley's original items plus a new "prayer experience index." The latter was intended to tap religious experiences of the 90 percent of the random sample of Akronites who reported engaging in personal prayer. The scale items included having a deep sense of peace, experiencing the presence of God, receiving answers to specific prayer requests, sensing a deep spiritual or biblical truth, and being led by God to perform some specific action. These items could be scaled according to the degrees of intimacy described in Stark's (1965) original taxonomy of religious experience, ranging from the human actor simply noting "the existence or presence of the divine actor" to perceiving him/herself as "a confidant of and/or a fellow participant in action with the divine actor."

Peak experiences, as Greeley (1975) suggested, were somewhat correlated with religious experiences but were not identical to them (r=.49). Neither the relationships between peak experiences nor prayer experiences *and* PSI or the occult were statistically significant. What is of some interest (and in need of further exploration) is that PSI and occult experiences tended to demonstrate inverse relationships from peak and prayer experiences when assessing their impact on subjective perceptions of well-being (SWB). While peak and prayer experiences tended to demonstrate positive relationships with SWB (life satisfaction, happiness, existential well-being), PSI and the occult correlations showed some weak negative relationships with SWB (Poloma and Pendleton, 1991).

Greeley's main contribution to social-science literature on religious experience may be to remind psychologists and others that paranormal experiences are normal. Polls conducted since Greeley's original work support his contention that "mystical" experiences are indeed widespread. Levin (1993), in analyzing Greeley's findings in light of the 1988 NORC survey, recently concludes that mystical experiences are more common today than they were twenty years ago. From 1973-1988, Levin (1993:511) notes:

> The percentage of respondents who reported ever having experienced mystical phenomena increased for four of the five indicators. Lifetime prevalence of déjà vu increased from 50 to 67.3%, ESP from 58 to 64.8%, clairvoyance from 24 to 28.3%, and spiritualism from 27 to 39.9%, while numinous experience declined from 35 to 31.5%.

Further support for the widespread nature of religious experience may be found in national Gallup surveys. Forty-three (43%) of the respondents affirmed that they had "been aware of, or influenced by, a presence or a power—whether [they called] it God or not—which is different from [their] everyday sel[ves]." The descriptions of this awareness varied from having a sense of the "presence of God," to receiving "guidance from God," to having an "indescribable feeling" (Gallup and Jones, 1989:164).

Despite the significance of these national surveys, it is fair to say that this pioneering work is just that—fledgling efforts to document the widespread presence of religious experience in American society and to demonstrate that these experiences are multifaceted. James Spickard (1993) appears to be somewhat critical of such studies in his recent appraisal of sociological contributions to the study of religious experience. He contends that the reason sociologists have not comprehended religious experiences well (and have consequently ignored them) is due to faulty conceptualization that has privatized them and thus removed them from the social sphere. As Spickard (1993:109) notes:

> Drawing upon a Protestant piety that can be traced back to Schleiermacher's late eighteenth-century defense of religion against its "cultured despisers" (Schleiermacher, 1958; see Proudfoot, 1985), James grounded religious experiences in feelings, which he treated as private. He drew a rigid distinction between these experiences and the "overbeliefs" by which they are labeled. Overbeliefs are clearly social. Treating experiences as private, however, removes them from the social sphere.

Since James, observes Spickard, "the sociology of religion has focused on religious institutions and religious ideas," often neglecting religion's experiential side. Spickard's discussion is worthy of some detailed summary.

Spickard's "For a Sociology of Religious Experience"

In his recent critique of the sociology of religious experience, Spickard (1993) discusses five different approaches to the topic. None of them is fully developed, but each contributes something toward the sociological discussion. Spickard identifies these five approaches as: Jamesian, labeling, constructivism, learning, and shared time.

Jamesian Approach

Building on the work of William James, this approach has been the most commonly used social-scientific perspective on religious experience. Spickard is critical of this model for its failure to wrestle with the social origins of religious experiences. Of the five perspectives, he judges the Jamesian approach to be the least useful for social science.

Spickard uses Poloma's analysis of charisma in the Assemblies of God (Poloma, 1989; Poloma and Pendleton, 1989a) as a prototype. In this analysis, I treat pentecostal experiences (glossolalia, prophecy, being "slain in the Spirit," healing, etc.) as having a quality *sui generis*. These experiences are seen as one (although certainly not the only) factor in the growth of the Assemblies of God. In a more recent work, I use a similar approach to demonstrate how such experiences may be a factor in local growth in some Episcopal churches (Poloma, 1993a). In other words, religious experiences are analyzed in terms of their effects on a religious institutions. I have also used a Jamesian approach in less institution-focused research that analyzed the impact of prayer experiences on diverse attitudes and behavior, including forgiveness of injuries, political activism, and subjective perceptions of well-being. I will defend the importance of this approach based on empirical findings in a following section.

Labeling Experiences

The labeling approach is akin to the Jamesian approach in that it fails to account for the social nature of religious experiences and tends to separate religious experiences from the beliefs used to frame them. Spickard uses Blackmore's (1983, 1984) work as exemplary.

According to Spickard's discussion of Blackmore, we do not experience the world directly. "Rather, our brains mold our perceptions into a model of reality; we then 'experience' this model." Although our vivid experiences are physiologically "real," they are "framed by labels that we attach to our experiences to explain them" (Spickard, 1993:111-112). The same physiological brain response may be labeled as "union with God" or as "nirvana," depending on the social context in which it is experienced.

Constructivism

While Jamesian and labeling approaches tend to separate religious experiences from beliefs, Spickard asserts that constructivists seek to explore the ways that experiences and ideas condition one another. He uses Neitz's (1987) research on Catholic charismatics as an empirical example and Proudfoot's (1985) critique of Schleiermacher and James as the best theoretical presentation of this approach.

According to Proudfoot, James assumes that religious emotions are simply "given." Proudfoot counters that emotions are not simply given but are matters of interpretation. Pure emotions are impossible, and James's attempt to base religion on pure feeling is absurd. Spickard contends that Proudfoot's own attempts to abolish the distinction between experiences and labels "merely pushed the labeling process back one step." The invaluable contribution that constructivists make to the discussion, however, is to recognize that "we cannot accept religious experiences simply as given; we must ask about their origins, to which religious beliefs may contribute" (Spickard, 1973:115).

Social Learning

While the Jamesian approach treats religious experience as *sui generis* and the labeling approach describes it as an "odd brain-state," the learning approach focuses on how religious experience is learned. According to this approach, people can learn to have religious experiences, and they can learn to produce certain brain states.

Spickard uses the example of Preston's (1988) analysis of the process by which "Zen reality" is transmitted to illustrate this approach. Learning techniques, rules, etc., does not induce meditation. Even ideas (except for the idea that ideas are meaningless) are regarded as meaningless. Yet "with extended practice—and an acceptance of the notion that ideas will not cause the Zen meditative state—the 'bodymind' becomes more attentive" (Spickard, 1993:117). Spickard feels that this same "nonconceptual training technique" exists for other religious settings and nonmeditative religious experiences. In sum:

> Clearly, this approach complements rather than contradicts the labeling and constructivist approaches to the social study of religious experiences. It locates a second way in which these experiences are socially formed, focusing on their nonconceptual aspects (Spickard, 1973:117).

Living in Shared Time

Following the thought of phenomenologist Alfred Schutz, Spickard emphasizes the importance of shared ideas for social ties. Schutz noted how people may be tied together by communal experiences—for example, sharing music. Spickard (1993:119) summarizes the sociality of music as follows:

> Music's peculiar sociality is not dependent on conceptual thought. Composers, performers, and audience all bring to music a socially generated stock of knowledge, which forms the ground of their experiences. *But musical experience is not reducible to that ground.* [Italics in original] Music generates a shared experience of inner time, what Schutz calls a "musical tuning-in relationship."

Spickard contends that this relationship can be the basis for a sociology of religious experience (see also, Neitz and Spickard, 1990), especially a study of religious rituals. "Experiences are patterns of inner time; like all patterns of inner time, they can be shared" (Spickard, 1993:119).[6]

Spickard (1991) has applied this approach to traditional Navajo religion, arguing that Navaho rituals "structure their participants' experiences of time." In taking this approach, Spickard takes what he calls "a more subtle version of James's thesis that religious belief grows out of experience." The difference is that rather than privatizing religious experiences (as Spickard claims James does), Spickard regards such experiences as primarily social.

Although Spickard says that all five of the approaches he has outlined can generate concrete research, he asserts that the James's model is probably the least useful. Spickard notes: "Though it finds religious experiences important, its portrayal of them as *sui generis* discourages detailed inquiry." I feel Spickard's critique overlooks the social dimension of James's theory. Without denying the importance of the other four approaches, I would like to respond with a case for the sociological relevance of the Jamesian model.

A Case for the Social Nature of the Jamesian Approach

Any critique of James's discussion of religious experience should recognize the nature of his discussion. James seems to try to refute some of the biases of the "scientific perspective" of his day. He warned against what may be called "scientific reductionism" or reducing all of reality to a particular scientific perspective. As James (1961:387) stated: "The individual's religion may be egotistic, and those private realities which it keeps in touch with may be narrow enough; but at any rate it always remains infinitely less hollow and abstract, as far as it goes, than a science which prides itself on taking no account of anything private at all." Scientific biases persist today, which may be one of the reasons for the neglect of the study of religious experience by sociologists. Although the scientific perspective is one that social scientists must embrace to "do" their research, humility dictates that we recognize the 1) there is diversity of thought within the scientific perspective itself and 2) there is (as Immanuel Kant noted well) tension between the noumena (spirit), and phenomena (empirical reality) that is not easily reconciled.

James may have overstated his case for "private" religion, but he did recognize that religious experiences have social consequences. James believed it was possible to judge religious experiences in terms of "fruits for life" (James, 1961:195). Conversion, for example, should produce *Saintliness*, "the collective name for the ripe fruits of religion" (p. 220). Saintliness, in turn, increased charity or "tenderness for fellow creatures." Whether religious experience is public or private, people who have them live in a social world which they help to create and modify. Thus, at least indirectly, they would appear to have social consequences.

None of the approaches described by Spickard raises this important question about the social functions of religious experience. It is precisely this question concerning the effects of religious experience that I have sought to make central in my own empirical research. Religious experience, my work suggests, has a range of both institutional and interpersonal consequences. Exploring these social consequences of religious experience is as important—if not more important—a task as identifying the social factors which help to promote them.

Institutional Consequences

My research on the Assemblies of God (Poloma, 1989; Poloma and Pendleton, 1989a) and my more recent work on the renewal movement within the Episcopal Church (Poloma, 1993a) both demonstrate that religious experience is a factor in institutional change. Research (cf. Hadaway, 1991) has shown evangelism to be related to church growth, but little empirical work has been done to explore motivating factors underlying evangelical efforts. Charismatic experience (speaking in tongues, healing, prophecy, etc.) was found to be the leading predictor of evangelism for adherents of the Assemblies of God. Their personal experiences, I argue, served as a dual motivating and empowering mechanism. Those who scored high on the "charismatic experience index" not only professed a belief in healing, prophecy, miracles, glossolalia, etc., they also experienced these paranormal phenomena and were able to use them in evangelism.

Charismatic experiences are not limited to pentecostal churches but have been part of many mainline churches for well over two decades (Poloma, 1980). In an attempt to study the institutional impact of these experiences on the Episcopal Church, I evaluated the "Leadership Training Institute," a program for priests sponsored by Episcopal Renewal Ministries. The degree to which priests reportedly had charismatic experiences during the Institute was significantly correlated with changes in their parishes, including church growth, level of outreach and evangelism, and charismatic manifestations within the congregation. More similar research needs to be done that explores the relationship between religious experience and institutional development, growth, and change.

Personal Consequences

My research on spiritual healing (Poloma and Pendleton, 1991:Chapter 4) and prayer experiences (Poloma and Pendleton, 1989a; 1991; Poloma, 1993b) explored the effects of religious experience on a variety of variables, including subjective perceptions of well-being (life satisfaction, happiness, and existential well-being), forgiveness, and political activism. In this research, religion was treated as a multidimensional phenomenon, with religious experience being but one dimension. The results of multivariate analysis showed that of the different dimensions of religiosity (ritual, devotion, belief, etc.), it was religious experience that was the best predictor of the different dependent variables.

In a local survey focusing on the relationship between religiosity and subjective perceptions of well-being, we found that respondents who scored higher on an index measuring religious experiences during prayer were more likely to perceive themselves to be happier, to have a greater sense of meaning and purpose in life, and to be more satisfied with life (Poloma and Pendleton, 1991, especially Chapter 3). [Poloma and Gallup (1991) found the same relationship between prayer experiences and life satisfaction for respondents in a national Gallup poll]. Of the different dimensions of religiosity, religious experience [through which God becomes a "significant other" (Pollner, 1989)] is clearly a most important predictor of well-being.

Poloma and Gallup (1991) explored the relationship between religiosity and forgiveness in a 1988 Gallup Poll. They found that those persons who reported more frequent prayer experiences were more likely to forgive those who had deliberately caused them injury. In a qualitative study of crime victims, Bulan (1993:91-94), building on Poloma and Gallup's survey, focused on three specific religious experiences: being born again, having an intense experience of the presence of God, and sensing protection from danger. Those victims claiming to have had such religious experiences were more likely to have forgiven their victimizers. Although these findings are social psychological in nature, I would argue they could have institutional consequences worthy of sociological investigation. Just as one might observe negative social consequences for vengeance (from crime to warfare), forgiveness may well sow seeds of peace and harmony within both micro and macro systems. In other words, religious experience has been found to influence attitudes which, in turn, influences behavior that can modify institutions.

In my research on religious experience, I have not attempted to discuss the origins of religious experience. Sociological searches for "origins," whether it be of family systems or religious experience, have not been particularly fruitful. I suggest that the "origins of religious experience" might better be pursued by other disciplines. As a "Jamesian," I am willing to accept the respondent's description of such experience as more real than many sociological (and psychological) accounts of them. Although I acknowledge the importance of studying how religious experiences are transmitted, I am wary of some of the untested assumptions made by some of the models that tend to repeat the Durkheimian error of explaining away religion. Despite this uneasiness, it is well within sociology's mandate to research the process of transmitting culture called for by Spickard. Personally I have found it more fruitful to accept religious experience as a "given" to move on to more interesting questions about its impact on social interaction and on the social order.

DUALITY AND RELIGIOUS EXPERIENCE: A SOCIOLOGICAL MODEL

I began this chapter by noting how sociologists increasingly are being called away from dualism—to bridge the chasm between so-called micro and macro approaches to the study of social reality (Collins, 1981) and between agents (or actors) and social structure (Giddens, 1984). I wish to conclude by emphasizing the potential of this integrative paradigm for the study of religious experience. Linking the micro and macro approaches—the actor with the social context—requires an interdisciplinary model with sociology and psychology working in tandem.

Religious experience and the social context in which it occurs are inseparable. While psychology hones in on elaborate exploration of the effects of religious experience on the individual, sociology studies the social stage upon which these experiences naturally take place. Social psychologists from both disciplines provide the bridge for linking seemingly private experiences to a larger social context. What Almond (1982:183) observes about "mysticism" may be applied equally to the more generic concept "religious experience":

> The mystical experience is *crucially* (although not *necessarily*) context dependent. A sociological, anthropological, and historical approach to particular mystical systems is consequently necessary if the mystical endeavor is to be placed within the societal and cultural framework as a whole. It is only in the recognition of the interplay between the retrospective and incorporated

> interpretations within specific cultural contexts that we may hope to generate accurate accounts of the mystical experiences that arise out of them.

Religious experience is (at least in part) dependent upon community, particularly upon the language of the community. In the words of Robert Ellwood (1980:141): "Sociology is present in religious mysticism in a way it might not be with 'raw' ecstasy, because what makes an experience religious is association with religious interpretative concepts derived ultimately from a socially transmitted language and world view." Emile Durkheim recognized the interface between community and religious experience in his discussion of "collective effervescence" in religious rituals. Max Weber (and Ernest Troeltsch) provided an equally important perspective in noting that not all religious experience arises in such a structured social context. There is prophet as well as priest; mystic as well as ritualist. In building on Weber, Troeltsch (1931) contended that mysticism was the third form of religious expression. Sociologists, trained in the Durkheimian perspective that emphasized social structure, embraced "church" and "sect," but rarely even noted the third form.

The Durkheimian perspective's emphasis on social structure is one that inspires the most basic question about religious experience, namely, is it normative? The answer to this question appears to be an affirmative one. The social facts paradigm also suggests questions about group differences in religious experience based on sex, age, race, and ethnicity. Existent research suggests that women, for example, are more likely to have religious experiences than men (Feltey and Poloma, 1991). Denominational affiliation appears to be related to religious experience, with conservative Protestants being more likely to report them than Catholics or mainline Protestants (Poloma and Pendleton, 1991; Chapter 7). Levin's (1993) recent work exploring age differences in the prediction of mystical experience suggests that different mystical experiences demonstrate different relationships based on age. Using Greeley indicants found in NORC data (déjà vu, ESP, clairvoyance, spiritualism and numinous experience), Levin reported that déjà vu, ESP, and clairvoyance declined slightly with age while numinous experience and spiritualism showed a slight increase. Poloma and Pendleton (1991: Chapter 5) similarly reported that age was positively related to peak and prayer experiences but negatively related to occult and PSI experiences. Clearly there is a need for more work that explores the social contexts of such experiences.

But social contexts are processes, modified through definitions and interpretations by actors. Social definitionists have long insisted on studying these definitions. Some sociologists with a phenomenological bent (particularly those using Spickard's "constructivist" and "living in shared time" approaches) have recognized the importance of capturing these processes through which religious experience is defined in social context. To paraphrase the quotation by Peter Berger used to open this article: "It is quite correct to say that the social context is an objective fact, coercing and even creating our religious experiences. But it is also correct to say that our own meaningful religious experiences help to support the edifice of society and may on occasion help to change it." Sociology's task is to study both the interface of the objective social context and its bearing upon religious experience as well as subjective interpretations of religious experience and how they impact the social world.

NOTES AND REFERENCES

1. One exception is the church-sect-mysticism typology developed by German sociologist Ernst Troeltsch. Troeltsch (1931), following his mentor Max Weber, developed a discussion of church and sect organization that is well known to scholars in the sociology of religion. What is less well known is that Troeltsch described another type of religious group, the mystics, that emphasizes nonrational personal experience as the cornerstone of religion.

2. This position stands in contrast to those who would insist on using the term mysticism to refer only to unitary experiences. Wainwright (1981:1), for example, states: "Mystical experiences should be distinguished from ordinary religious feelings and sentiments, from numinous experiences, and from visions, voices and such occult phenomena as telepathy, clairvoyance, and precognition. None of these experiences is unitary."

3. Scholars before and after Glock and Stark have discussed other dimensions, including social or fellowship aspect (Wach, 1944). Fukuyama (1961) elaborated on Glock's proposal, suggesting four major dimensions which he termed the cognitive, the cultic, the creedal, and the devotional. Glock and Stark's (1965) empirical project, however, identified the original four dimensions and added a fifth (the intellectual or religious knowledge). The original four dimensions discussed by Stark have become widely accepted as the major components of religiosity (cf. Faulkner and De Jong, 1966; Chalfant et al., 1987).

4. Although Glock and Stark's approach may be criticized for its failure to deal with nontheistic (monistic) experiences, this line of criticism does not really flaw the typology for most research in the United States. Given the U.S.'s overwhelmingly Judeo-Christian population, few nontheists find their way into research studies.

5. Glock and Stark (1965:62-64) also adapt this taxonomy to "evil experiences. Instead of the sacred, a general sense of evil, temptations, terrorizing experience, and possession may be experienced.

6. Yamane and Polzer's (1992) testing of what they call the "cultural-linguistic" theory appears to support Spickard's assertion about the importance of ritual for religious experiences. Rituals, particularly prayer and church attendance, were found to have a positive effect on the likelihood of having had an ecstatic experience.

Almond, P. C.
1982 *Mystical experience and religious doctrine: An investigation of the study of mysticism in world religions.* New York: Mouton Publishers.

Berger, P. L.
1963 *Invitation to sociology: A humanistic perspective.* Garden City, NY: Doubleday.
1967 *The sacred canopy: Elements in a sociological theory of religion.* Garden City, NY: Doubleday.
1979 *The heretical imperative: Contemporary possibilities of religious affirmation.* Garden City, NY: Doubleday.

Blackmore, S. J.
1983 Are out-of-body experiences evidence for survival? *Anabiosis* 3:137-55.
1984 Who am I? In *Beyond Therapy*, edited by G. Clason. London: Wisdom Publications.
Bulan, H. F.
1993 Victimization and forgiveness: The role of religiosity in the coping process. M.A. thesis, University of Akron.
Chalfant, H. P., R. E. Beckley, and C. E. Palmer
1987 *Religion in contemporary society*. Palo Alto, CA: Mayfield.
Collins, J. E.
1991 *Mysticism and new paradigm psychology*. Savage, MD: Rowman and Littlefield.
Collins, R.
1981 On the microfoundations of macrosociology. *American Journal of Sociology* 86:984-1014.
Deikman, A. J.
1982 *The observing self. Mysticism and psychotherapy*. Boston: Beacon Press.
Durkheim, Emile
1938 *The Rules of Sociological Method*, translated by S.A. Solovay and J.H. Mueller. New York: Free Press.
[1915]
1947 *The Elementary Forms of Religious Life*. New York: Free Press.
1973 *Emile Durkheim: On morality and society*, edited by R. N. Bellah. Chicago: University of Chicago Press.
Eisenstadt, S. N. (Ed.)
1968 *Max Weber on charisma and institution building. Selected Papers*. Chicago: University of Chicago Press.
Ellwood, R. S. Jr.
1980 *Mysticism and religion*. Englewood Cliffs, NJ: Prentice-Hall.
Faulkner, J. E. and G. E. De Jong
1966 Religiosity in 5-D: An empirical analysis. *Social Forces* 43:246-254.
Feltey, K. M. and M. M. Poloma
1991 From sex differences to gender role beliefs: Exploring effects of six dimensions of religiosity. *Sex Roles* 25:181-193.
Fukuyama, Y.
1961 The major dimensions of church membership. *Review of Religious Research* 2:154-161.
Giddens, A.
1984 *The constitution of society: Outline of the theory of structuration*. Berkeley, CA: University of California Press.
Glock, C. Y.
1959 The Religious Revival in America. In *Religion and the face of America*, edited by J. C. Zahn. Berkeley, CA: University Extension, University of California.
Glock, C. Y. and R. Stark
1965 *Religion and society in tension*. Chicago: Rand McNally.
Greeley, A.
1974 *Ecstasy: A way of knowing*. Englewood Cliffs, NJ: Prentice-Hall.
1975 *The sociology of the paranormal: A Reconnaissance*. Sage Research Papers in the Social Sciences (Studies in Religion and Ethnicity Series No. 90-023). London: Sage Publications.
1987 Mysticism goes mainstream. *American Health* 6:47-49.
Grönblom, G.
1984 *Dimensions of religiosity*. Abo. Abo Akademi.
Hadaway, C. K.
1991 From stability to growth: a study of factors related to the statistical revitalization of Southern Baptist congregations. *Journal for the Social Scientific Study of Religion* 30:181-192.
Happold, F. C.
1970 *Mysticism*. Harmondsworth. Penguin.

James, W.
[1902]
1961 *Varieties of Religious Experience*. New York: Collier.

Johnstone, R. L.
1992 *Religion in society*, 4th ed. Englewood Cliffs, NJ: Prentice-Hall.

Kass, J. D., R. Friedman, J. Leserman, P. C. Zuttermeister, and H. Benson
1991 Health outcomes and a new index of spiritual experience. *Journal for the Social Scientific Study of Religion* 30:203-211.

King, M. B. and R. A. Hunt
1972 *Measuring Religious Dimensions*. Dallas: Department of Research and Survey National Division. United Methodist Board of Missions.

Levin, J.S.
1993 Age Differences in mystical experience. *The Gerontologist* 33:507-513.

McCready, W. C., and A. Greeley
1976 *The ultimate values of the American population*. Beverly Hills, CA: Sage Publications.

Mullins, N.
1973 *Theories and theory groups in contemporary American sociology*. New York. Harper & Row.

Neitz, M.
1987 *Charisma and community*. New Brunswick, NJ: Transaction.

Neitz, J. and J.V. Spickard
1990 Steps toward a sociology of religious experience. *Sociological Analysis* 51:15-33.

Otto, R.
1932 *Mysticism East and West*. New York: Macmillan.

Parrinder, G.
1976 *Mysticism in the world's religions*. New York: Oxford University Press.

Pollner, M.
1989 Divine relations, social relations, and well-being. *Journal of Health and Social Behavior* 30:92-104.

Poloma, M. M.
1980 *The charismatic movement: Is there a new pentecost? Boston*. Twayne Publishers.
1989 *The Assemblies of God at the crossroads*. Knoxville, TN: University of Tennessee Press.
1993a Charismatic renewal in the Episcopal Church: Assessing the impact of the Leadership Training Institute. Paper presented at the society for the Scientific Study of Religion. Raleigh, NC. November.
1993b The effects of prayer on mental well-being. *Second Opinion* 18:37-51.

Poloma, M. M. and G. H. Gallup Jr.
1991 *Varieties of prayer: A survey report*. Trinity Press: Philadelphia.

Poloma, M. M. and B. F. Pendleton
1989a Religious experiences, evangelism, and institutional growth within the Assemblies of God. *Journal for the Scientific Study of Religion* 28:415-31.
1989b Exploring types of prayer and quality of life research: a research note. *Review of Religious Research* 31:46-53.
1991 *Exploring neglected dimensions of religion in quality of life research*. Lewiston, NY: Mellen Press.

Preston, D.
1988 *The social organization of Zen practice*. Cambridge: Cambridge University Press.

Proudfoot, W.
1985 *Religious experience*. Berkeley, CA: University of California Press.

Radhakrishnan, S.
1940 *Eastern religions and Western thought*. London: Oxford University Press.

Ritzer, G.
1992 *Contemporary sociological theory*. New York: McGraw Hill.

Schleiermacher, F. D. E.
1958 *On Religion*. New York: Harper & Row.

Schutz, A.
1964 Making music together. In *Collected Papers II: Studies in Social Theory*, edited by A. Broderson. The Hague: Nijhoff.
Simmel, G.
1905 A Contribution to the Sociology of Religion. *American Journal of Sociology* 11:359-376.
Smart, N.
1965 Interpretation and mystical experience. *Religious Studies* 1:75-87.
Spickard, J. V.
1991 Experiencing religious rituals. *Sociological Analysis* 52:191-204.
1993 A sociology of religious experience. In *A future for religion? New paradigms for social analysis*, edited by W.H. Swatos. Beverly Hills, CA. Sage.
Stace, W. T.
1961 *Mysticism and philosophy*. London: Macmillan.
Stall, F.
1975 *Exploring mysticism. A methodological essay*. Berkeley, CA: University of California Press.
Stark, R.
1965 "A Taxonomy of Religious Experience." Journal for the *Scientific Study of Religion*, 5:97-116.
Troeltsch, E.
1931 *The social teaching of the Christian churches*, 2 vols, translated by O. Wyon, with an introduction by H. Richard Neibuhr. New York: Macmillan.
Underhill, E.
1930 *Mysticism*. London: Methuen.
Wainwright, W. J.
1981 *Mysticism: A study of its nature, cognitive value and moral implications*. University of Wisconsin Press.
Warner, R.
1993 Work in progress toward a new paradigm for the Sociological Study of Religion in the United States. *American Journal of Sociology* 98:1044-93.
Weber, M.
1964 Basic concepts in sociology. New York. The Citadel Press.
Wolff, K. H. (translator and editor)
1950 The sociology of Georg Simmel. New York. The Free Press.
Yamane, D. and M. Polzer
1992 Ecstasy and Religious Organization: A Cultural-Linguistic View. Paper presented at the Annual Meetings of the Association for the Sociology of Religion. (August) Pittsburgh, PA.
Zaehner, R. C.
1961 Mysticism, Sacred and Prophane. London. Oxford University Press.

9

Phenomenological Psychology and Religious Experience

DAVID M. WULFF

Psychologists of religion at the turn of the twentieth century took it for granted that the object of their study was religious experience. If the phrase did not appear in the very titles of their books and articles, it was invariably conspicuous throughout their pages. These scholars assumed, furthermore, that to study such experience, their best tool was introspection, the results of which were usually obtained in the form of lengthy questionnaire replies.

Two revolutionary shifts in the intellectual climate undermined the experience-centered agenda of these early researchers. One, fostered by the new depth psychologies, was the growing conviction that virtually all significant psychological processes are unconscious and thus well out of the reach of introspective awareness. The other momentous shift came with the astonishingly successful rise of behaviorism, which disallowed any discourse that was not grounded in publicly accessible observations. Although at loggerheads on many issues, the depth psychologists and behaviorists at least agreed that the study of experience *per se* is radically insufficient, if not entirely futile, in the conduct of psychological investigation.

Phenomenological psychology is in large measure a response to these movements, particularly their denigration of human experience as an avenue of insight. To be sure, neither tradition has entirely succeeded in eliminating experience from psychological discourse. Just as free association and other forms of self-revelation are vital for the carrying out of depth psychotherapy, so various forms of self-report remain crucial to the conduct of much behavioral research. Yet in neither case is individual experience truly taken seriously, and in experimental and correlational research in particular, it is usually deprived of any voice beyond the investigator's sparse response categories. Phenomenological psychology seeks to reclaim for experience the preeminent position it possessed at the end of the last century, but without returning to a naive introspectionism.

THE PHENOMENOLOGICAL APPROACH IN PSYCHOLOGY

Contemporary psychologists use the term phenomenology with widely varying degrees of precision. Many employ it rather loosely, to designate any approach that gives prominence to subjective experience. Thus, for example, in many current psychology textbooks the personality psychologies of Rogers, Maslow, and Kelly are denominated phenomenological theories. The individual's experience, typically assumed to be unique, is then referred to as the individual's "phenomenology." In accord with the views of human nature put forward by Rogers and Maslow, the phenomenological perspective is also said to assume that human beings are self-determined, intrinsically good, and oriented toward growth.

Scholars more sensitive to the word's etymology and at least casually acquainted with the history of its usage reserve the term phenomenology to refer to essentially descriptive approaches to experience. They rightly recognize that phenomenology—which strictly means "the study of that which appears"—does not offer an alternative theoretical approach that can be compared to a variety of others. Rather, it designates a scholarly perspective that is essentially nontheoretical in its commitment to unalloyed description. It thus takes no particular stance on the inherent nature of human beings and may in fact limit itself to a much narrower range of phenomena than those that concern the personality psychologist.

Stricter still is the understanding of phenomenology that is embraced by its most dedicated practitioners. An essential component of phenomenology from their perspective is critical alertness for the assumptions, presuppositions, and prejudices that silently distort our understanding of what appears before us. Although it is most likely impossible to avoid all such predispositions, phenomenologists of the strictest variety argue that we must systematically strive to set them aside while acknowledging and taking into account all that are known to remain. Among the most critical of the presuppositions that the phenomenologists "bracket," or set aside, is the dogmatic notion that experience is subjective and private, and thus not properly the subject of scientific investigation.

Given both the widely varying understandings of phenomenology and the critical role that the investigator's own perspicacity plays in the outcome of any phenomenological analysis, it is not surprising that the literature is rather uneven. Complicating matters, too, is the widespread conviction among American proponents that other psychologists will take their work seriously only if their phenomenological procedures resemble traditional positivistic methods in certain basic respects. Thus, whereas European phenomenological psychologists have traditionally anchored their studies in their own personal experience, insight, and reflections, their American counterparts rely first and foremost on the verbal or written reports they elicit from "samples" of individuals thought in some way to be representative of larger populations. If the American work is thus more familiar to traditionally trained psychologists, it may also be limited in important respects by its dependence on naive and untrained observers.

CLASSICAL PHENOMENOLOGY OF RELIGION

The idea of a phenomenological approach to religion appeared at least as early as the 1880s, in Europe. At first it was little more than a reworking of the data of the history of religion in terms of specific themes. But with the emergence of the phenomenological movement inaugurated by Edmund Husserl at the beginning of the twentieth century and the related tradition of the human sciences instigated at about the same time by Wilhelm Dilthey, the proponents of the phenomenology of religion claimed for it certain virtues setting it apart from all earlier approaches. The study of religion, they maintained, would benefit substantially from Husserl's principle of *epoché*, the bracketing of presuppositions, including the evolutionary hypothesis that had led to pejorative comparisons among religious traditions. Furthermore, drawing on Dilthey's central notion of *Verstehen* (understanding), they saw in the phenomenological approach a new, more promising means for gaining access to the essence of religion in its various manifestations (Allen, 1989; Sharpe, 1986).

Preeminent among the contributors to this revised and more rigorous phenomenology of religion was the Dutch scholar Gerardus van der Leeuw, whose *Phänomenologie der Religion* (1933; translated as *Religion in Essence and Manifestation*, 1938) was, according to Sharpe (1986:220), "the first real milestone of the discipline in its newer form." Van der Leeuw stands out as well for his appreciation of psychology's potential contributions to the study of religion. Several years before his major work appeared, he published two extensive articles on the application of interpretive (*verstehende*) psychology to the history of religion and to theology (van der Leeuw, 1926, 1928); and conspicuous in the final, methodology, section of his 1933 book are the names of psychologist Eduard Spranger and psychiatrists Ludwig Binswanger and Karl Jaspers, all of whom were deeply influenced by Dilthey.

According to Dilthey's argument, to understand another's experience I must myself relive it or imaginatively reconstruct it, by drawing on similar experiences of my own. Furthermore, I must situate that experience within the structural whole that is constituted by the other's mental life. The carrying out of a phenomenology of religion, van der Leeuw says in like spirit, requires not only the meticulous collecting and classifying of historical religious phenomena but also a "psychological description" based on "a systematic introspection." What is required above all, he writes, is a description of "the experience born of what can only become reality after it has been admitted into the life of the observer himself" (quoted in Sharpe, 1986:231).

Similar requirements are placed on the reader of the phenomenologist's work. In a highly respected and extraordinarily influential work that is a study in the phenomenology and the psychology of religion, Rudolf Otto (1917:8) requests any reader who cannot recall "a moment of deeply-felt religious experience" to put the book down at once, for such a person, he maintains, is bound to misunderstand the analysis that follows. Because the nonrational experience of the holy, the object of his study, ultimately eludes every effort at articulation, we are forced, says Otto, to make do with carefully chosen analogies derived from everyday life. These analogical elements, which he calls ideograms, are merely pointers, which the religiously inexperienced will likely find incomprehensible.

Because of its continuing importance for the psychology of religion, Otto's famous analysis will serve here as an example of the phenomenological work of this earlier period. The experience of the holy—or what Otto calls the "numinous consciousness" in an effort to recover the original sense of the word holy—is a highly complex feeling state that possesses a dual structure. Acknowledging like other phenomenologists the "intentional," or content-centered, structure of consciousness, Otto characterizes this feeling state in terms of its object, the *mysterium*, which to the rational mind remains "wholly other." On the one hand, it is the *mysterium tremendum*, an awesome and unapproachable object characterized by awfulness, majesty, and energy. On the other hand, it is the *mysterium fascinans*, an alluring and fascinating object that is schematized by such notions as perfect love, mercy, and salvation. Subject in the course of human history to a process of maturation and purification, and expressed outwardly in gestures, words, and various forms of art, the numinous consciousness is said to be an inborn potential that is best evoked by the personal example of others. (See Wulff, 1991:528-532, 573-574, for a fuller account of Otto's analysis.)

PHENOMENOLOGICAL PSYCHOLOGY OF RELIGION

Given that some of the classic phenomenologists of religion were interested not only in religious experience but also in psychology, it is virtually impossible to draw a clear line between their work and what properly belongs to the psychology of religion. Granting that phenomenology is not easily separated from "the psychology of form and structure"—that is, the interpretive psychology of Dilthey and his followers—van der Leeuw (1933:686) suggests that all psychologies, and thus also all psychologies of religion, limit themselves to what is "psychical."

> But in religion far more appears than the merely psychical: the whole man participates in it, is active within it and is affected by it. In this sphere, then, psychology would enjoy competence only if it rose to the level of the science of Spirit—of course in its philosophic sense—in general which, it must be said, is not seldom the case. But if we are to restrict psychology to its own proper object, it may be said that the phenomenologist of religion strides backwards and forwards over the whole field of religious life, but the psychologist of religion over only a part of this (p.687).

If in principle it is difficult to distinguish the *phenomenology* of religion from the *phenomenological psychology* of religion, in practice the two differ substantially. Most obvious is the striking historical and cross-cultural perspective that phenomenologists—who are usually also historians of religion—have always brought to their work. Indeed, phenomenology was promoted at the outset as a new, more adequate means for gaining entrée into the spirit of other religious traditions, without distorting or judging them in terms of the investigator's own faith. Phenomenological psychologists, by contrast, most commonly investigate experience occurring within the context of a single tradition, usually one close at hand.

Furthermore, whereas phenomenologists of religion focus chiefly on one or more typical themes or categories that recur in various traditions—for example, power, demons and angels, sacred space, or sacred covenant—phenomenological psychologists are most interested in the experiences of particular individuals. Thus, whereas phenomenologists of religion rely chiefly on historical and anthropological materials, phenomenological psychologists of religion commonly base their work on interviews and personal documents.

It may also be said that, in spite of the widely embraced principle of *epoché*, it is usually the case that the primary identification of the investigator—whether it be theologian, historian of religion, psychologist, or psychiatrist—generally shines through at various points, in the kinds of comparisons that are made, the metaphors that are chosen, and even the conclusions that are drawn. Phenomenology often serves as a propaedeutic to other undertakings, which may already be foreshadowed in the phenomenological description.

In our review of studies of religious experience from the viewpoint of phenomenological psychology, we shall distinguish two main approaches: firsthand, or direct, phenomenology, in which the investigator draws first and foremost on his or her own experience; and indirect, or vicarious, phenomenology, for which the researcher turns to others as the source of self-observations. Phenomenological reports of the direct type are sometimes obviously so, as in the instance of Edward Casey's (1976) study of imagining. In many cases, however, the phenomenologist's personal contribution remains silently in the background. Vicarious studies, on the other hand, minimally provide some general characterization of the individuals from whom the reports were obtained as well as the means that were used to elicit their descriptions.

A DIRECT STUDY OF MYSTICAL CONSCIOUSNESS

Many proponents of phenomenology assume that, whenever possible, the investigator will begin with the experience that is closest at hand—his or her own. Indeed, some maintain that genuine comprehension of an experience is impossible if one has not had it oneself. James (1902), who is considered in certain respects to be a forerunner of modern-day phenomenology (see Edie, 1987), expresses this position when he writes: "One can never fathom an emotion or divine its dictates by standing outside of it." Rather, "one must have 'been there' one's self in order to understand [it]" (pp. 261, 260). Herbert Spiegelberg (1975), the preeminent historian and interpreter of the phenomenological movement (see Spiegelberg, 1965, 1972), remarks that phenomenology, "even in its broader senses, aspires to be a direct study of the phenomena as given to the phenomenologist himself without any intermediaries, personal or impersonal" (p.35). In fact, Spiegelberg says, the direct approach is properly taken to be "the decisive feature" of the phenomenological method (p.38).

An outstanding example of the direct approach in the phenomenological psychology of religion is offered by Carl Albrecht (1951, 1974), a physician-psychotherapist with training in theology, philosophy, and psychology and a deep professional and personal interest in mystical experience. While exploring the value for his patients of yoga and other forms of meditation, Albrecht was startled to discover the healing power of the state of consciousness that is attainable through such practices. As he explored this state with his patients, he happened upon a technique that allowed a few of them to describe their experience to him while still in the state of absorption. Mastering the technique himself, Albrecht drew on his own experience as well as his patients' to carry out a phenomenology of mystical consciousness.

Albrecht (1951:8) explicitly adopts "psychological phenomenology" as his method, which he distinguishes from philosophical phenomenology by quoting from Jaspers' *General Psychopathology* (1946:55): "Phenomenology sets out on a number of tasks: it *gives a concrete description* of the psychic states which patients actually experience and *presents* them *for observation*. It reviews the inter-relations of these, *delineates* them as sharply as possible, differentiates them and creates a suitable terminology." Whereas Jaspers proceeds, then, to acknowledge the indirectness of his approach to pathological states, Albrecht was privileged to have direct access to the phenomena he was investigating (Fischer-Barnicol, in Albrecht, 1974).

Albrecht (1951) divides his analysis into two parts, the first offering a detailed analysis of the process of "centering down" (*die Versenkung*) and the second, a description of the culminating end state, mystical absorption (*die Versunkenheit*). Revealing his background in medicine and psychology, Albrecht dedicates much of his analysis to contrasting ordinary states of consciousness—including bodily awareness, thinking, feeling, and acts of will—with those brought into being by the meditative process. Whereas, for example, centering down is ordinarily initiated through a conscious act of resolve, which establishes a "determining tendency," in none of the subsequent stages does one experience a genuine act of will. As centering down proceeds, consciousness is gradually emptied of its ordinary content, including its connections to the outer world as well as inner impulses and desires. The field of consciousness, becoming increasingly clear and unified, is pervaded by a mood of peacefulness.

The end-state of absorption is more remarkable still. Aware of psychology's long history of denigrating mystical consciousness, Albrecht carefully distinguishes this state of awareness from hallucinations and illusions as well as all ordinary modes of perception. Although consciousness retains its basic intentional structure, the "ego" is purely receptive and the content consists of an orderly but complex totality that is unique to this exceptional state. Albrecht carefully delineates the diverse forms this emergent whole may take, including the numinous "encompassing" (*das Umfassende*) that arrives from some foreign sphere and is sometimes—but not always—experienced as an invisible personal Thou (see Wulff, 1991:563-565, for more detail).

VICARIOUS PHENOMENOLOGICAL STUDIES OF RELIGIOUS EXPERIENCE

Albrecht's work, remarks Gerda Walther (1955:249) in another phenomenological study of mysticism, represents an astonishing step forward in this sphere, particularly in its depiction of mystical experience as "normal, healthy, [and] of the highest value." Regrettably, Albrecht destroyed all of his records before his death in 1965, thus leaving only tantalizing clues to the remarkable technique he used. Yet even if he had left detailed instructions, few researchers would likely themselves have personal access to the world of experience he describes. They would be forced, rather, to draw on the experience of other persons.

James's Varieties: Certainly that was James's situation. Although he once confessed to having enough of a "mystical germ" to respond sympathetically to the testimony of others, James declared in the *Varieties* that his constitution so limited his capacity to enjoy mystical states that he was forced to "speak of them only at second hand" (James, 1902:301). To allow himself to speak with some authority nevertheless, James turned to the writings of "experts" in the religious realm. From these diverse records of exceptional piety he eventually selected lengthy quotations to illustrate and make more compelling the types and principles that he abstracted from his various sources.

On the face of it, it may seem that the heart of the *Varieties* lies precisely in the delineation of these types and principles—the differentiation, for example, of two opposing temperamental types, the healthy-minded and the sick soul, or the four characteristics of mystical experience: ineffability, noetic quality, transiency, and passivity. More significant by far, however, is the assistance that James provides for an empathic understanding of religious experience, especially its less common and more dramatic variations. By using the method of serial study (see Wulff, 1991:481-483), James helps the serious reader pass over from familiar and more accessible phenomena to ones that might otherwise seem alien and incomprehensible.

Even though such empathic understanding was not James's only goal in writing the *Varieties*, it has won for the book a warm reception among phenomenologists of religion. James Edie (1987:52) declares that James was the first to undertake a strictly descriptive phenomenology of religious experience, without the biasing effects of some theory or doctrine. But set as he ultimately was on making a "spiritual judgment" about religion, James did in fact take guidance from "common sense" and confessed philosophical prejudices, including the pragmatic view of truth. He was capable, furthermore, of frank disdain for forms of piety that deviated from his own liberal Protestant heritage. We might note, too, that after the first few printings, he removed from the book the single mention of phenomenology, substituting for it "natural history." Nevertheless, major portions of the work are written in the spirit of modern-day phenomenology.

An Empirical Phenomenological Analysis of Spiritual Experience: Whereas James chose the vicarious approach because the direct one was not open to him, contemporary phenomenological psychologists elect the indirect avenue strictly as a matter of principle. Most influential in shaping this preference was Amedeo Giorgi, who, especially during his years at Duquesne University, wrote and edited a number of major works in phenomenological psychology. According to Giorgi's method of "empirical phenomenological analysis," the phenomenological researcher begins by gathering from a number of subjects written descriptions or transcribed interviews on the topic being researched. One then follows four "essential steps."

1) Each description is read through in its entirety, in order to get a general sense of it.
2) The description is read once again, this time with an eye to its "meaning units." These units, demarcated by shifts in meaning, are said to appear spontaneously when the researcher "assumes a psychological attitude toward the concrete description."
3) Each of the meaning units is subsequently transformed through a pro-

cess of reflection and imaginative variation, with the goal of translating the subject's everyday expression into language that more directly reveals the meaning unit's psychological insight.

4) The transformed meaning units are then synthesized into an integrated statement that reveals the "essential general structure" of the experience.

Implicit in the final step is the integration of meaning units across subjects, for Giorgi maintains that it is exceedingly difficult to arrive at such a structure on the basis of one subject only. "The more subjects there are, the greater the variations, and hence the better the ability to see what is essential." A single subject, on the other hand, is sufficient for discerning "specific situated structures" (Giorgi, 1985:10-19).

Christopher Aanstoos (1992), a former student of Giorgi, illustrates the approach as applied to an individual case of "spiritual experience." The subject, Michael, who wrote the description of his experience as a participant in one of Aanstoos's graduate seminars at West Georgia College, had with his wife been keeping a vigil at a hospital where their newborn daughter, Mia, was in critical condition. With arms and legs restrained, to keep her from pulling out the ventilating tube, and on a drug that, by paralyzing her, allowed the ventilator to maintain a proper rate of breathing, the young infant was not expected to live. Weary from their week-long vigil, they took a break at the nearby home of a friend, where Michael soon found himself alone on the bathroom floor, retching and in pain.

> I got the sense that Mia's pain was coming through to me. I felt happy about that, I felt it was coming out of Mia. I felt that God was behind it. I began praying to God to give me more of Mia's pain, to let it go out of her through me. I felt sure that I could handle it. . . . As I felt worse and worse, I felt happier, as I felt that my prayers were being answered (p.87).

Perhaps an hour later the nausea passed, and when Michael and his wife returned to the hospital that afternoon, Mia was doing better. She continued to progress steadily over the next several days and was out of intensive care within two weeks.

Applying Giorgi's method of phenomenological analysis to Michael's written description and his expansions during the subsequent interview by the seminar members, Aanstoos arrived at the following analysis.

> The structure of Michael's spiritual experience is one of being graced by the loving responsiveness of God. It happens when his encounter with the exigencies of birth and death has served to focus him beyond the mundane world of ordinary life, and into an ever more extraordinary situation. His life has been torn from its usual moorings, even its temporality and spatiality has become alien.

Following a more or less factual description of the events leading up to the severe attack of nausea, Aanstoos continues:

> The very time and space he occupies becomes a surreal irreality, a translucence rather than a boundary.
>
> At that moment, he feels the extraordinary pain of his newborn daughter, the terrible pain she is living. . . . He feels his pain as an embodied connection with her pain. Certain of this contact with her pain, Michael experiences the open pathway of this relationship as sacred, as the caring manifestation of God. He opens himself without question to this divine solicitude, feeling himself held within the hands of care. He acknowledges it and affirms his readiness and devotion to be its conduit and vessel to help his daughter by embracing and living her suffering more fully. . . . In the face of this most intense pain, Michael gratefully experiences God's loving responsiveness to his entreaty. Having deeply embodied that manifestation of the sacred, he feels sure that this experience has helped to relieve his daughter's suffering (p.89).

Such a formulation, says Aanstoos, when compared with other findings, could yield over time a taxonomy of spiritual experiences and an experiential foundation for a "psychology of religious issues."

A Phenomenology of Religious Doubt: An example of how Giorgi's method may be applied to a collection of protocols is offered by Lallene Rector (1987) in a doctoral dissertation she completed at Boston University. To describe phenomenologically the experience of religious doubt, Rector enlisted the help of seven "co-researchers," all of them partially or fully retired ministers of the United Methodist Church. After an initial orienting interview, each participant was asked to complete at his leisure a questionnaire consisting of six questions regarding religious doubt, religious commitment or faith, interpersonal relationships, and professional identity.

After Rector carried out a preliminary thematization of the questionnaire replies, two research assistants—with whom she had first discussed the project and their own experiences of religious doubt—reviewed her work in order to suggest additional perspectives, uncover unrecognized presuppositions, and identify points or topics that seemed to require further clarification. Together they also formulated a set of questions for the final interview. Special care was given to avoiding questions that would bias the respondent toward certain interpretations. The order in which these questions were posed during the final interview was determined by the flow of the discussion, which was carried out from the perspective and in the vocabulary of the co-researcher. The transcript from each final interview was integrated with the questionnaire replies to form the final protocol document.

Rector painstakingly subjected the seven protocols to the mode of analysis put forward by Giorgi, following which she collated the central themes and then formulated the following tentative phenomenological characterization of religious doubt.

> Religious doubt is a question or feeling of uncertainty about a tenet, an object of devotion, or a vocation which the individual understands to be religious. It is precipitated by cognitive dissonance and is intensified by the awareness of other persons' perceptions and experiences related to the particular question. It will entail years of resolution and may continue to be experienced throughout life.
>
> Religious doubt is experienced cognitively, affectively, and behaviorally and involves some form of interaction with other people. Motivation to seek a resolution is part of the experience of religious doubt. Resolutions can be final or ongoing and tend to be found in the formulation or adoption of a perspective which, for the individual, will adequately address the doubt. The experience of religious doubt is associated with changes in interpersonal relationships and modifications in the individual's experience of him or herself as a person and/or as a Christian. The individual experiences an increased awareness of what he or she can affirm with certainty (pp.580-581).

This definition, Rector acknowledges, will undoubtedly require modification when religious doubt is similarly investigated in a variety of other populations. Even now, however, she sees implications for religious education, pastoral care and counseling, and the training of ministers. Such research, she also suggests, promises to generate a host of new questions for those interested in the scientific study of religious experience.

A Phenomenology of Spiritual Gifts: An interview-based phenomenological study of religious experience was likewise the subject of William Sneck's (1981) doctoral dissertation, completed in the clinical program at the University of Michigan, but for this study of charismatic spiritual gifts, the methodological principles were derived from Spiegelberg rather than Giorgi, whose views, however, are also cited. The overall spirit of this undertaking is credited to James, whose "active emphasis on passionate searching" Sneck takes as a valuable addition to the phenomenological method of inquiry (p.80). The *Varieties*, he says, was his "concrete exemplar" (p.73).

In the final chapter of his magisterial, two-volume survey of the phenomenological movement, Spiegelberg (1965) identifies seven "steps" of the phenomenological method: 1) investigating particular phenomena by intuiting, analyzing, and describing them; 2) investigating general essences, perhaps by ordering particulars according to their similarities (much as James did in the *Varieties*); 3) apprehending essential relationships within and among essences, chiefly by means of imaginative variation; 4) watching modes of appearing, the way things present themselves to us; 5) watching the constitution of phenomena in consciousness, whether it be a spontaneous process or an active one; 6) suspending belief in the existence of the phenomena—a critical first step, according to some phenomenologists, but listed sixth here because not all accept or explicitly practice it; and 7) interpreting concealed meanings of the phenomena, a task that takes one beyond what is immediately given and into the realm of hermeneutic phenomenology (pp.659-695). Apart from the sixth step, which he elected not to take, Sneck explicitly uses Spiegelberg's outline to organize his analysis.

The nine men and thirteen women who were the subjects in Sneck's study were all members of the Word of God Community in Ann Arbor, Michigan, a charismatic group of Roman Catholics who patterned their communal lives after the first-century Christians. Sneck, a Jesuit priest, was involved with the community as a priest and counselor for a period of five years before he conducted this study. He became a novice in the community as well, but withdrew from that commitment after a year and a half over disagreement with the community leaders' policies. The subjects, recruited with a short advertisement in the community's weekly bulletin, were interviewed individually for about one and a half hours. Each was asked a flexible series of questions regarding his or her experiences of healing and prophecy and any theology of spiritual gifts used to understand such occurrences. Biographical data and earliest memories, particularly regarding father and mother, were also tape-recorded during these nondirective interviews.

The longest chapter in Sneck's book is given over to a narrative account of his subjects' and the group's experiences in three areas: prophecy, healing, and deliverance (from evil spirits). Individual experiences, which are frequently related by quoting the subjects' own words, are placed in the larger contexts of their personal lives and the history of the community. This chapter is offered in fulfillment of the first of Spiegelberg's seven steps.

The final chapter represents the five other steps of analysis that Sneck undertook. This material is too lengthy and complex to be summed up in its entirety here, but characterization of some major elements will give a flavor of it. In his quest for the essence of healing, for example, Sneck concludes that

> healing of memories includes calling to mind events which sometimes have been long forgotten, growing in insight concerning them, but also consciously forgiving oneself and any other participants, living or dead, present or absent, for inflicted pain. This healing is not considered complete until the event ceases to stir resentment, bitterness, anger, etc. Community members are taught the Pauline directive, "Rejoice in all circumstances" (Phil. 4:4-7), and are encouraged patiently to seek and pray for healing until they are actually able to thank God for the misfortune or pain which occurred.

Healing, even miraculous healing of illness, was considered to be "an ordinary and expected happening" in any community "relating to the Lord 'in the right way,' " (p.247).

In his search for essential relationships among essences, Spiegelberg's third step, Sneck identified five common elements or factors: 1) an ongoing, quasi-interpersonal relationship with "the Lord," which is characterized by reverence, familiarity, and trust; this relationship is the "core, essential experience of the spiritual gifts"; 2) an individual "sense from the Lord," instances of communication that are characterized by an element of surprise; 3) the need to "step out in faith," for these manifestations remain vague, and the Lord, hidden from one's eyes; 4) emotions, including peace and joy, and physical sensations, such as of anointing; and 5) the use of discernment—itself a gift, although one unusually vulnerable to social shaping—in deciding how to respond to the received communication (pp.254-254). Systematic removal of each of these factors by free imaginative variation substantially altered the religious experience of gifts, thereby demonstrating their essential quality.

For Spiegelberg's fourth step, watching modes of appearing, Sneck's focus is not on how a "sense of the Lord" presents itself to the individual, for example, but rather on the history of the community's changing response to the phenomena of gifts over the course of the five years that Sneck was associated with the group. The fifth step, watching the constitution of phenomena in consciousness, is likewise given an odd twist, so that instead of describing how each of the gifts is gradually constituted in the consciousness of the members, Sneck undertook to delineate five different ways that the gifts became incorporated into the members' life histories. And for the seventh step—Sneck declined the sixth one, we may recall—in place of attempting "to use the given as a clue for meanings which are not given" (Spiegelberg, 1965:695), Sneck briefly sums up the perspectives of several object relations theorists, as potentially nonreductionistic modes of interpretation.

We may wonder if Sneck's omission of the sixth step, suspending belief in the existence of the phenomenon, did not significantly limit the outcome of his study. There is no doubt that the reader learns much from this work about the charismatic movement and the phenomena of spiritual gifts. Yet the author's evident personal investment in the community, along with his convictions and outlook as a Roman Catholic priest, seems to have limited his appropriation of the phenomenological attitude. It is true that phenomenologists are expected to approach the objects of their study with sympathy and even a spirit of reverence, as Spiegelberg puts it. But the setting aside of preconceptions and other biases, in the act of *epoché*, is one of phenomenology's "chief tangible contributions" (Spiegelberg, 1965:657). Rather than leading to "philosophical wrangling" over "the question of the existence/nonexistence of the divine referent in the quasi-interpersonal relationship," as Sneck feared it would (p.276), the act of temporarily suspending belief, of systematically setting aside his own convictions for the purposes of this study, might have allowed him to carry out a more penetrating analysis.

A model of such bracketing, or at least of carrying out the search for factors in one's own life and outlook that might bias and distort one's seeing, is offered by Lewis Rambo (1992) in an essay on the phenomenology of conversion. "Unless the phenomenologist is keenly aware of his or her own assumptions, methods, values, and goals, the phenomenologist cannot pretend to the capacity to see, articulate, interpret, and clarify what is distinctive about someone else's experience," Rambo (p.245) says. He had good reason to be sensitive to the potential contribution of his own views and circumstances to this study, for the subject was not only a former student of his but also the spiritual advisee of an acquaintance of Rambo's from divinity school who was "to some degree a role model" of his (p.232). Furthermore, the protocols used for analysis were derived from repeated interviews with both Rambo and the subject's spiritual advisor. Rambo's courageous disclosures of his own background and continuing life circumstances at least alert the reader to potential biases in his report, if they did not also serve the author and his assistant as they worked through and analyzed the interview material.

Like others we have reviewed, Rambo took his methodological orientation chiefly from the Duquesne model developed by Giorgi. And in agreement with Malony (1981), another of Rambo's sources, he concludes that the phenomenologist must take "pretty much at face value" the subject's descriptions of experience as well as any interpretations and valuations the subject makes of his or her report (Rambo, 1992:247). Such an understanding, however, imposes a sharp and needless limitation on the phenomenological enterprise, even when it is carried out vicariously.

What is required in vicarious phenomenology is not simply textual analysis of what the subject says about his or her experience. Rather, phenomenologists are challenged to undertake what Spiegelberg (1975:48-52) calls "imaginative self-transposal." Such an act requires us to imagine ourselves as "occupying the real place of the other and view from there the world as it would present itself in this new perspective." In this process, "the transposing self has to submit to a transformation in which it not only divests itself of its congenital and historically acquired peculiarities, but adopts imaginatively as much as it can of the frame of mind of the other person," using as clues the other's reported perceptions and any available biographical material. A "complete fusion" must be avoided, however, for we must "shuttle back and forth between our own understanding self and that of the other who is to be understood" if we are to extend our own "phenomenological grasp." Once such a transposal is achieved, we begin "the actual work of constructing the other and his world on the basis of the clues which we find in the situation into which we have put ourselves imaginatively." Throughout this endeavor we must constantly check our imaginative construction against new evidence and be prepared to revise it whenever we find inconsistencies.

Facilitating the process of imaginative transposal and construction is what

Spiegelberg calls "the method of cooperative encounter." Given the indirectness of our access to the phenomenon, it behooves us to engage our co-researchers or participants in a process of cooperative exploration, which requires of us the "accepting and loving attitude" associated with any genuine encounter. We do not, however, accept the account of the other uncritically. Sympathetic probing may in fact lead to a modification of the other's report.

However well it is carried out, vicarious phenomenology nevertheless remains inferior to the direct variety, which, Spiegelberg notes, is itself hardly foolproof. Yet given the understandable reticence of most investigators about their own religious lives and the inevitable boundaries of their experience, we shall generally have to make do with an indirect approach. In doing so, we should be wary of conceiving of phenomenology merely as a method, a series of techniques by which to process textual data. When the outcome of such a conception is not simply a condensed restatement of what is obvious in the protocols, it is too often little more than an obscure translation of the textual material into the jargon of phenomenology and existential psychology. The methods, principles, and specialized vocabulary can be helpful, certainly; but they will not take us much beyond ordinary descriptive studies unless we first attain the phenomenological attitude and then seek to penetrate into the phenomenon on the basis of empathic understanding. No less challenging is the task of analyzing the phenomenon and finding the terms, including analogies and metaphors, that will allow us to convey to our readers what has been found and understood. Such an understanding is always provisional, of course, and it requires continued testing against further observations and the analyses carried out by others.

Most proponents of psychological phenomenology consider the approach sufficient in itself, an adequate resource for scientific understanding and clinical practice alike. But some also emphasize its value as a propaedeutic for alternate approaches in psychology, whether they be empirical ones of the statistical type or various of the interpretive psychologies, such as object relations theory. Thus, whether one is writing a questionnaire assessing religious experience or undertaking a depth interpretation of an individual's religious images, one is well advised to begin with a phenomenological interrogation of the material at hand.

Phenomenology is not "the master key to all locks," writes Spiegelberg (1975: xxiv). But it is enough, he says, "if it can unlock some doors and especially the front door." For the psychology of religion, which too often has seemed content to peer through but a single window or two, phenomenology promises a degree of access that has rarely been attained since James's *Varieties*. Indeed, systematically appropriated and developed by even a handful of contributors, phenomenological psychology could revolutionize the field. Short of that improbable outcome is the real possibility of improvement on virtually every front, a prospect that ought to rouse the interest of every researcher truly interested in religious experience.

REFERENCES

Aanstoos, C. M.

1992 Toward a phenomenology of spiritual experience. *Journal of the Psychology of Religion* 1:81-90.

Albrecht, C.

1951 *Psychologie des mystischen Bewußtseins*, Bremen: Carl Schünemann.

1974 *Das mystiche Wort; Erleben und Sprechen in Versunkenheit*, presented and edited by H.A. Fischer-Barnicol. Mainz: Matthias-Grünewald.

Allen, D.

1989 Phenomenology of religion. In *Encyclopedia of Religion*, Vol. 11, edited by M. Eliade. New York: Macmillan.

Casey, E. S.

1976 *Imagining: A phenomenological study*. Bloomington, IN: Indiana University Press.

Edie, J. M.

1987 *William James and phenomenology*. Bloomington, IN: Indiana University Press.

Giorgi, A.

1985 Sketch of a psychological phenomenological method. In *Phenomenology and psychological research*, edited by A. Giorgi. Pittsburgh: Duquesne University Press.

James, W.

[1902]

1985 *The varieties of religious experience; A Study in human nature*. Cambridge, MA: Harvard University Press.

Jaspers, K.

[1946]

1963 *General psychopathology*, translated by J. Hoenig and M. W. Hamilton, Chicago: University of Chicago Press, 1963.

Malony, H. N.

1981 Religious experiencing: A phenomenological analysis of a unique behavioral event. *Journal of Psychology and Theology* 9:326-334.

Otto, R.

[1917]

1950 *The idea of the Holy*, 2nd ed., translated by J. W. Harvey. London: Oxford University Press.

Rambo, L. R., with L. A. Reh

1992 The phenomenology of conversion. In *Handbook of religious conversion*, edited by H.N. Malony and S. Southard. Birmingham, AL: Religious Education Press.

Rector, L.

[1986]

1987 Toward a phenomenology of the experience of religious doubt. Doctoral dissertation, Boston University, *Dissertation Abstracts International*, 47, 2617A. (University Microfilms No. 86-24467)

Sharpe, E. J.

1986 *Comparative religion; A history*, 2nd ed. LaSalle, IL: Open Court.

Sneck, W.J.

1981 *Charismatic spiritual gifts; A phenomenological analysis*. Washington, DC: University Press of America.

Spiegelberg, H.

1965 *The phenomenological movement: A historical introduction*, 2nd ed. 2 vols. The Hague: Nijhoff.

1972 *Phenomenology in psychology and psychiatry*. Evanston, IL: Northwestern University Press.

1975 *Doing phenomenology; Essays on and in phenomenology*. The Hague: Nijhoff.

van der Leeuw, G.

1926 Ueber einige neuere Ergebnisse der psychologischen Forschung und ihre Anwendung auf die Geschichte, insonderheit der Religionsgeschichte. *Studi e materiali di storie della religioni* 2:1-43.

1928 Strukturpsychologie und Theologie. *Zeitschrift für Theologie und Kirche*, N.F. 9:321-349.

[1933]

1938 *Religion in essence and manifestation: A study in phenomenology*, translated by J.E. Turner. London: Allen & Unwin.

Walther, G.

[1955]

1976 *Phänomenologie der Mystik*, 3rd, enlarged ed. Olton: Walter-Verlag.

Wulff, D. M.

1991 *Psychology of religion: Classic and contemporary views*. New York: Wiley.

10

Freudian Theory and Religious Experience

EDWARD P. SHAFRANSKE

> Those ideas—ideas which are religious in the widest sense—are prized as the most precious possession of civilization, as the most precious thing it has to offer its participants. It is far more highly prized than all the devices for winning treasures from the earth or providing men with sustenance or preventing their illnesses, and so forth. People feel that life would not be tolerable if they did not attach to these ideas the value that is claimed for them. And now the question arises: What are these ideas in the light of psychology? Whence do they derive the esteem in which they are held? And to take a further timid step, what is their real worth? (Freud 1927:20).

We begin with Freud's own words, with his acknowledgment of the value culture ascribes to religion and, in the same breath, his challenge to its merits. The questions that Freud posed have relevance not only for the psychology of individual religious experience but, as we will see, form the basis of his critique of culture.

I will present in this chapter a summary of Freud's contributions to the study of religion. This examination will show that Freud intended, through his discussion of religion, to establish the primacy of unconscious psychic determinism and the universality of the Oedipus complex in the life of the individual and in the epigenesis of civilization. Freud's analysis led to a strident critique of civilization as one constructed of the strands of illusion and wish fulfillment. His motivation went beyond the heuristic to the political; he aimed at generating a paradigm shift (Kuhn, 1970) in which science would usurp the authority of religion in the culture. It will be argued that the crux of the Freudian critique rests on the interplay between the complementary perspectives of phylogenetic inheritance and ontogenetic experience. The emphasis for Freud, unlike that of contemporary psychoanalysts (Meissner, 1978, 1984, 1992; Jones, 1992; Rizzuto, 1974, 1976, 1979, 1986, 1989), was on the archaic, prehistorical heritage of humanity. The ontogenetic contribution, significant in its own right, yields to the forces of inherited prehistory (Freud, 1918:97).

To understand Freud we must appreciate the range of his ambition, intellect, and vision. We must suspend any prejudice and identify with the fluidity of his mind. His vision conjoined a microscopic view of the intrapsychic foundations of individual religious experience and a telescopic grasp of religion's influence within culture. We might conjecture that while attending to the Wolf Man, Freud was listening, as well, to the chants of prehistoric man, echoed in the anthropological works of Frazer or in the discourse of Darwin. His ambition and intellect demanded an analysis that would not only examine the psychology of personal faith but question the "real worth" of religious ideas for the sum of civilization past, present, and future. It was through his facile juxtaposing of clinical material, metapsychology, and evolutionary biology, together with investigations of anthropology and the humanities, that Freud (1925:72) constructed his views on civilization as he "returned to the cultural problems which had fascinated [him] long before when [he] was a youth scarcely old enough for thinking."

THE DEVELOPMENT OF FREUD'S CRITIQUE OF RELIGION

Although Freud was fifty years of age when he commenced his definitive studies of religion, the germ of his critique can be found in his early adult years. As an adolescent Freud was drawn to Feuerbach (1957:vi) who viewed the essence of religion as arising "from the needs, wishes, and lacks of human life" (Holt, 1988; Stepansky, 1986). Feuerbach's thesis that "God is merely the projected essence of Man" (1957:65) anticipated Freud's analysis of the role of projection in God-representations (Rieff, 1961:266). Freud remained interested in philosophical questions, and continued his studies at the university under the tutelage of Franz Brentano. Although highly challenged by the arguments of Brentano, Freud declared, in letter to Eduard Silberstein in 1875, that it was Feuerbach who "I revere and admire above all other philosophers, I respect the man and am happy to salute so steadfast a champion of 'our' truths" (Boehlich, 1990:76). Psychoanalysis was to later provide Freud with the empirical tools to examine the beliefs he formulated as a youth.

In the background of Freud's mind, as well, were the organizing principles of the scientific and medical education of his day. Among the ideas which psychoanalysis drew upon for its development, two points are central in Freud's consideration of individual development and cultural evolution: the primacy of reason and the role of phylogeny.

Freud was committed to a rational positivism which held reason and objectivity as its virtues and science its exemplar. Not yet eighteen years of age, Freud considered himself "a godless medical man and empiricist" (Boehlich, 1990:70), and, in the spirit of his teachers (Brucke, Hemholtz, Du Bois-Reymond, Claus), was "convinced that real progress in many fields was equivalent to the spread of science" (Breger, 1981:24). Logos, or reason, was his god (cf. Freud, 1961a: 68) for, "there [was] no appeal to a court above that of reason" (1961a: 35). Although "the riddles of the universe reveal themselves slowly . . . [and] there are many questions to which science today can give no answer . . . scientific work is the only road which can lead us to a knowledge of reality outside ourselves" (Freud, 1961a: 40).

It was through science, Freud believed, that the development of civilization would be forwarded. He speculated that a new epoch was at hand in which reason and science would usher civilization toward its ultimate destiny. It would be through an objective reading of individual psychodynamics and cultural history that Freud (1935:20) would address what he referred to as the "cultural problems that fascinated me long before, when I was a youth." He would come to see religion as the antithesis of this spirit, as a cultural neurosis, impeding the progress of civilization, in a fashion akin to that in individual psychoneurosis (cf. Freud, 1907:126-127).

Ideas concerning the evolution of the species contributed significantly to Freud's emerging theories on religion and psychoanalysis. The scholarship of Sulloway (1979), Ritvo (1970, 1990), and Grubrich-Simitis (1987) together with the recent discovery of an unpublished metapsychology paper, titled by Freud (1987), "Overview of the Transference Neuroses," now referred to as, "A Phylogenetic Fantasy," has brought renewed attention to the historicoscientific context of Freud's theory building. Following his failed attempt at reducing psychological phenomena to physical matter in the "Project for a Scientific Psychology" (1895), Freud then looked to evolutionary biology. Influenced by Darwin when a youth and by Carl Claus as a medical student, Freud was prepared to discover a developmental link between the past and the present which could be observed within primitive forms of the species. Sulloway (1979:365) concluded that there was "a shift from *proximate*-causal theory to *ultimate*-causal theory within Freud's lifetime ambition of attaining a synthetic, psychobiological solution to the problems of the mind." In keeping with the interrelated perspectives of Darwin and Lamarck, Freud (1913a:184) concluded, in 1913a, "that the principle 'ontogeny is a repetition of phylogeny' must be applicable to mental life." The influence of inherited prehistory within mental functioning remained a guiding principle throughout his life. To the end, following the major revisions in his work, including structural theory, Freud (1939:240-241) maintained a unique place for the "authority of the past" [to appropriate Rieff's phrase (1961:186)],

> We have no reason to dispute the existence and importance of original, innate distinguishing characteristics of the ego . . . we must not exaggerate the difference between inherited and acquired characteristics into an antithesis; what was acquired by our forefathers certainly forms an important part of what we inherit. When we think of an "archaic heritage" we are usually thinking only of the id and we seem to assume that at the beginning of the individual's life no ego is as yet in existence. But we shall not overlook the fact that id and ego are originally one; nor does it imply any mystical overvaluation of heredity if we think it credible that, even before the ego has come into existence, the lines of development, trends and reactions which it will later exhibit are already laid down for it. . . *Analytic experience has forced on us a conviction that even particular psychical contents, such as symbolism, have no other sources than hereditary transmission* and researches in various fields of social anthropology make it plausible to suppose that other, *equally specialized precipitates left by early human development, are also present in the archaic heritage* (italics added).

Freud's view of religion was clearly influenced by his belief in the transmission through heredity of precipitates of prehistorical, ancestral experience. Further, his analyses of religious beliefs and practices, together with his clinical studies, reinforced his perspective as a "cryptobiologist" (Sulloway, 1979) and, in Jones' epitaph, "Darwin of the mind" (Jones 1913a:xii). Any reading of Freud's texts must be taken within the perspective of the evolutionary biology of the late nineteenth century.

In addition to these intellectual influences, a number of personal, as well as political, considerations prompted Freud's attention to religion. He made the acquaintance of Oskar Pfister, a Protestant Swiss pastor, whom he described to Ferenczi as "a charming fellow who has won all our hearts" (April 26, 1909 Letter, Freud-Ferenczi Correspondence, Freud Collection, as cited in Gay, 1988:191). His ongoing correspondence with Pfister sharpened Freud's arguments as he prepared *The Future of an Illusion.* In addition, Freud developed a close relationship with the French writer and artist Romain Rolland who would figure prominently in his discussions of religious experience. Of this relationship Freud noted, "I may confess to you that I have rarely experienced that mysterious attraction of one human being for another as vividly as I have with you; it is somehow bound up, perhaps, with the awareness of our being so different" (E. Freud, 1960:406). These relationships contributed in some measure to Freud's consideration of religion. Of importance, as well, is Carl Jung, whose interest in mythology paralleled that of Freud himself. What began as mutual interest and regard soured with competition and vehement disagreement. The break between Freud and Jung threatened the psychoanalytic movement and contributed not only personally but politically as well to Freud's work on religion. It is to the political that we turn briefly.

In the second decade of psychoanalysis dissension arose within Freud's inner circle. The defections of Adler and most particularly of Jung, Freud's heir apparent, troubled the founder of this fledgling scientific movement. Whereas Adler's falling out could be tolerated, Jung's sedition could not be so easily dismissed. Jung's break struck at the heart of psychoanalysis. His disagreement with Freud concerned the essence of psychoanalysis, that being the sexual and aggressive origins of human motivation and pathogenesis. Jung's rejection of the centrality of sexual libido challenged the future of Freudian analysis. As we will see, Freud's rebuttal to Jung is contained in *Totem and Taboo*. Through a psychoanalytic reading of the beliefs and practices of primitive peoples, complemented by the analysis of the magical thoughts and obsessive rituals of neurotics, Freud could reassert the prime role of sexuality within civilization. Gay (1988:326) characterized Freud's text as "sweet revenge on the crown prince who had proved so brutal to him and so treacherous to psychoanalysis." He quotes Freud's comment to Abraham, that this paper would "serve to cut off, cleanly, everything that is Aryan-religious." His response to Jung, through the sword of the pen, typifies Freud's response to betrayal.[1] Freud's works may be seen as political documents, polemics aimed within psychoanalysis to maintain the authority of the father.

In addition to these personal and political influences, Freud's interest in religion was peaked by ongoing clinical work. Throughout the early 1900s Freud conducted analyses in which magical beliefs, private rituals, and personal religious identifications played a role. Through the study of Schreber's autobiography and the analyses of the Wolf Man, the Rat Man and others, Freud (1911, 1918, 1909) had the opportunity to observe closely the dynamics of paranoia and obsessional behavior. Simultaneously, Freud was reading the works of Frazer and Robertson-Smith that provided the anthropological data for his emerging model of the analogies between prehistory, the minds of primitives, and neurosis.

In keeping with the essential tenets of psychoanalytic theory, we would be remiss in not considering those personal, psychological aspects that contributed, as well, to the development of Freud's critique of religion. As Gay noted, "his private experience and his emotional evolution also left their deposits on his campaign." Although Judaism was an aspect of the Freud household, it did not occupy a prominent position. Freud, like his father Jacob, was conversant in the Bible; and in his autobiographical study he acknowledged its "enduring effect upon the direction of [his] interest" (Freud, 1925:8). Although Freud (Meng and Freud, 1963:63) referred to himself, "as a godless Jew," he was hardly dispassionate in his attitude toward religion.

Was Freud's enthusiastic allegiance to the scientific *Weltanschauung* sufficient to understand his disdain for religion of any form? Meissner (1984:64), for one, suggests not:

> The nature and content of any thinker's or creative artist's work reflect essential aspects of the dynamic configurations and conflicts embedded in the individual's personality structure. Freud is no exception, and his religious thinking unveils these inner conflicts and unresolved ambivalences more tellingly than any other aspect of his work.

Numerous scholars (Bakan, 1958; Diller, 1991; Gay, 1987, 1988; Jones, 1953-1957; Meissner, 1978, 1984; Rice, 1990; Scharfenberg, 1988; Schur, 1972; Vitz, 1988; Zilboorg, 1958) have pointed to features in Freud's development as having influenced his view of religion. These have included speculation that Freud was introduced to and drew from the mystical tradition in Judaism, conflicted identifications with his father, betrayal by the hands of a Catholic nanny, and the influence of anti-Semitism throughout his life. A comprehensive explication of the developmental material is beyond the scope of this presentation. Suffice it to conclude, in Meissner's (1984:vii) words:

> It seems clear that Freud's religious views, perhaps more than any other aspect of his work and his psychology, reflect underlying and unresolved ambivalences and conflicts stemming from the earliest psychic strata. Behind the Freudian argument about religion stands Freud the man, and behind Freud the Man, with his prejudices, beliefs, convictions, lurks the shadow of Freud the child.

Acknowledging the import of the emerging *Weltanschauung* of Freud's day, his early commitments and identifications with science, the personal relationships and political pressures which he faced, together with the intrapsychic rumblings which shaped his consciousness, let us commence our examination of Freud's thought. We approach his religious texts bearing particularly in mind his desire to demonstrate the primacy of sexuality as the progenitor of human motivation, and to provide a critique of religion while abridging psychoanalytic theory to evolutionary biology.

FREUD'S CRITIQUE OF RELIGION

Freud's critique of religion may be seen as constructed on a series of complementary postulates. A brief inspection of these postulates will serve as an introduction to our examination of Freud's cultural texts.

The first postulate concerns the accessibility of the unconscious through psychoanalytic interpretation. Following the completion of *The Interpretation of Dreams*, Freud could propose that there is a substrate of mental activity that could be interpreted through the lens of psychoanalysis. Although dreams were the quintessential locus for interpretation, they were not its limit. Jokes, parapraxes, and all manner of social behavior could be inspected. (Freud, 1901, 1905) Constructed on the principles of dream interpretation, religious ideas and practices could be interpreted from the perspective of depth psychology. Ricoeur (1970:6) articulates the relationship between the interpretation of dreams and interpretation of the products of culture.

> The interpretation is concerned with dreams: the word "dream" is not a word that closes, but a word that opens. It does not close in upon a marginal phenomenon of our psychological life, upon the fantasies of our nights, the oneiric. It opens out onto all psychical productions, those of insanity and those of culture, insofar as they are analogues of dreams, whatever may be the degree and the principle of that relationship.

The second postulate concerns Freud's use of analogy. Freud postulates throughout his theory building a number of analogous relations. These include the internal relationships between the compulsions of neurotics and the rituals of the religiously pious and between the beliefs of primitive peoples and ideas of children, to name but two. Freud's use of analogy goes beyond its common usage pertaining to a resemblance. Seen in the light of the id as a timeless, primordial structure, containing the vestige of prehistory and out of which all further psychological structure evolves, analogy becomes a particularly meaningful construct. In my reading, Freud goes beyond a depiction of similarity of form to propose an equality of essence. Within the realm of the unconscious mind, links between prehistorical events and contemporary psychodynamics are not addressed as points of comparison but rather are apprehended as repetitions. Such a view is intelligible in light of our earlier discussion of Freud's commitment to the principles of inherited characteristics. To clarify this point with an example, within Freud's conception of the Oedipus complex as rooted in both ontogeny and phylogeny, the son's rivalry with the father not only resembles that of Oedipus and Laius but recapitulates the essence of prehistoric events. It is upon this postulate that Freud constructs his theses in *Totem and Taboo* and *Moses and Monotheism*.

The third postulate establishes wish-fulfillment as the a priori central feature in all mental activity. All human enterprise is explained within the context of human desire and the fulfillment of wishes through action or illusion. Ricoeur (1970:6) defines this as the "semantics of desire." In all activity, including the religious realm of culture, is contained repressed wishes. There exists a double meaning in language and in action which represents the vicissitudes of these wishes. In an interesting point Ricoeur (1970:7) considers this "a semantics that centers around a somewhat nuclear theme: as a man of desires I go forth in disguise—*larvatus prodeo*." In all language and behavior lie the disguised, repressed wishes of humankind. We turn now to Freud's exegesis of culture in which his interpretations sought to penetrate the disguises religion offers.

Preliminary Works

Freud's analysis of religion commenced with a brief paper published in 1907, "Obsessive Actions and Religious Practices." In this work, he introduced an analytical device which appears throughout his major texts on religion. Freud compares contemporary religious beliefs and practices to the mental processes of children and neurotics and to the ceremonies of primitive peoples. He initiates his inquiry through the rhetoric of analogy and then deftly moves to equate an underlying common identity between the phenomena in question. He grants differences in manifest content only to persuade the equality in the latent content or psychical operation.

In this paper, Freud (1907:119) equates "neurotic ceremonials and the sacred acts of religious ritual." He suggests that obsessive actions and ceremonials serve to express unconscious motives and ideas which are derived from the most intimate, and for the most part sexual, experiences of the patient (cf. Freud 1907:120-123). Freud (1907:119-120) initially concedes that there are striking differences in the variability of "[neurotic] ceremonial actions in contrast to the stereotyped character of [religious] rituals." However, he then assails this seeming discrepancy.

> The fact that, while the minutiae of religious ceremonial are full of significance and have a symbolic meaning, those of neurotics seem foolish and senseless. In this respect an obsessional neurosis presents a travesty, half comic and half tragic, of a private religion. But it is precisely this sharpest difference between neurotic and religious ceremonial which disappears when, with the help of the psycho-analytic technique of investigation, one penetrates to the true meaning of obsessive actions. . . . It is found that the obsessive actions are perfectly significant in every detail, that they serve important interests of the personality and that they give expression to experiences that are still operative and to thoughts that are cathected with affect.

Analysis of obsessive actions reveals "an unconscious sense of guilt," the origin of which is hidden from consciousness. A "ceremonial starts as an action for defense or insurance, a protective measure" (Freud, 1907:123). Freud went on to assert that the obsessive actions of the neurotic, and equally so, the pious, serve protective functions and contain a representation of the original experience. Through displacements and other defensive operations of the mind (which he gleaned through his study of dreams), Freud (1907:126-127) deduced that over time

> the petty ceremonials of religious practice gradually become the essential thing and push aside the underlying thoughts. That is why religions are subject to reforms which work retroactively and aim at a re-establishment of the original balance of values.
>
> The character of compromise which obsessive actions possess in their capacity as neurotic symptoms is the character least easily detected in corresponding religious observances. Yet here, too, one is reminded of this feature of neuroses when one remembers how commonly all the acts which religion forbids—the expressions of their instincts it has suppressed—are committed precisely in the name of and ostensibly for the sake of, religion.
>
> In view of these similarities and analogies one might venture to regard obsessional neurosis as a pathological counterpart of the formation of a religion, and to describe that neurosis as an individual religiosity and religion as a universal obsessional neurosis.

At this level of analysis Freud was content to establish an analogy between the *practices* of neurotics and the pious. He proposes that the ideas which set particular observances and rituals in motion are forgotten. It is this point to which he will return in later works.

Freud introduces, as well, in this paper, his view of the demands civilization places on the individual to renunciate instinctual wishes. He writes: "A progressive renunciation of constitutional instincts, whose activation might afford the ego primary pleasure, appears to be one of the foundations of human civilization. Some part of this instinctual repression is affected by its religions, in that they require the individual to sacrifice his instinctual pleasure to the Deity" (Freud, 1907:127). He extends this point in a 1908 paper suggesting that "the single steps [in the progression of civilization through renunciation] were sanctioned by religion" (Freud, 1908:187). He further suggests that neurosis finds its etiology in the renunciation of instinct. Freud (1908:204) concludes this essay posing the question, "whether our 'civilized' sexual morality is worth the sacrifice which it imposes on us, especially if we are still so much enslaved to hedonism as to include among the aims of our cultural development a certain amount of individual happiness."

The wedding of renunciation, progress in civilization, religion, and neurosis form the nucleus of his critique of religion. He will go on in *Totem and Taboo, Moses and Monotheism, Civilization and Its Discontents*, and *The Future of an Illusion* to identify the ancestral event that is represented and enacted in religious ceremonies and identify religion as an agent of civilization in calling for the renunciation of instinct. He will further establish the ontogenetic contributions to religious ideas and to the renunciations religion demands.

Phylogeny and the Origin of Religion

Drawing on the works of anthropologists Frazer and Robertson-Smith, Freud (1913a) constructed in *Totem and Taboo* a speculative history of the origins of civilization. He regarded the taboos of primitive peoples to be analogous to the obsessional symptoms of neurotics. Further he posited that "there are men still living who, as we believe, stand very near to primitive man, far nearer than we do, and whom we therefore regard as his direct heirs and representatives" (Freud, 1913a:1). From the anthropological studies of such "savages," Freud inferred the mental contents and practices of primitive peoples. Homans (1989:283) considers this Freud's equation: savage = children = neurotic. He comments that this annuls the notion of timelessness and "ushers in the full-scale temporalization of life" (Homans, 1989:284).

He traced their development to particular epochs in the history of the species and divined the origin of the Oedipus complex to an historical event at the crossroads of civilization. In keeping with Darwin's thesis, this event concerned the murder of the tyrannical father by the primal horde. This act of parricide led to a disruption of the horde and eventuated in the establishment of a rudimentary social order built around two basic totemic laws concerning incest and killing the totem animal. This act of parricide was not an isolated event but rather consisted of a series of experiences within a given epoch of human existence. The murdered father became symbolized in the totem animal which held the authority within the horde. Through the sacrifice of the totem animal, the sons "could attempt, in their relation to this surrogate father, to allay their burning sense of guilt, to bring about a kind of reconciliation with their father" (Freud 1913a:144). Freud drew upon his clinical experience in which he observed the child's use of animals as displacements of the ambivalently held father. Freud (1913a:145) concluded that:

> Totemic religion arose from the filial sense of guilt, in an attempt to allay that feeling and to appease the father by deferred obedience to him. All later religions are seen as attempts to solve the same problem. They vary according to the stage of civilization at which they arise and according to the methods that they adopt; but all have the same end in view and are reactions to the same great event with which civilization began and which, since it occurred, has not allowed a moment's rest.

Religious ceremonies were enactments which contained the representations of the original murderous act. Freud agreed with Robertson-Smith's interpretations of the Christian Lord's Last Supper and Mass as a derivative of the totemic sacrificial meal. Keeping in mind the rituals of neurotics, Freud could conjecture that such religious ceremonies served defensive purposes and contained and represented the unconscious memory of the original act.

The injunctions following the epoch of parricide gave birth to civilization, religion, and the Oedipus complex (see Bergmann, 1992, for an alternative view implicating the sacrifice of children and its impact on religion and culture). Freud took from Robertson-Smith the principle of exogamy which protected the horde from a repetition of parricide. Freud suggests that each person, through inherited psychic endowment, carries under the veil of repression the original Oedipal "sin." Etched forever in the unconscious, the mnemonic image of the father prompted the formation of deistic religion and attracted generations removed from the historical event to the commemorative ritual of the totem meal. "Religion is not only repentance, it is also the disguised remembrance of the triumph over the father, hence a covert filial revolt; the filial revolt is hidden in other features of religion, principally in the son's efforts to put himself in the place of the father-god" (Ricoeur, 1970:242).

Through this formulation Freud placed religion within the context of phylogeny. The progressions of the totemic meal from animal sacrifice to the Christ sacrifice in the Catholic Mass represented not so much changes in the essence of the ritual as illustrations of the progression of civilization away from the prehistorical to the more abstract and symbolic. The functions of commemoration, appeasement, and renunciation of instinct remained integral to the cultural compromise the Oedipus complex expressed through religion.

Freud was able to assert a historical context for the universality of the Oedipus complex in keeping with the evidence provided by religion. Judeo-Christian beliefs and ceremonies contained and represented the history of the species and the contents of archaic inheritance. The transmission of his history was a product of inheritance. The influence of Lamarck is obvious as Freud (1923a:38) concluded: "Thus in the id, which is capable of being inherited, are harbored residues of the existences of countless egos; and when the ego forms the super-ego out of the id, it may perhaps only be reviving shapes of former egos and bringing them to resurrection." Rice (1990;147) comments:

> It should be noted that when Freud speaks of acquired characteristics he is not referring to physical aspects of the human organism but to the memory-traces of external events which, through repetition, become permanently embedded in the unconscious *id* through which, after a presumed saturation point is reached, is transmitted to further generations. It is the *id* of the progenitor that is inherited by the offspring.

Such a view is in keeping with nineteenth-century preformationist embryology, "which taught that organisms existed fully formed from the beginning" (Ritvo, 1990:18). This notion was popularized by Haeckel, in "ontogeny recapitulates phylogeny" (Ritvo, 1990; See also, Hoffer, 1992), and appears directly in *Beyond the Pleasure Principle*, "embryology in its capacity as a recapitulation of developmental history" (Freud, 1920:26). Rieff (1961:199-201) captures the importance of Freud's emphasis on inherited characteristics:

> Freud rejected the conscious transmission of culture for what he considered a more profound continuity. The deepest ancestral secrets are not rationally preserved and disseminated by parents and teachers; they are remembered. . . . On the conscious surface of a culture, the repressed content of the past is something "vanished and overcome in the life of a people." But this is just what defines the impact of memory: one's reaction to it, against it. Prototypical events—the primal crime and its repetitions, like the murder of Moses or the murder of Christ—take on the weight of tradition when they are repressed, and the reaction to them is, of course, unconscious. History, as the trail of the prototype, became for Freud a process of the "return of the repressed," distorting extensively yet eternally recapitulatory.

Freud locates religious thinking as a primitive form of thinking of a forgotten epoch in prehistory. Extending the thesis first explicated in his 1907 paper, Freud draws an analogy between the compulsions of obsessional neurotics and the rituals of totemic religion now within the context of the repressed primal event. Freud was able to reconcile the gap between the *private* character of the "religion of the neurotic" and the *universal* character of the "neurosis of the religious man" through the phylogenetic hypothesis (cf. Ricoeur, 1970:233). Further, in linking contemporary religious practices to the domain of the id, Freud could establish the universality of the Oedipus complex.[3] This accomplishment would safeguard the primacy of sexuality in human motivation and pathogenesis. Freudian psychoanalysis would be maintained.

In *Moses and Monotheism*, Freud (1939) returned to the thesis of *Totem and Taboo*. He sought to bring into line a further explication of the development of religion from animism, through the prophetic stage to monotheism. Freud deduced a repetition of the original parricide within the more immediate history of Judaism. Moses was the historical figure upon whom a mythology emerged which served to bring Judaism into existence. To encapsulate his argument: Moses was, in fact, an Egyptian; he introduced a strict, monotheistic religion to the Jewish people; for this he was murdered; after a period of time the tribes reunited under the tenets of monotheism which reflected Moses' original credo. The reemergence of monotheism occurs, in a fashion similar to that of the totem meal. After a period of social unrest, a compromise formation appears in which the murdered father, and now the murdered father-substitute, Moses, are commemorated and the parricide is symbolically undone. The resolution of the murder of Moses and the original sin is found in the form of a Messiah to expiate the murderous deeds. We see, in this explication, the Oedipal story retold now in a later epoch in history.

> It is worth noticing how the new religion dealt with the ancient ambivalence in relation to the father. Its main content was, it is true, reconciliation with God the Father; atonement for crime committed against him; but the other side of the emotional relation showed itself in the fact that the son, who had taken atonement on himself, became a god himself beside the father and actually, in place of the father. Christianity, having arisen out of a father-religion [Judaic monotheism], became a son-religion. It has not escaped the fate of having to get rid of the father (Freud, 1939:136).

Religion bears the imprint of these events and the ambivalence of its resolution through its rituals. Contained within religion exists the original deed and its legacy of the conflict between the father and the son. Freud (1913a:145) spoke of this earlier in *Totem and Taboo*:

> Another feature which was already present in totemism and which has been preserved unaltered in religion. The tension of ambivalence was too great for any contrivance to be able to counteract it; or it is possible that psychological conditions in general are unfavorable to getting rid of these antithetical emotions. However that be, we find that the ambivalence implicit in the father-complex persists in totemism and in religions generally. Totemic religion was not only comprised of expressions of remorse and attempts at atonement, it also served as a remembrance of the triumph over the father.

The emergence of Judaic monotheism marked a significant turn in the development of civilization. This turn consisted of the prohibition against making an image of God. For Freud (1939:113), "it meant that a sensory perception was given second place to what may be called an abstract idea; it was a triumph of intellectuality over sensuality, or strictly speaking, an instinctual renunciation." As we will develop in a moment, this turn from God representation toward abstraction foreshadowed, for Freud, an epoch in which instinctual renunciation would be achieved not through a relationship with a god but rather solely through the application of ethical precepts. Rizzuto (1979:28) succinctly captured the essence of this conceptual shift, "Freud is no longer concerned with images or ancestral 'precipitates' but with ideas."

Christianity, Freud assessed, retreated from Judaic monotheism in remaining fixed to a figure of God, Christ the Son of God. Recall Freud's earlier remark that "religions are subject to reforms which work retroactively and aim at a re-establishment of the original balance of values" (Freud, 1907:167). It is the Messiah of Christianity who is then sacrificed, to be commemorated in the Mass. The distinction that Freud is drawing has to do with the substitution of an idea of God for that of a representation or image of God. That Judaism maintained an ethical monotheism suggested a slight movement away from a reliance upon a wish fulfilling, God imago. The unifying thesis in these texts concerns the unconscious memory of the original parricide and the Oedipus complex which bears the imprint in perpetuity within the psyches of the horde's descendants. This event is the origin of civilization's progress and simultaneously the progenitor of psychological conflict.

Freud posits the centrality of this event for the development of neurosis and "bridges the gulf between individual and group psychology" (1939:100). It was through his analysis of religion that Freud was able to point to the universality of the Oedipus complex in both the individual and in the culture. Freud (1939:99) writes in *Moses and Monotheism*,

> The work of analysis has, however, brought something else to light which exceeds in its importance what we have so far considered. When we study the reactions to early traumas, we are quite often surprised to find that they are not strictly limited to what the subject himself has really experienced but diverge from it in a way which fits in much better with the model of a phylogenetic event and, in general, can only be explained by such an influence. The behavior of neurotic children toward their parents in the Oedipus and castration complex abounds in such reactions, which seem unjustified in the individual case and only become intelligible phylogenetically—but their connection with the experience of earlier generations. . . . Its evidential value seems to me strong enough for me to venture one further step and to posit the assertion that the archaic heritage of human beings comprises not only dispositions but also subject-matter—memory-traces of the experience of earlier generations. In this way the compass as well as the importance of the archaic heritage would be significantly extended.

The veracity of Freud's account has been challenged repeatedly. Freud was not unaware of the difficulties in putting forth his historical hypothesis. It is evident in his correspondence during the writing of this work that Freud was aware of the problem of "poetic license versus historical truth" and originally intended *Moses and Monotheism* to be subtitled 'Ein historischer Roman' (a Historical Novel). He wrote to Arnold Zweig, "Where there is an unbridgeable gap in history and biography, the writer can step in and try to guess how it all happened" (Yersuhalmi, 1989:377). Bolstered by his discoveries of the Oedipus complex in clinical psychoanalysis, Freud applied psychoanalytic thinking to the figure of Moses. We may also discern in *Moses and Monotheism* the workings of Freud's own mind in his resolution of the Oedipus complex. Freud (1935:71), in a postscript to *An Autobiographical Study*, reveals that "two themes run through these pages: the story of my life and the history of psychoanalysis. They are intimately interwoven." Freud (1914:233) is, perhaps, unconsciously self-referential, in ascribing to Michelangelo's Moses, "the highest achievement that is possible in a man, that of struggling against an inward passion for the sake of a cause to which he has devoted himself." *Moses and Monotheism* brings to a close Freud's longstanding interest of Moses and explicates, perhaps, the nature of his identification with this historical figure.[4] Meissner (1984:50) suggested: "In a sense, Freud's writing of *Moses and Monotheism* was the final attempt to work through and resolve this deep-seated conflict and ambivalence about his father. Jacob [Freud] had destroyed Freud's image of the omnipotent father, and Freud never forgave him. The work was an act of rebellion and revenge, a rising up against the religion of the father and a smashing of it with the power of the mind." Echoing the primordial theme, perhaps, we may find the Freud's attempt at Oedipal resolution: the father-religion of Judaism and Christianity yields to the son-religion of psychoanalysis. We turn now to Freud's examination of individual psychodynamics and religious experience.

The Ontogenetic Contribution to Religion

Complementing Freud's phylogenetic explanation of the origins of religion is his discussion of ontogeny, the development of the individual member of the species. In "A Phylogenetic Fantasy," Freud (1915:10) considers the relationship between phylogeny and ontogeny:

> One can justifiably claim that the inherited dispositions are residues of the acquisition of our ancestors. With this one runs into (the) problem of the phylogenetic disposition behind the individual or ontogenetic, and should find no contradiction if the individual adds new dispositions from his own experience to his inherited disposition on the basis of earlier experience.

His description of individual development is anchored within the structure of the Oedipus complex which as we've seen finds its genesis in the prehistory of humanity. Freud's analysis of religion concerns religious practices, religious experience, and religious ideas. As we have discussed Freud (1907, 1913a, 1939) viewed religious practices from the perspectives of analogy to the individual neurosis and repetition of totemic ritual. Religious practices are seen as processes of atonement and undoing related to ancestral parracide and the psychodynamics of obsessive actions. We turn now to his examination of religious experience and religious ideas.

Religious Experience

Having declared himself to be a "infidel Jew," and, although, by his own admission, emotionally moved by religious art and architecture and fascinated by superstition and the "uncanny," Freud (1928:170) reported having never had an experience he considered religious (see Gay, 1987). Our discussion commences with Freud's analysis of his friend Rolland's description of religious experience.

> This, he says, consists of a peculiar feeling, which he himself is never without, which he finds confirmed by many others, and which he may suppose is

> present in millions of people. It is a feeling which he would like to call a sensation of "eternity," a feeling as of something limitless, unbounded as it were, "oceanic." This feeling, he adds, is a purely subjective fact, not an article of faith; it brings with it no assurance of personal immortality, but it is the source of the religious energy (Freud, 1930:64).

Freud reports that he cannot discover such an experience in himself and admits that it is not easy to deal scientifically with such feelings. He goes on to consider such feelings within the context of the ego's relation to the world. Freud conjectures that the child seeks an object cathexis with the mother, in part, to ensure her protection from the dangers of the external world. The origin of religious inclination is found in the child's helplessness in the face of the crushing powers of nature. He suggests that the primary ego-feeling, described by Romain Rolland, as limitlessness and a bond with the universe, finds its origin in the child's nascent ego relating prior to the formation of the more sharply demarcated ego-feeling of maturity (Freud, 1930, 1936; see also Fisher, 1991). Freud (1930:72) writes:

> A feeling can only be a source of energy if it is itself the expression of a strong need. The deviation of religious needs from the infant's helplessness and the longing for the father aroused by it seems to me incontrovertible, especially since the feeling is not simply prolonged from childhood days, but is permanently sustained by fear of the superior power of Fate. I cannot think of any need in childhood as strong as the need for the father's protection. Thus the part played by the oceanic feeling, which might seek something like the restoration of limitless narcissism, is ousted from a place in the foreground. The origin of the religious attitude can be traced back in clear outlines as far as the feeling of infantile helplessness.

The "oceanic" feeling is located within childhood and is understood as a telling complement of the regressive, wish-fulfilling aspect upon which religion is based. Such infantile feelings are far more intense and inexhaustibly deep than those of adults; only religious ecstasy can bring back that intensity[5] (cf. Freud, 1939:134). Kovel (1990:71, 76) argues that Freud's view is unnecessarily reductionistic.

> What is not possible—within the framework of Freud's worldview—is that the experience can have any transcendent qualities. . . . The infantile version of the oceanic experience is simply that—a *version*, or to use another term, an occasion. . . . Thus we need not assume that later occasions of the oceanic experience are somehow produced by the memory of the first one.

Freud's reading of such experiences was delimited to interpretations based on wish-fulfillment within the individual and universal context of the Oedipus complex. Explications of alternative versions of the meanings of religious experience were left to future writers, e.g., Meissner (1984). These feelings contribute and set the stage for the development of religious ideas (cf. Freud, 1930:72).

Religious Ideas

For Freud (1927) religious ideas are illusions tethered to human desire. In keeping with his analysis of religious practices and religious experience, wish-fulfillment is progenitor, as well, of religious sentiment and belief. Within the context of ontogeny, as the child shifts attachment from the mother to the father, who is perceived as stronger and better able to protect the child from the forces of nature, ideas of the father-god are formed. The construction of the god imago is a product not only of ontogeny, however, but phylogeny as well.

> To begin with, we know that God is a father-substitute; or, more correctly, that he is an exalted father; or, yet again, that he is a copy of a father as he is seen and experienced in childhood—by individuals in their own childhood and by mankind in its prehistory as the father of the primitive and primal horde . . . *the ideational image belonging to his childhood is preserved and becomes merged with the inherited memory-traces of the primal father to form the individual's idea of God*" (Freud, 1923a:85)(italics added).

Freud saw the creation of the father-god as serving an important function in the economics of the resolution of the Oedipus complex. In dealing with the rivalry of the Oedipus complex, an ambivalence exists in the wish to maintain the bond with the father-protector. This is accomplished through projection in which the child shifts cathexis to a now more powerful father-god with whom the Oedipal drama is played out. "It is an enormous relief to the individual psyche if the conflicts of its childhood arising from the father-complex—conflicts which it has never wholly overcome—are removed from it and brought to a solution which is universally accepted" (Freud, 1927:38-39). In his somewhat autobiographical reflection, "On Schoolboy Psychology," Freud (1914) writes: "Of all the imagos of a childhood which, as a rule is no longer remembered, none is more important for a youth or a man than that of his father. . . . A little boy is bound to love and admire his father, who seems to him the most powerful, the kindest and the wisest creature in the world. God himself is after all only an exaltation of this picture of a father as he is represented in the mind of early childhood."

Religion finds its dynamic impetus in motives similar to the child's investment in the father. The individual comes to realize that in many respects he or she will remain a child forever, helpless to the forces of nature. Realizing "that he can never do without protection against strange superior powers, [he] lends those powers the features belonging to the figure of his father;

he creates for himself the gods whom he dreads, whom he seeks to propitiate, and whom he nevertheless entrusts with his own protection. . . . [This reaction to helplessness is] "precisely the formation of religion" (1927:24). Religion is an illusion which stems from the individual's wish for protection and favor and out of fear of destruction and injury. "By representing the hostile presence of nature in human form, man treats nature as a being that can be appeased and influenced; by substituting psychology for a science of nature, religion fulfills the deepest wish of mankind" (Ricoeur, 1970:251). The essence of religion does not derive from the content of its beliefs but rather from the strength of the wish. Freud goes beyond Feuerbach's (1841) thesis, "God is merely the projected essence of man," in identifying the psychodynamics of the propelling force of the wish. Freud (1927:31) wrote: "Thus we call a belief an illusion when a wish-fulfillment is a prominent factor in its motivation, and in doing so we disregard its relations to reality, just as the illusion itself sets no store for verification."

Freud (1927) does not state that illusion is necessarily false; he intends, however, to place emphasis on wish fulfillment which is expressed within the structure of belief. At this level of analysis Freud does not assume a pejorative view but rather understands religious inclination within a psychoanalytic appreciation of wish-fulfillment. Religious beliefs express, using Ricoeur's phrase, "a semantics of desire." In other words, he does not fault religion its motivational wellspring. Freud did not overstate his case by attempting to disprove the validity of religious beliefs; he never crossed the line between arguments of persuasion and those of scientific assertion. Grunbaum (1987:152) claims that Freud "did *not* fall prey to the well-known genetic fallacy." He drew short of claiming a disproof of religion, "all I have done—and this is the only thing that is new in my exposition—is to add some psychological foundation to the criticisms of my great predecessors" (Freud, 1927:35). That religious beliefs find motivation from human desires and psychodynamics does not constitute disproof. Critics sympathetic to religion, e.g., Meissner (1984) and Kung (1979), do not object to examination of the psychodynamic vicissitudes that contribute to faith.

It is only when religion asserts truth claims, as Hood (1992) noted, that Freud, takes up the cause of reality, proposing religion to be a delusion. Freud (1925:72) concluded: "Later, I found a formula which did better justice to [religion]: while granting that its power lies in the truth it contains, I showed that the truth was not a material but a historical truth." Freud's argument again rests on the phylogenetic thesis.

Freud places the ontogenesis of religious experience and religious beliefs within the same context: the fulfillment of the infantile wish for protection and favor. In this location, the adult believer, and a culture built upon religious illusion, is fixed within the developmental sequence of the Oedipal child. In his placement of religion within the context of the child's relationship with the father, he amplifies the importance of the Oedipus complex for both the individual and for civilization. The ambivalence of this period and the inclination to the regressive pull of the pleasure principle supersedes the mature attention to the reality principle. Further, religious inclination is based, as well, on the influence of inherited prehistory. The dynamics of religious belief extend beyond personal history to the history of civilization. Freud's understanding of the complementary forces of ontogeny and phylogeny contribute to his critique of religion and culture.

The Problem of Religion and the Renunciation of Instinct

We turn, now, from Freud's explication to his critique of religion. He, "invite[s] the reader to take a step forward and assume that in the history of the human species something happened similar to the events in the life of the individual. That is to say, mankind as a whole also passed through conflicts of a sexual-aggressive nature, which left permanent traces, but which were for the most part warded off and forgotten; later, after a long period of latency, they came to life again and created phenomena similar in structure and tendency to neurotic symptoms"[6] (Freud, 1939:80). His thesis rests on the merits of the proposed relationship between ontogeny and phylogeny. "What is today an act of internal restraint was once an external one, imposed perhaps, by the necessities of the moment; and, in the same way, what is now brought to bear upon every growing individual as an external demand of civilization may some day become an internal disposition to repression" (Freud, 1913b:188-189).

The problem with religion, for Freud, is that it establishes the renunciation of instinct based on an illusion tied to Oedipus complex and residue from prehistory. "It now became the task of the gods to even out the defects and evils of civilization, to attend to the sufferings which men inflict on one another in their life together and to watch over the fulfillment of the precepts of civilization, which men obey so imperfectly" (Freud, 1927:22). Responsibility for one's fate is entrusted to the gods; wish supersedes personal responsibility. The disposition of the instinctual life is meted out not only within the Oedipal complex of personal history but within one of phylogenic origin, as well. "Instinctual renunciation [occurs] through the presence of the authority which replaced and continued that of the father (Freud, 1939:120). Further, instinctual renunciation becomes internalized as a psychological structure. This ego ideal or super-ego is formed through the process of identification of one's parents. "When we were little children we knew these higher natures, we admired them and feared them; and later we took them into ourselves" (Freud, 1923a:36). This internalization enjoins the preexisting, archaic heritage. Renunciation of instinctual life finds its origin in the confluence of ontogency and phylogeny, within the personal history of the individual and the prehistory of civilization.

For Freud this meant that the basis of personal intentionality was not located in the reasoning capacities of the individual but rather was found in archaic prehistory. As long as these forces held sway in the lives of individuals, civilization could not progress. As in individual neurosis, the conflicts and resolutions of the past preempted further development. The culture was fixated and mired within the throes of the Oedipal conflicts of a long forgotten time. Further, the problem with religion was that it was potentially a Trojan horse and may eventually undermine the civilization and social order which it supports (cf. Roazen, 1968:160; See also Trilling, 1955; Rieff, 1966; DeLuca, 1977). Ricoeur (1970:243) concludes:

> The striking thing about this history is that it does not constitute an advance, a discovery, a development, but is a sempiternal repetition of its own origins. Strictly speaking, for Freud there is no history of religion: religion's theme is the indestructibility of its own origins; religion is precisely the area where the most dramatic emotional configurations are revealed as unsurpassable.

While acknowledging the positive influence of religion on culture, Freud (1927:44), asserted that there was a greater risk in maintaining the "present attitude towards religion than [in giving] it up."

> Religion has clearly performed great services for human civilization. It has contributed much to the taming of asocial instincts. But not enough. It has ruled society for many thousands of years and has had time to show what it can achieve. If it had succeeded in making the majority of mankind happy, comforting them, in reconciling them to life and in making them into vehicles of civilization, no one would dream of attempting to alter the existing conditions (Freud, 1927:47).

Cultural progression, which for Freud was based on instinctual renunciation, was forestalled as long as the renunciation was based on religious, father-god prohibitions rather than on a thoughtful, deliberate, and rational assessment.

The end result of renunciation based on religion is that the restriction of instinctual expression: 1) occurs within the vicissitudes of a personal and primeval Oedipal setting; 2) is achieved not through a rational assessment which would foster healthy pride but rather through the expression of the wish for favor and through oppression and repression; and 3) may be overly restrictive due to sexual and aggressive wishes being apprehended within the context of the aforementioned dynamics (Jay, 1973). Wishes are not transformed within the course of their appearance but rather are wishfully maintained, repressed, or inappropriately acted upon. Religion does not lead to the reality principle but rather maintains the wished for benevolence to allow for the expression of such instinctual drives. "Its essence is the pious illusion of providence and a moral world order, which are in conflict with reason" (Meng and Freud, 1963:129). The dynamics of religion were seen as analogous to the psychodynamics of neurosis in which both originated in the compromise formations under the sway of the unresolved Oedipus complex [see for example Freud's (1918:114-111) case of the Wolf Man].

This view led to a strident assay of religion and a juxtaposition of psychoanalysis and religion. Of the powers within culture that "may contest the very soil of science," he judged, "religion alone is the serious enemy" (1933:160). As we have seen, in anchoring culture to the wish fulfillments that religious illusions offer, Freud argued that religion prohibited rationality from asserting its influence in human affairs. Human activity was swayed by the regressive pull of infantile wishes which religion nurtured. Faith and religious belief were inimical, in Freud's thinking, to reason and objectivity. "Religion, was quite simply the enemy" of the progression of society (Gay, 1988:533). Jones reflected Freud's thinking on this matter in responding:

> "Obviously" the study of religion "is the last and firmest stronghold of what may be called the anti-scientific, anti-rational, or anti-objective Weltanschauung, and no doubt it is there we may expect the most intense resistance, and the thick of the fight" [Jones to Freud, August 31, 1911, as cited in Gay (1988:534)].

What Freud called for was a religion of science to supersede the old religion of illusion [Freud to Eitington, 1927, as cited in Gay (1987:12)]. Freud called for an evaluation of instinctual expression in accordance to the reality principle. Logos (reason) and Anake (necessity) were to be the guiding principles of the progress of civilization. This progress clearly reflected Freud's own resolutions of psychic conflict. Van Herik (cf. 1982:59) argues that Freud establishes his critique on a gender-biased formula in which renunciation is seen as progressive and fulfillment as regressive. Further, "intellectual primacy is not only the psychological but also the masculine and the cultural ideal" (Van Herik, 1982:166). As we have seen, Freud's discussion of religion went beyond an assessment of its psychological constituents. In fact, individual religious experience, or what today we might refer to as God representation, took a back seat to Freud's critique of culture. He wrote: "my discoveries are a basis for philosophy. There are few who understand this; there are few who are capable of understanding this" [Freud, cited in Van Herik (1982:9]. Religion was for Freud the stumbling block civilization would have to master to develop further. As Gay (1987:56) summarized:

> Freud would have been the first to admit that his indefatigable harassment of that illusion, religion, was anything but disinterested, anything but detached scientific investigation. Immersed as he was in European culture, he wove his commitment to the supremacy of science into the very texture of his intellectual style.

Freud (1933:161) was aware that science "can be no match for [religion] when it soothes the fear that men feel of the vicissitudes of life, when it assures them of a happy ending and offers them comfort in unhappiness." Freud, having endured much suffering through his own life (see Schur, 1972; Gay, 1982), seems to have found through the life of the intellect a means of personal resolution. In these cultural texts we may discern his application of psychoanalysis to a critique of culture and glean an understanding of Freud's personal solutions to the problems in living.

CONCLUSION AND COMMENTARY

Freud demonstrated through his cultural texts the utility of applying psychoanalytic theory and clinical method to investigations beyond the consulting room. These expositions on religion contributed not only to an examination of unconscious dynamics in religious observance and belief but also provided, in Freud's view, additional support for the tenets of psychoanalysis. First, the universality of the Oedipus complex could be demonstrated through the study of the religious beliefs and ceremonies of primitive peoples and their analogous ceremonies in contemporary religious observance. The parallels between the past and the present, the primitive and the contemporary, suggested to Freud the existence of a universal intrapsychic dynamic. The thread of the Oedipus complex, which he perceived as woven throughout the history of the individual and the culture, was clarified in his speculation concerning the origins of Judeo-Christian religion. As in neurosis, the cultures beliefs and practices were shaped by long repressed conflictual events; however, derivatives of the events could be discovered through an analysis of the symbolism contained within the rituals. *Totem and Taboo* and *Moses and Monotheism*, in particular, present the findings of such an analysis. Second, clinical experience furnished empirical evidence of the workings of unconscious mental processes which contributed to Freud's appraisal of religion as a disguised wish fulfillment and illusion. The latent content of religious ideas and practices could be inferred in keeping with the principles of psychoanalysis as practiced in the consulting room. These investigations served one hierarchical purpose: the demonstration of unconscious psychic determinism within human existence. Through these texts Freud could assert the workings of primeval history in the unconscious life of the individual. He could peer into the heart of the culture through his inspection and analysis of religious experience. His view that religion contains truth, but that this truth was of the veracity of a past event, and not the material truth of the existence of a deity, paralleled his understanding of neurosis and prepared the way for his radical critique of culture and "after education" (Freud, 1925:72).

In his critique, Freud placed religion at the nexus of cultural development. He viewed religion as contributing to an immature mode of instinctual renunciation that was established in the Oedipal complex and was in response to the repressed guilt and anxiety originating in prehistory. (Freud, 1927:7) called for

> a re-ordering of human relations . . . which would remove the sources of dissatisfaction within civilization by renouncing coercion and the suppression of instincts, so that, undisturbed by internal discord, men might devote themselves to the acquisition of wealth and its enjoyment."

For Freud, religion was the cultural expression of neurosis. The influence of the rational was overshadowed by the claims of the irrational. Civilization was held captive by the dynamics of Oedipal conflict enshrined within religion. This examination concludes with a final question to which we now turn: "What is the value of Freud's critique of religion today?"

As we have seen, Freud's critique was established on the interplay between phylogeny and ontogeny. His acceptance of the phylogenetic hypothesis remained immutable throughout his life. Anna Freud remarked in a letter to Lucille Ritvo, "Personally, I remember very well how imperturbed my father was by everyone's criticism to his neo-Lamarkianism. He was quite sure that he was on safe ground" (Ritvo, 1990:frontispiece). The phylogenetic basis of Freud's understanding of religion is untenable. Although an appreciation of evolutionary biology in psychological functioning is developing (see Slavin and Kriegman, 1992) Freud's reliance upon specific Lamarkian principles of inherited characteristics is not supported. His view of religion as the cultural expression of an archaic event, *as transmitted through biological inheritance*, is unfounded. It was Freud's examination of ontogeny that has been the springboard for contemporary psychoanalytic study of religion.

Ontogeny was conceived by Freud as psychosexual development culminating in the resolution of the Oedipus complex. In a footnote to *Three Essays on Sexuality*, Freud (1905:226) asserted:

> It has been justly said that the Oedipus complex is the nuclear complex of the neuroses, and constitutes the essential part of their content. . . . Every new arrival on this planet is faced by the task of mastering the Oedipus complex. . . . With the progress of psycho-analytic studies the importance of the Oedipus complex has became more and more clearly evident; its recognition has become the shibboleth that distinguishes the adherents of psycho-analysis from its opponents.

In keeping with this view, Freud's critique of religion rests firmly on the cornerstone of the Oedipus complex. Belief in god finds its origin in the child's desire for maternal protection and care. From this origin, religious belief evolves into the form of a father-god in keeping with the increased focus and conflict with the father within the Oedipal constellation. Is Freud correct in his reduction? In my view, Freud was both correct and limited in this assessment. He was correct in illustrating the dynamics of identification and projection in God-representational processes. He was also correct in placing emphasis on God-representational processes in the Oedipal phase. Further, there are instances in clinical practice in which the leitmotif of the Oedipal, ambivalently held God the Father, articulates accurately an individual's God representation, its dynamic origin and the compromise formations that it serves. As salient as this model is, it is inadequate to describe the legion of self and object representations and the multiple dynamics which are contained in religious experience. Freud's view was limited by his unidimensional understanding of the Oedipus complex.

Freud brought both the method and theory of psychoanalysis to bear on Feuerbach's critique of religion as a human enterprise of projection. Psychoanalysis views these processes of identification and projection within the context of unconscious conflict. It is its approach to religion as a solution to an intrapsychic conflict as well as a response to humanity's ontological situation that marks a significant contribution. Freud's analysis leads to an appraisal of the function of God-representations and religion, in toto, along topographic, structural, economic, genetic, and dynamic lines. This perspective posits religious experience to be a dynamic, multidimensional process. For example, within the structural approach, the influence of religion, vis-à-vis, processes of internalization and projection, may be seen to contribute significantly to superego functioning. Religious experience, seen in this light, is far more than theistic beliefs; rather, as an ingredient of the structure of the psychic apparatus it contributes to the psychological equilibrium of the human organism. Religion participates silently in the mental operations which dictate behavior and consequence. Religious ideas and object relations serve a multiverse of functions. This view expands the horizon of inquiry into the nature of religious experience. In Freud's analysis, however, this horizon was contained within the Oedipus complex. This leads to a consideration of the Oedipus complex: its universality and comprehensiveness.

For Freud the Oedipus complex referred to specific libidinal and aggressive conflicts centered around the gradual triangulation of child's relationship with his or her parents. Anthropological studies for the most part have not substantiated Freud's thesis of the universality of the Oedipus complex; debate continues to ensue regarding the interpretation of such investigations (see Malinowski, 1927 and Spiro, 1982). The failure to support the universality of the Oedipus complex necessarily calls into question the claim that all religious experience bears the mark of Oedipus. This leads to a second concern regarding the comprehensiveness of the Oedipus complex as a template for understanding religious experience.

The Oedipus complex remains for many psychoanalysts today the cornerstone of psychoanalytic work and theory (see Panel, 1985; Feldman, 1990; Greenberg, 1991; Loewald, 1979; Simon, 1991; Wisdom, 1984); however, for many theorists it refers to processes that go beyond the categories of drive theory. For example, Loewald (1983:439) points to its function as "a watershed in individuation" in which drive conflict is seen within the context of the developing self. In his view emphasis is placed on object relations that become internalized as structures of the self within the Oedipal phase. Chasseguet-Smirgel (1988), although not convinced of its phylogenetic nature, nevertheless views the Oedipus complex as an innate schema through which the capacity for establishing categories and classifying impressions leads to structure formation. Kohut (1977, 1984), although rejecting the psychobiology of drive theory, maintains the importance of the Oedipus complex in terms of the parents' attunement to the child's emerging Oedipal self. When we examine the validity of the Oedipus complex as a template for religious experience we must first establish which Oedipus complex do we mean?

Freud's understanding of the Oedipus complex is restrictive and inadequate to capture *all* of the facets of development and conflict. However, his theory does articulate important constituents of God-representational processes as related to drive conflict and structural theory. He locates religious belief and experience within the intrapsychic realm of conflict and compromise and demonstrates the utility of God-representations in the economy of psychic operation and structure. Although Freud did not develop a comprehensive understanding of object relations, his inquiries into internalization and the processes leading to the formation of the superego anticipated a more complete explication of the internal world of objects.[7] Was Freud incorrect in positing that a God-representation is a displacement from the Oedipal father vis-à-vis processes of identification and projection? No, Freud was not wrong, however, he was limited by the metapsychology that he invented. His limitation lies in the narrowly conceived catalogue of meanings for religious experience posited by drive theory. In a more contemporary view of psychological functioning, considering multiple developmental lines within the realms of pre-Oedipal and Oedipal experience, religious experiences are seen to hold the potential to express a host of meanings and serve a number of functions. Rizzuto (cf. 1979), in her landmark study, *The Birth of the Living God*, proposed that the formation of the image of God is an object representational process that originates within the transitional space and that occurs, shaped by ever-present psychodynamics throughout the life of the individual. Although God-representations may derive in part from the processes which Freud described in terms of identification and projection of the father, her understanding goes beyond Freud's in asserting that "[God-representation] is more than the cornerstone upon which it was built. It is a new original representation which, because it is new, may have the varied components that serve to soothe and comfort, provide inspiration and courage—or dread and terror—far beyond that inspired by the actual parents" (Rizzuto, 1979:46). It may be concluded that Freud initiated an inquiry into the psychodynamics which are involved in God-representations.

His view of wish fulfillment as the basis for religious illusions represents a partial understanding. If the notion of wish is construed beyond the parameters of drive, then Freud's thesis accounts for many aspects of religious motivation. Psychoanalysis does not have the ability to reduce all religious motivation and experience to the determinants of wish. Nor would a demonstration of such an occurrence establish or deny the veracity of religious beliefs or experience. Psychoanalysis provides a unique perspective and method, however, to examine a particular class of influences. This leads us to his critique of culture. Does religion serve the function of renunciation? A definitive answer cannot be found outside of an individual's psychodynamics. Freud's analysis of the function of religion as renunciation, and his comparison of religious practices to the obsessive actions of neurotics, in certain instances yields a valid appraisal. However, as Meissner (1991, 1992b, in press) and Vergote (1988) have convincingly argued, it is not religion per se but rather how an individual is religious that determines the function of religious belief and practice. It is within the consulting room that the nature of the influence of religion in the resolution of conflict and the formation of identity can be surmised.

Freud's contributions to the study of religion are significant in terms of the perspective that he offers; it is one which posits the crucial influence of unconscious processes in religious experience. Although Freud's reliance on phylogeny and his exclusive focus on the Oedipus complex is inadequate, in light of our current knowledge, these speculative texts nevertheless demonstrate the potential of applied psychoanalysis in which insights gleaned from clinical investigation may be employed in the study of culture. His contributions offer a perspective and a method of inquiry into the unconscious constituents of religious experience. His significance lies not in his definitive analysis of religion and culture but rather in commencing the psychoanalytic study of religion.

NOTES AND REFERENCES

1. We may get a glimpse of his sublimation in his comments on Michelangelo's Moses (with whom he appears to have closely identified). He interprets the placement of the hands of Moses as reflecting restraint of his wrath at the Israelites for their betrayal in worshiping false idols. Freud (1914:233), perhaps is unconsciously self-referential in ascribing to Michelangelo's Moses, "the highest achievement that is possible in a man, that of struggling against an inward passion for the sake of a cause to which he has devoted himself" (see Freud, 230, regarding Jones's original interpretation).

2. In reference to this case, Meissner (1984:59) commented, "Piety had won a victory over sadistic and masochistic sexuality. But the victory was won at the cost of blasphemous thoughts and the obsessive exaggeration of religious ceremonial."

3. In the development of structural theory, Freud extends this notion by reminding that the ego originates in the id and, further, the superego develops out of the ego. Prehistory influences and is contained in each system.

4. Freud visited Michelangelo's Moses throughout his visits to Rome; he reveals the intensity of his identification with Moses in a letter to Jones who was visiting Rome at the time, "I envy you for seeing Rome so soon and so early in life. Bring my deepest devotion to Moses and write me about him" (Gay, 1988:314). See also, *The Moses of Michelangelo*, (Freud, 1914) and *Freud and Moses* (Rice, 1990).

5. In this instance I am drawing upon the translation of *Moses and Monotheism* by Katherine Jones, New York: Vintage Books, 1967:172.

6. In this instance I am drawing upon the translation of *Moses and Monotheism* by Katherine Jones, New York: Vintage Books, 1967:101.

7. An excellent illustration of the utility of Freud's theory, in consort with the expansion of his ideas in ego psychology, can be found in W.W. Meissner's *Ignatius of Loyola, The Life of a Saint.*

Baken, D.
1958 *Sigmund Freud and the Jewish mystical tradition*. Princeton, NJ: Van Nostrand.
1991 Is the Oedipus complex still the cornerstone of psychoanalysis? Three obstacles to answering the question. *Journal of the American Psychoanalytic Association* 39:641-668.

Bergmann, M. S.
1992 *In the shadow of Moloch. The sacrifice of children and its impact on western religions*. New York: Columbia University Press.

Black, D.
1993 What sort of thing is a religion? A view from object-relations theory. *International Journal of Psycho-analysis* 74:613-625.

Boehlich, W. (Ed.)
1990 *The Letters of Sigmund Freud to Eduard Silberstein* 1871-1881, translated by A. Pomerans. Cambridge, MA: The Belknap Press of Harvard University Press.

Breger, L.
1981 *Freud's unfinished journey: Conventional and critical perspectives in psychoanalytic theory*. London: Routledge & Kegan Paul.

Chasseguet-Smirgel, J.
1988 From the archaic matrix of the Oedipus complex to the fully developed Oedipus complex. *Psychoanalytic Quarterly*, 57:505-527.

DeLuca, A. J.
1977 *Freud and future religious experience*. Totowa, NJ: Littlefield, Adams.

Diller, J.
1991 *Freud's Jewish identity*. London: Associated University Presses.

Dunn, J.
1993 Psychic conflict and the external world in Freud's theory of the instinctual drives in light of his adherence to Darwin. *International Journal of Psycho-analysis* 74:231-240.

Feldman, M.
1990 Common ground: The centrality of the Oedipus complex. *International Journal of Psycho-analysis* 71:37-48.

Feuerbach, L., E. G. Warning, and F. W. Strothmann (Eds.)
[1841]
1957 *The essence of Christianity*. New York: Frederick Ungar.

Fisher, D. J.
1991 *Cultural theory and psychoanalytic tradition*. New Brunswick, NJ: Transaction.

Freud, E. L.
1960 *Letters of Sigmund Freud*, translated by T. Stern and J. Stern. New York: Basic Books.

Freud, S.

[1886-1940]
1955- *The Standard Edition of the Complete Psychological Works*, edited and translated by
1974 J. Strachey. London: The Hogarth Press and the Institute of Psychoanalysis.
[1895]
1950 Project for a scientific psychology. In *SE*, vol.1,283-397.
[1901]
1960 The psychopathology of everyday life, In *SE*, vol.6,1-239.
[1905]
1960 Jokes and their relation to the unconscious. In *SE*, vol.8,3-238.
[1902]
1959 Obsessive actions and religious practices. In *SE*, vol.9, 115-127.
[1908]
1959 'Civilized' sexual morality and modern nervous illness. In *SE*, vol.9,177-180.
[1909]
1955 Notes on a case of obsessional neurosis. In *SE*, vol.10,153-318.
[1911]
1958 Psycho-analytic notes on an autobiographical account of a case of paranoia. In *SE*, vol.12,3-82.
[1913a]
1958 *Totem and taboo*. In SE, vol.13,1-162.
[1913b]
1958 The claims of psycho-analysis to scientific interest. In *SE*, vol.13,165-190.
[1914]
1958 *The Moses of Michelangelo*. In *SE*, vol.13,211-236.
[1918,1914]
1955 From the history of an infantile neurosis. In *SE*, vol.17,3-122.
[1919a]
1955 The 'Uncanny.' In *SE*, vol.17,217-252.
[1919b]
1955 Preface to Reik's *Ritual: Psychoanalytic Studies*. In *SE*, vol.17,257-263.
[1920]
1955 *Beyond the pleasure principle*. In *SE*, vol.18,3-64.
[1923a]
1961 The ego and the id. In *SE*, vol.19,3-66.
[1923b]
1961 A seventeenth-century demonological neurosis. In *SE*, vol.19,69-105.
[1924]
1961 A short account of psychoanalysis. In *SE*, vol.19,191-209.
[1925,1924]
1959 An autobiographical study. In *SE*, vol.20,7-70.
[1927]
1961 *The future of an illusion*. In *SE*, vol.21,5-56.
[1928]
1961 *A religious experience*. In *SE*, vol.21,167-172.
[1930,1929]
1961 *Civilization and its discontents*. In *SE*, vol.21,59-145.
[1933,1932]
1964 Lecture XXXV. The question of a *weltanschauung*. In *SE*, vol.22,158-182.
[1935]
1959 Postscript. An autobiographical study. In *SE*, vol.20,71-74.
[1936]
1964 A disturbance of memory on the Acropolis. In *SE*, vol.22,239-248.
[1937]
1964 Analysis terminable and interminable. In *SE*, vol.23,216-253.
[1939]
1964 *Moses and monotheism*. In *SE*, vol.23,3-139.

[1987]
1915 Overview of the transference neuroses. In *A phylogenetic fantasy. Overview of the transference neuroses*, edited by I. Grubrich-Simitis. Cambridge, MA: The Belknap Press of Harvard University Press.

Gay, P.
1987 *A Godless Jew: Freud, atheism and the making of psychoanalysis.* New Haven, CT: Yale University Press.
1988 *Freud. A life for our time*. New York: Norton.

Greenberg, J.
1991 *Oedipus and beyond.* Cambridge, MA: Harvard University Press.

Grunbaum, A.
1987 Psychoanalysis and theism. *The Monist* 70:152-192.

Hoffer, P.
1992 The concept of phylogenetic inheritance in Freud and Jung. *Journal of the American Psychoanalytic Association* 40:517-530.

Holt, R.
1988 Freud's adolescent reading: Some possible effects on his work. In *Freud Appraisals and Reappraisals. Contributions to Freud Studies*, vol.3, edited by P. Stepansky. Hillsdale, NJ: The Analytic Press.

Homans, P.
1970 *Theology after Freud: An interpretive inquiry*. New York: Bobbs-Merrill.
1989 *The ability to mourn. Disillusionment and the social origins of psychoanalysis.* Chicago: University of Chicago Press.

Hood, R. W., Jr.
1992 Mysticism, reality, illusion, and the Freudian critique of religion. *The International Journal for the Psychology of Religion* 2:141-160.

Jay, M.
1973 *The dialectical imagination: A history of the Frankfurt School and the Institute of Social Research*, 1923a-1950. Boston: Little Borwn.

Jones, E.
1913a *Papers on psychoanalysis*. New York: William Wood.

Jones, J.
1992 *Contemporary psychoanalysis and religion*. New Haven, CT: Yale University Press.

Kohut, H.
1977 *The restoration of the self.* New York: International Universities Press.
1984 *How does analysis cure?*, edited by A. Goldberg. Chicago: University of Chicago Press.

Kovel, J.
1990 Beyond the future of an illusion: Further reflections on Freud and religion. *Psychoanalytic Review* 77:69-87.

Kuhn, T.
1970 *The structure of scientific revolutions*, 2nd ed. Chicago: University of Chicago Press.

Kung, H.
1979 *Freud and the problem of God*. New Haven, CT: Yale University Press.

Loewald, H.
[1979]
1980 The waning of the Oedipus complex. In *Papers on Psychoanalysis*, H. Loewald, 384-404. New Haven, CT: Yale University Press.
1983 Oedipus complex and development of self. *Psychoanalytic Quarterly* 54:435-443.

Malinowski, B.
1927 *Sex and repression in savage society*. New York: Harcourt Brace.

Meissner, W. W.
1978 Psychoanalytic aspects of religious experience. *Annual of Psychoanalysis* 6:103-142.
1984 *Psychoanalysis and religious experience.* New Haven, CT: Yale University Press.
1991 The phenomenology of religious psychopathology. *Bulletin of the Menninger Clinic* 55:281-298.
1992a *Ignatius of Loyola. The Life of a Saint.* New Haven, CT: Yale University Press.

1992b The pathology of belief systems. *Psychoanalysis and Contemporary Thought* 15:99-128.

in press The pathology of beliefs and the beliefs of pathology. In *Religion and the clinical practice of psychology*, edited by E. Shafranske. Washington, DC: American Psychological Association.

Meng, H. & Freud, E. (Eds.)
1963 *Psychoanalysis and faith: Letters of Sigmund Freud and Oskar Pfister*. New York: Basic Books.

Panel
1985 The Oedipus complex revisited. *Journal of the American Psychoanalytic Association* 33:201-216.

Pfister, O.
1928 *Die illusion einer zukunft* (The illusion of a future). *Imago* 14:149-184.

Rice, E.
1990 *Freud and Moses. The long journey home*. Albany, NY: State University of New York Press.

Ricoeur, P.
1970 *Freud and philosophy: An essay on interpretation*, translated by D. Savage, New Haven, CT: Yale University Press.

Rieff, P.
1961 *Freud: Mind of the moralist*. New York: Doubleday.
[1966] 1987 *The triumph of the therapeutic: Uses of faith after Freud*. Chicago: University of Chicago Press.

Ritvo, L.
1990 *Darwin's influence on Freud*. New Haven, CT: Yale University Press.

Rizzuto, A-M
1974 Object relation and the formation of the image of God. *British Journal of Medical Psychology* 47:83-99.
1976 Freud, God, the Devil and the theory of object representation. *International Review of Psycho-analysis* 31:165.
1979 *The Birth of the Living God*. Chicago: University of Chicago Press.
1986 Religious experience and psychoanalysis. Paper presented as William James Lecture, The Divinity School, Harvard University, Cambridge, MA.
1989 Interview. In *APA Division 36 Newsletter*, edited by E. Shafranske.

Roazen, P.
[1968] 1986 *Freud: Political and social thought*. New York: Da Capo Press.

Scharfenberg, J.
1988 *Sigmund Freud and his critique of religion*, translated by O. C. Dean, Jr. Philadelphia: Fortress Press.

Schur, M.
1972 *Freud: Living and dying*. New York: International Universities Press

Simon, B.
1991 Is the Oedipus complex still the cornerstone of psychoanalysis? Three obstacles to answering the question. *Journal of the American Psychoanalytic Association* 39:641.

Slavin, O. & Kriegman, D.
1992 *The adaptive design of the human psyche. Psychoanalysis, evolutionary biology, and the therapeutic process*. New York: Guilford Press.

Spiro, M.
1982 *Oedipus in the Trobriands*. Chicago: University of Chicago Press.

Stepansky, P.
1986 Feuerbach and Jung as religious critics—with a note on Freud's psychology of religion. In *Freud appraisals and reappraisals: Contributions to Freud studies*, vol.1, edited by P. Stepansky. Hillsdale, NJ: The Analytic Press.

Sulloway, F.
1979 *Freud, biologist of the mind*. Cambridge, MA: Harvard University Press.

Trilling, L.
1955 *Freud and the crisis of our culture.* Boston: Beacon Press.
Van Herik, J.
1982 *Freud on femininity and faith.* Berkeley, CA: University of California Press.
Vergote, A.
1988 *Guilt and desire,* translated by M.H. Wood. New Haven, CT: Yale University Press.
Vitz, P.
1988 *Sigmund Freud's Christian unconscious.* New York: Guilford Press.
Wisdom, J.
1984 What is left of psychoanalytic theory? *International Review of Psycho-analysis* 11:313-326.
Yerushalmi, Y.
1989 Freud on the 'Historical novel': From the manuscript draft (1934) of *Moses and Monotheism. International Journal of Psycho-analysis* 70:375-395.
Zilboorg, G.
1958 *Freud and religion.* Westminster, MD: Newman Press.

11

Jungian Theory and Religious Experience

FREDRICA R. HALLIGAN

> The psychologist, inasmuch as he[1] assumes a scientific attitude, has to disregard the claim of every creed to be the unique and eternal truth. He must keep his eye on the human side of the religious problem, in that he is concerned with the original *religious experience* quite apart from what the creeds have made of it (Jung, 1938:7, emphasis added).

Jung's analytic psychology attempts to approach the realm of "soul" objectively, annexing to science a region that lies at the intersection between religion and psychology. Jungian dreamwork may occur on many levels, but it is uniquely different from most other psychoanalytic approaches in that the numinous quality of certain dreams is acknowledged and often interpreted in terms of spiritual, rather than regressive, understandings. For Jung, the *teleological* or forward-pull of the psyche is of paramount importance. Consider this case example: A young woman was exhausted and depressed. She had finally completed her dissertation in theology and had graduated in May. But she was grieving deeply for her beloved who had recently died, when he finally succumbed after a lengthy bout with cancer. Emotionally dealing with his death was just too much. She felt her life had no purpose now. Until recently all her energy had gone into caring for him and into scholarly exploration of the medieval mystics. But now she was burned out, and so she took a summer day off—to meditate and swim and refresh her soul. She felt herself deeply in touch with her past loves, joys, and sorrowful losses.

That night she could not sleep. She awoke with fear. She had heard the words: *"The thunder of the far distant future."* She knew she was dealing with death and the specter of her own mortality and powerlessness. Again she prayed and meditated—resting all her fears and sadness "in the lap of the Lord." Finally, she slept. When she awoke, she recorded this dream:[2]

> *I was terribly lost. I was traveling with a man I know only slightly (a professor who had helped with my research). I realized I'd left my purse behind and would have to return and get it. So we parted, and I found I was lost in a huge railway station. Back and forth I went through many terminals, not knowing where I was, where I'd been, or where I was going. I had a few coins in my pocket, and I knew I could call Sally (a friend who had been there for me when mother died). But I couldn't even find a phone booth. So I sat down on some steps to wait and catch my breath. Suddenly, from around the bend, Sally arrived with Sr. Elaine (a charismatic prayer group leader who befriended and helped me in difficult times many years ago). I jumped up and embraced them both with the words: "It just goes to show,* you have to wait on the Lord."

With this dream, she felt better immediately. She awoke with a sense that somehow she would be all right and would be guided to find her direction again. That very afternoon, she picked up the phone to hear an unexpected invitation to teach a course in mysticism at a neighborhood college.

A dream such as this has a powerful impact on the individual. When it is viewed in the context of her directionless state and her quest for guidance, the dream can be viewed spiritually as an answer to prayer (Sanford, 1989). When combined with the unexpected job offer that occurred that same afternoon, this dream would be interpreted by Jungians as an example of *synchronicity*, i.e., the meaningful connection of events in the universe (Von Franz, 1980).

"But," the reader may exclaim, "that's not scientific!" As scientists of the mind, we psychologists can make no definitive assertions as to the nature of the godhead or of divine action in the world, but we can (and I believe we must!) faithfully record what we observe and hear as people describe their religious experience. In discussing a similar case, Jung wrote: "He felt it as a revelation of the Holy Ghost, whose life and procreative power no church could bring to a stop. The numinosity of this feeling was heightened by the temporal coincidence—'synchronicity'" (Jung, 1968b:85). The *felt experience* of divine action was what both of these individuals were reporting. In the case of our dreamer, her concerns over her future direction and her potentials for employment are symbolized both by the feeling of being lost and by having left her purse behind. The real-life job offer then provided both some sense of future direction and financial remuneration. Hope and purpose returned, and these changes were foreshadowed by the dream that encouraged her to have patience and trust: "You have to wait on the Lord."

Jungian analytic psychology would take a dream such as this and work with it on many levels. For example, the manifest content would be taken at face value and the symbolic references would be explored at both personal and archetypal levels. Personal history, including latent Oedipal striving, would not be ignored, of course, but the dream content would also be explored in terms of spiritual aspects of the dreamer's libidinal yearnings. Her sense that this dream was transformative, and an answer to prayer, would be understood by the therapist with full respect for her belief system and empathy for her joyful relief.

Tomas Agosin, a leader in the contemporary movement to acknowledge and welcome spiritual issues into the mental health environment and therapeutic dialogue, has written from a Jungian perspective about exploring sacred elements of dreams when they appear in clinical practice. He emphasizes open acceptance and validation:

> There is not much exploration that can be done when the sacred appears; it needs to be recognized as such, validated and then left alone. It is not to be analyzed or reduced to anything else—just to be cherished for what it is. When the Divine appears, or better said, when the person becomes aware of the spiritual presence, this dimension will always have a powerful impact on the individual. It is the recognition of this presence that is so important (Agosin, 1989:8).

The purpose of the present chapter is to outline ways in which a broad understanding of the work of Carl Jung can facilitate the therapeutic dialogue when spiritual issues emerge. To accomplish that end, we will first situate Jung in relation to his early mentor, Sigmund Freud. A brief *history* will, therefore, be followed by presentation of a *four-stage model* of levels of consciousness. The following sections will then center on *Jungian theory, techniques* of working with dreams, and *implications* for the study of psychology of religious experience and mysticism.

HISTORY

Carl Gustav Jung was born in 1875 and grew up in Basel, Switzerland, amid a poor but refined culture where his parents' strict Protestantism contrasted with a rich multicultural heritage dating back to Roman times. He came from a family that abounded in ministers (on the paternal side) and psychics (on the maternal side). Jung was introverted and intuitive (both concepts that he himself first described). He rejected his father's form of rigid

Christianity and set out to become an independent explorer in the territory of psyche and spirit. He studied medicine and was employed as a psychiatrist working with Bleuler at the Burgholzi. He was well respected by his colleagues before he ever encountered Sigmund Freud (Ellenberger, 1970).

In 1907 Jung and Freud met after Jung had written a long letter complimenting Freud on the exciting new ideas found in *The Interpretation of Dreams*. Their first meeting was mutually stimulating, and they talked for thirteen hours. This led to a close relationship, but one that was marred by numerous vicissitudes (Donn, 1988; Jung, 1973; McGuire, 1974).

In 1912 the differences between these two brilliant men began to surface in ways that led, in 1914, to an irrevocable break between them, a rupture in their friendship that was excruciatingly painful for both Jung and Freud. The beginning of that conflict was heralded by a lecture series that Jung gave in New York, at Fordham University. In those lectures, he continued to honor Freud and psychoanalysis, but he added new emphasis on some concepts of his own. Libido, he stated, was not simply sexuality but was "passionate desire" (Jung, 1961:111) in all its forms. Whereas Freud could not accept the broadening of his key concept of libido, for his part Jung found this central energic concept of sufficient richness to empower his own lifelong search into the collective unconscious and the spiritual domains within the psyche (e.g., see Jung 1967, 1968a, 1968b, 1969, 1970). Thus a bifurcation of psychoanalytic thought occurred.

THE MULTILEVELED PSYCHE

Today, when we compare these two dramatically different schools of psychoanalytic thought, we see that the major ideological differences between Freud and Jung are perpetuated in their respective schools; and yet, some evidence of rapproachement is also to be found (Halligan and Shea, 1992). A unifying schema requires respect for the differing contributions of Freud and Jung and a way to conceptualize the relationship between their two theories that will be useful in the therapeutic endeavor, and in understanding the relationship between psychotherapy and spirituality.

A useful heuristic device is a multilevel model of the psyche that was originally proposed by psychologists and psychiatrists and later developed by theologian Ewert Cousins (1992), who writes:

> Where can we find a model of the psyche comprehensive enough to encompass Teresa [of Avila's] interior castle and Jung's [archetypal] dream? Or to put it in more general terms, a model of the psyche to encompass the areas of the psyche explored in spirituality and those explored in psychotherapy. I do not believe that we will find such a model either in classical spiritual writings or in the investigations of twentieth-century psychotherapy. Yet there is such a model at hand. I am referring to the model that has emerged out of the

> research into altered states of consciousness pursued in the 1960s and 1970s, especially the investigations of the team of Robert Masters and Jean Houston, and later of Stanislov Grof . . . [who] used psychedelic drugs to explore these states of consciousness. After the first phase of their research using drugs, Masters and Houston explored altered states without the use of drugs for some ten years. Through such techniques as hypnosis, sensory deprivation, and sensory overload, they were able to explore the major realms of the psyche as effectively as with psychedelic drugs. . . .
>
> The model of the psyche that emerges out of this research can provide precisely what we need at the present time to investigate the complex relation between spirituality and psychotherapy. I am not proposing that this is the ultimate model of the psyche . . . for, the psyche is far too vast and multidimensional to be encapsulated in that fashion. It is a model, however, that can throw light on that borderline area where spirituality and psychotherapy contact and interpenetrate each other.
>
> The most important finding from their research is that the psyche has distinct levels or horizons of consciousness. . . . The levels that their subjects explored were the following:
>
> (1) The sensorium, the realm of heightened sense experience;
>
> (2) The ontogenetic realm, where subjects explored their personal past on a level of deep affect. This realm is comparable, but not limited to, the areas explored in Freudian psychoanalysis;
>
> (3) The phylogenetic level, where subjects explored the great archetypal symbols, myths, and rituals that are the heritage of the human community as a whole. This is similar to the collective unconscious of Jung;
>
> (4) The level of the mysterium where subjects experience ultimate reality or the highest levels of consciousness. This realm is similar to that experienced by the mystics of the world's religions (133-134).

It has been my own clinical experience that each of these realms is also tapped, at varying times, by dreams. For this reason, I find this four-stage model to be extremely useful for conceptualizing the psychospiritual state and progress of individuals seen in psychotherapy. Two examples of dreams at the level of the *sensorium* would be, first, the focused dream of: *"beautiful autumn leaves, nothing else. I was simply walking down a road surrounded by all the beautiful autumn colors."* Another example is a similar dream experience of: *"simply watching the clouds drift by against a clear blue sky."* Such heightened sensory experience can also result from various meditative techniques; and many spiritual paths induce trance or altered states of consciousness by use of hypnotic-like guided imagery in which sensory details are vividly described.

At the second or *ontogenetic* level of consciousness, the whole psychodynamic therapeutic endeavor finds its place. As Freud discovered, free association is a potent method for eliciting elements of personal history that continue to be relevant to the individual. Just as in Freudian psychoanalysis, so also in Jungian analytical psychology, the major portion of psychotherapeutic time is spent exploring the personal unconscious in relation to current life issues. In the dream first presented in this chapter, for example, it would be necessary to explore all the dreamer's personal associations and feelings (Whitmont and Perera, 1989). These would include aspects of the recent relationship with the theology professor and the relationship with the two supportive friends from the more remote past. The therapist must always wonder where a mother-figure or father-figure might be symbolized (e.g., the professor and Sr. Elaine, both of whom were authority figures). On the other hand, a Jungian approach would also look at the persons depicted in the dream as possibly symbolizing certain aspects of the dreamer's own psyche.

Jungian psychotherapy differs from its Freudian precursor where the third or *phylogenetic* level emerges. Dreams at this level are relatively rare.[3] It was Jung's genius, fascination, and persistence that enabled him to discover and exemplify vast numbers of dreams that are suggestive of the common human condition. These dreams, which Jung called *archetypal*, contain symbols from the *collective unconscious* which Jung described in 1914 as

> an unconscious not consisting only of originally conscious contents that have got lost, but having a deeper layer of the same universal character as the mythological motifs which typify human fantasy in general. These motifs are . . . typical forms that appear spontaneously all over the world, independently of tradition, in myths, fairy-tales, fantasies, dreams, visions, and the delusional systems of the insane (Jung, 1960:180).

Because of its dream access to the archetypal symbols, the Jungian approach to psychotherapy provides a bridge to the spiritual domain of the psyche. Here is an example of a dream at the interface between the collective unconscious and the realm that religionists have called "spirit," and mystics have described as the inner chamber of the psyche. The dreamer was a man in midlife transition who was trying to discover new directions in relation to family, career, and general meaning or purpose in life. Of the dream, he said:

> *At first I was walking around a great amphitheater. (It reminds me of the coliseum but did not appear to be in Rome.) At the far side our parish priest (a deeply spiritual and beloved pastor) was celebrating the Mass. I did not linger, but moved on around the perimeter to a place that seemed to be ancient Iran. There I found a junk pile and began rummaging in it. It seemed very important that I find a treasure that was hidden on that spot. Finally I found it: it was an ancient, wizened head, like an Iranian icon. It had pine cones for ears. A critical friend stopped by and could not understand the value of what I had uncovered. But I knew somehow that this was an icon representative of the great god of the ancients.*

The dream had a numinous feeling, and exploration of the spiritual associations led to the recognition that this dreamer's spiritual vocation no longer was associated with Rome, nor even with his ("good father") parish priest who was celebrating Eucharist. Rather, he needed to move farther, toward the holy land, where exploration of the junk pile would yield a sacred image of real psychospiritual energy. In terms of therapy, the junk pile symbolized his need for continued, courageous encounter with his own inner "junk" (including the critical aspects of his own personality). But the discovery of the icon also had a spiritual dimension in terms of "finding the sacred in the ordinary." Here, amidst the seeming trash of life, he would find a symbol of the god-image or Self that governs his psyche. He held the image of that sacred icon as a guiding principle over a number of years. Often he wondered why the icon had pine cones in place of ears; finally he felt a spiritual insight emerge when he realized that pine cones (seed pods of the evergreen tree) represented simple, natural ways in which he should listen for the sacred messages from the Self.

Following Jung's lead, a number of scholarly compendiums of archetypal symbols have been published and can be extremely useful for amplifying the meaning of symbols that reflect the collective unconscious.[4] It is not necessary to determine which exact meaning the pine cone represents in this patient's dream, but presentation to him of the array of cross-cultural meaning allows him to get a broader sense of the archetype that has manifested itself in his dream. In this case, the amplification of the pine cone symbol served to strengthen his sense of awe and numinosity that accompanied the finding of his sacred god image.

At the fourth level, deeper dreams that enter the *mysterium*, are even more rare than archetypal dreams. They do occur, however, in working with individuals who are committed to a spiritual path, and usually at key transition points in their lives. Often dreams at the mystical level may be very simple. For example, a Jewish man described a dream by saying, *"It was just pure white light—almost blue-white and very luminous. I had a sense that God was manifesting to me in that light."*

Another dreamer spoke of an image of *"black swirling energy"* that had a numinous sense of beneficient power. In this case, the dream of darkness could easily be differentiated from a depressive image because the individual felt such peace and joy when the dark energy circled around him. Jungian analyst Ann Ulanov (1992), writes beautifully of such dark mystical images of God:

> If it is really true that the unconscious is another medium through which God touches us, what do we do when the God in hiding there approaches? All our hard-won insight, our enlarged seeing-into falls under the great shadow of the Holy. We are brought into an illuminating darkness. Ignorance, as a cloud of unknowing, overcomes us, for this God is so much bigger than any-

thing we have conceived. Our eye is overwhelmed. . . .

Darkness is the necessary way, for the God who draws near lies outside our God-images. It is not so much that our images of God are wrong or our religious practices mistaken. They are simply too small in their finiteness. The dark side of God is a merciful one, effacing useless images, stretching, pushing us beyond even the best of what we have found in our traditions and created in our prayers (p.157).

Just as pure light, or a pregnant darkness can be representative of the mysterium, so also dreams of intense, luminous energy would be manifestations of the mystical level of consciousness. Occasionally one may encounter a powerful spiritual experience, such as the following, where the energy of a dream continues into waking consciousness:

I felt a burst of energy in the back of my head. My body, too, was in a totally different feeling: tingling, like a pulsating vibrancy. . . . I could feel energy pouring out into my head. Then I felt a total collapsing and tumbling of time and space. It was another reality, another dimension. It was similar to a vortex with things tumbling into it. I was the observer and also part of it. I was going down into the vortex, gazing through historical time periods, all different ages. There was a collapsing of history, not governed by time or measured space (see Halligan, 1992:176).

This dreamer was Episcopalian and an ex-nun, but her experience is very similar to those described as the awakening of Kundalini energy in Hindu and Tantric Buddhist traditions (Krishna, 1985; see also Grof, 1985). As therapists, pastoral counselors, and spiritual directors explore the religious experience of the people we see, we must open ourselves to a variety of unexpected mystical or even paranormal experiences. Jung's analytical psychology, as a bridge to the spiritual aspects of dreamwork, allows us to situate such dreams within the full range of human religious experience, acknowledging their validity and their transformative power for the individual.

JUNGIAN THEORY

James Hillman writes: "Living religion, experienced religion, originates in the human psyche and is as such a psychological phenomenon" (1967:42). It must be emphasized too that Jungian theory is primarily a psychological theory. Religious or spiritual experiences are but one end of the experiential spectrum that is anchored, at the other end, in clinical observation of psychopathology.[5]

To sum up Jungian theory in a few pages is virtually a "mission impossible." Several good, succinct books have addressed this task (e.g., Bosnak, 1988; Hall, 1983; Singer, 1973; Stein, 1984; Whitmont, 1969) and so I will confine myself to a brief overview in order to mention a few of the key archetypes that typically emerge in psychotherapy, pointing to their impact on our understanding of religious experience. Jung himself writes:

> The seat of faith . . . is not consciousness but spontaneous religious experience, which brings the individual's faith into immediate relation with God.
>
> Here we must ask: Have I any religious experience and immediate relation to God and hence that certainty which will keep me as an individual, from dissolving in the crowd?
>
> To this question there is a positive answer only when the individual is willing to fulfill the demands of rigorous self-examination and self-knowledge. . . . He will have . . . taken the first step toward the foundations of his consciousness—that is, toward *the unconscious, the only accessible source of religious experience.* This is certainly not to say that what we call the unconscious is identical with God or is set up in his place. It is the medium from which the religious experience seems to flow (Jung, 1957:100ff, emphasis added).

Here we have intimations of the essence of the Jungian quest. As leading theorist, Edward Edinger (1973) posits, the aim of analysis is to build a bridge between consciousness, with ego as its center, and the Self or true center of the entire personality. Self is an archetype at the center of the unconscious, so the aim of therapy is to build what Edinger calls the "ego-Self axis." In this process, "individuation" occurs, i.e., the healthy recognition and acceptance of who one truly is, in one's essence and totality.

According to Jung, the primary evolution during the first half of life is development of one's gender identity and adaptation to the environment. This requires certain compromises between what we naturally are and what society expects us to be. This compromise, which involves role-playing and a certain degree of falsification, is known in Jungian circles as the *persona* (from the Greek word for theatrical mask).

Opposite the persona, and held in the unconscious, are all those elements of our personalities that we think of as dark and foreboding. These aspects known as *shadow* are often depicted in dreams by an unappealing figure who is the same sex as the dreamer. As Miller (1981) writes:

> By definition, the shadow is the opposite of the persona. . . . The shadow is like a foreign personality—a primitive, instinctive, animalistic kind of being. It is the collection of uncivilized desires and feelings that simply have no place in cultured society. The shadow is everything we don't want to be. Or rather it is perhaps everything we would like to be but don't dare. The shadow is everything we don't want others to know about us. It is everything we don't even want to know about ourselves and have thus conveniently "forgotten" through denial and repression (p.22f).

Individuation or the journey toward wholeness requires the humble acceptance and courageous integration of the shadow elements into the conscious view of one's whole personality. Often among religiously oriented people, the shadow side includes narcissistic and exhibitionistic qualities as well as repressed rage. Occasionally, shadow may even include unrecognized strengths, and when shadow is integrated, all the previously feared aggressive potentialities are modified in the direction of socially appropriate assertiveness rather than the primitive extreme rage that may have been evident at the start.

In the healthy developmental sequence, by midlife one's gendered identity is also well formed, and the locus of the individuation path takes a point of inflection, changing direction toward personality unification and wholeness. To accomplish this developmental task, the contrasexual elements of personality that were previously held in the unconscious must be brought to consciousness and integrated into one's sense of identity. It is time for the "inner marriage" to begin.

In the case of a man, the internal aspects of his personality that are usually associated with feminine feelings and behavior will usually be projected in his dreams as female figures that Jung describes as representative of the *anima* archetype. For a woman, the opposite is true: her conscious female identity is compensated within by unconscious qualities often attributed to males in our society. These prototypical qualities are pictured as men in her dreams and as such they are representative of the *animus* archetype.[6] The important point is that all humans have elements in their personalities that are gotten genetically and behaviorally from both the male and female progenitors (as well as teachers, mentors, and friends). Jung emphasizes at midlife (beginning around age thirty-five), a major developmental task is to bring to consciousness the contrasexual elements and integrate them into the whole personality. This theory fits well with ample developmental research that suggests that men tend to become more feeling-oriented and women tend to become more assertive at midlife.

What Jung calls the "conjunctio" (a term taken from medieval alchemy) represents, on one level, the inner marriage or emergence of wholeness (see Halligan, 1992). There are many facets to this emerging unity. In Jungian psychotherapy, for example, consciousness and the unconscious must meet and dialogue. This includes the meeting of persona and shadow; as well as conscious gender identity and the animus or anima. This individuation process is not a one-time event, although dreams may dramatically herald its onset and progress. Whitmont (1969) says about the process:

> Even though the shadow is strange and remote, it is still somehow within reach and can, at least to quite a considerable degree, be charted or sketched out, but the anima and animus are forever defiant of complete understanding or taming. After we think we have found out everything there is to be found out, they

may appear in entirely new and unexpected forms, and there is never an end to this. They connect us with the limitlessness of the psyche itself. The shadow, one might say, is an unknown inland lake, animus and anima the ocean. This realization is extremely important from a practical standpoint, for it implies that only constant attention to the unconsciousness, an inner devoted tribute, is sufficient to enlist its cooperation. The unconscious realms cannot be analyzed away, cannot be defeated in battle, but, at best by conscious confrontation, can be taken into account within the limits of one's individual capacity (p.215).

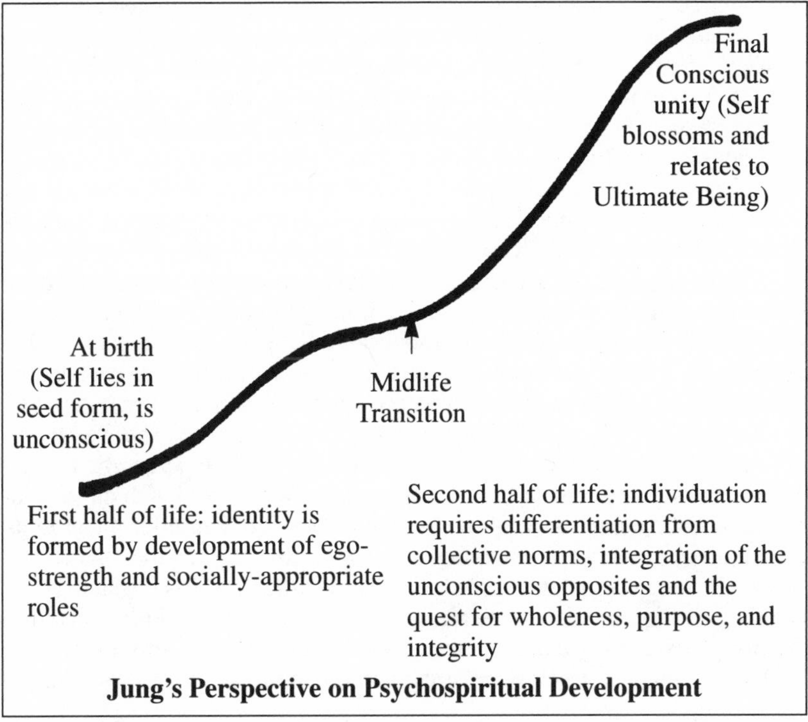

Jung's Perspective on Psychospiritual Development

The final conscious unity to which Jung repeatedly points is the *Self*, the teleological aim of individuation, often described as the *union of opposites* within the psyche. For Jung the Self is the central archetype of great primacy. Self represents the centering tendency of the psyche and also its wholeness. As Jean and Wallace Clift (1986) describe it:

> In Jung's terminology, the Self is the ordering and unifying center of the total psyche (conscious and unconscious), while at the same time the Self is the whole sphere—the Self is both center and circumference of the psyche. The Self thus incorporates all the other archetypes into a paradoxical unity, transcending any attempt to contain or define it (p.133).

Self is the destination and individuation is the path of psychospiritual development. Self is the focal point and goal of personality development. Individuation is the process of differentiating oneself from collective norms so that one's unique personality can be manifest. Although Jung viewed this process as occurring primarily in the second half of life, and as facilitated by a course of Jungian analysis, some individuals (especially those over-invested in persona values) never come to discover their own true Self, whereas others may begin the process sooner than Jung predicted.

For example, a thirty-year-old oriental graduate student was studying computer science in an American university. She felt conflicted about her career goals, and so she sought counseling with this Jungian-oriented therapist. We spent months weighing the alternatives and watching her dreams. The identity conflict as she was experiencing it was closely related to her parents' personalities and expectations, along with her habitual pattern of playing both sides and trying to please everyone. Her father, who was a successful businessman, wanted her to complete her doctorate in computer science. Her mother, an artist, had always encouraged her daughter to develop her musical abilities. The daughter loved the sense of freedom, affectivity, and beauty that she associated with flute playing (which she practiced faithfully). Should she give up graduate school and make a serious effort to support herself as a musician? She also respected the discipline and power she experienced in computer work. It made "practical sense" to her to get her doctorate, but she feared she would ultimately hate the work since it was "too dry."

Clearly, thinking and feeling were two of the opposites she was trying to integrate in her own career plans, but since they were personified in her dreams as male and female figures, respectively, we worked with those manifestations of the unconscious, always aiming toward conscious integration. It took many sessions of wavering back and forth between the "male" and "female" elements in her dreams before some gradual shifts began to occur naturally. For instance, there was less rigidification of the difference between the two poles. Finally a dream emerged that marked both a turning point in her therapy and the emergence of the archetype of Self. Of the dream, she reported:

> *My boyfriend and I were walking in the forest. We had left my parents behind. We came to a place where some tree houses were built on huge pine trees. It was built like a maze. We start at the outer edge of the trees on the ground and walk around in concentric squares that grow smaller and smaller toward the center, while at the same time rising higher and higher into the trees with each square. As we walk we hear a guide telling the story that this tree house used to be the final test for a secret, exclusive society. Each prospective member had to walk this path and when they reached the top (the space gets smaller and smaller as you go), they had to stay in a tiny room for several hours.*

Here the mandala figure, which is symbolic of the Self archetype, emerges in a totally natural setting. The "temenos," or sacred space within, is depicted as a place to enter for a period of time. She is with her boyfriend (a caucasian American) who represents a positive animus figure, and so the union of opposites is implied. Most significantly, she has left her parents behind. The quest has become her own, and she is no longer torn by those conflicting energies and their internalized pressures. She is becoming her own woman, her own Self.

Simultaneously with this dream, a new sense of her career direction occurred. She would continue her graduate studies in the applied mathematics department, at least until she completed her masters. Meanwhile, she would accept a job as an usher in a New York Theater (returning to a job she had held the previous summer) and would work toward obtaining a position in theater or concert management. The integration of arts and business felt uniquely her own. I have observed that whenever Self dreams occur in young people, it often marks a time of significant differentiation from the family of origin (as in this case); or else it marks a time when the psyche is striving to integrate a trauma, or is otherwise making a major therapeutic change.

The emergence of Self symbolism was marked here by the mandala imagery of the square maze in the woods. Jung wrote extensively of the power and ubiquity of mandala figures. They represent the centering tendency within the psyche and are clear evidence of the individuation process.

Typically the Self archetype manifests in beautiful dreams where there is a numinous affect, and the imagery includes very balanced figures (mandalas based on circles, squares), quadrated figures, emphasis on the number four (which Jung ascribed to the four functions: thinking, feeling, sensation, and intuition), and a great tree, mountain, or column (representation of the *axis mundi* in medieval symbology). Self may also be implied in very beneficent guide figures such as the "Wise Old One," or as central authorities such as "The President," "The Queen," "The Director," "The Ship's Captain." Positive references to places of centrality or significant authority are also suggestive of the dwelling place or presence of Self. These include: "The White House," "Buckingham Palace," "Canterbury Cathedral," "Grand Central Station," "Central Park," "Center City," "Rome," "Jesusalem," "Mount Fujiyama," and "The Mountain of the Grail." The "Divine Child" and the "Great Fish" also represent the Self and are manifestations of the Christ archetype (Clift and Clift, 1986; Edinger, 1987; Jung, 1967, 1968a, 1968b, 1969, 1970; Whitmont, 1969).

Jung viewed the image of Christ as a representation of Self, the incarnate God dwelling within. He conceptualized the Self archetype as a psychic matrix into which the Christ figure was assimilated over the course of Western history. In 1951 he wrote:

> Had there not been an affinity—magnet!—between the figure of the Redeemer and certain contents of the unconscious, the human mind would never have been able to perceive the light shining in Christ and seize upon it so passionately. The connecting link here is the archetype of the God-man which on the one hand became historical reality in Christ, and on the other, being eternally present, reigns over the soul in the form of a supraordinate totality, the Self (Jung, 1968b:181f).

In a similar manner, he viewed the symbol of the fish as a connecting link to this greatest of all the archetypes. The fish is an element that swims in the sea, which represents the unconscious; it is also a symbol of Christ dating back to earliest Christian times. Jung theorized how the image of the fish, arising from the depths of the unconscious, became connected to the person of Jesus:

> The fish symbol is thus the bridge between the historical Christ and the psychic nature of man, where the archetype of the Redeemer dwells. In this way Christ became an inner experience, the "Christ within. . . ." In as much or in as little as the fish is Christ does the Self mean God. It is something that corresponds, an inner experience, an assimilation of Christ into the psychic matrix, a new realization of the divine Son (p.183).

In his elegant small volume, *Jung's Quest for Wholeness: A Religious and Historical Perspective*, Curtis Smith (1990) gives a most readable and yet complete scholarly account of Jung's intellectual development, centering around the concept of Self. Smith writes:

> The individuation process can be thought of as a "rite of passage" in which the opposites of conscious and the unconscious collide and struggle with one another in an attempt to give birth to psychic wholeness. . . .
>
> For Jung, the Self is the psychological equivalent of the Upanisadic conception of the Atman, which is both the center of the individual and the cosmos itself. . . . Thus Jung's understanding of the self includes the oneness of the cosmos and the individual. More precisely, Jung believes that at the farthest reaches of the psyche, its individuality merges into the materiality of the world. At some point the boundary between psyche and world blurs to the point of extinction so that . . . psyche and world appear as points on a continuum, forming an indivisible whole (p.98).

Here is reference to one of the many places where Jung's thought moves from the personal level, through the archetypal layer of the unconscious, and seems to address the level of the mysterium. At some points Jung seems quite mystical in his outlook (Jaffee, 1989), but at other times he seems to misread clear references to mystical union and interpret them (reductively) at the archetypal level. In general, it is in his references to the archetype of Self that Jung transcends, moving from the purely psychological into the realm of spiritual or mystical experience.

To return briefly to the case of the young oriental student who found Self at the intersection of her business goals and artistic inclinations, it is interesting to note that the very next step in her path of individuation led toward opening to the religious dimension of her psyche. Although she was an avowed atheist, she began to express an interest in meditation. Since she came from a Buddhist/Taoist culture, it was an easy step to begin spiritual practice. Encouraged by her boyfriend, she chose a kataphatic method of envisioning herself bathed in white light. As her therapist, I was unaware of this shift into a spiritual dimension until she reported a dream of *"swimming in very blue water toward a white temple that wasn't really religious but just very pure and very white."* She said the place reminded her of Greece, which again is evidence of the multicultural aspects of the archetypal level of the psyche.

Each case is different, of course, but it is not unusual for emergence of Self symbolism to be accompanied by, or immediately followed by, powerful religious symbolism. As Jung views it, the Self is the spiritual aspect within the psyche, and its manifestation may have much or little to do with the symbolism and iconography of the dreamer's own religious culture. Dreams of Self that mark a deeper opening to the spiritual dimension often appear at midlife.

One such dream sequence occurred for a Catholic laywoman who was studying to become a spiritual director. She and her husband were about to be transferred to another country. She was anxious and felt resistant about the move because she abruptly had to terminate her therapy, as well as leaving her community of friends. She dreamt first of *being inside a huge human body where she initially felt frightened and disgusted by the anatomical parts in living color. Then she realized that she must help others who were there and, as she began to do so, a sense of peace and calm returned to her*. In discussing the dream, we talked of the archetypal image of "the body of Christ" which is a metaphor for all God's people. The following week she returned, jubilant, for what had to be her termination session of therapy. She related the following dream:

> *I saw a young couple who were anxious. Each of them was carrying a blue velvet cushion. The husband noticed a bead in her cushion and, when he pulled on it, a beautiful diamond necklace emerged. I've never seen anything like it: fiery diamonds, sparkling on velvet!*
>
> *Then he placed the necklace around her neck and it began to glow even more. It transfigured her! Then, in glowing light she began to rise up and up; and she was lifted out somewhere into the cosmos.*

She finished recounting her dream by saying how amazed she continued to feel, and my own countertransferential reaction was one of awe and wonder. Here we were witnessing a Self figure, a female god-image, a divinization or internal representation of the Divine. The dreamer felt filled with grace and ready to move on to her new location. A sense of intense numinosity marks such dreams, and they are often described as being incredibly beautiful. The usual psychospiritual result is empowerment and a sense of deep gratitude and purpose.

TECHNIQUES

Jung often writes of his deeply held belief in the guidance of the Self archetype when it emerges. He conceives of Self as the inner wisdom that produces dreams. Working with dreams then is the paramount method in Jungian analysis. In 1928-1930 Jung gave a series of lectures specifically devoted to methodology of dream analysis. He estimated some 20 percent of dreams may be viewed objectively, that is, the figures in the dream may represent themselves if they are currently significant in the dreamer's life. On the other hand, Jung claimed that 100 percent of dream content can also be viewed subjectively, i.e., as symbolic of intrapsychic elements in the dreamer's personality (Jung, 1984).

Typically, Jungians use a variety of techniques for working with dreams in order to elicit the associations and underlying archetypal symbolism. While some do dreamwork in groups (Greene, 1984; Halligan and Shea, 1991; Ullman and Zimmerman, 1979), most dreamwork is in the context of individual psychotherapy (Stein, 1984; Whitmont and Perera, 1989) where transference and countertransference are as important in Jungian analytical psychology as in Freudian psychoanalysis (Jung, 1966; Jacobi, 1984). One major difference, however, is that in addition to the free association method as Jung initially learned it from Freud, Jungians generally tend to deal more concretely with the imagery manifest in the dream. Hillman (1967, 1983, 1989) in particular, emphasizes the importance of staying with the affective power of the visual image rather than moving to the intellectual level of interpretative discourse.

In Jungian dreamwork, the power of the manifest dream images is accentuated. Every person depicted in a dream is viewed as a facet of the personality. For example, a dream image of the "class clown" remembered from grade school might be symbolic of the "trickster" archetype within the dreamer's psyche. To elicit the personal symbolic meaning of a specific person known to the dreamer, the therapist may ask about the personality of the dream figure, e.g., "What is the first thing you think about when you think of that person?" These associations are continued until the affective connection is made.

The connection between meaning and image is central for Jung. He felt that a dream symbol can never be grasped in terms of what the dreamer already knows; i.e., that its very nature is to take one beyond. In 1934 Jung wrote of the importance of giving attention to the manifest content of the dream:

> Interpretation must guard against making use of any other viewpoints than those manifestly given by the content itself. If someone dreams of a lion, the correct interpretation can lie only in the direction of the lion; in other words, it will be essentially an amplification of this image. Anything else would be an inadequate and incorrect interpretation, since the image "lion" is a quite unmistakable and sufficiently positive presentation (Jung, 1966:162).

One of the key ways to elicit meaning from the dream symbols is through use of *active imagination*. For example, one may dialogue with the dream image or, through fantasy, *be the image*. A woman whose dream included *a bouquet of pink daisies* imagined herself as one of the flowers and said: "I am a small pink daisy; I am very centered. I am fragile and feminine. I am a separate individual, yet I live and grow amongst a community of others much like me." This dreamer was a feminist and, through this bit of dream-work, she recognized both the mandala shape of the flower as representing her Self, and the value of her women's spiritual community as the context that supported her growth.[7]

Mary Watkins (1984) has written in her beautiful book, *Waking Dreams*, of the numerous creative ways dream images can be incorporated into life, allowing their affective power and deep wisdom to enrich one's understanding of the meaning, purpose and direction of one's life. She writes, "We must learn . . . to deepen ourselves into the context of the individual image. By spending time with it, trying to feel it, to slip into it, we can try to note where and how it lives" (p.141). Watkins gives a scholar's compendium of historical approaches that were precursor to and contemporary with Jung's dream interpretation; and yet she also offers an artist's appreciation of the dramatic and creative processes that are rooted in the unconscious and surface in dreams and active imagination. She writes, for example:

> Theodore Flournay (1854-1920), a disciple of Wundt's, studied this myth making propensity of the unconscious. . . . He came to feel that the weaving of myths goes on continuously in the unconscious. . . . The "creative function" of the unconscious he saw as that which enables one to receive insights and wisdom not attributable to the conscious personality. . . . Flournay felt that the unconscious also had a protective function which would creatively offer warnings and comfort (p.33).

Jung would heartily agree with Flournay's viewpoint as presented by Watkins: Dreams creatively provide both warnings and comfort necessary for the development of the dreamer's central Self. In so eloquently articulating Jung's use of active imagination, Watkins creates an important bridge to the work of contemporary cognitive psychology in its efforts to understand the function and purpose of dream imagery and its dramatic unfolding processes.

IMPLICATIONS FOR THE PSYCHOLOGY OF RELIGIOUS EXPERIENCE

> *Out of the sea the young man emerges, his brow crowned by a circlet of fresh green seaweed. What representation of the gods of the ancients is active at this moment in his soul? Poseidon lives herein despite centuries of Judeo-Christian repression. In the mystery of the deep unconscious, the God of the Sea is still manifest.*

Jungians would look at such a dream image with playfulness, spontaneity, and often reverence. When we look into Jung's experience of religion, we see that he was pantheist, Christian, alchemist, and pagan; gnostic, esotericist, and a seeker into mystical experience in Eastern, Western, primitive and Third World traditions (e.g., see Coward, 1985; Edinger, 1987; Grant, Thompson, and Clark, 1983; Moore, 1988). In recognizing and naming the archetypes, he provided access to the deeper realms of the psyche where the human spiritual yearning and capacity for religious experience arises. Jung cast his scholarly net widely, and he found examples of a great variety of divine images within the psyches of those whose dreams and fantasies he studied. He was particularly influenced by the Ancient Greeks and found the Olympian pantheon broadly applicable for expressing images of both gods and goddesses, as well as human characteristics. The Olympian deities provide a comprehensive view of god images manifest in early Western thought;[8] yet, for Jung, each such god image would be representative of only part-processes. For Jung, true sacrality lies in wholeness, the union of the opposites.

The concept of conjunctio, or mystical marriage, permeates Jungian thought and research into religious experience (Jung, 1970; Dourley, 1987; Wehr, 1990). Like Eastern philosophy, Jung emphasized the union and comingling of all opposites within the world and within the psyche. Coward (1985) writes:

> In Hindu or Brahmanical thought, the pairs of opposites are experienced as a continuum extending from external opposites such as heat and cold to the fluctuations of inner emotion and the conflict of ideas such as good and bad. The Hindu . . . path aims at freeing the individual completely from entanglement in the opposites, which seem inherent in human experience so that he can experience oneness with Brahman. . . . What is meant, says Jung, is a union of opposites in which they are canceled out. . . . This transcendence of opposites involves the systematic withdrawing of libido or attention from both. . . . This eventually . . . opens the way for rising up of images from the

> collective unconscious. . . . symbols with the power to regulate and unite the destructive tensions of the pairs of opposites (p.15).

From the Western Christian perspective, Bonaventure, a thirteenth-century mystic, expressed this same idea well when he wrote:

> For what is supremely one
> is the universal principle of all multiplicity.
> (Bonaventure, 1978:99)

Religious experience, from the Jungian perspective, is based on a progressive psychospiritual path where all facets of the soul are first differentiated and then integrated. Male and female characteristics, leading to agentive and receptive spiritual processes (Hood and Hall, 1980), are equally important. Kataphatic or image-based spirituality, and apaphatic spirituality of emptiness are two opposite paths that may ultimately lead to a similar state of mystical union or samadhi, i.e., the ultimate psychological result may simply be two sides of the same coin. As Hayao Kawai (1988), first Zurich-trained Jungian analyst in Japan, has pointed out, the Eastern mind is dominated by the idea of emptiness whereas the Western mind is permeated by an aim of fulfillment or fullness. For Kawai, however, these seeming opposites *can* be integrated so that the apparent differences are transcended. For each spiritual seeker this transcendence is an individual process and quest.

The path of individuation is unique and yet broadly anchored in the archetypes of the collective unconscious. It is not unusual for Catholic nuns quite literally to dream of ordination and celebrating the Eucharist. More unusual, but not rare, is for those same nuns to dream of leading a fire dance, partaking in an underwater ritual, or dancing an initiation rite as an Indian princess. With Oriental students dreaming of Greek temples and North American priests dreaming of Shamanic rituals in Africa, there is ample empirical evidence of the existence of the collective unconscious. It behooves those of use who study contemporary psychology of religion to recognize the importance of these unconscious primary processes for nourishing spiritual practice and religious experience.

When the numinous arises, are we open to it? Are we ready to soar with it? To sail across the sea of the imagination in order to follow its beckoning call? Are we ready to float in a state of open awareness, ready to receive enrichment from the deepest sources of spiritual power?

When the numinous arises, we must let go of our preconceptions of the way things are, or the way things ought to be. We must temporarily let go of our scientific attitudes in order to get glimpses of what lies beyond our ordinary abilities to perceive. The ego with its propensity to judge, to measure and to conceptualize, must surrender to the Self. As a gift from the Self, a dream image tells its own story, when we are open to receive:

An absolutely beautiful, silver tree was glistening in the light. It was upside down! It had a luminosity such as I have never seen in waking life.

This tree is easily recognized as a manifestation of the archetypal tree of life. Upside down, as it is here, the glistening tree presents the spiritual insight that its roots are in heaven.

The wisdom of the psyche often manifests in pictures that portray deep truths as well as sometimes extraordinary beauty. But even in the ordinary—the soaring of a seagull, or a pine cone resting on the path—the sacred is ready to give glimpses of itself to the spiritually oriented dreamer. Just as in the Christian myth of the stable at Bethlehem, the divine fecundity incarnates as deeply moving religious experience. The unmanifest becomes manifest; the spirit becomes matter. If we open ourselves to see, we can begin to grapple, as Jung did, with a psychology of religious experience that stretches all the way from the depths of the individual soul into the realms of mystical experience.

NOTES AND REFERENCES

1. Inclusive language is used in this chapter except in direct quotes. Jung was of a different era. The present author acknowledges the feminist critique of Jung as valid and appropriate. His theory, however, including the often criticized anima and animus archetypes, leaves ample room for reconceptualizing the androgenous aspects of human personality. Furthermore, Jung's emphasis on the union of opposites as central to the Self, allows for re-theologizing in ways such that the "female face of God" (Englesman, 1987:94) comes readily into focus.

2. All dreamers described in this chapter have given consent for use of their dream material. Identifying characteristics have been altered to preserve confidentiality, but the essence of the dream content has been retained.

3. It has been my observation that the well-known saying the "people in Freudian analysis have Freudian dreams and people in Jungian analysis have Jungian dreams" is not completely true. I have observed Jungian archetypal dreams to occur among people, even young adults and children, who have never heard of Jung; and typically Oedipal dreams do occur, on occasion, in Jungian-oriented psychotherapy. The emphasis of the therapist does have influence, however, due to the power of transference. In practice, most dreams would profitably be explored for possible elements of both the personal unconscious and the collective unconscious.

4. Cirlot (1971), for example, writes of the pine-tree symbol: "Like other evergreen trees the pine is a symbol of immortality. Conifers . . . also partake of the symbolism corresponding to that of the cabbalistic . . . sacred tree, associating it with the cult of Attis. Pine-cones were regarded as symbols of fertility (p.256)."

And Cooper (1978) notes the meaning attributed to pine cones in various cultural traditions: "The pine cone represents the masculine creative force, and good luck. . . . Chinese: Longevity; courage, faithfulness; constancy in adversity; emblem of Confucius. Greek: Emblem of Zeus. The pine cone as phallic and fecundity was an attribute of Dionysos and surmounted his Thyrsus. . . . As prophylactic it is associated with Aesculapius. . . . Semitic: The cone is a life symbol, fertility. The tree is sacred to the Phrygian Attis" (p.131f).

5. For those interested in a comparison of mystical and psychotic experience, see Agosin, 1992.

6. Although Jung, being a Victorian male, tended to idealize the man's anima and denigrate

the woman's animus, those value judgments need no longer be applied today.

7. The archetype of the Great Mother is Neumann's (1955) Jungian contribution to our contemporary understanding of the feminist spiritual quest. For a thorough discussion of the comparable development of male consciousness, see Neumann (1954).

8. Many contemporary Jungians are active in the recent explorations of god images within the psyche. Jung (1973) felt that genuine spirituality cannot flourish if wrapped in the defensive strictures of organized religion. Freedom to worship naturally implies freedom to feel and to experience spontaneously the loving fecundity of the universe. Recently Pope John Paul II spoke out against the nature spirituality of numerous American women, many of whom are strongly influenced by Jungian concepts of goddesses and gods within the psyche (A. Cowell, *NY Times* July 3, 1993:1). Conservative religionists are understandably threatened and defensive in relation to neo-pagan rituals, but fearing and labeling "witchcraft" without a comprehensive understanding of archetypes within the collective unconscious leads only to polarization that is divisive, rather than unitive, and that leads away from, rather than toward, genuine spiritual experience.

Agosin, R. T.
1989 Exploring the Divine in psychotherapy. *Seeds of Unfolding* 6:8-11.
1992 Psychosis, dreams and mysticism in the clinical domain. In *The fires of desire: Erotic energies and the spiritual quest*, edited by F.R. Halligan and J.J. Shea. New York: Crossroad.

Bonaventure, St.
[1259]
1978 *The soul's journey into God*, in Bonaventure, translated and introduced by E. Cousins. New York: Paulist.

Bosnak, R.
1988 *A little course in dreams*, 2nd ed., translated from the Dutch by M.H. Kohn, Boston: Shambhala.

Cirlot, J. E.
1971 *A dictionary of symbols*, 2nd ed., translated from the Spanish by J. Sage with a forward by Herbert Read. New York: Philosophical Library.

Clift, J.D., and W.B. Clift
1984 *Symbols of transformation in dreams*. New York: Crossroad.

Cooper, J. C.
1978 *An illustrated encyclopedia of traditional symbols*. London: Thames and Hudson.

Cousins, E. H.
1992 States of consciousness: Charting the mystical path. In *The fires of desire: Erotic energies and the spiritual quest*, edited by F.R. Halligan and J.J. Shea. New York: Crossroad.

Coward, H.
1985 *Jung and eastern thought.* Albany, NY: State University of New York Press.

Cowell, A.
1993 Pope issues censure of nature worship among American women. In *New York Times*, July 3, 1993:1.

Donn, L.
1988 *Freud and Jung: Years of friendship, years of loss*. New York: Macmillan.

Dourley, J. P.
1987 *Love, celibacy and the inner marriage*. Toronto, Inner City Books.

Edinger, E.F.
1973 *Ego and archetype: Individuation and the religious function of the psyche*. Baltimore: Penguin Books.
1987 *The Christian archetype: A Jungian commentary on the life of Christ*. Toronto: Inner City Books.

Ellenberger, H. F.
1970 Carl Gustav Jung and analytical psychology. In *The discovery of the unconscious*, by H.F. Ellenberger. New York: Basic Books.

Engelsman, J. C.
1987 Beyond the anima: The female self in the image of God. In *Jung's challenge to contemporary religion*, edited by M. Stein and R. L. Moore. Wilmette, IL: Chiron.

Grant, W. H., M. Thompson, and T. E. Clark
1983 *From image to likeness: A Jungian path in the gospel journey*. Toronto: Inner City Books.
Greene, T. A.
1984 Group therapy and analysis. In *Jungian analysis*, edited by M. Stein. Boulder, CO: Shambhala.
Grof, S.
1985 *Beyond the brain: Birth, death and transcendence in psychotherapy*. Albany, NY: State University of New York Press.
Hall, J.A.
1983 *Jungian dream interpretation: A handbook of theory and practice*. Toronto, Inner City Books.
Halligan, F.R.
1992 Keeping faith with the future: Toward final conscious unity. In *The fires of desire: Erotic energies and the spiritual quest*, edited by F.R. Halligan and J.J. Shea. New York: Crossroad.
Halligan, F. R., and J. J. Shea
1991 Sacred images in dreamwork: The journey into Self as journey into God. *Pastoral Psychology*, 40, 371-380.
1992 Whither the divine fire: Beginning the quest. In *The fires of desire: Erotic energies and the spiritual quest*. New York: Crossroad.
Hillman, J.
1967 *Insearch: Psychology and religion*. London: Hodder and Stoughton.
1983 *Archetypal psychology: A brief account*. Dallas: Spring Publications.
1989 *A blue fire: Selected writings*, introduced and edited by T. Moore. New York: Harper & Row.
Hood, R. W., and J. R. Hall
1980 Gender differences in the description of erotic and mystical experiences. *Review of Religious Research* 21:195-207.
Jacoby, M.
1984 *The analytic encounter: Transference and human relationship*. Toronto: Inner City Books.
Jaffee, A.
1989 *Was C.G. Jung a mystic? And other essays*, translated by D. Duchler and F. Cairns, edited by R. Hinshaw. Einsiedeln, Switz: Daimon Verlag.
Jung, C. G.
1953-1979 The Collected works of C. G. Jung (20 vols.), edited by H. Read, M. Fordham, and G. Adler; translated by R. F. C. Hall (except for Vol. 2, translated by L. Stein and D. Diviere). Princeton, NJ: Princeton University Press, Bollingen Series.
[1907-1958]
1960 *The psychogenesis of mental disease*, Collected Works, Vol. 3.
[1913]
1961 The theory of psychoanalysis, in *Freud and psychoanalysis*, Collected Works, Vol. 4.
[1911-1913 & 1952]
1967 *Symbols of transformation*, Collected Works, Vol.5, 2nd ed.
[1934-1954]
1968a *The archetypes and the collective unconscious*, Collected Works, Vol.9, Part I, 2nd ed.
[1951]
1968b *Aion: Research into the phenomenology of the Self, Collected Works*, Vol.9, Part II, 2nd ed.
[1928-1954]
1969 *Psychology and religion: West and East, Collected Works*, Vol.11, 2nd ed.
[1955-1956]
1970 *Mysterium Coniunctionis, Collected Works*, Vol.14, 2nd ed.
[1908-1944]
1966 *The practice of psychotherapy, Collected Works*, Vol.16, 2nd ed.

[1909-1944]
1938 *Psychology & religion*. New Haven, CT: Yale University Press.
1957 *The undiscovered Self*, translated from the German by R.F.C. Hull. New York: New American Library.
1973 *Memories, dreams, reflections*, recorded and edited by A. Jaffe, translated by R. and C. Winston. New York: Random House.
1974 *Dreams* (excerpted from Collected Works, Vols.4,8,12,16), Princeton, NJ: Bollingen.
1984 *Dream analysis: Notes of the seminar given in* 1928-1930, edited by W. McGuire, Princeton, NJ: Bollingen.

Kawai, H.
1988 *The Japanese psyche: Major motifs in the fairy tales of Japan*, translated from the Japanese by H. Kawai and S. Reece. Dallas, TX: Spring Publications.

Krishna, G.
1985 *Kundalini: The evolutionary energy in man*, with psychological commentary by J. Hillman. Boston: Shambhala.

McGuire, W. (Ed.)
1974 *The Freud/Jung letters*, translated by R. Manheim and R.F.C. Hull. Princeton, NJ: Bollingen.

Miller, W.A.
1981 *Make friends with your shadow*. Minneapolis: MN: Augsburg.

Moore, R.L. (Ed.)
1988 *Carl Jung and Christian spirituality*. New York: Paulist.

Neumann, E.
1954 *The origins and history of consciousness*, translated by R.F.C. Hull. New York: Bollingen Series XLII.
1955 *The Great Mother*, translated by R. Manheim. New York: Bollingen Series XLVII.

Sanford, J.A.
1989 *Dreams: God's forgotten language*. San Francisco: Harper & Row.

Singer, J.
1973 *Boundaries of the soul: The practice of Jung's psychology*. Garden City, NY: Doubleday.

Smith, C.D.
1990 *Jung's quest for wholeness: A religious and historical perspective*. Albany, NY: SUNY Press.

Stein, M. (Ed.)
1984 *Jungian analysis*, 2nd ed. Boulder, CO: Shambhala.

Ulanov, A.B.
1992 The holding self: Jung and the desire for being. In *The fires of desire: Erotic energies and the spiritual quest*, edited by F.R. Halligan and J.J. Shea. New York: Crossroad.

Ullman, M., and N. Zimmerman
1979 *Working with dreams*. Los Angeles: Tarcher.

Von Franz, M.L.
1980 *On divinization and synchronicity: The psychology of meaningful chance*. Toronto: Inner City Books.

Watkins, M.
1984 *Waking dreams*, 3rd ed. Dallas, TX: Spring Publications.

Wehr, G.
1990 *The mystical marriage: Symbol and meaning of the human experience*, translated from the German by J. Sutcliff. Northhamptonshire, England: Crucible/Aquarian Press.

Whitmont, E.C.
1969 *The symbolic quest: Basic concepts of analytical psychology*. Princeton, NJ: Princeton University Press.

Whitmont, E.C., and S.B. Perera
1989 *Dreams: Portal to the Source*. New York: Routledge.

12

Object Relations Theory and Religious Experience

BENJAMIN BEIT-HALLAHMI

Our first task is to define psychoanalytic object relations (or "relational") theory and to show how it differs, and how distant it really is, from classical psychoanalytic theory. Two assumptions were suggested by Freud himself to characterize his approach. The first states that all psychic processes are strictly determined (no accidents, chance events, or miracles), the second that unconscious mental processes exist and exert significant influences on behavior. These unconscious forces shape much of the individual's emotional and interpersonal experiences. Rapaport (1960) summed up the structure of classical psychoanalytic theory through five orientations: the dynamic, economic, structural, genetic, and adaptive points of view. The dynamic point of view states that the ultimate determinants of all behavior are to be found in the drives. The economic states that all behavior disposes of psychic energy, and is regulated by it. The structural point of view states that all behavior has structural determinants. The genetic states that all behavior is part of a sequence, and the present form of the personality was created by antecedents. The adaptive point of view states that all behavior is determined by reality.

Psychoanalysis draws our attention to a universal sequence of psychological development, which becomes a basic epistemological ordering of the world and of individual personality, culture, and humanity. The universal experience of the human infants includes a developing awareness of three realms, always in the following order: first, knowledge of one's body and its experienced needs. Second, awareness of the existence of another. Third, knowledge of relations between ourselves and others.

All further experiences must be based on these early experiences and reactions, acquired in that order, and will be assimilated into that order. The existence of such a universal sequence cannot be challenged, and here lies the attraction of psychoanalysis for those wanting to understand, not only human personality, but also human society and culture.

If we want to explain the success and the attraction of psychoanalytic theories of personality, despite their speculative nature and their reliance on private experiences, one major factor emerges from the preceding discussion. Psychoanalytic theories of personality follow an essentially biological rationale.

All psychoanalytic theorists agree that personality development is organized through predetermined stages, with continuities from earlier to later ones. All theorists in the psychoanalytic tradition also agree that personality structures formed during critical periods in early childhood are almost irreversible, short of successful psychotherapy, which is not easy to achieve. The notion of a sensitive period, during which enduring patterns of behavior may be learned, is intrinsically attractive, since it fits our knowledge about the development of behavior.

No one will argue with the assumption that the organism is most open to influence during childhood, and that the impact of early learning will be long-lasting. We all agree with the notion that what is sensitive during critical periods is the central nervous system, and we have much anatomical evidence to support that thesis. Psychoanalysis is a theory that does not easily lead to good measurement or good prediction, but is nevertheless immensely attractive to a large number of psychologists. The reason for this attraction must have something to do with the basic biological rationale of the theory, as shown above. Psychoanalysis, even when it is most speculative, is anchored in a biological model, or a biological analogue, which we find intuitively attractive and persuasive.

Defining Object Relations Theory

The concept of "object relations" in psychoanalytic writings of the last two generations means relations with significant others and their internal representations, starting with mother. Moreover, this approach emphasizes internal representations resulting from actual relations, and these representations as projected later on. Primitive, early object relations are the starting point for personality development.

> In broadest terms, psychoanalytic object-relations theory represents the psychoanalytic study of the nature and origins of interpersonal relations, and of the nature and origins of intrapsychic structures deriving from, fixating, mod-

> ifying, and reactivating past internalized relations with others in the context of present interpersonal relationships. Psychoanalytic object-relations theory focuses upon the internalization of interpersonal relations, their contribution to normal and pathological ego and superego development, and the mutual influences of intrapsychic and interpersonal object-relations (Kernberg, 1976:56).

According to this theoretical school, personality is formed through object relations patterns which are set up in early childhood, become stable in later childhood and adolescence, and then are fixed during adult life, and reflected in transference patterns. The functioning of the adult personality depends on the maturity of one's object relations. Object relations theorists propose a personality structure and a drive system which are radically different from the classical systems. Thus, according to Guntrip (1969), the structure revolves around a central ego which is the "conscious self." It has various relationships with objects (external) and internal object representations. The ego seeks objects, and this is the basic drive animating the personality system.

As Ryan and Bell (1984:209) put it, the assumption in modern object relations theory is that "the quality of this representational world then becomes the mental template for the development of all future psychic structures and, thus, for the basic structure of a person's character." Object relations theory rejects the classical notions of innate instincts and the id-ego-superego personality structure. It assumes no instincts except object-seeking. The basic assumption in object relations theory, as opposed to classical instinctual structural psychoanalysis, is that the crucial determinant of personality consistencies, whether normal or pathological, is the relations between self and others, real or imagined by the self. Object relations theory agrees with classical instinctual structural theory on the importance of early childhood. As Ryan and Bell observed (1984:210), "The explicit or implicit suggestion in much of this work is that object-relations patterns are set down in early childhood, become consolidated through late childhood and adolescence, and remain relatively fixed throughout adult life as the transference paradigms of character. Adult functioning, whether normal, neurotic, or psychotic, is assumed to be dependent on the maturity of one's object relations, that is, on the relatively stable level one has achieved along the developmental continuum."

While classical psychoanalytic theory viewed the personality as an information processing system, or a drive-based system, in touch (or out of touch) with reality, in object relations theory the emphasis is on introjection and projection, leading to a total distortion of reality. Compared with classical approaches, object relations theory is more pessimistic. It views personality as less reality-oriented, and its structure as determined earlier in life. One way of highlighting the differences between the two approaches is by looking at their concepts of a "critical period" in personality development. Theoretical debates and theoretical changes have hinged on the following two questions: First, when is the critical period? Second, what is learned during this period? The original answer to the first question, provided by Freud, was age 3-6. The original answer to the second question was the handling of instincts. Object relations theory moved the critical period back to age birth-2, and changed the answer to the second question to "object relations" or "the self." For Freud, all of childhood is a critical period, because of the greater fluidity of behavior, and every psychological stage is a critical period for the learning of specific behaviors. During the oral period the child will learn to deal with oral impulses. During the anal stage he will deal with anal impulses, and the ego will learn to integrate those with earlier ones. During the phallic-Oedipal period the issue is basic genital identity, and this is why it becomes the critical period par excellence. While the whole of childhood is a rehearsal for adulthood, the Oedipal stage is the final dress rehearsal.

Nagera (1966:57), representing the traditional instinctual-structural approach, echoes that "the 'phallic-oedipal' phase is in fact an essential turning point in human development."

The mere notion of personality implies the assumption of consistency over time and situations. So the question is not one of reversibility, but one of stability in behavior. Psychoanalytic approaches assume that structures acquired during the critical period of childhood will endure, and the results of early learning will be irreversible because no similar learning experience is likely to occur later on in life. In object relations theory, the critical period in personality development has been moved earlier, from age 3-6 years to birth-2 years.

The classical theory stated that what the child learned during the critical period was a way of handling instincts, whereas the latest modern version states that the child learns attitudes toward the self and others. The relational theoretical formulations, to use the classical terms, choose to place the critical period in pre-Oedipal or pre-genital stages. This focus immediately reduces the importance of sexual drives, assumed by Freud to be crucial in the shaping of personality, and increases the importance of interpersonal behavior.

According to object relations theory, what is learned during the critical period of infancy is a way of relating to objects (i.e., other people) and of imagining these objects (or "significant others") internally. The debate, so to speak, between the traditional Freudian approach and the more recent views is whether the crucial sensitive period is in the Oedipal stage of personality development, i.e., age 3-5, or in the pre-Oedipal stage, age birth-3. Using Freud's original terminology, the historical change among theorists has been from the emphasis on the phallic-Oedipal period (3-6 years) to the oral stage (birth-1). This historical sea change has been a movement for focusing attention, not on the Oedipal stage (3-6 years) and "Oedipal neurosis," but to earlier years, and to other, more serious kinds of psychopathology, namely borderline and psychotic conditions. The change is tied to the names of Melanie Klein, W.R.D. Fairbairn, D.W. Winnicott, Michael Balint, and others, who formed the "British school of object relations."

It was Melanie Klein (1948) who claimed for the first time that crucial processes for personality development take place during the first few months of life. Klein (1948), Fairbairn (1952), and Guntrip (1968) focused on object relations and object representations during the first two years of life. Kernberg (1975, 1976) followed their footsteps and suggested an emphasis on the internal representations of self and others. Mahler (1963:307) defined her own starting point in looking at object-relations by basing it on a psychological-biological observation:

> The fact that a lifelong, albeit diminishing, emotional dependence on the mother is a universal truth of human existence. The biological unpreparedness of the human infant to maintain his life separately conditions that species-specific prolonged phase which has been designated "the mother-infant symbiosis."

According to Mahler, crucial events for eventual personality development take place during the first year of life. The critical period is one during which the child is preverbal and essentially passive. As Langman and Kaplan (1978:362) observed,

> The preverbal child is said to experience a variety of tension states but is most limited in its capacity to relieve these tensions through action or thought. With the exception of some reflexes and simple sensori-motor schematas, the child is ill-equipped to organize experience, much less master or change events.

In all versions of psychoanalytic theory, from Freud to Kohut (Kohut, 1971), parents play a central role and are really the most important factors in events during the critical period. The mother, of course holds dominance in the child's emotional world. "When we distill some of the main points of psychoanalytic self-theorists, we see that maternal empathy is to healthy development of the self as early cognitive stimulation is to later intelligence or calcium intake to skeletal growth" (Langman and Kaplan, 1978:361-362).

The common core of instinct (i.e., classical) theory and object relations theory can be summarized in the two concepts of desire (for an object or for instinctual gratification), and separation (from the object or from life), through thanatos. Both approaches agree that our style of dealing with the world all starts with the small child and its (mis)understanding of sex, birth, family, with the resulting confused ideas that stay with us for life. Object relations theory says that the process starts very early, which means that the cognitive confusion is greater and deeper.

The rise of object relations theory and the attention given to pre-Oedipal experiences have broadened the scope of the basic psychoanalytic view of personal and cultural phenomena. Object relations theory, arguably the most important theoretical development in psychoanalysis since Freud (Guntrip, 1968; Winnicott, 1971), provides the best theoretical basis for understanding the externalized world of spirits (and imagined interactions with them) in relation to the internal world of objects.

The Object Relations Approach to Religion

Interpretations of religion along the theoretical lines of object relations theory have been articulated and reviewed by Beit-Hallahmi (1989, 1992, 1994), Finn and Gartner (1992), Guntrip (1968, 1969), Rizzuto (1979), and Wulff (1991), among others. We should realize that such interpretations are not a recent fad. As soon as such ideas first started to be discussed in psychoanalytic circles, they were applied to religion and to religious experiences. Thus, Weigert-Vowinkel (1938) suggested that the phenomenon of prehistoric mother worship is to be interpreted (following Melanie Klein) as the result of an unbroken mother tie, which increases the danger of castration, and of a general manic-depressive disposition.

Roheim (1939) interpreted the ancient ritual of convenating through the cutting of a victim through the middle, mentioned in the Hebrew Bible but known elsewhere, by offering an object relations explanation. The fantasy of opening up the mother's body, appearing in analysand's free associations, is tied to a fantasy of finding "good body contents" inside. The ritual, sublimating these early fantasies, reinforces feelings of security and fantasies of reparation, as destruction is followed by the promise of future life. Here Roheim seems to anticipate the theoretical ideas of Melanie Klein and Margaret Mahler.

Milner (1987) offers this view of religion:

> It seems that the elusive inner realities of feeling are continually taking to themselves the form of outer realities. It seems that the discovery of the inner life is made in terms of the outer world. . . . This symbolizing capacity of the mind, its infinite capacity for using metaphor in expressing psychic realities, flows out in a tremendous stream which has many branches: the imaginative play of childhood, art, symbolic rituals, religion. Words become the central mode of expression for most people, after early childhood, and bridge the gulf between the inner and outer realities. But words also become caught up in the original confusion between the two realities and are too often given an absolute value" (Milner, 1987:14).

Inspired by relational concepts, Pruyser (1983) suggested a model of three psychological worlds, each of which deals with fantasy differently: 1) the autistic world of uncontrolled fantasy and omnipotence; 2) the realistic world of reality testing and sense perceptions; 3) the illusionistic world of tutored fantasy. The third world clearly includes religion as well as other cultural products. Religion is defined as "the illusionist enterprise par excellence."

These early and later examples seem to convey the flavor and the rationale of object relations explanations for religious behaviors and religious commitment. What we find in these attempts is a significant level of continuity with classical psychoanalytic theory. Object relations theory offers its own articulation of classical projection theory. The question regarding specific religious behaviors or religious experiences becomes that of the nature of the specific projected object. According to the classical view, it is an Oedipal object; according to the relational view, it is just an "object," in general, or an early infancy ("pre-genital") object.

Relational theory views religion as a means of relating to a projected object. In fantasies, cultural and individual, we try to relive the encounter between infant and mother, as well as other encounters with our internalized significant others. Rizzuto (1979) found that the image of God is created not only through the projection of early father-child relations, but also through the impact of other early relationships, such as mother-son, daughter-father, daughter-mother. Still, father projection was found to be highly relevant to the development of religious beliefs.

Splitting as a Basic Mechanism

The phenomenon of splitting, proposed by Klein (1948), is assumed to take place in early infancy. It is hypothesized that the infant passes through a stage of splitting the object into good one and bad one, occurring between the age of 3 months and 12 months. This notion has been used to explain numerous religious ideas and experiences (cf. Prince, 1961; Henderson, 1975). Descriptions of mystical state read like infancy fantasies of the good breast or the fantasied good object.

Fauteux (1981) suggested that early infancy splitting of the mother into good/bad object is reflected in religious belief systems about God and the Devil. The same splitting mechanism operates in converts to various new religions who reach a state of complete euphoria, denying negative impulses and negative realities, which are found to resurface nevertheless. Bychowski (1958) described splitting as the basic and earliest ego mechanism. It in turn leads to a later yearning for unity, expressed through culturally defined religious experiences.

One such experience is the stigmata, interpreted according to object relations theory by Carroll (1987). The stigmata which have appeared most often in Catholic females, are characterized by reported pain, observed recurrent bleeding, and reported inedia (persistent fasting). Classical psychoanalytic explanations suggest that stigmata represent hysterical behavior. Klein's theory, which assumes such complex processes as splitting and depression in early infancy, is offered as a substitute. It is hypothesized that the stigmata represent 1) the infant's desire to incorporate father, 2) the infant's desire for milk from mother's Good Breast, and 3) the infant's desire to make reparation for the imagined oral sadistic attack on mother. Looking at five documented cases of the stigmata, it is suggested that the imitation of the mythological Christ's wounds satisfies the desire for the father (that is why there are more such cases among women, and Catholicism involves "swallowing" the Christ). Bleeding is interpreted as expressing the desire for milk.

The Mystical "Encounter"

The experience of communion, merger, or "encounter," reported in many religious traditions, is to be interpreted as either a return to what once was infantile reality, or, more likely, an attempt to recreate imagined infantile bliss that never was.

Winnicott (1965) referred to the mystical experience as a communication with a subjective satisfying object. The perception of fusion with loved objects in "higher" mystical states, which are characterized by an indescribable ecstasy, and not by concrete visions was interpreted by Lewin (1950) as a regression to the early infant-mother symbiotic relationship in nursing. Similarly, Pollock (1989) suggested that the imagined symbiosis with God equals symbiosis with the early pregenital mother, an imagined pregenital paradise. Prince and Savage (1966) interpreted the mystical state of "union" as a regression to an infantile level of experience, a fantasied return to the nursing situation.

The idea of the "encounter" is expressed sometimes on a group level. The history of a unique medieval religious movement was presented and interpreted by Cohn (1961). This movement, in existence all over Europe, taught freedom from conventional morality and economy through the achievement of unity with God, following neoplatonic teachings. It was opposed to monogamy and private property, and advocated nudism. This episode is interpreted as expressing total regression to early childhood behavior and psychic functioning.

Winnicott's (1971) idea of a transitional state and transitional objects has been regularly used, and often misused, in writing about religion (see Beit-Hallahmi, 1989, 1992). Horton (1973, 1974) proposed an interesting and original theoretical idea: that the mystical experience itself may have the character of a potential transitional phenomenon. It becomes a "reliably soothing inner experience" that the individual may wish to return to. Denial and projected rage, resulting from the pain and disappointment of a ruptured symbiosis (i.e., pre-Oedipal), lead to mystical experiences. The mystical affective experience, sometimes accompanying conversion, is an attempt to repeat the transitional state, as conceptualized by Winnicott, through an upsurge of residual primary narcissism.

Ostow (1969) offered a comparison of mysticism and schizophrenia. Both are precipitated by an ambivalent situation, followed by a retreat from reality. In both cases the immersion of internal psychic life is interpreted as the experience of a hidden universe. The content of the mystical fantasy, psychically determined just like the schizophrenic fantasy, is that of a union with the beloved parent.

Kakar (1991) proposed an important and original view of visions as transient reactions lessening the agony of separation. The guru-disciple relationship in Asian traditions is described as being much like the mother-child attachment, and much like certain forms of modern psychotherapy.

Religious Experience, Conversion, and Personality Dynamics

Is there a way in which we can predict, or post-dict, the personality dynamics of individuals reporting mystical experiences? A general conceptualization, based on an intensely studied case of adolescent conversion, has been proposed by Allison (1969). Adolescent conversion is interpreted as changing the perception of one's actual father as weak, ineffective, or absent, and creating an internal representation of a strong and principled substitute father, with clear values and firm judgment. This paternal image is crucial in helping the adolescent to achieve individuation and differentiation, and avoiding a sense of undifferentiated union with the maternal figure. Similar suggestions were made by Olsson (1983), who stated that adolescent preoccupation with "supernatural" objects is actually a mental representation of failed symbolic attempts to create separation from maternal and paternal objects. Olsson presented three case studies to illustrate this diagnostic generalization, whose validity should be supported by other reports.

Following more recent development in North American relational theory, Capps (1985) proposed viewing Augustine as a narcissistic personality, as defined by Heinz Kohut. If traditional psychoanalytic portraits of Augustine emphasized Oedipal problems, the analysis presented here emphasizes pre-Oedipal personality development. What happed in Augustine's conversion should be described as a narcissistic transformation, rather than an Oedipal resolution.

Ostow (1988) suggested that the "gnostic journey" represents an imagined return to physical intimacy with the mother, or with both parents. This may be in the form of a return to the mother's body, sitting in her lap, being in a parents' arms, or in the parental bed. Religious groups offering such journeys attract psychotics, depressives, and borderlines, as well as others escaping harsh reality. Ostow speculated that organized religion, by offering an illusion sponsored and controlled by the collectivity, tries to discourage irresponsible and self-defeating mysticism.

Spero (1982) suggested that individuals who had undergone a conversion to minority religions were characterized by severe ambivalence and an intolerance of this feeling, and of any ambiguity, projections of hate and self-hate, and splitting. Similarly, Meissner (1988) suggested that the sources of psychological energy for the creation of deviant religious groups are found to reside in followers' personal difficulties, formulated in the language of object relations theory and psychoanalytic self theory.

Object Loss as Predictor

Atwood (1978) and Stolorow and Atwood (1973) suggested that strong religious commitments result from an identification with an early lost object. Messianic salvation fantasies appear in individuals who have experienced one or more traumatic disappointments or losses in relationships with early love objects. Then, a regression to fantasy is followed by the developing image of the lost object as a deity. Later on, an identification with the lost object leads to the individual's declaring himself to be the saving messiah. Taking on lesser religious roles than that of the messiah is also predicted by early object relations (Masson, 1976). Indian ascetics have typically suffered one of three major childhood traumas: loss of a parent, seduction, or physical abuse. The resulting dynamics are one of extreme aggression toward internalized objects, expressed through the choice of an ascetic career.

The connections and similarities between mysticism and mourning were explored by Aberbach (1987) through testimonials and literary works. Mysticism is said to provide an effective outlet for grief, satisfying the need for an orderly, goal oriented form of mourning. Severe childhood loss is found in the lives of many mystics, and of those who expressed mystical feelings in their poetry. Greenberg, Witztum, and Buchbinder (1992) show how personal losses may lead troubled individuals to pursue mystical practices and experiences which are normative in their cultures.

Ullman (1982, 1989) carried out a comparative study of 40 converts (to Catholicism, Orthodox Judaism, ISKCON, and Bahaism) and a control groups of thirty nonconverts (members of the same groups) by means of intensive interviews. The aim was to test the psychoanalytic explanation for conversion, which emphasizes problems in the relationship with one's father, against the "cognitive quest" hypothesis. Almost one-third of the converts reported the loss of their fathers by death or divorce before age ten. About half of them reported unsatisfactory and stressful relations with their fathers. The findings were interpreted as showing that the most significant determinant in cases of conversion is found to be the role of the father, and conversion seemed like a means of attaining an idealized father-attachment. Converts experience identification with the divine, a form of narcissism, because they wish to merge with an extension of the self.

Integration: Projection, the Sacred, and Religious Experience

"Religious experience is so very much an expression of human nature as rooted in the primary need for good personal relationship" (Guntrip, 1961:255). Later on, Guntrip stated that "it may well be that integration, maturity, mental health, and religious experience are all closely related" (1969:324). "The need of the human being to retain a fundamental sense of organic unity which is at the same time a latent sense of relationship, and which will develop through a good mother-infant experience into a specific capacity for ego-object relationship, ultimately with the universe itself, the final reality, must have been the core of religious experience all down the ages . . . i.e., Buber's 'yearning for the cosmic connexion' as something entirely different from projecting a father-image on to the universe" (Guntrip, 1974:267). This is one attempt to separate relational interpretations of religion and religious experiences from the classical "Oedipal" view. How successful are such attempts, and how different are they actually? How can a new theoretical integration be achieved?

It seems that what Guntrip said about the yearning for a connexion is very similar to what was described by Roheim (1943), who stated that all culture represents attempts to protect us from object loss. Similarly, Ross (1968) stated that the need for religious faith represents the dread of object loss, and that religious phenomena represent projections of the need for the sustained, eternal existence of an immutably protective loving object. Such projections also contain the most archaically ambivalent attitudes toward the earliest object, maneuvers of various obsessive and propitiatory acts, all serving the purpose of trying to retain the lost object.

We realize again that any relational approach to religion is basically a variation on classical projection theory. However, since the Oedipal explanation of the sacred object does not seem satisfactory, we need to move to pre-Oedipal stages. The challenge before a new theoretical integration is not only explaining religious experience, but dealing with the essence of the religious phenomenon in its many manifestations. If the religious experience is the royal road to humanity's eternal yearning, what is the secret of this yearning?

One answer has been offered by Lutzky (1991), who suggested that the "numinous" experience stems from early object relations, and in this way proposes a solution to the mystery of the origins of the sacred. There is a connection between the sacred and the internal object, between early experience and the numinous.

Following Fairbairn, the internal object (world) is proposed as the prototype of the sacred. The dichotomies between the internal/external object and the sacred/profane are analogous, as the splitting of the maternal object and the ego is the prototype of the sacred/profane dichotomy. Moreover, the preservation of the bond with the mother by the constitution of the internal object as psychic structure is proposed as the prototype of the preservation of the social bond by the relation of the sacred to the social structure (cf. Durkheim). The individual phenomenology of the sacred is similar to the distortion of reality in schizoid pathology. The closedness of the internal object world is the prototype of the inviolability of the sacred. This theoretical solution demonstrates the use of the theory toward the understanding of religion in the most basic way. The proposed connection between the sacred and the internal object, between early experience and the numinous is a major discovery. It aims, and succeeds, at illuminating religion as a basic human experience.

Independently, Hutch (1990) suggested that the hub of sacred authority in life is a powerful mother-imago. Moreover, the experience of the sacred stems from the *residuum*, which is a carryover from the earliest psychological experiences. The *residuum* "is the psychological origin of all religious myths, rituals, doctrines, communities, and ethics" (p.85). "The *residuum* is the sum total of prototypical affect-laden traces or images . . . which, arising from infancy, remains the person's more or less fixed projection on the world and others" (p.84).

But don't some of these ideas remind us of Freud's "oceanic feeling"? Indeed, Harrison (1979) elucidates this connection, as he discusses biographical and (hypothesized) psychodynamic differences between Romain Rolland and Freud, which in turn might have led to their different views of the "oceanic." Rolland denied the pre-Oedipal "bad mother" and infancy traumas by adopting a hallucination of a divine mother, representing lost primary narcissism. Freud isolated childhood traumas through aversion, in his fear of merging with the ambivalent mother.

The object relations theoretical enterprise seems to aim at dethroning the father-imago in two ways: First, by replacing the Oedipal situation and the Oedipal father image with the mother-imago of early infancy. Second, by replacing Father Freud with other parental figures. Observations of intense religious behaviors are in fact a serious challenge to classical notions of the origins of religion. If it is the omnipotent father (or self) that we project, why the yearning to merge with this awesome object? Early experiences of the mother seem much more conducive to imagined symbiosis cum ecstasy. And so we move to pre-Oedipal levels, only to encounter again Freud's "oceanic feeling." We realize again that relational ideas started very early on in the history of psychoanalytic theory, and that these ideas grew out of empirical observations. Freud was first and foremost a great, though selective, collector of observed facts. Even when dethroned, Father Freud is always behind our back, looking over our shoulders with his knowing smile.

REFERENCES

Aberbach, D.

1987 Grief and mysticism. *International Review of Psychoanalysis* 14:509-526.

Allison, J.

1969 Religious conversion: Regression and progression in an adolescent experience. *Journal for the Scientific Study of Religion* 8:23-38.

Atwood, G. E.
1978 On the origins and dynamics of messianic salvation fantasies. *International Review of Psychoanalysis* 33:85-96.

Beit-Hallahmi, B.
1978 Critical periods in psychoanalytic theories of personality development. In *Sensitive periods in development: Interdisciplinary perspectives*, edited by M. H. Borstein. Hillsdale, NJ: Erlbaum.
1989 *Prolegomena to the psychological study of religion*. Lewisburg, PA: Bucknell University Press.
1992 Between religious psychology and the psychology of religion. In *Object relations theory and religion*, edited by M. Finn and J. Gartner. Westport, CT: Praeger.
1994 The psychoanalytical study of religion: Critical assessment and annotated bibliography. Westport, CT: Greenwood Press.

Bychowski, G.
1958 The ego and the introjects: Origin of religious experience. *Psychoanalysis and the Social Sciences* 5:246-279.

Capps, D.
1985 Augustine as narcissist. *Journal of the American Academy of Religion* 53:115-127.

Carroll, M. P.
1987 Heaven-sent wounds: A Kleinian view of the stigmata in the Catholic mystical tradition. *Journal of Psychoanalytic Anthropology* 10:17-38.

Cohn, N.
1961 The cult of the free spirit: A medieval heresy reconstructed. *Psychoanalysis and the Psychoanalytic Review* 48:51-68.

Fairbairn, W. R. D.
1952 An object relations theory of personality. New York: Basic Books.

Fauteux, A.
1981 "Good/bad" splitting in the religious experience. *American Journal of Psychoanalysis* 41:261-267.

Fenichel, O.
1945 The psychoanalytic theory of neurosis. New York: Norton.

Finn, M., and J. Gartner (Eds.)
1992 *Object relations theory and religion: Clinical applications*. Westport, CT; Greenwood Press.

Greenberg, D., E. Witztum, and J. T. Buchbinder
1992 Mysticism and psychosis: The fate of Ben Zoma. *British Journal of Medical Psychology*.

Guntrip, H.
1961 *Personality structure and human interaction*. New York: International Universities Press.
1968 *Schizoid phenomena, object relations and the self.* New York: International Universities Press.
1969 Religion in relation to personal integration. *British Journal of Medical Psychology* 42:323-333.
1974 *Schizoid phenomena object relations and the self.* London: Hogarth Press.

Harrison, I.
1979 On Freud's view of the infant-mother relationship and of the oceanic feeling—some subjective influences. *Journal of the American Psychoanalytic Association* 27:399-421.

Henderson, J.
1975 Object relations and the doctrine of "Original Sin." *International Review of Psycho-Analysis* 2:107-120.

Horton, P. C.
1973 The mystical experience as suicide preventive. *American Journal of Psychiatry* 130:294-296.
1974 The mystical experience: Substance of an illusion. *Journal of the American Psychoanalytic Association* 22:364-380.

Hutch, R. A.

1990 *Religious leadership: Personality, history and sacred authority.* New York: Peter Lang

Kakar, S.

1991 *The analyst and the mystic: Psychoanalytic reflections on religion and mysticism.* Chicago: University of Chicago Press.

Kernberg, O.

1975 *Borderline conditions and pathological narcissism.* New York: Jason Aronson.

1976 *Object relations and clinical psychoanalysis.* New York: Jason Aronson.

Klein, M.

1948 *Contributions to psychoanalysis.* London: Hogarth Press.

Kohut, H.

1971 *The analysis of self.* New York: International Universities Press.

Langman, L., and L. V. Kaplan

1978 The circis of self and state under late capitalism: A critical perspective. *International Journal of Law and Psychiatry* 1:343-374.

Lewin, B. D.

1950 *The psychoanalysis of elation.* New York: International Universities Press.

Lutzky, H.

1991 The sacred and the maternal object: An application of Fairbain's theory to religion. In *Psychoanalytic reflections on current issues,* edited by H. B. Siegel, L. Barbanel, I. Hirsch, J. Lasky, H. Silverman, and S. Warshaw. New York: New York Universities Press.

Mahler, M. S.

1963 Thoughts about development and individuation. *The Psychoanalytic Study of the Child,* 18:307-324.

Masson, J. M.

1976 The psychology of the ascetic. *Journal of Asian Studies* 35:611-625.

Meissner, W. W.

1988 The cult phenomena and the paranoid process. *The Psychoanalytic Study of Society* 12:69-95.

Milner, M.

1987 *The suppressed madness of sane men: Forty-four years of Exploring Psychoanalysis.* London: Routledge.

Nagera, H.

1966 *Early childhood disturbances, the infantile neurosis, and the adulthood disturbances.* New York: International Universities Press.

Olsson, P. A.

1983 Adolescent involvement with the supernatural and cults. In *Psychodynamic perspectives on religion sect and cult,* edited by D. A. Halperin. Boston: John Wright.

Ostow, M.

1969 Antinomianism, mysticism and psychosis. In *Psychedelic Drugs,* edited by R. E. Hicks and P. J. Fink. New York: Grune & Stratton.

1988 Four entered the garden: Normative religion versus illusion. In *Fantasy, myth, and reality: Essays in honor of Jacob A. Arlow,* edited by H. P. Blum, Y. Kramer, A.K. Richards, and A.D. Richards. New York: International Universities Press.

Pollock, G. H.

1989 *The Mourning-Liberation Process.* Madison, CT: International Universities Press.

Prince, R.

1961 The Yoruba image of the witch. *British Journal of Psychiatry* 107:795-805.

Prince, R., and C. Savage

1966 Mystical states and the concept of regression. *Psychedelic Review* 8:59-75.

Pruyser, P.

1983 *The play of the imagination: Toward a psychoanalysis of culture.* New York: International Universities Press.

Rapaport, D.

1960 The structure of psychoanalytic theory. In *Psychological Issues,* monograph 6, edited by G. S. Klen. New York: International Universities Press.

Rizzuto, A. M.
1979 *The birth of the living god.* Chicago: University of Chicago Press.
Roheim, G.
1939 The covenant of Abraham. *The International Journal of Psychoanalysis* 20:452-459. [1943]
1971 *The origin and function of culture.* Garden City, NY: Doubleday.
Ross, N.
1968 Beyond "The future of an illusion." *Journal of the Hillside Hospital* 17:259-276.
Ryan, E. R., and M. D. Bell
1984 Changes in object relations from psychosis to recovery. *Journal of Abnormal Psychology* 93:209-215.
Spero, M. H.
1982 Psychotherapeutic procedure with religious cult devotees. *Journal of Nervous and Mental Disease* 17:332-244.
Stolorow, R., and G. Atwood
1973 Messianic projects and early object relationships. *American Journal of Psychoanalysis,* 33:213-215.
Ullman, C.
1982 Cognitive and emotional antecedents of religious conversion. *Journal of Personality and Social Psychology* 43:183-192.
1989 *The transformed self: The psychology of religious conversion.* New York: Plenum Press.
Weigert-Vowinkel, E.
1938 The cult and mythology of the Magna Mater from the standpoint of psychoanalysis. *Psychiatry* 1:347-378.
Winnicott, D. W.
1965 *The maturational process and the facilitating environment.* London: Hogarth Press.
1971 *Playing and reality.* New York: Basic Books.
Wulff, D. M.
1991 *Psychology of Religion: Classica and contemporary views.* New York: Wiley.

13

Developmental Theories and Religious Experience

KALEVI TAMMINEN AND KARI E. NURMI

INTRODUCTION

In the empirical research on religion, religious development, especially in childhood and adolescence, has been a very central focal point (see Hyde, 1990). Religious education has increased research interest in the problems of religious development. Large parts of this research have described religiousness in terms of age-related changes, but often it has been linked to or taken its starting point from developmental theories. Already at the turn of this century, G. Stanley Hall (1900; 1904) created a modern psychological theory of religious development with evolutionary developmental stages based on the *recapitulation theory*, i.e., the thought that the ontogenetic development of the individual recapitulates the phylogenetic development of the human race and religions. His phases extended from fetishism in early childhood to Christian love and altruism in adolescence (see Wulff, 1991). Hall's theory affected later theories and research in the field of religious development. For instance, Ronald Goldman (1964) related some traits of his theory of religious thinking to the concepts of the recapitulation theory.

Goldman based his conceptualization, however, mainly on Jean Piaget's *theory of operational thinking*, which has been largely applied to religious development as well as to many other aspects of development. The growing interest in Piaget's ideas since the 1960s was one of the reasons why research in this field has emphasized the cognitive aspects of development. During recent decades several authors have presented critical remarks, corrections, and alternative formulations to Piaget's theory and also to its application in the area of religious thinking. Instead of or in addition to the Piagetian paradigm some researchers have proposed for the study of religious thinking *a linguistic viewpoint*. Also Oser's and Gmünder's (1988) theory is linked to the cognitive-structural theories and in part to the Piagetian paradigm. At the same time it gives to the examination of religious thinking its own flavor, viz., *religious judgment* in the lifespan of the human being.

The cognitive domain is central to the above-mentioned theories, the emotional domain and everything else remaining in the background. Emotions and actions are important for the *motivation* for religious behavior and they have been considered in *theories of attitude* (often also called theories of cognitive consistency), which have also been used as a frame of reference for the study of religious development. In addition, *emotions and affects* are important for *intense religious experiences*, which has been one of the foci of research, although not a very central one.

Depth psychology, initiated by *psychoanalysis*, has brought many fruitful impulses to the study of religious experience and its development. In the field of religious research the *"psycho-social" theory* of Erikson (1950; 1968) has been used especially to describe crises of identity during adolescence. It also provided a starting point for Fowler's (1981) *structural theory* of faith development covering the entire life-span. In addition, Fowler linked to his theory several other domains, such as Piaget's genetic epistemology and Lawrence Kohlberg's conceptualization of the development of moral judgment.

We will present in this chapter the main ideas of some of the *most central theories* used in the study of religious development and also review some of the *empirical research* based on them or describing phenomena related to them. A natural point of departure is the question of what is meant by religious development and what by research concerning it.

PROBLEMS OF CONCEPTUALIZATION AND DESCRIPTION OF RELIGIOUS DEVELOPMENT

Development of Religious Experience as a Concept

The development of religious experience refers to an underlying sequence of age-related changes that is typical for the human life-span. Religion is here understood on the one hand as a personal relation toward the ultimate value-base of action (in Christianity toward God), on the other hand as a social phenomenon: an organized movement with doctrine and acting as a reference group for the individual's self-understanding. This development is constrained by human biological potential and its interaction with the attempts at socialization by family and other parts of society. Socialization follows models which may be denominationally religious, indifferent toward religion, or atheistic. These cultural models define the normal and the deviant patterns for individual development.

The central phenomenon for developmental explanations is systematic change. Not all changes are developmental. Many of them are incidental and have only a chance relation to any pattern. We are here looking mainly for age-related changes without necessarily expecting them to be directional in relation to any "goal" of development. In fact, many of the age-related changes in old age are deteriorations in comparison to the levels attained during earlier years.

One obvious question concerns the generality of religious development: is it different for various religions or is there a general common core? The history of research might favor at least a minimal common pattern following an order of general cognitive stages. On the other hand, the emphasis previously laid on culturally based models of socialization favors a differentiated hypothesis. Unfortunately we do not at present know the answer. The question is straightforwardly empirical and can only be answered in relation to a sufficient database of evidence gathered from different cultures and denominations. Until recently and despite the widespread interest in comparative religion very few studies have dealt with other than Christian religions, and most of those that have still show a Christian or Western origin. Consequently, a lot more research is needed, even to see the ramifications of this question, let alone the answers.

Paradigms of Research

There are several ways to try to capture the essence of religious development. Even while remaining within the boundaries of various psychological or educational explanations, a number of paradigms can easily be discerned. They may perhaps not be Kuhnian in the sense that obvious shifts from an earlier, less accurate conceptualization of the object of study (development of religious experience) has been superseded by a later theory with more explanatory power. As in other areas of research on human action, they tend to exist side by side, their ups and down determined more by governed marketing processes than by the advancement of knowledge. Most of them can rather easily be classified according to the various schools of psychological personality research, although the overlapping is not complete. As a preliminary list, five paradigms could be proposed: biographical, depth psychological, behavioristic, trait theoretical, and cognitive.

The *biographical tradition* was very influential during the time William James wrote his lectures on the varieties of religious experience (James, 1902), and depth psychological schools, especially psychoanalysis, have made use of it. Erikson's psychological studies of Luther (1958) and Gandhi (1969) are prime examples of this approach. This narrative paradigm will always complement other paradigms in the form of historical research. The form of biography makes it interesting and easily understandable. The main problems of this approach from the point of view of psychology are its often atheoretical and ipsative rhetoric (although not in the aforementioned cases) and its unrepresentative choice of both subjects and situations.

The depth psychological research tradition uses special forms of biographical techniques. In *psychoanalysis and analytical psychology* ordinary autobiographical stories are enriched by various associative and interpretative means to bring unconscious associations into light. Analytical techniques are utterly time consuming, based on repeated discussions and use of the customer-therapist relationship to its limits. The tradition of defining developmental stages owes much to Sigmund Freud's concepts of the development of sexuality, and C. G. Jung was a pioneer in describing individuation during later years. Despite Freud's natural science view of research, much of the analytical literature on religion has been of the relatively impressionistic sort. The return to the original intentions of the paradigm has only been realized with the object relations theory (McDargh, 1983).

Most of the proponents of *behaviorist psychology* have not been interested in religion, some seem even hostile to it. This is understandable from the experimental-deductive nature of this paradigm. Religion is, of course, individually a mentalistic entity, the essence of which escapes S-R and S-O-R considerations. Behaviorist studies will not be handled in this chapter, but behaviorist psychology must be mentioned with reference to methodology. Often-used research techniques, such as the semantic differential, have been designed by behaviorists. The modeling theories and research techniques of social behaviorism must be taken into account in relation to the research on the influence of different social agencies on religious experience. Certainly behaviorism's strict methodological stance has also had a sobering influence on research done with other paradigms.

The *psychometric trait paradigm* is an outgrowth of early questionnaire research in the field of religious research. Factor analytic methodology, developed among others by L. L. Thurstone, is with minor variation still often used in empirical multivariate research. During the 1970s it was adapted to longitudinal lifespan studies. The trait paradigm has also produced one of the most influential theoretical contributions, that of Allport (1950). His writings have made an impact, and his definition of intrinsic and extrinsic types of piety are currently used in empirical studies.

Since the 1960s the dominant paradigm, even in the field of religion, has been the *cognitive stage theory*, developed according to Piaget's model that he himself applied, among other areas, to his studies of moral judgment. It must be remarked, however, that the dominance of the cognitive paradigm is not caused by the definition of developmental stages that is so characteristic for Piaget and later for Goldman, Kohlberg, Fowler, and Oser. Cognitivism is rather a convergent trend of psychology, a common historical denominator toward which the various paradigms tend to gravitate. In biographical research it can be seen as the emphasis of narrative patterns, in depth psychology as the emergence of ego theories, in behaviorism as the acceptance of internal stimulus-reaction chains. Of course, also most of the trait theoretical edifice is based on cognitive measures and an increasing share of work is done on ever more complex representations of cognitive structures.

The five entries used here do not cover all research in the field of religious development. One might suggest for instance that a new feminist paradigm is emerging to counterbalance this realm of male rhetoric. We would, however, like to see it as a variety of the biographical paradigm.

At any rate, much of the research work done on religious development is eclectic research rather than narrowly paradigmatic normal research. Perhaps more than in some other fields scholars have been aware of work done in other paradigms, and this has served mutual understanding. In relation to religion this is important, because in itself religion has been a dividing factor in the world. It would be very valuable if this attitude could be extended to scholars from traditions other than the Judeo-Christian, Western tradition.

Ways of Describing Development

There are but few ways age-related description and explanation have been done (if the anecdotal narration of an individual biography is, for the moment, disregarded). The patterns that are used either alone or in combination are 1) characterization of a single phenomenon or a unidimensional trend, 2) characterization of the age group by age group description of multidimensional changes, 3) description of relatively age-independent developmental stages, and 4) conceptualizing the various mechanisms that generate and control developmental changes.

1) Most of the developmental studies of religious experience belong to the first category on this list. They are studies on one particular type of action or a *unidimensional trend*. In fact many researchers have conceptualized religiousness itself as a unitary dimension of variation, which means that (as is the case with general intelligence) people could be divided on a continuum ranging from atheists and areligious to pious saints, most people being probably neither but moderately consensually religious. Actually this is the impression one easily gets when gathering empirical data on a random population. Such a crude measure can sometimes be used in a denominationally relatively homogenous population, but a mere developmental curve of this kind is from the theoretical point of view uninteresting. This type of description can be used in developmental studies with respect to various manifestations of religiousness, such as prayer or reading the Bible, but even in these cases the possibility of experimential associations producing multidimensionality must be taken into account.

2) The description of development *from the point of view of age* is of course one of the first and easiest ways to approach the subject. It is fairly common in the field of general development, the best known examples being

the studies of children and adolescents by Gesell, Ilg and Ames. It has seldom been done with respect to religion with the same systematic persistence, but there are broader characterizations of religiousness in children, adolescents, young adults, etc., which use essentially the same principles of description. In reading this kind of literature it must be kept in mind that such descriptions based on—as they mostly are—cross-sectional data contaminate age differences with cohort differences. This distorts the picture in ways that are usually impossible to untangle.

There is no generally accepted multivariate model of religious experience. So far, the multivariate descriptions of religiousness have rather been collections of categories or indicators belonging to the single phenomenon category, and even for the most developed of them it is conceivable that some of the dimensions themselves are decomposable or that there are important interdimensional phenomena that one should take into account in developmental studies. Many studies use a multivariate model, but only for structural purposes. The descriptions of development for which, e.g., a factor analytic model could be used are instead constructed as stages relatively independently of the factor model.

3) In developmental research in the *Piagetian tradition*, the multivariate descriptions are usually constructed from the point of view of *the states of cognitive structure*. The concept of sequence is usually seen as an important one, and it is customary to make a distinction between "hard" and "soft" stages. A model contains hard stages if they are qualitatively different, follow an unchanging sequence which at a later stage exhibits greater complexity and improved problem-solving capacity. A hard stage model is usually seen as universal. The alternatives are variously called functional (with various outcomes) or soft (alternative or probability-based sequences, fuzzy limits, later stages can also be regressive). The stages defined by Goldman are relatively hard, those of Erikson functional, and those of Oser and Gmünder relatively soft (Reich, 1993).

4) Any model of religious experience alone is not enough to explain development; the various factors influencing experience should also be presented. Many of the studies take into account such processes and factors as learning, family and group influences, effects of schooling, church activities, media effects, etc. Still they are usually conceptualized in an oversimplified manner, and most studies show very little understanding for their systemic character and various interactions. For some time an urgent need for interdisciplinarity has been felt among the researchers in this field.

Research Methods

Religious experience is a very sensitive field and presents special requirements and difficulties in relation to the methods used for documentation and interpretation. The normal requirements for scientific research, such as objectivity, systematization, and exactitude, are not easily adaptable in any kind of experience-related research. By their very nature experiences are subjective, situational, holistically diffuse, and impulse-driven. The relation to the numinous creates almost insurmountable difficulties, as we must accept an ontological premise according to which the divine part of the relation to be researched in most cases does not lend itself to observation at all. Still, the data gathered to document the experiences and the theoretical explanations offered for these data must be relevant. They must make sense from the point of view of the experiencing person, from the point of view of those who are trying to facilitate their development by educational means, and of course also from the point of view of research workers who are committed to the specific kinds of paradigms referred to above. Even humanistic psychology is closely tied to the academic experimental tradition.

As has been noted before, the different paradigms tend to favor different methods for documenting and interpreting experiences and related facts. The use of biographical methods shows this clearly. As a developmental research methodology they were all but abandoned in the wake of quantitative and semiquantitative measurement methods after the World War II. Earlier research made frequent use of written biographical sources, in addition to spontaneously written diaries, letters, and autobiographies, e.g., especially requested conversion stories and other researcher-dependent products. The revival of qualitative methods, which took place gradually after the mid-sixties, has brought these techniques again to the forefront of research. Especially biographical interviews are now used in new, sophisticated ways, as can be seen in Fowler's (1981) research, which uses detailed but still personal interview data. German social-science research has presented sophisticated theories of human biographical processes (Schütze, 1981; 1984; Schweitzer, 1987:13-35), and this, together with the use of more general considerations on the narrative qualities inherent in oral presentation, can be expected to lead to new insights in research on religion.

Truly experimental, controlled research methods have so far been outside the limits of developmental research on religious experience. Despite the difficulties, the main corpus of research on these matters has adopted the quasi-experimental approach. According to this approach, phenomena which cannot be reproduced in laboratory are studied in their natural settings with as much control as is possible without doing away with the object of study. The main techniques used are psychometric measurement, careful selection and comparison of representative samples of relevant research groups, and extensive use of sophisticated statistical techniques to separate influences of the numerous covarying factors. Psychometrics is based on the idea of giving the subjects to be studied a number of preestablished small tasks, which have been scaled according to criteria guaranteeing maximum reliability and validity for scales combined of such tasks. The same idea can also be extended to assessments made by external judges giving their evaluations as reactions to limited tasks. For instance, in attitude measurement the subjects characteristically have been asked to assess their degree of acceptance toward a set of sentences or short texts, usually so-called attitude statements like

Every story of the Bible is absolutely true
I cannot believe everything written in the Bible
The Bible can provide help in difficult situations

It is common to give the subject alternatives ranging from "I totally agree" to "I totally disagree." Even a scale constructed from such relatively synonymous or antonymous propositions is seldom entirely unidimensional.

In addition to statements, a number of other stimuli have been used in similar ways: pairs of adjectives in relation to some religious concepts, names of affects, emotions or values, role constructions, descriptions of religious action. Common to many of these item-types is that the subject must state his or her religiousness in relation to the stimuli chosen before-hand by the researcher. As a result, these measurements are notoriously incapable of distinguishing strongly religious, ordinary persons from committed, creatively religious persons. To catch the personal character of religious experience and its associations, a number of projective or semi-projective techniques have been constructed. The stimuli of these measurements are intentionally vague. Among them are the beginning words of open sentences, artistic pictures, classical melodies. In research on religious experience they may have open or hidden religious referents, but it is essential that the subject of research is relatively free to choose both the content and style of his or her personal expression. Typical examples of this variety are pictures used to elicit relatively natural thoughts of children and adolescents (Godin and Coupez, 1957; Robinson, 1961; Tamminen, 1991). The interpretation of expressions becomes increasingly difficult when the procedure allows more open verbal strategies, similar to those used in an interview. Projective techniques widen the perspective, but can also be criticized—and partly on the same grounds as the more structured methods. They are still very dependent on the researcher's religious intentions, and, in addition to that, the results obtained tend to be less reliable (even if not necessarily less valid) than with previous types of measures.

The judgmental tasks of the Piagetian type of research depart somewhat from the above mentioned item-types. They consist of two parts, a relatively complicated and well-formed narrative structure, a dilemma that is known to be problematic to the age group under scrutiny, and a clinical interview which is based on the subject's reactions to the dilemma. One of the best known is Oser's "Paul dilemma," which describes a young man's hesitation between a promise given to God during adversity and a more mundane plan which would cause him to break his vow (Oser and Gmünder, 1988). The purpose of a dilemma is to awaken a cognitive conflict which makes the subject give serious consideration to existing alternatives and the grounds that may exist for a decision. At its best the interview comes close to normal discussion, which brings this method relatively close to various biographical methods in the production of data. On the other hand, the analysis is usually restrictive, as the researcher's aim is a general assessment of the level of judgment, and major parts of the material are considered mainly in this respect.

It must be stated that the longitudinal approach, in which the same persons have been followed up during a number of years, is rare. In theory the researchers are aware that such data is necessary, either as natural description or as quasi-experimental longitudinal measurement. Few examples can be mentioned: Koppe (1973) followed American Lutheran children and adolescents over a period of four years, studying the effects of congregation on learning. Helve (1993) used repeated measurement on a school-based group of suburban Finnish adolescents. Tamminen (1991) also repeated the battery of religiousness measures with part of the Finnish group of schoolchildren he studied. The effects of educational strategies can be adequately ascertained only by longitudinal approach, and more are sorely needed.

THE APPLICATION OF PIAGETIAN COGNITIVISM TO RELIGIOUS DEVELOPMENT AND ITS ALTERNATIVES

Goldman's Piagetian Formulation

Goldman's (1964) formulation is the best known and most expansive application of Piaget's paradigm of operational thinking in the area of religious thinking. Goldman tested it by using three Bible stories and three projective religious pictures in semiclinical interviews with 200 British persons aged 6 to 17. According to Goldman the general Piagetian sequence of 1) pre-operational, 2) concrete operational and 3) formal operational stages is applicable also to the development of religious thinking. Goldman called the stages intuitive (up to 7/8 years), concrete (7/8-13/14) and abstract religious thinking (13/14). In a later book (1965) he talked about prereligious, subreligious and personal religious thinking. Between the stages proper Goldman placed periods of transition, during which new thinking gradually breaks through the boundaries of the earlier stage. The age limits of stages were, especially with respect to the change from concrete to abstract religious thinking, higher than in Piaget's stages in other areas of thinking. Goldman proposed that the delay was due to the secondary nature of religious thinking and the manner in which religion was taught at school. In his later book Goldman adjusted the age limit of the last stage at 11-12, the same as Piaget.

There are, according to Goldman, great personal differences both in the age limits and in the pace of development. Piaget (1972) thought that all adults do not reach the stage of formal operations and that few adults can apply it in all areas of knowledge and in every situation (see Waern, 1982). Similarly, Goldman (1964) stated that many young people and adults remain at the concrete level in their religious thinking. This may lead to the abandonment of religion or to an indifferent attitude toward it.

On the basis of Goldman's study Peatling (1973) created a multiple-choice measure *Thinking about the Bible* for the stories of the Bible used by Goldman. Each of the stories had four answer alternatives representing different levels of religious thinking. Four scales of religious thinking were defined: very concrete, concrete, abstract, and very abstract. On the basis of his empirical study of American children and adolescents Peatling considered that the intermediate stage between concrete and abstract religious thinking was clearly longer than Goldman stated, i.e., abstract thinking began later. When comparing the results of the studies of Goldman and Peatling we must, however, remember the differences in the methods used.

Peatling's measure has been used in several studies (e.g., Peatling and Laabs, 1973; Greer, 1981a; Kay, 1981; Tamminen, 1976; 1991; McGrady, 1990). The general line of development of these studies is similar: abstract thinking increases with chronological and mental age. In general the development of abstract thinking progresses rather evenly from one age group to another. No sharp turning points can be seen. In Peatling's original study (1973) the change was greatest between ages 12 and 16, but, e.g., in Tamminen's study (1983a) among Finnish students of the same age groups (9-20), only between ages 9/10 and 11/12 was the change a little more pronounced than between other age groups. There were no great systematic differences between girls and boys in the development of abstract thinking. Peatling (1977) stated that religious thinking continues to develop during the adult years.

The Development of Religious Concepts

Religious concepts, like the concept of God, of the Bible, of prayer, of death, are central in religious thinking. They are extensive totalities containing many smaller concepts, metaphors, and analogies. They comprehend a large part of the content and object of religious thinking.

The Piagetian research paradigm, with the dimensions concrete-abstract, undifferentiated-differentiated, magic-realistic, has been very central also in the study of the development of religious concepts. For instance, David Elkind (1961; 1962; 1963) noticed clear Piagetian stages in the development of children's understanding of their religious identity revealed in their conception of their own religious denomination: 1) global undifferential concepts in the ages of 5-7, 2), concretely differentiated concepts (ages 8-9), and 3) abstractly differentiated concepts (10-12). Long, Elkind, and Spilka (1967) found similar stages in the development of prayer. Goldman (1964) stated that the Piagetian developmental stages could be observed in the development of many religious concepts.

The development of religious concepts shows also other aspects and dimensions than those typical for Piagetian thought. They require theological interpretation, as was seen also in Goldman's research. Even though the formal development of thinking affects them, they are—as concepts in general—first and foremost the result of social learning. They are formed in an individual's mind gradually on the basis of information, perceptions, and experiences. Every individual gives his or her own stamp to these concepts.

We deal here only with three religious concepts: image of God, concept of the Bible and concept of prayer.

The *image of God* is unquestionably the most central in the development of an individual's personal religiousness, at least in Christianity. It is understandable that during the past few decades the concept of God has also been investigated more than any other religious concept. The results, however, are partially contradictory. This is mostly due to the fact that the viewpoints and research methods have varied and also to the fact that the concept of God is very complex. Harms (1944) grounded his whole presentation, one of the first models of religious development, on the development of the image of God. With the help of drawings of 3-18 year old children and adolescents he distinguished three stages in religious development: fairytale (ages 3-6), realistic (7-12), and individualistic (after the age of 12) stage.

One of the developmental lines of the image of God, according to the studies, is that the concept of God becomes more *internalized*, which can be seen in the characteristics associated with God (Babin, 1964; Ludwig, Weber, and Iben, 1974). Through word association tests Deconchy (1965; 1967) distinguished three dimensions in the associations with the word "God" which were emphasized in different age groups: 1) the peak of attributivity phase—typical themes such as Greatness, Goodness, Justice—was during the age of 9-10, 2) in the personalization phase (peak in ages of 12-13) the themes Sovereignty, Redeemer, Fatherhood were most typical, and 3) in the internalization phase (peak in ages of 15-16) such subjective themes as Love, Obedience, Trust, but to some extent also Doubt and Fear were emphasized.

Anthropomorphism is a characteristic that has been given special emphasis in the studies on children's concepts of God. It means that external, physical human traits or in a very broad sense also that human, psychological characteristics, such as "kind," "gentle," "helpful," are attributed to the nature of God. It has often been regarded as a central characteristic of the concept of God, especially at the preschool age, decreasing gradually after that (Vianello, 1980; Vianello, Tamminen, and Ratcliff, 1992).

This trait was central also in Goldman's (1964) presentation of the concept of God in childhood. According to him, a child's concept of God is anthropomorphic up to the age of 10-11. The symbolic concept of God starts to develop at the age of 12. God is still described in anthropomorphic terms, but they are used metaphorically. Children talk about God as goodness, love, and an invisible spirit. Hilliard's (1960) study based on the essays of children ("My Idea of God") shows a similar developmental line. Between ages 11 and 16 the number of anthropomorphic descriptions clearly decreased, whereas spiritual and abstract descriptions increased. However, there are other studies with very few anthropomorphic descriptions by children (e.g., Graebner, 1960). This was true also in Tamminen's (1991) study, in which the concept of God of children and young people ages 7-20 was investigated by several different measures. Coarsely anthropomorphic, i.e., human physical descriptions of God, were fairly uncommon in all age groups (in answers to a fill-in sentence "When I think about God" and essays on the subject "What is my God like?"). They were even a little more common in the age group 13-16 than among younger respondents. For many young people the coarsely anthropomorphic view is clearly a remnant from an earlier age expressing a slighting attitude toward God. This relates to Goldman's (1964) thought that where negative attitudes develop, poor concepts tend to form.

Another trait that has often cropped up in the research is *legalism*, a conception of God in which God is seen as one who demands, carries out justice, and punishes. From the point of view of human behavior, it can mean trying to please God by living properly, according to God's will. Often, especially in earlier research—in part reflecting the thought of the recapitulation theory—the God concept of late childhood remained legalistic, in keeping with the Old Testament outlook (Hall, 1990; Gruehn, 1956, Hilliar, 1960). Klingberg's (1959) view was different. On the basis of material consisting of essays written by Swedish schoolchildren, he concluded that there are not grounds for the argument that the image of God in later childhood is legalistic. Both ideas of God, the strict and punishing as well as the loving and forgiving, are found side by side in later childhood. In many studies made recently on the image of God in later childhood and adolescence, the respondents' emphasis has been clearly on the *loving, forgiving idea of God*. However, with some children and young people this is also connected to an image of God as one who punishes (Potvin, Hoge, and Nelsen, 1976; Nelsen, Potvin, and Shiels, 1977; Potvin, 1977). In Tamminen's (1991) study God was seen in all age groups as trustworthy, forgiving, loving, and helpful. These characteristics were most emphasized with the 7- to 13- year-olds, and were a little less frequently mentioned among the older students. The loving, forgiving God was slightly less emphasized by boys than by girls. Instead, the boys placed a little more emphasis on God's omnipotence and power than did the girls. These characteristics were emphasized more in later childhood than in adolescence, which is consistent with the results of other studies.

The concept of God is not only cognitive; it also has a belief-related dimension. In many studies, critical assessment and doubt increase at the age of puberty, which is the case also in relation to the image of God. For many, God becomes more distant and less real (Hilliard, 1960; Hutsebaut and Verhoeven, 1991; Tamminen, 1991). Also the *problem of theodicy*, the contradiction between God's goodness and the suffering and evil of the world, becomes important in this age (Nipkow, 1988).

Rizzuto (1979; 1991) has studied the development of the representation of God from an object relations viewpoint. According to her the representation of God in the Western world follows the same psychological rules as the development of representations in general. According to Rizzuto the ideal developmental sequence, which also agrees with the seven phases of life described by Erikson (1959), is: "(1) a fully trustworthy being, (2) a good, tolerant companion, (3) a lovable and loving (even if a bit frightening) being, (4) a knowledgeable good protector, (5) a being that can tolerate questioning and doubt while believers face the contradictions of life and the evil in the world, (6) a being who is there and who lets believers be themselves, and (7) a trustworthy being whose mysterious existence is not challenged" (Rizzuto, 1991:56). For Rizzuto this is an ideal sequence that is never completely found in actual life.

Scholars have been very interested in the relation between *children's concept of God and their image of and relationship with their parents*. The central starting point was Freud's (1927) view that a child's idea of God reflects the idea that the child has of his or her father, which Piaget also (1929) agreed with. The results of empirical studies of the relationship between a child's idea of God and his or her parents, and which parent's traits are more reflected in the idea of God, have been contradictory. According to some researchers, the father figure is more dominant in the idea of God (Vergote et al., 1969), whereas other results show that the mother's influence is more decisive (Strunk, 1959; Godin and Hallez, 1965; Deconchy, 1968). It has also been claimed that the father has more influence on a girl's idea of God and the mother more influence on a boy's idea of God. On the other hand, it has been hypothesized—as Alfred Adler did—that the parent who is closer to the child has more effect on the child's idea of God (Nelson, 1971; Spilka, Addition, and Rosensohn, 1975). Scholars have also found that cultural differences affect the results (Vergote et al., 1969; Vergote, 1981).

These studies were mainly made of adults and young people and only rarely of children. Vianello and his colleagues found that the father/God relationship was dominant for 9- to 10-year-old Italian children. The correlation between the image of mother and the concept of God was higher for girls than for boys. (Vianello, Tamminen, and Ratcliff, 1992.)

Among others, Godin and Hallez (1965) observed that the connection between the idea of God and the idea of parents weakens with age. The subjects of their study were young people and adults. In Tamminen's study (1991) children and adolescents evaluated in many different ways their own relation to each of their parents. A close relationship with parents was in semantic differential connected to evaluations of God as being close, real, caring, and forgiving. The correlations were strongest in the youngest ages.

The development of the concept of the Bible has been investigated only in a few studies. Goldman (1964) clarified the concept of the Bible among children and adolescents (ages 6-16) from several perspectives. He based this part of his investigation on the interpretation of three biblical stories and on a drawing, in which a child looked at a damaged Bible.

In Goldman's view the understanding of the nature of the Bible develops through four central developmental phases: 1) (up to about 10 years of age) children talk about the appearance and use of the Bible. 2) (Up to about 12:6 years) attention has shifted to the content of the Bible: a completely true or old book, from which we learn about God and Jesus. 3) (-14:8 years) the religious significance and the message of the Bible. 4) (After 14:8) the spiritual meaning and significance of the Bible. Goldman also presented three developmental phases in children's views about *how the Bible came to be written*: 1) (-9 years of age) the origin of the Bible is, basically, understood in a magical way. 2) (about -14:5) the Bible, written by several authors, is based upon either the accounts of eyewitnesses or an oral tradition. 3) The authors of the Bible are recognized to be more "inspired" than "accurate." Goldman's three developmental phases of the *truthfulness of the Bible* are 1) (up to about 10:5) the Bible is considered to be literally true. 2) (-12:5) the "truth" of the Bible is affirmed on the basis of the authority of God and his omnipotence. 3) The veracity of biblical stories is based upon the fact that they are eyewitness accounts, or they are in accord with one's own inner experience. A certain critical attitude is likely to appear in this phase.

Tamminen (1983a; 1991) studied the concept of the Bible of 7-16-year-old schoolchildren, among other things, with the help of two projective photographs: In the one photograph "The girls and the Bible" a girl was looking at the Bible with her little sister by her side. The text ran: "Helen was looking at the big family Bible. Her little sister came to her and asked: 'What sort of a book is it?' Helen said it was the Bible and continued: 'The Bible is . . .'" In the other picture "Wondering about the Bible" a boy, or a girl, was looking at the Bible and the following text was attached: "This is Mark/Mary. He/she is reading the Bible and wondering about something that has been in his/her mind before. He/she is thinking about . . ." The results differed in many respects from those of Goldman. No clear-cut developmental phases connected to age levels were discerned. All in all, responses focusing upon the physical appearance of the Bible were few. They were most common with the youngest pupils (i.e., 7-8 year olds), and declined in frequency rapidly until puberty (i.e., the age of 13-15 years). Finnish schoolchildren had almost no tendency to credit the Bible with magical traits.

The clearest developmental line was seen in a change in the tendency to question the truthfulness of the Bible from the age of 9-10 years to the age of 15-16. In response to the photograph "Wondering about the Bible," 5 percent of 9-10 year old pupils and 20 percent of 15-16 year olds gave responses in the category "Is the Bible true?" The problem seems to become still more current after this age. Pirinen (1983) used a quite similar photograph in his study of life questions of 16- to 18-year-old Finnish students, but the verbal stimulus was different indicating to that "the Bible sometimes seems to be a problematic book." Almost half the responses concerned the truthfulness of the Bible. Actually 36 percent of the responses raised this question, while 6 percent affirmed the Bible's truthfulness and 4 percent denied it.

Tamminen (1991) also applied Peatling's Literalism Scale (1973). The interpretation of the Bible changed from the youngest to the oldest age groups straightforwardly from a literal to a more nonliteral attitude. The result corresponded on the whole to Peatling's (1973) results among American pupils. The religiously active, committed students had the most literal position among Finnish students. But also their opinion became a little more liberal with age until the age of 15-16.

Some research has been done also on children's and young people's *concept of prayer*. Long, Elkind, and Spilka's (1967) study using Piagetian stages was mentioned above. According to them the understanding of prayer goes through three stages: 1) Between 5 and 7 a child has only a vague and indistinct understanding of the meaning of prayer. Prayer is connected to the word God and to some adopted modes of action. 2) Between 7 and 9 children are able to distinguish prayer from other actions, but it is still connected to a certain concrete, verbal action and to the external form of prayer. 3) In this phase (ages 9-12) requests have only a secondary significance in prayer. It is understood first and foremost to be a personal conversation with God. The inner activity connected to it is understood to be more important than the form.

Many of these aspects came out in Tamminen's (1983b; 1991) studies of Finnish 7-20 year olds, who arranged by order of importance five definitions of prayer and completed the sentence "I think prayer is . . ." Seven to eight year olds answered an open question: "What do you feel is most important in prayer?" There were differences in the results gained by these different methods. When the definitions were ranked in order of importance the external form of action, folding one's hands, and the presenting of requests and wishes to God were clearly more important for 9-10 year olds than for other age groups. Conversation with God and thanksgiving to him were, however, the most important characteristics of prayer in all age groups. When the pupils were asked to describe prayer ("I think prayer is . . ."), they mentioned external forms of prayer—folding one's hands and staying quiet—very seldom and generally not by the youngest age groups but mostly by such adolescents who themselves prayed very seldom or not at all. Instead, now one-third of the subjects described prayer in terms of petitionary prayer. This was the most central trait up to the age of puberty. Conversation with God and reliance on him was now in general the second most popular, but among the oldest adolescents (ages about 16-20), the most often mentioned trait of prayer.

Goldman's (1964) view of the concept of the fulfillment of prayer is based on the Piagetian tradition. In his three stages the concept of "magic" is central: 1) In the magical phase (up to about the age of 9) prayer is seen as the only cause of events without other factors. The child expects God to answer prayer immediately. 2) In the semimagical phase (9-12), the child sees that other factors apart from prayer have an effect on events. 3) In the non-magical, religious phase (12-), the children are no longer sure whether prayer has an effect or not. Praying is based upon reliance on God. More rational explanations are connected to the effect of prayer, and especially the spiritual effect on the praying person is emphasized.

Some other scholars have also emphasized magical traits in the prayer concept of children (e.g., Gruehn, 1956; Virkkunen, 1975). This view was obviously affected by the recapitulation theory emphasizing parallels between the development of children and primitive peoples and religions (Zeininger, 1929). Tamminen (1983b; 1991), however, found among Finnish subjects 7-20 years old that their free descriptions of prayer and their reports of their experiences of prayers being heard contained only very few thoughts that clearly tended toward the magical. Much depends, of course, on the definition given to the word "magical."

According to Thun (1963; 1964) a small child expects all prayers to come true; if this is not the case, it is because of the child's behavior, for example because he or she may not have followed the commandments or gone to church. Young people between ages 14 and 20 believed that God hears prayers that come from the heart, and they doubted the effectiveness of prayer if their prayers were not answered. In Brown's studies (Thouless and Brown, 1965, Brown, 1966, 1967) as well as in Tamminen's (1983b; 1991), children thought that the effect of petitionary prayer between age groups was reflected also in the fact that the youngest group, 7 to 10-year-olds, thought God acted for the most part directly. From the age of 11-12 children and adolescents saw God as acting indirectly, for example, through medication. Rosenberg (1989) stated that in evaluations of the effectiveness of prayer older adolescents emphasized more than younger respondents the value of prayer in itself and its effect on the praying person.

Scarlett and Perriello (1991) studied in the United States the concept of prayer with the help of prayers which Catholic adolescents and young adults wrote for hypothetical situations and with their responses to questions. As a result they stated, e.g., that "the seventh graders provided examples of a naive faith not only in a God 'out there' but also in a self 'out there' and visible to all," whereas "the ninth graders and especially the undergraduates shifted the focus to the inner world of feelings and to an awareness of how difficult it is to know what is true and best" (p.74).

According to the psychoanalytic object relation view, prayer develops because images of God and images of self and other develop. A more "mature" prayer, in which the person searches for God's will, or strives to have a change in feelings or to become closer to God, presumes an autonomous, responsible self and a God who is more friend than parent (Rizzuto, 1979; see Scarlett and Parriello, 1991).

The Linguistic Point of View

The criticism directed recently against Piagetian theory has already been mentioned. Its main point has been directed toward the centrality of formal thinking in the development of personality: cognitive development is more complex than Piaget's model supposes. Also Piaget's view that formal thought is acquired independently of the content and context of cognitive activity has been questioned (Brown and Desforces, 1979). From the point of view of religious thinking, Piaget's model has been considered too limited and one-side (Slee, 1987).

Instead of or in addition to the Piagetian theory *a linguistic viewpoint*, the central significance of language and especially of its characteristics metaphors, has been emphasized (Murphy, 1979; Slee, 1987; McGrady, 1987; 1990). This problem has a long history connected to the classical Aristotelian theory of similes and metaphors. According to this theory, if the ideas connected to a metaphor are too remote, the metaphor becomes too difficult to understand; if they are too close, however, it is not interesting enough to be effective. This view of social influence through language has again become relevant with the linguistic turn of cognitive science since the sixties.

Some researchers have developed a model in which they distinguish between *general core cognitive elements*, which refer to and affect all aspects of human thinking, and *distinctive cognitive elements*, which distinguish one field from other forms of thought. Piaget's stages of intellectual development and the ability to understand a variety of language forms belong to the general core cognitive elements. Thus, in religious thinking the operation component is only one of several components. According to McGrady (1990) religious thinking is distinguished from other areas of discourse especially by its dependence on metaphors and extended metaphors systems called models. In fact, metaphors and models are crucial also to many other areas of thinking and language in which complex phenomena cannot be directly apprehended and which must be approached indirectly through analogy. In religious thinking metaphors portray the relationship of the human being with the uttermost basis of life, with the divine and transcendence.

Biblical parables and their analogies and metaphors have been the subject of several studies during recent decades. This research has, however, not, as McGrady (1990) states, really applied the cognitive theory of metaphor or reflected the recent debates concerning the role of metaphor in religious language. Many of these studies have been linked to Piaget's paradigm (Ainsworth, 1961; Martinsson, 1968; Pettersson, 1969; Beechick, 1974).

Chiefly the results show development of religious thinking from the concrete to the abstract, as, e.g., in Beechick's (1974) study. She distinguished four levels in the understanding of parables: 1) the child cannot answer the question; 2) the child can repeat the details and the concrete aspects of the story (intuitive stage, up to 7); 3) the child can apply the parable in a simple way (concrete operational stage, 8-10); 4) the child can understand the parable at an abstract level and relate it to his or her own life situation in some way; the child understands the spiritual meaning of the parable (formal operational stage, 11-).

The central result of Beechick's work shows that the understanding of parables is essentially connected to the child's age. Also other studies, such as that of Murphy (1979), show that the understanding of the analogies and metaphors of parables clearly increases with age.

The studies mentioned above were limited to children of ages 7-13. It seems that at the age of 12-13, most of them have reached the abstract level of thinking necessary for understanding the meaning of parables. In Tamminen's (1983a; 1991) study subjects 9-20 years old interpreted two parables (the prodigal son, and the speck and the log) with the help of answer alternatives (four of them represented concrete level, four human-ethical, and four abstract interpretation) and gave free interpretations to some central metaphors of the mentioned two parables. The most clear increase in understanding of parables took place between age groups 9/10 and 11/12, but after that the development continued with smaller changes until late adolescence.

The understanding of parables is reflected by the aforementioned general core cognitive elements, the development of abstract thinking and linguistic abilities, but it also presumes interaction with the content of parables. The understanding of parables depends on the level of the difficulty and the type of parable and on the familiarity of the parable's content to the listener. Several different parables have been used in the studies. The ethical message of a parable seems to be easier for children to understand than the religious message; maybe it is often closer to everyday life and the children's own sphere of experience (Murphy, 1979; Tamminen, 1991). The understanding of parables requires also their theological interpretation, which is affected, e.g., by the religious attitudes and experiences of the respondent.

The empirical research done on the understanding of parables has been criticized on the basis of new perspectives opened on the explanation of parables. The parables have been viewed primarily as narratives and as poetic metaphors, the understanding of which assumes that the listener empathizes with parables. The essential question is what happens in the listener when he or she enters the spirit of the parable (Slee, 1983).

McGrady (1990) linked his investigation to *the comparison of metaphoric and operational paradigms in the development of religious thinking*. He distinguished six categories in the metaphoric religious thinking (metaphoric recognition, comprehension, production, elaboration, interrelation, and validation). As a result he stated that operational thinking is not a necessary prerequisite for all aspects of metaphoric religious thinking. He proposed that there may be three phases in the application of metaphorical religious thinking to biblical material. Phase 1 is its application to short statements (such as the metaphor "camel through the eye of a needle") based upon displaced metaphoric concepts that are within the experience of the individual. Phase 2 is the application of metaphorical thinking to the interpretation of extended metaphors, models, including more complex parables. Phase 3 is "the application of metaphorical thinking as a broad, generalized paradigm extending the range of valid interpretative possibilities that can be appealed to generally and specifically when conflict arises with a scientific worldview." Formal operational thought does not seem to be a prerequisite for phase 1 and for some aspects of phase 2, but it would be firmly established for phase 3 (McGrady, 1992:16).

More research along these lines is needed to explain the relationships between the development of religious thinking and the understanding of metaphoric language. It would be important also for religious education.

DEVELOPMENTAL VIEWS FROM THE ANALYTICAL TRADITION

Modern developmental thinking received strong impulses from Freud's theory of libido and ego development. He divided the childhood developmental process into oral, anal, oedipal, and latency periods. The classical terminology is partly retained in the modern object-relation versions of psychoanalytic theory, although its content has been undergoing a relatively thorough revision, in which many of the obvious differences between it and mainstream cognitive stage approaches have markedly diminished.

Freud's theory is one of the first to define the developmental sequence in terms of natural bio-psychological rather than age-related units. Most of the earlier discussions were conceptualized with the traditional seven-year units, with various philosophical and dogmatic connotations, whereas the Freudian discussion allows some latitude for changes to take place. Freudian theory also contains the notions of regression and fixation—the child can for various reasons revert to an earlier stage or remain innerly fixated to a latent early stage which can only be inferred from some seemingly irrational indications in his or her action. These have been constant themes for discussions also in relation to the developmental stage theories of religiousness and morality (the "hardness" vs. "softness" issue). In her analysis of early oedipal development Klein (1932) also put forward the idea that sometimes indications of a later stage can be anticipatorily detected—a theme also found in discussions of religious development.

Although original Freudian theory was concerned mainly with childhood and puberty, its influence on research on later development should be kept in mind. The first important proponent of a theory of adult development in the analytical tradition was Jung. He calls the process of self-fulfillment *individuation* . This process unites the individual and extrapersonal dynamics of the human psyche and is realized mainly by moral decisions. It is inherent in man and follows a regular pattern. Jung's developmental concept is relatively undifferentiated in the sense that he discerns only two main stages. According to him the first half of life can be characterized as initiation into outward reality and the second half as initiation into the inner reality. It is (or, in a normal developmental sequence, should be) a "reflectio," a turning back to the personality traits that have either remained or become unconscious during earlier development. The attainment of a broader personality can also be seen as a preparation for death. There is no doubt that Jung sees in this later individuation a kind of religious maturation, albeit in psychological terms. He explains it (e.g., Jung, 1943) as the formation and manifestation of archetypal symbols.

The meeting of the archetypes, one by one, is a scientific system of psychic experience. In recent practice it has created a multiplicity of popular courses based on Jungian views on the personal mythology (e.g., Feinstein and Krippner, 1988; Larsen, 1990). On the other hand, there is but little controlled empirical research supporting this view, so at least for the moment it seems to be more a part of the general Aquarian movement of the New Age than scientific study on the development of religious experience.

Erikson is the one psychoanalytic research worker after Freud who has had the most definitive influence on developmental studies in general and studies on religious experience in particular. In *Childhood and Society* (1950) he describes the complex interplay between the value-basis of society and the epigenetic psychic growth of the individual. His conceptualization consisting of eight well-defined and qualitatively different stages extended over an entire life-span. One of the central tenets of this comprehensive theory is that every stage is tied to the development of a particular psychic strength: 1) Basic Trust, 2) Autonomy, 3) Initiative, 4) Industry, 5) Identity, 6) Intimacy, 7) Generativity, and 8) Ego Integrity (Erikson, 1982).

The arrest of any of them will necessarily hinder the later stages. The attainment of these strengths requires the successful resolution of a psychic crisis. All the qualities preexist in a preliminary form from the beginning of development, and they are inseparably related to bodily functions, personal experiences and communal social relationships. For nonpsychoanalytic developmental conceptualizations, Erikson's ideas about adolescence, adulthood, and old age have become especially important.

If the adolescent task of identity formation is not achieved, serious identity confusions or role diffusions will disturb the later stages of development. The crisis is to a large extent created by growth and sexual maturation, which make an adolescent to question his or her sameness as an individual. The adult roles ahead require also a stable social identity in addition to the experience of personal continuity and self-worth (Erikson, 1950; 1964).

In *Childhood and Society* Erikson sees generativity in adulthood as the socially most important of all the developmental tasks or "virtues." It is characterized by care, whether that is induced by love or by obligation. In considering this stage he refers also to the monastic institutions. They serve as an example of the need for understanding, an important concomitant to generativity as a cultural necessity. The counterforce to care is called rejectivity, and it is essential to Erikson's vision of crisis that generativity cannot be achieved without learning to deal with the need to reject selectively.

Erikson's description of old age integrity comes very close to Jungian thinking in its emphasis on the attainment of coherence and wholeness. It is a synthesis of mature ego qualities, with distinctly spiritual overtones. Courage in facing death is one of its landmarks. Wisdom is often provided by a religious or philosophical tradition. The counterforce of this serene development is despair, which threatens to dispossess the individual of almost everything that has been valuable to him or her before.

Erikson's theory has been used as a general frame of reference for descriptions and studies of the mental development and identity crisis of youth. It has also given starting points for some studies concerned with the life questions of children and adolescents. Strommen (1974) conducted a broad study of 14- to 18-year-old U.S. high-school students and their life situations. Strommen summarized his results on the basis of factor analyses into five major factors, each of which was represented in one set of questions of a profound nature. As examples, two of these factors, self-relations and religious identity, are briefly presented here.

With regard to the first category, awareness of personal faults and lack of self-confidence, undermine feelings of self-esteem. This seems to be a cycle, in which self-regard drops lower and lower. Human relationships, including attitudes toward the opposite sex, parents, and academic problems were correlated to this cycle. Self-esteem was also related to faith, and the lack of it was related to awareness of distance and alienation from God. Youth suffering from low self-esteem expected help from the church in learning how to make a friend and be a friend (78 percent) and also in finding meaning and purpose in life (also 78 percent).

Strommen also describes the 30 percent of the sample that participate actively in congregational activities, pray for people needing God's special help, seek religious guidance for their moral decisions, and are interested in church social work. More than others they were conscious of God's presence and believed in his love and care. It was very interesting to notice that despite this they were as much as the others bothered by lack of self-confidence, academic problems, personal faults, classroom relationships, and national issues. Their self-esteem, however, was much higher. The most religiously committed were also the ones wanting to grow in faith and service.

Tamminen (1975; 1988) and Pirinen (1983) studied life questions of Finnish children and adolescents using projective photographs and open-ended texts. Tamminen focused on age groups 7-16 and Pirinen on age groups 16-18. Their studies received impetus from some Swedish studies, in which life questions of 10- to 13-year-old children had been studied with almost similar projective measurements (Hartman, Pettersson, and Westling, 1973; Hartman, 1985).

Pirinen was especially interested in the extent to which the life questions of young people reflect Erikson's theory of adolescence as an age of identity formation and identity crisis. Pirinen affirms that the most general life questions clearly show that the formation of the adolescent identity is integral to the process of maturation, with the ego, family, friends, and dating being the most frequently mentioned items. Reflections on the past and the future express the experience of inner sameness and continuity in identity. This same context includes the maturation process, which reflects the young person's struggle to become independent of parental authority, while at the same time joining in dating and binding oneself to friends.

The results of Tamminen's (1975; 1988) study and of its replication (Jaakkola, 1988; Tamminen, 1991) reveal the search for identity upon entering adolescence as an increase in questions dealing with the future and, to some extent, as questions of the purpose of life. In studies of this type it is impossible to achieve absolute results with regard to the generality of various life problems at different ages. The results depend to some degree on the instrument and the stimuli. Nevertheless, they do disclose tendencies in the weighing of existential questions at diverse ages.

RELIGIOUS DEVELOPMENT FROM THE POINT OF VIEW OF MOTIVATION, ATTITUDES, AND EXPERIENCES

Attitudes as Motivational Structures

The concept of motivation refers, on the one hand, to the initiating and energizing of the forces of action, on the other hand, to their control. Motivation can be seen as a composite consisting of a basic stratum of needs and of a superstructure of attitudes. From this point of view it is natural to ask first whether there is a biological need for religion, or whether it is just a socially conditioned, habitual phenomenon. Second, a major part of our discussion arises from the fact that religiousness has often been discussed in terms of attitude theories. They relate directly to experiences gained by human action.

There is only insufficient evidence available for the discussion of the biological nature of religious experience. In some sense it may be meaningful to say that a human being needs religion. We have a kind of spiritual "need" for personal security, deeper explanations, and an all-encompassing unity, as well as a need to identify with a personally held value-base. It has sometimes been said that the presence of religion in all societies proves religiousness to be based on an innate need for religion in man.

There has been some research on the heritability of attitudes which may be of interest in this respect. It has mainly been done as studies of twins, and religiousness has usually been taken into account within the context of conservative attitudes. The results are inconclusive. The present relatively vague conceptualizations do not really allow the kind of assessment needed. But with procedures similar to those used with, e.g., general intelligence, extraversion, and anxiety, it seems that the relative heritability is by far the lowest for social attitudes, not exceeding 30 percent. The safest assumption at the moment seems to be that there is a genetically determined readiness to form religion-related cognitive structures, but it is general in nature, not specifically tied to any particular religion.

Religion is an extraordinarily complex, many-faceted, symbolic superstructure. A person's religion determines his or her festival and ritual experiences, is reflected in many everyday actions and transforms some of them to instances of supernatural significance. In order to explain such regularities and experiential transformations, a relatively general and pervasive theoretical basis is necessary. Usually this is done in terms of attitude theory.

The Development of Religious Attitudes

Although theories of social attitudes are not mainly developmental, the concept of attitude has been important in describing development during childhood and adolescence. In the studies of religious development the descriptions of changes in religious attitudes have been one of the dominant points of view. In some studies they have even provided the basis for the describing of religious development as a whole (e.g., Virkkunen, 1975).

Attitude is one of the most central concepts in social psychology, but there has been a lot of disagreement about its definition. Olson and Zanna (1993:119) suppose that "most attitude theorists agree that (a) evaluation constitutes a central, perhaps predominant, aspect of attitudes, (b) attitudes are represented in memory, and (c) affective, cognitive, and behavioral antecedents of attitudes can be distinguished, as can affective, cognitive, and behavioral consequences of attitudes."

Thus, usually three dimensions have been distinguished in an attitude: the affective component represents a person's feelings toward the attitude object and his or her evaluation of this object. The cognitive component represents knowledge about the object. The behavioral component points to the action with respect to the object. There is often, however, a significant difference between attitudes and real actions. The defining component in an attitude is its affective or evaluating emphasis (Abelson and Rosenberg, 1967; Olson and Zanna, 1993). The object is evaluated as positive, neutral, or negative. Scholars are, however, not unanimous about the interrelations of these components of an attitude.

The components of an attitude have usually been regarded as being to a large extent intertwined. Some scholars have, however, distinguished more strongly between them. Fishbein and Ajzen (1975), e.g., limit attitude to the affective dimension, and belief forms the cognitive component. According to them, beliefs are the basis of an attitude, they determine it. They represent the information and knowledge that the person has about a given object. Fishbein and Ajzen divide the third, behavioral or conative, component into two parts: intention or intended action and action itself toward a given object of the attitude.

Attitudes thus always have a content-related aspect. Stressing this side we can talk either about attitudes and their development or about the development of beliefs. Beliefs are not only representations of knowledge, but an accepting or rejecting evaluation is always connected to them (Rokeach, 1972): "I believe that . . .", "I insist that . . .", "I doubt that . . .".

Oerter (1969) presented an interesting view on the development of religious attitudes. According to it the hypothesized three components do not develop simultaneously at an equal rate but are merged into a unity only gradually. First the child learns religious habits (like prayer, making the sign of the cross), then the affective component becomes attached to action. Usually a child adopts a positive attitude toward religion. Gradually the cognitive content of the attitude also crystallizes. This is also accompanied by conflicts between the dimensions. Oerter's view gains some indirect support from later research, but no attempts have been made to specify and test it directly.

Meadow and Kahoe's (1984) developmental conception, although not related to age or to a three-component model, comes close to Oerter's suggestion. Meadow and Kahoe's model is based on two motivational dimensions. The first of them is the empirically much researched extrinsic (instrumental, utilitarian, using God to own ends) vs. intrinsic (individual serving religion rather than the other way round) religiousness (Allport, 1950; Allport and Ross, 1967) or consensual vs. committed (Allen and Spilka, 1967) religiousness. The second one proposed by Meadow and Kahoe (1984) themselves is observant or other-directed vs. autonomous religiousness. Meadow and Kahoe hypothesize that when a person comes under the influence of a religious institution he or she has often extrinsic reasons for this, such as stress, crises, or anxieties. The institution then inspires observance (beliefs, ceremony, rituals) among its members. The shift to intrinsic religiousness continues the movement away from self-centered instrumentality and may also contain freedom of dogmatism. The concept of autonomous faith is proposed as a higher stage reached by but a few individuals. The theorists note that such autonomy is not usually promoted by religious institutions. They speculate that mystical experience, intelligence, and education, especially in philosophy, might be influential for this rare shift.

The attitudes toward religion and religious beliefs of children and young people have in recent times quite often been the subject of scholarly research. The results show in general a similar line of development: attitudes toward religion become clearly more negative at the age of puberty, about between ages 13 and 15 (e.g., Hyde, 1963; 1965; Richmond, 1970; Turner, 1970;

1980; Hyde, 1992). These results are consistent with those of earlier studies: the beginning of doubts usually occurs at early puberty, approximately at the ages of 11 to 13 (see Argyle and Beit-Hallahmi, 1975; Turner, 1970).

Francis (1979; 1987; 1989), in whose study the spread of age was quite large, 8-15/16, stated that the change of attitudes to religion among British children and young people clearly began already before the age of puberty. The change toward more negative attitudes was fairly even throughout these ages. No special turning point could be seen. However, Gibson (1989), who used Francis' attitude measure among Scottish secondary-school pupils aged 11 to 16 years, stated that the greatest change occurred between 13 and 14/15. In Greer's study (1981a), according to the same measure, the attitudes of North Irish children from ages 8 to 16 became even a little more positive in 8 to 10 year olds, but afterwards more negative in fairly even increments.

The above-mentioned studies measured a general attitude toward religion or Christianity. Tamminen (1991) arranged the beliefs of his statement measure into nine scales on the basis of factor analyses. For some belief scales, such as "Trust in God" and "Belief in the veracity of the Bible," the developmental lines of 7- to 20-year-old Finnish pupils were similar as in previous studies. The change toward a more negative attitude began already at the age of 9-10, but most noticeable estrangement from the Christian religion took place during puberty, at age 13-15. After that the changes were slight. However, the changes of all beliefs did not follow a uniform line. For instance, a clear change toward denying the legalistic concept of God occurred already in age groups 7/8 and 9/10; after that the change was slight. No noticeable change occurred in the belief in life after death and in the emphasis on religion as the basis of ethics.

The change toward more negative attitude in puberty and thereafter does not necessarily mean denial of religious beliefs but usually an increase in doubt and critical thinking (Turner, 1970; Tamminen, 1991; Hyde, 1990).

The period of puberty, years 12-15, has thus been shown to be a period of transition in the development of religious attitudes—and in religious development in general. Values and attitudes that were considered self-evident in childhood are now being reevaluated. Many factors are related to this critical phase of puberty.

Hyde (1965) and Richmond (1970) see the negative development of attitudes toward religion linked to the development of thinking from the concrete to the abstract. A change in thinking results in criticalness toward earlier beliefs and toward concepts that are too concrete. This phase means also the widening of the social sphere and orientation toward peer groups, gangs and various other forms of youth culture. With age and experience the adolescent learns to recognize new kinds of social values and opinions. Young people also notice the contradiction of values and norms evident in a pluralistic society.

Gender differences in the rhythm of development are discernible in the observation that girls' attitudes start to change on the average earlier than those of boys' (Tamminen, 1991). Universally, in all the studies, girls'—and women's—attitudes toward religion are, on the average, more positive than those of boys and men.

There are denominational differences in the development of religious attitudes—not so much in the direction as in the pace. This is the case in Greer's (1981a) study of the differences between Catholic and Protestant pupils. However, even within the same denomination there are differences between different religious cultures, as in the responses of the Catholic children in church schools in England, Northern Ireland, and the Irish Republic, which may reflect the different position religion occupies in these societies (Kay, 1981; Hyde, 1990).

The development of religious attitudes varies greatly between different individuals. There are also young people whose positive religious attitudes are strengthened at the age of puberty and in adolescence. It is easily understandable that there is no negative attitude change for those who continue to take part in congregational activities, at least not as clearly as for others (Hyde, 1965; Kay, 1981). In fact, this only shows that the various dimensions or components of religiousness are closely related.

The religious atmosphere of home and parents' religiousness seem to explain religious attitudes better in younger children. The development of religious attitudes is also connected to many other factors, such as the peer group, the school community, and the religious education given them at school and in their religious community (Turner, 1970; Francis, 1976; 1979; Tamminen, 1991).

Fishbein and Ajzen (1975) distinguished two basic strategies in transforming attitudes: active participation and persuasive communication. Small group participation and living with others in situations ranging from homes to peer groups, class, and school play a very important part in the transforming of attitudes of schoolchildren. Source of communication and information are abundant, ranging from television and the press to instruction in school and in the religious community. Some of the above-mentioned links with religious attitudes found in the studies fit these strategies. There is only meager evidence of the influence of TV and press on changes of religious attitudes, but they are said to be among the causes for the secularization of at least the European youth during recent decades (Nembach, 1987; Francis, 1988; Tamminen, 1991). Mass media influence is, however, not an independent phenomenon but an aspect of more general modern changes of cultural atmosphere and the influence of various youth cultures.

Ordinarily attitudes change rather slowly, depending of course on their strength and centrality. It is natural that strong and salient attitudes change more slowly than weaker and shallower attitudes. During times of crisis the attitudes toward religion may undergo rather rapid and profound changes.

These have been explained in a variety of attitude change models that are generally known as theories of cognitive consistency. One of the most often quoted is Leon Festinger's theory of cognitive dissonance, which predicts changes of thinking or action as a result of becoming aware of psychological dissonance relations between cognitive elements. It has been used also in relation to some religious phenomena (e.g., Festinger, Riecken, and Schacter, 1956). It can in part also clarify attitude changes in puberty and adolescence.

Religious Experiences in Childhood and Adolescence

In this handbook religious experience is presented in its widest sense and it covers practically the full diversity of religiousness. Religious experiences can also be discussed in a more limited sense. Religious concepts are always based on experiences and these are used as building blocks. It is also common to speak of *intense religious experiences*, which are attached to critical points or decisions arising out of individual, emotionally charged peak experiences, and which may determine the future course of an entire life.

Children's religious experiences have been studied but seldom. At the beginning of the century religious experiences were often considered, but the research focused especially on unusual or extremely strong experiences, such as conversion. According to this early research religious experiences could occur at the earliest only with sexual maturity in puberty (e.g., Hall, 1900). Other, more recent studies have also found that religious experiences take place especially during adolescence. This response was given by most university students in Hay's study (1979). Similarly, in Paffard's (1973) study only few high-school and university students reported religious experiences before adolescence.

This view was supported especially by earlier studies \concerning religious awakening or—often sudden—conversion (Starbuck, 1899; James 1902; Hall, 1904). In many of them the peak of the age distribution of conversions was found to be at the ages of 12-18, a bit later for boys than for girls. Thus in Clark's (1929) study the peak of conversions was on the average at the age of 12.7. Many of the studies were made of subjects belonging religious communities which required conversion. In some denominations conversion or salvation experiences are still normative (see Stark, 1965; Hoge and Smith, 1982). The conversion experiences seem to have become less numerous. In fact, however, the number of such experiences is still quite high according to some new American surveys (see Hoge and Smith, 1982; Meadow and Kahoe, 1984; Benson, Donahue, and Erickson, 1989). In Hay's (1979) British study only four out of 109 university students reported a conversion experience. In Greer's studies (1981b; 1982) among North Irish children and adolescents the proportion of conversion experiences was higher (about 11 percent in 1981 and 4 percent in 1982). Very few Finnish adolescents reported conversion or salvation experiences (Tamminen, 1991). On the other hand, significantly more of their parents told that they had experienced "a religious awakening." About 11 percent (36) of mothers answered the relevant question affirmatively. For only one third of them did this happen between the ages of 12 and 18, for 10 percent at 8-10, and for about 60 percent after age of 18. Correspondingly 3 percent (6) of fathers had experienced "an awakening," the age varying between 6 and 27. Meadow and Kahoe (1984) stated that conversion experiences were also frequently reported to have occurred before and after adolescence. It seems, that though for many the puberty and adolescence years are a time of clear religious decisions, conversion and salvation experiences are not concentrated at that age, but are dispersed over almost the entire age range.

In empirical studies of older adolescents and adults, a great number of respondents claimed to have had "a religious or mystical experience," felt the "presence of God" or experienced "close contact with something holy and sacred" (Hay, 1979, 1987, 1990; Glock and Wuthnow, 1979; Hay and Morisy 1978). But what about religious experiences in childhood?

Bovet (1929) stated early on that all religious experiences typical of adolescence can be found among children. Later empirical studies also seem to show that religious experiences are very common already in childhood. Gote Klingberg (1959) strongly dismissed the earlier notion that late childhood is a religious "cold" phase. After analyzing essay material written by Swedish boys and girls between 9 and 13 years of age on the theme "When I once thought about God . . ." Klingberg considered that religious experiences were very common in childhood. Much the same conclusion was drawn in Elkind and Elkind's (1962) study. Most of their subjects, American fifth-grade students, reported direct experiences of God's presence. In Greer's study (1982) 33 percent of 12-17 year old secondary and grammar school boys and 51 percent of girls expressed that they had sometimes had "an experience of God, e.g., his presence or his help or anything else." He did not find differences between age groups. In another study Greer (1982) found that 38 percent of sixth form boys and 51 percent of girls aged 18-19 years replied affirmatively to the same question. In Tamminen's study (1991) children and adolescents aged 7-20 years were asked the question "Have you at times felt that God is particularly close to you?" According to the responses religious experiences were especially abundant in childhood. The study showed a clear declining trend based on age: many adolescents confirmed in their reports that they had experienced God's nearness in their childhood but not after that. The results concerning experiences of God's guidance and experiences of answers to prayers were similar. In all age-groups religious experiences were more common among girls than among boys. All these studies deal with numinous experiences, feelings of God's nearness.

It may be that the experiences of young children and older adolescents differ qualitatively from each other in some way. However, we have very little research about such differences. Some studies have clarified the circumstances with which children and young people connect their religious experiences. In Klingberg's (1959) study about two-thirds of (9-13 years old) pupils mentioned an emergency situation, such as illness, an accident, danger, loneliness, or encounter with death. Less usual were experiences in nature, moral experiences and pre-arranged devotional experiences. Elkind and Elkind (1962) asked American pupils in the 9th grade two questions. They thought that the replies to the first question ("When do you feel closest to God?") described *"repeated experiences."* The most common answers were: 1) church experiences (45 percent); 2) solitary experiences (17 percent); 3) anxiety and fear experiences (14 percent). The replies to the second question: ("Have you ever had a particular experience of feeling especially close to God?") were characterized *"as acute experiences."* They formed the following groups: 1) appreciation experiences (36 percent); 2) meditation experiences (20 percent); 3) activities in church (15 percent); 4) sorrow experiences (14 percent); and 5) revelation experiences (5 percent). Clearly these results indicate that the way a question is formulated may greatly affect the observed results. Paffard (1973) stated that among young adults the most common situation of a religious experience was loneliness in the evening. In Hay's (1979) study of university students mentioned above, three situations were most often connected to a religious experience: 1) solitude and silence, 2) times of anxiety and 3) times of decision.

In fact, these studies did not deal with the changes of situations by age. Tamminen (1983c; 1991) compared by age groups (7-20) the situations and contexts of God's closeness and guidance which children and adolescent presented in their reports. The most common situations of God's closeness were in almost all age groups those involving an emergency. In puberty, with 13-15 year olds, more than 50 percent of the responses belonged to this category. However, when children in age groups 7-14 said more about the concrete situations of escaping or avoiding danger, older students spoke more frequently of various internal difficulties or encounters with death and sorrow. This tendency may reflect on the one hand the development of thinking from a concrete level to a more abstract level, on the other hand the struggle with inner problems typical for adolescents. Especially younger respondents often described situations of loneliness, being alone or afraid, as situations of God's nearness. In adolescence, among 15-year-olds and older, experiences connected with devotion, e.g., with prayer, and church situations, such as confirmation school and confirmation, became more important. Thus at this age fewer pupils reported experiences of God's closeness, but their experiences were more connected with clearly religious activities and congregational situations. More than children, adolescents talked about experiences connected to inner problems and difficulties. Children had a tendency to focus on a single concrete event, whereas adolescents tended to focus on a larger generality, which is probably related to the normal development of thinking.

There were gender differences in reported personal religious experiences. Girls mentioned encounters with death, prayer and meditation, and church activities clearly more often than boys did, whereas boys told about escaping or avoiding danger and various other difficulties more often than girls (Tamminen, 1991).

Religious Development over the Life Cycle

Early theories and descriptions of religious development focused almost solely on childhood and adolescence. Even in these the earliest, preschool age was very seldom studied. There is still but little research on religious development during the *preschool age*, due partly to the difficulties in collecting data (see Ratcliff, 1988).

Religiousness in *adults* was also almost neglected in early research. Only since the fifties has the entire life span become increasingly the object of researchers' interest. Comprehensive theories have been developed, the best known of them being Erikson's epigenetic theory and Kohlberg's theory of moral development.

Two structural theories concerning life-span religious development have drawn much attention and discussion in recent years: Fowler's (1981) theory of faith development and Oser and Gmünder's (1988) theory of the development of religious judgment. These theories have much in common. They are both structural and they both hypothesize a development in stages. The stages follow each other hierarchically in a certain sequence, each of them forming its own structural unity. The theories also have some common starting points, especially Piaget's work and Kohlberg's theory of the development of moral judgment. Both Fowler and Oser use evidence based on the semi-clinical interview method.

On the other hand, they also have some distinguishing traits. An essential difference appears already in the most central concepts that determine the contents of the development: in Fowler the concept of "faith" and in Oser the concept of "religious judgment."

Faith has, according to Fowler, a very large content. It is the most fundamental category in the human quest for relation to transcendence. It is a dynamic and generic human experience, not only religious. In this definition, Fowler is mainly relying upon Paul Tillich, Richard Niebuhr, and W.C. Smith. Faith is "an orientation of the total person, giving purpose and goal to one's hopes and strivings, thoughts and actions" (Fowler, 1981:14). It is 1) "a dynamic pattern of personal trust in and loyalty to a center or centers of value." It is trust and loyalty 2) "to images and realities of power" and 3) "to a shared master story or core story" (Fowler, 1991:32).

Fowler's theory is eclectic, combining, on the one hand, structural-developmental theories of Piaget and Kohlberg, and on the other hand, psychosocial theories, especially those of Erikson and Levinson (Fowler, 1981). Later, he also incorporated into his theory viewpoints on the development of the self (Kegan, 1982; see Fowler, 1987).

Fowler (1981, 1984, 1987, 1991) considers faith development from several aspects, the form of logic (Piaget), social perspective taking (Selman, 1980), the form of moral judgment (Kohlberg), the bounds of social awareness, the locus of authority, the form of world coherence, and symbolic function.

According to Fowler faith development is "a sequence of stages by which persons shape their relatedness to a transcendent center or centers of value" (Moseley, Jarvin, and Fowler, 1986:1). The stages not only refer to cognitive development, they also reflect the interpretation of cognition and affection. Fowler (1981; 1991) differentiates six stages of faith development. Preceding these is the stage of primal, undifferentiated faith, which covers the first two years of life, corresponding to Erikson's first stage. The following traits are typical for Fowler's six stages:

1) Intuitive-Projective Faith: Stories, gestures, and symbols stimulate imagination combined with emotions to create long-lasting faith images representing both the protective and threatening powers of surrounding one's life.

2) Mythic-Literal Faith: Literally interpreted narratives, myths, beliefs and observances symbolize belonging to the community. God rewards good deeds and punishes bad deeds.

3) Synthetic-Conventional Faith: Composing "a story of my stories," the meaning of life; synthesis of beliefs and values derived from one's significant others. These are not yet objectified for critical reflection.

4) Individuative-Reflective Faith: Individuality and autonomy and, at the same time, a third person perspective. A critical examination of inherited beliefs and values.

5) Conjunctive Faith: A "second naivete," a postcritical readiness for participating in the reality brought to expression in symbol and myth. Combining of deep commitments with openness for the truths of other traditions.

6) Universalizing Faith: Beyond paradox and polarities, oneness with the power of being or God. Passionate, yet detached, spending of the self in love, living in effective anticipatory response to the reality of an emerging commonwealth of love and justice.

Fowler states that stage 2 begins usually at the beginning of school age, stage 3 at early adolescence, stage 4 for many people at the beginning of young adulthood (about age 20) and stage 5 for some people at mid-life (age 35 and beyond). For a great number of adult persons the third stage is the last one. The sixth stage is practically unknown in empirical studies.

The Fowlerian semi-structured interview deals with the life story of the research subjects, their centers of value, and the guiding stories of their lives. The interview broadly charts the development of personality, with religion being only one part of the whole.

Essential in *Oser's theory* is the interpretation of the human being's relation to Ultimate Being (God) and the action of Ultimate Being in human life. As a person interprets the experiences of his or her life, discusses them or prays, as he or she studies religious texts and takes part in the life of a religious community, he/she actualizes the system of rules that concern his/her relationship to the Ultimate Being (Oser and Gmünder, 1988; Oser, 1991). This relation appears in verbal form in "religious judgment," which is "some kind of cognitive pattern of religious knowing of reality" (Oser, 1980:283). Behind the verbal expressions there are religious (narrative) deep structures, latent models for religious knowing. Oser and Gmünder (1988) borrowed the concept of "mother structure" from Piaget. By the "mother structure," they mean the basic religious cognitive structure that is typical for the whole human life span, for all religions, even for atheists. It cannot be reduced to some other thought structure.

Individuals produce religious judgments especially in times of crisis in their lives. Therefore, based on Piaget's and Kohlberg's model, Oser and Gmünder use in the study of the development of religious judgment hypothetical dilemmas, imagined situations in which the relationship to an Ultimate Reality is under stress (Oser, 1980; Oser and Gmünder, 1988).

Oser (1980; 1991; Oser and Gmünder, 1988) distinguishes seven dimensions, which an individual has to balance and relate to each other in order to produce a religious judgment. Each of these dimensions forms a continuum and has its own developmental course. These dimensions are: 1) Freedom versus dependence: At a lower stage an individual tends to see dependence as immediate; and conversely, individual freedom as given directly by God. The higher the stage, the more an individual sees both types of experience as mutually dependent. 2) Transcendence vs. immanence, 3) Hope vs. absurdity, 4) Explanation (transparency) vs. mystery (opacity), 5) Faith (trust) vs. fear (anxiety), 6) The holy versus the profane, 7) Eternity vs. ephemerity.

As an individual relates his or her experience to God, he or she does this in qualitatively different ways during the life cycle, depending on his/her developmental stage. Oser (1991; Oser and Gmünder, 1988) differentiates five stages, which form a hierarchal sequence:

1) Orientation of religious heteronomy (deus ex machina). God is understood as active, intervening unexpectedly in the world, the human being is reactive. The ultimate Being is all-powerful and makes things happen.

2) Orientation of "do ut des" ("give so that you may receive"). God is still an all-powerful being, who may either punish or reward. The human being can, however, influence him by good deeds, promises, and vows.

3) Orientation on absolute autonomy (deism). Transcendence and immanence are separated from each other. The human being is autonomous, responsible for his or her life and the world. Religious and other authorities are often rejected.

4) Orientation on autonomy and salvation plan (Correlation). The human being has an indirect relationship with the Ultimate Being, which gives

meaning and hope and the possibility of human freedom. Many various forms of religiousness emerge, all accepting a divine plan that brings things to a good end.

5) Orientation to religious intersubjectivity and autonomy, universal and unconditional religiosity. Transcendence and immanence interact completely. The Ultimate Being is present in every human commitment and in intersubjective actions. Solidarity with all human beings.

Oser does not present any clear age limits for his stages. The empirical studies made on the basis of the dilemmas, however, show some degree of development of religious judgment with age. In general, the third stage is not possible before the phase of abstract thinking has been reached. For some people the third stage is the final point. Oser and Gmünder (1988) state that this stage can include various forms of religiousness from atheism to extreme religiousness. Schweitzer and Bucher (1989) think that in the case of religiously oriented persons this stage is a transition from stage two to stage four; it can mean the differentiation of personal from congregational religiousness. For nonreligious persons it is the final stage, and it has atheistic and agnostic traits. The scholars have also been interested in the development of "atheists" through these stages, but this research still needs more clarification (Reich, 1993). The fourth stage is in general located at middleage, but it is possible to reach it already in young adulthood (Oser and Gmünder, 1988; Tamminen, 1992). In empirical studies only very few persons have been found at the fifth stage.

Different dilemmas have been used with success in these studies. They do not, however, give exactly identical results, and the story makes a difference. It is essential that the dilemma and its situation are relevant for different persons of various ages.

Besides age, many other things seem to influence the development of religious judgment. Oser (1991:21-22) states that "the courses of individual development strongly depend on biographical circumstances," as on the religious and positive educational climate in the family. There are in the theory still open questions which wait for more empirical research.

One of these questions is the universality of the theory. Cross-cultural data have indicated age-related development across samples. The rates of growth, however, depend on cultural and religious contexts (Oser, 1991).

Oser's theory has also certain philosophical and theological connections. This is shown most clearly in the fifth stage. True, Oser (1991) states that the theory does not say anything about theological models representing the fifth stage. On the other hand, religion gets here a certain meaning and content. Oser (1991:50) points to Tillich, who said that to be religious means to question passionately the meaning of life and to be open for answers even if they trouble us. Such a position makes religion something universally human, even if this is not the usual meaning of the word religion.

One of the credits of Fowler's and Oser's theories is that they have paid attention to and provoked discussion and empirical research concerning religious development in adulthood and in the entire life span (see Bucher and Reich, 1989; Fowler, Nipkow, and Schweitzer, 1991).

Concluding Remarks

Religious development has been described from the point of view of several different theories, even of different paradigms. These theories, and empirical studies based on them, complement each other, creating a total image of religious development; but there are also conflicting notions. There is no "United Grand Theory" of religion or religious development, such as Reich (1991, 1992, 1993) has been looking for on the basis of existing theories. It would be very important and useful to create one, but it seems exceedingly difficult, perhaps entirely impossible. Different theories have very different points of departure, also from the standpoint of their philosophical and theological background. It does not seem probable that they could be resolved in near future. Also the empirical evidence is relatively unsatisfactory. More longitudinal data are needed, and there are many religious cultures outside the Judeo-Christian sphere of influence, as well as subcultures inside it, that have hardly been touched by researchers at all. Any generalizations across the cultures are, in this situation, premature. Even the existing measurements and descriptions are in many cases still relatively inaccurate or artificial.

All these reservations and criticisms do not, however, change the impression that sound research has been accumulating. Its integration has also created interesting perspectives. We expect that future developments in general psychology will lead to further progress also with respect to the development of religious experience.

REFERENCES

Abelson, R. P., and M. J. Rosenberg

1967 Symbolic psycho-logic: A model of attitudinal cognition. In *Readings in attitude theory*, edited by M. Fishbein. New York: Wiley.

Abou-Allam, A.

1964 *A study of difficulty of different forms of verbal analogies*. Doctoral dissertation, Mohammed College, Ann Arbor, MI.

Ainsworth, D.

1961 *A study of some aspects of the growth of religious understanding of children aged between 5 and 11 years*. Dipl. Ed. Thesis, University of Manchester.

Allen, R. O., and B. Spilka

1967 Committed and consensual religion: A specification of religion & prejudice relationships. *Journal for the Scientific Study of Religion* 6: 341-348.

Allport, G. W.

1950 *The individual and his religion*. New York: Macmillan

Allport, G. W., and J. M. Ross
1967 Personal religious orientation and prejudice. *Journal of Personality and Social Psychology* 5: 432-443.
Argyle, M., and B. Beit-Hallahmi
1975 *The social psychology of religion*. London: Routledge & Kegan Paul.
Babin, P.
1964 The idea of God: Its evolution between the ages 11 and 19. In *From religious experience to religious attitude*, edited by A. Godin. Brussels: Lumen Vitae.
Beechick, R. A.
1974 *Children's understanding of parables: A developmental study*. Doctoral dissertation, Arizona State University.
Benson, P. L., J. D. Donahue, and J. A. Erickson
1989 Adolescence and Religion: A Review of the Literature from 1970 to 1986. *Research in the Social Scientific Study of Religion* 1: 153-181.
Bovet, P.
1929 *Le sentiment religieux et la psychologie de l'enfant* (The psychological sentiment and child psychology). Neuchatel - Paris.
Brown, G., and C. Desforces
1979 *Piaget's theory: A psychological critique*. London: Routledge & Kegan Paul.
Brown, L. B.
1966 Egocentric thought in petitionary prayer: A cross-cultural study. *The Journal of Social Psychology* 68: 197-210.
1967 Some attitudes underlying petitionary prayer. In From cry to word, edited by A. Godin. Brussels: Lumen Vitae.
Bucher, A.
1985 *The development of religious identity: Religious judgment, its stages and its genesis.*
Bucher, A. A., and K. H. Reich
1989 *Entwicklung von Religiositat. Grundlagen - Theorienprobleme - Praktische Anwendung* (Development of religiousness. Bases - problems of theory - practical applications). Freiburg: Universitatsverlag.
Clark, E. T.
1929 *The psychology of religious awakening*. New York: Macmillan.
Clark, W. H.
1971 Intense religious experience. In *Research on religious development: A comprehensive handbook*, edited by M.P. Strommen. New York: Hawthorn.
Deconchy, J-P.
1965 The idea of God: Its emergence between 7 and 16 Years. In *From religious experience to a religious attitude*, edited by A. Godin. Chicago: Loyola University Press.
1967 *Structure genetique de l'idee de Die* (Structural development of the concept of God). Brussels: Lumen Vitae.
1968 God and parental images. The masculine and feminine in religious free associations. In *From Cry to Word*, edited by A. Godin. Brussels: Lumen Vitae.
Dykstra, C., and S. Parks
1986 *Faith development and Fowler*. Birmingham, AL: Religious Education Press.
Elkind, D.
1961 The child's conception of his religious denomination I: The Jewish child. *Journal of Genetic Psychology* 99: 209-225.
1962 The child's conception of his religious denomination II: The Catholic child. *Journal of Genetic Psychology* 101: 185-193.
1963 The child's conception of his religious denomination III: The Protestant child. *Journal of Genetic Psychology* 103: 291-304.
1964 Piaget's semi-clinical interview and the study of spontaneous religion. *Journal for the Scientific Study of Religion* 4: 40-47.
1971 The development of religious understanding in children and adolescents. In *Research on religious development: A comprehensive handbook*, edited by M.P. Strommen. New York: Hawthorn.

Elkind, D., and S.F. Elkind
1962 Varieties of religious experience in young adolescents. *Journal for the Scientific Study of Religion* 2: 103-111.
Erickson, J. A.
1992 Adolescent religious development and commitment: A structural equation model of the role of family, peer group, and educational influences. *Journal for the Scientific Study of Religion* 31: 131-152.
Erikson, E. H.
[1950]
1963 *Childhood and society*, 2nd ed. New York: Norton.
1958 *Young man Luther: A study in psychoanalysis and history*. New York: Norton.
Erikson, E. H.
1959 *Identity and the Life Cycle*. New York: International Universities Press.
1964 *Insight and responsibility. Lectures on the ethical implications of psychoanalytic insight.* New York: Norton.
1968 *Identity: Youth and crisis*. New York: Norton.
1969 *Gandhi's Truth: On the origins of militant nonviolence*. New York: Norton.
1982 *The life cycle completed: A review*. New York: Norton.
Feinstein, D., and S. Krippner
1988 Personal mythology. *The psychology of your evolving self. Using ritual, dreams, and imagination to discover you inner story*. Los Angeles: Jeremy P. Tarcher.
Festinger, L., H. W. Riecken, and S. Schachter
1956 *When prophecy fails*. New York: Harper.
Fishbein, M., and I. Ajzen.
1975 *Belief, attitude, intention and behavior: An introduction to theory and research.* Reading, MA: Addison-Wesley.
Flavell, J. H.
1985 *Cognitive development*, 2nd ed. Englewood Cliffs, NJ: Prentice-Hall.
Fowler, J.
1981 *Stages of faith. The Psychology of human development and the quest for meaning*. San Francisco: Harper & Row.
1984 *Becoming adult, becoming Christian: Adult development and Christian faith.* San Francisco: Harper & Row.
1987 *Faith development and pastoral care*. Philadelphia: Fortress.
1991 Stages in faith consciousness. In *Religious Development in Childhood and Adolescence*. edited by F. K. Oser and W. G. Scarlett. San Francisco: Jossey-Bass.
Fowler, J. W., K. E. Nipkow, and F. Schweitzer (Eds.)
1991 *Stages of faith and religious development: Implications for church education, and society*. New York: Crossroad.
Francis, L. J.
1976 *An enquiry into the concept "readiness for religion."* Doctoral dissertation, University of Cambridge.
1977 Readiness for research in religion. *Learning for Living* 16: 109-114.
1978 Attitude and longitude: A Study in measurement. *Character Potential: A Record of Research* 8: 119-130.
1979 Measurement Reapplied: Research into the child's attitude toward religion. *British Journal of Religious Education* 1: 45-51.
1984 Roman Catholic schools and pupil attitudes in England. *Lumen vitae* 39: 99-108.
1987 The decline in attitudes toward religion among 8-15 year olds. *Educational studies* 13: 125-134.
1988 Monitoring attitude towards Christianity during childhood and adolescence. *Kasvatus ja uskonto*. Toim. M. Pyysiäinen. Porvoo: WSOY, 230-247.
1989 Drift from the churches: Secondary school pupils' attitudes toward Christianity. *British Journal of Religious Education* 11: 76-86.
Freud, S.
[1927]

1961 *Die Zukunft einer Illusion*. Gesammelte Werke XIV, London. (The future of an illusion. In Standard Edition, Vol. 21).

Gibson, H. M.
1989 Attitudes to religion and science among schoolchildren aged 11 to 16 Years in a Scottish city. *Journal of Empirical Theology* 2: 5-26.

Glock, C. Y., and R. Wuthnow
1979 Departures from convential religion: the nominally religious, the nonreligious, and the alternatively religious. In *The religious dimension*, edited by R. Wuthnow. New York: Academic Press.

Godin, A., and A. Coupez
1957 *Religious projective pictures. Research in religious psychology*. Brussels: Lumen Vitae

Godin, A., and M. Hallez
1965 Parental images and divine paternity. In *From religious experience to a religious attitude*, edited by A. Godin. Chicago: Loyola University Press.

Goldman, R.
1964 *Religious thinking from childhood to adolescence*. London: Routledge & Kegan Paul.
1965 *Readiness for religion*. London: Routledge & Kegan Paul.

Graebner, O. E.
1960 *Child concept of God*. Seventeenth yearbook 1960, Lutheran Education Association. River Forest, IL.

Greer, J. E.
1980 Stages in the development of religious thinking. *British Journal of Religious Education* 3: 24-28.
1981a Religious attitudes and thinking in Belfast pupils. *Educational Research* 23: 177-189.
1981b Religious experience and religious education. *Search* 4: 23-34.
1982 The religious experience of Northern Irish pupils. *The Irish Catechist* 6: 49-58.
1990 *The persistance of religion. A study of sixth form religion in Northern Ireland, 1968-1988*. A paper at ISREV VII, Dronningen.

Gruehn, D. W.
1956 *Die Frömmigkeit der Gegenwart* (The piety of the present). Grundtatsachen der empirischen Psychologie. Munster: Aschendorfsche Verlagsbuchhandlung.

Hall, G.S.
1900 The religious content and the child-mind. In *Principles of religious education*, edited by N.M. Butler et al. New York: Longmans, Green.
1904 *Adolescence, its psychology, and its relations to physiology, anthropology, sociology, sex, crime, religion, and education*, 2 vols. New York: D. Appleton.

Harms, E.
1944 The development of religious experience in children. *American Journal of Sociology* 50: 112-122.

Hartman, S. G.
1985 *Children's philosophy of life*. Dissertation Malmö: GWK Gleerup.

Hartman, S. G.
1986 *Children's philosophy of life*. Studies in Education and Philosophy 22. Stockholm: CWK Gleerup.

Hartman, S. G., S. Pettersson, and G. Westling.
1973 *Vad funderar barn på?* (What do children think about?) Stockholm: Utbildningsforlaget.

Hay, D.
1979 Religious experience amongst a group of post-graduate students: A qualitative study. *Journal for the Scientific Study of Religion* 18: 164-182.
1987 *Exploring Inner Space: Is God still possible in the twentieth century*. London: Mowbray.
1990 *Religious Experience Today: Studying the facts*. London: Mowbray.

Hay, D., and A. Morisy
1978 Reports of ecstatic, paranormal or religious experience in Great Britain and the United States: A comparison of trends. *Journal for the Scientific Study of Religion* 17:255-268.

Helve, H.
1993 *The world view of young people. A longitudinal study of Finnish youth living in a suburb*

of metropolitan Helsinki. Annales Academiae Scientiarum Fennica B 267. Helsinki: Suomalainen tiedeakatemia.

Heywood, D.
1986 Piaget and faith development: A true marriage of minds? *British Journal of Religious Education* 8: 72-78.

Hilliard, F. H.
1960 Ideas of God among secondary school children. *Religion in Education* 27: 14-19.

Hoge, D. R., and E. I. Smith
1982 Normative and non-normative religious experience among high-school youth. *Journal for the Scientific Study of Religion* 43: 69-82.

Hutsebaut, D., and D. Verhoeven
1991 The adolescents representation of God from age 12 to 18. *Journal of Empirical Theology* 4: 59-72.

Hyde, K. E.
1963 Religious concepts and religious attitudes I and II. *Educational Review* 15: 132-141, 271-226.
1965 *Religious learning in adolescence*. Educational Monographs VIII. University of Birmingham, Institute of Education, Edinburgh: Oliver & Boy.
1990 *Religion in childhood and adolescence: A comprehensive review of the research.* Birmingham, AL: Religious Education Press.
1992 Adolescents and religion. In *Handbook of youth ministry*, edited by D. Ratcliff and J.A. Davies. Birmingham, AL: Religious Education Press.

Inhelder, B., and J. Piaget
1958 *The growth of logical thinking from childhood to adolescence*, translated by A. Parsons and S. Milgrom. New York: Basic Books.

Jaakkola, M.
1988 *Peruskoululaisten elämänkysymykset* (Life questions of schoolchildren). Master thesis, Faculty of Theology, University of Helsinki.

James W.
1902 *Varieties of religious experience*. New York: Longmans.

Jung, C. G.
1943 *Die Psychologie des Unbewussten*. (English in Collected Works, Vol. 7). Zurich: Rascher.
1944 *Psychologie und Alchemie*. (English: Psychology and alchemy. Collected Works. Vol. 12) Zurich: Rascher.

Kay, W.
1981 *Religious thinking, attitudes and personality among secondary pupils in England and Ireland*. Doctoral dissertation. Reading.

Kegan, R.
1982 *The evolving self: Problems and process in human development*. Cambridge, MA: Harvard University Press.

Klein, M.
[1932]
1975 *The psycho-analysis of children*, translated by A. Strachey and revised by H.A. Thorner in collab. with A. Strachey. New York: Delacorte Press.

Klingberg, G.
1959 A Study of religious experience in children from 9 to 13 years of age. *Religious Education* 54: 211-216.

Koppe, W. A.
1973 *How persons grow in Christian community*. Philadelphia: Fortress.

Larsen, S.
1990. *The mythic imagination: Your quest for meaning through personal mythology*. New York: Bantam.

Long, D., D. Elkind, and B. Spilka
1967 The child's conception of prayer. *Journal for the Scientific Study of Religion* 6: 101-109.

Ludwig, D.J., T. Weber, and T.D. Iben

1974 Letters to God: A study of children's religious concepts. *Journal of Psychology and Theology* 2: 31-35.

Martinsson, E.
1968 *Religionsundervisning och mognad* (Religious education and maturity). En jämförande studie av förmågan att tänka abstrakt, förstå liknelser och religiösa begrepp hos barn i årskurserna 2, 4 och 6. Lärarhögskolan i Stockholm.

McDargh, J.
1983 *Psychoanalytic object relations theory and the study of religion: On faith and the imaging of God.* Lanham, MD: University Press of America.

McGrady, A. G.
1987 A Metaphor and model paradigm of religious thinking. *British Journal of Religious Education* 2: 136-141.
1990 *The development of religious thinking: A comparison of metaphoric and Piagetian operational paradigms.* Doctoral dissertation.
1992 *Metaphorical and operational aspects of religious thinking: A discussion in the light of research with Irish Catholic pupils.* A paper at ISREV VIII in Banff, Alberta, Canada.
1993 Glimpsing the divine: Metaphor and religious thinking. In *Religion and culture in dialogue*, edited by D. Line. Dublin: Columba Press.

Meadow, M. J., and R. D. Kahoe
1984 *Psychology of religion: Religion in individual lives.* New York: Harper & Row.

Moseley, R. M., D. Jarvin, and J. W. Fowler
1986 *Manual for faith development research.* Atlanta, GA: Center for Faith Development, Candler School of Theology.

Murphy, R. J. L.
1979 *An investigation into some aspects of the development of religious thinking in children aged between six and eleven years.* Doctoral dissertation, St. Andrews University.

Nelsen, H. M., R. H. Potvin, and J. Shields
1977 *The religion of children.* Boys Town Center for the Study of Youth Development. Washington D.C.: United States Catholic Conference.

Nelson, M. O.
1971 The concept of God and feelings toward parents. *Journal of Individual Psychology* 27: 46-49.

Nembach, U.
1987 *Jugend und Religion in Europa* (Youth and religion in Europe). Frankfurt am Main: Peter Lang.

Nipkow, K. E.
1988 The issue of God in adolescence under growing post-Christian conditions: A Württenbergian survey. In *Kasvatus ja uskonto.* Toim. M. Pyysiäinen. Porvoo: WSOY, 187-200.

Oerter, R.
1969 *Moderne Entwicklungspsychologie* (Modern developmental psychology). Donauwörth: Verlag Ludwig Auer.

Olson, J. M., and M. P. Zanna
1993 Attitudes and attitude change. *Annual Review of Psychology* 44: 117-154.

Oser, F.
1980 Stages of religious judgment. In *Toward moral and religious maturity.* The First International Conference on Moral and Religious Development. Morristown, NJ: Silver Burdett.
1991 The development of religious judgment. In *Religious development in childhood and adolescence*, edited by F.K. Oser and W.G. Scarlett. San Francisco: Jossey-Bass.

Oser, F., and G. Gmünder
1988 *Der Mensch: Stufen seiner religiosen Entwicklung* (The human being: The stages of his religious development). Gütersloh: Gütersloher Verlagshaus Gerd Mohn.

Oser, F., K. H. Reich, and A. Bucher
1991 *Development of belief and unbelief in childhood and adolescence.* A Paper at 5th Symposium for Psychology of Religion, Leuven.

Paffard, M.
1973 *Inglorious Wordsworths: A study of some trancendental experiences in childhood and adolescence*. London: Hodder & Stoughton.

Parks, S.
1986 *The critical years: The young adult search for a faith to live by*. San Francisco: Harper & Row.

Peatling, J. H.
1973 *The incidence of concrete and abstract religious thinking in the interpretation of three bible stories by pupils enrolled in grades four through twelve in selected schools in the Episcopal Church in the United States of America*. Doctoral dissertation, New York University.
1974 Cognitive development in pupils in grades four through twelve: The incidence of concrete and abstract religious thinking in American children. *Character Potential: A Record of Research* 7: 52-61.
1977 Cognitive development: Religious thinking in children, youth and adults. *Character Potential: A Record of Research* 8: 100-115.

Peatling, J. H., and C. W. Laabs
1973 *A comparison of data from a Lutheran sample of students and the original Episcopalian sample results, with some reference of other analyses undertaken using Laabs' Lutheran data*. Doctoral dissertation.
1975 Cognitive development of pupils in grades four through twelve: A comparative study of Lutheran and Episcopalian children and youth. *Character Potential: A Record of Research* 7: 107-115.

Peatling, J. H., C. W. Laabs, and T. B. Newton
1975 Cognitive development: A three-sample comparison of means on the Peatling Scale of Religious Thinking. *Character Potential: A Record of Research* 7: 159-162.

Pettersson, S.
1969 *Mognad och abstract stoff* (Maturation and abstract material). En studie av barns sätt att uppfatta visst abstrakt stoff vid en lektionsserie i religionskunskap i årskurs fyra. Pedagogisk-psykologiska institutionen. Lärarhögskolan i Stockholm.

Piaget, J.
[1929]
1977 *The child's conception of the world*, translated by J. and A. Tomlinson. St. Albans: Frogmore.
1972 Intellectual evolution from adolescence to adulthood. *Human Development* 15: 1-12.

Pirinen, H.
1983 *Nuorten elämänkysymykset identiteetin etsimisenä* (English summary: Life problems in adolescence: Young peoples search for identity) Doctoral dissertation, Helsinki: Suomalaisen teologisen kirjallisuuden seura 135.

Potvin, R. H.
1977 Adolescent God images. *Review of Religious Research* 19: 3-53.

Potvin, H., D. H. Hoge, and H. M. Nelsen
1976 *Religions and American youth: with emphasis on Catholic adolescents and young adults*. Washington D.C.: United States Catholic Conference.

Ratcliff, D. (Ed.)
1988 *Handbook of preschool religious education*. Birmingham, AL: Religious Education Press.

Reich, K. H.
1991 Integrating different theories. The case of religious development. *Journal of Empirical Theology* 6: 39-49.
1992 Religious development across the life span: Conventional and cognitive developmental approaches. In *Life-Span Development and Behavior* 11: 145-188.
1993 Cognitive-developmental approaches to religiousness: Which version for which purpose? *The International Journal for the Psychology of Religion* 3: 145-171.

Richmond, R. C.
1970 *Maturity of religious judgments and differences of religious attitudes between the ages*

of 13 and 16 Years. Dipl. in psychology of childhood. University of Birmingham.
1972 Maturity of religious judgments and differences of religious attitude between the ages of thirteen and sixteen years. *Educational Review* 24: 225-236.

Rizzuto, A.-M.
1979 *The birth of the living God. A psychoanalytic study*. Chicago: University of Chicago Press.
1991 Religious development: A psychoanalytic point of view. *Religious Development in Childhood and Adolescence* 52: 47-60.

Robinson, M. P.
1961 The "Lumen Vitae" religious projective pictures, Presented as A group Test on Lantern Slides. *Child and Adult before God*, edited by A. Godin. Brussels: Lumen Vitae.

Rokeach, M.
1972 *Beliefs, attitudes and values. A theory of organization and change*. San Francisco: Jossey-Bass.

Rosenberg, M. J.
1967 Cognitive structure and attitudinal affect. In *Readings in attitude theory and measurement,* edited by M. Fishbein, New York: Wiley.
1989 Die Entwicklung von Gebetskonzepten. (Development of the concepts of prayer). In *Entwicklung von Religiosität: Grundlagen - Theorieprobleme - Praktische Anwendung,* edited by A. A. Bucher and K. H. Reich. Freiburg: Universitatsverlag.

Scarlett, W. G., and L. Perriello
1991 The development of prayer in adolescence. *Religious Development in Childhood and Adolescence* 52: 63-76.

Schutze, F.
1981 Prozessstrukturen des Lebenslaufs (The structures of biographical processes). In *Biographie in handlungswissenschaftlicher Perspektive*, edited by J. Matthes, A. Pfeifenberge, and M. Stosberg. Nürnberg: Verlag der nürnberger Forschungsvereinigung.
1984 Kognitive Figuren des autobiographischen Stegreiferzählens (Cognitive figures of autobiographical narration). In *Biographie und soziale Wirklichkeit. Neue Beiträge und Forschungsperspektiven,* edited by M. Kohli and G. Robert Stuttgart: J.B. Metzlersche Verlagsbuchhandlung.

Schweitzer, F.
1987 *Lebensgeschichte und Religion* (Life story and religion). Religiose Entwicklung und Erziehung im Kindes- und Jugendalter. München: Chr. Kaiser.

Schweitzer, F., and A. A. Bucher
1989 Schwierigkeiten mit Religion. (Difficulties with Religion). Zur subjektiven Wahrnehmung religiöser Entwicklung. In *Entwicklung von Religiösität: Grundlagen - Theorieprobleme - Praktische Anwendung*, edited by A. A. Bucher and K. H. Reich. Freiburg: Universitatsverlag.

Selman, R. L.
1980 *The growth of interpersonal understanding*. New York: Academic Press.

Slee, N.
1983 Parable teaching: Exploring new worlds. *British Journal of Religious Education* 5: 134-138, 146.
1987 The development of religious thinking: Some linguistic considerations. *British Journal of Religious Education* 9: 60-69.

Spilka, B., J. Addison, and M. Rosensohn
1975 Parents, self, and God: A test of competing theories of individual-religion relationships. *Review of Religious Research* 16: 154-165.

Starbuck, E. D.
[1899]
1911 *The psychology of religion: An empirical study of the growth of religious consciousness*, 3rd ed. New York and Melbourne: Walter Scott.

Stark, R.
1965 Social context and religious experience. *Review of Religious Research* 7: 17-28.

Strommen, M. P.
1974 *Five cries of youth*. New York: Harper & Row.
Strunk, O.
1959 Perceived relationships between parental and deity concepts. *Psychological Newsletter*. New York University, 10.
Tamminen, K.
1975 *Lasten ja nuorten elämänkysymykset uskontokasvatuksessa* (Life questions of children and young people in religious education). Suomalaisen teologisen kirjallisuusseuran julkaisuja 99. Helsinki.
1976 Research concerning the development of religious thinking in Finnish students: A report of results. *Character Potential: A Record of Research*: 7, 206-219.
1981a *Lasten ja nuorten uskonnollinen kehitys 1* (The religious development of children and young people I). Helsinki: University of Helsinki, Institute of Practical Theology, Uskonnonpedagogiikan julkaisuja (Publications on Religious Education) B 5.
1981b *Lasten ja nuorten uskonnolliset kokemukset* (Religious experiences of children and young people). Helsinki: University of Helsinki, Institut of Practical Theology, Uskonnonpedagogiikan julkaisuja (Publications on Religious Education) B 6.
1983a *Lasten ja nuorten uskonnolliset käsitteet kouluiässä 1: ajattelu ja käsitys Raamatusta* (Religious concepts of children and young people in school-age 1: Thinking and the concept of the Bible). Helsinki: University of Helsinki, Institute of Practical Theology, Uskonnonpedagogiikan julkaisuja (Publications on Religious Education) B 9.
1983b *Lasten ja nuorten uskonnolliset käsitteet kouluiässä 2: jumalakuva, rukouskäsitys ja käsitys kuolemasta* (Religious concepts of children and young people in school-age 2: Image of God, concept of prayer and concept of death).
1983c *Religious experiences of children and young people*. Research Reports on Religious Education C 2, Institute of Practical Theology, University of Helsinki.
1985 *Mihin koululaiset ja heidän vanhempansa uskovat?* (What do pupils and their parents believe in?) Helsinki: University of Helsinki, Institute of Practical Theology, Uskonnonpedagogiikan julkaisuja (Publications on Religious Education) B 14.
1988 *Existential questions in early* youth and adolescence. Research Reports on Religious Education C5/1988. Institute of Practical Theology, University of Helsinki.
1991 *Religious development in childhood and youth. An empirical study*. Annales Academiae Scientiarum Fennicae B 259. Helsinki: Suomalainen tiedeakatemia (Distribution: Helsinki: Tiedekirja).
1992 *Comparing Oser's and Fowler's developmental stages on the basis of empirical studies among Finnish young adults and adults*. A paper presented at ISREV VIII, August, in Banff, Alberta, Canada.
Tamminen, K., R. Vianello, J-M Jaspard, and D. Ratcliff
1988 The religious concepts of preschoolers. In *Handbook of preschool religious education*, edited by D. Ratcliff. Birmingham, AL: Religious Education Press.
Thouless, R. H., and L. B. Brown
1965 Petitionary Prayer: Belief in its approriateness and causal efficacy among adolescent girls. In *From religious experience to a religious attitude*, edited by A. Godin. Chicago: Loyola University Press.
Thun, T.
1963 *Die religiöse Entscheidung der Jugend* (The religious decision of adolescents). Stuttgart: Enst Klett.
1964 *Die Religion des Kindes* (The religion of a child). Zweite, durchges. Aufl. Stuttgart: Ernst Klett.
Thurstone, L. L., and E. J. Chave
1929 *The measurement of attitude: A psychophysical method and some experiments with a scale for measuring attitude toward the church*. Chicago: University of Chicago Press.
Turner, E. B.
1970 *Religious understanding and religious attitudes in male urban adolescents*. Doctoral dissertation, The Queen's University of Belfast.
1980 General cognitive ability and religious attitudes in two school systems. *British Journal*

of Religious Education 2: 136-141.

Vergote, A.
1981 Overview and theoretical perspectives. In *The parental figures and the representaiton of God*, edited by A. Vergote. The Hague: Mouton.

Vergote, A., A. Tamayo, L. Pasquali, M. Bonami, M. R. Pattyn, and A. Custers
1969 Concept of God and parental images. *Journal for the Scientific Study of Religion* 8: 79-87.

Vianello, R.
1980 *Ricerche psicologiche sulla religiosita infantile* (Psychological research on the religion of children). Firenze: Giunti.

Vianello, R., K. Tamminen, and D. Ratcliff
1992 The religious concepts of children. In *Handbook of childrens' religious education*, edited by D. Radcliff. Birmingham, AL: Religious Education Press.

Virkkunen, T.P.
1975 *Yksilön uskonnollinen kehitys* (The religious development of an individual). Suomalaisen teologisen kirjallisuusseuran julkaisuja 94. Helsinki.

Waern, Y.
1982 Ymmärtämisprosessit (The processes of understanding). In *Johdatus kognitiiviseen psykologiaan* (Introduction to cognitive psychology), edited by E. Hjelmquist, L. Sjöberg, and H. Montgomery. Vaasa: Gaudeamus.

Zeininger, K.
1929 *Magische Geisteshaltung im Kindesalter und ihre Bedeutung fur die religiöse Entwicklung* (Magical spirituality and its meaning for religious development). Leipzig.

Wulff, D. M.
1991 *Psychology of religion. Classic and contemporary views.* New York: Wiley.

14

Cognitive Theory and Religious Experience

BEVERLY J. (MACY) McCALLISTER

LIMITATIONS AND AMBITIONS

The cognitive "revolution" is now more than thirty years old. Now the interests of many cognitive psychologists are directed toward topics of particular interest to the scientific study of religious experiences: recollected experiences (Tulving, 1987), emotions (Zajonc, Murphy, and Inglehart, 1989) and how goals shape possible selves (Markus and Nurius, 1986). How could such quintessential human characteristics as these have been ignored for so long? After all, hadn't William James, lauded by cognitive psychologists as well as psychologists of religion, insightfully described these characteristics, long before the "revolution"? But during the early years in cognitive psychology, it was important that time be spent in laboratories identifying the general cognitive processes and experimental paradigms that would define cognitive psychology as a field. Recently the significance of this laboratory work has been called into question by ecologically oriented psychologists. They object that experimental procedures such as learning a list of words contributes very little to understanding remembering in the "outside world" (Neisser, 1988:356). Lab workers respond that, remembering in the laboratory and in the real world share both similarities and differences (Tulving, 1983:145-146). Rememberers in experiments do not "leave their minds outside the laboratory doors." Both general process and applied approaches are necessary for the advancement of a scientific discipline. One challenge facing an applied field such as the psychology of religion is to consider whether or not the general processes identified in the laboratory are operative in religion and how they, perhaps with otherwise heretofore undetected processes, function in a particular individual's performance on a task within a specific context (Isen and Hastorf, 1982).

While some cognitive psychologists cite the contributions James made to psychology in his *Principles of Psychology*, the contributions James made to psychology as expressed in *The Varieties of Religious Experience: A Study of Human Nature* have generally been ignored by cognitive psychologists. But James maintained that the "religious propensities of man must be at least as interesting as any other facts pertaining to his mental constitution" (James, 1902:22). Furthermore, "No account of the universe in its totality can be final which leaves these other [nonrational/mystical] forms of consciousness quite disregarded . . . they forbid a premature closing of our accounts with reality" (James, 1902:305). Therefore, as the cognitive accounts with reality and in particular our psychological understanding of religious experiences are far from closed, the application of cognitive research to the scientific study of religion could be useful to both fields. In the scientific study of religion, cognitive psychologists could find sought-after examples among religious individuals who are self-consciously aware of vividly recollected experiences, who feel profoundly moved by emotive experiences, who are committed to keeping memories of the past alive and who act out the ultimate concerns/goals according with their self-concepts (schemas). Such religious examples could help refine such conceptually fuzzy notions as self-schemas, since many religious self-schemas are particularly salient; and salience is important in measuring the effects of schemas (Taylor and Crocker, 1981). Among psychologists of religion, the scientific psychologist of religion who only focuses on behavior, motives, and attitudes without accounting for mental operations has not accounted for reality. For instance, attribution theory has figured prominantly in the psychology of religion, but unless, as Rogers, Kuiper, and Kirker (1977) point out, the cognitive conditions under which self-related information is made available are known, attributions can not be understood.

For depth psychologies of religion, what Freud described as transcontextual associations of concepts and what Jung described as innate transcontextual archetypes ("a kind of readiness to produce over and over again the same or similar mythical results," Jung, 1943:63) may alternatively be described in terms of other cognitive processes which also influence the availability of personal knowledge and performance, but which depend more on the immediate context and task demands than most depth psychologists tend to acknowledge. How much, for example, is the first word that comes to mind during free association influenced by a repressed childhood experience, or by cognitive processes which affect a word's availability such as encoding specificity (Tulving and Thomson, 1973), serial position (Greene, 1986), or mood dependency (Bower, 1981)?

Integrating cognitive research into the study of religion is fraught with challenges. The interpretive validity of a psychological understanding of religious experiences will not begin to be realized until it has been shown how cognitive processes and structures interact not only with motives, emotions, and behavior but with social and somatic influences as well (Isen and Hastoff, 1982). Even James seemed to be of two minds about the study of cognition and religion. The James of *Principles of Psychology* seemed to ignore the James of *Varieties*. For example, the theory of emotion/cognition that James expounded in *Principles*—perceptions prompt bodily changes which prompt feeling (James, 1890:13)—was not even mentioned in *Varieties,* despite the central role James awarded to feelings associated with religious experiences (Wulff, 1991). James's interest in both cognition and religious experiences will not be furthered by psychologists who, perhaps because they confound religious method (theology/philosophy) with religion as a subject matter, avoid the subject as they avoid the method. But neither will James's interests in both cognition and religious experiences be furthered by narrow understandings of metaphysical issues. For instance, when the cognitive psychologists Lachman, Lachman, and Butterfield (1979) described religious methods in general as being based on divinely revealed axioms, they ignored the refutations of such propositional theology that dominated twentieth-century theology (Hick, 1967). Nor will James's interest in both cognition and religious experiences be furthered by cognitive psychologies not rooted in empirical research. For instance, Watts and Williams' (1988) "relating" of an unrepresentative cognitive psychology to religious knowing in order to discuss "direct religious knowing" (p.3) suggests a more metaphysical than psychological agenda.

The multidimensional nature of religion and the variety of religious experiences require a certain sensitivity; and this sensitivity needs to be extended to cognition where the relatively subtle effects of mental activities are often disputed and confused. Mood-dependency, for example, is a subtle effect: the effect occurs in some mood-dependent studies but is absent in other similar experiments (Bower and Mayer, 1989). Mood-dependency occurs when recall performance under mood congruent conditions (i.e., happy-happy) exceeds performance under incongruent conditions (i.e., happy-sad). Mood-dependency effects may disappear depending upon the intensity of the moods, perceived event-mood causality, or whether the event was mentally generated (i.e., imagining). Describing such a basic mental act as remembering is disputed and occasionally confused. Cognitive psychologists disagree about how many memory systems there are and about the relationship between these hypothetical systems (Tulving, 1983; Cohen, 1984). Moreover, definitions of key cognitive concepts differ. For instance, Tulving (1993) wrote that episodic memory mediates people's ability to remember personally experienced events in a "certain situation at a certain time" (p.67), while Nelson (1993) states that the "specific identification of time and place does not seem to be necessarily part of episodic recall" (p.7). All told, sensitivity to the variety and controversies in the study of religion and cognition may help avoid the Skinnerian creation of a variety of religious mental experiences ex nihilo.

In general, cognitive psychology investigates how people think, learn, perceive, remember, and represent knowledge. Many of the contemporary cognitive psychologists considered in this chapter start with three basic assumptions: the existence of mental processes, that people actively process knowledge, and that mental processes are inferred from behavioral measures of the time taken to complete a task and how accurately the task was completed (Ashcraft, 1989). The cognitive research in this chapter uses mental processes as an independent variable, measuring how processing affects remembering, reaction times, word pairs and word/paragraph fragment completion tasks. Much of the cognitive research applied to the study of religion does not manipulate cognitive processes, and instead uses such indirect measures as content analysis or paper and pencil tests.

This chapter will consider how aspects of the four following religious experiences as interpreted by selected psychologists might be reinterpreted in light of some new research in contemporary cognitive psychology: religious training (including fundamentalism and prayer) as interpreted by Ronald Goldman and his followers, religious rituals as interpreted by Sigmund Freud, dramatic conversion as interpreted by William James, and altered states as interpreted by Carl Jung. The cognitive research presented was taken from a much larger body of work and was selected for its possible relevance to the study of religious experiences. The primary objective of this chapter will be to suggest how, at this fetal stage of integrating a contemporary cognitive approach into the scientific study of religion, the intrapsychic aspects of four religious experiences might be interpreted. To engage in such an enterprise at this point will be to "pick at" more comprehensive theories, while not being able to provide equally comprehensive cognitive alternatives, and to speculate beyond what many consider to be the primary advantage of using a cognitive approach, namely, its experimental orientation. However, since as some claim the scientific psychology of religion long ago lost its "soul" (theological terminology is rarely used) and has focused too many of its resources on describing behavior (e.g., church attendance), some attempt should be made to reclaim scientific psychology of religion's interest in the mind. Mental processes are, after all, essential to understanding humans.

In particular this chapter will consider the following. According to Goldman some types of religious training create a gap between religious cognitive development and nonreligious cognitive development, both described by Jean Piaget. Subsequent researchers reported that some denominations fall behind others in their religious cognitive development. In light of later cognitive research, this difference might be reinterpreted as the goal-related preference of a particular denomination for a particular cognitive style (Schmeck, 1983). Why this alternative? In part, because the methods of testing religious mental development used by Goldman and his followers analyzed the content of the religious material in a way that favored a liberal Christian bias. But when a standard experimental memory test, relatively content free, was given, the presence of two different denominationally specific cognitive styles was detected that did not have to be interpreted in terms of some supposed denominationally based cognitive deficiency. Just as the architecture of a religious building may reflect its teachings, so might the socially shared processing styles of a religious group reflect the processes through which those teachings were acquired. Also considered in this section are suggestions concerning some possible cognitive outcomes of receiving literal or fundamentalist training as well as some cognitive interpretations of children's concepts of prayer.

While Goldman saw differences in religious training, Freud saw similarities between religious ritual and obsessional behavior. Freud's theory of obsessional behavior is based on his theory of childhood amnesia. However, recent cognitive research on childhood amnesia questions Freud's interpretation. According to this research, children can recall early childhood experiences, but only after they learn how to narratize general events. Consequently, ritual acts may not serve to protect childhood amnesia, as Freud supposed, but serve as mnemonics, to elaborate existent religious schemas, enhance self-focus, and subsequently elaborate religious self-schemas by identifying with the variants of personal attributes (James's wider self) recognized in fellow ritual devotees.

Moving from internalizing the processing style of a religious tradition through enriching that style in ritual experiences comes the often more intense experiences: dramatic conversion and altered states. William James described a dramatic conversion experience as the destruction of an accumulated self-construct (schema) with a dramatic emotional experience. For James the original schema becomes the bedrock for the new. In keeping with James's description of a conversion experience, recent research in cognition indicates that extreme emotional occasions, unlike their milder counterparts, may actually restrict what can be remembered about an experience. Since the memorial fragments of that event can not be effectively encoded they might be replaced by an adopted narrative. James wrote that following an emotive experience, ideas once peripheral to consciousness will take center stage. Such a replacement may best be accomplished by those with a tendency to use the narratives of others when describing themselves. Some current research indicates that when dramatic converts want to describe themselves they use narrative accounts that describe others. Converts can process recollective experiences like others when properly self-focused, but what distinguishes them from nonconverts is that they usually rely upon narratives describing others to describe themselves. Conversion may not, as is frequently proposed, be a mental restructuring of an existant self-schema but is, as James described, a rearrangement.

Jung emphasized that altered states such as dreams and mystical experiences provide an important source of information about ourselves. From the perspective of contemporary cognitive psychology, Jung's description of dreams (i.e., sources of unconscious knowledge that oppose our conscious selves) and their method of interpretation may not be as Jung described. Instead, dreams may be a part of our normal processing of conscious knowledge. Recently investigated cognitive processes such as learning how to enhance memory performance without consciously recollecting the learning experience (implicit memory) and the inability to discriminate between information presented previously and imaged information (reality monitoring) raise questions about the effectiveness of Jung's method of identifying unconscious archetypal motifs. In interpreting dream motifs Jung maintained that parallel symbols found in similar contexts would function in the same way. However, recent cognitive research demonstrates the dependence of items presented in a specific context on that context (Tulving and Thomson, 1973). Consequently, we may learn about ourselves, not by identifying unconscious archetypes as Jung proposed, but rather by comparing how we remember functioning in one context with how we remember functioning in a different context. Dreaming may best be described as the processing of conscious material; and mystical experiences may reflect a preference for knowledge stored in the visual, implicit, or procedural memory systems.

Before looking at how these four religious experiences might be reinterpreted from a cognitive perspective, it will be useful to consider what key elements constitute an experience and how an experience might be investigated. What can be learned about a "practically ineffable" experience is illustrated by Dennett (1988:70). In Dennett's illustration a birdwatcher has never experienced hearing an osprey cry but would like to. To paraphrase Dennett, a bird book's description of the properties of an osprey's cry—"a series of short, sharp, cheeping whistles, cheep, cheep or chewk chewk, etc.; sounds annoyed" (from Peterson, 1947:69)—however inadequate, serves the purpose of limiting the range of bird cries from all possible cries that can be heard, to those with some descriptive similarity to the osprey. But even with this limitation, the remaining range is large. A visual sighting of an osprey further limits the logical space of possible osprey cry experiences in a way the verbal description could not.

Hearing the sighted osprey—"So *that's* what it sounds like" (Dennett, 1988:70)—reveals how the description failed to capture the experience. But after hearing only one cry, the birdwatcher may not be able to describe his new-found ability to discern an osprey's cry any better than before. The birdwatcher doesn't even know what it was that his property detectors detected. However, what the birdwatcher has now, that he did not have before, is the ability to *refer* to the detected property: *it* is the property detected in *that event*.

This initial experience, then, serves as a reference point, against which subsequent, similar encounters can be compared. Examining the variation in performance over subsequent similar encounters is often described as improving one's ability to detect experiential properties (e.g., training one's ear, educating the palate). However, it is not the birdwatcher's ability *itself*, that changes. What seems different and erroneously called change is the birdwatcher's subjective experience of now hearing an osprey cry, as compared to what he remembered experiencing before. For since every experience is as 'directly apprehended' as the one before, and since every subjective experience happens only once, the experience of hearing the first cry does not change. In addition, "The properties of the 'thing experienced' should not be confused with the properties of the event that realizes the experiencing" (p.72). In other words, form (experiencing) should not be confused with its content. The highly informative complexity of experiences makes them practically ineffable and prohibits determining whether there are "absolutely indescribible properties in our experience" (p.74).

From this illustration, it appears that experiences should be described in terms of at least four elements: 1) structured representations obtained from prior experiences (e.g., bird book description, other mental abstractions); 2) experiencing the event in a particular context (e.g., hearing an osprey); 3) the processes operative in the interaction between existent representations and incoming information (e.g., the act of differentiating the osprey's cry from others) and when applicable, 4) the drivers of these processes (e.g., wanting to hear an osprey).

This example also illustrates how mental processes can only be inferred from external indicators of processing performance (what can be known about the process of identifying an osprey's cry was inferred from remembering previous encounters). The best descriptions of processing would be those that rely least upon the medium (e.g., the English language) used to identify it. For example, if Peterson's bird book description actually identified what an osprey sounds like, a person who spoke Japanese should be able to use Peterson's book as effectively as an English speaking person. And despite how content-free the guide on differentiating may be, the description will be of little use, if it fails to consider the conditions of the event itself (e.g., the chances of hearing an osprey are better outside).

All of these elements (structured representation, event in context, processes, motive/goals) interact with each other. Many theories tend to focus on only one element (schema), while disregarding the rest. This provides a rather inadequate account of the experience. Moreover, placing too much weight on the descriptive capabilities of one element may tend to overestimate its influence. However, as cognitive psychology develops, the ability to take on additional complexities will improve. For the present purpose, most of the cognitive paradigms under discussion will deal with only one cognitive element at a time. Each religious experience discussed will only be able to focus on one element at a time.

PSYCHOLOGICAL INTERPRETATIONS OF RELIGIOUS TRAINING: FROM "COGNITIVELY" CHALLENGED TO EPISODIC STYLE

Training has been included as a type of experience, despite the common tendency to consider experiences mediated by institutions as second-order substitutes for 'first' hand experiences. It is often overlooked that James, who lionized subjective, directly apprehended experiences, nevertheless noted "the whole universe of concrete objects, as we know them, swims . . . in a wider and higher universe of *abstract ideas* that lend it its significance" (James, 1902:61). Similarly, Jung who described individual experiences as more immediate and convincing than the best tradition also wrote, "Even the sum total of the series of dreams could not compare in beauty and expressiveness to any part of a traditional creed. A creed is always the result and fruit of many minds and many centuries, purified from all the oddities, shortcomings and flaws of individual experience" (Jung, 1938:63).

Zachry (1990) should be credited with drawing attention to a questionable conclusion: according to results from several sources, Missouri Synod Lutherans, Baptists, Protestants in Belfast, and Finns were found to be more "cognitively challenged" (sub-formal operational thinkers) than Catholics, Catholics in Belfast, and Episcopalians, respectively. The subformal thinkers in these studies with ages ranging from five to thirty supposedly think like children most often between the ages of seven to eleven. Why these individuals may be 'cognitively challenged' has been attributed either to the liberal bias in the instruments used, to the conservatism/fundamentalism among the subjects, to how poorly these instruments operationalize Piaget's concrete and abstract stages of cognitive development or to the conviction that Piaget's stages simply do not exist. What these apparent differences between these religious groups may represent has yet to be determined.

This line of research began when Goldman (1964) adopted Piaget's stages of logical development (described below) to investigate the effect of religious training on how children think about religion. Goldman proposed that Piaget's stages of cognitive development represented only one of four essential ingredients of thinking. The other three ingredients are 1) the materials selected by perception and stored as mental categories; 2) the motive for thinking such as feelings, needs, or attitudes; and 3) abilities such as habits. With these four ingredients Goldman could have accounted for many of the elements necessary to describe an experience as outlined above. However, his application (and that of his followers) of Piaget's stages nevertheless received the most attention. Noam (1990) observed when other theories are applied they are transformed (psychoanalytic to attachment theory) but when Piagetian theory is applied it is not transformed; instead it is filled with more issues, dimensions, processes, and content.

In adopting Piaget's stages to the study of religion, Goldman selected on the basis of pilot studies three Bible stories: Moses and the burning Bush, the Crossing of the Red Sea, and the Temptation of Jesus, as well as five questions about each story. Theologically trained judges used a standardized scale of theological concepts to analyze the content of the children's verbatim responses. The children's responses were then rated by judges trained on how to identify Piagetian stages of logical development. The theological scale reflected the views of many liberals concerning the Bible (e.g., "Scripture is the inspired but not the infallible Word of God," Goldman, 1964:49). Goldman acknowledged the decidedly liberal slant of his scoring but realized that some common standard was needed. The problem that would plague Goldman and all the researchers who followed was, as Hyde (1984:5) stated: "Can there be a test of theological thinking devoid of theological content?"

For Piaget, the stages of cognitive development are products of the ongoing processes of *assimilating* information to conform to our way of thinking (i.e., pretending) or *accommodating*, changing ourselves to fit the world (i.e., imitation). Critics of Piaget argue that stages do not exist: rather it is only the underlying processes of assimilating and accommodating that create the impression of stages (Brainerd, 1978). Instead of proposing stages, the suggestion has been made that cognitive development reflects the child's continuously improving capacity to mentally retain information (Grusec, Lockhart, and Walters, 1990).

Goldman begins his analysis of religious thinking with Piaget's preoperational stage. During this stage, which usually occurs between the ages of two and seven, the child is incapable of adopting the perspective of others (egocentrism) according to Piaget. But contrary to Piaget's description, Borke (1975) and others demonstrated that young children can exhibit the capacity for perspective-taking, albeit with some difficulty. According to Piaget, it is also during this stage that children cannot solve a conservation task which requires the understanding that underlying physical properties can remain unchanged (weight) despite superficial changes in appearance (shape). They fail to realize that changing the shape of a quantity, such as pouring water from a tall glass to a short glass, can be reversed and does not affect the amount (reversibility). In addition, children at this level cannot concentrate on two properties of objects (weight and shape) simultaneously. For Goldman, because these children can only see one problem at a time, they simplify solutions. This simplification leads to inconsistent and fragmentary conclusions. But Gelman (1978) demonstrated that conservation can be taught to preoperational children and that by simplifying the task many conservation problems can be solved.

In the concrete operational stage between the ages of seven and eleven the child learns how to manipulate objects mentally and can therefore overcome the problems of reversibility and egocentrism. Goldman proposed that the child's thinking about religion at this age was "limited to concrete situations, visual experience, and sensory data" (Goldman, 1964:55-56). Children will judge the stories only in "light of their own experience" and thought is limited to those "features visibly or tangibly present in the situation" (p. 56).

During the final stage of formal operations (twelve years and beyond) the adolescent begins to think in abstract terms. Adolescents begin to develop the ability to compare current situations with imaged possibilities. Goldman describes thinking at this stage as being able to think symbolically and as being liberated from concrete elements and situations.

Goldman concludes from his research that children think religiously along the lines of these three operational stages. However, the age at which their religious thinking develops lags behind their development in other areas (Goldman, 1964:25). Goldman attributes some of this lag to the figurative language used in the Bible that can only be understood by someone with a sufficient breath of experiences and propositional thinking to decode its metaphors. Children forced to deal with material beyond their comprehension will crystallize their thinking too quickly and will then adhere to these inadequate forms for so long that they will interfere with the normal development of their religious thinking. Both Piaget and Goldman agree that some adults never reach the level of formal operations. But if religious development lags behind, many adults will eventually reject religious thinking as childish (Goldman, 1964:115). Goldman recommends that children must be helped in passing beyond literal interpretations of the Bible.

John Peatling, one of Goldman's followers, observed that Goldman's research does not directly measure Piaget's stages of religious development. So, Peatling (1973) in his own study used Goldman's Bible stories but offered the subjects four forced-choice responses to questions asked about the Bible stories (e.g., "How would you explain the bush burning and yet not being burnt?" (p.596). The four objective responses ostensibly identified Very Concrete (e.g., "God was protecting the bush," p.598), Concrete, Abstract and Very Abstract operational thinking (e.g., "This is the kind of story that does not need to be 100% correct to give it meaning," p.598). Peatling named his forced-choice test *Thinking About the Bible* (TAB). Using this measure on Episcopalian children between the ages of nine and nineteen, Peatling reported a stage-like sequence of development away from the concrete and toward more abstract thinking. But Spilka, Hood, and Gorsuch (1985) doubted that cognitive thinking is being researched when Peatling's measures are used, for liberal religious responses could be concretely acquired by children and their abstract responses would not reflect abstract processing. Similarly, Kohlberg (1969) felt that particularly when children are forced to choose between alternative answers, "Piaget's dimensions are really matters of content rather than cognitive form" (p.375).

Nevertheless, Peatling's measures were next applied to different denominations and countries. Peatling and Laabs (1975) reported that Missouri Synod Lutherans scored less abstractly than Episcopalians. They proposed that conservative religious education may facilitate concrete religious thinking. In a large study of students living in Belfast between the ages of eight and sixteen, Greer (1981) reported that Roman Catholics scored higher on Peatling's measure of abstract thinking than Protestants. The *TAB* scores measuring the preference for abstract thinking among the Irish in Greer's study, and among the Finns in McGrady's research (1983) are lower than they were for Peatling's American Episcopalians (Tamminen, 1991). Greer attributed this difference to the religiosity of his subjects and the theological bias of Peatling's measure. The literal bias issue is further supported by Tamminen (1991) who reports finding a correlation between Peatling's *Religious Thinking Very Abstract* scale and a nonliteral measure of interpreting the Bible (Peatling's Literalism scale).

Hoge and Petrillo (1978) report the results of an abstract-only subsection of Peatling's measure *The Religious Thinking Total Abstract* which they found to be a more reliable measure than Peatling's entire instrument. Their results contradict Goldman's findings that religious thinking lags behind general cognitive ability and will eventually lead to a rejection of religion; but they do obtain significantly lower scores for Baptists than for both Catholics and Methodists on their measure of abstract thinking. After correlating Peatling's measures with other factors dealing with religious behavior, religious attitudes and general cognitive ability, Hoge and Petrillo (1978) concluded that "the impact of religious education [on abstract thinking] was quite strong while the impact of overall cognitive capacity was weaker than expected" (p.153). This conclusion is in keeping with other criticisms of Piaget that his cognitive theory failed to account adequately for the influence of social context (Donaldson, 1978), experiences (Higgins and Parsons, 1983) and personal conviction (Fowler, 1986) on cognitive development. The factors Hoge and Petrillo (1978) correlated with Baptists' concrete thinking included strongly held beliefs, religious interest, peer influence, church attendance, and prayer habits.

Finally, Zachry (1990) investigated the relationship between a simplified version of Peatling's measure of abstract thinking (BIBLE) and a paper and pencil test of Piaget's level of formal operational reasoning (Formal Operational Reasoning Test, FORT). Drawing subjects from different denominations, Zachry reported a modest positive correlation between FORT and BIBLE. The "high operational" (abstract) subjects (n=54) held significantly higher BIBLE scores than the "low operational" (concrete) subjects (n=16). The difference between these groups was significant when a t test was used, but failed to be significant when the more stringent F test was applied. As

Flavell (1993) noted, the variability within one of Piaget's cognitive stages often exceeds the variability between stages. In conclusion, while Zachry considered whether literal interpretations of the Bible should be regarded as evidence of subformal thinking, he suggests that new cognitive measures be used; and he asks whether the phrase intelligent literalist/fundamentalist might be an oxymoron.

The consideration of the cognitive ability of literalists and fundamentalists that follows is not intended to provide a cognitive justification for any one theological orientation but rather to consider alternative interpretations to the Piagetian-based research just presented of the cognitive differences found between religious groups.

Because of the importance placed upon literal readings of the Bible, a literalist may value knowing portions of the Bible by heart. Material learned verbatim is generally acquired by repeating it over and over again until it is retained: so-called rote memorization. For the most part, items acquired by rote are quickly forgotten. For the most part rote memorization is a poor way of learning. To learn an item effectively, it should be elaboratively and/or distinctively encoded. An elaboratively encoded item is related to other stored knowledge, thereby "enriching" its informational value. A distinctively encoded item is contrasted with existing information. Both processes increase the probability that an item will be recalled. However, there may be different levels of rote memorization. A closer examination of the effects of rehearsal reveals that subtle differences in how the repetitions are executed produce different results.

Craik and Jacoby (1985) distinguish between maintenance processing and maintenance rehearsal. Maintenance processing occurs when "subjects maintain an item continuously in mind by rehearsal" (p.151). Items processed in this way are not retained for very long, nor will they lead to a greater acquisition of knowledge (Mandler, 1979). Maintenance rehearsal, on the other hand, is the explicit repetition of an item, often with spaced intervals between repetitions. Maintenance rehearsal may modestly improve retention (Nelson, 1977). Such rehearsal may increase "the integration or coherence of an item" (Craik and Jacoby, 1985). Over time, aspects of the word which remained constant across contexts will be reinforced. These now more coherent words may become the necessary building blocks for the construction of more complex mental structures (Mandler, 1979).

Rubin (1982) discussed the importance of literal recall and how it might be preserved. "It just isn't Hamlet's soliloquy if it's paraphrased, no matter how well the paraphrase may preserve the original meaning" (Rubin, 1982:300). Based on an analysis of how well-known passages are retained, Rubin concluded that such passages are retained by chaining surface structure units (e.g., how a word looks). But if one link is lost, the whole phrase is lost. An intact chain of well integrated items might be quite resistant to subsequent interference. If the task of attending to the surface structure (how a word looks) is made more difficult (how a word looks upside down and backwards), difficult pattern-analyzing skills can be retained for some time (Kolers, 1976).

Among certain unique individuals, the ability to recall information verbatim is accomplished by visualization. The mnemonist "S" studied by Luria (1987) would mentally convert a series of words into graphic images. When asked to recall the list, even many years later, "S" would literally 'read' the mental image he created, backwards or forward. It has been amply demonstrated elsewhere that concrete words (e.g., apple) are more memorable than abstract words (e.g., honor) because concrete words elicit images (Paivio, Yuille, and Madigan, 1968; Sasson and Fraisse, 1972). According to the dual coding theory (Paivio, 1990), words which elicit images will store two representations; one imaginal and one verbal, thereby improving this word's accessibility. Yeatts (1988) demonstrated the superior memorability of concrete over abstract sentence fragments/words taken from the Bible. He did so by first having students rate how well these fragments/words elicited an image. Then Yeatts administered a free recall test and found that concrete fragments/words were recalled significantly more often. Considering, too, that expert chess players encode larger perceptual chunks of familiar subconfigurations of chessmen than novices (Chase and Simon, 1973), could an expert user of concrete words elicit not only images but chunk these images into larger groups, thereby consolidating large amounts of information?

The extensive elaboration of a word through maintenance rehearsal and the distinctiveness of imagery may endow some words with more abstract capabilities than a literal answer might suggest. Have intelligent literalists mastered some expert level of maintenance rehearsal? Or are they high visualizers, so that words, as they use them, convey more cognitive knowledge to them than what appears on the surface? When Karl Barth, the prolific twentieth-century theologian and erudite author of *Church Dogmatics*, was asked late in life, what is the most important thing you know about the Christian faith? Barth replied, "Jesus loves me this I know, for the Bible tells me so." A very concrete answer.

How have the cognitive capabilities of fundamentalists or religiously orthodox been examined? One idea popular among psychologists is that more (mental structure) is better. Better because more structure is thought to allow for greater flexibility and adaptability in the processing of new information. One structure under consideration is the hierarchically ordered cognitive model of Schroder, Driver, and Struefert (1967). This hierarchical model focuses attention on two elemental ideas (differentiation and integration). Unfortunately, as with a structurally based model, the influence of context is too often minimized. When Batson and Ventis (1982) write "the reality we construct is based on our cognitive structures" (1982:68), they slight contextual influences. Batson and Raynor-Prince (1983) were the first to use a modified version of Schroder, Driver, and Streufert's Paragraph

Completion Test (PCT) to measure religious complexity. In the Religious PCT (RPCT) test, subjects are asked to write paragraphs in response to five existential sentence stems (e.g., "When I am trying to decide whether to do something that may be morally wrong . . ." [p. 43] and four PCT stems. The content of the answers was then rated for complexity (e.g., openness, tolerance, uncertainty). Batson found an expected positive relationship between complexity and the quest orientation (.37) and a negative relationship with Orthodoxy (-.37). But as Hunsberger et al. (1990) noted, the positive correlation between this measure of cognitive complexity and quest is not surprising, since both measures share similar assumptions.

Hunsberger, Pratt, and Pancer (1992) measured the relationship between fundamentalism and complexity of thought. Other dispositional variables included in this study were right-wing authoritarianism, dogmatism, Christian orthodoxy, and a Need for Cognition measure. Since the authors realized the importance of accounting for not only dispositional but situational variables as well, Hunsberger et al. (1992) included three situational factors: familiarity with the dilemma, content, and prompting for complexity. They found no overall relationship between fundamentalism and complexity of thinking. In general, the four remaining dispositional measures were unrelated to cognitive complexity. Among the situational variables, however, familiarity with the topic, and asking prodding questions, influenced cognitive complexity across all content domains. Perhaps this measure of cognitive complexity failed to interact with fundamentalism overall because not all cognitive processes are thought to operate with equal effectiveness across specific content domains (Brown and Desforces, 1979).

Another way to explore the structural aspects of fundamentalism might be to liken the mental representation of fundamentalist principles to a type of schema. Schemas are generalizations developed from repeated categorization and evaluation of behavior of oneself and others within a particular domain (Markus and Smith, 1981). The work by Sherif and Hovland (1961) on latitudes of rejection and acceptance suggests a possibly useful way to measure the supposed rigid thinking about religious issues believed to characterize some fundamentalist individuals (Hunsberger et al., 1990). Applying Sherif and Hovland's theory, if *particular ego-involved* persons develop a religious self-schema, they would be expected to be intolerant of slight deviations from their religious domains. Information opposing their self-schema will be resisted (Markus and Smith, 1983). Judgments made about the attitudes or behaviors of others with similar religious domains would be over-evaluated or under-evaluated. Moreover, because self-schemas develop in areas that individuals care about, relevant incoming information may take on affective qualities (Markus and Smith, 1981). In short, ego-involved individuals with religious self-schemas may exhibit a certain cognitive narrowness on religious topics.

Goals and tasks are believed to be intimately involved in schema development (Markus and Nurius, 1986). If the goals or values are shared by group members, then these group members may also process information in common domains in similar ways, i.e., they have socially shared cognitions. If there are religious schemas, then it should be possible to demonstrate cognitive differences between different religious groups. A study by Markus et al. (1982) found evidence of cognitive differences between groups of individuals with different gender schemas.

There are, however, many areas that cannot be accommodated by a schematic approach. For example, Anderson and Pichert (1978) asked subjects to adopt the perspective of a burglar or a potential homebuyer. Subjects were then given a narrative about two boys playing in a house. In the house were objects that would interest a homebuyer and objects that would interest a burglar. Following a distractor task, subjects were then asked to name every item in the house. They found that subjects tended to recall items relevant to their perspective. For example, a burglar would remember the jewelry in the house. After this first recall test, subjects were asked to shift their perspective to the alternative one and then without consulting the narrative, once again recall as many of the items in the house from this new perspective. Anderson and Pichert reported that subjects recalled "additional, *previously unrecalled* information following a shift in perspective" (p.10). If, as supposed, schemas attend primarily to relevant information, why was the extraneous information encoded? But self-schemas may give only a partial, dispositional account of how people experience their world.

How might situational variables such as how a person is affected by the act of experiencing, the location in which it occurred and the moment when it occurred, be encoded? Neisser (1988) wrote that ordinary memory consists of what Tulving (1972) described as episodic and semantic memory. Tulving's two memory systems are, according to Brown (1975), roughly equivalent to what Piaget meant by "memory in the strict sense" and "memory in the broad sense." According to Tulving (1972, 1983, 1985), the semantic memory system "registers and stores generic/abstract knowledge" (Tulving, 1983:40). So schemas, by definition, are part of the semantic system. The episodic memory system registers and stores a person's consciously experienced and personal events which happen in a particular place, and at a particular time (Tulving, 1993). Taken together many dispositional and situational variables can be accounted for with these two memory systems. As a theory, the episodic/semantic distinction has its critics (Tulving, 1985), but almost all agree about the heuristic usefulness of this distinction.

Can the episodic and semantic distinction account for the processing differences between Baptists and Catholics as described by Hoge and Petrillo (1978)? Since the episodic system is represented concretely, perhaps the Baptists' tendency toward answering questions about Bible stories by selecting concrete interpretations may be an artifact of Baptists' thinking about themselves and their interpretations in terms of their concrete personal episodes. If so, a cognitive measure of a concrete versus an abstract task should not differentiate between the two denominations, while a measure of episodic and semantic memory should. Other studies have found differences between groups on episodic-like measures. Ross and Holmberg (1990) found that females recalled more detailed and vivid memories than did their husbands—a result which Ross and Holmberg attribute to the possibility that females learn how to be relationship experts. Schmeck and Meier (1984) describe "naturally" occurring differences among the learning styles of students. Some, but not all, students use a self-reference learning style conceptually similar to episodic processing. Other differences in processing styles and the evidence supporting the mnemonic effectiveness of episodic processing can be found in several other studies (e.g., Brooks, Simutis, and O'Neil, 1985; Brown, Keenan, and Potts, 1986).

One experiment was designed to measure if Baptists (n=50) or Catholics (n=57) would demonstrate a preference for either episodic or semantic processing or using a concrete or abstract task (McCallister, 1988). In this experiment, subjects were asked questions about twenty-four personality trait adjectives (e.g., honest) under four different conditions. The four conditions were: episodic-self-concrete ("Can you think of a particular personal experience in which you would use this adjective to describe yourself?"), semantic-self-abstract ("Does this adjective describe you?"), semantic-other-concrete ("Can you think of a particular story told to you about your mother about which you could use this adjective to describe her?") and semantic-other-abstract ("Does this adjective describe your mother?"). Each set of adjectives was balanced for frequency of use, affect, meaning, and concreteness (Anderson, 1968). Then, following a distractor task, subjects were asked to recall as many of the adjectives as possible. Both groups were about the same age, were raised in their denomination and had parents in the same denomination. As in other experiments of this kind (Bower and Gilligan, 1979), possible serial position effects and rate of yes response were accounted for.

The experiment is based on four premises. First, how an item (word) is processed will affect the probability that it will be remembered (Craik and Lockhart, 1972). Second, the more extensively an item is related to other knowledge (elaboration) or contrasted with other items (distinctiveness), the more recall is enhanced (Craik and Jacoby, 1985). Third, the probability that an adjective will be recalled depends on how well a retrieval cue matches the stored memory engram/trace (Tulving and Thomson, 1973). In this experiment, the subject's retrieval cue is the subject's ability to reconstruct what they thought about while they answered questions about adjectives. The memory engrams are the adjectives stored in memory. The fourth premise assumes the existence of an episodic and a semantic memory system, and that the effect of these systems is being measured in this experiment.

The hypothesis that Baptists would use their episodic memory when describing themselves more than Catholics was supported. Baptists recalled significantly more episodically encoded words than Catholics. Although not measures of Piaget's operations, Baptists and Catholics did not differ in how effectively the abstract or concrete tasks were used in this study. Both groups also differed in the religious and pedagogical values they held. Baptists valued personal religious experiences, while Catholics valued religious experiences in community. The pedagogical methods found to be associated with these values may have helped shape these processing styles. Baptists valued the direct transmission of religious knowledge and teachers who live a life of Christian witness (Hoge and Thompson, 1982). The 'concreteness' measured by Hoge and Petrillo (1979) may perhaps reflect the cognitive style of the group. Of course, within these denominations, cognitive styles will vary. Theoretically, everyone uses both their episodic and semantic memory systems. How dramatic converts in this experiment processed knowledge differently than their nonconvert counterparts is discussed below.

One religious experience with close institutional ties is the experience of learning how to pray. Long, Elkind, and Spilka (1967) used Piaget's stages of cognitive development as an interpretive tool to study prayer, and, like Goldman, they used a semistructured interview to measure the level of cognitive development. Adding to Goldman's method, Long et al. included sentence fragments ("Sometimes I pray for . . . p.102) in their semistructured interviews. Long et al. were cognizant of the theological positions implied in their sentence fragments. Moreover, they were cognizant of the difference between processing form and the content of prayer concepts. Unfortunately, however, cognitive form was at times confounded with the content of prayer concepts in their discussion. In their study, they rated the content from the interview for levels of Piagetian differentiating and abstracting. A subsequent analysis suggested five "more or less distinct age level clusterings" (p.103) of the eight age levels measured. Ages five, eight, and twelve seemed clearly to represent global-undifferentiated, concrete differentiation, and abstract differentiation, respectively, while the remaining five age levels were described as transitional stages between levels.

Confounding processing form and prayer concepts lead the authors to an "apparently contradictory development" (p.108). They grappled with why the "*form* of the prayer concept, the child's understanding, becomes increasingly differentiated and abstract and increasingly divorced from personal elements" while the "*content* of prayer becomes increasingly personal and loses the stereotyped and rote quality which it has in childhood" (p.108). The real contradiction is that they identify as a cognitive form "being divorced from personal elements" which instead describes the content of the child's concepts; and they identify as content a "rote quality" which instead describes a cognitive way of processing information. As stated above, in describing experiences it is important not to confuse the properties of the thing experienced (the prayer concepts) with the event that realizes the experiencing (rote learning).

Applying alternative cognitive research to the results found here, the prayers of the so-called "global undifferentiated" child may be fragmentary and vague because the child is still learning how to order events (Hudson, 1990). Memorizing a prayer gives them a standard. The so-called concrete differentiated child may equate what they say while praying with what prayers are (e.g., Prayers are God bless mommy and daddy) because the only way the child knows how to describe prayers at this age is in terms of a generalized narrative that reports the prayer activity. Hearing religious stories again and again about prayers may help solidify what the sequence of the prayer scripts (Schank and Abelson, 1977). The prayers of the "abstract undifferentiated" child may contain personal content because at about the age of seven children start to form separate and distinct memories and can therefore distinguish one event from another. Learning to describe the prayer activity provides the basis from which the child will eventually learn how to describe their more autobiographical prayers (Farrar and Goodman, 1990).

The concern of the authors about the theological presuppositions inherent in their sentence fragments (Sometimes I pray *for* . . .) may be well-founded. Loftus and Zanni (1975) conducted a series of experiments on the effect questions asked about witnessed events have on how the subject later remembered the event. They found that using an indefinite article (Did you see *a* . . .?) instead of a definite article (Did you see *the* . . .) produced fewer instances of subjects reporting seeing objects which had not been presented. And since information presented after an event may be integrated with the memory of that event (Loftus, Miller, and Burns, 1978 vs. Berkerian and Bowers, 1983), asking the same question of a child before and after a suggestive question may produce inconsistent answers that overall may be interpreted as being vague.

PSYCHOLOGICAL INTERPRETATIONS OF RITUAL EXPERIENCES: FROM RITUAL AMNESIA TO MNEMONIC RITUAL

Freud used two models when he described the mental activities operating during a religious ritual. In Freud's repression model, childhood memories of sexual fantasies are repressed, resulting in an adult amnesia for childhood events. The only events that adults can recall from their childhood are displaced events whose only connection to the original emotional events is some spatial, temporal, or contextual similarity. Obsessive religious ritual acts are described as behavioral symptoms of displaced physical intensity. For example, the devotee kneels excessively before the idol of Vishnu with his mother/consort and so helps repress his infantile desire to possess his own mother.

In Freud's second, screen model, adult memories of childhood experiences are reconstructed out of fragments of powerful and significant events.

Only fragments remain because children are incapable of narratizing an event. Children will not develop the ability to narratize until they are about six years old. Pathologies occur when these childhood fragments are not sufficiently reconstructed to mask the true nature of these memorial fragments, or when the fragments are displaced (White and Pillemer, 1979). Because of the discontinuity between the nature of childhood memories and the nature of adult memories, the actual childhood fragments of memories cannot be accessed. Elaborate memories supposedly recalled from childhood are actually reconstructions.

Instead of proposing, as Freud does, that childhood memories are forgotten because of childhood amnesia, or an insurmountable discrepancy between how children remember and how adults remember, Fivush and Hammond (1990) report that even young children can recall events, but this ability is not generally detected because children do not respond well to direct questioning (Fivush, 1988). Also because children must first learn how to represent general events (Hudson, 1990) and only then can they learn how to mentally represent personal experiences, many childhood events are memorial fragments rather than narratives and are consequently "forgotten" in adulthood.

Children learn how to narratize by talking with their parents. Until that time, children depend upon their parents to provide them with retrieval cues. Eventually, children will have to learn how to provide their own retrieval cues to recall personal experiences. Farrar and Goodman (1990) demonstrated that young children are more dependent on general event representation, when recalling specific episodes, than are older children. The ability to generate a narrative varies between children. Parents who converse with their children in an elaborative manner (e.g., "And then what did you do?") build a better foundation for the later recall of episodes (Hudson, 1990). This line of research undermines the premise upon which Freud's interpretation rests. How might a religious ritual be understood in light of some research in cognitive psychology? First, there is probably no one cognitive mechanism that can account for the entire ritual.

Freud identified ritual repetition as obsessional acts fueled by unconscious motivations; but alternatively, the function of repeating a religious act may be like acquiring a skill. When a skill (flying a plane) is first acquired, the learner will be given a description of the procedure and will watch how others perform this task. Procedural descriptions form part of the declarative memory, the system that mediates *what* is known (Anderson, 1987). For exacting rituals, a great deal of attention would be required initially. For less structured ceremonies, a script, a generalized event memory, might suffice (Schank and Abelson, 1977).

As the ritual is repeated, the descriptions and models needed initially will be needed less and less. Knowledge about how to perform the ritual will be transferred from the declarative memory system to procedural memory which mediates the "automatic" performance of a procedure or skill.

Once registered in procedural memory the ritual is no longer accessible to direct conscious awareness. Consequently, it might become difficult after a long time to remember why a particular act is being performed at a particular time. Repeating ritual acts, then, might serve to make the actions, which were once conscious, more "unconscious." Actions are made subconscious in the service of conscious awareness. Learning a ritual would add to the reservoir of subconscious material, rather than compensating for unconscious instincts, as Freud supposed. Because repeating a ritual will eventually make performing this ritual "automatic," the previously engaged conscious awareness will eventually be freed to attend to other matters. Under the right circumstances, conscious awareness may be redirected to the religious environment and oneself.

Once these procedures become "automatic," they are less prone to modification and it might be difficult to suppress the impulse to perform portions of the ritual act, particularly in the original learning context. Changing the ritual performance requires that the devotees must once again become conscious of what they are doing—which would tax whatever conscious self-reflection in which they may be engaged. Consequently, the idea of a change in the ritual may be meet with some resistance, particularly from those for whom the procedures are the most "automatic." But if the ritual becomes too routine, it may lose its mnemonic effectiveness and become what Neisser (1967) labeled a repisode, an event so common, like brushing your teeth, that the event itself is no longer memorable nor consequently considered to be significant. Occasional and moderate changes in the ritual may serve to keep conscious awareness at hand although not totally consumed with procedural details.

As the mental representation of the ritual procedure is transferred to procedural memory, the conscious processes can attend to the religious environment and the devotee's reflections. Environmental context and mood-congruent effects may conspire to direct the devotee's conscious awareness toward the eventual elaboration of the devotee's religious self-schema by providing the occasion for the devotee's religious schema to interact with an enhanced self-focus.

Typical of an environmental context effect would be when knowledge learned in context "A" is not successfully retrieved in context "B" but subsequently retrieved when context "A" is reinstated. The research on such environmental context effects can be impressive, because even when the difference between contexts is slight this effect can be demonstrated. As returning to an old familiar context like a childhood home can "bring to mind" information not thought about anywhere else, a religious setting may serve as a mnemonic for religious information and contribute to the activation of an individual's religious schema. However, environmental context effects are not always reliably produced. For instance, in one experiment subjects were instructed to recall context "A" while in context "B" and the environmental effect disappeared (Smith, 1979). Environmental context effects may be brought under conscious control. Spradlin and Malony (1981) failed in their experiment to obtain a religious context effect. This may have occurred because the effect of their religious context (religious art in a gallery) may have been offset by their imaginary physiological state manipulation (instructions to get excited or become relaxed). In an earlier study, another arousal agent, caffeine, was also ineffectual (see Spradling and Malony, 1981). It is possible that these physiological agents were ineffective because the effect of the arousal agents was only assessed by monitoring the main task (how the experience was described). But because there may be two arousal systems active in any one arousal condition (one system creates a disequilibrium while the second works to reestablish a equilibrium) the effects of arousal will not be felt on the main task. For example, if a sleep-deprived subject (low arousal) is aroused by being asked to perform a demanding task (drive a car), the low arousal will be compensated for by extra-vigilant driving. Consequently, the main task (how the car was driven) might not show the effects of the arousal. However, the effect of increased arousal should be indicated on some secondary task because so much extra energy is being expended on the main task (Eysenck, 1976).

Mood congruence might also contribute to direct conscious awareness toward religious material and self-focus. Brown and Taylor (1986) demonstrated that moods activate self-schemas. Devotional music may contribute to the creation of a mood which may subsequently initiate a mood-congruent effect. A mood-congruent effect occurs when the mood of a devotee biases the availability of memories in favor of memories which complement the devotee's mood. Contemplative devotional music may elicit a contemplative mood which prompts the recollection of events that occurred during other contemplative moods (Snyder and White, 1982). But mood-congruent effects, like environmental effects, are subject to conscious control. Devotees must sustain being in a particular mood during the recall of memorial material to bias that recall.

Repeating certain sounds during rituals may also contribute to putting devotees into a particular subjective feeling state which may prompt a mood-congruent effect. Zajonc, Murphy, and Inglehart (1989) in a series of experiments showed that the muscular movement of specific facial muscles similar to what occurs during smiling or frowning altered subjective feeling, but *not* because of how the muscular movement was interpreted. Two facial movements respectively cooled or heated the sensitive nasal cavity which subsequently lowered or raised the temperature of the subject's blood, a change which then, theoretically, prompts the release of emotion-linked neurotransmitters which in turn influence whether the subjects rated their subjective feeling state positively or negatively. In some of the experiments, for example, German-speaking people pronounced the German "umlaut," which affected the zygomatic muscle enough to increase their blood temperature and these subjects tended to describe their current subjective state negatively. When other subjects pronounced the phoneme "ah" (as in Allah and Amen) a marginally significant drop in blood temperature was recorded.

How long these moods or feeling states can be sustained depends in part upon how the ritual is sequenced. For if the ritual is not continuous but there are segments in the activity, participants might be more accurate in being able to describe the activity and might rate the experience as being more intelligible (Newston and Enquist, 1976). A more cerebral group, therefore, might be expected to have more breaks in their ceremonies than a more charismatic one. The punctuations in a service might interrupt experiencing the ceremony as a single entity. Context, mood and sounds might coalesce to activate a devotee's preexistent religious schema.

The effect that activated religious schemas or frames of reference have on how religious experiences are described has been consistent. Hood and Morris (1981) found that intrinsically oriented individuals reported seeing more religious imagery in an isolation tank when instructed to do so, than did extrinsically oriented individuals. The effectiveness of some religious schemas was further emphasized when these same intrinsically oriented people reported seeing more religious imagery than those extrinsically oriented, even when the intrinsics were instructed to imagine seeing cartoon characters. Similarly, van der Lans (1985) found that subjects with a religious cognitive structure or schema and with an experimental variable designed to arouse their religious schema, described more of their meditational experiences as being religious than did subjects with weaker or nonexistent religious schemas. But, however necessary religious schemas and other experimental variables might be, they are not sufficiently influential to prompt subjects to describe their experiences as being religious. As van der Lans points out, the subjects must be personally motivated or engaged to be aware of their religious schema's applicability to a particular experiential moment. In other words, to make the religious schema a religious self-schema, the semantic material must become part of the individual's personal past. The individuals might not be able to identify or describe what they consider to be religious, but they can refer to a moment when they felt religious. When the self is engaged, the use made of material related to the self changes. When investigating how a religious schema affects the way religious sermons are heard, Morlan (1950) and Pargament and DeRosa (1985), found that familiarity and consistency between subject and sermon improved memory performance. To see oneself acting in a moment is more likely to occur as self-focus increases. Self-focus is thought to increase when subjects disclose personal information (Hull and Levy, 1979), when subjects are the focus of attention, when they are asked to perform some act such as to make a decision, when they view their image, or when they are moderately aroused.

What might enhancing one's self-focus accomplish? Self-focused attention was shown to "increase a person's responsiveness to their affective state (Scheier and Carver, 1977) and to make the subject feel more engaged in the events (Duval and Wickland, 1973). Self-focus can make internal states relevant to the context seem more salient, and help participants more effectively remember material that has been related to themselves (self-reference effect; Rogers, Kuiper, and Kirker, 1977). People with high self-consciousness are also more aware of how they are being perceived by others (Fenigstein, 1979) and may develop a better articulated self-schema (Nasby, 1985) which in a religious context would be a better articulated religious self-schema.

Because self-focus may make the devotee more aware (of the present moment, relevant material, and how they are seen by others), during a ritual an individual's religious self-schema may be enhanced by identifying one's existent self-schema with the perceptions of one's wider religious self that the devotee sees in other ritual participants (James, 1890; Markus and Nurius, 1986). It was James who offered an early expanded view of the self. James saw the self as the sum total of all—people, possessions, ideas, work, etc.—that individuals could call their own, because what happens to these "others" is part of the individual (James, 1890). For James there existed a social self which was not the "result of *remaking* a preexisting self into a social being, but of *creating* a self from the beginning that is social in nature" (Leary, 1990:109-110). For Markus and Nurius (1986), following James, others function as possible selves which serve as incentives for what the individual might become. So, if others are part of our social selves or are our possible selves, then interacting communally with other devotees in rituals may elaborate one's religious schema. The development of a religious self-schema and the opening up of one's self-schema may further sensitize the devotees to the impact of other experiences.

As the ritual act was learned and was transferred to the "subconscious" procedural memory, the conscious declarative system of religious ideas about the self may be elaborated through the collected efforts of the situational cognitive variable found in contexts and ritual acts, religious schemata, self-focus, and wider selves. That some future elaboration of one's self-schema with one's wider self will halt production of this particular current system of ideas is considered by William James. It was *through* the wider self that James envisioned that "saving experiences" would come (James, 1902:398).

PSYCHOLOGICAL INTERPRETATIONS OF DRAMATIC CONVERSION: FROM ENHANCED SELF TO NARRATIZED SELF

The enhanced self emerging from the ritual is represented internally by a system of ideas that has been added to, or subtracted from, over time. James envisions the collapse of this system during an emotive occasion:

> The collection of ideas alters by subtraction or by addition in the course of experience. . . . A mental system [of ideas] may be undermined or weakened by this interstitial alteration just as a building is, and yet for a time keeps upright by dead habit. But a new perception, a sudden emotional shock, or an emotional occasion which lays bare the organic alteration, will make the whole fabric fall together; and then the center of gravity sinks to a new attitude, more stable, for the new ideas which reach the center in the re-arrangement seem now to be locked there, and the new structure remains permanent (James, 1902:166).

During this conversion experience, the previous structure (system of ideas) was not restructured, but, falling and sinking, becomes the bedrock for a new structure. The primary actors in James's description are the emotions and the event. The emotions destroyed the existing system of ideas which were built over time through previous experiences. The idea that high levels of arousal are the antithesis of the structure of ideas is supported by some recent research. High arousal may facilitate long term memory, but *inhibit* short term memory among subjects (Levonian, 1972). Imagine Leon Festinger waiting for the moment when prophecy fails; but when it happens, believers in the prophecy cannot remember anything about what just happened but may *construct* something for Festinger later! Add to this temporary inhibition produced by the emotive experience, that a state of high arousal might even restrict the kind of information that will be recalled later. Information recalled while a subject is aroused might be organized around physical characteristics rather than words with associative potential (Eysenck, 1976). High levels of arousal may further limit subsequent recall to central details while peripheral ones, such as the location of the event, are forgotten (Christianson and Loftus, 1990). Consequently, the information rendered from a highly arousing event may be fragmented. Since the fragments remaining from a highly arousing event might be insufficient to recollect much about the experience itself, external analogies and narratives might be relied upon to replace the previous structure.

In James's description of a dramatic conversion experience the old structure falls down and new ideas take center stage. After the emotion subsides what memorial fragments that do remain are forgotten, similar to the way children will forget their experience until they learn how to describe events in general. In this respect, the dramatic conversion experience described by James is like a rebirth. The emotional experience destroyed the previous schema and now the converts must rely on a received religious narrative to describe the event. James does not indicate where the new peripheral ideas come from or which peripheral ideas are likely to reach the center. Possibly, since these religious ideas were previously peripheral to consciousness, emotion, and events ("the habitual center of his personal activity," James, 1902:165), they were learned secondhand. Religious material used for religious instruction is often presented in story form. As Hjalmar Sundén proposed, people use religious narratives as role models (Kallstad, 1987; van der Lans, 1987).

Do converts use narratives to describe themselves? Hudson (1990) proposed that children first learn how to remember general event representations. Then, if the parents encourage conversational elaboration, children will learn how to represent their own personal experiences. Being able to narratize as one gets older corresponds to Tulving's ideas that the episodic memory system does not develop until the child matures. But if children are not encouraged to elaborative conversations, they might continue to favor narrative forms of representation. Lack of encouragement might reflect a lack of communication between a parent and child, or that elaboration was not a pattern of behavior that characterizes their household (children are to be seen and not heard). If the parents are more authoritarian, children might be expected to adopt, rather than debate, their parents' point of view.

Ullman (1982) reported that the belief system of dramatic converts was judged to be more impermeable. Does this impermeability reflect the more generalized quality of a narrative which, relative to how recollected experiences are usually represented, would be less resistant to change? Ullman also found that dramatic converts described their childhoods as being unhappy ones. Perhaps the children were not encouraged to be who they were, to represent themselves by describing their experiences.

The idea that dramatic converts might tend to use narrative accounts when describing themselves was also explored in the experiment described above (McCallister, 1988). It was found that both Baptist and Catholic converts remembered fewer adjectives related to personal experiences (encoded episodically) than did the nonconverts in their respective denominations, but did recall more adjectives under the encoding condition in which subjects were asked to relate to-be-remembered items to a story they had heard about their mother.

Converts in this study also differed from nonconverts in the significantly higher value they placed on "living each day with a sense of Divine forgiveness" (Hoge et al., 1982). Does this higher value reflect that they have a sense of what James described as the "inner or subjective awareness . . . taken concretely" (1890:283)?

However, it is also possible that the convert's recall pattern does not reflect a general preference for using narratives but the inability to process episocally. A manipulation in this second experiment was used to test converts' proficiency at relating material to episodes. The mood manipulation, playing of devotional music, was introduced to enhance self-focus and possibly activate the convert's religious schema. It was found that under this music condition, the convert's recall performance was like the nonconvert's: high episodic and lower semantic-other-concrete encoding. Converts, it seems, can process experiences like nonconverts under the right conditions. What might then distinguish converts from nonconverts is not some qualitatively different experience but that the episodic processing of personal information in a dramatic conversion experience represents a departure from the semantic way converts usually think about themselves. Nothing in the convert's cognitive structure may have actually been *restructured*. Instead, personal knowledge was replaced.

Since during the convert's conversion experience it seems reasonable to expect that self-focus was high, the convert might have (uncharacteristically) encoded this experience episodically. Consequently, whatever personal information was obtained during that experience might seem to be unusually (for the convert) affect-laden and convincing (Tulving, 1983). But since the conversion experience was not only self-focused but emotive, what the converts might remember about their conversion experiences might simply be the *recollective* awareness of themselves at that moment. As James wrote: "An objective person, known by passing subjective Thought and recognized as continuing in time" (James, 1890:371). An awareness that will later adopt a narrative.

But how have other psychologists interested in cognition described dramatic conversion? Bartlett, so instrumental in developing the concept of schemata, describes a religious conversion as "the completion of what appears to be unfinished evidence . . . by an intuitive leap" (Bartlett, 1932). Bartlett states that turning around upon one's own schema occurs with increased conscious awareness (Bartlett, 1932:206). Batson and Ventis (1982) place less emphasis on structure than Bartlett. They describe religious experience as a "cognitive restructuring in an attempt to deal with one or more existential questions" (p.86). Unfortunately, they do not explain exactly how the restructuring takes place, or how their two key processes, integration and differentiation, interact with each other. They do, however, provide three examples of momentous change: when solutions come in "aha" moments, Gestalts, and moments of scientific discovery. Taken together, Bartlett's "consciousness," Batson and Ventis's examples, and James's "emotional occasion," could be describing a conscious, novel, vivid, and emotional moment, which once stored in memory could be described as a recollected awareness (Tulving, 1983).

Aside from the impact that high arousal and self-focus have on recollective events, other characteristics of recollective experiences may shed light on conversion experiences to the extent that conversion experiences are like other recollected events.

When an experience is recalled an image quite often comes to mind. Images related to an experience are most likely stored in a visual system (Paivio, 1990), and these visual representations may be ordered spatially. Indeed, the relationship between temporal and spatial representations may be quite close. Time is often described using spatial metaphors: being ahead or behind time (Neisser, 1967). Consequently, a recollective experience may be accessed using a temporal cue (When did you?) or a spatial cue (Try to imagine where it happened). This greater accessibility may increase the frequency with which the experience is recalled. Being able to recall an event more often will make it seem more memorable and important (Linton, 1982). Rubin and Kozin (1984) found that clear memories about autobiographical experiences were judged to be more surprising, consequential, and emotional.

The quintessential characteristic associated with a recollected event is what James described as its "warmth and intimacy" (1890) and a sense of pastness. With that "warmth and intimacy" comes a confidence about what happened during that event (Gardiner, 1988). For example, you remember what happened to you yesterday with a greater degree of confidence than you may "know" anything else you learned yesterday. Consequently, whatever converts may remember about their conversion experience, the confidence characteristic of all recollective experiences might tinge the information associated with their experiences with a special confidence and a resiliency to change.

Once the experience is over, the new system of ideas is subject to the same adding and subtracting of associated ideas described earlier by James. This emotional occasion will serve as a baseline against which subsequent events will be judged. But because this experience was so emotional, subsequent events will be judged as being less significant than they were before. Eventually the subject will habituate to whatever they gained from this experience (Brickman, Coates, and Janoff-Bulman, 1978).

PSYCHOLOGICAL INTERPRETATIONS OF RELIGIOUS EXPERIENCES IN ALTERED STATES: THE NARRATIZED SELF COMPARED BETWEEN STATES

For Carl Jung, the narratized selves who persisted in identifying with one generalized representation of themselves (persona) would be arresting their further self-realization (individuation). The ego represents only one part of the self and its manifestation in one context should not be equated with the self. The process of self-realization never ends. For Jung, individuals can learn more about themselves by interpreting such altered states as dreams and mystical experiences. The interpretation of these states is central to analytic psychology.

Cognitive research on the content of dreams raises doubts about how Jung described dreams and how he described the process of dream interpretation. Dreams, he wrote "are a spontaneous manifestation of the unconscious mind, based upon contents which are not to be found in consciousness" (Jung, 1945:24). But many studies demonstrate a relationship between the contents found in dreams and in consciousness. For example, Rados and Cartwright (1982) found that the content of dreams was most clearly related to presleep thoughts, ones held in mind just before the sleeper falls asleep. But what can be known about the content of dreams? Perhaps the proposed similarity between the content in dreams and consciousness can be attributed to the effect presleep instructions have on the dream reports, rather than the effect presleep instructions have on dreams. Bellicki and Bowers (1982) investigated the problem of differentiating between the content of the dream and what the dream reports. They reasoned that if sleep instructions (e.g., notice how many times you are alone in your dream) influenced dream reports, then postsleep instructions should also affect dream reports. But they found that dream changes were reported only following presleep instructions. No changes were reported with postsleep instructions.

Jung also proposed that the "meaning of most dreams is not in accordance with the conscious mind but shows peculiar deviations" (Jung, 1945:287). Jung recognized that there were some similarities between conscious content and dreams. In dreams there are "memory-images" which correspond with conscious concerns, and occasionally the content of dreams and the concerns of consciousness will simply coincide (Jung, 1938). But Cohen (1976) reported that *most* of the research on the relationship between personality and dream content have focused on, and found support for, the continuity between the personality and the dream content. From Cartwright's (1990) examination of the similarity between conscious concerns and dream content, she concluded that dreams are part of our normal cognitive processing. Dreams "relate waking experiences to past emotional experiences" (p.188).

How independent are dreams from external influences? Jung claimed that "the dream not only fails to obey our will but very often stands in flagrant opposition to our conscious intention" (Jung, 1945:287). However, the "flagrant opposition" of dreams may have had some conciliatory moments. Jung suggested that motifs related to the individuation process would appear "chiefly and predominately in dream-series recorded under analysis" (Jung, 1945:290). Badia (1990), after reviewing the literature, found substantial evidence that "material learned while awake can be transferred to sleep, retrieved from long term memory and worked upon" (p.72), while Eich (1990) found that subjects who were instructed to learn while asleep did so. Sleepers who were not similarly instructed failed to learn. Both articles indicate that sleepers do comply with conscious intentions.

But are dreamers and their dreams influenced by external instructions? LaBerge (1990) and his colleagues in a series of studies demonstrated the voluntary control of breathing and eye movements during lucid dreaming (all other skeletal muscle groups are inhibited during REM sleep). LaBerge also demonstrated that lucid dreaming can improve with training. They presented external cues (e.g., light) to dreamers to "remind" subjects they were dreaming and once the cues were incorporated into their dreams these external cues served as reminders. But if dreams are related to conscious concerns why are some dreams disturbing? Don't vivid dreams indicate some imbalance between the consciousness and unconsciousness? Physiologically, dream images may appear as vivid perceptual images because the neurons that normally inhibit vivid hallucinations while awake are not inhibited during dream sleep (Mandell, 1980). Dreams then may correspond with conscious concerns more than Jung suggests in his statement "*dreams* . . . have the advantage of being involuntary, spontaneous products of the unconscious psyche and are therefore pure products of nature not falsified by any conscious purpose" (Jung 1936: p.48).

But Jung, as mentioned, recognized that some dream material coincided with conscious material, so when he interpreted a dream he tried to identify a dream motif that reflected an archetypal form and not conscious concerns. To do this, Jung tried to select a dream motif that the dreamer does not remember encountering while conscious and one that the dreamer is not likely to have encountered. However, as the research on implicit memory indicates, we may learn material and demonstrate a facility at using some knowledge without being aware we possess this information or when we could have learned it. Specifically, implicit memory occurs when task performance (e.g., word completion) is enhanced by a previous learning (e.g., associating two words) during a previous experience but *without* the subject being consciously aware that the learning event happened (Schacter, 1987). It is possible therefore, that dreamers may not always recognize that they have seen a particular motif before.

Another method Jung used to investigate archetypal motifs was to have the analysand imagine a sequence of different contexts about a dream fragment until the meaning of the dream motif became clear (Jung, 1936:49). But finding contextual associations for archetypal motifs produced in this way may, over the course of analysis, make it difficult to discriminate between what was imagined by the analysand from mythic images introduced by the analyst. Johnson, Raye, Wang, and Taylor (1979) found that repeated exposure to *perceived* items and imagined items makes it difficult for subjects to discriminate between items that were initially internally produced, from those that were initially externally produced (reality monitoring). But since for Jung both internally and externally produced associations may provide interesting material about archetypal motifs, this concern may seem minor. However, the origin of the associations is a concern when the effect that cultural influences have on analysis is not adequately accounted for; and archetypal motifs are presented not as the products of a culture but as immutable innate sources of personal revelation and this method is thought to demonstrate the existence of the collective unconscious. Archetypal motifs elaborated in this way may not have originated in the unconscious. Even Jung expressed a concern that this method might take the analysand too far away from reality.

A third technique Jung used to interpret archetypal motifs was to take a dream motif and find a valid mythological parallel for that motif. Jung wrote that "in order to draw a valid parallel, it is necessary to know the functional meaning of the individual symbol, and then to find out whether the apparently parallel mythological symbol has a similar context and therefore the same functional meaning" (Jung, 1936:50). But can a functionally similar symbol (money), in a similar context (in someone else's pocket) ever have the same functional meaning to the original owner of the money?

The idea that items function differently in similar contexts is illustrated in the following experiment (Tulving and Thomson, 1973). First, subjects were asked to learn twenty-four pairs (one cue and one TARGET) of weakly associated words (e.g., fruit FLOWER). Following other tasks, subjects were then given twenty-four cues strongly associated with the targets presented earlier (e.g., bloom). Subjects were then asked to generate six words associated with this strong cue (e.g., bloom). Next, subjects were asked if, among the words they had generated, they recognized any of the generated targets as ones that they had seen during the initial presentation. Tulving and Thomson found that even though some of the generated words were target words (e.g., FLOWER) they were not always recognized as original targets, but when the original weakly associated cues (e.g., fruit) were presented again and subjects were asked to recall the originally associated target word, some of the original target words were recalled (e.g., FLOWER). Some targets (e.g., FLOWER) that subjects failed to *recognize* among the words they generated in the context of a strongly associated cue (e.g., bloom) were *recalled* in the presence of the weakly associated cue (e.g., fruit). Consequently, the same item did not function in the same way in a similar context as it had before. Subjects failed to recognize the item in the strong cue context but could recall the same item in the original weak cue context.

Consequently, what Jung described as the functional identification of parallel symbols in similar contexts might more accurately be described as comparing how what-was-identified-as-the-ego functioned in one context with how what-was-identified-as-the-ego functioned in a different context. It is by comparing how what we remember as aspects of ourselves functioned differently in different contexts that the self is realized. What "transcends" similar contexts is not the identification between functions but the memory for, and the conscious identification with, other "moments" from our remembered past.

Despite how he described the process, Jung knew that no interpretation was final. New contexts must be constantly taken up, "dream the myth onward" (Jung, 1951:160); and regardless of how the method was described, some analysands feel that these interpretative techniques worked for them. But realizing that because dreams do reflect our current concerns and cultural inheritance and not because they may be contrary to consciousness and innate as Jung suggested, comparing how we function in different states might free our "true" selves from the confines of how we are defined by any one historical context, culture or supposedly innate psychological inheritance.

For Jung, "the aim of individuation [self-realization] is nothing less than to divest the self of the false wrappings of the persona on the one hand, and of the suggestive power of primordial images on the other" (Jung, 1935:173-174). Redefined, Jung's process of self-realization is making the comparison between how we remember functioning in contexts that were dreamt, imagined, social or historical/mythical. It is how we function in different contexts that defines us, particularly in our relationships with others and in the tasks we undertake. How we functioned in one context should not mean that we should be defined in, or by, that context.

The aim of the self-realization/individuation process Jung described as the "divesting the self of the false wrappings of the persona on the one hand, and the suggestive power of the primordial images on the other" (Jung, 1935:173-174). However, the process of self-realization may not be best described as trying to battle between two opposing fronts. For the chronic harkening back to how the narratized self functioned in one historic context (persona) might portend a restriction of immediate experiential awareness until no one can *recall* who they are now. On the other hand, the mindless (nonrational, see Hillman, 1975) accumulation of new associations in the hope of divesting primordial images of their power portends the ultimate blurring of the narratized self beyond present *recognition*. For both trying to bring back (recall) who we may have been, or trying to see (recognize) all that we may be, are in the end chimeras and of secondary importance to *remembering*: becoming more consciously aware of the cognitive processes and other noncognitive variables that now shape how we image our past and future.

Mystical Experiences

From a cognitive perspective, the perceptual unity that supposedly characterizes the extrovert's mystical experience (Stace, 1960) may reflect an ability at visualizing. Bartlett differentiated between verbalizers and visualizers. High visualizers found it difficult to verbalize their experiences. Is it in part because mystics are high visualizers that they find it difficult to describe mystical experience, and so claim that their experiences are ineffable? Other research suggests that high visualizers comprehend abstract sentences better than low visualizers: does this supposed ability make more intelligible the affinity of some mystics for paradoxes?

The benefit mystics seem to derive from their experience stands in sharp contrast to the little they claim that can be said about their experiences. Are some mystics able to dissociate and retain what they learn from experiences without remembering the experiences themselves? Since meditation is an acquired skill, learning how to meditate would be stored in procedural memory (the how-to system). Cohen and Squire (1980) demonstrated that even those lacking conscious awareness (e.g., amnesics) can acquire procedural skills. Amnesics, it has been shown, demonstrate enhanced abilities at numerous tasks, even operating a computer, unaccompanied by the conscious awareness of knowing how they know what they know. Do mystics regard as their source of knowledge what they store in their procedural, implicit, and visual memories, instead of their episodic and semantic memory systems?

Religious Experiences and Cognitive Theory

From Dennett's (1988) illustration of a practically ineffable experience, four elements were identified: the structured representation obtained from prior experiences, an event occurring in a context, processes operative in this interaction, and the drivers of these processes.

Relative to each other, the religious self-schema is the structured semantic representation of the received tradition, and the event is the ritual or dramatic conversion experience. Among dramatic converts, their supposed preference for narrative forms of self representation distinguished how they experience their tradition. However, all of the religious experiences considered, training, ritual, conversion, and being in an altered state, have the capability for becoming occasions in which we distinguish *between* how we remember functioning in different temporal and spatial contexts.

Identifying the drivers and processes in religious experience is often most influenced by the investigator's philosophical/theological orientation. Since the drivers and processes can only be inferred from observed performance, investigators tend to identify and design measurements of those processes that reflect their orientation. Consequently, examining the methods a researcher employs is particularly important in the psychological study of religion. With more exacting methods, the tendency for bias is not eradicated, but only becomes more subtle.

In the psychological study of religion, it may be relatively preferable to focus on processes and drivers, rather than using measures of performance that assess content, since assessing content necessitates interpreting that content out of its original philosophical/theological context. One of cognitive psychology's contributions to the study of religion can be to offer more refined methods that may be less content-dependent than other methods. In any case, focusing on mental operations is one essential part of understanding religious experiences with the caveat that understanding how a religious experience functions should not become a forum for equating how a religious experience functions with the significance it holds for the religious practitioner. But neither should understanding how a religious experience may function be dismissed as being of secondary importance to appreciating it. For the act of considering how something is "made" can enhance one's appreciation of it.

REFERENCES

Ackerman, B., and S. Freedman
1988 The relation between conceptual elaboration and retrieval access to episodic information in memory for children and adults. *Journal of Experimental Child Psychology* 46:100-128.
Alba, J., and L. Hasher
1983 Is memory schematic? *Psychological Bulletin* 2:203-231.
Anderson, J.
1987 Skill acquisition: Compilation of weak method problem solutions. *Psychological Review* 94:192-210.
Anderson, N.
1968 Likableness ratings of 555 personality-trait words. *Journal Personality and Social Psychology* 9:272-279.
Anderson, R., and J. Pichert
1978 Recall of previously unrecallable information following a shift in perspective. *Journal of Verbal Learning and Verbal Behavior* 17:1-11.
Ashcraft, M.
1989 *Human memory and cognition*. New York: Harper Collins.
Badia, P.
1990 Memories in sleep: old and new. In *Sleep and Cognition*, edited by R. Bootzin, J. Kihlstrom, and D. Schacter. Washington, DC: American Psychological Association.
Bartlett, R.
1950 *Remembering: A Study in Experimental and Social Psychology*. Cambridge: Cambridge University Press.
Batson, C., and L. Raynor-Prince
1983 Religious orientation and complexity of thought about existential concerns. *Journal for the Scientific Study of Religion* 22:38-50.
Batson, C., and L. Ventis
1982 *The Religious Experience*. New York: Oxford University Press.
Begg, I., and A. Paivio
1969 Concreteness and imagery in sentence meaning. *Journal of Verbal Learning and Verbal Behavior* 8:821-827.
Bellicki, K., and P. Bowers
1982 The role of demand characteristic and hypnotic ability in dream change following a presleep instruction. *Journal of Abnormal Psychology* 91:426-432.
Berkerian, D. and J. Bowers
1983 Eyewitness testimony: Were we misled? *Journal of Experimental Psychology: Learning, Memory and Cognition* 9:139-145.
Blaney, D.
1986 Affect and memory: A review. *Psychological Bulletin* 99:229-246.
Borke, H.
1975 Piaget's mountain revisited: Changes in the egocentric landscape. *Developmental Psychology* 11:240-243.
Bower, G.
1981 Mood and memory. *American Psychologist* 26:129-148.
Bower, G., and S. Gilligan
1979 Remembering information related to one's self. *Journal of Research in Personality* 13:420-432.
Bower, G., S. Gilligan, and K. Monteiro
1981 Selectivity of learning caused by affective states. *Journal of Experimental Psychology* 110:451-474.
Bower, G., and J. Mayer

1989 In search of mood dependent retrieval. *Journal of Social Behavior and Personality* 4:121-156.

Brainerd, C. J.
1978 The stage question in cognitive-developmental theory. *The Behavioral and Brain Sciences* 2:173-213.

Bransford, J., and M. Johnson
1972 Contextual prerequisites for understanding. *Journal of Verbal Learning and Verbal Behavior* 11:717-726.

Brickman, P., D. Coates, and R. Janoff-Bulman
1978 Lottery winners and accident victims: Is happiness relative? *Journal of Personality and Social Psychology* 36:917-927.

Brooks, L., Z. Simutis, and H. O'Neil
1985 The role of individual differences in learning strategies research. *Individual Differences in Cognition* 2:219-251.

Brown, A.
1975 The development of memory: Knowing, knowing about knowing, and knowing how to know. In *Advances in child development and behavior*, edited by H. Reese. New York: Academic Press.

Brown, G., and C. Deforces
1979 *Piaget's theory: A psychological critique*. London: Routledge and Kegan Paul.

Brown, J., and S. Taylor
1986 Affect and the processing of personal information: evidence for mood-activated self-schemata. *Journal of Experimental Social Psychology* 22:436-452.

Brown, P., J. Keenan, and G. Potts
1986 The self-reference effect with imagery encoding. *Journal of Personality and Social Psychology* 51:897-906.

Cacioppo, J., R. Petty, and J. Sidera
1982 The effect of a salient self-schema on the evaluation of proattitudinal editorials: top-down versus bottom-up message processing. *Journal of Experimental Social Psychology* 18:324-338.

Cartwright, R.
1990 A network model of dreams. In *Sleep and cognition*, edited by R. Bootzin, J. Kihlstrom, and D. Schacter. Washington, DC: American Psychological Association.

Cermak, L., and F. Craik
1979 *Levels of processing in human memory*. Hillsdale, NJ: Erlbaum.

Chapman, L.
1967 Illusory correlation in observational report. *Journal of Verbal Learning and Verbal Behavior* 6:151-155.

Chase, W., and H. Simon
1973 Perception in chess. *Cognitive Psychology* 4:55-81.

Cheesman, J., and P. Merikle
1985 Word recognition and consciousness. In *Reading research: Advances in theory and in practice*, edited by D. Besner, G. MacKinnon, and T. Waller, New York: Academic Press.

Christianson, S., and E. Loftus
1990 Some characteristics of people's traumatic memories. *Bulletin of the Psychonomic Society* 28:195-198.

Cohen, C.
1981 Goals and schemata in person perception: Making sense from the stream of behavior. In *Personality, cognition and social interaction*, edited by N. Cantor and J. Kihlstrom. Hillsdale, NJ: Erlbaum.

Cohen, D.
1976 Dreaming: experimental investigations of representational and adaptive properties. In *Consciousness and self-regulation advances in research*, edited by G. Schwartz and D. Shapiro. New York: Plenum Press.

Cohen, N.

1984 Preserved learning capacity in amnesia: evidence for multiple memory systems. In *Neuropsychology of memory*, edited by L. Squire and N. Butters. New York: Guilford Press.

Cohen, N., and L. Squire
1980 Preserved learning and retention of pattern analyzing skill in amnesia: dissociation of knowing how and knowing that. *Science* 210:207-210.

Craik, F., and L. Jacoby
1985 Elaboration and distinctiveness in episodic memory. In *Perspectives on learning and memory*, edited by L.-G. Nilsson and T. Archer. Hillsdale, NJ: Erlbaum.

Craik, F., and R. Lockhart
1972 Levels of processing: a framework for memory research. *Journal of Verbal Learning and Verbal Behaviour* 11:671-684.

Dennett, D.
1988 Quining qualia. In *Consciousness in contemporary science*, edited by A. Marcel and E. Bisiach. Oxford: Clarendon Press.

Donaldson, M.
1978 *Children's minds*. London: Fontana.

Duval, S., and R. Wicklund
1973 Effects of objective self-awareness on attribution of causality. *Journal of Experimental Social Psychology* 9:17-31.

Eich, E.
1990 Learning during sleep. In *Sleep and cognition*, edited by R. Bootzin, J. Kihlstrom, and D. Schacter. Washington, DC: American Psychological Association.

Eysenck, M.
1976 Arousal, learning, and memory. *Psychological Bulletin* 83:389-404.

Farrar, M., and G. Goodman
1990 Developmental differences in the relation between scripts and episodic memory: Do they exist? In *Knowing and remembering in young children*, edited by R. Fivush and J. Hudson. New York: Cambridge University Press.

Fenigstein, A.
1979 Self-consciousness, self-attention and social interaction. *Journal of Personality and Social Psychology* 37:75-86.

Fivush, R.
1988 The functions of event memory: Some comments on Nelson and Barsalou. In *Remembering reconsidered: Ecological and traditional approaches to the study of memory*, edited by U. Neisser and E. Winograd. New York: Cambridge University Press.

Fivush, R., and N. Hammond
1990 Autobiographical memory across the preschool years: Toward reconceptualizing childhood amnesia. In *Knowing and remembering in young children*, edited by R. Fivush and J. Hudson. New York: Cambridge University Press.

Flavell, J.
1993 *Cognitive development*. Englewood Cliffs, NJ: Prentice-Hall.

Fowler, J.
1986 Faith and the structuring of meaning. In *Faith development and Fowler*, edited by C. Dykstra and S. Parks. Birmingham, AL: Religious Education Press.

Freud, S.
1907 Obsessive actions and religious practices. In *The standard edition of the complete psychological works of Sigmund Freud*, Translated from the German under the general editorship of J. Strachey. London: Hogarth Press and the Institute of Psycho-Analysis.

Gardiner, A.
1988 Functional aspects of recollective experience. *Memory and Cognition* 16:309-313.

Gelman, R.
1978 Cognitive development. *Annual Review of Psychology* 29:297-332.

Goldman, R.
1964 *Religious thinking from childhood to adolescence*. London: Routledge and Kegan Paul.

Greene, R.

1986 Sources of recency effects in free recall. *Psychological Bulletin* 99:221-228.

Greer, J.
1981 Religious attitudes and thinking in Belfast pupils. *Educational Research* 23:177-189.

Grusec, J., R. Lockhart and G. Walters
1990 *Foundations of psychology*. Toronto: Copp Clark Pitman.

Hick, J.
1967 Revelation. In *The Encyclopedia of Philosophy*, edited by P. Edwards. New York. Macmillan.

Higgins, E., and J. Parsons
1983 Stages as subcultures: Social-cognitive development and the social life of the child. In *Social cognition and social development: A socio-abilities perspective*, edited by E. Higgins, W. Hartup, and D. Ruble. New York: Cambridge University Press.

Hillman, J.
1975 *Re-visioning psychology*. New York: Harper & Row.

Hoge, D., E. Heffernan, E. Hemrick, H. Nelsen, J. O'Connor, P. Philibert, and A. Thompson
1982 Desired outcomes of religious education and youth ministry in six denominations. *Review of Religious Research* 23:230-253.

Hoge, D., and G. Petrillo
1978 Development of religious thinking in adolescence: A test of Goldman's theories. *Journal for the Scientific Study of Religion* 17:139-154.

Hoge, D., and A. Thompson
1982 Different conceptualizations of goals of religious education and youth ministry in six denominations. *Review of Religious Research* 23:297-304.

Hood, R., and R. Morris
1981 Sensory isolation and the differential elicitation of religious imagery in intrinsic and extrinsic persons. *Journal for the Scientific Study of Religion* 20:261-273.

Hudson, J.
1990 The emergence of autobiographical memory in mother-child conversation. In *Knowing and remembering in young children*, edited by R. Fivush and J. Hudson. New York: Cambridge University Press.

Hull, J., and A. Levy
1979 The organizational functions of the self: An alternative to the Duval and Wicklund model of self-awareness. *Journal of Personality and Social Psychology* 37:756-768.

Hunsberger, B.
1978 The religiosity of college students: Stability and change over years at university. *Journal for the Scientific Study of Religion* 17:159-164.
1982 The "generation gap": Parent-university student agreement on current attitudes and retrospective reports, and parental estimates of children's current attitudes. Paper presented to the Canadian Psychological Association, Montreal.

Hunsberger, B., M. Pratt, and S. Pancer
1992 Thinking about religious and nonreligious topics: Does fundamentalism affect complexity? Paper presented at the annual meeting of the Society for the Scientific Study of Religion, Washington, DC.

Hunsberger, B., M. Pratt, S. Pancer, B. McKenzie, and J. Lea
1990 Does religiosity affect the way we think? Integrative complexity of thought and religious orthodoxy. Paper presented at the annual meeting of the Society for the Scientific Study of Religion, Virginia Beach.

Hyde, K.
1984 Twenty years after Goldman's research. *British Journal of Religious Education* 7:5-7.

Isen, A.
1984 Toward understanding the role of affect in cognition. In *Handbook of social cognition* (3 Vols.), edited by R. Wyer and T. Srull. Hillsdale, NJ: Erlbaum.

Isen, A., and A. Hastorf
1982 Some perspectives on cognitive social psychology. In *Cognitive social psychology*, edited by A. Hartorf and A. Isen. New York: Elsevier.

Jackson, L., and B. Hunsberger

1992 The religiosity/integrative complexity relationship: an examination of the roles of religious fundamentalism, topic and social identification. Paper presented at the annual meeting of the Society for the Scientific Study of Religion, Washington, DC.

James, W.
1890 *The principles of psychology* (2 Vols.) New York: Dover, 1950.
1902 *The varieties of religious experience*. New York: Collier, 1961.

Johnson, M., C. Raye, A. Wang, and T. Taylor
1979 Fact and fantasy: the roles of accuracy and variability in confusing imaginations with perceptual experiences. *Journal of Experimental Psychology: Human Learning and Memory* 5:229-240.

Jung, C. G.
1935 The relations between the ego and the unconscious. In *The collected works of C. G. Jung*, edited by H. Read, M. Fordham, and G. Adler; translated by R.F.C. Hull. Princeton, NJ: Princeton University Press.
1936 The concept of the collective unconscious. In *The collected works of C. G. Jung*, edited by H. Read, M. Fordham, and G. Adler; translated by R. F. C. Hull. Princeton, NJ: Princeton University Press.
1938 *Psychology and Religion*. New Haven, CT: Yale University Press.
1945 On the nature of dreams. In *The collected works of C. G. Jung*, edited by H. Read, M. Fordham, and G. Adler; translated by R. F. C. Hull. Princeton, NJ: Princeton University Press.
1951 The psychology of the child archetype In *The collected works of C. G. Jung*, edited by H. Read, M. Fordham, and G. Adler; translated by R. F. C. Hull. Princeton, NJ: Princeton University Press.

Kallstad, T., H. Sundèn, N. Holm, O. Wikstrom, and J. van der Lans
1987 Symposium on Hjalmar Sundèn's role-theory of religion. *Journal for the Scientific Study of Religion*. 26:366-412.

Kihlstrom, J.
1980 Posthypnotic amnesia for recently learned material: interactions with 'episodic' and 'semantic' memory. *Cognitive Psychology* 12:227-251.

Kohlberg, L.
1969 Stage and sequence: The cognitive-developmental approach to socialization. In *Handbook of socialization theory and research*, edited by D. Goslin. New York: Rand McNally.

Kolers, P.
1976 Reading a year later. *Journal of Experimental Psychology: Human Learning and Memory* 2:554-565.

Kuiper, N., and P. Derry
1981 The self as a cognitive prototype: An application to person perception and depression. In *Personality, cognition and social interaction*, edited by S. Cantor and J. Kihlstrom. Hillsdale, NJ: Erlbaum.

Kuiper, N., and A. Paivio
1977 Incidental recognition memory for concrete and abstract sentences equated for comprehensibility. *Bulletin of the Psychonomic Society* 9:247-249.

LaBerge, S.
1990 Lucid dreaming: Psychophysiological studies of consciousness during REM sleep. In *Sleep and cognition*, edited by R. Bootzin, J. Kihlstrom, and D. Schacter. Washington, DC: American Psychological Association.

Lachman, R., J. Lachman, and E. Butterfield
1979 *Cognitive psychology and information processing: An introduction*. Hillsdale, NJ: Erlbaum.

Larsen, S.
1988 Remembering without experiencing: memory for reported events. In *Remembering reconsidered: Ecological and traditional approaches to the study of memory*, edited by U. Neisser and E. Winograd. New York: Cambridge University Press.

Larsen, S., and K. Plunkett
1987 Remembering experienced and reported events. *Applied Cognitive Psychology* 1:15-26.

Leary, D.
1990 William James on the self and personality: clearing the ground for subsequent theorists, researchers, and practitioners. In *Reflections on The Principles of Psychology: William James after a century*, edited by M. Johnson and T. Henley. Hillsdale, NJ: Erlbaum.

Levinson, H.
1981 *The religious investigations of William James*. Chapel Hill, NC: University of North Carolina Press.

Levonian, E.
1972 Retention over time in relation to arousal during learning: an explanation of discrepant results. *Acta Psychologia* 36:290-321.

Linton, M.
1982 Transformations of memory in everyday life. In *Memory observed: Remembering in natural contexts*, edited by U. Neisser. San Francisco: Freeman.

Loftus, E., D. Miller, and H. Burns
1978 Semantic integration of verbal information into a visual memory. *Journal of Experimental Psychology: Human Learning and Memory* 4:19-31.

Loftus, E., and G. Zanni
1975 Eyewitness testimony: The influence of the wording of the question. *Bulletin of the Psychonomic Society* 5:86-88.

Long, D., D. Elkind, and B. Spilka
1967 The child's conception of prayer. *Journal for the Scientific Study of Religion* 6:101-109.

Luria, A.
[1986]
1987 *The mind of a mnemonist*, translated by L. Solotaroff. Cambridge, MA: Harvard University Press.

Mandell, A.
1980 Toward a psychobiology of transcendence: God in the brain. In *The psychobiology of consciousness*, edited by J. Davidson and R. Davidson. New York: Plenum Press.

Mandler, G.
1979 Organization and repetition: Organizational principles with special reference to rote learning. In *Levels of processing in human memory*, edited by L. Cermak and F. Craik. Hillsdale, NJ: Erlbaum.

Mandler, J., and N. Johnson
1997 Remembrance of things parsed: Story structure and recall. *Cognitive Psychology* 9:111-151.

Markus, H., M. Crane, S. Bernstein, and M. Siladi
1982 Self-schemas and gender. *Journal of Personality and Social Psychology* 42:38-50.

Markus, H., and P. Nurius
1986 Possible selves. *American Psychologist* 41:954-969.

Markus, H., and J. Smith
1981 The influence of self-schemata on the perception of others. In *Personality, cognition and social interaction*, edited by N. Cantor and J. Kihlstrom. Hillsdale, NJ: Erlbaum.
1983 Self-knowledge: an expanded view. *Journal of Personality* 51:541-565.

McCallister, B.
1988 How individuals from denominations with divergent goals remember self-related information differently. Paper presented at the Annual Meeting of the Society for the Scientific Study of Religion, Chicago.
1991 Personal recollections and religious experiences. Paper presented at the Annual Meeting of the American Psychological Association, San Francisco.
1993 Remembering religious experiences. Paper presented at the Annual Meeting of the American Psychological Association, Toronto.

McGrady, A.
1983 Teaching the Bible: Research from a Piagetian perspective. *British Journal of Religious Education* 5:26-133.

McSpadden, M., J. Schooler, and E. Loftus

1988 Here today, gone tomorrow: The appearance and disappearance of context effects. In *Memory in context: Context in memory*, edited by G. Davies and D. Thomson. New York: Wiley.

Moeser, S.
1976 Inferential reasoning in episodic memory. *Journal of Verbal Learning and Verbal Behavior* 15:193-212.

Morlan, K.
1950 An experiment on the recall of religious material. *Religion in Life* 16:589-594.

Morris, C., J. Bransford and J. Franks
1977 Levels of processing versus transfer appropriate processing. *Journal of Verbal Learning and Verbal Behavior* 16:519-533.

Nasby, W.
1985 Private self-consciousness, articulation of the self-schema, and recognition memory of adjective traits. *Journal of Personality and Social Psychology* 49:704-709.

Neisser, U.
1967 *Cognitive psychology*. New York: Appleton-Century-Crofts.
1986 Nested structure in autobiographical memory. In *Autobiographical memory*, edited by D. Rubin. New York: Cambridge University Press.
1988 What is ordinary memory the memory of? In *Remembering reconsidered: Ecological and traditional approaches to the study of memory*, edited by U. Neisser and E. Winograd. New York: Cambridge University Press.
1982 Snapshots or benchmarks? In *Memory observed: Remembering in natural contexts*, edited by U. Neisser. New York: Freeman.

Nelson, T.
1977 Repetition and depth of processing. *Journal of Verbal Learning and Verbal Behavior* 16:151-171.

Nelson, K.
1993 The psychological and social origins of autobiographical memory. *Psychological Science*, 4:7-14.

Newston, D., and G. Enquist
1976 The perceptual organization of ongoing behavior. *Journal of Experimental Social Psychology* 12:436-450.

Noam, G.
1990 Beyond Freud and Piaget: Biographical worlds-interpersonal self. In *The moral domain: Essays in the ongoing discussion between philosophy and the social sciences*, edited by T. Wren. Cambridge, MA: M.I.T. Press.

Ozorak, E.
1989 Social and cognitive influences on the development of religious beliefs and commitment in adolescence. *Journal for the Scientific Study of Religion* 28:448-463.

Paivio, A.
1990 *Mental representations: A dual coding approach*. New York: Oxford.

Paivio, A., J. Yuille, and S. Madigan
1968 Concreteness, imagery, and meaningfulness values for 925 nouns. *Journal of Experimental Psychology: Monograph Supplement* 76:1-25.

Pargament, K., and D. DeRosa
1985 What was that sermon about? Predicting memory for religious messages from cognitive psychology theory. *Journal for the Scientific Study of Religion* 24:119-236.

Peatling, J.
1973 The incidence of concrete and abstract religious thinking in the interpretation of three Bible stories by pupils enrolled in grades four through twelve in selected schools in the episcopal church in the U.S.A. Doctoral dissertation, New York University.
1974 Cognitive development in pupils in grades four through twelve: The incidence of concrete and abstract religious thinking. *Character Potential* 7:52-61.
1974 Finn and American: reflections on a comparison. *Character Potential* 7:220-225.

Peatling, J., and C. Laabs
1975 Cognitive development of pupils in grades four through twelve: A comparative study of

Lutheran and Episcopalian children and youth. *Character Potential* 7:107-115.

Peterson, R.
1947 *A field guide to the birds*. Boston: Houghton Mifflin.

Pratt, M., B. Hunsberger, S. Pancer, D. Roth, and N. LaPointe
1990 Reflections on religion: aging and cognitive style variations in adult thinking about religious issues. Paper presented at the annual meeting of the Society for the Scientific Study of Religion, Virginia Beach.

Rados, R., and R. Cartwright
1982 Where do dreams come from? A comparison of presleep and REM sleep thematic content. *Journal of Abnormal Psychology* 91:433-436.

Rogers, T., N. Kuiper, and W. Kirker
1977 Self-reference and the encoding of personal information. *Journal of Personality and Social Psychology* 35:677-688.

Ross, M. and D. Holmberg
1990 Recounting the past: Gender differences in the recall of events in the history of a close relationship. In *Self-Inference processes: The Ontario symposium, Volume 6*, edited by J. Olson and M. Zanna. Hillsdale, NJ: Erlbaum.

Rubin, D.
1982 Very long-term memory for prose and verse. In *Memory observed: Remembering in natural contexts*, edited by U. Neisser. New York: Freeman.

Rubin, D., and M. Kozin
1984 Vivid memories. *Cognition* 16:81-95.

Sasson, R., and P. Fraisse
1972 Images in memory for concrete and abstract sentences. *Journal of Experimental Psychology* 94:149-155.

Schacter, D.
1987 Implicit memory: history and current status. *Journal of Experimental Psychology: Learning, Memory and Cognition* 13:501-518.

Schank, R., and R. Abelson
1977 A case study in the development of knowledge structures. In *Scripts, plans, goals and understanding*, edited by R. C. Schank and R. P. Abelson. Hillsdale, NJ: Erlbaum.

Scheier, M., and C. Carver
1977 Self-focused attention and the experience of emotion: attraction, repulsion, elation, and depression. *Journal of Personality and Social Psychology* 35:625-636.

Schmeck, R.
1983 Learning styles of college students. In *Individual differences in cognition* 1, edited by R. Dillon and R. Schmeck. New York: Academic Press.

Schmeck, R., and S. Meier
1984 Self-reference as a learning strategy and a learning style. *Human Learning* 3:9-17.

Schroder, H., M. Driver, and S. Streufert
1967 *Human information processing*. New York: Holt, Rinehart and Winston.

Schwartz, S.
1975 Individual differences in cognition. *Journal of Research in Personality* 9:217-225.

Sherif, M., and C. Hovland
1961 *Social Judgment: Assimilation and contrast effects in communication and attitude change*. New Haven, CT: Yale University Press.

Smith, S.
1979 Remembering in and out of context. *Journal of Experimental Psychology: Human Learning and Memory* 5:460-471.

Snyder, M., and P. White
1982 Moods and memories: Elation, depression and the remembering of the events of one's life. *Journal of Personality* 50:149-167.

Spilka, B., R. Hood, and R. Gorsuch
1985 *The psychology of religion: An empirical approach*, Englewood Cliffs, NJ: Prentice-Hall.

Spiro, R., and C. Sherif

1975 Consistency and relativity in selective recall with differing ego-involvement. *British Journal of Social Clinical Psychology* 14:351-361.

Spradlin, W., and H. Malony
1981 Physiological state deviation, personal religiosity, setting variation and the report of religious experience. Paper presented at the Annual meeting of the Society for the Scientific Study of Religion, Baltimore.

Stace, W. T.
1960 *Mysticism and philosophy*. Philadelphia: Lippincott.

Tamminen, K.
1991 *Religious development in childhood and youth*. Helsinki: Suomalainen Tiedeakatemia.

Taylor, S., and J. Crocker
1981 Schematic bases of social information processing. In *Personality, cognition and social interaction*, edited by N. Cantor and J. Kihlstrom. Hillsdale, NJ: Erlbaum.

Toulmin, S.
1972 *Human understanding: The collective use and evolution of concepts*. Princeton, NJ: Princeton University Press.

Tulving, E.
1972 Episodic and semantic memory. In *Organization of Memory*, edited by E. Tulving and W. Donaldson. New York: Academic Press.
1983 *Elements of episodic memory*. New York: Oxford University Press.
1985 Memory and consciousness. *Canadian Psychology* 26:1.
1987 Multiple memory systems and consciousness. *Human Neurobiology* 6:67-80.
1993 What is episodic memory? *Current Directions in Psychological Science* 2:67-70.

Tulving, E., and D. Thomson
1973 Encoding specificity and retrieval processes in episodic memory. *Psychological Review* 80:352-373.

Ullman, C.
1982 Cognitive and emotional antecedents of religious conversion. *Journal of Personality and Social Psychology* 43:183-192.

van der Lans, J.
1985 Frame of references as a prerequisite for the induction of religious experience through meditation: an experimental study. In *Advances in the psychology of religion*, edited by L. B. Brown. New York: Pergamon Press.
1987 The value of Sundén's role-theory demonstrated and tested with respect to religious experiences in meditation. *Journal for the Scientific Study of Religion* 26:401-412.

Watts, F., and M. Williams
1988 *The psychology of religious knowing*. New York: Cambridge University Press.

White, S., and D. Pillemer
1979 Childhood amnesia and the development of a socially accessible memory system. In *Functional disorders of memory*, edited by J. Kihlstrom and F. Evans. Hillsdale, NJ: Erlbaum.

Wickland, R., and S. Duval
1971 Opinion change and performance facilitation as a result of objective self-awareness. *Journal of Experimental Social Psychology* 7:319-342.

Wulff, D.
1991 *Psychology of religion: Classic and contemporary views*. New York: Wiley.

Yeatts, J.
1988 Variables related to recall of the English Bible: comprehensibility, structural importance, meaningfulness, interest, specificity of denotation and abstract-concreteness. *Journal for the Scientific Study of Religion* 27:593-608.

Zachry, W.
1990 Correlation of abstract religious thought and formal operations in high school and college students. *Review of Religious Research* 31:405-412.

Zajonc, R., S. Murphy, and M. Inglehart
1989 Feeling and facial efference: implications of the vascular theory of emotion. *Psychological Review* 96:117-123.

15

Affective Theory and Religious Experience

PETER C. HILL

"Two things you should never discuss: politics and religion." Many people have taken this advice to heart for fear that in the passion of discussion, one may regret what was said. It is hardly an insight to claim that religion often involves strong feelings. But, the affective base of religion is what this chapter is all about. So again we will explore religious experience—this time with feeling.

One conclusion drawn quickly after a perusal of the professional literature is that there is little consensus about how to conceptualize the terms affect and emotion. Likewise, there may be considerable confusion about the term religious experience. But even if for the sake of agreement we conceptualize religious experience in rather broad terms, such as a confrontation with some sort of ultimate transcendent dimension, certainly then we must consider the role of affect in such experience.

My first concern is not to discuss specific emotional qualities such as anger, anxiety, fear, comfort, disgust, etc., in terms of religious experience. While a discussion of some of these qualities is interspersed throughout this chapter, I am more interested in reviewing efforts that explain the conditions under which we experience such emotional qualities. My contribution then is to identify implications from those experiences that can be labeled religious. In other words, I am concerned more with the structure and function of emotions as they pertain to religious experience, something curiously absent in the professional literature, than I am in the specific emotions themselves. Without a broader theoretical framework, we are left with small smatterings of research on specific emotions in relation to religious experience, with little to tie that research together. The lack of a general integrative theory of affect in the psychology of religion may seem somewhat surprising since emotions play a prominent role in religious experience.

THE PROMINENCE-ABSENCE PARADOX

The Prominence of Affect

Some religious groups, including many traditional churches and other organizations within the mainstream of major world religions, place a major emphasis on the private experience and even the public display of intense feelings. Consider the case of Stephen Bradley (from James, 1902), a common man who encountered what some orthodox Christian groups might consider an experience of the power of the Holy Spirit. In Bradley's own words from a scarce 1830 pamphlet recounted by James:

> At first, I began to feel my heart beat very quick all of a sudden, which made me at first think that, perhaps, something is going to ail me, though I was not alarmed, for I felt no pain. My heart increased in its beating, which soon convinced me that it was the Holy Spirit from the effect that it had on me. I began to feel exceedingly happy and humble, and such a sense of unworthiness as I never felt before. . . . It took complete possession of my soul, for I am certain that I desired the Lord, while in the midst of it, not to give me any more happiness, for it seemed I could not contain what I had got. My heart seemed as if it would burst, but it did not stop until I felt as if I was unutterably full of the love and grace of God (1902:188).

James (1902) himself, concerned with the philosophical justification of religious faith, suggested that what distinguishes religious states from other states of experience is the transforming influence on lives of the persons who experience them. Arguing that the significance of religion is an intensely private and individual matter, James affirmed the centrality of feeling in religious experience. In his twentieth and concluding Gifford lecture in Edinburgh which collectively make up the *Varieties* (1902), James proclaimed:

> By being religious we establish ourselves in possession of ultimate reality at the only points at which reality is given us to guard. Our responsible concern is with our private destiny, after all. You see now why I have been so individualistic throughout these lectures, and why I have seemed so bent on rehabilitating the element of feeling in religion and subordinating its intellectual part. Individuality is founded in feeling; and the recesses of feeling, the darker, blinder strata of character, are the only places in the world in which we catch

real fact in the making, and directly perceive how events happen, and how work is actually done (1902:491-492).

Given that the *Varieties of Religious Experience* is indisputably considered the single great classic of the psychology of religion and given James's insistence that the personal significance of religious experience is grounded in the recesses of our emotions, one may expect that psychologists of religion have emphasized—indeed, become even preoccupied with—the study of affect. What is maintained here is that this is far from the case.

The Absence of Theory

The reader of this chapter will find the following thesis, sometimes implied and sometimes explicit, throughout: namely, that there are no general overarching theories of affect guiding research on religious experience. Hardly can psychologists of religion be blamed for this state of affairs, however, since the general study of affect is in considerable disarray. Leventhal and Tomarken (1986) attributed this disarray to psychology's "begrudging" attitude to grant independent conceptual status to emotion, blaming in particular the behaviorist tradition and it's suspicion of subjective concepts, the cognitive-arousal tradition of emotion with its heavy emphasis on cognitive components (Schachter, 1964; Schachter and Singer, 1962), and the reluctance of cognitively oriented scientists to view emotion as anything more than an "interrupt rule" of mental operations. Nevertheless, Leventhal and Tomarken were cautiously optimistic about "the promise of new theoretical integrations that pervade the field" (1986:566), suggesting that the concept of affect may finally achieve independent status.

In a presentation such as this it is virtually impossible to lay out a comprehensive theory (even if I had one in mind) of affect in religious experience. But, in fact, this is precisely what is needed. To date, there is little in the scientific investigation of religion that even hints at explaining why some religious experiences are intensely affectual while others are not. Nor has much attention been paid to how religious interpretation of events lead to different emotions and to emotions of varying intensity. Nor has there been much systematic research on how different emotions within the context of religious experience are related to each other. For example, to what extent might an orthodox believer of any of a number of religious traditions, who interprets homosexuality as a morally reprehensible or "sinful" lifestyle, find the practicing homosexuality of a close friend to be disgusting, distressful, and yielding conflict—all distinct affectual states? It is premature to answer questions such as these in this chapter. But these questions point out new and potentially valuable avenues of theory and research in the psychology of religion.

On a more positive note, however, one can find within the psychology of religion the recent development of what I will call middle-level theories, the type that derive empirically testable hypotheses that are clearly affectual in nature. Examples include Kirkpatrick's adaptation of attachment theory (Kirkpatrick, 1992; Kirkpatrick and Shaver, 1990) to religious experience and Pargament's (1990) religious coping theory. These theories are exceedingly useful in their own right; however, their value could be even more beneficial and appreciated if they were further integrated within a broader affective-based theoretical framework. In the absence of an integrative framework on religious affect and a corresponding sparcity of research, the discussion here must necessarily be characterized more as general and speculative than precise and conclusive.

CONCEPTUALIZING AFFECT

Affect, Attitude, and Emotion

Historically, the concept of affect has been distinguished from cognition, volition, and even emotion. Whereas the concept of cognition has embraced forms of knowing, including perceiving, reasoning, and imagining, and whereas volition has involved the process of deciding upon a course of action, affect has generally been viewed as a broad class of processes that include feelings, moods, and emotions. When I use the term *affect*, I am referring to an overall positive/negative subjective feeling which closely resembles what some social psychologists (e.g., Zanna and Rempel, 1988) have called *attitude*.[1] Affect is thus a more general (and, some would argue, less complex) concept than *emotion*, which refers to differentiated states of positive and negative affect such as happiness, joy, fear, and anger. Although there has been considerable disagreement about a precise definition of emotion, we will borrow the definition provided by Folkman and Lazarus as "complex, organized psychophysiological reactions consisting of cognitive appraisals, action impulses, and patterned somatic reactions" (1990:315), with the understanding (as intended by Folkman and Lazarus) that what is included within these components are subjective feelings.

But as one begins to analyze these concepts more thoroughly, it becomes readily apparent that any bifurcation, particularly between cognition and affect, is somewhat artificial. Hilgard's (1980) trilogy of mind—cognition, motivation, and emotion—are interwoven in such a complex fashion that Lazarus suggested that the best way to conceptualize affect is to consider "how motivation and cognition produce emotions in adaptationally relevant encounters" (1991:352). Not everyone has agreed with Lazarus, however, and the result has been an extended interchange, most notably between Lazarus (1982, 1984) and Zajonc (1980, 1984), on the relationship specifically between cognition and emotion.

Zajonc (1980, 1984) has argued that although cognition and affect usually operate in conjoint fashion, they are essentially separate and somewhat independent systems, such that affect can operate without cognition. In contrast,

Lazarus (1982, 1984, 1991) has suggested that emotion and cognition are by their very nature intertwined in that emotion must involve cognitive processes. Hence, Lazarus has argued for the primacy of cognition while Zajonc has maintained that feeling can (though not necessarily will) precede thinking.

Current Theory on Emotion

Many emotion theories can be categorized along the lines of the Lazarus-Zajonc debate. There are those theories which take a *biosocial* approach to emotion. The other broad category is what can be referred to as the *appraisal* or *constructivist* theories. The differences between the two approaches are most noted in terms of the role they assign to cognition (Vanman and Miller, 1993).

Biosocial Theories: Biosocial theories of emotion (e.g., Ekman, 1984; Izard, 1977; Zajonc, 1980, 1984) deemphasize the role of cognition and rely more on biological processes and evolutionary function, generally offering "evidence" for a "basic" set of innate emotions. This evidence has been provided by the universality of distinct emotional meanings in a small set of facial expressions, suggesting that certain expressions of emotion (e.g., anger, fear, surprise, happiness, sadness, disgust) are hardwired (Ekman, 1984). Though research suggests that the expression of certain emotions are universal, there has been considerable disagreement among biosocial theorists as to what comprises this set of basic or primary emotions and the precise role of the face in generating such emotions (Vanman and Miller, 1993).

If the claim of biosocial theorists is true and there is a set of basic emotions universal in their experience and expression, the implications for the psychology of religion are significant. Such universality would imply an overlap of "pure" (i.e., uncontaminated by religious teaching, cultural values, etc.) basic emotional experience across religious traditions and would, at first glance, simplify the study of religion and affect considerably. This still does not suggest an easy task, however, for researchers must also consider the interaction of religious teaching and other transmissions of religious and cultural values with the primary set of emotions. But the possibilities are numerous and provocative. For example, if the universal characteristics and causes of a basic emotion such as fear can be articulated, then how that fear interacts with the teachings of religious traditions can be investigated. Thus a universal emotion such as fear may be experienced quite differently within a religious tradition that emphasizes a wrathful or punitive God than teachings within a tradition which stresses a patient, loving, and forgiving God.

Appraisal Theories: Appraisal theorists (e.g., Lazarus, 1982, 1984, 1991; Ortony, Clore, and Collins, 1988; Schachter, 1964), on the other hand, emphasize that emotions require cognitive interpretations or appraisals. Two people, therefore, may respond to the same event or object and yet experience different emotions. Differences among appraisal theorists are accounted for primarily in terms of the specific dimensions defined as relevant to emotional appraisals (Vanman and Miller, 1993). For example, Ortony et al. (1988) specified three dimensions upon which an emotional appraisal is determined: 1) whether the action agent is self or other; 2) whether the action is approved or disapproved; and 3) the extent to which the action affects personal well-being. Thus the difference between feeling guilty or angry when, for example, a close friend is hurt by another's actions may be determined by the first dimension. If the action agent is one's self, a sense of guilt may be experienced. But if another person performed the hurtful behavior, anger may result.

The Ortony et al. (1988) dimensions are useful for religious appraisals as well. For instance, one could make a valenced evaluation of an action (i.e., approval/disapproval) in terms of whether it is pleasing to God. If the appraisal is "God approved," then, if the agent is the self, one can feel comfort and/or pride (unless prohibited by religious teaching), much as a child may feel upon pleasing his or her parents. If the agent is other, one can feel admiration or gratefulness. Similar emotional distinctions depending on whether the action agent is self or other may occur if the religious appraisal is negatively valenced (i.e., displeasing to God) as well.

With regard to religious appraisals, Bassett et al. (1990) conducted a study with implications for the third dimension suggested by Ortony et al. (1988): the extent to which personal well-being is involved. As an indirect test of Narramore's (1984) theory contrasting the emotional experiences of guilt (a destructive emotion) and "Godly sorrow" (a constructive emotion), Bassett et al. (1990) found that one of the major distinctions is the extent to which the self (as compared to another) becomes the focus of attention. Christian respondents within their study said that if, for example, after hurting another person, the agent is concerned primarily about his or her own feelings, then that would be the cause of guilt. If, however, the agent's focus of concern was the feelings of the wronged person, then that is characteristic of Godly sorrow.

Rather than advocating a general biosocial or appraisal approach to the study of emotion in particular, and affect in general, both perspectives will be used to discuss the role of affect in religious experience. What will serve as the structural organization for the next two sections of this chapter then are ways in which affect and cognition influence each other within the realm of religious experience. Some of the research reviewed could be discussed in either section, depending upon the point of origin within this reciprocal causal relationship.

COGNITIVE INFLUENCE ON AFFECT

Certainly how a person understands his or her religion will influence the affective nature of the religious experience. It is therefore important to identify cognitive antecedents of the affective experience of religion. Since another entire chapter (McCallister) is devoted to the cognitive basis of religion, the review here will be brief and necessarily selective.

Religion-as-Schema

A potentially valuable conception of religious experience is to consider religion in terms of cognitive schemas (McIntosh, 1991). Though conceived in a variety of ways, schemas are typically said to be "cognitive structures of organized prior knowledge, abstracted from experience with specific instances" (Fiske and Linville, 1980:543). Such structures are useful in that they influence what in the environment is perceived and how it is perceived.

It is apparent that people conceive their environment in terms of their schematic organization (Taylor and Crocker, 1981; McIntosh, 1991). Thus, a devoutly religious person may impose a religious interpretation on events and this, in turn, may influence an affective response. So, for example, a religious individual who interprets abortion as a violation of "God's law" may possess unusually strong feelings—anger, disgust, grief—because the issue is interpreted through a self-defined relevant and important schema. An excellent example relating schema to affect is provided in McIntosh's (1991) discussion of research results reported by Gorer (1965). Gorer found that the Spiritualists and Christian Scientists in his sample do not appear to experience even inward grief following the death of a loved one. McIntosh interprets Gorer's findings in schematic terms by suggesting that for these people, death is not worthy of grief because of a religious schema that denies the importance of death.

Cognitive-Arousal Theory

Yet another perspective with major implications for the psychology of religion, which demonstrates the effect of cognition on emotion, is what is known as cognitive-arousal theory (Schachter, 1964). Schachter and Singer's (1962) classic study of the combined effects of an injected drug, epinephrine, with available external factors on emotional experience provided the impetus for this well-known theory of emotion. This theoretical framework suggests that emotions are products of bodily arousal interpreted within the context of emotion-eliciting circumstances that require cognitive assessment. The basic premise is that if no immediate explanation is apparent for a physiological arousal, the individual will label the state in terms of whatever cognitions are available. Further, it is the subsequent level of physiological arousal that determines the extent to which the individual later experiences the emotion in reaction to the same cognitive circumstance. The emotion itself then is not experienced until both the arousal and cognitive components are engaged.

Among some of the most relevant research of cognitive-arousal theory for the psychology of religion can be found in the *mis*attribution literature. If an individual is in an active search for labeling an emotion and if such a search is dependent on salient contextual cues, then the individual may mislabel the arousal. For such mislabeling to occur outside the laboratory, Olson and Ross (1988) suggested that the alternative cause must also be without ambiguity, highly plausible, and perceived to be of considerable strength.

The extent to which misattributions are found in religious experience is unclear. But it does seem that religious (mis)attributions could on occasion meet the Olson and Ross (1988) criteria. What is clear, however, is that *contextual effects* alone are not likely to lead to religious (mis)attributions (Lupfer, Brock, and DePaola, 1992). Therefore, mere presence in a worship service, for example, may not lead to a religious assessment of a physiological arousal. However, if the actual arousal is unclear and a worship leader earnestly invokes the presence of God, there is greater likelihood of a religious (mis)attribution.

Religious Coping

The biblical writer Paul's admonition to the Christians at Philippi to "be anxious for nothing" (Philippians 4:6) is a forerunner of psychologists' recent interest in religiousness as a potential buffer to stress. Given 1) the well-documented relationship between negative affect and negative health outcomes (Scheier and Carver, 1985), 2) that many people turn to religion as a coping resource (Koenig, George, and Siegler, 1988), and 3) the complex relationship between affect, religious orientation, and religious coping style (Schaefer and Gorsuch, 1991), the role of religious coping as a mediator of affect is a topic well worth investigating.

Emotion and coping occur in a dynamic mutually reciprocal relationship. Central to this relationship is the role of cognitive *appraisal* (Folkman and Lazarus, 1990; Pargament, 1990). That is, when a transaction with the environment is appraised as significant to a person's well-being—threatening, beneficial, challenging—the individual engages in a coping response that changes the person-environment relationship, and hence the emotional reaction (Folkman and Lazarus, 1990). In this sense, then, coping can be viewed as a mediator of emotional response.

Effective Religious Coping: A growing body of research indicates that people are likely to turn to religion for comfort when confronting events appraised as threatening, especially to the physical self, such as serious accidents (Bulman and Wortman, 1977), severe illness (Jenkins and Pargament, 1988), chronic pain (Kotarba, 1983), and bereavement (Maton, 1989; Rosik, 1989). The likelihood of using religion to cope may be partially determined by the extent to which religious schemas are already in place. Given that schemas seem to expedite cognitive processing and facilitate the finding of meaning in an event (McIntosh, 1991), we can expect that religious schemas often help in coping.

Research suggests that at least some types of religious coping strategies are especially effective in reducing depression following bereavement (Mattlin, Wethington, and Kessler, 1990) and in situations of uncontrollable stress (Park, Cohen, and Herb, 1990). Schaefer and Gorsuch (1991) found that a collaborative coping strategy (Pargament et al., 1988), where the self and God are viewed as a dynamic problem-solving partnership, mediated the relationship between religious belief and anxiety. In particular, collaborative intrinsics with images of God as benevolent, stable, and powerful appeared to be better adjusted psychologically, at least in terms of reduced anxiety.

What is religion's distinctive that can provide such coping benefits? The prevalence and apparent utility of religious coping can be expected for a number of reasons, many of which tie to the three basic coping themes discussed by Taylor (1983) and echoed by Spilka, Shaver, and Kirkpatrick (1985): a search for meaning, an attempt to regain mastery or control, and an effort to restore or enhance self-esteem.

Sense of mastery. Since some forms of physical threats (e.g., life-threatening diseases, naturalistic disasters, etc.) are at best only partly amenable to individual problem-solving, coping efforts may necessitate belief in something beyond naturalistic conventional wisdom to provide a sense of mastery. The tendency to involve the supernatural dimension appears to be a function of how threatening an event is. Some dimensions, such as physical and financial, appear to be more important to the individual and, in turn, more distress-producing when threatened, than other dimensions, such as the psychological and social. Religious individuals are prone to see God as a causal agent for the more important physical and financial domains, especially when the outcomes are positive (Gorsuch and Smith, 1983).

Religious coping, particularly of the collaborative variety (Pargament et al., 1988), therefore, may offer a sense of control (Spilka, Shaver, and Kirkpatrick, 1985; Taylor, 1983). The collaborative coper, who otherwise may sense a lack of control over personal destiny, may find solace that the "team" (i.e., God and self) *is* in control.

Sense of meaning. An individual may alter his or her emotional state by changing the meaning or significance of the threatening event (Folkman and Lazarus, 1990). In this case, the religious individual may reframe a threat to either as a test of one's faith that will eventually result in spiritual growth or as an accomplishment of God's will. Such reframing can transform a negative feeling, such as anger or depression, into a positive affectual state, such as a sense of challenge, personal growth, or even gratitude. Thus, religious coping may allow an individual to focus on controlling unpleasant emotions in the face of threatening conditions (Ellison, 1993). Bijur et al. (1993) found that men and women differ in the affective benefits of religious coping. Both genders affectively benefit, just in different ways. For women, the use of religion in coping was inversely related to negative affect, such as feeling anxious, angry, overwhelmed, and ashamed. For men, religiously coping was positively related to positive affect such as feeling interested or involved, feeling in control, and feeling challenged. These results suggest that gender may be an important moderator in the relationship between stress, the impact of stress on health and functioning, and the use of religion in coping.

Sense of optimism. Religion, especially of a more fundamental variety (such as Orthodox Judaism or Calvinism), may promote more optimistic explanations of events (Sethi and Seligman, 1993). Religious conservatives may use a different attributional logic that encourages optimism. Smith and Gorsuch (1989) reported that conservatives are more likely to 1) attribute greater responsibility to God, 2) view God as active through multiple channels rather than a single modality, and 3) see God work conjunctively with (or through) natural causes, including one's own personal behavior (i.e., the individual sees him or herself as an "agent" of God). Not only does such a perspective provide greater religious influence on daily life, but it also encourages religious involvement and provides a sense of hope, factors empirically identified by Sethi and Seligman as central to optimism.

Ineffective Religious Coping: The ledger presented thus far suggests that religion can be used in constructive and beneficial ways. But critics of religion have long contended that religious beliefs can also be used as a crutch and can negate other effective coping strategies, possibly by immobilizing the person as he or she "waits on the Lord."

To help determine whether religion is part of the problem or part of the solution, Pargament et al. (1993) have recommended three broad types of warning signs, or "red flags," of ineffectual religious coping: when religious coping reflects and even encourages an imbalance between self-concern and concerns beyond the self ("Wrong Direction"); where the religious coping strategy is inappropriate to the threatening life event ("Wrong Road"); and where the individual experiences religious conflict in the coping process ("Against the Stream"). "Wrong Direction" can include the chronically self-sacrificial person, the self-devalued person, and the self-glorified person. Typical of a "Wrong Road" approach is the use of religion to deny a negative event or to use the event as a means to unjustly punish one's self. An example of "Against the Stream" is the use of religion to cope while simultaneously either doubting the religion's validity or feeling angry with God.

Initial research on the warning signs produced mixed results (Pargament et al., 1993). Indeed, some signs were red flags; feelings of being punished by God, doubts about one's religion, and anger with God correlated positively with indicators of poorer mental health and event outcomes. Some signs, however, were anything but red flags. Signs of sacrificial commitment and religious denial were associated with *better* mental health and event outcomes. Concluding that psychologists of religion should take a closer look at the meaning of religious phrases that are commonly used in coping, the researchers found, for example, that religious denial could also be thought of as a religious "reappraisal." In other words, denial may not be so much of the negative event itself, but of the event's negative emotional impact. So, again, *how* an event is appraised in religious terms appears to be a crucial factor in determining the efficacy of religious coping strategy.

AFFECTIVE INFLUENCE ON COGNITION

Cognitive impact on affect is only half the story. A growing body of research suggesting that feelings influence cognitions also has a variety of applications to religious experience.

Attributional Processes

Research on cognitive-arousal theory and the person's vulnerability to misattributions, whether of the religious variety or not, may lead the reader to ask why might an individual make a religious attribution in the first place. Drawing from the rather extensive social-psychological literature, Spilka et al. (1985) have suggested that people may utilize religious attributions when their sense of meaning, control, and self-esteem are undermined. Clearly, then, religious attributions are "hot" cognitions.

It is in the area of emotional experience that attributional processes were first introduced to the psychology of religion (Proudfoot and Shaver, 1975) and one area, among others, in the study of religious experience, where attribution theory continues to generate research (Spilka, Brown, and Cassidy, 1992). One of the limits of cognitive-arousal theory, misattribution research, and Proudfoot and Shaver's analysis of religious conversion is that the attribution processes described are data-driven. That is, such processes are determined by immediate situational information to the exclusion of information brought by the individual to the situation.

Affective experience, however, is also determined by top-down theory-driven judgments such as people's knowledge about the situation they are entering (Weiner, 1985), schematic memories of affect (Leventhal, 1980, 1984), and affective expectations brought to the situation (Wilson et al., 1989). It is therefore important to account for affective factors in the process by which the individual arrives at a situational context.

Storage of Affect

An Independent Mechanism: Many biosocial theorists, most notably Leventhal (1980, 1984), have proposed that emotions are represented in an independent memory system distinct from cognitively based memories. The existence of a separate memory mechanism suggests that religious development not only consists of held cognitions and beliefs from religious teachings, but also includes separate representations of felt emotions toward religion.

An independent mechanism storing affectively based memories may create an "emotional readiness" toward religious experience. Ozorak's (1992) conception of religious faith as "an emotional landscape of primordial strength and simplicity upon which we erect structures of more reasoned belief" (p.1) contends that one's religion is largely based on an emotional framework through which religious teachings are assimilated. The framework itself, whether influenced by genetic factors (Waller et al., 1990) or early emotional experiences (Ozorak, 1992), becomes an anchoring base for later religious belief, including the typical adjustments of belief during adolescence (Ozorak, 1989). Thus, even though an adolescent's set of beliefs may reflect modification from parental teachings, rarely is there wholesale rejection of the belief system and, conversely, the framework often becomes even more firmly established (a polarization effect).

Emotion memories may also be more difficult to change than cognitive memories (Leventhal, 1980). One might infer then that a faith commitment rooted in affective-based memories may be more resistant to change (Ozorak, 1992). Though not a direct test of this hypothesis, Hunsberger's (1980; Hunsberger and Brown, 1984) research on apostasy has found that one of the key predictors of later "keeping the faith" is the emphasis on religion in the childhood home environment. The "staying-power" of emotion-based memories may help explain why a majority of United States Catholics wish to remain a part of the Catholic church despite serious differences with the church on such social issues as clergy marital status, abortion, and the morality of sex outside of marriage ("How U.S. Catholics," 1993).

Affective Schematic Memories: Our affective response to a stimulus may be influenced by memories of affect in similar situations. This does not suggest that our memories are always correct; evidence indicates, to the contrary, that memories are often distorted. Sometimes the memories themselves are distorted (Hasher, Attig, and Alba, 1981) and sometimes the relative significance of the memory to current experience is distorted, such as when memories are used in a selective fashion to confirm a belief (Snyder and Cantor, 1979). When strong feeling is involved, such as what may be found in religious experience, distortions are potentially magnified.

Nevertheless, people's memories of emotional experiences, whether distorted or not, oftentimes trigger an affective reaction to the same or similar stimulus. When a person encounters an emotion, a schema is created and represented in memory in terms of perceptual, motor, and subjective feelings which, when confirmed through subsequent experiences, becomes an emotional prototype (Leventhal, 1980, 1984). Such *schematic processing* is automatic and does not require higher-level *conceptual processing*. Emotions may be processed at a conceptual level, where the individual reflects upon experiences and draws conclusions, sometimes in abstraction, about a proper affective response, but such processing relies more on the volitional use of memories and is thereby under the relative control of the individual. Since underlying feelings are often stronger when they haven't been analyzed (Millar and Tesser, 1986), schematic memories may be especially powerful.

It is contended that schematic memories are central to religious experience. Two interrelated lines of research will be considered here as support: people's images of God and the role of attachment in religious experience.

God images. It is likely that many images of God are rooted in affective schematic memory. For example, Jubis (1991, as reported in Kirkpatrick, 1994) found that God-images among Catholic fourth-graders correlated highly with parent-images, which were undoubtedly influenced by schematic memory. For instance, a maternal image of supportive reassurance, affectionate support, and tolerant helpfulness correlated positively with an image of God who "listens to me" and "pays attention to me." Similarly, the prevalence of paternal images of God (Roof and Roof, 1984) may be influenced by the memories or images of a father who, in the mind's eye of the child, could do just about anything. On the other hand, one's image of God may be negative if an affective schematic memory of a father (or mother) is unpleasant.

Attachment processes. Attachment processes in religious experience (Kirkpatrick, 1992, 1994; Kirkpatrick and Shaver, 1990) also utilize affective schematic memory. Based on Bowlby's (1969) notion that the infant is motivated to maintain attachment with it's caregiver and that such attachment tendencies exert influence on behavior throughout the lifespan, Kirkpatrick and Shaver contend that "the God of most Christian traditions seems to correspond very closely to the idea of a secure attachment figure" (1990:318). The authors further maintain that "this theoretical perspective offers a potentially powerful framework for integrating research findings in the psychology of religion concerning such diverse topics as images, sudden religious conversions, prayer, and glossolalia" (1990:318). An underlying premise of their application of attachment theory to religion is what they have labeled the "mental model hypothesis" where one's working models of early attachment relationships become the basis for constructing images of God and other religious beliefs. A potential convert, thus, may assess his or her attachment relationships, conclude they are wanting, and see God as a substitute attachment figure. An empirical investigation by Kirkpatrick and Shaver (1990) supported this "compensation hypothesis"; higher religious adult sentiment was associated with avoidant maternal attachments. Seeking God as a substitute attachment for avoidant human attachments requires that the individual have affective-based memories, perhaps unconsciously, of the parent-child relationship. Similarly, Kirkpatrick's (1994) conceptualization of religious longing as seeking closeness (a proximity function), care (a haven function), and security (a secure base function) from God as a substitute attachment figure necessitates the presence of strongly felt schematic memories.

The more we investigate the role that affective memories play in religious experience, the more we may understand such phenomena as how religious belief is anchored in early socialization processes, why people maintain certain images of God, and how God is used as a substitute attachment. A broadly based theoretical approach that incorporates affective memory may help researchers integrate a number of these important psychological processes that appear central to religious experience.

Affective Expectations: People's affective memories influence their expectations of how they will feel about a given experience or behavior (Fiske, 1982; Wilson et al., 1989) which, in turn, influences their actual reaction. "Going forward" at a Billy Graham crusade, for example, can be thought of as a conscious, planned conversion (Beit-Hallahmi, 1993) in that the individual most likely knew (simply by attending) what he or she was getting into in the first place.

Jones and McGillis (1976) differentiated between *target-based expectancies*, where expectations are based on prior responses to the object or event, and *category-based expectancies*, which rely on knowledge of how other people reacted to the object or event. Target-based expectancies may often be determined by schematic memories of affect. Thus, under conditions of conflict or turmoil the individual may suddenly experience relief when remembering prior positive benefits of leaving similar circumstances "in the Lord's hands." Likewise, religious category-based expectancies may be influenced by the affective schematic memories from testimonials of others, what Tversky and Kahneman (1973) refer to as the "availability bias."

What happens if affective expectations are disconfirmed by experience? Traditional dissonance theory (Festinger, 1957) suggested a resulting cognitive tension which is often resolved by altering the beliefs (in this case, expectations) to fit the experience. But initial research on affective expectations (Wilson et al., 1989) found that people with strong affective expectations were more likely to examine the stimulus relatively quickly, rate the stimulus consistently with the expectation, and engage in less conscious thought about the stimulus while evaluating it. What results is that often the discrepancy between expectation and experience either goes unnoticed or the size of the discrepancy is downplayed. By this time the emotional commitment may be so strong that it would be virtually impossible for the individual to alter beliefs for the sake of reducing discrepancy (Abelson, 1988).

Of course, there will be times when the discrepancy between expectation and reality cannot be denied. In such cases, the methods of cognitive tension reduction suggested by dissonance theory (Festinger, 1957) may apply. Religious beliefs often involve strongly affective expectations and are highly resilient to change, even in the face of negative major events (Calhoun, Tedeschi, and Lincourt, 1992). Because of their resiliency, religious beliefs may be in the unique position to offer ways of assimilating negative events. Thus, following the death of a loved one despite fervent prayer for healing, the efficacy of prayer may not be questioned. Rather, the belief system is modified to accommodate the actuality of death (i.e., "it was God's will").

Religious Convictions

Religious beliefs and attitudes, like any other belief or attitude, can be firmly held with passion or can be just superficially maintained. Abelson

(1988), arguing that certain beliefs, including many religious beliefs, can have a possessive-like quality (i.e., something you "own," not something you merely "have"), suggests that the study of strong belief, or conviction, has much to offer the field of psychology. His research suggests three underlying factors: emotional commitment, ego preoccupation, and cognitive elaboration. There is clearly an affective base to strong belief.

Suggesting a similar core with two important attitude research traditions, attitude centrality and attitude accessibility, Abelson (1988) prefers the term conviction because it is often used in a phenomenonological sense to describe strong feeling. People talk about their "convictions" rather than the centrality or accessibility of their attitudes. Conviction is also sometimes used as a religious term and is therefore a favored term for this discussion. Yet the research traditions of attitude centrality and accessibility can enrich our understanding of religious convictions.

Attitude Centrality: Attitudes associated with strong religious beliefs or convictions are likely to be *central* attitudes in that the self and the attitude object (i.e., elements of one's religious faith) are closely linked. Among other things, such highly central attitudes a) are associated with stronger affective reactions, b) are more consistent and interlinked with other attitudes and values, c) are more resistant to change, and d) have greater impact on subsequent evaluations and judgments (Krosnick, 1989). The centrality of religious attitudes may be a key indication of how personally involving one's religious experience is.

Construct and Attitude Accessibility: Another way of thinking about religious conviction is in terms of construct and attitude accessibility. In his seminal work, Kelly (1955) coined the term construct[2] as a category used by necessity to effectively handle an overabundance of social information. Kelly suggested that people develop a somewhat limited framework of constructs based on frequent experience with detectable characteristics of social behavior (e.g., kindness, cruelty) typically found in one's environment. This framework results in the habitual or chronic use of certain categories to interpret social interaction. The religious person may utilize religious concepts as a construct system, thereby interpreting observed behavior, for example, as sinful or righteous. The words of a popular song during the Jesus movement of the 1970s entitled "They will know we are Christians by our love" communicates a religious construct. In this song, Christian social behavior ("love") is construed as demonstrating unity by guarding each other's dignity and saving each other's pride.

Recent derivations of Kelly's theory, with important implications for the study of religious experience, have focused on the *accessibility* of social constructs. For example, research has suggested that if a religious construct is highly accessible, it a) is likely to be stable (Dornbusch et al., 1965), b) is likely to have greater impact on subjective impressions and social recall (Higgins, King, and Mavin, 1982), c) has been frequently activated (Higgins and King, 1981), and d) can occur in response to both momentary, context-dependent cues as well as chronic, context-independent stimuli (Bargh et al., 1986).

Hill (in press; Hill and Bassett, 1992) has suggested that construct or attitude accessibility may be a useful indicator of the importance and strength of religious belief (i.e., conviction). Based upon the model offered by Fazio and his associates (Fazio, 1989; Fazio et al., 1986), Hill maintained that some religious attitudes are automatic; that is, an attitude may be activated automatically without conscious control upon the mere presentation of a religious attitude object (e.g., a cross or a statue of Mary).[3] Such occurrence may be descriptive of what a highly religious person may experience. In contrast, a less religious person may require considerable effort (a "controlled" process) in constructing an attitude toward the object.

An initial test of religious automaticity (Hill, Jennings, Haas, and Seybold, 1992) has been conducted. It was predicted that although attitude strength of religious and nonreligious people toward religiously neutral objects (e.g., kitten, smile, crime, etc.) would be similar, attitude strength toward religious objects (e.g., Bible, salvation, damnation, etc.) would be greater for religious people. This prediction was supported. Using introductory psychology students with the highest and lowest twenty-five measures of religiosity from a scale administered in class two weeks earlier, it was found that religious students could identify a religious object presented on a computer screen as "good" or "bad" faster than could nonreligious students. However, as expected, no differences were found among religiously neutral words.

Hill (in press) maintained that an attitude process model of religious experience has much to offer the psychology of religion. First, he suggested that this model may fill a void in the psychology of religion literature on unconscious decision-making models, a concern articulated by Gorsuch (1986) when discussing "reasoned action" models of religious experience. Second, given Kirkpatrick and Hood's (1990) concern about an over-reliance on the intrinsic-extrinsic (I-E) religious orientation paradigm, the attitude process model may provide an alternative conception of the importance and centrality of religion within psychological experience. Third, the concept may introduce a useful unobtrusive measure (response latency) in the psychology of religion. The measure is currently rather awkward to implement; however, software programs designed for such a measure are becoming common. Fourth, the model may have predictive validity of attitudes' resiliency to counterinfluence and thus may be useful in predicting religious apostasy. Finally, the model may provide insight into attitude-behavior discrepancies which, like most other behavioral domains, may also plague religious behavior.

Reasoning Bias: People with strongly held religious beliefs may be prone to biased reasoning, despite the fact that research has failed to find a consistent relationship between religiousness and rationality (Baither and Saltzberg,

1978). Considerable research indicates that when people hold a strong opinion on a matter, they are more likely to demonstrate biased reasoning on that matter. For example, studies (Feather, 1964; Lynn and Williams, 1990) have found syllogistic reasoning to be influenced by prior attitude toward syllogism content. Syllogisms were judged to be more logical by people who agreed with their content and less logical by those who disagreed. People without strong opinions either way were the most accurate (Lynn, 1987). The only investigation of syllogistic reasoning with religious belief was Feather's (1964) study. He found that religious beliefs were no different than other beliefs in distorting reasoning processes.

Lynn and Williams (1990) discovered that strong beliefs toward labor unions were vulnerable to three types of reasoning bias: judgment of plausibility, contrast effects, and social attribution. It is likely that these same reasoning biases exist in the presence of other strong beliefs, including religious beliefs (Lynn, 1987).

A PROTOTYPE APPROACH TO EMOTION

In the opening paragraphs of this chapter, it was pointed out that affect and emotion are difficult terms to define, that there is little consensus about how they should be conceptualized, and that there is the lack of a general integrative theory of affect as it applies to religious experience. One reason for this disarray may be the rather strong adherence to a classical view of emotion which requires that to know the meaning or intension of a concept, one must know its necessary and sufficient features (Russell, 1991). Markman (1989) claimed that classical definitions require that categories have both intension (attributes or features that define a category) and extension (a set of objects or members of a category that fulfill the intensional criteria) that determine one another. Some (Averill, 1980; Kagan, 1978), including James (1902), questioned whether classical definitions of emotion are even a possibility. If these individuals were correct, then my call in the introduction for a comprehensive theory of affect in religious experience will be nothing more than an unfulfilled dream.

But an alternative and provocative approach to emotion theory, with implications for religious experience, has been surfacing recently in the literature (Lysak, Rule, and Dobbs, 1989; Russell, 1991). These authors promote a prototype analysis of emotion. In this approach, members of a category are determined by sufficient resemblance to prototypical exemplars, which can be empirically determined. For emotion concepts, a prototypical exemplar may be determined by a sequence of subevents, or a script (Russell, 1991). Thus, there may be a prototypical script for anger (e.g., harmful intention by offender, victim glares and scowls, victim feels tension and agitation, victim desires retribution, victim strikes at offender) by which an actual event is compared. The closer the resemblance between the script and actual event, the more appropriate is the script label.

The feasibility of the prototype approach to emotion concepts have been empirically explored in a number of studies. Initial research reported by Russell (1991) suggested that although the emotion concept has fuzzy boundaries, some emotions (e.g., happiness, love, anger) are more prototypical than others. Russell concluded that although further work needs to be done, a prototypical approach to the study of affect warrants consideration.

What does this approach offer the psychology of religion? Most importantly, a prototype approach allows the religious experience itself to help define the emotion. This may mean (with obvious measurement implications), for example, that the *content* of the religious beliefs may help define the affective experience.

An indirect application of the prototype approach to the study of religious experience has been offered by Bassett and his colleagues (Bassett et al., 1993). Their approach is a modified version of Schachter and Singer's (1962) theory of emotion where a particular emotion is a function of physical arousal ("A"), cognitive interpretation ("C"), and expression ("E"). The "ACE" model suggests that what determines the moral direction of the emotion are factors associated with the cognitive and expressive, but not arousal domains. Hence, what might be construed by a highly religious person as a negative (and therefore, problematic) emotion, such as anger, may in fact be justified if experienced for the "right" reason (cognition) and in an appropriate manner (expression).

Based upon an earlier investigation (Bassett et al., 1989) which surveyed Christian therapists regarding their personal and professional experiences with anger, four factors were identified and subsequently empirically verified that discriminated "righteous" from "sinful" anger: a) whether or not the person overreacted in anger; b) whether or not the person was following specific Godly principles; c) whether or not the individual experienced initial negative results from the anger; and d) whether or not another person was being mistreated. Results from research on other potentially "problematic" emotions for the religious person such as guilt (Bassett et al., 1990) and anxiety (Hill, Bassett, and Rowe, 1989), as well as a positive emotion such as love (Bassett et al., 1993 Study 2), support the ACE model.

The prototype approach to the study of religious experience has obvious limitations. Most notably, a religious emotional prototype may reflect only a particular religious tradition. Thus, the ACE model may reflect only an orthodox Christian perspective. But this very limitation is also what makes the prototype approach intriguing and a potentially fertile means for studying religious experience. For example, one evident program of research would be to apply the ACE model to other religions. Indeed, one may find that a certain body of emotions, regardless of religious identity, is viewed as either morally positive or negative and that similar criteria across religions are used in making such distinctions. The extent to which distinguishing elements in other religions are a function of the cognitive and expressive domains, as Bassett et al. (1993) found among Christians, is a topic that requires empirical determination.

CONCLUSION

"You see now . . . why I have seemed so bent on rehabilitating the element of feeling in religion and subordinating its intellectual part" (James, 1902:492). These words by James are every bit as appropriate today as they were at the turn of the century. It has been contended throughout this chapter that a consideration of recent advances in affect theory and research will greatly enrich the study of religious experience. The growing literature on affect, only briefly reviewed here, has yet to make a significant impact on either prevailing theory or on current methodology in the psychology of religion.

Research in the psychology of religion has been dominated by Allport's (1950; Allport and Ross, 1967) intrinsic-extrinsic paradigm. Though it remains unclear precisely what intrinsic and extrinsic religious orientations are (Kirkpatrick and Hood, 1990), Allport originally posited affectively based motivational processes. Similarly, research today on religious experience involves affect through dynamics such as human attachment and coping processes. But whether we are talking about religious orientation, attachment, or coping, little is being said directly about underlying emotional experience.

What has been suggested here is that there is certain value of "getting back to the basics" in studying the affective component of religious experience. At the same time, it is admitted that the task won't be easy given the historic state of disarray in the study of emotion. But with the demonstrated renewed interest in affect, the time may be ripe for contemporary psychologists of religion to "go back to the future" and acknowledge what James (1902) was trying to tell us all along.

NOTES AND REFERENCES

1. It is common for attitude researchers to define an attitude as a "categorization of a stimulus object along an evaluative dimension" (Zanna and Rempel, 1988:319). In so doing, some attitude theorists (e.g., Fishbein and Ajzen, 1975) confuse the terms attitude and affect in that both involve evaluation. In contrast, Breckler and Wiggins (1989) convincingly argue that affect and evaluation are distinct and are both components of an attitude, implying that affect and attitude are not isomorphic. They maintain that the affective component refers to the emotional responses toward an attitude object, whereas the evaluative component engenders thoughts, beliefs, and judgments about an attitude object. In this sense, attitude is a more general term than affect. While it is tempting to use the terms affect, emotion, and attitude interchangeably, I have tried to carefully use the term most appropriate along the lines differentiated here.

2. The nomenclature here is somewhat confounded. The term "construct" is used because it is a term found frequently in the literature when discussing accessibility. The term is similar to attitude in that constructs frequently employ evaluative criteria. The distinction between the terms construct and schema is even more muddled. In fact, it sometimes appears that the term schema has replaced the term construct. Schemas, as earlier defined in this paper, are a broader classification of cognitive structures than are constructs. Stillings et al. (1987) suggest that schemas for people's personalities and social behavior (the way the term construct is used here) is just one of many types of schemas. Thus, "person schemas" or "self-schema" can be thought of as constructs. McIntosh (1991), in conceptualizing religion as schema, has suggested that religious schemas could include, for example, perspectives on God's nature as well as how God's nature affects the God-person relation. Such schemas could also be called religious constructs, especially given their implication for social relationships and behavior.

3. The concept of automaticity has been useful to the field of cognitive psychology (Shiffrin and Dumais, 1981) but has been only recently applied to the affective domain (Fazio, 1989; Isen and Diamond, 1989). An automatic cognitive process is differentiated from a "controlled" cognitive process in that the former, among other differentiating characteristics, either: a) does not require as much use of cognitive resources nor does it decrease processing capacity; or b) is activated upon the presentation of an external stimulus regardless of any attempt to ignore the stimulus (Shiffrin and Dumais, 1981). So two sufficient features of automaticity are its effortlessness and its inescapability.

Abelson, R. P.
1988 Conviction. *American Psychologist* 43:267-275.

Allport, G. W.
1950 *The individual and his religion.* New York: Macmillan.

Allport, G. W., and J. M. Ross
1967 Personal religious orientation and prejudice. *Journal of Personality and Social Psychology* 5:432-443.

Averill, J. L.
1980 A constructivist view of emotion. In Vol. 1 of *Theories of emotion*, edited by R. Plutchik and H. Kellerman. San Diego: Academic Press.

Baither, R. C., and L. Saltzberg
1978 Relationship between religious attitude and rational thinking. *Psychological Reports* 43:853-854.

Bargh, J. A., R. N. Bond, W. J. Lombardi, and M. E. Tota
1986 The additive nature of chronic and temporary sources of construct accessibility. *Journal of Personality and Social Psychology* 50:869-878.

Bassett, R. L., P. C. Hill, C. Hart, K. Mathewson, and K. Perry
1993 Helping Christians reclaim some abandoned emotions: The ACE model of emotion. *Journal of Psychology and Theology* 21:165-173.

Bassett, R. L., P. C. Hill, M.C. Pogel, M. Lee, R. Hughes, and J. Masci
1990 Comparing psychological guilt and Godly sorrow: Do Christians recognize the difference? *Journal of Psychology and Theology* 18:244-254.

Bassett, R. L., P. Ridley, P. Swan, L. Lehmann, V. Crothers, H. Nielsen, B. Peters, R. Robson, J. Rosko, M. Ryan, and C. Stiefler
1989 Righteous and sinful anger from the perspective of Christian therapists and college students. *Journal of Psychology and Christianity* 8:47-56.

Beit-Hallahmi, B.
1993 *Mystery of private salvation: Learning from James and Freud.* Paper presented at the meeting of the American Psychological Association, Toronto, ON (August).

Bijur, P. E., K. A. Wallston, C. A. Smith, S. Lifrak, and S. B. Friedman
1993 *Gender differences in turning to religion for coping.* Paper presented at the annual meeting of the American Psychological Association, Toronto, ON (August).

Bowlby, J.
1969 Attachment. Vol. 1 of *Attachment and loss.* New York: Basic Books.

Breckler, S. J., and E. C. Wiggins
1989 On defining attitude and attitude theory. Once more with feeling. In *Attitude structure and*

function, edited by A. R. Pratkanis, S. J. Breckler, and A. G. Greenwald. Hillsdale, NJ: Erlbaum.

Bulman, I., and C. Wortman
1977 Attributions of blame and coping in the "real world": Severe accident victims react to their lot. *Journal of Personality and Social Psychology* 35:351-363.

Calhoun, L. G., R. G. Tedeschi, and A. Lincourt
1992 *Life crises and religious beliefs: Changed beliefs or assimilated events?* Paper presented at the annual meeting of the American Psychological Association, Washington, DC (August).

Dornbusch, S. M., A. H. Hastorf, S. A. Richardson, R. E. Muzzy, and R. S. Vreeland
1965 The perceiver and the perceived: Their relative influence on the categories of interpersonal cognition. *Journal of Personality and Social Psychology* 1:434-440.

Ekman, P.
1984 Expression and the nature of emotion, In *Approaches to emotion*, edited by K. R. Scherer and P. Ekman. Hillsdale, NJ: Erlbaum.

Ellison, C. G.
1993 Religious involvement and self-perception among Black Americans. *Social Forces* 71:1027-1055.

Fazio, R. H.
1989 On the power and functionality of attitudes: The role of attitude accessibility. In *Attitude structure and function,* edited by A. R. Pratkanis, S. J.Beckler, and A. G. Greenwald. Hillsdale, NJ: Erlbaum.

Fazio, R. H., D. M. Sanbonmatsu, M. C. Powell, and F. C. Kardes
1986 On the automatic activation of attitudes. *Journal of Personality and Social Psychology* 50:229-238.

Feather, N. T.
1964 Acceptance and rejection of arguments in relation to attitude strength, critical ability, and intolerance of inconsistency. *Journal of Abnormal and Social Psychology* 69:127-136.

Festinger, L.
1957 *A theory of cognitive dissonance*. Stanford, CA: Stanford University Press.

Fishbein, M., and I. Ajzen
1975 *Belief, attitude, intention, and behavior: An introduction to theory and research*. Reading, MA: Addison Wesley.

Fiske, S. T.
1982 Schema-triggered affect: Applications to social perception. In *Affect and cognition*, edited by M. S. Clark and S. T. Fiske. Hillsdale, NJ: Erlbaum.

Fiske, S. T., and P. W. Linville
1980 What does the schema concept buy us? *Personality and Social Psychology Bulletin* 6:543-557.

Folkman, S., and R. S. Lazarus
1990 Coping and emotion. In *Psychological and biological approaches to emotion*, edited by N.L. Stern, B. Leventhal, and T. Trabaso. Hillsdale, NJ: Erlbaum.

Gorer, G.
1965 *Death, grief, and mourning in contemporary Briton*. London: Cressent Press.

Gorsuch, R. L.
1986 *BAV: A possible non-reductionistic model for the psychology of religion*. Paper presented at the meeting of the American Psychological Association, Washington, DC (August).

Gorsuch, R. L., and C. S. Smith
1983 Attributions of responsibility to God: An interaction of religious beliefs and outcomes. *Journal for the Scientific Study of Religion* 22:340-352.

Hasher, L., M. S. Attig, and J. W. Alba
1981 I knew it all along—or did I? *Journal of Verbal Learning and Verbal Behavior* 20:86-96.

Higgins, E. T., and G. King
1981 Accessibility of social constructs: Information-processing consequences of individual and contextual variability. In *Personality, cognition, and social interaction*, edited by N. Cantor and J. F. Kihlstrom. Hillsdale, NJ: Erlbaum.

Higgins, E. T., G. A. King, and G. H. Mavin
1982 Individual construct accessibility and subjective impressions and recall. *Journal of Personality and Social Psychology* 43:35-47.
Hilgard, E. R.
1980 The trilogy of mind: Cognition, affection, and conation. *Journal of the History of the Behavioral Sciences* 16:107-117.
Hill, P. C.
in press Toward an attitude process model of religious experience. *Journal for the Scientific Study of Religion.*
Hill, P. C., and R. L. Bassett
1992 Getting to the heart of the matter: What the social-psychological study of attitudes has to offer psychology of religion. In Vol. 4 of *Research in the social scientific study of religion*, edited by M. L. Lynn and D. O. Moberg. Greenwich, CT: JAI Press.
Hill, P. C., R. L. Bassett, and R. Rowe
1989 *Understanding the role of anxiety in the Christian experience: An empirical analysis.* Paper presented at the annual conference of the Christian Association for Psychological Studies, Philadelphia (April).
Hill, P. C., M. A. Jennings, D. D. Haas, and K. S. Seybold
1992 *Automatic and controlled activation of religious attitudes*. Paper presented at the meeting of the American Psychological Association, Washington, DC (August).
How U.S. Catholics view their church. (1993, August 10). *USA Today*, 6A.
Hunsberger, B. E.
1980 A re-examination of the antecedents of apostasy. *Review of Religious Research* 21:158-170.
Hunsberger, B. E., and L. B. Brown
1984 Religious socialization, apsotasy, and the impact of family background. *Journal for the Scientific Study of Religion* 23:239-251.
Isen, A. M., and G. A. Diamond
1989 Affect and automaticity. In *Unintended thought*, edited by J. S. Uleman and J. A. Bargh. New York: Guilford Press.
Izard, C. E.
1977 *Human emotions*. New York: Plenum.
James, W.
1902 *The varieties of religious experience: A study in human nature*. New York: Modern Library.
Jenkins, R., and K. I. Pargament
1988 Cognitive appraisals in cancer patients. *Social Science and Medicine* 26:625-633.
Jones, E. E., and D. McGillis
1976 Correspondent inferences and the attribution cube: A comparative reappraisal. In Vol. 1 of *New directions in attribution research*, edited by J. H. Harvey, W. J. Ickes, and R. F. Kidd. Hillsdale, NJ: Erlbaum.
Jubis, R.
1991 *An attachment-theoretical approach to understanding children's conceptions of God.* Doctoral dissertation, University of Denver.
Kagan, J.
1978 On emotion and its development: A working paper. In *The development of affect*, edited by M. Lewis and L. A. Rosenblum. New York: Plenum Press.
Kelly, G. A.
1955 *The psychology of personal constructs*. New York: Norton.
Kirkpatrick, L. A.
1992 An attachment-theory approach to the psychology of religion. *International Journal for the Psychology of Religion* 2:3-28.
1994 The role of attachment in religious belief and behavior. In *Advances in personal attachment relationships, Vol. 5: Adult attachment relationships*, edited by K. Bartholomew and D. Perlman. London: Jessica Kingsley.
Kirkpatrick, L. A., and R. W. Hood

1990 Intrinsic-extrinsic religious orientation: The boon or bane of contemporary psychology of religion? *Journal for the Scientific Study of Religion* 29:442-462.

Kirkpatrick, L. A., and P. R. Shaver
1990 Attachment theory and religion: Childhood attachments, religious beliefs, and conversion. *Journal for the Scientific Study of Religion* 29:315-334.

Koenig, H. G., L. K. George, and I. C. Siegler
1988 The use of religion and other emotion-regulating coping strategies among older adults. *Gerontologist* 28:303-310.

Kotarba, J. A.
1983 Perceptions of death, belief systems, and the process of coping with chronic pain. *Social Science and Medicine* 17:681-689.

Krosnick, J. A.
1989 Attitude importance and attitude accessibility. *Personality and Social Psychology Bulletin* 15:297-308.

Lazarus, R. S.
1982 Thoughts on the relations between emotion and cognition. *American Psychologist* 37:1019-1024.
1984 On the primacy of cognition. *American Psychologist* 39:124-129.
1991 Cognition and motivation in emotion. *American Psychologist* 46:352-367.

Leventhal, H.
1980 Toward a comprehensive theory of emotion. In Vol. 13 of *Advances in experimental social psychology*, edited by L. Berkowitz, 139-207. New York: Academic Press.
1984 A perceptual-motor theory of emotion. In Vol. 17 of *Advances in experimental social psychology*, edited by L. Berkowitz. New York: Academic Press.

Leventhal, H., and A. J. Tomarken
1986 Emotion: Today's problems. *Annual Review of Psychology* 37:565-610.

Lupfer, M. B., K. F. Brock, and S. J. DePaola
1992 The use of secular and religious attributions to explain everyday behavior. *Journal for the Scientific Study of Religion* 31:486-503.

Lynn, M. L.
1987 *How strong beliefs bias reasoning: An exploring model.* Paper presented at the annual meeting of the Religious Research Association, Louisville, KY (October).

Lynn, M. L., and R. N.Williams
1990 Belief-bias and labor unions: The effect of strong attitudes on reasoning. *Journal of Organizational Behavior* 11:335-343.

Lysak, H., B. G. Rule, and A. R. Dobbs
1989 Conceptions of aggression: Prototype or defining features? *Personality and Social Psychology Bulletin* 15:233-243.

Markman, E. M.
1989 *Categorization and naming in children: Problems of induction.* Cambridge, MA: MIT Press.

Maton, K.I.
1989 The stress-buffering role of spiritual support: Cross-sectional and prospective investigations. *Journal for the Scientific Study of Religion* 28:310-323.

Mattlin, J. A., E. Wethington, and R. C. Kessler
1990 Situational determinates of coping and coping effectiveness. *Journal of Health and Social Behavior* 31:103-122.

McIntosh, D. N.
1991 *Religion as schema: Implications for the relation between religion and coping.* Paper presented at the annual meeting of the American Psychological Association, San Francisco (August).

Millar, M. G., and A. Tesser
1986 Effects of affective and cognitive focus on the attitude-behavior relationship. *Journal of Personality and Social Psychology* 51:270-276.

Narramore, S. B.
1984 *No condemnation*: Grand Rapids, MI: Zondervan.

Olson, J. M., and M. Ross
1988 False feedback about placebo effectiveness: Consequences for the misattribution of speech anxiety. *Journal of Experimental Social Psychology* 24:275-291.
Ortony, A., G. L. Clore, and A. Collins
1988 *The cognitive structure of emotions*. Cambridge: Cambridge University Press.
Ozorak, E.W.
1989 Social and cognitive influences on the development of religious beliefs and commitment in adolescence. *Journal for the Scientific Study of Religion* 28:448-463.
1992 *In the eye of the beholder: A social-cognitive model of religious belief development*. Paper presented at the annual meeting of the Society for the Scientific Study of Religion, Washington, DC (November).
Pargament, K. I.
1990 God help me: Toward a theoretical framework of coping for the psychology of religion. In Vol. 2 of *Research in the Social Scientific Study of Religion*, edited by M. L. Lynn and D.O. Moberg. Greenwich, CT: JAI Press.
Pargament, K. I., J. Kennell, W. Hathaway, N. Grevengoed, J. Newman, and W. Jones
1988 Religion and the problem-solving process: Three styles of coping. *Journal for the Scientific Study of Religion* 27:90-104.
Pargament, K. I., P. Stanik, P. Crowe, K. Ishler, L. Friedel, J. Possage, R. Rowiller, M. Ward, and M. Weinborn
1993 *Red flags and religious coping: Identifying some religious warning signs among people in crisis*. Paper presented at the annual meeting of the American Psychological Association, Toronto, ON (August).
Park, C., L. H. Cohen, and L. Herb
1990 Intrinsic religiousness and religious coping as life stress moderators for Catholics verses Protestants. *Journal of Personality and Social Psychology* 59:562-574.
Proudfoot, W., and P. Shaver
1975 Attribution theory and the psychology of religion. *Journal for the Scientific Study of Religion* 14:317-330.
Roof, W. C., and J. L. Roof
1984 Review of the polls: Images of God among Americans. *Journal for the Scientific Study of Religion* 23:201-205.
Rosik, C. H.
1989 The impact of religious orientation on conjugal bereavement among older adults. *International Journal of Aging and Human Development* 28:251-261.
Russell, J. A.
1991 In defense of a prototype approach to emotion concepts. *Journal of Personality and Social Psychology* 60:37-47.
Schachter, S.
1964 The interaction of cognitive and physiological determinants of emotional state. In Vol. 1 of *Advances in experimental social psychology*, edited by L. Berhowitz. New York: Academic Press.
Schacter, S., and J. E. Singer
1962 Cognitive, social, and physiological determinants of emotional state. *Psychological Review* 69:379-399.
Schaefer, C. A., and R. L. Gorsuch
1991 Psychological adjustment and religiousness: The multivariate belief-motivation theory of religiousness. *Journal for the Scientific Study of Religion* 30:448-461.
Scheier, M. F., and C. Carver
1985 Optimism, coping and health: Assessment and implications of generalized outcome expectancies. *Health Psychology* 4:219-247.
Sethi, S., and M. E. P. Seligman
1993 Optimism and fundamentalism. *Psychological Science* 4:256-259.
Shiffrin, R. M., and S. T. Dumais
1981 The development of automatism. In *Cognitive skills and their acquisition*, edited by J. R. Anderson. Hillsdale, NJ: Erlbaum.

Smith, C. S., and R. L. Gorsuch
1989 Sanctioning and causal attributions to God: A function of theological position and actors' characteristics. In Vol. 1 of *Research in the social scientific study of religion*, edited by M. L. Lynn and D. O. Moberg. Greenwich, CT: JAI Press.

Snyder, M., and N. Cantor
1979 Testing hypotheses about other people: The use of historical knowledge. *Journal of Experimental Social Psychology* 15:330-342.

Spilka, B., G. A. Brown, and S. A. Cassidy
1992 The structure of religious mystical experience in relation to pre- and postexperience lifestyles. *The International Journal for the Psychology of Religion* 2:241-257.

Spilka, B., P. Shaver, and L. A. Kirkpatrick
1985 A general attribution theory for the psychology of religion. *Journal for the Scientific Study of Religion* 24:1-20.

Stillings, N. A., M. H. Feinstein, J. L. Garfield, E. L. Rissland, D. A. Rosenbaum, S. E. Weisler, and L. Baker-Ward
1987 *Cognitive science: An introduction*. Cambridge, MA: MIT Press.

Taylor, S. E.
1983 Adjustment to threatening events: A theory of cognitive adaption. *American Psychologist* 38:1161-1173.

Taylor, S. E., and J. Crocker
1981 Schematic bases of social processing. In Vol. 1 of *Social cognition: The Ontario symposium*, edited by E. T. Higgins, C. P. Herman, and M. P. Zanna. Hillsdale, NJ: Erlbaum.

Tversky, A., and D. Kahneman
1973 Availability: A heuristic for judging frequency and probability. *Cognitive Psychology* 5:207-232.

Vanman, E. J., and N. Miller
1993 Applications of emotion theory and research to stereotyping and intergroup relations. In *Affect, cognition, and stereotyping*, edited by D. M. Mackie and D. L. Hamilton. New York: Academic Press.

Waller, N. G., B. A. Kojetin, T. J. Bouchard, D. T. Lykken, and A. Tellegen
1990 Genetic and environmental influences on religious interests, attitudes, and values: A study of twins reared apart and together. *Psychological Science* 1:138-142.

Weiner, B.
1985 An attributional theory of achievement motivation and emotion. *Psychological Review* 92:548-573.

Wilson, T. D., D. J. Lisle, D. Kraft, and C. G. Wetzel
1989 Preferences as expectation-driven inferences: Effect of affective expectations on affective experience. *Journal of Personality and Social Psychology* 56:519-530.

Zajonc, R. B.
1980 Feeling and thinking: Preferences need no inferences. *American Psychologist* 35:151-175.
1984 On the primacy of affect. *American Psychologist* 39:117-123.

Zanna, M. P., and J. K. Rempel
1988 Attitudes: A new look at an old concept. In *The social psychology of knowledge*, edited by D. Bar-Tal and A. W. Kruglanski. Cambridge: Cambridge University Press.

16

Behavioral Theory and Religious Experience

H. NEWTON MALONY

Sometimes the terms "behavior" and "experience" in the title to this chapter are given restricted meanings when applied to religious phenomena. When such meanings are used "behavioral" has been limited to *observable* events such as who did or did not stop to help an apparently injured man in Darley and Batson's (1973) attempt to replicate the conditions of the parable of the Good Samaritan. "Experience," on the other hand, has been limited to subjective, nonobservable events such as the apprehension of being in a mystical religious state by women who went through different art galleries (Malony, 1992). My intent, in this discussion of behavioral theory and religious experience, is to broaden the definitions of these terms.

DEFINITION OF TERMS

Behavior

"Behavior" in "behavioral theory" has, through most of this century, referred to acts that can be overtly observed via the five senses (cf. Skinner, 1953). Although I, too, will tend to focus on actions and words that can be publicly seen and heard, I intend, nevertheless, to maintain that "behavior" also includes religious thoughts and religious feelings which cannot be seen so readily. By defining behavior in this fourfold manner, i.e., thoughts, feelings, words, and actions, I do not mean, thereby, to imply a necessary sequence—as if actions were preceded by words, words by feelings, and feelings by thoughts. While such an implied causation is commonly assumed and even prescribed by Jesus in his admonitions that "whosoever looks on a woman to lust after her has committed adultery with her already in his heart" (Matthew 5:28), I will not make this presumption. Instead, I conclude that religious thoughts, words, feelings, and actions are independent behaviors and can be studied separately even though they may often be related. I think this presumption is supported by a survey of the literature which demonstrates that the correlations among these four behaviors are not necessarily high (Spilka, Hood, and Gorsuch, 1985). Thus, they may be considered to be independent of each other, to some degree.

Experience

The understanding of "experience" will also be broadened in this chapter. I will consider the *trait* of religiousness to be of equal importance to the *state* of religious ecstasy. Both are religious experiences.

Religious Experience as TRAIT: On the one hand, there is the common, everyday, routine "experience of religion" which is a trait that ebbs and flows over extended periods of time in many persons. This is religious experience as a "trait." This type of religious experience is frequently referred to in a somewhat negative way as "religiosity" (Kawamura and Wrightsman, 1979). In this discussion, my hope would be to resurrect religiosity from the ill-repute into which it might have fallen because I am convinced that religiosity is, by far, the most common form of religious experience today. In spite of the fact that Uren (1928) opined that such study of religion in its institutional, habitual form was not "psychology" because it dealt with, what he called, "externals," as a psychologist, I am convinced that the personal and individual dimensions of these experiences of religion can be profitably investigated. Furthermore, religiosity is the type of experience that most readily meets the typical understanding of religious behavior, namely observable actions.

Religious Experience as STATE: However, on the other hand, there are those ecstatic, unique, but sometime recurring, often transforming "religious events" to which persons refer when they report they have been "born again" or had a "mystical revelation." These religious experiences are *states* that exist for a time but do not persist over time. They are often remembered with great nostalgia and the feelings they evoke are yearned for with great anticipation.

Such religious states have captivated the attention of psychology since early in this century (cf. Starbuck, 1899; Ames, 1910). The persistence of psychology's interest in mystical and conversion states (cf. Hood, 1978; Malony and Southard, 1992, for example) has, perhaps, been due to the fact that their idiosyncratic, highly subjective expression appeals to the discipline's focus on individual dynamics rather than social conformity. Of course, the anti-institutional mood of many in Western societies tends to feed this fascination with non-normative experience. I expect the Alister Hardy Center's planned survey of religious experience in the United Kingdom and America to elicit much the same enthusiastic response as did its original survey earlier in this century (Hay, 1994). I also expect that the data will be dominated again by reports of mysticism and conversion.

Religious Experience as EVENT: There is yet another, somewhat more technical way in which I will refer to "experience" in this discussion. Instead of defining religious experience as either a set of behaviors over time, as in the trait of religiosity, or as a momentary event of intense feeling and insight, like in the states of religious mysticism or conversion, I would like to join them together in what might better be termed a religious "event." In an earlier essay (Malony, 1985), I depicted this combination of state and trait understandings of religious experience in an "S-O-R" model.

For those acquainted with learning theory, this S-O-R model can be readily recognized as the application of conditioning theory to religion. Later in this chapter I will contend that a significant part of religious experience can be understood from a classical conditioning, S-R, point of view in which there is little inner thought or reflection and the response is reactive or even instinctual. However, I am convinced that in most religious experiencing there is a heavy "O" component which means intrapsychic reflection that leads to thoughtful perception and decision. Nevertheless, there is room for thinking of religious experience as encompassing classical, instrumental, operant, and respondent conditioning events in religious experience, as later will be seen.

In the aforementioned S-O-R model, the "S" stands for the "Stimulus" aspect of the event. The stimulus is the environment or situation which catches the attention of the individual. The stimulus is always present, as can be seen in William James's well-known definition of religion as "the feelings, acts, and experiences of individual men in their solitude, so far as they stand *in relation to whatever they may consider divine* (1902, 31; italics not in the original). The phrase in italics indicates that there is always a stimulus dimension to religious experience, no matter whether that stimulus is the preaching of a revivalist, the coincidence of paranormal insight, the smell of incense, the church edifice on the corner, a strikingly beautiful sunset, or the picture of a starving child. According to James, the unique trans-empirical, super-natural quality of the stimulus was what made an experience "religious." I agree (cf. Malony, 1981). In regard to this characteristic of its stimulus, religious experience is unique. In other ways, religious experience resembles common, everyday events.

The "O" in this S-O-R model stands for those internal, intrapsychic processes of perception, reflection, and decision which occur within the individual in response to the religious stimulus, the "S." While many of these internal processes become habitual and less conscious in more trait-type religious experience, I am convinced that self-awareness is always present and that in many cases of religious experience there is a hyper-alterness as to what is going on. James (1902) wrote of the intensity of religious experience and I contend that this referred to a greater conscious awareness than was typical of normal experience.

Certainly, the role theory model of the Swedish psychologist Hjalmar Sundén (1959, 1966) reflects this contention. He suggested that in religious experience, persons consciously adopted the role of one of the classic figures in their religious tradition, e.g., the disciple Peter, and played out, in that role, a socio-dramatic interaction with God or some other divine figure. This kind of conscious decision making clearly reflects the kind of inner reflection which makes the "O" in this model so crucial. Psychodynamic processing is essential to religious experiencing, at least in its inception.

No doubt, there is an interaction between personal needs and the religious stimulus in all religious experience (cf. Lofland and Stark, 1965). All religious reflection occurs at a time and place in the worshiper's life. Thus, the very choice of which classic figure on which to base one's interaction with God, as seen in Sundén's (1959, 1966) model, is grounded in the life experience of a person at that moment.

There is a sense in which it could be said that religious experience is always idiosyncratic and that it would not occur if it did not meet human needs. The very act of conscious perception, as contrasted with sensation, has been conceived to be "need based." Persons only perceive that which they are motivated to perceive. While individuals sometime report religious experiences resembling Moses and the burning bush, Samuel in the temple, and Paul on the Damascus road, all of which seem unprovoked, analyses of these experiences have contended that they, too, resulted from deep-seated expectations or frustrations (cf. Malony, 1986; Rambo, 1992; Kildahl, 1965).

Out of this internal reflection, the "O" in the S-O-R model, comes the "R" or response of the individual. It should be noted that usually these responses in religious experience are not "reactions," as they are typically conceived in classical conditioning experiences. They are "responses" which require thought and decision. Reactions are thought to be natural, instinctual behaviors that are innately present within organisms in a fully developed form. The excretion of saliva in the presence of food, as in Pavlov's experiments with dogs, is an example. The dog did not initially learn to salivate. What was learned was salivation to the sound of a bell which had been paired with the presentation of food. This was termed a secondary reaction. The dogs mastered a discrimination problem in that they identified the bell with food, but they did not learn a new behavior. The behavior, salivation, remained the same and appeared as it did the first time, in full, instinctive fashion.

Religious "responses," in contrast to reactions, are not innate and do not appear full-blown the first time they are expressed. Take, for example, the response of receiving the Holy Communion. In many liturgical churches this requires both a discrimination of when and how to perform the act. I well remember my four-year-old son going along the communion rail after the morning service and draining each of the cups left there. He knew that some of the people had had something to eat, and he wanted to join them. But he had no idea of the meaning or the way in which that should be done. Some time later he could be seen filing forward, waiting his turn to kneel, opening his hand in reception, dipping the wafer into the wine, and putting it to his lips—i.e., consciously mastering the various moves in the religious response. This was a response, not a reaction. It resulted from decision, imitation, and learning.

The "R" might be conceived as the result or effect of the experience of interaction between the "O" (organism) with the "S" (stimulus). This is not incorrect because if one conceives of religious experience as an "event," then the event is not complete without some result. The religious event is, thus, a complete religious experience in that it includes the three components of a stimulus, with which a person interacts, and to which a person responds as the result of the interaction. The diagram to follow illustrates this composite understanding. It should be noted that the diagram includes a theological perspective which I believe includes aspects which parallel this type of S-O-R behavioral analysis.

RELIGIOUS EXPERIENCE AS RELIGIOUS EVENT

	S (Stimulus)	O (Organism)	R (Response)
Theological Perspective	God	Faith	Work
Behavioral Perspective	Sensation	Perception	Behavior
Phenomenological Perception	Need	Reflection	Action

(Adapted from Malony, 1990:81)

Religious experience as "event," thus encompasses these three behavioral experiences of perception, thought, and action. And the action that results as a response to the "S" and the "O" of the S-O-R formula completes the event by demonstrating that religious experience demands action both to confirm and affirm it. The response can be as mild as a report to others that it has happened and as dramatic as the dedication of one's life to sacrificial service because of it.

In sum, my discussion of behavioral theory and religious experience will focus on overt actions but will also include thoughts, words, and feelings in its understanding of behavior. Likewise, it will assume that religious experience includes the trait of religiosity as well the state of religious enthusiasm.

Furthermore, the discussion will contextualize religious experience within an event model in which persons both perceive themselves in interaction with, and responding to, a trans-empirical or super-natural stimulus. I believe these understandings provide a perspective on religious experience that is in accord with Dittes' (1971) comments about a need to balance the historical and non-historical aspects of religion in his discussion of the Intrinsic/Extrinsic Religious Orientations and Oden's 1971 suggestion that institutional and charismatic expressions have been normative in religious history.

In an interesting manner, there is warrant for saying that trait, state, and event forms of religious experience all include "altered states of consciousness" to one degree or another. Even in its most ritualistic and/or institutional expressions, religious experience includes a sense of being in the presence of transcendent reality. Although routinized for the regular worshiper who may find the experience uninspiring, there is, nevertheless, a presumption that something trans-empirical is occurring.

Sundén (1959, 1966) poignantly noted this essential quality in his aforementioned role theory description of these events. He suggests that religious experiences differ only in the duration and intensity of "phase alterations" between times of being in the presence of the supernatural and times of being in one's normal state of consciousness. Perhaps religious experience as "trait" might be said to be situated more toward the end of a continuum in which awareness of normal social reality dominates over and alternates less intensely with transcendent reality. Contrariwise, religious experience as "state" might be said to be situated more toward the opposite end in which the balance of mental states is less on social and more on transcendent reality. Religious experience as "event" would encompass both equally in that, while the perception, reflection, decision states of mind usually occur during an altered state of consciousness, the behavioral result, or the response, occurs in a more normal state of intentional action after the fact. It is still important to remember, however, that the human acts of perception, reflection, thought, decision making, words, feelings, as well as overt acts are all "behavior" from my viewpoint. I turn now to the ways in which behavioral theory has dealt with these issues.

BEHAVIORAL THEORY AND RELIGION

There is a long history of the application of behavioral theory to religious experience. Beginning with John Watson in the early years of this century, behaviorism has adopted a decidedly biocentric, objective, environmentalistic viewpoint that has discounted the functional, anthropocentric, introspective approach (Sexton, 1978). Quite correctly, in my opinion, is the opinion that psychology's move from the Structuralism of Titchener and others at the turn of the century to the Behaviorism of Watson and his contemporaries, was a change from chemistry to biology as a basic model. Early behaviorists pushed this biological approach to its most radical conclusion, according to Randall (1940). He summed up this approach by stating that these behaviorists "made of psychology the study of the physiological reactions of the human organism as a whole . . . the biological reactions of the nervous system to specific stimuli" (p.481).

Wulff (1991:113) quoted Bower and Hilgard's summary of this position by writing that behavioral theory assumes

(1) **sensationalism** . . . all knowledge is derived through sensory experience;
(2) **reductionism** . . . complex ideas are . . . reducible to . . . simple ideas;
(3) **associationism** . . . ideas . . . are connected through the operation of associationism of experiences that occur closely together in time; and
(4) **mechanism** . . . the mind is like a machine built up from simple elements with no mysterious components.

These elements have important implications for the study of religious experience.

BEHAVIOR IS LEARNED

Probably most crucial for religious experience has been behavioral theory's contention that all human behavior is *learned*; i.e., no behavior is innate or instinctive. Although not all psychologists would consider themselves "behaviorists" in any radical, or ontological, sense, most contemporary psychologists would consider themselves convinced that human behavior, in all its expressions from language to worship, was a result of associative learning of some sort. Psychologists from Wundt to the present consider themselves at least to be "soft," even "methodological," behaviorists in their focus on learning.

One could say of Freud that his seminal contribution was to bring all the content of mental life, including the unconscious, under a learning paradigm—thus destroying any claim to innate ideas, such as "God." The idealists had contended that the thought of God would never have crossed human minds had there not been such a supernatural being to inspire the thought. The "God-thought" was a copy, or reflection, of the "real-God" who existed somewhere in some realm. Freud contended God was a projection resulting from a learned interaction of internal psychodynamics with environmental forces (1964, 1927).

The contribution of Piaget, in turn, could be thought to be the bringing of conscience under a learning paradigm. Kant had contended that the "moral law," or conscience, was innate; an awareness that was as natural as the categories of the mind through which the brain organized sensations. Piaget (1932, 1965) contended that morality was a result of experience, i.e., learning, and that conscience served the function of adjustment. These are ideas which evoke almost universal support today.

Of most importance, however, in the convictions of, at least, early behaviorists, was that consciousness itself was epiphenomenal. By consciousness being epiphenomenal is the contention that the real events are at the level of reflexive motor movements. In the case of thought, thought can be explained as the nerve excitations in the brain resulting from the exercise of the larynx in speech. Spoken words, which are muscularly determined, are the real events; they are behavior. Thought is a secondary result; it is not real. As Watson (1928) stated it, "Psychology, as the behaviorist views it, is a purely objective, experimental branch of natural science which needs consciousness as little as do the sciences of chemistry and physics. . . . This suggested elimination of states of consciousness as proper objects of investigation in themselves will remove the barrier which exists between psychology and the other sciences" (p.27).

Since religion has usually been based on the truth claims of beliefs about supernatural events, these ideas have resulted in a behaviorism's suspicion of self-reports about such experiences. Even William James, who would identify himself more as a pragmatist than a behaviorist, questioned whether reports of religious experience, which were always after-the-fact, ever portrayed the actual event (James, 1902). Behaviorists have gone one step farther by either seeing these reports as illusions, projections, or outright fabrications.

As noted above, behaviorists have also been skeptical of assertions that there is an instinctive need for religion and they have doubted the truth claims that religious behavior is due to the intervention of supernatural realities. Saying does not make things so but saying can create false ideas. There are no innate ideas in behaviorism. The mind is filled with the superfluous reflections or after-effects of the larynx and is not to be trusted or studied.

However, this does not mean that behavioral theory has not dealt with religious experience. It has, but it has explained it in terms different from those offered by religionists. As Casler (1968) stated, "One's religious convictions may . . . be regarded as nothing more than a complex set of learned responses to a complex set of stimuli" (quote in Wulff, 1991:112). Although neither would consider themselves behaviorists nor be as doubtful about religion's truth claims as some, both Holm (1987) and Samarin (1969) illustrate this option by contending that ecstatic glossolalia, i.e., speaking in tongues, is learned behavior rather than an altered state of consciousness resulting from extrasensory perception.

Samarin (1969) observed that the "glossas," or sounds of glossolalic speech within groups of persons who met together in this form of worship, showed similarities that were not purely random even though they lacked the recognized structures of language. He concluded that this indicated that imitative learning was going on in that the glossolalic style of one group would differ from that of another. If the character of individual glossolalic speech was due to the unique inspiration of a given person by God, idiosyncratic features would result. Since these were not typical and since there were group distinctives, Samarin hypothesized that glossolalia was a result of learning. This type of religious experience was imitative rather than expressive; it resulted from group influence rather than an altered state of supernatural inspiration.

Holm (1987), writing almost two decades after Samarin, came to a similar conclusion. In a study of Pentecostal movements in Sweden, he concluded that glossolalia could be understood as social learning. Using Sundén's role theory (1959, 1966) he described a process that was somewhat more complex than Samarin's (1969) imitative model but which, nevertheless, was similar in its basic thesis that glossolalic utterances were learned rather than inspired.

Although Holm admitted that speaking in tongues was based on a universal human capacity to imitate, he suggested that this type of religious expression was more typically based on the social expectation that persons could reexperience the baptism of the Holy Spirit such as was recounted in the Bible after the resurrection of Jesus. The adoption of this role, a la Sundén, most often occurred, according to Holm, in a atmosphere of intercessory prayer where the social influence and expectation was intense.

In an interesting manner, similar to the early behaviorists contention that thought resulted from nervous excitations delivered to the brain from the larynx as one spoke, Holm concluded that glossolalic speech in the presence of loud shouts, songs, exhortations, provided "the impetus which releases the chain of perceptions leading the individual to interpret this speech as the gift of God" (p.385). At this moment the person feels they have been baptized by the Holy Spirit and they adopt for themselves the role of the early disciples gathered together on the day of Pentecost. Thus, observable behavior shapes perception; the though follows the act. Social learning rather than divine action provides the basis for understanding the event.

The conclusions of Holm and Samarin about glossolalia illustrate the basic premise of behavioral theory, namely, that behavior is learned. While, as Wulff (1991) noted, not all behaviorists after Watson would contend that thought is epiphenomenal, they would all agree that religious experience results from some kind of associative learning rather than innate tendencies. This is true regardless of whether theorists emphasize readily "observable habits" or less transparent "cognitive structures," as some contemporary behaviorists are prone to do.

Interestingly enough, this contention that religion is learned behavior is shared by others who would not consider themselves behaviorists in any sense. The theologican George Lindbeck (1984) is an example. He compares "experiential-expressive" with "cultural-linguistic" models of religion. Although he might agree with those who contend, from an apologetic point of view, that the capacity for religious experience is part of what it means to be created in the image of God (cf. Genesis 1:26-27), Lindbeck opts for a cultural-linguistic understanding of religion. He asserts that religion is "like a culture or language . . . a communal phenomenon that shapes the subjectivities of individuals rather than being primarily a manifestation of those subjectivities (Lindbeck, 1984:33). In other words, he is suggesting that religion is not an impulse as much as it is a shaped capacity that would not be known apart from what is learned in cultural formation. Experience does not produce religion; religion produces experience. In a similar way, it is well known that basic "intelligence" can never be observed in a pure sense; it can only be measured by "achievement," which reflects what one has learned from culture.

The "experiential-expressive" point of view is summarized by Lindbeck in a manner similar to that to which the early behaviorists so strongly objected. He states that this viewpoint sees different religions as varied expressions of a common core experience which is present in all people. Most importantly, the "experiential-expressive" option believes that this common impulse underlying religious experience of the "mysterium tremendum" is that which validates religion for most people.

Lindbeck opposes this experiential-expressive view that religion is a common core experience which emerges in concrete expressions in various cultures but which is essentially the same across all diversity. Religion is not so much a experience as it is a cultural-linguistic event. Lindbeck is correct, in my opinion, in concluding that religious traditions make possible "the description of realities, the formulation of beliefs, and the experiencing of inner attitudes, feelings, and sentiments" (1984:33). The very words used to report and frame the religious experience are themselves the product of social experience within a given religious tradition. A better statement of behavioral learning would be hard to find.

LEARNING CONCEPTS

Having established the centrality of the learning paradigm for a behavioral understanding of religious experience, I turn now to a more detailed discussion of several processes of learning theories that I feel have import for the acquisition of religious behavior. Although I shall discuss concepts from various theorists, there is a unifying concern in all of them for the acquisition, the maintenance, the generalization, and the change of behavior as a result of individuals' interaction with their environment. Following Wulff's (1991) outline, I will consider the Associationist theory of Guthrie (1952, 1959), the Operant theory of Skinner (1953, 1974), and the Social Learning theory of Bandura, (1977). I am indebted to Wulff for his treatment of these issues in his monumental text *Psychology of Religion: Classic and Contemporary Views* (1991).

Associationism: The Associationist theory of Guthrie (1952, 1959) was an attempt to reconstrue the learning event in terms of the timing of the response in relation to the stimulus as distinct from the supposed satisfaction of a need which the response supposedly satisfied. It will be remembered that in an earlier reference to Pavlov's classical conditioning paradigm, the response of salivating was thought to be an instinctive, unlearned reaction to the presentation of food which would satisfy the hunger drive. Extrapolating from that basic need, Dollard and Miller (1950), among others, had contended that more complex behaviors were learned only when responses to stimuli relevant to social or cognitive needs were made. Thus, they were called "drive reduction" theorists. In contrast, Guthrie suggested that learning was not dependent on behavior which reduced needs.

These alternatives have relevance for a behavioral understanding of religious experience. On the one hand, Dollard and Miller's (1950) theorizing could be extended to the idea that there is a innate need for meaning and purpose in life which religion meets. Fowler (1981) is one among many who postulate such a basic drive. If this is true, then religious experience is learned in just as automatic and reactive a manner as was the salivation of Pavlov's dogs to the bell. The satisfaction that comes from worship, from conversion, from prayer, or from a myriad of other religious acts is a "conditioned reflex" which reduces this to a drive to find meaning and purpose.

Guthrie's position contradicts this drive reduction understanding of religious experience, however. He believes that habits are built up, not because they meet basic needs, but because the behavior occurs near to the time that the stimulus is presented. "Contiguity," or coincidental occurrence, is sufficient to explain religious behavior. Worship, etc., does not require the postulation of an intermediary drive for meaning. Religious experience occurs because persons behave religiously at the time that they are in certain stimulating environments.

Guthrie goes one step further. Not only does he *not* believe that behavior reduces drives, he neither believes in the term "habit strength," as if a habit becomes stronger with practice. He concluded that habits are at full-strength the first time a behavior occurs in the presence of a given stimulus. What does occur over time is that the behavior becomes more discriminated because the person becomes attuned to more and more aspects of the stimulus event to which they can respond in an already full-blown responsive manner. These so-called "cues" become the signals for the response to occur. In terms of religious ecstasy, Guthrie might contend that a feeling of reverence and religious ecstasy might occur the first time when one was with one's parents in church but that, over time, the feeling might occur as one rode by the church or even when one's parents were dressed in the same way they were when the experience first occurred.

The question of what underlying purpose behavior serves was not considered by Guthrie. He was what has been termed a "peripheralist" in that he attended only to the overt response to a clearly observed stimulus and did not infer any underlying cause as to why the behavior occurred at that time and that place. The issue is the degree to which religious experience functions to reduce innate religious needs (a la Dollard and Miller, 1950) or is an entirely situationally defined event—completely culturally, or situationally, dependent (a la Guthrie).

Our earlier discussion of Lindbeck's (1984) contrast between the "experiential-expressive" and the "cultural-linguistic" options is yet another expression of this debate. The underlying question of whether a given religious expression or tradition represents an absolute or a relative reality is another form of the question. One alternative would be to suggest that there was a basic religious need, but that culture gave it its form. Another alternative would be to suggest that there was only a secondary need for religion among some but not all people. If this latter alternative is taken, then Guthrie's position of contiguity would offer a sufficient explanation for the appearance of religion in one form, but not another. Further, if pure associationism is accepted as the underlying process, it would also offer a sufficient explanation of why, within the same culture, some people were religious and others were not.

According to Wulff (1991), there has been at least one thorough analysis of religion from an Associationist point of view, i.e., that of Vetter (1948). Using Skinner's accounts of "superstitious" conditioning in pigeons and dogs, Vetter contended that religious behavior followed similar patterns. "Like these less complicated species, human beings tend to respond to unpredictable or uncontrollable situations with ritualistic behaviors" (Wulff, 1991:120). Since humans, as contrasted with pigeons and dogs, have verbal abilities, these irrational, ritualistic behaviors become supported by beliefs. In a hard-to-comprehend manner, the more contradictory the evidence for a belief, the stronger it is held. "When a belief is held with an unusual intensity unrelated to the amount or quality of evidence for it, Vetter identifies it as 'faith'" (Wulff, 1991:120). Thus, does Vetter, remaining true to Guthrie's "contiguity" hypothesis, conceive of religious experiences as resulting from coincidental connections between stimuli and responses.

Operant Conditioning: Turning to the second set of concepts, Operant conditioning theory basically agrees with Guthrie and Vetter that religious behavior is superstitious but disagrees with them in other ways. The first disagreement has to do with order of events. Whereas Guthrie was an S-R theorist, Skinner was an R-S theorist. Better said, Skinner was an R-R theorist; he thought of environmental events as "reinforcements" not "stimuli." They occurred after the response, not before it. Behavior occurred first. If the environment responded in a reinforcing way, the likelihood of the behavior occurring again was increased. Behavior was the way that humans sought reinforcement by "operating" on their environment; thus, Skinner's synonym for response was "operant." Yet, in order to distinguish these acts from Associationist, Guthrie-type behavior, Skinner labeled his behavior "emitted" by the organism instead of "elicited" by a stimulus. The implication of these ideas for religious behavior will become clearer after consideration of the another way in which Skinner disagreed with Guthrie.

Whereas Guthrie thought that behavior appeared in full strength the first time it occurred, Skinner (1953) contended that behavior was "shaped" or grew in strength over time. Shaping means that a behavior increases in frequency, intensity, quickness, or duration. The environment is reinforcing if it increases the likelihood that the operant behavior will increase in one or more of these four ways. Like Guthrie, Skinner does not infer that behavior satisfies some underlying purpose. He considers the environment reinforcing after-the-fact; meaning after the observation that the behavior increases. He does not contend that it increases because a need has been met.

Nevertheless, Skinner asserted that the growth in habit strength was a much more varied and complex process than Guthrie believed. Not only did behavior develop from weak to strong but its strength was a function of whether and when the reinforcer was present. "Ratio" and "interval" were the terms used to refer to how often the environment reinforced an operant behavior.

Ratio schedules pertained to the number of behaviors that had to occur before the environment reinforced the response, as for example in how many times would prayer have to occur before it was answered. Interval schedules pertained to the length of time that had to pass before the environment reinforced the response, as for example in how often would a person experience euphoria in the middle of a revival meeting.

According to Operant conditioning, each of these can vary in terms of whether reinforcement is fixed or variable. For example, one could experience a sense of guidance every time, or every other time, or every five times one opened the Bible to read it. This would be a fixed ratio schedule which one could come to expect or count on. On the other hand, one could experience guidance one time, then after six times, then after eight times, then after nineteen times. This would be a variable ratio schedule.

Interval schedules would differ in regard to the amount of time that would pass before reinforcement. If it occurred every other day, or every five days, or every other week, these would be fixed intervals. If, however, reinforcement occurred on the sixth, seventh, ten, twenty-first, and twenty-seventh days, this would be a variable interval schedule.

These ideas have much relevance for religious experience because of the different manners in which persons feel their behavior is or is not reinforced. Terms often used for these reinforcements are "answers to prayers," "feelings of closeness to God," "experiencing forgiveness," "knowing God's will," "feeling inspired," "being given consolation and courage," etc. In accordance with research on other behaviors, one might expect that religious experience would shape up or be strengthened quickest by ratio reinforcement, particularly constant reinforcement but would persist longest in the presence of interval reinforcement, particularly variable reinforcement. .

It is rare, except in the ideal case of young children who are nurtured and experience God's love through their parents and others with no break in reinforcement, to think that religious experience has been shaped by ratio reinforcement of any kind. Religious reinforcement is rarely, if ever, constant or predictable. No one has a religious experience every time they go to church. Even charismatic experiences vary in their effect. At best religious reinforcement is on an interval basis. From time-to-time religious experience occurs on, what might best be termed, a variable schedule.

This is what makes religious experience so tenacious, according to Skinner. It is superstitious to begin with in that the behavior is reinforced in just as irrational a way as the dog who urinated and looked for food because the two events had coincidentally occurred some time in the past. Further, religious behavior is hard to extinguish because it has been reinforced every now and then on a completely accidental and nonsensical basis.

Skinner (1971) is just as critical of religious behavior as is Vetter, although he does plan for quasi-religious events in his utopian society, Walden Two, because he thinks religion has a cohesive effect on culture. These events, however, would be quite different from typical religious experiences.

Nevertheless, even those whose attitude toward religious experience is more positive than Skinner's would do well to consider his analysis of how behavior is developed. Bufford (1981) illustrates this possibility. He avoids the pitfall of overgeneralizing Skinner's doubts about the validity of religion and, instead, reflects on the value of operant thinking for understanding behavior in general and religious behavior in particular. Bufford affirms the validity of many operant insights about how habits are formed. He suggests that religionists can apply many of these understandings to the task of religious education and character formation. While Bufford (1981) expresses some concerns about the question of whether humans always initiate contact with divine, i.e., operate on the religious environment, yet he strongly affirms the interactive and functional quality of the divine-human event. He agrees with Skinner that reinforcement strengthens action and that most religious experience is instrumental in its intent.

Yet another example of a constructive application of Skinnerian thinking is Sundén (1959, 1965). He clearly notes that the religious experience of role taking is significantly dependent on the extent to which children have been immersed in their religious tradition. He also notes that there are striking differences among families in the manner in which they share and teach their religious traditions. Even where the emphasis has been the same, those families where the teaching has been empathic and age-related can expect their offspring to be able to enter into religious role playing in more effective and satisfying ways than those families where the teaching has been dogmatic and authoritarian, according to Sundén.

These reflections on the importance of developing strong habits which eventuate in vital religious experience could be understood in terms of Operant shaping and schedules of reinforcement. Without debating the underlying ontological reality of the supernatural, which Skinner would reject, the differences between adults who are and who are not able to assume prominent religious roles in their religious experiences can be explained completely through the concepts of situational contingencies stemming from Operant constructs. It is possible to be a "methodological" behaviorist even if one is not an "ontological" behaviorist.

Social Learning Theory: These comments about the importance of the home environment in creating situations where religious learning occurs leads naturally into a discussion of Social Learning theory (Bandura, 1977). In Social Learning theory, the central meaning of the word "social" refers to the interpersonal environment in which most personality formation occurs, according to these theorists. In the other two theories heretofore discussed the implication has been that stimuli or reinforcements with which learners interact are cold, hard, factual realities. While Associationist and Operant theorists would acknowledge the reality of human influence on habit formation, imitation of other people becomes the primary focus in Social Learning theory. This means that the kinds of stimulus-response or response-reinforcement bonds which Associationist and Operant models contend are established by specific, individual, repeated events are superseded by more global, complex human acts which learners attempt to imitate in a global manner. Thus, the formation of habits which might lead to religious experience would be based on the imitation of parents and others who generally behaved in a way that made such events possible.

Yet another distinctive aspect of Social Learning theory is its emphasis on the importance of cognition, or thought. Although both of the previously discussed theories of behavior agree that habits are imprinted on the nervous system, neither of them accords as much importance to thought as does Social Learning theory. In fact, Skinner would probably be closer to Watson in contending that thought is epiphenomenal, although his opinion would probably be more methodological than ontological. Social Learning theory, however, emphasizes the centrality of such cognitive processes as attention, memory, motivation, and self-direction in its description of how imitation functions in habit formation.

This emphasis on mental events makes Social Learning theory compatible with other neuropsychological understandings of how crucial thinking is to human experience. McKay (1978) speaks for this point of view in his well-known distinction between the "I story" (personal, self-conscious) and the "O story" (organic, biological). He contends that whatever else is happening at the physical level of existence, the crucial aspects of human life are at the mental, or "I story," level. Thought is central and determinative. Most religious experiencers would agree wholeheartedly, even though they would admit that a considerable part of their thinking is afterthought, as James (1902) so poignantly reminds us.

Wulff (1991) reported a fascinating example of these imitative processes in his text. He described the behavior of Duffey Strode, a North Carolina ten-year-old boy, who, along with his younger brother and sister, began standing outside their school and preaching hellfire to other students as they arrived for class. Duffey's brother, five years old, "could recite Bible passages before he was able to read, waved a Bible at passersby and shouted at them about adultery, damnation, and hell" (Wulff, 1991:135).

The behavior of these children is readily understandable from a Social Learning point of view. Their father had been doing the same thing. He modeled for them by standing at street corners and shouting threats of damnation to motorists as they drove by. He took his children with him when he went to football games and shopping districts. He called the Pope a child molester and told a local television talk-show host that she was going to hell. Without question, the behavior of the Strode children was an imitation of their father's actions. If a close analysis had been done all the processes described by Bandura (1977) could likely be observed.

What was probably true in a negative sense in the behavior of the Strodes is also true in a positive sense in other cases. Wulff (1991) notes that the famous book *The Imitation of Christ* and the accounts of altruism in those who sheltered Jews during the Nazi occupation both attest to the conviction that allegiance to high ideals is grounded in the imitation of other persons.

Religious experience, therefore, could be readily conceived within the constructs of Social Learning theory. The importance of heroes, models, and personal examples is widely attested to in the accounts people give of the influences on their lives—both in religious and nonreligious aspects. Many theorists have concluded that there is an innate drive to imitate in the human being. Common sense has known this for centuries. Social Learning theory speaks for much scientific reasoning in affirming it. Religious experience is imitative at its core. This explains the differences among devotees to different religious traditions as well as provides an understanding of various emphases within religious traditions. Although there are numerous examples of deviations from models, these deviations can often be explained in terms of learning principles which made imitation difficult.

CONCLUSION

This chapter has considered religious experience from the viewpoint of behavioral theory. Hopefully the definitions of "behavior" and "experience" provided in the beginning section clarified my approach to both the general issues and specific processes considered in the text. I am convinced that behavioral theory, which is grounded in learning processes, has much to say that is important in an understanding of religious experience. The detailed discussion of associationist, operant, and social learning theories was intended to provide the reader with an appreciation for the different ways behaviorists have approached the acquisition of habits. While many religionists would have difficulty in accepting the anti-metaphysical tenets of some behavioral theorists, I feel sure that reflection on many of their ideas can lead to affirming "methodological behaviorism" as a stance in both understanding and even promoting religious experience.

REFERENCES

Ames, E.S.
1910 *The psychology of religious experience*. Boston: Houghton Mifflin.

Armstrong, J. R.
1977 Trends in American eschatalogy: An application of Skinnerian concepts in an analysis of changes in religion and culture. *Dissertation Abstracts International,* 37, 3575B-3576B. Boston College, University Microfilms No. 76-30, 375.

Bandura, A.
1977 *Social learning theory*. Englewood Cliffs, NJ: Prentice-Hall.

Brown, L. B. (Ed.)
1985 *Advances in the psychology of religion*. New York: Pergamon Press.

Bufford, R. K.
1981 *The human reflex: Behavior psychology in a biblical perspective*. San Francisco: Harper & Row.

Casler, L.
1968 Instrumental learning. *International encyclopedia of the social sciences,* vol. 9, edited by D. L. Sills. New York: Macmillan and the Free Press.

Darley, J. M., and C. D. Batson
1973 "From Jerusalem to Jericho": A study of situational and dispositional variables in helping behavior. *Journal of Personality and Social Psychology* 27:100-108.

Dittes, J. E.
1971 Typing the typologies: Some parallels in the career of church-sect and extrinsic-intrinsic. *Journal for the Scientific Study of Religion* 10:375-383.

Dollard, J., and N. Miller
1950 *Personality and psychotherapy*. New York: McGraw-Hill.

Fowler, J. W.
1981 *Stages of faith: The psychology of human development and the quest for meaning*. San Francisco: Harper & Row.

Freud, S.
[1927]
1964 *The future of an illusion*. Garden City, NY: Doubleday.

Guthrie, E. R.
1952 *The psychology of learning* (rev. ed.) New York: Harper & Row.
1959 Association by contiguity. In *Psychology: A study of a science. Vol. 2*, edited by S. Koch. New York: McGraw-Hill.

Hay, D.
1994 The biology of God. *International Journal for the Psychology of Religion*.

Hollingworth, H. L.
1926 *The Psychology of thought, approached through studies of sleeping and dreaming*. New York: Appleton.

Holm, N. G.

1987 Sundén's role theory and glossolalia. *Journal for the Scientific Study of Religion* 26:383-389.

Hood, R. W. Jr.

1978 Anticipatory set and setting: Stress incongruities and elicitors of mystical experience in solitary nature situations. *Journal for the Scientific Study of Religion* 17:279-287.

James, W.

[1902]

1985 *The varieties of religious experience*. Cambridge, MA: Harvard University Press.

Kallstad, T.

1974 *John Wesley and the Bible: A psychological study*. Stockholm: Nya Bokforlags Aktiebolaget.

Kawamura, W. I., and L. S. Wrightsman Jr.

1969 The viability of religious belief: A factorial study of religious attitudes, values, and personality. Paper presented at the Southeastern Regional Convention of the Society for the Scientific Study of Religion, Atlanta, Georgia, January 1969.

Kennedy, E. C.

1974 *Believing*. Garden City, NY: Doubleday.

Kildahl, J. P.

1965 The personalities of sudden religious converts. *Pastoral Psychology* 16:37-44.

King, W. P. (Ed.)

1930 *Behaviorism - A battle line*. Nashville, TN: Cokesbury Press.

Leuba, J. H.

1912 *A psychological study of religion: Its origins, function, and future*. New York: Macmillan.

Lindbeck, G. A.

1984 *The nature of doctrine: religion and theology in a postliberal age*. Philadelphia: Westminster.

Lofland, J. and R. Stark

1965 Becoming a world-saver: A theory of conversion to a deviant perspective. *American Sociological Review* 30:862-875.

Malony, H. N.

1981 Religious experiencing: A phenomenological analysis of a unique behavioral event. *Journal of Psychology and Theology* 9:326-334.

1985 An S-O-R model of religious experience. In *Advances in the psychology of religion*, edited by L. B. Brown. New York: Pergamon Press.

1986 Conversion: The sociodynamics of change. *Fuller Theological Seminary: Theology News and Notes*, June, 16-19,24.

1990 The conception of faith in psychology. In *Handbook of faith*, edited by J. M. Lee. Birmingham, AL: Religious Education Press.

1992 Analogue measures of religion: Experimental psychology of religion revisited. *Irish Journal of Psychology* 13:316-326.

Malony, H. N., and S. Southard (Eds.)

1992 *Handbook of religious conversion*. Birmingham, AL: Religious Education Press.

McKay, D.

1978 *Science, chance, and providence*. Oxford: Oxford University Press.

Oden, T. A.

1972 *The intensive group experience: The new pietism*. Philadelphia: Westminster.

Ostow, M.

1958 Biologic basis of religious symbolism. *International Record of Medicine*, 171:709-717.

Piaget, J.

1965 *The moral judgment of the child*, translated by M. Gabian. New York: Free Press.

Pratt, J. B.

1920 *The religious consciousness: A psychological study*. New York: Macmillan.

Rambo, L. R.

1992 The psychology of conversion. In *Handbook of religious conversion*, edited by H. N. Malony and S. Southard. Birmingham, AL: Religious Education Press.

1993 *Understanding religious conversion*. New Haven, CT: Yale University Press.

Randall Jr., J. H.
1940 *The making of the modern mind: A survey of the intellectual background of the present age*, rev. ed. New York: Houghton Mifflin.
Samarin, W. J.
1969 Glossolalia as learned behavior. *Canadian Journal of Theology* 15:60-64.
Sexton, V. S.
1991 American psychology and philosophy, 1876-1976 Alienation and reconciliation. *In Psychology of religion: Personalities, problems, possibilities*, edited by H. N. Malony. Grand Rapids, MI: Baker.
Skinner, B. F.
1953 *Science and human behavior*. New York: Macmillan.
1971 *Beyond freedom and dignity*. New York: Knopf.
Spilka, B., R. W. Hood Jr., and R. L. Gorsuch
1985 *The psychology of religion: An empirical approach*. Englewood Cliffs, NJ: Prentice-Hall.
Starbuck, E. D.
1899 *The psychology of religion: An empirical study of the growth of religious consciousness*. New York: Scribner's.
Sundén, H.
1959 *Religionen och rollerna e (Religion and Roles)*. Stockholm: Svenska Kyrkans Diakaonistyrelse Bokforlage.
Trout, D. M.
1931 *Religious behavior: An introduction to the psychological study of religion*. New York: Macmillan.
Uren, A. R.
1928 *Recent religious psychology: A study in the psychology of religion*. New York: Scribner's.
Vande Kemp, H., and H. N. Malony
1984 *Psychology and theology in western thought 1672-1965: A historical and annotated bibliography*. Millwood, NY: Kraus International Publications.
Vetter, G. B.
1958 *Magic and religion: Their psychological nature, origin, and function*. New York: Philosophical Library.
Watson, J. B.
1914 *Behavior: An introduction to comparative psychology*. New York: Holt.
Wulff, D. M.
1991 *Psychology of religion: Classic and contemporary views*. New York: Wiley.

17

Role Theory and Religious Experience

NILS G. HOLM

INTRODUCTION

Role theory belongs to that area of scientific knowledge which attempts to understand individual behavior by an analysis of social conditions. There is not one single role theory but several, all interlinked and yet each slightly different. While role theory, on the one hand, implies a complex theoretical argument centered on individual behavior, several of its ideas have become universal and passed into everyday currency. This development may be an advantage, but can also be regarded as a drawback when one aims for precision in the use of theoretical concepts.

Role theory is one element in a number of more extensive theoretical context. The theory occurs in pure sociology and cultural anthropology, in learning psychology, in the contexts of cognition, field-theory, and social psychology, as well as in depth psychology. There can be no question here of attempting to cover the entire field of role psychology, and the present chapter is therefore restricted to theories of particular relevance for religious experience.

Historically, the term "role" has been borrowed form the theater. As early as the Greeks and the Romans, the characterization of a dramatic text made by an actor was described as a role. At the turn of this century, the term was gradually adopted by the social sciences to denote the function acquired by an individual in a specific social context. A distinctive feature of all role theory is that roles do not exist in isolation, but are always inserted into social patterns, which means that most roles are inscribed in what is at least a two-way interaction.

Many of the classics of the psychology and sociology of religion came to use the term "role" or other concepts very close to it. We may, for example, cite William James whose major work, *The Principles of Psychology*, from 1890, approached the concept when he tried to pin down the notion of "self" in psychology. Something of the same tendency is also apparent in the work of Durkheim (1893). One of the greatest contributions was made by Mead in the 1930s, when he analyzed the origins of the social "me," and his theoretical arguments have greatly enriched research in the study of social psychology. Most social psychologists to date have been inspired by Mead. Another scholar to have analyzed roles in the 1930s was Linton, and the latter's contribution within social anthropology has also had great significance for the development of role theory. It may also be observed that role theory is closely associated with theories of social learning.

After the Second World War, social psychology went through a particularly flourishing period. Many of the great classics of the field appeared at this time, including the work of Parsons (1951), Merton (1968), Dahrendorf (1959), Newcomb (1952), Sarbin (1954), Goffman (1986), Sherif and Sherif (1969), Rocheblave-Spenlé and Habermas (1973). This period also saw the publication of comprehensive textbooks in social psychology, in which role theory acquired central importance. These include the *Handbook of Social Psychology* by Lindzey (1954), and *Social Psychology* by Newcomb (1952), as well as *Role Theory: Concepts and Research* by Biddle and Thomas (1966) (cf. Shaw and Costanzo, 1970).

In Scandinavia the concept of role followed a quite unique direction, under the inspiration of Hjalmar Sundén, who, in his book *Religionen och rollerna* [Religion and Roles] in 1959, borrowed the notion in an attempt to understand religious experience. The book was published in German in 1966 under the title *Die Religion und die Rollen*. In a number of subsequent works, Sundén returned to the concept of role, and we shall later pay closer attention to his way of using it. Several of Sundén's pupils have also used role theory, modifying or refining it to some extent in the process (cf. Holm, 1987a). Within the field of folkloristics, Lauri Honko in Finland has also used role theory in a manner similar to Sundén.

A broad survey of the vast area within which role theory has been used suggests that research may be divided into three main directions. These are not, of course, mutually exclusive, although they reflect rather different focuses of interest. First, we have the *structural analytical* school, where the main concern is to discover the different roles of a social unit. The second school might be called the *interactionist* school, since its prime interest is to study the interaction between two or more individuals and examine how these individuals fulfill socially given roles (cf. Waller, 1977; Dreitzel, 1979). The third group, concerned with what I would like to call *perceptual role theory* school, is primarily represented by Sundén and his pupils. This tendency develops and incorporates the two earlier models, but at the same time places another kind of emphasis on the function of roles in the individual mind. It furthermore points up the importance of roles in generating new impressions within the individual. These impressions also influence perception. The following account will consider Sundén's use of role theory in some detail, since his theory aims explicitly at explaining religious experience.

First, a few words about religious experience. The latter refers to the individual's total capacity to register events within his or her own field of perception. These experiences have many different qualities, including emotional, cognitive, behavioral, and other possible aspects of mental activity. The fact that the experience is religious in character presupposes a mental system which reckons with supernatural forces capable of influencing an individual's life. Such mental systems are always social and are normally shared by a number of other individuals within the same social unit.

THE STRUCTURAL-ANALYTICAL MODEL

As representatives of the structural-analytical model we may cite Linton (1945), Parsons (1951), and Dahrendorf (1959). These scholars are mainly concerned with discovering the social role structures operating in a given social context. They are less interested in examining the role achievements of single individuals, but pay attention to the description of roles as social quantities. Every society and group thus consists of a series of functions or roles which must be present for a group's continued existence and development. In different situations, roles thus emerge within a given social unit. It then becomes important to study different leader roles, official roles, pedagogical roles, sex roles, status roles, etc. The role represents a division of labor within a certain group or social unit.

Linton speaks of societies as aggregates of individuals, whose behavior and relations are controlled by given patterns. Within these patterns, there are fixed positions occupied by different individuals. Certain rights and duties are bound up with these positions, and Linton refers to such a position as a "status." The dynamic aspect of the latter is the role. When an individual is assigned a "status," and thereby uses his rights or carries out his duties, he is playing a role. The role, in other words, is the behavior connected with a particular status or position within a given group. The analysis pays particular attention to the association of roles with position in the group, and individual distinctive features are not emphasized. Linton does speak of personality, but sees this principally as the individual experiences a person undergoes as a participant in a specific culture.

If one examines the research based on this model, one notes that religion is mentioned as one example among many others of how social interaction functions. It is difficult to find research concerned exclusively with the study of religious experience. Very often, it confines itself to the social description of the units within the group, although it is interesting to see how religious groups tackle new situations which society at large creates for them. Which roles or functions acquire greater importance in a situation characterized by difficulties or adversities? Which roles emerge in churches and communities where secularization and materialism gain the upper hand? What is required of a new sect with an Indian philosophy, for example, for it to be able to succeed in Western society? Which roles should be developed in a church or religious community which aims at growth and success? These and many other questions may be asked from a structural-analytical perspective when one studies how groups in a society function.

One research contribution within the sociology of religion may be said to adhere to this model, even if the term "role" is not mentioned with any frequency. This is Wach's major study, *The Sociology of Religion* (1944), which analyzes in depth the functions and official representatives of various religious groupings. It is the role spectrum of these groups which receives particular emphasis. One advantage of Wach's study is that it covers several different religions.

THE INTERACTIONIST MODEL

The interactionist model emphasizes the analysis of situations from daily life. It attempts to isolate different roles which the individual plays and study how individuals function in different everyday situations. The question here is how given roles are executed within the social context. Names that may be identified with this school include Mead (1934), Turner (1962), Goffman (1986), Habermas (1973), Sarbin (1954), Newcomb (1952), Berger and Luckmann (1966). One of the most important theoretical contributions comes from Mead (cf. Kellner, 1979; Falk, 1979), while for a description of role and personality, Thomas (1963) should be consulted.

According to Mead, the fundamental process in the social context is the interaction between individuals. Language is perhaps the most important means of communication, but there are also nonverbal forms such as gestures and facial expressions. All of these are symbolic behaviors which function as stimuli for the human being at which they are directed. But the symbols must acquire content in order to function as means of communication. This operation occurs through the transmission of a symbol—linguistic or otherwise—which receives a response from the receiver. By a repeated series of exchanges, the symbol acquires meaning. The process may be described by saying that the sender puts himself in the position of the receiver, and in this way tries to understand the content of his own symbol, as the receiver might be thought to understand it. But the receiver, in turn, must familiarize himself with the transmitter's intentions. Each party must, in other words, adopt the other one's role. This means that one enters into the other's situation as completely as possible, identifying with his expectations, attitudes, and feelings.

A feature of this role-taking, according to Mead, is the development of the self. The experience that an individual acquires through this communication of symbols Mead calls the "self." The distinctive feature of this self is that it can be an object in relation to itself. In this way, the self is separated from other objects and from the body.

Mead makes a further distinction. He separates the "I," which is the active function of the individual, from the "me" which is the perceiving, reflective, and judgment-forming dimension of an individual. It is this "me" which makes it possible to enter other people's situations and take on their roles. According to Mead, all of this is primarily a cognitive process. Through role-plays, the child for example is able to enter into the experience of how others see it. The child can be both child and mother in one and the same game. By means of such games, the child learns to internalize other people's evaluations of itself. The child, in other words, acquires its conscious knowledge of generalized others.

Having studied Mead's fundamental account of how symbolic interaction works, we may now turn to more strictly socio-psychological theorists. We may first of all consider how Sarbin presents the issue. In order to be able to discuss roles, Sarbin first clarifies what is meant by social position. To cite his own words: "A position is a cognitive organization of expectation, a shorthand term for a concept embracing expected actions in persons enacting specified roles. These expectations, organized as they are around roles may justifiably be called role expectations. Thus, a position is a cognitive organization of role expectations" (Sarbin, 1954:225). He therefore defines role in the following way: "A role is a patterned sequence of learned actions or deeds performed by a person in an interaction situation" (p.225). According to Sarbin, then, social roles have an existence independent of the individual, but the essential point here is that the role is understood not merely as a socially given quantity, where the individual can be varied and exchanged. It is also intimately related to different individuals' ways of integrating roles. One may therefore, according to Sarbin, speak of how one takes roles upon himself, what qualities roles have, what expectations are present in single individuals, and how the latter perceive roles of different kinds. Roles, in other words, approach the concept of attitudes.

It is now possible to study carefully how individuals understand roles, how they take on roles, and how under varying conditions they play these roles. What may also be described as the organismic dimension becomes an important factor. Sarbin thus refers to different degrees of proximity between the role and the self. He specifies seven different levels, all the way from a situation where the self and the role are remote from each other, to the seventh level where the role and the self are united in deep trance. To this seventh stage, Sarbin reckons different mystical states, possession, and religious conversion, situations in which the conscious will of the individual has been suspended. These are states which do not occur in ordinary daily life. What does really emerge from the account is the reason why the self sometimes becomes deeply involved and sometimes only slightly.

In Sarbin's discussion of role-taking the self acquires very great significance. It is the self which ensures that role perception, role enactment, and taking-the-role-of-the-other function in different ways. The self is in turn the result of social interaction. In Sarbin's own words: "The self develops out of interaction between the organism and stimulus objects and events" (p.238). Depending on how the self has developed, role enactment varies in character. It is generally regarded as a positive quality if the self has the capacity for taking on the role of the other, for placing itself in the other's position, and thus coming to understand the other. A rigid personality does not have the capacity for role empathy in this sense but lives inside its own role-play.

It should be noted that the interactionist role model reckons with socially given roles, learned by the individual during social interaction in the course of his life. The self thus becomes an intermediate variable which can either facilitate or inhibit role-taking. Taking on another's role thus becomes a function of the development of the self.

Newcomb (1952) describes role-taking in much the same way as Sarbin. Starting from Mead, he discusses children's role-playing and observes that the child in this way learns to anticipate the behavior of others. He goes on to explain: "Children learn to 'take the role of the other' because it is necessary for them to do so. Only by anticipating his mother's responses to himself can a child make sure of the responses which he wants from her and avoid those which he does not want. But since his mother does not behave with machine-like predictability, he sooner or later discovers that the best guide to her behavior is his own estimate of her present attitudes. This, in fact, is the strict meaning of 'taking the role of the other'—i.e., anticipating the response of another person who is perceived as having attitudes of his own" (p.321).

The essential part of Newcomb's argument is that another's role has in a way become integrated into the personality, into the self. In this way, individuals can anticipate another's behavior and also influence it over the course of time by their own. Individuals thus achieve an internal communication between their own role and an internalized, sometimes generalized, role of others. The more internalized the role in the individual, and the more consistently the other party plays out its role or roles in reality, the more intensive becomes the communication between individuals. In other words, one acquires common norms and frames of reference, leading to good communication between individuals.

A consistent deployment of the interactionist model is provided by Berger and Luckmann, who in their much-cited book, *The Social Construction of Reality* (1966), give an account of the theory. It has also been elaborated here into a sociological theory, although it still retains its psychological consequences. Berger and Luckmann build on the European tradition of the sociology of knowledge, as represented, among others, by Scheler (1960) and Mannheim (1949). The authors begin from three fundamental concepts: externalization, objectivization, and internalization.

They believe that human beings, because of their specific disposition, build up social activity and a world of human experience. This they call externalization. People give this world the status of an objective reality. Through a process of socialization it comes to be internalized by new generations and is thus experienced by individuals as objectively given. The relation between the internalization and the externalization process is dialectic, making continuous change possible.

When people externalize their way of thinking and acting, a process of typification always occurs. This accounts for the origins of institutionalized activity. Institutions in turn develop different systems of legitimization to explain and justify their own existence. One of the most important ways of legitimizing social reality is through dialogue, and language therefore acquires great significance in the social context. Institutions not only have typified ways of thinking, but also typified ways of acting, or roles. When people take over a role, they identify with one of the socially objectified action patterns. In this way, the objective world becomes subjectively real for them. "The actor embodies the roles and actualizes the drama by representing it on the given stage" (p.92), as Berger and Luckmann express it.

The legitimization of social reality occurs in different ways and at different levels. The highest level is constituted by what are known as "symbolic universes," among which may be counted religions. These attempt to provide people's actions and thoughts with meaningfulness and a sense of reality. They are primarily "universes of meaning." Such meaning systems also create situations where people acquire plausibility structures for their thought and action, that is to say necessary conditions for "reality-maintenance." Symbolic universes are all-embracing, giving meaning to birth, life, and death, as well as providing man with an identity. Mythology, theology, and philosophy are regarded as "machineries of universe-maintenance." They are institutionalized means of keeping plausibility structures intact.

The objective world becomes real for individuals through a socialization process in two phases, the primary one occurring in childhood and the secondary one at a more adult age. By means of people close to the individual, significant others as they are called, the internalization of a certain universe of meaning takes place. The individual thus achieves knowledge of a "subworld," becoming a participant in its ideology and its roles, acquiring in the process his or her own place in the system. There are various ways, although constant communication with others is the main one, in which the reality character of such a "sub-universe" is maintained. As Berger and Luckmann define it: "Reality-maintenance and reality-confirmation thus involve the totality of the individual's social situation, though the significant others occupy a privileged position in these processes" (p.171).

When one moves from one symbolic universe to another, the authors speak of alternation. The socialization process which occurs in this process is essentially equivalent to the primary one. Strengthening the reality character of a sub-universe in an individual by different kinds of legitimization, the authors refer to as therapy. They call its opposite nihilation. When a plausibility structure has been well learned, a person experiences identity and integrity. He possesses explanations for the events he has already encountered, goes on encountering, and is expected to encounter.

As will be apparent, Berger and Luckmann treat people's perception of reality in very broad terms. They do not attempt any detailed interpretation of individual activities. From our own point of view, it is nonetheless interesting to note here that individual behavior is regarded as a function of the plausibility structure which a society or a group has developed for itself, and as a result of each individual's specific internalization of this structure.

Berger and Luckmann's theoretical model has been widely used within the sociology of religion, but it has also received some attention in the psychology of religion. It has been employed, above all, to explain how individual groups, such as the Pentecostal movement, create a special universe for themselves and their interpretations of the world (Holm, 1976). But the theory has also been used to explain the ability of single individuals to create their own mystical frame of experience. Constant reinforcement of the special interpretative frame, by reading, letter-writing, or meditation, for example, helps to maintain a symbolic universe of this kind (Geels, 1980).

If we make a survey of the interactionist models, we thus find that they emphasize communication between individuals via symbols, normally linguistic ones. This means that these theories have also come to be known as symbolic interactionism. One must reckon with norms and frames of references formed by communication, but also with action patterns or roles. These roles acquire their realization in different ways, depending on a number of factors, including completely individual-centered ones. The self becomes, in other words, a kind of intermediate variable, acquiring considerable significance in the process of role enactment.

As we have seen, the religious perspective is incorporated into these models. Different religious experiences, such as conversion, ecstasy, possession, etc., are treated as important role experiences. The everyday roles which are part of normal religious life do not however receive satisfactory treatment. The perspective offered by Berger and Luckmann does consider everyday roles but tends to over-standardize and thus perhaps over-simplify the role-play of daily life. That there are individual churches and religious communities which aim for a totalization of the symbolic universe is quite clear, but in daily life there are several different perspectives constantly in conflict with each other. This is at least the case with developed Western societies. How people choose between competing symbolic interpretative frames is something which the theory does not consider. On this point, deeper analysis is required of the reasons why particular individuals choose a specific symbolic universe, as well as how and why they strive to maintain it.

THE PERCEPTUAL MODEL

In Scandinavia or the Nordic countries, role theory has been of special use in both the psychology of religion and folkloristics. Since role theory has been explicitly adopted to explain religious or supernatural experiences, I shall give a detailed account of how the theory has been used. I therefore begin by presenting its most celebrated application, that by Hj. Sundén (1908-1993), after which I give some consideration to how others have used role theory.

Sundén studied theology at the University of Uppsala and wrote his doctoral thesis on "La théorie bergsonienne de la religion" (1940). As the title suggests, the dissertation dealt with the problem of religion in the French philosopher, Henri Bergson. While working as a teacher of religion and psychology in various schools during the following decades, Sundén became increasingly engrossed in psychology, perhaps above all social psychology, which was then making great advances. At this point Sundén seized upon the notion of role, seeing great potential in the use of the concept in order to understand how a religious experience comes into being.

It should be noted that in his use of role theory Sundén addresses himself primarily to theologians and students of religion. His working method might perhaps be characterized as phenomenological. He does not operate with experiments or statistics but with arguments in favor of the approach he finds viable. There are thus no conventional proofs for his hypotheses.

Another necessary consideration for understanding his use of role theory is the notion prevalent in his day of what a religious experience was. The dominant theory was that of Otto (1917), according to which the inner core of religion was a numinous experience stripped of its social ingredients. The experience was mainly understood as a movement of feelings within the individual mind. Sundén reacted against this way of seeing things and believed that a religious experience captured all of a person's mental qualities. From a psychological point of view, he therefore wished to illustrate how a religious experience could come into being. To this end, he used the conceptual apparatus of social psychology, available above all from such theorists as Newcomb, Sarbin, Linton, and Young. He did not, however, adopt the use of concepts exactly as they had been presented by these writers but came instead to place an emphasis on role as a perception pattern. At the same time, he shifted the implications over to the study of religious experience. Although Sundén is chiefly known for his so-called role theory, it is important to point out that he also used and developed other theoretical insights, perhaps above all those of depth psychology. But it is not the purpose of the present article to present these sides of Sundén's research profile.

The earliest use of role theory in Sundén is to be found in the collection, *Sjuttiotredje Psalmen och Andra Essayer* [The Seventy-third Psalm and Other Essays] from 1956. Here Sundén describes how this personal experience of Paris before and after the second World War came to be affected by the seventy-third psalm. German superiority came to a terrifying end, just as that described in the psalm. The latter thus functioned as a kind of interpretative model for the terrible events which had engulfed Europe during the Nazi period. Germany, which had caused havoc by its cruel acts of violence, fell to the judgment of history, which was the same as that of God, as interpreted in the words of the psalmist.

In a separate section of the above-mentioned book, Sundén explains how he thinks religious experience comes into being. In his opinion, it is not simply a matter of numinous feelings but far more a question of learned preparedness. As he himself writes: "To take on a role, therefore, does not mean merely to appropriate certain gestures and replies, but means at the same time, and this is the most important aspect in our context, to anticipate someone else's activity. Role-taking does not merely imply a preparedness for action but also a preparedness for perception. A role means a perception system or a frame of reference in the sense of psychological perception" (p.152-153).

In the same chapter we also find several of the important literary examples which Sundén uses to describe role-taking in the context of the psychology of religion. Here he analyses the German poet Max Dauthendey, who while traveling alone in the Pacific shortly before his death has the experience of meeting the merciful God on reading the Book of Psalms; Lewi Pethrus, grand old man of the Swedish Pentecostal movement with the experiences he describes in his memoirs; and Juan de la Cruz, who after a difficult period in prison experiences God and all of creation as a single simple being. Sacred literature, the Bible, Sundén believes, "opens up for us a world of experience, deeper and richer than all the role creations of human art combined." Or, as he also maintains: "It allows the experience of God to be made real. It is in complementary relation to that of science. In what can be experienced, God and world are one" (p.175).

In his *magnum opus, Religionen och rollerna* from 1959 (1966), Sundén further develops his discussion of role theory. It should however be noted that the book not only discusses role theory, but also deals with a large number of other important questions within the psychology of religion.

Depth psychology, both Freud's and Jung's, is thus the subject of detailed discussion. The main elements of the study are included in Sundén's textbook, called quite simply *Religionspsykologi: Problem och metoder* [The Psychology of religion: Problems and methods] (1977), which appeared in several editions during the 1970s. In his study *Barn och religion* [Children and religion] (1970), Sundén also draws on his use of role theory, although the concept is not central in the latter work. Role theory is also presented in a number of other articles. I would above all like to mention "Die Rollenpsychologie und die Weisen des Religions-Erlebens" (1969), included in the *Festschrift* for Wilhelm Keilbach entitled *Wesen und Weisen der Religion*, and the article "Saint Augustine and the Psalter in the Light of Role-Psychology" (1987).

In the more detailed presentation of Sundén's use of role theory that follows, I shall combine the accounts offered in these various books and articles. The discrepancies to be found between these texts are not, in my opinion, large enough to warrant a chronological review of the different versions (Holm, 1987a; Wikstrom, 1987).

The main question for Sundén is how a world of religious experience is psychologically possible. In the same way that physicists must use various instruments and apparatus to understand the intrinsic properties of matter, so too must the human mind be "prepared" for a religious experience to take place. Man must "devote himself to a religious tradition and in certain cases to a ritual apparatus" (p.47) writes Sundén in the introduction to the section on roles in his major study.

He also goes on to ask why natural scientists are allowed to use all kinds of instruments and apparatus in order to study "reality," whereas a religious individual is not allowed to be prepared for his experience without this being misunderstood. He believes that religious experience can only come into existence through preparation, a process of learning, and then the experience is similar in principal to what occurs in the natural sciences. The two experiences, in other words, become complementary. They do not cancel each other out, but actually reinforce each other to produce a comprehensive perception of reality.

Sundén observes that an experience occurs by one or more of our senses being influenced. The neural processes thus produced are interpreted and completed in a way that is conditioned by the entire formative situation. This also includes the state of preparedness of the organism affected. It is this preparedness which decides what becomes of the actual stimulus. This may be regarded as the most important aspect of Sundén's line of argument. In order to illustrate what he says, Sundén has in several of his works used the example of a police force pursuing dangerous criminals. I shall briefly describe this example as it frequently appears in Nordic contexts in discussions of Sundén's role theory.

In Northern Sweden the criminal police received knowledge of a criminal league from Finland which was wreaking havoc on the Swedish coast. A search party set out. It was discovered that a weekend cottage had been broken into and that the thieves had stolen a couple of rifles, together with ammunition. A rowing-boat had also disappeared. The latter was discovered on an island. Therefore the thieves were also probably present on the island. The search party disembarked and moved forward over the open countryside. Suddenly the commander leapt behind a rock for shelter. He had seen a man pointing a gun at him. He waited for the whistle of bullets, but nothing happened. Finally, he got up and searched carefully over the terrain. He found a beer-bottle lying on the ground, with the neck pointed toward him, and this shape corresponded to an element in the preparedness that the commander had built up: the gun barrel which he had been expecting to see (p.48).

The course of events in psychological terms is described by Sundén as follows:

1. There is an actual excitation of the senses. There are many stimuli, but only one of these is actualized in accordance with the individual's set.
2. Processes in the internal nervous system are set in motion. These reach the brain, where
3. The search for a pattern begins, often leading to the actual discovery of one. This process is unconscious. Only the result itself is conscious.
4. The discovered pattern now structures the perception content and gives meaning to the stimuli which affect the organism (Sundén, 1977:27).

In the above example the discovered pattern is an armed criminal. Because of the nature of the pattern, the policeman must deal with a "partner" or human counterpart, although there is actually only an object, the neck of a bottle. "The object perceived can become a partner if the perception pattern of the moment is a role," Sundén concludes (1977:27).

For his definition of role, Sundén has drawn partly on Linton, and partly on A.M. Rocheblave-Spenlé. According to the latter: "A role is a behavior model which the individual adopts in an interactional ensemble" (Sundén, 1977:27). We find this definition in the supplement to later editions of *Religion och rollerna*, and also in the different versions of *Religionspsykologi*. Sundén also refers to the arguments developed, above all, by Newcomb on position, role, set, frame of reference, and anticipation.

He cites a large number of religious experiences which may be analyzed from the perspective of role psychology. Sundén's most important contribution here is to regard the individual contacts with God described in the sacred texts as roles. We are thus dealing with roles which belong to the human party and roles which belong to God. Sundén thus transfers the term "role" from a social context to a mythical one, to the descriptions that occur in the sacred texts. Here we have specific roles for different situations where people have been in direct contact with God, but we also find generalized roles both for God and for the individual. The roles are thus absorbed in a process of dual interplay. All religion, Sundén points out, has a dual character. As a result of the careful reading of sacred texts, a role set is coded in man, who thus acquires the potential for specific role experience and for generalized role contact.

I would like once more to stress the point of Sundén's use of role. He is not concerned simply with socially given roles, but regards the mythical textual roles in linguistic form as possibly more important. By these means, succeeding generations build up similar role patterns internally and thus acquire frames of reference with strong common features. A modern individual can thus feel a sense of togetherness with previous generations and with biblical figures. As deployed by Sundén, roles are as it were internalized in the individual's mind and are stored there as potential experience patterns.

For a religious experience to be able to materialize, a learning process is required. The individual must draw on the socially given tradition in which the mythical roles are included. When the person has done this, there is a range of latent roles which constitute a set for religious experience.

In order to understand Sundén's subsequent line of argument, it is necessary to refer to perception psychology. In this context, Sundén usually cites an example from optics. When we see something, we absorb certain light stimuli which are interpreted by our brain and thus acquire meaning. In the brain there are previously coded experiential structures which ensure that the stimulus of the moment can find interpretation models and become meaningful. This is a process common to all of our senses. As we grow up, we construct interpretative models which ensure that we can experience the world meaningfully. Without these models, we experience chaos, panic, and anxiety.

The mythical roles function in the same way as ordinary frames of experience. They are learned and remain as potential experiential structures. What is required for a religious experience then to occur is, on the one hand, an external stimulus in the experienced world, but also a source of motivation. All sources of excitation in the external world may act as stimuli, but so also may those that are internal, inside our own bodies. Motivation is normally provided by a situation of crisis or necessity, but a special motive is often required for a specific mythical role to be applied. The everyday frames of reference are then insufficient, and the search for an alternative interpretation is necessary.

If there is a stimulus and a motivation of a particular kind, the search and discovery of a model can occur in the individual mind, with the result that the mythical roles structure that individual field of perception. What then occurs is that the individual *takes the role* of the human party in a mythical role play, and simultaneously *adopts* God's role, which unconsciously structures perception so that what happens in or around the individual is actually experienced as the action of God. For a brief instant, the person can quite concretely experience the action of God. A *phase shift* has taken place, and the individual field of perception has become structured by a mythical role. Important qualities in experiences of the more intensive kind are *intention-*

ality and *totality*. The person encounters an intimate figure with a message for humanity, and the experience becomes a *total* one. It takes possession of that individual entirely. A phase shift back to more secular and everyday experiential models then normally occurs after a certain period.

It is perhaps important to point out that perceptual role-taking does not imply a slave-like repetition of the role model. There is often some variation, depending on personality factors and external circumstances. A blending of different mythical roles may also take place. The essential point, however, is that the individual identifies what has occurred as an act of God, in accordance with a certain religious tradition.

It is thus clear that Sundén's use of roles implies that the latter may be regarded as hypothetical variables in an individual's mind. They are latent structures of experience which are actualized in certain situations and even structure perception for the individual by an unconscious process. They become processes just as automatized as those we receive from sight or sound stimuli. Religious experience becomes just as real for the individual as secular or everyday experience ever was. After the phase shift has taken place, the individual can of course reflect over his experience and find it unusual, perhaps even surprising. Doubts may then arise, which threaten the religious experience. Generally the latter is reinforced, however, by renewed experiences and by further reading of mythical narratives.

In Sundén's writings there are a number of examples of religious experiences which could be interpreted by means of role theory, and I shall cite one of these in order to illustrate the argument. The example comes from seventeenth-century England and concerns a certain James Nayler. He had returned from fighting in the parliamentary army and was deeply disappointed with the result. In 1652, he underwent the following experience: "I was at the plough and thinking on those things which belong to God. I then suddenly heard a voice saying: 'Go out from your family and from your forefathers' home.' And a covenant was then made with me. I was overjoyed to have heard God's voice which I had known since childhood but never perceived" (quoted by Sundén, 1966). Abraham's story in the Old Testament had transferred itself to Nayler's life. He identifies with Abraham, and at the same time adopts the role of God. His organism has anticipated this process. Nayler leaves wife, home, and children. In everything he encounters he now sees a busily active "other," the God who had dealings with people in the Bible: "This God is for Nayler and experienced reality" (1966:58), Sundén concludes.

Sundén has also dealt with the major experiences of Martin Luther (1982), and of St. Augustine (1987). He is surprised that previous study has not noted the importance assumed by the Book of Psalms in the lives of both. Role theory in its perceptual sense nevertheless draws attention to the influence exerted by the Book of Psalms, with its intensive roles for both man and God, on the origins of the central experiences undergone by these important Christian figures.

As we have seen, Sundén regards roles as perception patterns; he deals principally with mythical roles from the sacred scriptures. Through a learning process—reading, listening, meditation—these roles are encoded in a person. By a process of regular contact with religious models, there emerges a generalized role for God and a generalized role for a person. The latter can then experience himself or herself as God's partner. When special motivation is present, specific roles can be actualized to structure the individual's field of perception, so that what happens in and around him or her is literally experienced as the action of God. A person may thus encounter a "Thou"—the divine partner. This occurs through an unconscious and automatic process in the human mind or nervous system. This process, according to Sundén, runs completely parallel with what constitutes our normal, everyday experience.

THE USE OF PERCEPTUAL ROLE THEORY

After Sundén had won recognition in the Nordic countries through his book, *Religionen och rollerna*, the Swedish government created a personal chair for him in psychology of religion within the faculty of theology at the University of Uppsala. This occurred in 1967. It was then that the study of the psychology of religion really began in the Nordic countries. Since then, the chair has been transformed into a permanent one, and another chair has been founded at the University of Lund. Elsewhere in the Nordic countries there are no special chairs in the psychology of religion, but the interest for the subject has been maintained, sometimes in departments of applied theology and elsewhere within those of comparative religion. Within general psychology there has been only sporadic interest for the psychology of religion as a subject of research.

Sundén's role theory has exerted great influence on psychologists of religion in the Nordic countries. Källstad (1974) completed a doctoral dissertation on John Wesley, the founder of Methodism, using role theory in combination with L. Festinger's theory of cognitive dissonance. Källstad claimed that Wesley was a keen reader of the Bible, but was also devoted to spiritual literature, such as Thomas à Kempis's *The Imitation of Christ*. Through contact with his spiritual models, Wesley constantly took on different roles, including that of a despised disciple of Jesus (Källstad, 1974).

Hans Åkerberg (1975) at the University of Lund has also used role theory to explain the spiritual experiences of the young Nathan Söderblom, the well-known religious scholar, archbishop, and ecumenicist. At the end of the nineteenth century, Söderblom underwent a deep crisis originating in the conflict he experienced between Bible-based evangelical piety and the historico-critical view of the Bible. By identifying with biblical roles, Söderblom saw parallels to his own life and was thus able to experience the merciful God. He went through a kind of conversion experience, which left him with a strong conviction of God's grace and mercy. After this, he could carry on with his research according to historico-critical methods.

When Åkerberg analyzed Söderblom's spiritual awakening, he also applied the theories of William James. In a later article (1985:111-146), Åkerberg makes a thorough analysis of the similarities between James's method of analyzing conversion and the gains provided by role theory. Åkerberg concludes that the concept of role-taking should be combined with an important observation made by James, namely, the importance of self-surrender. For perceptual role-taking to occur, conscious self-surrender is required, which is an essential element of traditional conversion.

Another important work is Unger's doctoral thesis entitled *On Religious Experience* (1976). The dissertation is mainly an internal analysis of Sundén's way of using role theory. It demonstrates clearly how Sundén moves from the use of role as a social quantity to the use of role to describe a mythical quantity and how this becomes linked with the person-centered, hypothetical variables in the perception process. Wikstrom (1975) uses the theory to explain the experience of God's guidance in older people. He suggests that a lifetime of contact with biblical roles creates a generalized role of God as partner, which in turn gives the sense of being guided by a good and loving God. Even negative experiences thus achieve positive integration into the religious cognitive system.

Holm (1976; 1978; 1987b; 1991; 1991a) used role theory to explain the Pentecostalist experience of baptism in the Holy Spirit with subsequent glossolalia. This study demonstrates that the biblical models, above all those in the Acts of the Apostles, provide Pentecostalists with a mythical model. By means of various facilitating processes, the speech apparatus is then set into motion at what is an optimal moment for each individual, resulting in the production of a kind of "abracadabra" language, similar in some aspects to authentic language. This speech process then becomes the incitement which initiates total role-taking. The individual believes that he is the object of an act of God. He feels quite concretely that it is God who has given him the gift of tongues and therefore enters the role as one who has been baptized in the Holy Spirit.

At the University of Nijmegen Jan van der Lans (1978; 1987) has used role theory to study meditation experiences. He regards meditation as a technique that activates previously learned patterns, which then come to structure the individual's perceptual experience. By adopting the Lotus position, for example, and concentrating on a mandala, the Buddhist can adopt Buddha's role. A phase shift from secular to religious interpretation then takes place. Van der Lans then sets up an experiment to test his theory. His subjects are made to undergo a four-week course in Zen meditation, after which they report religious experiences to a considerably higher degree than those who have not undergone any such preparation. Van der Lans's study is probably the only one to date to have tested perceptual role theory by statistical significance.

A number of other researchers have also used role theory. In this respect, I may briefly mention Pettersson (1975), who has used the theory in the dynamics surrounding the retention of religious experiences; Capps (1982), who used it to study the experiences of John Henry Newman and also in the context of petitionary prayer (1982a); Geyer (1989), who critically analyzed the theory while studying the effect of confirmation teaching in the Swedish Church; and Järvinen (1991), who used the theory to analyze the fantasies of psychotics. The perceptual theory developed by Sundén has been presented and discussed in many other contexts (Wulff, 1991; Luoma, 1965), sometimes with critical reservations (Björkhem, 1977; Belzikoff, 1992). Generally speaking, however, the theory has given notable fresh impetus both to research into the psychology of religion, but also to public debate on religious questions.

FOLKLORISTIC MATERIAL

Folkloristic studies attempt, among other things, to establish the various types of folk narrative material by means of genre analysis. One genre that has been studied a great deal is the *memorat*. By memorat, we mean a narrative that contains a rich supply of individual features and describes a personal experience. Memorats may change in the course of time and become narratives in other genres.

In connection with his discussion of the memorat, Lauri Honko, professor at the Finnish University of Turku, has studied how such a narrative originates. His analysis has features in common with the concept of role theory as presented by Sundén. There are, however, a number of differences. Honko has worked primarily with folkloristic material from the Finno-Ugric language area, and I offer a brief account of one of his analyses (Honko, 1969; 1971; 1972).

Honko describes one supranormal experience as follows: in the evening a man goes to warm the kiln. He is rather tired since the heating process has gone on for two days without interruption. He is individually responsible for the drying of the grain; he must supervise the storing of the sheaves, keep the temperature at the right level, and see to the ventilation. The oven must not become too warm, however, since this will obviously create a fire risk. He must also ensure that no children trample the grain, and that no thieves steal it when it is threshed. As he sits by the fire, he wants to stretch out for a moment. Against his will, he falls asleep. Suddenly, he hears the barn door creak and looks in that direction: there stands an old man with a grey beard and white coat, looking at him with displeasure. In the same instant, this creature disappears. The man goes to the door; there are no tracks in the snow outside. He looks into the oven, and sees that the fire is on the point of going out. He puts on more wood and goes off immediately to the house. There he describes his experience to the others. They consider what has happened and reach the conclusion that the sprite had appeared to wake up the person tending the fire, because the fire was going out.

Drying the grain was an important task for a man. It was forbidden to fall asleep on such occasions and neglect one's duties. This was an important requirement. The man's falling asleep was a source of concern to him, so that he was expecting some form of correction. The sound that released the process was the creaking of the door. It was a familiar sound for the man, but at that instant it seemed strange to him and woke him up. The poor light (it was dusk) facilitated the appearance of the vision. The man had learned from tradition that it was the task of the sprite to watch over those carrying out their duties on the farm. He thus possessed clear cognitive models for a supranormal experience. The motivation, combined with the model (the role), thus released a vision in him. The next moment, everything had disappeared. His perception was restructured and returned to a more everyday way of understanding things around him.

Honko claims that what the man saw was clearly formed in a cognitive sense before he heard the opinions of the others and that together they formed an idea of who it was that had actually appeared. The creature, which had not been given a clear interpretation, Honko refers to as *numen*. He suggests that many supranormal experiences are diffuse and therefore remain at the numen stage. It is only subsequent reflection, perhaps in the company of others, which can clearly identify a being and give it a name. The others verify and legitimize this interpretation.

We see that Honko stresses the diffuse aspect of the vision itself. Sundén, on the other hand, emphasizes the primary task of the religious role in structuring the field of perception in a clear way. In the case of Christianity, there is seldom any doubt about who it is one meets in the context of the experience. The folkloristic tradition is probably more ambivalent in character and does not therefore function so immediately as a explicatory perceptual role. In both cases, however, continuing legitimation through contact with like-minded individuals assumes great importance for preserving the event as a socially acceptable experience.

Honko has also used the concepts of role-taking in his excellent article of the Siberian Shaman (Honko, 1969). An important study drawing on Honko's insights is Siikala's doctoral dissertation, *The Rite Technique of the Siberian Shaman* (1978), based on extensive first-hand data. Siikala claims that the activity of the shaman may be characterized as a role. It has great significance within the community, above all so that people can understand the reasons for illness and other occurrences. Before a shaman is accepted, a long learning process takes place. This imparts both the role for the active shaman as well as that of the spirits, which the shaman will play in the course of his trances. The depth of the trance may vary considerably, and in order to reach such a state, the shaman uses rhythmic stimuli. As Siikala writes: "Connected with the rhythmical, sensory stimulus slowly gaining momentum and directly influencing the central nervous system is the gradual actualization of the supranormal conter-roles and a deepening by degress of the taking of supranormal roles in step with the sensory stimulus" (p.333).

She distinguishes between three different role identifications: a) the shaman identifies completely with the spirit role (role-identification), b) manifesting both his own role as a shaman and that of the spirit (dual role), and c) the shaman creates an image of the role performances of his spirit-helpers purely verbally (description of counter-role) (p.335). In his role identification, the shaman must never forget the aim of his art, that is, try to find answers to the questions posed by the individual or group. When the shaman does this, he or she balances between an identification with the spirit roles and the response which the listeners give. In other words, the depth of the trance fluctuates. Or as Siikala writes: "The mental process of the trance induction stage can be regarded as a gradual deepening of role-taking directed at the supranormal" (p.340).

In her role analysis Siikala relies heavily on the interactionist model presented above. She refers to and leans on the classic role theorists. Great significance is attached to Sarbin's account of the "organismic dimension," but Siikala also draws on role theory in the perceptual sense and then refers, among others, to Honko, who claims that myths, legends, prayers, etc., provide models for the "constructing of supranormal roles" (p.62). Siikala's dissertation is perhaps the most comprehensive analysis of supranormal experience with the use of role theory in its different forms.

DISCUSSION

My presentation has featured three principal models of role analysis: the structural-analytical, the interactionist, and what I have called the perceptual. The three models represent a development in both chronological and conceptual terms. Role analysis has been shifted from a social context to an internal, perceptual process; or what began as a socio-psychological context evolved towards the analysis of intrapsychic events.

Although the models may be regarded as building on each other, none of them may actually be regarded as superseded or unproductive. The structural-analytical model is a prerequisite for the analysis of how the group functions in society. Time and again it is necessary to study what role set a group must follow in order to survive and develop within society at large. Here, as I see it, there is considerable potential for analysis, since in today's pluralistic environment we constantly see new groups emerge and evolve, either to survive or gradually to disappear. One of the prerequisites for group survival is the specification of objectives, that is to say the building up of roles.

The interactionist model brings the individual into the discussion. Now it is no longer merely a question of analyzing the social role set, but the potential of the self for role-taking must also be considered. Personality variables are seriously introduced into the discussion, and we being to study how experienced reality has been constructed and is currently legitimated. We address questions of identity and integrity. To regard supranormal roles as learned behavior models is an important advance in this process. In a religious context it is not only socially created roles that interact, but there are also supranormal dimensions, as in the case of possession or trance. The typically religious roles of priest, miracle-worker, shaman, etc., condition both the content of the role and its enactment. The experiences which this provides in individuals will naturally have a strongly religious character.

The perceptual model thus implies a radical advance at the same time as it includes the previous models: roles are also descriptions of individual contacts with God, text roles in linguistic form. The whole thing can be an intrapsychic process which occurs through the reading of sacred texts and meditation on them. When there is a particular motivation, these roles can structure perception so that what happens to the individual is experienced by him as God-given, as a divine act. Then the person *takes* the human roles in the myth and simultaneously *adopts* God's role, which constitutes the important part of the perception process. Through the role of God, the individual makes contact with a role which allows the experience of a living, active, and eternal God. The experience becomes "verifiable," in the sense that it can be checked against the experiences of previous generations, but also—and this is many times more important—against the models in the holy myth.

It is not, however, a question of slavishly repeating the experiences of the models. A variation and even a mixture, or generalization, of role models can take place. Individual factors—the "self"—acquire meaning in any case in the origin of the experience.

The perceptual model has proved productive for the understanding of religious experience. No comprehensive formalization of the theory has yet appeared, however, and using it in experimental situations is not therefore easy. The theory thus acquires a more phenomenological-hermeneutical character.

Many of the individual elements of the theory could be developed. I would like to draw attention to the motivation side. It has generally been assumed that some kind of special need must exist for the perceptual process to begin. Several of the examples discussed have featured extreme external adversity of some kind. One may also suggest, however, that the motivation factor may include far deeper issues such as the mother, the father, the child, the lost son, the bridegroom, the bride, the singer, the musician, etc. Behind such motives may lie a series of early emotional experiences which have created a lasting desire for a certain kind of role identification. The mythical role spectrum of religions is so large that it can cater to almost everybody's personal needs. A perceptual role identification may thus conceal basic mental structures of this kind. Within the frame of religion, these can be reinforced or compensated. When the mythical and symbolic formalizations of human experience interact with the needs of a concrete individual and his motivation factors, a reinforcement and stimulation may occur which contributes to a lasting religious experience in the individual. These experiences then genuinely acquire a crucial meaning for that individual's life. They become guarantees for the life view he has formed for himself.

Other elements which could be further studied are the relation between the individual's God role and the generalized one. One may ask, for example, what purely social and mental factors lie behind the generalized role of God. That it is reinforced by individual role sets is clear, but what, ultimately, is the relation between momentary experiences and a more total experience in spiritual dimensions? At this point, we must also consider the significance of meditation and practice. Is there, for example, an unstructured and impersonal mythical experience, independent of role sets?

Role theory does not answer all the questions connected with religious experience. It nonetheless provides an essential contribution to the understanding of experiences which clearly belong to the theistic theological tradition.

REFERENCES

Åkerberg, H.
1975 Omvändelse och kamp. Lund: Studia psychologiae religionum lundensia 1.
1985 Tillvaron och religionen. Lund: Studia psychologiae religionum lundensia 7.

Belzikoff, B.
1991 Nazism och kristendom ur ett judiskt perspektiv. Stockholm/Stehag: Brutus Östling bokförlag Symposion.

Berger, P.L., and T. Luckmann
1966 *The social construction of reality*. London: Penguin.

Biddle, J., and E. J. Thomas (Eds.)
1966 *Role theory: concepts and research*. New York: Wiley.

Björkhem, Ö.
1977 Hjalmar Sundéns tidiga rollteori. En analys av några huvudpunkter. Svensk Teologisk Kvartalsskrift nr 3.

Capps, D.
1982a Sundén's role-taking theory: the case of John Henry Newman and his mentors. *Journal for the Scientific Study of Religion* 21:58-70.
1982b *The psychology of petitionary prayer. Theology Today* 39:130-141.

Dahrendorf, R.
[1959]
1971 *Homo sociologicus*. Köln: Opladen.

Dreitzel, H. P.
1979 *Rollentheorie*. In *Die psychologie des 20. Jahrhunderts VIII*. Zürich: Kindler.

Durkheim, E.
1893 *De la division du travail social*. Paris: Alcan.

Falk, G.
1979 *Über die theorie der symbolischen interaktion*. In *Die psychologie des 20. Jahrhunderts VIII*. Zürich: Kindler.

Geels, A.
1980 *Mystikern Hjalmar Ekstrom 1885-1962*. Malmö: Doxa.
Geyer, K.
1989 *Att dana människor*. Uppsala: Doctoral dissertation.
Goffman, E.
1986 *Frame analysis*. Boston: Northeastern University Press.
Habermas, J.
1973 *Kultur und Kritik*. Frankfurt: Suhrkamp Verlag.
Holm, Nils G.
1976 *Tungotal och andedop*. Uppsala: Acta universitatis upsaliensis, Psychologia religionum 5.
1978 Functions of glossolalia in the Pentecostal Movement. In Källstad. *Psychological studies on religious man*, edited by To. Uppsala: Acta universitatis upsaliensis, Psychologia religionum 7.
1987a Scandinavian psychology of religion. Åbo Akademi university: Religionsvetenskapliga skrifter nr 15.
1987b Sundén's role theory and glossolalia. *Journal for the Scientific Study of Religion* 26:383-389.
1991 Pentecostalism: Conversion and charismata. *The International Journal for the Psychology of Religion*. 1:135-151.
1991a Sundén's role theory and glossolalia. In *Psychology of religion: Personalities, problems, possibilities*, edited by H. N. Malony. Grand Rapids, MI: Baker.
Honko, L.
1969 Role-taking of the Shaman. Temenos 4.
1971 Memorat och folktroforskning. In Folkdikt och folktro. Lund: Gleerups.
1972 *Uskontotieteen näkökulmia*. Porvoo & Helsinki: Werner Soderstrom osakeyhtio.
James, W.
1890 *The principles of psychology*. New York: Holt.
Järvinen, P.
1991 *Psykos och religion*. Åbo: Åbo Academy Press.
Källstad, T.
1974 *John Wesley and the bible*. Uppsala: Acta universitatis upsaliensis, Psychologia religionum 1.
Källstad, T. (Ed.)
1978 *Psychological studies on religious man*. Uppsala: Acta universitatis upsaliensis, Psychologia religionum 7.
Kellner, H.
1979 Der Beitrag von G. H. Mead zur Sozialpsychologie. In *Die psychologie des 20. Jahrhunderts VIII*. Zurich: Kindler.
Lindzey, G. (Ed.)
1954 *Handbook of social psychology*. 2 vols. Cambridge, MA: Addison-Wesley.
Linton, R.
1936 *The study of man: An introduction*. New York: Student's edition.
1945 *The cultural background of personality*. New York: Appleton-Century-Crofts.
Luoma, M.
1965 *Uskonnonpsykologia eilen ja tänään*. Tampere: Acta Academiae Socialis ser. A vol. 1.
Mannheim, Karl
[1936]
1949 *Ideology and utopia*. London: Routledge and Kegan Paul.
Mead, G. H.
1934 *Mind, self, and society*. Chicago: University of Chicago Press.
Mead, R. K.
1934 *Mind, self, and society*. Chicago: University of Chicago Press.
Merton, R. K.
1968 *Social theory and social structure*. New York: Free Press.
Newcomb, T. M.

1952 *Social psychology*. London: Tavistock Publications.
Otto, R.
1917 Das Heilige. Über das Irrationale in der Idee des Göttlichen und sein Verhältnis zum Rationalen. Bresl.
Parsons, T.
1951 *The social system*. Glencoe, IL: Free Press.
Pettersson, T.
1975 The retention of the religious experience. Uppsala: Acta universitatis upsaliensis, Psychologia religionum 3.
Rocheblave-Spenlé, A.-M.
1962 *La notion de rôle en psychologie sociale. Thèse*. Paris: Universite de Paris. Faculte des lettres et sciences humaines.
Sarbin, T. R.
1954 Role theory. In *Handbook of social psychology*, Vol. 1, edited by G. Lindzey. Reading, MA: Addison-Wesley.
Scheler, M.
1960 *Die Wissensformen und die Gesellschaft*. Bern: Francke.
Shaw, M. E., and P. R. Costanzo
1970 *Theories of social psychology*. New York: McGraw-Hill.
Sherif, M., and C. W. Sherif
1969 *Social psychology*. New York: Harper & Row.
Siikala, A-L
1978 *The rite technique of the Siberian shaman*. Helsinki: Academia Scientarum Fennica.
Sundén, Hjalmar
1940 *La théorie bergsonienne de la religion*. Uppsala: Almqvist & Wiksells förtryckeri Ab.
1956 *Sjuttiotredje psalmen och andra essäer*. Stockholm: Svenska kyrkans diakonistyrelses bokförlag.
[1959]
1966 *Religionen och rollerna*, 4th ed. Stockholm: Svenska kyrkans diakonistyrelses bokförlag.
1966 *Die Religion und die Rollen*. Berlin: Alfred Töpelmann.
1969 Die rollenpsychologie und die weisen des religions-erlebens. In *Wesen und Weisen der Religion*, edited by Charlotte Hörgl, Kurt Krenn, and Fritz Rauh. Munchen: Max Hueber Verlag.
1970 *Barn och religion*. Stockholm: Verbum.
1977 *Religionspsykologi. Problem och metoder*. Stockholm: Proprius förlag.
1982 Luther's Vorrede auf den Psalter von 1545 als religions-psychologisches dokument. In *Archiv für Religionspsychologie* 15:36-44.
1987 Saint Augustine and the psalter in the light of role-psychology. *Journal for the scientific study of religion* 26:375-382.
Thomas, E. J.
1968 Role theory, personality, and the individual. In *Handbook of personality theory and research*, edited by E. F. Borgatta and W. W. Lambert. Chicago: Rand McNally.
Turner, R. H.
1962 Role taking: process versus conformity. In *Human behavior and social processes: An interactionist approach*, edited by A. M.Rose. Boston: Houghton-Mifflin.
Unger, J.
1976 On religious experience. Uppsala: Acta universitatis upsaliensis, Psychologia religionum 6.
van der Lans, Jan
1978 Religieuze ervaring en meditatie. Nijmegen. Doctoral dissertation.
1987 The value of Sundén's role-theory demonstrated and tested with respect to religious experiences in meditation. *Journal for the Scientific Study of Religion* 26:401-412.
Wach, J.
1944 *Sociology of religion*. Chicago: Phoenix Books.
Waller, M.

1977 Rollenanalytische. Perspektiven der empirischen Persönlich-keitsforschung. In *Die psychologie des 20. Jahrhunderts V*. Zürich: Kindler.

Wikström, O.

1975 Guds ledning. Uppsala: Acta universitatis upsaliensis, psychologia religionum 4.

1987 Attribution, roles and religion: A theoretical analysis of Sundén's role theory of religion and the attributional approach to religious experience. *Journal for the Scientific Study of Religion* 26:390-400.

Wulff, D. M.

1991 *Psychology of religion*. New York: Wiley.

Young, K.

1946 *Handbook of social psychology*. London: Appleton-Century-Crofts.

18

Attribution Theory and Religious Experience

BERNARD SPILKA AND DANIEL N. MCINTOSH

To most people terms like religious, spiritual, ecstatic, transcendental, or mystical experience convey an air of awe, reverence, and mystery. Many wonder whether those who report such events have really encountered a divine presence. Psychologists are likely to view such claims differently. Those who specialize in cognition might focus on altered states of consciousness and talk about selective attention, the topography of conscious states, focus deautomization, disinhibition, etc. (Martindale, 1981; Wallace and Fisher, 1983). In contrast, clinicians might hypothesize that such phenomena relate to some form of mental disturbance, possibly transitory, but more likely, chronic (Group for the Advancement of Psychiatry, 1976). An alternative view was advanced by Maslow (1964) who identified religious experiences as peak experiences that tend to be associated with good mental health. Though some data support both positions, there is no definitive evidence to suggest that most people who report such events are abnormal or exceptional in either a positive or negative sense. In fact, depending on the way the question of having such experiences is phrased, anywhere from 25 to 50 percent of the American and English populations report these encounters (Greeley, 1974; Hardy, 1979; Hay and Morisy, 1978; Thomas and Cooper, 1978). The implication is that the overwhelming majority of those who relate such incidents are quite normal.

THE NATURE OF RELIGIOUS EXPERIENCE

After a century of psychosocial writing on religious experience, this remains a topic which invites more questions than answers: For example, to what degree are nature, aesthetic, and religious experiences similar (Back and Bourque, 1970)? There is much reason to believe that they are alike. As Stark (1965) points out, "events or feelings are only 'religious' if a person *defines* them as such" (p.99). Malony (1973) also claims that "the constructs one brings to experience help shape its meaning" (p.78). Bourque and Back (1971) detail this possibility by contending that "the availability of language determines the individual's ability and willingness to describe feeling states" (p.1). Noting much similarity between religious and aesthetic experiences, Bourque (1969) suggests that they are largely determined by the context in which they occur. Environmental influence is also stressed by Dittes (1969).

Does each religious tradition have its own form of experience? This is implied by those who, for example, distinguish specifically Christian experience from other possibilities (Godin, 1985). Stace (1960) identifies a variety of experiences associated with particular religious traditions; however, he stresses similarities across the faiths. Again, the difference may be one of subjective experiential content rather than of objective form and process. Malony (1973) holds this view, suggesting that "religious experience, while it may differ in content, is nevertheless identical with other experiences in terms of the underlying processes involved" (p.77).

The information we have on factors associated with the induction of religious experiences demonstrates primarily correlation rather than causation. Lists of "triggers" are suggestive, but generally remain poorly integrated into our understanding of these states. The prime difficulty is the lack of organizing theoretical perspectives that may direct research. A few possibilities have been advanced (Group for the Advancement of Psychiatry, 1976; Kirkpatrick, 1992; Proudfoot and Shaver, 1975; Pruyser, 1968), but little or no work has been undertaken to assess and develop such views.

The purpose of the present effort is to offer some guidelines from the vantage point of attribution theory, a major perspective in contemporary social psychology (Fiske and Taylor, 1991; Hewstone, 1983; Proudfoot and Shaver, 1975; Ross and Nisbett, 1991; Spilka, Shaver, and Kirkpatrick, 1985). Proudfoot and Shaver (1975) note that "attribution theory is attractive to the student of religion because . . . it deals directly with a person's interpretation of his own experience" (p.322). As a first step, this approach offers the potential of a definition for religious experience. We suggest that religious experience refers to a cognitive-emotional state in which the experiencer's understandings involve attributions or references to religious figures, roles, or powers. These explanations may involve perceptions of oneself in relation to a religious framework or to religious agents (e.g., God, angels, divine forces, Satan). In other words, as Proudfoot (1985) recommends "religious experience must be characterized from the perspective of the one who has that experience. It is an experience that the subject apprehends as religious" (p.181). A pertinent element in this is that research indicates that experiences, as occurrences that happen to people, elicit attributions to external forces. They are not perceived as being produced by oneself (Brown and Fish, 1983).

FORMS OF RELIGIOUS EXPERIENCE

Before exploring the processes that may cause individuals to have various types of experiences they understand as religious, it is important to address the variation in types of religious experiences. One initial distinction likely to be made by the person having the experience is whether there is an interpersonal or relational component to the experience. Is there "another" present?

Scholars themselves have struggled with the question of whether a sense of a supernatural "other" is necessary for an experience to be considered religious. James (1902), Stark (1965), and Hardy (1979) claim that the distinguishing feature of religious experience is a sense of contact with a supernatural agency. An event has occurred (experience), and its meaning is sought in interpersonal relational terms within the domain of religion. This perception includes the assumption that there is a real other there to be perceived, and with whom the experiencer interacts.

Not all forms of religious experience, however, include this relational component. Another concept enters this picture, namely the notion of mysticism, a term and concept that Clark (1973) calls vague and elusive. Some conceptions of mystical experience include an interpersonal element. Otto (1923) restricted the idea of mystical to an experience of unification of one's self and the divine. In most schemes, such a sense of unity is a major criterion for religious experience. Without denoting an "other," James (1902) asserted that mystical experience is noetic and ineffable. New knowledge is gained and the experience cannot be adequately put into words. He thus states that "mystical states are more like states of feeling than like states of intellect" (p.380).

More recently, definitions of mystical experience have broadened to include experience with nonpersonal or anthropomorphic powers such as "belief in a power (supernatural or other) that plays a key role in helping to produce what appears to be an altered state of consciousness" (Wallace and Fisher, 1983:138). This broadens the referential scheme to the nonsupernatural, meaning naturalistic. One could argue that modern theologies such as Process, Liberation, and Feminist leave room for such a view. In any event, attributions are made to a "power."

Some scholars make distinctions between religious and mystical experiences. Calling mysticism "a basic–if not *the* basic–experiential core or essence to human religious experience," Hood (1975:29) presents evidence that not all forms of mystical experience are interpreted religiously. He operationalized mysticism utilizing eight of Stace's (1960) criteria for such experiences. Statistically, these collapsed into two forms: 1) intense experience "not interpreted religiously and not necessarily positive" (p.34), and 2) "a joyful expression of more traditionally defined religious experiences which may or may not be mystical but which are interpreted to indicate a firm source of objective knowledge" (p.34). Mysticism per se becomes "intense experience," and Hood concludes that "some religious experiences may in fact not be mystical and some mystical experiences may in fact not be interpreted as religious" (p.34).

Thomas and Cooper (1978) distinguish mystical experiences from those they define as psychic and of faith and consolation. The last two include "religious or spiritual elements, but no indication of the extraordinary or supernatural" (p.435.) Mystical is reserved for "awesome emotions, a sense of the ineffable feeling of oneness with God, nature or the universe" (p.435). This sounds very much like the positions of James and Hood. Even though workers in this area agree that the core of mystical experience involves intense emotion, they still vary in what they place under the rubric, mystical. Nevertheless Stace's criteria have, in the main, gained support (Hardy, 1979; Spilka, Brown, and Cassidy, 1993).

There are apparently no reliable dividing lines between religious experience per se and mystical experience. Suggestions of greater emotion for the latter may founder on the subjectivity of making such distinctions. Therefore, for our purposes, Stark's (1965) broad experiential avenue will best suffice. He states that "the term religious experience covers an exceedingly disparate array of events: from the vaguest glimmerings of something sacred to rapturous mystical unions with the divine, or even to revelations" (p.97). This is certainly suggested by Hardy's forty-eight categories of experience. To go beyond this is to justify some version of partisanship, the evidence for which is dubious. We thus leave to the person having the religious experience the decision whether to understand it as including a supernatural other or a paranormal or natural force. This is one dimension on which attributions for such events will vary.

Other than rather inconclusive efforts to separate religious experience in general from mysticism in specific, the various expressive criteria proposed by Stace (1960), Hardy (1979), Hood (1975) and Spilka, Brown, and Cassidy (1993), have not been formally employed to identify different forms of religious experience. Stark (1965), however, has offered one taxonomy that appears fruitful. This includes two broad sets of attributions that are designated divine and diabolic, the former largely to God, the latter to the Devil. Both patterns hold for the four kinds of experience that are theorized.

The most common kind of experience is termed *confirming*. The prime attribution is to the truth of the experience. Two subtypes are hypothesized in which attributions are to 1) "*a generalized sense of sacredness*" (p.100), and 2) to "*a specific awareness of the presence of divinity*" (p.100). In the case of Satan, sacredness becomes evil with an attendant presence "*of an evil supernatural being or force*" (p.113).

The second form of experience is termed *responsive*, and the attribution is to *mutual awareness* on the part of both the person and the supernatural. Mutuality may occur three ways—through *salvation, positive miracles*, or *negative sanctions*. One may be saved or born-again, be miraculously healed, or make attributions to receiving divine punishment. With regard to the sphere of the diabolical, the corresponding explanations are termed *temptational, damnational*, and *accursed*. One is thus tempted by the Devil, "The Devil made me do it"; rewarded by Satan, "The Devil takes care of his own"; or suffers because the Devil victimizes good people who reject his offerings.

The third form of experience, denoted as *ecstatic*, includes both the confirming and responsive kinds but extends these to a deep intimate relationship with the supernatural. This often contains sexual imagery and utilizes the language of physical love. Relative to the Devil and demonic attributions, reference is to the *terrorizing* experience and its frightening, shocking, and horrifying sexual potential.

Last, the most infrequent type of experience is called *revelational*. Here the person is selected usually via a vision to carry a divine message to others or to receive secret information regarding the future. Good spirits have their counterpart in evil spirits that may take *possession* of the individual to carry out their commands. This is another way the Devil is said to make one do his bidding.

Stark (1965) has provided a religious experiential framework that is widely used by both the devout and the general public to explain events and their own thoughts and behavior in a variety of situations and circumstances. It is rife with attributional material relative to the divine or diabolical referent that is seen as involved in the process. This is formulated in relational terms, the domain in which attributional theory was initially conceptualized and most extensively developed. There is a clear need to realize these ideas in research, something that has not been done in the more than quarter century since they were advanced by Stark.

Mention should be made of a form of religious experience that has been overviewed historically from biblical times to the present, and also cross-culturally, namely glossolalia or "speaking in tongues" (Goodman, 1972; Kelsey, 1964; Kildahl, 1972). Despite the fact that glossolalia may be distinguished behaviorally, we will not afford it special analysis, as the same attributional elements appear to characterize all of these experiential forms.

In addition to the initial question of why people perceive some experiences (and not others) as religious, there are subsequent questions of when they experience the presence of a supernatural other, and what motives they impute to that other. Further, these attributions are likely to have consequences. Our task is thus to comprehend why religion is selected, what factors might influence the type of religious experience that is elicited, and what religious attributions portend for the person reporting such occurrences.

ATTRIBUTION THEORY AND RELIGIOUS EXPERIENCE

In general attribution theory as applied to the psychology of religion there are four basic elements: the person, the context in which the person exists, the event, and the context of the event. In the case of a religious experience (event), the context of the person and the event are the same. Attributional explanations will be restricted to the characteristics of the experiencer, the experience, and the context. For the first, attention must be afforded not only lasting and permanent features of the individual who is the actor-experiencer in this situation, but also the momentary and transitory features of the setting that may have stimulated the experience.

Emotion Attribution and the Context

Among the more significant early uses of attribution theory were its applications to emotional experience (Schachter, 1964; Schachter and Singer, 1962). Given the importance of the emotional component in religious experience, it is necessary to consider what attributional processes may be involved in the experience of emotion. It has been theorized that persons in a state of physiological/emotional excitation who lack understanding of what is happening to them will have their "evaluative needs" aroused. They will then search the environment for cues to the source of their arousal. Salient cues should furnish them with identifying labels (e.g., a happy person in a room with the subject would provide a cue to the latter that the appropriate feeling is happiness). People would then label their physiological arousal "happiness," and would subjectively experience this emotion. In other words, a given set of physiological sensations could be labeled—and experienced as—any number of emotions. "Knowledge" is thus a function of the attributions made. What one felt was theorized as being controlled by the cues in the environment. As Dienstbier (1979) points out, the origin of the emotional state which will be attributionally explained may actually be unknown and quite irrelevant to the interpretation that is made. In situations likely to occur outside the laboratory—when arousal is caused by something other than surreptitious manipulations by the experimenter—it is not easy to make individuals missattribute their feelings to a source other than its actual cause. For people to misattribute their arousal, its actual source must be ambiguous, and the alternative cause must be salient, unambiguous, plausible, and perceived by the person as stronger in impact than it actually is (Olson and Ross, 1988; Ross and Olson, 1981; Sterling and Gaertner, 1984). Nonetheless, under the proper circumstances, people will mistakenly attribute their emotional state to a source other than the actual cause.

The circumstances that increase the probability of misattribution of arousal may well be those likely to confront a person undergoing a religious or mystical experience. Proudfoot and Shaver (1975) claim that "religion functions as a cognitive system to reduce anxieties over problems of interpretability raised by 'boundary situations'—anomalous experiences and events" (p.318). They further suggest that "at least some religious experiences are due to emotional states that are given a particular interpretation" (p.319). In essence, they conclude that "the attributional or interpretative component appears to be the crucial factor in an experience that is felt to be religious" (p.324). From this perspective, a person who has a religious or mystical experience is probably physiologically (or emotionally) aroused by some ambiguous or unnoticed source (e.g., being in a large crowd, greater than usual physical exertion). Further, there should be a *salient* alternative *religious cause* in the environment (e.g., a preacher telling the person that they are about to be infused with the spirit of God, or a ritual such as prayer that is purported to cause encounters with mystical powers). This potential cause must be one that is believable to the person. Simply to be present in a religious context may not be enough to spur a religious misattribution of arousal (and thus a religious experience).

General Attribution

The distinctions made in emotion-attribution research are consistent with evidence from a more general attributional framework. Specifically, attribution theory indicates that people should view a particular cause as responsible for an occurrence when there are fewer competing explanations available. In the domain of social perception, Kelley (1972) noted the *discounting principle*. For example, this rule recognizes that if you know that Maria always eats lunch at the city's one Ethiopian restaurant, you will be less likely to conclude that this is because she loves Ethiopian food if you also know that it is the only restaurant within walking distance of her office building. If one knows of two plausible causes, one is less likely to view only one of them as the single cause. If the only plausible explanation for a sensation is a religious one, a person will be more likely to make an attribution to that cause than if there are other possible explanations available.

A number of studies from developmental and social psychology have isolated a few basic principles of causation used by both children and adults (see Fiske and Taylor, 1991, for discussion). They are especially likely to be used when events happen in domains in which there is little knowledge. We can assume that when these basic principles point toward a religious explanation for an occurrence, the probability that a religious attribution will be made will be increased. First, not only do we assume that a cause will precede an effect, but we are more likely to see something as the cause of an event if the potential cause and the effect have *temporal contiguity*. That is, if a person feels elated immediately after a religious ritual, the ritual is more likely to be seen as the cause than if there were a twenty-minute gap between the ritual and the elation. Second, consistent with the work on emotion attribution, perceptually salient stimuli are more likely to be considered as the cause of an event.

In sum, then, the context or situation appears likely to influence the probability that a religious attribution will be made—and that the perceiver will have a "religious experience." Though there are some grounds for suggesting that a religious environment increases the probability of a *religious* experience (Greeley, 1974), in the main, support for this position has been problematic in studies of religious attributions. Neither Spilka and Schmidt (1983) or Lupfer, Brock, and Depaola (1992) were able to demonstrate contextual effects. It may be that, although there were religious components of the situation, they did not meet the criteria discussed above for being truly influential candidates for attribution. Another possibility for the apparent lack of situational influence may be based on self-monitoring before a possible religious experience. Just as Samuel Johnson observed that hanging "concentrates one's mind wonderfully," so may such self-monitoring of self-focusing cause the individual to become less sensitive to environmental stimuli. In other words, the person, in becoming "cognitively busy" may be "less able to make use of situational information" (Fiske and Taylor, 1991:72). Future research should examine directly the role of potential religious causes that are salient, plausibly powerful, temporally congruent with the effect, and which occur in the absence of competing causal explanations.

Motivational Influences

Though further work on the effects of religious environmental stimuli is indeed in order, the motivational-emotional framework should also be afforded consideration. Apparently in most circumstances cognitive recourse is initially made to naturalistic possibilities for understanding; however, for some people in some situations, religious attributions are offered. For the latter, there may be times naturalistic reference is cognitively and emotionally unsatisfying. For example, medical situations are much more likely to elicit religious attributions than economic or social problems, intimating a shift from naturalistic to religious explanations (Lilliston and Brown, 1981; Loewenthal and Cornwall, 1993). This implies that there are motivational reasons for making attributions that better meet personal needs and goals.

Basic Human Needs: Meaning, Control, and Esteem

The search for basic human motives has occupied philosophers and psychologists for over two thousand years. Aristotle's opening line in *De Anima* "All men by nature desire to know" implies the existence of innate, higher order basic motives such as a "search for meaning." In 1788, Thomas Reid asserted that the three fundamental human desires are for knowledge, power, and esteem (Reid, 1969). The modern counterpart is to imply intrinsic needs for meaning, mastery or control, and self-esteem (Spilka, Shaver, and Kirkpatrick, 1985; Taylor, 1983). It has been theorized that conditions that challenge these three elemental motives stimulate attributional activity to help the person make sense out of what is or has happened, to maintain or enhance one's sense of control, and/or to sustain or augment self-esteem (Spilka, Shaver, and Kirkpatrick, 1985). In some situations, these goals may be met better with religious attributions than with naturalistic explanations. Early attribution theory held to the premise that people make attributions because they have a need to predict the future and control events (e.g., Heider, 1958; Kelley, 1967). Prediction itself may be a form of control—implicit and vicarious.

The tendency mentioned above to shift to religious attributions in medical situations may be because most people are not privy to specialized medical knowledge, hence medical problems usually possess a high degree of ambiguity. In addition, satisfactory meanings may be at a premium for those affected, and the associated dependency on medical professionals increases one's sense of powerlessness. Ambiguity is often supplemented by other intimations of danger. Few things are more forbidding than physical health problems. Pain, illness, weakness, and infirmity can intimate permanent disability or possibly death, even if the doctor offers a favorable prognosis. Despite assurances by physicians, patients and their families may feel the "best face" is being put on the situation. We note, for example that about 90 percent of breast cancer patients pray and/or offer religious attributions once they receive their diagnosis (Ladd and Spilka, 1992). We suggest that ambiguity and threat concurrently increase emotional arousal and reduce the meaningfulness of naturalistic attributions.

Though the absence of meaning parallels a lack of control, there are many situations where one understands what is happening, but cannot master the problem. Control per se becomes the central issue. In our recent work with breast cancer patients, 74 percent of the women saw much or total control as being in the hands of God (Spilka, Ladd, and David, 1993).

Generally, powerlessness reduces as religious commitment and action (e.g., prayer) increases (Krause and Van Tranh, 1989; O'Brien, 1982). Research clearly indicates that deprivation of control stimulates attributional activity (Pittman and Pittman, 1980). Our work suggests that this is true for the offering of religious attributions. Their expression in confirming, responsive, or even ecstatic religious experiences must be highly gratifying to those obtaining such "authentication." This is seen in what has been termed *predictive control* (Weisz, Rothbaum, and Blackburn, 1984). An example of a confirming sign from God is presented in Eliach's *Hassidic Tales of the Holocaust.* A devout Jew was brought into the death camp at Auschwitz where the number 145053 was tattooed on his arm. He looked at it, and immediately "knew" that he would survive. In a cabalistic manner, he added the digits to obtain a sum of 18 which in Judaism signifies life. His future was assured.

The above needs for meaning and control are easily supplemented by a like requirement to maintain or enhance one's self-esteem. Certainly, the absence of meaning and powerlessness are in themselves blows to esteem that people attempt to counter. Taylor (1983) and Bulman and Wortman (1977) among others note the self-serving nature of attributions in that they are invariably directed toward restoring or improving one's self-concept. A considerable literature affirms that religion can make people feel good about themselves, and the positive attributions to both the self and God that overwhelmingly result from intense religious experiences testifies to this observation (Clark, 1929; Greeley, 1974; Spilka, Brown, and Cassidy, 1993; Starbuck, 1899).

We are by no means saying that deprivation, frustration, threat, or personal troubles are the only motivators of religious experience, for many triggers that are cited by workers in this area have a positive quality to them (e.g., music, beauty, nature, etc.) (Greeley, 1974; Hardy, 1979; Hood, 1977a). Unfortunately, lists of such triggers speak to the immediate precipitating circumstances and not possible underlying preparatory conditions which might activate religious schemas and experiential attributions (Hood, 1977b). Even in rather desired and favorable triggering situations, we wonder if we are not looking at settings in which there are "crises" of meaning, control, or esteem that need resolution and are resolved by the making of religious activated experiential attributions.

The Person: Influences and Dispositions

Each individual-situation transaction has its own idiosyncratic character. Still, we may ask if there are not more fundamental levels for understanding a person's actions and experiences. Though many situational elements are referred to as "triggers" for religious experience, we must also look at the qualities of the person that may make the probability of religious attributions—and thus having a religious experience—greater. These individual differences follow the categories of factors we have discussed above. Thus, there are likely to be individual differences in the plausibility or salience of religious causes, in the availability of religious understandings, and in the strength of underlying motives. The concept of personality is often used as an intra-individual dynamic when seeking such cross-situational consistencies, but on a broader social level, we must be aware of cultural and group influences.

Cultural and Group Factors

The individual is the central figure in a matrix of forces that temporally include past, present, and future-predictive elements. Concomitantly, the person, across time, has been and is the repository of socio-cultural and group influences. The interpretive attributions one makes reflect these factors.

Our culture and the groups and people which translate the ethos into individual terms have taught us what is acceptable and what is not for a broad range of circumstances. Our attributions are thus patterned. Religious explanatory possibilities pervade American mass culture. Whether it be called "public piety" or "civil religion," the language of traditional faith, primarily of Protestant Christianity, infuses our social order (Bellah and Hammond, 1980). Whether such allusions are in the pledge of allegiance or in the standard remarks at the opening of a meeting, religious potential is kept before people at almost every turn.

In conservative religious circles, naturalistic explanations for individual actions are regarded as appropriate within a more limited sphere than in modernist or liberal milieus. The situation is reversed for religious attributions. Research tells us that attributions to God are more proper for the good things that happen to us than for the bad, except under extreme conditions (Bulman and Wortman, 1977; Lupfer et al, 1992; Spilka and Schmidt, 1983). Literal diabolical attributions to the role of the devil are common among Protestant Fundamentalists, but essentially unknown among Jews. Stace (1960) notes major differences in the content of Christian, Indian, Islamic, and Jewish mysticisms which reflect these cultural traditions and the personal expectations of those upholding such legacies. Stace accepts variation in experiential content, but not in process across cultures.

One must also consider attributional variation to be a function of subcultural differences among those claiming adherence to the same faith. Hasidic Jews are miles apart in their understandings and experiences from Reform Jews (Himmelfarb, 1973). The spectrum of Protestantism is equally broad. Regional and class factors are also influential but have not been studied to any extent.

In like manner, people are definable in each and every situation in terms of position-role complexes. Of widest import, one may think of age and sex roles. In recent years, gender differences in religious experience have been highlighted, but age effects have yet to be solidly researched even though much speculative advice has been offered (Fecher, 1982; Meadow and Rayburn, 1985).

The Concept of Schema

One way of understanding how these differences are activated in specific circumstances is available from the work done on the concept of cognitive schemas. A schema is a cognitive structure or mental representation containing organized, prior knowledge about a particular domain, including a specification of the relations among its attributes (Fiske and Linville, 1980; McIntosh, 1991; Taylor and Crocker, 1981). People have schemas for many domains including objects, events, roles, persons, and the self, and these will influence situational interpretations (Taylor and Crocker, 1981).

Specifically, many people possess organized knowledge about religion and religious issues. These may be called religion schemas, and they are presented, reinforced, and implied on many levels from the sociocultural to the family and individual experience. Obviously a wide variety of forms and contents exist among religion schemas. Some people probably have schemas for religion that encompass a broad spectrum of events, situations, outcomes, etc. Such individuals should be more prone to deduce religious causes for many events (see McIntosh, 1991, for further discussion of religion schemas).

Kelley (1972) notes that people have causal schemas that they use to infer the origin of single events. This is "knowledge" a person has regarding how certain types of causes interact to produce a particular type of effect. When we have incomplete or ambiguous information about the whys and wherefores in a particular instance, we can use these schemas to go beyond the information given to infer the reasons for an event. Because people share heavily overlapping experiences with causality, their schemas are likely to be similar in many ways. However, there may be relatively different "experiences" or learning about causality in the religious domain. Thus, people will fill in the gaps in information about causality differently, depending on their experience with similar events. Because causal schemas tend to be used when information about event origins are sketchy, individual differences are more apt to appear in attributions in ambiguous circumstances.

Individual differences in schemas are cognitive ways in which people can vary in their likelihood of understanding an experience as religious. Relative to motives, there is often evidence of underlying personal problems of one sort or another. Clark (1929) claimed that 7 percent of his sample had "definite crisis awakenings" in which immediate conflict and turmoil was evident. Still what he termed "emotional stimulus" and "gradual" awakenings indicated longer preexisting turmoil in over 50 percent of those he studied. Similar signs dominate in the work of Beardsworth (1977), Conway and Siegelman (1978) and Spilka, Brown, and Cassidy (1993). Ellwood (1980) speaks of "internal triggers caused by a need for alleviation" (p.40). Starbuck (1899) emphasized "the sense of sin and depression and sadness" (p.66). Niebuhr (1972) refers to "fearing/dreading," and commented that "we note as the salient mark of this affection the sense of powerlessness . . . a sense of the presence of power that one is unable to annex to oneself or to master" (p.90). Kildahl (1972) cites the work of a colleague to the effect that "more than 85 percent of the tongue-speakers had experienced a clearly defined anxiety crisis preceding their speaking in tongues" (p.57). In other words, one may have a problem which "only God can resolve." Fichter's (1981) assertion that "religious reality is the only way to make sense out of pain and suffering" (p.20) thus carries a lot of truth. A religious experience (making religious attributions) often confirms this underlying belief with noteworthy effects. Religious or mystical experience not only frequently solves personal dilemmas, but also represents attributions that corroborate one's religious stance (Kulik, 1983).

Background Factors

Though schemas are often generally shaped by sociocultural influences, individual variation in the breadth and strength of various schemas, hence their perceived utility in everyday life, is apt to be a function of socialization processes. A home in which religious rituals, ideas, and language are extensively employed should increase the probability that religious language and notions are available for attributional use. The same would be expected of early religious schooling and attendance at church services and activities.

Language. Language is the sine qua non of attributions. It shapes and directs thinking along certain lines. The more familiar we are with certain areas, the more rapidly we visually and auditorially recognize words relating to these topics, and the more readily we employ this language (Howes, 1957, Howes and Solomon, 1951). As Bernstein (1964) observes, "Language marks out what is relevant, affectively, cognitively and socially, and experience is transformed by what is made relevant" (p.254). Laski (1961) and Bourque and Back (1971) have thus shown that religious people possess a religious language with which they describe their experiences. The attributions they make are a function of this language which, as might be expected, reflects one's background and interests. To a considerable degree, thought is indeed a slave of language (Carroll, 1956).

Attitudes and Personality

This broad category includes virtually everything that cannot be assigned to situation and context. One thinks primarily of dispositional factors—long-lasting individual characteristics such as traits. Relative to attributions and religious experience, only a few areas have been extensively researched, namely, self-esteem, locus of control, and form of personal faith. Attribution researchers perceive such work as illustrating *attributional styles* which are patterned individual differences in the making of attributions (Ickes and Layden, 1978; Metalsky and Abramson, 1981). These probably influence whether or not people have religious experiences plus the form of the experience they report. In other words, the three areas just cited may be treated as attributional styles. For example, people with low self-esteem experience God differently than those with high self-esteem (Benson and Spilka, 1972). Much of personality thus becomes the study of attributional tendencies and their ramifications.

Self-esteem. As a rule, people with high self-esteem attribute their problems to external factors while those with low self-esteem perceive themselves to be the cause of what adversely affects them (Ickes and Layden, 1978). We know that cancer patients overwhelmingly deny that God had a role in causing their cancer and perceive the deity as performing supportive and curative functions (Johnson and Spilka, 1991). Some research indicates that self-blame constitutes a major attribution when one contracts a serious illness (Abrams and Finesinger, 1953; Taylor and Levin, 1976). In our work the tendency is not to see oneself as causing cancer. Attributions are largely made to unknown influences or genetic and other medical possibilities over which the patient cannot exert control. Since these have the quality of being external factors, and self-blame is essentially absent, they suggest high self-esteem. Concurrently, we have a picture of patients who seek to identify with their God, considering the frequency with which they pray, attend church, and report how helpful their faith is in their struggle with cancer (Spilka, Ladd, and David, 1993). Anecdotal comments picture God experiences of a strong and positive quality in the sense of God answering questions (providing meaning), or providing the strength to face their illness (enhancing their sense of control). Earlier work further suggests that positive images of the deity go with like concepts of the self (Benson and Spilka, 1972), and favorable God attributions work to maintain self-esteem. Though we did not directly assess the presence of religious experiences per se, there was no doubt that the women in our studies felt quite close to their God. Their experiences through prayer in particular caused many to feel that they would be successful in their trials.

Two independent studies of those who report intense or mystical religious experiences reveal low self-satisfaction or esteem in pre-experience time. As a rule, the experience attributions countered negative self percepts (Jackson and Spilka, 1980; Spilka, Brown, and Cassidy, 1993). Hay (1985) and Hood (1977a) suggest a similar pattern in that those who stated that they had undergone religious experiences seemed to be more "self-actualized" or "realized" than others who did not have such encounters. This finding also holds for persons whose experiences resulted in conversion with the post-conversion state picturing high self-satisfaction compared to the convert's prior life (Jones, 1937; Ullman, 1982).

There is a potential bias in this work, namely, that those assessed are evaluated after having undergone a major life-event, usually a profound, intense religious experience. Their feelings, outlooks, and beliefs can be radically changed. Frequently pre- (as recounted) and post-experience attributions to the self and world deviate sharply. A "contrast" effect has been produced, and memories may be distorted; current perceptions, expectations, and attributions become the creators of a possibly divergent past. Such effects are well-documented (Conway and Ross, 1984), and Snow and Machalek (1984) consider "biographical reconstruction" to be a formal property of conversion. In any event, the feeling of having experienced God places one in a very special category that should do wonders for self-esteem.

Locus of control. One of the best researched attributional styles deals with how people perceive power and control in their lives. Do they see themselves as the repository of control or are attributions made to powerful others, fate and chance, or to God (Kopplin, 1976; Levenson, 1973; Pargament et al., 1988)?

Even though religious experiences have not been conceptualized in the language of control and mastery, they invariably include attributions in which power is a central force. The words chosen may be the terminology of love, adoration, unity, peace, joy, and the like, but the "other present" is a "force," "something more," "the father," "infinite dimension," and, of course, God, the divine, Holy Spirit, etc. (Beardsworth, 1977). This is no relationship among equals. What has occurred is due to an agent that implicitly, if not explicitly, connotes omnipotence, omniscience, and omnipresence.

But how does one relate to such power? You can compete with it as in resisting "temptation offered by Satan," who is, of course, an opponent who will often "have his way." Sin is not attributed to the self, though reference to one's "weakness" may have to be recognized. The blame, however, could be assigned to the "Devil, who made me do it" (Hunsberger and Watson, 1986). In contrast, success has often been attributed to Jesus, God, or Elijah who comes to the aid of those in distress by providing the necessary strength to resist the lure and overcome adversity.

Pargament et al. (1988) point out that the control attributions people make to God involve various relational patterns. If divine power is accepted, one may defer to it. God is active and the person takes a passive role. Here is the prayerful entreaty for help, the petition that places one's hopes and desires totally in the "hands of God." Weakness is the self-attribution; strength and decision, the lot of the deity. Finally, the attribution may be to collaboration. "God helps those who help themselves," hence potency is mutual. A cooperative, supportive association is postulated.

We were unable to locate research directly tying religious experience to locus of control, yet noted that much contradiction has been observed in relationships between religious and control variables. The most consistent finding is that God control and personal control tend to be negatively related (Kopplin 1976; McIntosh, Kojetin, and Spilka, 1985; Pargament, Sullivan, Tyler, and Steele, 1982; Spilka and Schmidt, 1983). This possibility may be combined with an extensive literature that suggests profound religious experiences, especially those involving sudden conversion, are frequently preceded by considerable personal stress in what may be viewed as crises of meaning and control. Havens (cited in Malony, 1973) speaks of persons being "prepared" (p.81) for religious experiences. Such preparation may often be great personal turmoil over a long period of time (Clark, 1929; Lofland and Skonovd, 1981; Spilka, Brown, and Cassidy, 1993). These people are seeking a way out of their difficulties and they apparently unite this need with inclinations that permit them to attribute to God the power and willingness to alleviate them of their burden. Lofland and Skonovd (1981) see this in their "mystical" conversion motif in which "the level of emotional arousal is extremely high" (p.378). A door is thus opened to emotional attribution. Variations on attributional explanations of religious experiences that lead to conversion may be applied to the other themes identified by these authors.

Hypothetically, attributions of one's lack of personal power are countered by experiential indications of divine control that imply a potential mastery of one's troubles. Such problems may take many forms as illustrated by Glock's (1964) discussion of "deprivations" which he identifies as economic, social, organismic, ethical, and psychic. These can be regarded as crises of control. Identifying with God and being able to make attributions of divine intervention via religious experience could be quite effective in maintaining or enhancing one's sense of mastery. This is strongly indicated in Sales (1972) study of conversion to authoritarian churches in times of economic distress.

In summary, there is strong evidence that preparation for religious experience often involves pre-experience stress which one is unable to master. Religious experiences that permit attributions to divine power can counter feelings of powerlessness, probably through the adoption of either God-deferring or collaborative modes of problem-solving. Since the collaborative approach permits a greater degree of personal control, this attributional perspective may be of more benefit to the individual than utilization of a deferring strategy (McIntosh and Spilka, 1990).

Form of personal faith. From the viewpoint of how people express their personal faith, one scheme has been studied relative to religious experience. Allport's distinction between Intrinsic and Extrinsic religious orientations has dominated this literature. These tendencies represent very different ways of looking at religion and responding to others and the world (Donahue, 1985; Hunt and King, 1971). They therefore bear both cognitive and motivational implications that tie to different attributional patterns. Intrinsic religion is said to be a faith in which the goals of determining the truth and locating oneself in the scheme of things dominates. In contrast, an extrinsic outlook stresses religion-as-means; it is a utilitarian orientation, a faith of convenience to be called upon when needed.

In general, an intrinsic perspective associates with attributions to a forgiving and benevolent God that is very much involved in human affairs, and is a causal agent in the world (Spilka and Mullin, 1977; Watson, Morris, and Hood, 1990). This outlook parallels positive self-attributions (Kahoe, 1976; Spilka, 1976). An extrinsic orientation is likely to take an opposing avenue, perceiving the self as relatively helpless, a victim of circumstances and external forces (Kahoe, 1974; Minton and Spilka, 1976; Strickland and Shaffer, 1971). The attributional style of intrinsics is also more complex than that of extrinsics (Watson, Morris, and Hood, 1990).

Intrinsic-extrinsic differences extend to the domain of religious experience. In two separate studies, the trend was for intrinsics to report more religious experiences than extrinsics (Hood, 1970; Hood and Morris, 1981). This may be because intrinsics more readily than extrinsics meet the criteria of being "truly" religious in terms of religious ideals. If so, as has also been suggested, intrinsics may be more likely to manifest a perceptual set that utilizes religious attributions in both religious and nonreligious settings (Hood and Morris, 1981).

THE EVENT: RELIGIOUS EXPERIENCE

As noted earlier, the range of religious experience is extremely broad. The individual who prays is having an experience, so is the Bible reader, and the person attending a religious service; one who is "born again" or "saved" also has an experience. To say the last is much more profound than the others may be to succumb to the influence of its overt apparent impressiveness. The test may be in the "fruits" of the occurrence, but the limits of the psychological versus the theological are unclear in this situation. Confining ourselves, as best we can to the former, we have been largely restricting ourselves to the more "impressive" expressions that have been the focus of investigation and reference by Greeley, Hood, Hardy, James, and Stace. These are "big effects" to which people infer and attribute "big causes" (Fiske and Taylor, 1991), and there can hardly be a bigger cause or attribution than to God or the Devil, hence our restriction to events of this character.

These attributions can be viewed as examples of the *fundamental attribution error* in that inferences are solely made to the "dispositions" or qualities of the deity for both the components of the experience and its results. Situational influences or possibilities are invariably ignored. Fiske and Taylor (1991) note that "a dispositional attribution leads one to generate a prediction for the situation, whereas an attribution to situational factors would not" (p.72). Such a dispositional attribution is also said to be "a relatively spontaneous and simple process, whereas the use of situational information to qualify or discount the role of dispositional factors is a more complex process" (Fiske and Taylor, 1991:71). This process has also been treated as twofold in nature: identification and inferential (Fiske and Taylor, 1991). Identification is based upon immediate factors—behavioral, informational, and situational. "Dispositional-relevant categories" are created and expectancies and cues are utilized toward the goal of having an experience in a situation that is "facilitating." One may thus see God as the only explanatory possibility and then infer divine motives and goals such as God's dispositional qualities in terms of love, forgiveness, salvation, and the like.

For our purposes, these points further translate into the position that the experiencer gains much by not qualifying this attribution. To slightly paraphrase Fiske and Taylor (1991), "Because (God) is dominant in the perceiver's thinking, aspects of (God) come to be overrated as causally important" (p.67). Meaning, control, and esteem are thereby not "diluted."

There is much variation among religious experiences. A multiplicity of feelings, physical reactions, and cognitive interpretations have been identified. The reasons for such diversity are essentially unknown though some theoretical and empirical correlations have been advanced. Not discussed thus far is the potential role of the expectations of the experiencer. Currently research along these lines is under way. One must ask to what degree the content and outcome of religious experience is in line with what one expects of such an occurrence.

The experience per se represents a plethora of attributions in its assumed qualities and effects, most of which are regarded as positive and of a healing nature. A number of these have been consistently reported. For example, prominent is a sense of unity—unity within oneself where conflict is resolved, unity with the world and nature whereby one is in harmony with all things. This has been observed for both religious and nonreligious mysticism (Morris and Hood, 1980), and constituted the strongest factor in the work of Spilka, Brown, and Cassidy (1993). Some representative illustrations from Beardsworth (1977) are: "All things were working together for good" (p.48); "I and what I watched were one" (p.53); "I was extending into my surroundings and was becoming one with them" (p.50). To such unity is attributed: "Beginning to understand the true meaning of the universe" (p.50); "the power to do anything" (p.50)1; "a strange feeling of expansion" (p.50). Again, meaning, control, and esteem enter the picture.

The widespread finding of perceptions of peace, joy, happiness, and well-being comprised the second most frequently reported response by Hardy (1979). Though he found a "sense of security, protection, and peace" (p.26) to be the feeling composite most often experienced, items relating to both of the foregoing patterns loaded on one factor in the work of Spilka, Brown, and Cassidy (1993). Even though Hardy theoretically distinguished these feelings in his work, chances are that great overlap across these two configurations exists in his data. Unfortunately, the minimal quantification he provided precludes such an analysis. Greeley (1974) notes that one "finds himself in the possession of a power much greater than he, which overwhelms him with joy" (p.24). The attribution is that this "power" produces the joy.

This sensing of an external power or presence is the third strongest percept offered by Hardy's respondents. It comes across as a truly central theme of which James (1902) concluded: "It is as if there were in the human consciousness *a sense of reality, a feeling of objective presence, a perception* of what we may call '*something there*'" (p.58). Leuba (1929) infers that "the sense of presence may refer to a particular person, or to an undefined person whose sex is not known; it may indeed refer to a physical agent" (p.292). He then anticipates attribution theory by noting that "the idea of this Agent sets off in the subject reactions which themselves contribute to the nature of the Agent and to the certainty of his presence" (p.293). Though Stark (1965) saw the external agent as divine or diabolical, Hardy's data indicates that divine influence is reported over ten times more often than that of an evil force. The outcome is overwhelmingly a new "sense of purpose or new meaning to life" (p.99). Like views were earlier espoused by James (1902), Leuba (1929), and Starbuck (1899).

This analysis of the components of experience can easily be detailed through the many categories and responses that researchers have specified since Starbuck initiated such efforts in 1899. A number are consistently found such as impressions of awe, reverence, sacredness, and holiness; awareness of new knowledge, and various emotional and physical reactions including sensory stimulation and hallucinatory behavior. Hardy's (1979) listing of forty-eight elements constitutes a truly exhaustive breakdown. In his work, the most common attributions are to the self for initiating the process such as through prayer, but to the "beyond" (p.77) for causing the response. Greeley (1974) interprets this to mean that "the goal is not so much loss of self...as it is the transformation of the self for its return to even more vigorous involvement" (pp.132-133). By itself, this is an interesting predictive attribution. As important as it is to understand the factors that make for attributions to positive and negative agents, there is much evidence in Hardy's work for our hypothesis that divine intervention via experience is largely a function of preexperience distress. Despair and depression are given as the most common triggers for religious experience, and the outcome is generally quite favorable from the viewpoint of those affected. Though they have not been analyzed as such, the "triggers" for experience given by Greeley (1974), Hardy (1979), and Laski (1961) are obviously multiform in nature, and if these are theoretically and/or quantitatively dimensionalized the various groupings may be shown to be instrumental in eliciting different attributions.

Religious experience as we have conceptualized it may reflect the operation of an altered state of consciousness. In recent years cognitive and neuro-psychologists have been undertaking solid research on this topic. Insofar as such states may sensitize or desensitize individuals selectively to themselves or their environment, the attributions they make could be a function of the experienced state. This, as so much else that remains unknown about religious experience, must be left to future researchers.

CONCLUSION

We have attempted to show that attribution theory is a potentially fruitful way of studying religious experience. Considering the massive amount of work that attribution researchers have produced in mainstream social psychology, we feel that this is an area which remains to be explored in depth as far as religious thinking and behavior is concerned. A number of social psychologists of religion have already recognized these opportunities and have undertaken pioneer work. As is so often true in our profession, we seem to be taking our first steps along "the yellow brick road" to the knowledge we eagerly seek. As psychologists we take the path of science but may paraphrase Leuba's (1929) belief that the experience we seek to understand "is one of the outstanding expressions of the creative power working in humanity. It is paralleled in the realm of reason by the development of science. Both lead, if in different ways, to physical and spiritual realization" (p.299).

REFERENCES

Abrams, R. D., and J. E. Finesinger
1953 Guilt reactions in patients with cancer. *Cancer* 6:474-482.

Back, K. W., and L. B. Bourque
1970 Can feelings be enumerated? *Behavioral Science* 4:87-496.

Beardsworth, T.
1977 *A sense of presence*. Manchester College, Oxford, England: Manchester College Religious Experience Research Unit.

Bellah, R. N.
1967 Civil religion in America. *Daedalus* 96:1-21.

Bellah, R. N., and P. E. Hammond
1980 *Varieties of civil religion*. New York: Harper & Row.

Benson, P. L. and B. Spilka
1972 God image as a function of self-esteem and locus of control. *Journal for the Scientific Study of Religion* 13:297-310.

Berenstein, B.
1964 Aspects of language and learning in the genesis of the social process. In *Language in culture and society*, edited by D. Hymes. New York: Harper & Row.

Bourque, L. B.
1969 Social correlates of transcendental experiences. *Sociological Analysis* 30:151-163.

Bourque, L. B., and K. W. Back
1971 Language, society, and subjective experience. *Sociometry* 34:1-21.

Brown, R. D., and D. Fish
1983 The psychological causality implicit in language. *Cognition* 14:237-273.

Bulman, R. J., and C. B. Wortman
1977 Attributions of blame and coping in the real world: Severe accident victims react to their lot. *Journal of Personality and Social Psychology* 35:351-363.

Carroll, J. B. (Ed.)
1956 *Language, thought, and reality: Selected writings of Benjamin Lee Whorf*. New York: Wiley.

Clark, E. T.
1929 *The psychology of religious awakening*. New York: Macmillan.

Clark, W. H.
1973 The influence of religious experience. In *Religious experience: Its nature and function in the human psyche*, edited by W. Clark, N. H. Malony, J. Daane, and A. R. Tippett, Springfield, IL: C. C. Thomas.

Conway, F., and J. Siegelman
1978 *Snapping*. Philadelphia: Lippincott.

Conway, M., and M. Ross
1984 Getting what you want by revising what you had. *Journal of Personality and Social Psychology* 47:738-748.

Dienstbier, R. A.
1979 Emotion-attribution theory: Establishing roots and exploring future perspectives. In *Nebraska symposium on motivation*, edited by R. A. Dienstbier. Lincoln, NB: University of Nebraska Press.

Dittes, J. E.
1969 The psychology of religion. In *The handbook of social psychology*, Vol. 5, edited by G. Lindzey and E. Aronson. Reading, MA: Addison-Wesley.

Donahue, M. J.
1985 Intrinsic and extrinsic religiousness: Review and meta-analysis. *Journal of Personality and Social Psychology* 48:400-419.

Eliach, Y.
1982 *Hassidic tales of the holocaust*. New York: Avon.
Ellwood Jr., R. S.
1980 *Mysticism and religion*. Englewood Cliffs, NJ: Prentice-Hall.
Fecher, V. J.
1982 *Religion & aging: An annotated bibliography*. San Antonio, TX: Trinity University Press.
Fichter, J. H.
1981 *Religion and pain*, New York: Crossroads.
Fiske, S. T., and P. W. Linville
1980 What does the schema concept buy us? *Personality and Social Psychology Bulletin* 6:543-557.
Fiske, S. T., and S. E. Taylor (Eds.)
1991 *Social Cognition*. 2nd ed. New York: McGraw-Hill.
Glock, C. Y.
1964 The role of deprivation in the origin and evolution of religious groups. In *Religion and social conflict*, edited by R. Lee and M. E. Marty. New York: Oxford.
Godin, A.
1985 *The psychological dynamics of religious experience*. Birmingham, AL: Religious Education Press.
Goodman, F. D.
1972 *Speaking in tongues: A cross-cultural study of gossolalia*. Chicago: University of Chicago Press.
Greeley, A.
1974 *Ecstasy: A way of knowing*. Englewood Cliffs, NJ: Prentice-Hall.
Group for the Advancement of Psychiatry
1976 *Mysticism: Spiritual quest or psychic disorder*. New York: Group for the Advancement of Psychiatry.
Hardy, A.
1979 *The spiritual life of man*. New York: Oxford.
Hay, D.
1985 Religious experience and its induction. In *Advances in the psychology of religio*n, edited by L. B. Brown. New York: Pergamon.
Hay, D., and A. M. Morisy
1978 Reports of ecstatic, paranormal, or religious experience in Great Britain and the United States: A comparison of trends. *Journal for the Scientific Study of Religion* 17:255-268.
Heider, F.
1958 *The psychology of interpersonal relations*. New York: Wiley.
Hewstone, M. (Ed.)
1983 *Attribution theory: Social and functional extensions*. Oxford: Basil Blackwell.
Himmelfarb, M.
1973 *The Jews of modernity*. New York: Basic Books.
Hood Jr., R. W.
1970 Religious orientation and the report of religious experience. *Journal for the Scientific Study of Religion* 9:285-292.
1975 The construction and preliminary validation of a measure of reported mystical experience. *Journal for the Scientific Study of Religion* 14:29-41.
1977a Differential triggering of mystical experiences as a function of self-actualization. *Review of Religious Research* 18:264-270.
1977b Eliciting mystical states of consciousness with semistructured nature experiences. *Journal for the Scientific Study of Religion* 16:155-163.
1985 Theoretical confrontations with mysticism. *Psychologists Interested in Religious Issues Newsletter*: 1-2, 6-7.
Hood Jr., R. W., and R. J. Morris
1981 Sensory isolation and the differential elicitation of religious imagery in intrinsic and extrinsic persons. *Journal for the Scientific Study of Religion* 20:261-273.

Howes, D. H.
1957 On the relationship between the intelligibility and frequency of occurrence of English words. *Journal of the Acoustical Society of America* 29:296-305.
Howes, D. H., and R. L. Solomon
1951 Visual duration threshold as a function of word probability. *Journal of Experimental Psychology* 41:401-410.
Hunsberger, B., and B. Watson
1986 The devil made me do it: Attributions of responsibility to God and Satan. Paper presented at the Convention of the Society for the Scientific Study of Religion, Washington, DC.
Hunt, R.A., and M. B. King
1971 The intrinsic-extrinsic concept: A review and evaluation. *Journal for the Scientific Study of Religion* 10:339-356.
Ickes, W., and M. A. Layden
1978 Attributional styles. In *New directions in attributional research*, Vol. 2, edited by J. H. Harvey, W. Ickes, and R. Kidd. Hillsdale, NJ: Erlbaum.
Jackson, N. J., and B. Spilka
1980 *Correlates of religious mystical experience: A selective study*. Paper presented at the Convention of the Rocky Mountain Psychological Association. Tucson, AZ.
James, W.
1902 *Varieties of religious experience*. New York: Longmans, Green.
Johnson, S., and B. Spilka
1991 Religion and the breast cancer patient: The roles of clergy and faith. *Journal of Religion and Health*, 30, 21-33.
Jones, W. I.
1937 *A psychological study of religious conversion*. London: Epworth.
Kahoe, R. D.
1974 Personality and achievement correlates of intrinsic and extrinsic religious orientations. *Journal of Personality and Social Psychology* 29:812-818.
1976 The intrinsic and extrinsic dimensions: A value base for evaluating religious behavior. In *Research in mental health and religious behavior*, edited by W. J. Donaldson. Atlanta, GA: Psychological Studies Institute.
Kelley, H. H.
1967 Attribution theory in social psychology. In *Nebraska symposium on motivation*, Vol.15, edited by D. Levine. Lincoln, NB: University of Nebraska Press.
1972 Causal schemata and the attribution process. In *Attribution: Perceiving the causes of behavior* edited by E. E. Jones, D. E. Kanouse, H. H. Kelley, R. E. Nisbett, S. Valins, and B. Weiner. Morristown, NJ: General Learning Press.
Kelsey, M. T.
1964 *Tongue speaking: An experiment in spiritual experience*. Garden City, New York: Doubleday.
Kildahl, J. P.
1972 *The psychology of speaking in tongues*, New York: Harper & Row.
Kirkpatrick, L. A.
1992 An attachment-theory approach to the psychology of religion. *International Journal for the Psychology of Religion* 2:3-28.
Kopplin, D.
1976 *Religious orientations of college students and related personality characteristics*. Paper presented at the Convention of the American Psychological Association, Washington, DC.
Krause, N., and T. Van Tranh
1989 Stress and religious involvement among older Blacks. *Journal of Gerontology*: 44:S4-S13.
Kulik, J. A.
1983 Confirmatory attribution and the perpetuation of social beliefs. *Journal of Personality and Social Psychology*, 44:1171-1181.
Ladd, K., and B. Spilka
1992 *Threat and ambiguity as factors eliciting religious attributions*. Paper presented at the Convention of the Society of the Scientific Study of Religion, Washington, DC.

Laski, M.
1961 *Ecstasy*. Bloomington, IN: University of Indiana Press.
Leuba, J. H.
1929 *The Psychology of religious mysticism*. London: Kegan, Paul, Trench, & Trubner.
Levenson, H.
1973 Multidimensional locus of control in psychiatric patients. *Journal of Consulting and Clinical Psychology* 41:397-404.
Lilliston, L., and P. M. Brown
1981 Perceived effectiveness of religious solutions to personal problems. *Journal of Clinical Psychology* 37:1181 22.
Loewenthal, K. M., and N. Cornwall
1993 Religiosity and perceived control of life events. *International Journal for the Psychology of Religion* 3:39-45.
Lofland, J., and N. Skonovd
1981 Conversion motifs. *Journal for the Scientific Study of Religion* 20:373-385.
Lupfer, M. B., K. F. Brock, and S. J. DePaola
1992 The use of secular and religious attributions to explain everyday behavior. *Journal for the Scientific Study of Religion*, 31:486:503.
Malony, H. N.
1973 Religious experience: Inclusive and exclusive. In *Religious experience: Its nature and function in the human psyche*, edited by W. H. Clark, H. N. Malony, J. Daane, and A. R. Tippett. Springfield, IL: C. C. Thomas.
Martindale, C.
1980 *Cognition and consciousness*. Homewood, IL: Dorsey.
Maslow, A. H.
1964 *Religions, values, and peak-experiences*. Columbus, OH: Ohio State University Press.
McIntosh, D. N.
1991 *Religion as schema, with implications for the relation between religion and coping*. Presented at the Convention of the American Psychological Association, Washington, DC.
McIntosh, D. N., B. A. Kojetin, and B. Spilka
1985 *Form of personal faith and general and specific locus of control*. Paper presented at the Convention of the Rocky Mountain Psychological Association, Tucson, AZ.
McIntosh, D. N., and B. Spilka
1990 Religion and physical health: The role of personal faith and control beliefs. *Research in the Social Scientific Study of Religion*. Vol. 2. New York: JAI Press.
Meadow, M. J., and C. A. Rayburn (Eds.)
1985 *A time to weep, a time to sing*. Minneapolis, MN: Winston.
Metalsky, G. I., and L. Y. Abramson
1981 Attributional styles: Toward a framework for conceptualization and assessment. In *Cognitive-behavioral interventions; Assessments and methods*, edited by Kendall and S. D. Hollon. New York: Academic Press.
Minton, B., and B. Spilka
1976 Perspectives on death in relation to powerlessness and form of personal religion. *Omega* 7:261-267.
Morris, R. J., and R. W. Hood Jr.
1980 Religious and unity criteria of Baptists and nones. *Psychological Reports* 46:728-730.
Niebuhr, R. R.
1972 *Experiential religion*. New York: Harper & Row.
O'Brien, M. E.
1982 Religious faith and adjustment to long-term hemodialysis. *Journal of Religion and Health* 21:68-80.
Olson, J. M., and M. Ross
1988 False feedback about placebo effectiveness: Consequences for the misattribution of speech anxiety. *Journal of Experimental Social Psychology* 24:275-291.
Otto, R.
1923 *The idea of the holy*. New York: Oxford University Press.

Pargament, K. I., M. S. Sullivan, F. B. Tyler, and R. E. Steele
1982 Patterns of attribution of control and individual psychosocial competence. *Psychological Reports* 51:1243-1252.
Pargament, K. 1., J. Kennell, W. Hathaway, N. Grevengoed, J. Newman, and W. Jones
1988 Religion and the problem-solving process: Three styles of coping. *Journal for the Scientific Study of Religion* 27:90-104.
Pittman, T. S., and N. L. Pittman
1980 Deprivation of control and the attribution process. *Journal of Personality and Social Psychology* 39:377-389.
Proudfoot, W.
1985 *Religious experience*, Berkeley, CA: University of California Press.
Proudfoot, W., and P. Shaver
1975 Attribution theory and the psychology of religion. *Journal for the Scientific Study of Religion* 14:317-330.
Pruyser, P.
1968 *A dynamic psychology of religion*. New York: Harper & Row.
Reid, T.
[1788]
1969 *Essays on the active powers of the human mind*. Cambridge, MA: MIT Press.
Ross, L., and R. E. Nisbett
1991 *The person and the situation: Perspectives of social psychology*. New York: McGraw-Hill.
Ross, M., and J. M. Olson
1981 An expectancy-attribution model of the effects of placebos. *Psychological Review* 88:408-437.
Sales, S. M.
1972 Economic threat as a determinant of conversion rates in authoritarian and nonauthoritarian churches. *Journal of Personality and Social Psychology* 23:420-428.
Schachter, S.
1964 The interaction of cognitive and physiological determinants of emotional states. In *Advances in experimental social psychology*, Vol. 1, edited by L. Berkowitz. New York: Academic Press.
Schachter, S., and J. E. Singer
1962 Cognitive, social, and physiological determinants of emotional state. *Psychological Review* 69:379-399.
Snow, D. A., and R. Machalek
1984 The sociology of conversion. In *Annual Review of Sociology*, Vol. 10, edited by R. Turner. Palo Alto, CA: Annual Reviews.
Spilka, B.
1976 The compleat person: Some theoretical views and research findings for a theological-psychology of religion. *Journal of Psychology and Theology*, 4:15-24.
Spilka, B., and M. Mullin
1977 Personal religion and psychosocial schemata: A research approach to a theological-psychology of religion. *Character Potential* 8:57-66.
Spilka, B., and G. Schmidt
1983 *Stylistic factors in attributions: The role of religion and locus of control*. Paper presented at the Convention of the Rocky Mountain Psychological Association, Snowbird, UT.
Spilka, B., G. A. Brown, and S. E. Cassidy
1993 The structure of mystical experience in relation to pre- and post-experience lifestyle correlates. *International Journal for the Psychology of Religion* 2:241-257.
Spilka, B., K. Ladd, and J. David
1993 *Religion and coping with breast cancer: Possible roles for prayer and form of personal faith*. Unpublished paper.
Spilka, B., P. Shaver, and L. A. Kirkpatrick
1985 A general attribution theory for the psychology of religion. *Journal for the Scientific Study of Religion* 24:1-20.

Stace, W. T.
1960 *Mysticism and philosophy*. Philadelphia: Lippincott.
Starbuck, E. D.
1899 *The psychology of religion*. New York: Scribner's.
Stark, R. A.
1965 A taxonomy of religious experience. *Journal for the Scientific Study of Religion* 5:97-116.
Sterling, B., and S. L. Gaertner
1984 The attribution of arousal and emergency helping: A bidirectional process. *Journal of Experimental Social Psychology* 20:586-596.
Strickland, B. R., and S. Shaffer
1971 I-E, I-E, and F. *Journal for the Scientific Study of Religion* 10:366-369.
Taylor, S. E.
1983 Adjustment to threatening events: A theory of cognitive adaptation. *American Psychologist* 38:1161-1173.
Taylor, S. E., and J. Crocker
1981 Schematic bases of social processing. In *Social cognition: The Ontario symposium*, vol 1, edited by E. T. Higgins, C. P. Herman, and M. P. Zanna. Hillsdale, NJ: Erlbaum.
Taylor, S. E., and S. Levin
1976 The psychological impact of breast cancer: Theory and practice. In *Psychological aspects of breast cancer*, edited by A. Enelow. San Francisco: West Coast Cancer Foundation.
Thomas, S. E., and P. E. Cooper
1978 Measurement and incidence of mystical experiences: An exploratory study. *Journal for the Scientific Study of Religion* 17:433-437.
Ullman, C.
1982 Cognitive and emotional antecedents of religious conversion. *Journal of Personality and Social Psychology* 43:183-192.
Wallace, B., and L. E. Fisher
1983 *Consciousness and behavior*. Boston: Allyn & Bacon.
Watson, P. J., R. J. Morris, and R. W. Hood Jr.
1990 Attributional complexity, religious orientation, and indiscriminate proreligiousness. *Review of Religious Research* 32:110-121.
Weisz, J. R., F. M. Rothbaum, and T. C. Blackburn
1984 Standing out and standing. In The psychology of control in America and Japan. *American Psychologist* 39:955-969.

19

Attachment Theory and Religious Experience

LEE A. KIRKPATRICK

Psychodynamic approaches to the study of human experience and behavior from the beginning have been replete with speculations on the nature of religious belief and behavior. As reviewed in other chapters in the present volume, much has been written on religion from the standpoint of Freudian, object relations, and other psychoanalytic theories. At the same time, but almost entirely independently, a voluminous research literature on psychology of religion has evolved based on behavioral and cognitive approaches to the topic. It is as if two independent psychologies of religion coexist in mutual isolation—the psychoanalytic study of religion and the "empirical" study of religion—and never the twain shall meet. Indeed, this chasm reflects the larger world of psychology generally, in which psychoanalysis has long been estranged from the empirically research-oriented fields of social, developmental, personality, and even clinical psychology.

This is an unfortunate state of affairs for the psychology of religion, because the strengths of each approach are the weaknesses of the other. In short, psychoanalytic approaches to religion are generally strong on theory and weak on data, whereas behavioral/empirical approaches to the topic tend to be strong on data but weak on theory. Of course, psychoanalytic work is not entirely devoid of empirical data, but the case studies and projective techniques favored in this discipline are viewed with suspicion by experimentalists who prefer "objective" behavioral measures and nomothetic forms of data analysis. Likewise, empirical research in psychology of religion is not entirely devoid of theory, but few of these theoretical approaches offer much depth of analysis or capture the extraordinary breadth and depth of religious experience and belief in a compelling way. The dominant intrinsic-extrinsic paradigm, for example, offers little more than a descriptive typology and fails to provide much in the way of an explanatory framework for understanding the emotional, cognitive, and behavioral variability of religious experience (Kirkpatrick and Hood, 1990).

In the present chapter I will not, and indeed could not, detail the varied and complex reasons for this state of affairs. I will, however, offer what I believe to be a potential solution. I wish to argue that *ethological attachment theory*, as developed by John Bowlby (1969, 1973, 1980) and extended and refined by a host of other researchers, offers a rich and powerful theoretical perspective for understanding religious experience—one that may help to bridge the enormous gulf between contemporary psychoanalytic and social-psychological perspectives. Attachment theory represents a psychodynamic approach to lifespan personality development that rivals psychoanalysis in terms of scope and theoretical depth, but at the same time is grounded in, and continues to generate, a strong empirical research base.

In contrast to many topics covered in the present volume, including psychoanalytic approaches, the attachment approach to religion is barely in its infancy. This chapter will therefore be forward-looking rather than retrospective. My goal will be to provide a theoretical basis for new research rather than review existing research and to offer some examples of how the theory might be brought to bear on a few of the many varieties of religious experience. I conclude with some remarks on what I regard as some crucial points of difference between the attachment approach and psychoanalytic theorizing about religion.

The Ethological Theory of Attachment

A psychiatrist trained in the British object relations school of psychoanalysis, John Bowlby (1969) set out explicitly to construct a new theory to replace psychoanalysis in view of what he regarded as a variety of conceptual and empirical shortcomings. First, Bowlby found these previous approaches inadequate to explain the data with which he was initially concerned, particularly regarding the effects of maternal deprivation and separation among children raised in institutional environments. Second, Bowlby argued for a prospective theoretical approach in contrast to the retrospective orientation (from adult experience backwards toward childhood) favored by psychoanalysts. Third, and most important in my view, he sought to update psychoanalytic theory in light of modern developments in evolutionary biology and ethology—a goal with which Freud undoubtedly would have been the first to agree.

Attachment theory postulates the existence of a behavioral system in human and other primates that has been "designed" by natural selection to maintain proximity between infants and their caregivers. The evolutionary function of the system, according to Bowlby, was (and is) the protection of helpless infants against predation and other natural dangers. Bowlby (1969) argued persuasively that the attachment system is distinct from, but on a par with, other behavioral/motivational systems concerned with reproduction and nutrition.

Influenced by the control-systems approach to motivation favored by modern ethologists, Bowlby (1969) conceptualized the dynamics of attachment as a homeostatic or *goal-corrected system.* Figure 1 provides a graphical depiction of the system in flow-chart format. As represented by the diamond at the top of the figure, the infant continually monitors the environment to determine whether a primary caregiver or attachment figure is sufficiently attentive and responsive to provide protection and comfort if needed. If the answer is yes (upper right of figure), the resulting state of "felt security" (Sroufe and Waters, 1977a) leads to activation of an *exploration system* (Bretherton 1985): The perceived availability of the attachment figure provides a *secure base* for confident interaction with the environment. If the answer is no (bottom left of figure), anxiety increases and a hierarchy of attachment behaviors is activated. The infant searches visually, cries or calls, or physically moves toward the attachment figure to reestablish proximity. (It is assumed that a complementary *caregiving* system causes adult caregivers to be receptive to these signals.) Felt security is restored when sufficient proximity has been established.

Figure 1

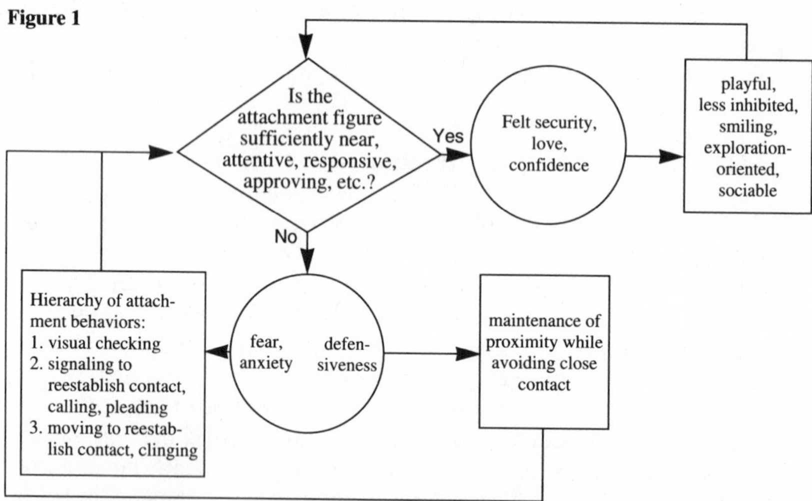

Schematic representation of the attachment system. Reprinted from Shaver and Hazan (1993).

According to Bowlby's model, the degree of proximity considered to be "sufficient"—the *set goal* of the system—is itself variable. Signals of perceived danger, illness or injury, or other forms of distress serve to increase the desired level of proximity to the attachment figure. At such times the attachment figure functions as a *safe haven* from potential danger. The set goal varies also as a function of age: In situations in which young children would require physical contact for felt security, for example, older children may be comforted by visual or verbal contact. For adolescents and adults, with their greater cognitive and conceptual abilities, mere psychological availability (e.g., knowing that the attachment figure is just a phone call away) may suffice in many circumstances, although in times of severe distress physical proximity may be required.

The description above summarizes the normative functioning of the attachment system. However, due to consistent experience with differential levels of parental responsiveness to the infant's signals, relatively stable individual differences in the functioning of the attachment system begin to emerge over time. When the attachment figure is consistently responsive and attentive—i.e., the infant's experience is characterized by repeated flow through the upper-right loop in the figure—the infant develops a *secure* pattern of attachment characterized by *mental models* (or *internal working models*) of attachment figures as trustworthy and dependable. If the attachment figure is instead *inconsistently* responsive, the lack of confidence and trust in the attachment figure's availability can lead to a state of chronic activation of the attachment system—the lower-left loop of the figure. This pattern of insecure attachment has been labeled alternatively as *anxious, ambivalent*, or *anxious/resistant* attachment.

Finally, if the infant's attempts to gain or restore proximity are repeatedly rebuffed, the infant may learn to essentially shut down activation of the attachment system. Bowlby (1969) described a variety of ways this may be accomplished, including *defensive exclusion* of information (which Bowlby relates to several of Freud's defense mechanisms). This pattern of *avoidant* attachment is represented by the lower-right loop of Figure 1.

Empirical research on attachment was pioneered by Mary Ainsworth and her colleagues, who developed a laboratory procedure known as the *Strange Situation* to assess individual differences in infant-mother attachment (Ainsworth, Blehar, Waters, & Wall, 1978). In addition to describing and labeling the three patterns summarized above, Ainsworth et al. demonstrated empirically links between parental behavior and infant attachment classification.

In brief, *secure* infants are distressed by brief separation from their mothers but are quickly comforted upon her return. Their mothers are characterized by sensitive and appropriate responding to the infants' signals of distress and attempts to gain and maintain proximity. Anxious/ambivalent infants are generally highly anxious and are severely distressed by separation. Upon reunion they are difficult to calm and alternate between clinging, proximity-promoting behaviors and resistant, angry behaviors. Mothers of anxious/ambivalent babies are characterized by insensitivity to the infant's signals, being inconsistently available when proximity is desired and sometimes intrusive at inappropriate times. Avoidant infants behave as if they were indifferent to separation and reunion in the Strange Situation, although physiological measures indicate they are no less distressed by these episodes than other children (Sroufe and Waters, 1977b). Their mothers tend to reject the infant's attempts to gain proximity and largely try to avoid physical contact with the infant.

An enormous body of research in developmental psychology has since emerged to replicate these findings and further demonstrate the ability of infant classification to predict prospectively individual differences in personality, sociability, and other behavioral indices during childhood (see Bretherton 1985, 1987 for review of this literature). Theoretically, Bowlby asserted that young children develop *mental models* (or internal working models) of attachment figures that, although malleable, tend to be resistant to change. This continuity of mental models is thought to account for the stability of individual differences across childhood and point toward the possibility of continuity of such differences into adolescence and adulthood (Main, Kaplan, and Cassidy, 1985). In essence, mental models represent the child's answer to the question: "Can I count on my attachment figure to be available and responsive when needed?" The three possible answers are yes (secure), no (avoidant), and maybe (anxious/ambivalent) (Shaver and Hazan, 1994).

The phenomenology of attachment: Although attachment is conceptualized, as depicted in Figure 1, as a goal-corrected behavioral system, from the standpoint of the attached person it is experienced as a psychological or affectional *bond* (Ainsworth, 1985; Bretherton, 1985). To be attached is to love and to feel loved.

Successful maintenance of the system at the level proscribed by the set goal is experienced as *felt security* (Sroufe and Waters, 1977a). In Bowlby's (1973:202) words, "When an individual is confident that an attachment figure will be available to him whenever he desires it, that person will be much less prone to either intense or chronic fear than will an individual who for any reason has no such confidence." The secure base provided by the attachment figure gives rise to a sense of security and confidence with which to approach and master one's environment. In the face of threat, the haven of safety provided by the attachment figure offers solace and comfort.

The dynamics of attachment are experienced to large extent in terms of the major emotions. Many of the most intense emotions, according to Bowlby, are associated with attachment dynamics: "In terms of subjective experience, the formation of a bond is described as falling in love, maintaining a bond as loving someone, and losing a partner as grieving over someone" (Bowlby, 1979:69). The threat of potential loss of the relationship causes anxiety (Bowlby, 1979: Ainsworth, 1985).

It is important to note that attachment represents only one of many kinds of psychological bonds. Ainsworth (1985) distinguished attachment from a variety of other kinds of affectional bonds, noting that the distinguishing features of an attachment bond are the experience (or seeking) of comfort and security and the ability to use the other as a secure base. From a functional perspective, Weiss (1982) distinguished six different provisions offered by various kinds of close relationships. While attachment relationships are characterized by the provision of security, other relationships offer such provisions as affiliation or social integration, opportunity for nurturance (caregiving), collaboration and reassurance of worth, a sense of persisting alliance, and obtaining help or guidance.

Attachment in Adulthood

Although from the beginning Bowlby regarded attachment as an important basis of personality development across the lifespan, empirical research on attachment in adulthood is a rather recent development. Weiss's (1973) theoretical extension of attachment to adult loneliness received empirical support from Cutrona and Russell (1987). Main and her colleagues (e.g., George, Kaplan, and Main, 1985) have examined the orientations toward relationships among adults that predict attachment classification of their own infants. However, it was not until the publication of articles by Hazan and Shaver (1987) and Shaver, Hazan, and Bradshaw (1988) that social and personality psychologists began in earnest to empirically extend attachment theory to the study of adult relationships.

According to Shaver et al. (1988), adult love relationships involve the interaction of three behavioral systems: attachment, caregiving (the complement of attachment), and sexual mating. Hazan and Shaver (1987) showed empirically that adults could reliably classify themselves into three categories paralleling Ainsworth's three patterns of infant attachment and that these three groups differed in theoretically expectable ways in their experience of love relationships. A sizable literature has quickly accumulated examining differences among the three adult attachment styles in terms of relationship quality and satisfaction (Collins and Read, 1990; J. Feeney and Noller, 1990; Levy and Davis, 1988, Simpson, 1990), relationship stability and breakups (Kirkpatrick and Davis, 1994; Kirkpatrick and Hazan, 1994); behavior toward romantic partners in a stressful situation (Simpson, Rholes, and Nelligan, 1992), and physiological responses in the presence and absence of partners in a stressful situation (B. Feeney and Kirkpatrick, 1993). For thorough reviews of this literature, see Hazan and Shaver (1994) and Shaver and Hazan (1993).

Attachment and Religion

The most obvious point of departure for an attachment approach to religion is the observation that for many people God functions psychologically as an attachment figure. Elsewhere I have argued that a wide range of research findings in the psychology of religion literature can be meaningfully interpreted within this framework (Kirkpatrick, 1992a). In the discussion below I focus specifically on the interpretation of religious experience from an attachment perspective. Although the primary focus will be American Christianity, I will briefly address the question of cross-cultural generality in a subsequent section.

Love and the experience of a relationship with God: In the building in which I work, a poster advertising a meeting of the Inter-Varsity Fellowship on our campus recently announced: "Christianity is not a religion: It is a *relationship*." According to Greeley (1981:18), "just as the story of anyone's life is the story of relationships—so each person's religious story is a story of relationships." National survey data confirm that having a close relationship with God (versus finding meaning in life, church membership, or a set of beliefs) is central to the faith of a majority of Christians (Gallup and Jones, 1989). Psychologically, this relationship meets all of the defining criteria of a true attachment relationship (Kirkpatrick, 1994).

From an attachment perspective, the experience of a relationship with God is the experience of a deep emotional bond: According to an oft-cited phrase: "God is love." This is why religious emotion is so often expressed "in the language of human love," particularly among mystics (Thouless, 1923:132), and why religious conversions have frequently been likened to "falling in love" (James, 1902; Pratt, 1920; Thouless, 1923; Ullman, 1989). It may also be why religious experience is so often described as ineffable, and why religious emotion is so widely expressed in song and other art forms. The experience of being in love is an extraordinarily powerful emotional state which, as any poet will quickly attest, words are woefully inadequate to describe. Song, dance, and other nonverbal expressions have proven for centuries to be infinitely better suited than language for the communication of such emotional states.

Although the idea that a relationship with God is a love relationship is probably as old as the idea of God itself, deeper analysis of the analogy typically runs into a snag. As summarized by Greeley (1990:249): "The usual reaction . . . to a comparison of human love with divine love is to insist that it is utterly different from sexual attraction ('not at all physical,' my students tell me)." That is, an important component of adult romantic relationships—and perhaps the one of which people are most acutely aware—is sexual attraction, but this component is absent entirely from most people's experience of a relationship with God.

The answer to the dilemma is that divine love experienced by the worshiper is, in effect, a more "pure" form of attachment than adult romantic relationships (Kirkpatrick, 1992). Whereas adult romantic love involves the integration of at least three behavioral systems—attachment, sexual mating, and caregiving (Shaver et al., 1988)—perceived relationships with God generally tap only the first of these. Here we see the significance of Bowlby's conceptualization of the attachment system as distinct from the sexual mating system. Psychologically, love for God is more akin to a child's love for her mother or father than to an adult's love for a romantic partner or spouse. Conversely, God's love for oneself is perceived in terms analogous to a mother's love for her child. In the words of an anonymous woman quoted by Greeley (1990:252): "If you've ever held in your arms a child you have just given life to and been filled with love for that wondrous little being, you know that's how God feels about us."

Although the preceding discussion has focused on perceived relationships with God per se, in different religious traditions other deities may instead fulfill the role of attachment figure. In many Protestant churches, for example, worshipers perceive themselves to have a personal relationship with Jesus, whereas God is more distant and less directly accessible. Wenegrat (1989) argues that, in contrast to Protestantism, Catholicism offers a kind of psychological division of labor in which the desexualized maternal image of Mary provides an ideal vehicle for attachment concerns, whereas God and Jesus play somewhat different roles.

Wenegrat's observation receives strong theoretical and empirical support from the work of Andrew Greeley. Although he never cites attachment theory, Greeley's understanding of this process is clearly consonant with the attachment perspective. In *The Mary Myth*, for example, he writes that

> Mothering is part of any intimate human relationship in the sense that we expect those who love us to be at least on occasion passionately tender toward us, to assume the responsibility of "taking care" of us. In marriage, then, a spouse does indeed mother the other (Greeley, 1977:108).

In Greeley's view, the image of Mary as fulfilling this role is a crucial, defining aspect of Catholicism; it is an image of great power with deep psychological and biological roots. "The Mary Myth's powerful appeal is to be found . . . in the marvelous possibility that God loves us the way a mother loves her baby" (Greeley, 1990:252). Drawing heavily on Greeley's work, Donahue (this volume) concludes that the power of this Mary image constitutes an important reason why modern Catholics remain Catholic despite doctrinal dissention.

Individual differences in the experience of God: Individual differences in people's beliefs about God have been explored in a wide variety of factor analytic and correlational studies. Factor analyses of such questionnaires invariably yield a large factor resembling a secure attachment dimension (e.g., Benson and Spilka, 1973; Broen, 1957; Gorsuch; 1968; Spilka, Armatas, and Nussbaum, 1964; Tamayo and Desjardins, 1976) that has been labeled by different investigators as *Benevolent Deity* (Gorsuch, 1968), *Availability* (Tamayo and Desjardins, 1976), *Nearness to God* (Broen, 1957) and *Loving*

God (Benson and Spilka, 1973). In attachment terms, these measures assess one's mental models of God as an attachment figure. Moreover, consistent with attachment theory, these models tend to complement people's models of self: loving God images tend to be positively correlated with self-esteem and positive self-concepts (Benson and Spilka, 1973; Flakoll, 1974; Jolley, 1983; Spilka, Addison, and Rosensohn, 1975). As Bowlby (1969) observed, people who think of their attachment figures as available and responsive tend also to regard themselves as worthy of care and love.

Recent evidence also suggests that images of God and perceptions of one's relationship with God may parallel one's orientation to other adult attachment relationships. Kirkpatrick and Shaver (1992) and Kirkpatrick (1993) showed that people who classified themselves as secure rated God as significantly more loving, less controlling, and less distant/inaccessible than those classifying themselves as one of the insecure styles. In other words, people tend to perceive God in a manner consistent with their concurrent mental models of attachment relationships.

The presence of a secure-attachment factor in these studies suggests that not everyone views his or her attachment relationship with God as a *secure* one. Kirkpatrick and Shaver (1992) asked respondents to classify their perceived relationships with God by choosing among three paragraphs designed to represent secure, avoidant, and anxious/ambivalent attachments. Although few respondents chose the avoidant (cold, distant, indifferent) description, a sizable proportion selected the anxious/ambivalent paragraph describing God as inconsistently supportive and somewhat unpredictable. These perceptions were empirically correlated with several measures of loneliness, depression, psychosomatic symptoms, and low life satisfaction. Moreover, these images of God were related to parallel measures of adult attachment styles vis-à-vis relationships, at least for some subjects. A perceived relationship with God that includes negative emotions and insecurity does not necessarily mean a lack of attachment, but rather, as in infant-mother or adult love relationships, a different pattern or style of attachment.

In general, attachment theory would predict that one's relationship with God is constructed from the building blocks of one's own actual experiences in close relationships (Wenegrat, 1989), just as adult love relationships are thought to be shaped by early childhood experience with attachment relationships (Sroufe and Fleeson, 1986). However, despite the theoretical parallels drawn here, there are important differences between perceived relationships with God and relationships with people. Chief among these is the fact that interpersonal relationships are influenced by the behavior of the partner as well as one's own behavior; the partner's behavior, in turn, is influenced in part by one's own behavior. An anxious person can easily drive away a human relationship partner with excessive dependency and demands for closeness (which, in turn, confirms the anxious person's mental model of others as being insufficiently close and responsive); an avoidant person can drive a partner away by failing to meet the partner's desire for intimacy and closeness. A person desiring greater intimacy from a spouse or lover can easily be frustrated by an intimacy-avoiding partner; a person wishing to maintain emotional distance can feel smothered by a clingy, dependent partner.

These interactive processes often lead to a kind of self-fulfilling prophecy in which a person elicits the kind of behavior from the partner that confirms the mental models one brought into the relationship. (See Caspi and Bem, 1990 for an interesting theoretical discussion of ways in which person-environment interactions contribute to the stability of individual differences.) Moreover, this kind of process may be largely responsible for the fact that attachment styles tend to remain remarkably stable across time (Hazan and Shaver, 1994; Kirkpatrick and Hazan, 1994). It is difficult for insecure individuals to break out of such cycles, in large part because potential opportunities for a secure relationship are easily undermined by one's own self-defeating behavior.

Perceived relationships with God, in contrast, are presumably not influenced directly by God's "actual" behavior; nor is God's behavior influenced by that of the worshiper. A perceived relationship with God characterized by the desired level of intimacy can be maintained over time without being undermined by either "partner's" behavior. An individual might well be able to invent or reinvent his or her perceived relationship with God in secure terms without inadvertently undermining the process through previously established, counterproductive patterns of behavior.

This observation is important because it means that some people with insecure attachment histories might be able to find in God—but perhaps not in human relationships—the kind of secure attachment relationship (and the provisions it offers) they never had in human interpersonal relationships. Ainsworth (1985) argued that children with insecure attachment histories are likely to turn to "parent surrogates," such as older siblings and teachers, for this purpose. Although Ainsworth did not mention God in her list of potential surrogates, it seems reasonable to suppose that God or other deities may play this role for many individuals. A perceived relationship with God, then, potentially could be of substantial therapeutic value in helping persons with insecure attachment histories break out of a self-defeating cycle of unsatisfactory close relationships.

The experience of a haven of safety: Once God has taken a place in an individual's hierarchy of attachment figures, the answer to the critical question in the diamond (Figure 1) at any given point in time is more likely to be "yes." In times of distress, the experience of God as a safe haven gives rise to the same feelings of comfort and security provided by secure human attachments. If we take seriously the self-reports of committed Christians, the haven of safety provided by a relationship with God is experienced in very much the same terms as in human attachment relationships.

The experience of God as an attachment figure may be particularly important when the attachment system is strongly activated: that is, a) when human attachment figures are either temporarily or permanently unavailable and b) under conditions of severe stress in which human attachments may be inadequate. Many writers have noted the particularly important role taken on by religion in terms of crises (e.g., Argyle and Beit-Hallahmi, 1975; Pargament and Hahn, 1986; Spilka, Hood, and Gorsuch, 1985). Perhaps "there are no atheists in foxholes" because the soldier in the field experiences simultaneously the absence of one's primary human attachments (i.e., a spouse or parent back home) and extraordinary stress.

In some ways, God may serve as a particularly effective attachment figure—perhaps even more effective than a human caregiver. Allport (1950:57) concluded from his research with combat veterans that "the individual in distress craves affection and security. Sometimes a human bond will suffice, more often it will not." For the soldier in combat, the psychological closeness of a parent or spouse at home may be inadequate in the most stressful moments; instead, belief in a God who is immediately present and capable of intervening in ongoing events may provide far greater comfort. In the words of Kaufman (1981:67), "The idea of God is the idea of an absolutely adequate attachment figure. . . . God is thought of as a protective and caring parent who is always reliable and always available to its children when they are in need." That is, whereas even the best of human attachment figures are ultimately fallible, God is not perceived as being constrained by such human limitations.

Of course, not everybody turns to God in times of distress. For some persons, the psychological safe haven provided by a secure attachment may be sufficiently strong to transcend physical separation. (Recall that the need for physical proximity per se tends to wane with increasing cognitive development.) The point was illustrated nicely by a battle veteran interviewed by Gordon Allport who reported that "there were atheists in foxholes, but most of them were in love" (Allport 1950:56).

The experience of a secure base: In the absence of danger, the secure base provided by an attentive attachment figure gives rise to confident exploration of one's environment. Belief that God represents a responsive, available attachment figure, then, should result similarly in feelings of confidence, high self-esteem, and an absence of anxiety. Christian hymns and language are replete with references to God or Jesus being by one's side, holding one's hand, and holding one in his arms or hands. Consistent with this account, empirical research suggests that religious commitment is related to lower levels of trait anxiety (Baker and Gorsuch, 1982; McClain, 1978) and fear of death (Kahoe and Dunn, 1975) and greater internal locus of control (Kahoe, 1974; Strickland and Shaffer, 1971). Batson, Schoenrade, and Ventis (1993) found religious commitment (intrinsic religious orientation) to be positively correlated with "freedom from worry and guilt" and "personal competence and control" but, notably, not other aspects of mental health. In this way belief in God as an attachment figure is experienced as a source of strength and confidence.

Another manifestation of belief in God as a secure base should be reduced levels of loneliness. In a recent study my students and I found the distinction between secure and anxious attachments to God to predict a significant amount of variance in loneliness scores, even after controlling for a host of general and specific social support variables as well as general religiosity (Kirkpatrick, Kellas, and Shillito, 1993).

The experience of prayer: Reed (1978:15), incorporating some of Bowlby's ideas into his "oscillation theory" of religion, noted that

> crying and calling [by an infant] find a close parallel in supplicatory prayer. The prominent place of prayer in most religions is perhaps the most striking point of contact with Bowlby's observations.

Prayer is a direct manifestation of the perception of having a relationship with an immediate, personal God (Heiler, 1932). Such communication can take a variety of forms under different circumstances.

Young children use their attachment figures as a secure base while exploring their environment by periodically checking back with their mothers visually, verbally, and/or physically to reassure themselves that they are still available and attentive. Such behavior has been labeled *social referencing* by Campos and Stenberg (1981). Similarly, prayer may frequently be characterized as a kind of "God referencing" in which the goal is to maintain proximity and reassure oneself of God's continued presence and availability. A consequence of such prayer should be a sense of confidence and security and, concomitantly, a reduction in general anxiety.

In times of perceived danger or distress, however, prayer may reflect instead the haven function of attachment. Stouffer et al. (1949) showed that soldiers in battle pray frequently and feel that such prayer is beneficial. Loveland (1968) showed that bereaved persons (i.e., people who have suffered the loss of an attachment figure) engaged in increased prayer activity. Summarizing the role of religion in times of crisis, Argyle and Beit-Hallahmi (1975) and Spilka et al. (1985) concluded that prayer in particular plays an especially important role on such occasions. Such prayer should be experienced as providing comfort, solace, and reduced anxiety.

The experience of dramatic religious conversion: Although a quest for answers to existential questions undoubtedly plays an important role in many people's religious development (e.g., Batson et al., 1993), this does not appear to be the stuff of sudden and dramatic religious conversions. Ullman (1989:xvi) came to this conclusion, much to her own surprise, on the basis of an in-depth study of forty religious converts:

> What I initially considered primarily a change of ideology turned out to be more akin to a falling in love. . . . Conversion pivots around a sudden attachment, an infatuation with a real or imagined figure which occurs on a background of great emotional turmoil. The typical convert was transformed not by a religion, but by a person. The discovery of a new truth was indistinguishable from a discovery of a new relationship, which relieved, temporarily, the upheaval of the previous life. This intense and omnipresent attachment discovered in the religious experience promised the convert everlasting guidance and love, for the object of the convert's infatuation was perceived as infallible.

In fact, religious conversion has been likened to "falling in love" since the earliest days of psychology of religion (James, 1902; Pratt, 1920; Thouless, 1923). This striking parallel has led many researchers to postulate that religious beliefs are linked to puberty or sexual instincts (Coe, 1916; Thouless, 1923). As discussed in a preceding section, I would argue instead that it is activation of the attachment system, not the sexual mating system, that is most closely associated psychologically with religious belief and conversion.

A variety of studies point to the conclusion that dramatic religious conversions are most likely among people with a history of poor parental relationships (Deutsch, 1975; Ullman, 1989). In a study designed explicitly within an attachment framework, Kirkpatrick and Shaver (1990) showed that adults who described (retrospectively) their childhood attachments to their mothers as avoidant were four times more likely to experience a dramatic conversion later in life than those who classified their maternal relationships as secure or anxious/ambivalent. For these individuals, God may be functioning as a kind of "parent surrogate" in Ainsworth's (1985) terms.

Research also suggests that dramatic religious conversions are most likely to occur at times of severe distress, depression, and high stress. Clark (1929), Galanter (1979), Kirkpatrick and Shaver (1990), and Ullman (1989) all noted the frequency with which converts described their preconversion lives as rife with emotional trauma. According to the attachment model, these are the times at which the set goal of the attachment system is adjusted and desire for proximity to an attachment figure is heightened. Particularly if adequate human attachments are seen to be unavailable, "finding God" as an attachment figure is most likely to occur in moments of intense anxiety and distress.

Moreover, if people are most likely to "find God" when their attachment systems are activated, the individuals most likely to have this experience at a given point in time should be those whose attachment systems are chronically or most readily activated. As discussed previously, this is a defining feature of the anxious/ambivalent attachment style. Consistent with this prediction, I have found in two longitudinal studies that anxious/ambivalent adults are more likely than others to find a new relationship with God over a four-month (Kirkpatrick, 1993) or four-year (Kirkpatrick, 1992b) interval.

The powerful emotions associated with such dramatic conversions are understandable within this framework. As argued above, to "find God" is to fall in love—and most of us are well aware of the emotional power of this experience. In addition however, this experience (at least in a sudden, dramatic form) appears most likely to occur to individuals who have histories of insecure or absent attachments. For such a person, the conversion experience may well represent the first time he or she has ever experienced the sense of security, confidence, and solace associated with secure attachment. It is no wonder that the emotions associated with such an experience are extraordinarily powerful.

It is also worth noting that attachment theory offers a new interpretation for the long-recognized fact that religious conversions are disproportionately common during adolescence. Because adolescence represents such a unique developmental period, it is not surprising that a wide range of explanations have been advanced for the prevalence of conversion at this time, including postulated links to puberty and sexual instincts (Coe, 1916; Thouless, 1923), the need for meaning, purpose, and sense of identity (Starbuck, 1899), and self-realization (Spilka, Hood, and Gorsuch, 1985). From an attachment perspective, however, it is important to note that adolescence represents a period of major *transition* between primary attachment figures. According to Weiss (1982), relinquishing the parents as attachment figures has a number of important implications for the adolescent, including vulnerability to loneliness—and for Weiss, loneliness "indicates the absence from one's internal world of an attachment figure" (p.178). At such a time, many adolescents may turn to God (or perhaps a charismatic religious leader) as a substitute attachment figure.

Glossolalia: One of the most remarkable examples of religious behavior within the Christian tradition is that of speaking in tongues, or glossolalia. In this section I offer an (admittedly speculative) account of the phenomenon from an attachment perspective.

Despite repeated efforts by researchers to demonstrate a pathological basis for glossolalia, a considerable body of evidence suggests that glossolalics do not differ significantly from non-glossolalics on most indices of psychopathology (Hine, 1969; Richardson, 1973). However, a number of studies suggest that persons who speak in tongues may differ from others in terms of quality of their interpersonal relationships. Plog (1965) found that a dimension of interpersonal relationships was the only component of the California Psychological Inventory on which glossolalics differed from nonglossolalics, and Wood (1965) suggested that glossolalics "have an uncommon degree of uncertainty concerning interpersonal relationships." Vivier (1960; cited in Richardson, 1973) found glossolalics to come disproportionately from "disturbed" homes and to "cling to objects in the environment for emotional support."

In terms of the adult attachment literature, these individual differences seem to parallel closely the anxious/ambivalent adult attachment style. The empirical data suggest that such individuals characterize their close relationships as being insufficiently intimate; they describe relationship partners as failing to meet their needs for closeness and intimacy. In addition, they are likely to say that their strong desire for closeness may sometimes drive partners or potential partners away (Hazan and Shaver, 1987). Especially among women, the close interpersonal relationships of anxious/ambivalent adults tend to be characterized by emotional highs and lows, jealousy, conflict, and dissatisfaction (see Shaver and Hazan, 1993 for a complete review). From an attachment perspective, this constellation of interpersonal characteristics describes the individual most likely to turn to God to meet their attachment needs.

As illustrated in Figure 1, the attachment systems—and hence attachment behaviors—of anxious/ambivalent individuals tend to be chronically activated (Main and Goldwyn, 1984; Simpson and Rholes, 1994). Glossolalia, which sounds to the outside observer much like infant babbling or a "child-like form of language" (Oates, 1967), might then be viewed as an attachment behavior reminiscent of infant attachment behavior. The parallel is particularly striking when, as is common in Pentecostal or charismatic services, the speaker raises his or her arms to the sky in manner reminiscent of an infant waiting to be picked up by its mother. I hasten to add that although this may sound, in Freudian terms, like a form of "infantile regression," infant-like attachment behaviors such as cooing, talking "baby-talk," and cuddling are quite common between adult love partners as well (Shaver, Hazan, and Bradshaw, 1988). Glossolalia, then, can be seen as a parallel form of attachment behavior directed toward God. In fact, Kirkpatrick and Shaver (1992) found that adult respondents who classified themselves as anxious/ambivalent were significantly more likely than other respondents to report having had a glossolalic experience.

As discussed above in the case of religious conversion, activation of the attachment system (and hence attachment behavior) is especially likely in times of distress. Kildahl's (1972) observation that the vast majority of tongue-speakers had experienced a "clearly defined anxiety crisis" preceding their speaking in tongues is clearly consistent with this interpretation. Kildahl further reported that these crises typically involved feelings of worthlessness and powerlessness. To quote one of his research respondents, "I felt like a child who could only say 'Goo'" (p.64).

Kildahl's (1972) observations concerning the psychological effects of speaking in tongues also fit neatly with an attachment interpretation. Kildahl (1972) reported that the glossolalic experience invariably resulted in increased feelings of confidence and security, which he attributed to worshipers' perception that they had proof that they were loved and protected by God. In terms of Figure 1, this means that the attachment behavior (glossolalia) is perceived by the speaker as having been successful in restoring proximity to the attachment figure, which in turn leads to deactivation of the attachment system and an increased level of felt security.

The darker side of religious beliefs: It has probably occurred to many readers that the preceding discussion of religion from an attachment perspective paints an unrealistically rosy picture of religion by focusing exclusively on perceived relationships with loving, benevolent deities. How can it be, the reader might ask, that many people's religious beliefs include a large dose of fear and negative emotions? The God of the Old Testament, for example, is hardly a picture of warm fuzzies; indeed, this depiction of God clearly includes (among other images) an angry, vindictive, and sometime jealous God with whom a secure attachment relationship would seem difficult to attain. Moreover, measures of images of God frequently detect two factors—a loving, caring, protective image and an angry, controlling image (e.g., Benson and Spilka, 1973). If the former dimension captures the essence of a secure attachment figure (see Kirkpatrick, 1992a, for a review and discussion), what of the latter dimension?

First, a theoretical extension of the individual differences described in the infant and adult attachment literatures would suggest that although God may serve as an attachment figure, this perceived relationship need not necessarily be a secure one. As discussed above, research suggests that such individual differences do exist, although there are reasons to expect that insecure attachments to God might be less common than insecure attachments to other people. Nevertheless, there are many cases in which people hold negative and maladaptive beliefs about God and one's relationship to God. Such cases are often described in the psychoanalytic literature on religion (e.g., Rizzuto, 1979) and frequently appear to be symptomatic of pathological childhood histories of various sorts.

Second, perceptions of God as an attachment figure and as a punitive, frightening being are not necessarily mutually exclusive. In fact, the latter may actually serve to reinforce the former. Bowlby (1969) noted that lambs and puppies develop and maintain attachments despite receipt of unpredictable punishments from their "attachment figures" and, moreover, that attachment behaviors actually increase as a result of such treatment. Similarly, human infants are attached to parents who mistreat them (Egeland and Sroufe, 1981). The basis for this seemingly paradoxical behavior is that the punishments, like other sources of fear and distress, activate the attachment system and hence the seeking of proximity to the primary attachment figure. The same individual is, in a sense, both the source of the problem and the solution.

Belief in a god that rains fire and brimstone upon the world, but who also serves as an attachment figure, may function in a similar manner. In fact, this may explain why beliefs about vindictive, frightening gods have persisted throughout the history of humankind despite the negative emotions they elicit. It may also help to explain why conservative Christian churches, which generally give greater attention to this aspect of God, are growing while mainline and liberal denominations continue on a downward spiral.

Attachment and Other Religious Traditions

The preceding discussion has focused primarily on Western Christianity in which the parallels between attachment and a loving Christian God are fairly straightforward. The question remains, however, as to whether religious experience in other cultures can be meaningfully described or explained in attachment terms. As an in-depth analysis of these issues would take us far beyond the scope of the present chapter, I will offer just a few preliminary observations on this issue below.

Other theistic religions: First, it seems reasonable to suppose that most theistic religions are potentially understandable in terms of attachment dynamics. Insofar as one perceives oneself to have a *relationship* with a god or gods, particularly one that provides a secure base and/or a haven of safety, the attachment model may prove useful in understanding religious belief and experience.

In Islam, for example, to put faith in God is to entrust in and submit to God. The root of the Arabic word for faith (*amn*) means "to be secure, trust, and entrust." Those who have faith experience security from God (Woodberry, 1992). Although the God of Islam may differ in important ways from the God of Christianity or of Judaism, similar psychological processes rooted in attachment dynamics may well be involved. Specifically, the *experience* of a relationship with God as an attachment figure may be defined in large part by operation of the attachment system within a given cultural milieu. Empirical examination of these applications of attachment theory in other monotheistic religions would be invaluable to assess the universality of attachment dynamics in religious experience around the world.

Cultural differences in parenting: Second, it is important to note that although religious belief systems vary widely across cultures, so do child-rearing practices and other cultural influences on attachment processes. Research on infant-mother attachment using Ainsworth's Strange Situation has been conducted in Japan, Germany, and Israel. The relative proportions of the three primary attachment styles were observed to differ considerably across cultures. Compared to American samples, for example, German samples contain (as classified by the Strange Situation) higher proportions of avoidant babies, whereas Japanese samples yield higher proportions of anxious/resistant babies. These differences seem to reflect, at least in part, cultural differences in child-rearing techniques: For example, Japanese babies are rarely separated from their mothers for extended intervals of time, and hence find the separation episodes in the Strange Situation unusually stressful. At the same time, cross-cultural research suggests that the *patterns of association* between parenting behavior and infant attachment classification are universal. Although the typical member of one culture may differ considerably from the typical member of another, the underlying attachment dynamics appear to be very much the same. (See Bretherton, 1985, for a more thorough discussion and review.)

Research suggests that differences across cultures with respect to predominant parenting styles (e.g., generally rejecting versus accepting of children) are correlated with personality differences between children and adults in these cultures (Rohner, 1975). As summarized by Bretherton (1985:26), "In societies where children are rejected, children and adults tended to be emotionally unresponsive, more dependent, less emotionally stable, and less able to become involved in affectionate relationships and to show more aggressive behavior and hostility." Moreover, a number of studies have shown that such cross-cultural differences in parenting behavior are also correlated with differences in religious beliefs. Studies by Rohner (1985) and Lambert, Triandis, and Wolf (1959) suggest that societies predominated by an "accepting" parenting style are more likely than others to embrace benevolent deities, whereas those with "rejecting" styles are characterized by belief in malevolent deities.

In short, cross-cultural differences in parenting styles, as well as other cultural influences on the formation and development of interpersonal relationships, may result in cross-cultural differences in people's experience of close relationships. These differences, in turn, may influence the degree to which various forms of religious beliefs and experience are perceived to be believable and acceptable. In addition, as other cultural practices change with time, acceptance of new religious beliefs may follow. To understand these differences, historical analyses of the childrearing practices of various cultures, in conjunction with attachment theory, might yield valuable insights into the religious histories of those cultures.

To illustrate with a single example, consider the childhood experiences of young boys raised in India. (The following discussion is adapted from Wulff, 1991). These boys are raised until age 4 or 5 in the nearly constant presence of their mothers, who are unusually available and responsive to the boys' needs and wants. Suddenly, around age 5, the boy is abruptly separated from the mother, and this relationship is replaced with lesser attachments to other family members. Kakar (1978:128) interprets this pattern of upbringing as providing the basis for "a heightened narcissistic vulnerability, an unconscious tendency to 'submit' to an idealized omnipotent figure." As summarized by Wulff (1991:356), Kakar surmises that

> the young boy compensates by activating the grandiose self and its convictions "I am perfect" and "I do not need anyone." This attitude finds mythic embodiment in the image of the solitary Shiva meditating high in the remote Himalayas.

An analysis of this scenario in attachment terms would differ in several respects from Kakar's account: For example, Bowlby (1973) speaks of *compulsive self-reliance* (rather than narcissism) as one common response to separation, and Kakar's discussion of phallic symbolism and other psychoanalytic speculations would have no place in an attachment account. However, the central idea is much the same: Cultural patterns of childrearing may lead to dramatic differences in orientations to close relationships (in this case, an avoidant attachment style), which in turn may influence the acceptability and attraction of various religious belief systems.

Attachment and Eastern religions: A natural question to pose for an attachment account of religious beliefs concerns the applicability of the model to Eastern religious traditions, which typically are conceived as being more or less nontheistic. This question was addressed in part in the preceding section: Some of the major differences between Western and Eastern religious traditions may owe in part to differences in childrearing practices and other cultural influences on the development and maintenance of close relationships, which in turn influence religious belief and experience.

However, it is important to realize that many Eastern religions are considerably less devoid of attachment figure-like gods than is commonly thought. According to Hiebert (1992), for example, Hinduism presents adherents with three alternative roads to enlightenment. Two of these fit the Westerner's common conceptions of Eastern religion: the path of duty (*karma marga*) is largely ritual-based, and the path of wisdom (*jnana marga*) is philosophical and metaphysical. However, according to Hiebert, an estimated 90 percent of Hindus follow the path of devotion (*bhakti marga*). This path "offers immediate, unconditional salvation to those who throw themselves on the mercy of God," where God refers to the god of one's caste and/or a personal god chosen by the individual (p.11). Moreover, Hiebert (p.11) observes that

> conversion in the path of *bhakti* is similar to that in Christianity. A person must choose a god or goddess and surrender totally to this deity. The god then saves all those who call on him or her (p.11).

Although Westerners typically think of Hinduism more as a nontheistic, metaphysical philosophy than a personal religion in the Western sense, Hiebert's analysis suggests that many (if not most) Hindus may be experiencing a personal relationship with God psychologically in much the same way as their Christian counterparts.

Several of Hiebert's (1992) observations on Buddhism point in a similar direction. For example, Heibert contrasts the two major traditions of Buddhism by noting that

> for the masses caught in the struggles of life, [*Theravada*] Buddhism was too austere. . . . They were used to worshiping the many gods of India.

> Consequently, when sculptors began to carve images of the Buddha, the common people took to worshiping these images. . . . By the third century A.D. the idea of Buddha as the Suffering Savior emerged. It is *Mahayana* that won the Chinese with their belief in spirits and gods, and, through them, the Koreans and Japanese (p.17).

Again, it is the metaphysical *Theravada* tradition (along with Zen) that most of us readily associate with Buddhism, but it is the theistic *Mahayana* tradition that touched the hearts and minds of everyday people. Moreover, in countries dominated by *Theravada* Buddhism, such as Thailand and Sri Lanka, the beliefs of the average person include a variety of personal gods rooted in the ancient folk religions that historically preceded the advent of Buddhism (Hawkins, personal communication, 1993).

Of course, there are countless doctrinal and philosophical differences between most Western and Eastern religions, but in many important ways the psychological similarities may be greater than most of us might imagine. Specifically, it seems that the idea of a personal god to whom one submits and in whom one places one's faith—in return for salvation and a sense of security—is practically irresistible to human beings around the globe. To the extent that religious beliefs include such a component, it seems reasonable to assert that attachment dynamics may lie behind and shape the religious experiences of these individuals. Although empirical research to support these conjectures is sorely needed, it seems reasonable to maintain that attachment may be far more universally applicable to the understanding of religious belief and experience than one might initially suspect.

Attachment Theory and Freud

It will be obvious to many readers that the central thesis of the attachment model of religious experience has a decidedly Freudian flavor. Religious beliefs, as argued by Freud, are seen to provide comfort and perceived protection against a dangerous and sometimes cruel world. God is regarded as a parental image though, in attachment terms, this is conceptualized as a kind of "exalted attachment figure" rather than an exalted father figure. Despite these superficial similarities, however, the theories differ in important ways. Indeed, Bowlby explicitly developed attachment theory in large part to remedy what he regarded as errors in Freudian theory—errors that became apparent only after Freud's time. I suspect Freud himself would take attachment theory quite seriously were he alive today.

In his excellent review of the Freudian approach to religion, Shafranske (this volume) organizes his essay around two themes: biological (phylogenetic) evolution and the centrality of sexual motivation. It is with respect to these very issues that the differences between Bowlby and Freud are most apparent. Moreover, I submit that it is on the basis of these differences that the Bowlbian approach is to be preferred as a general psychodynamic model of human personality development and, hence, of religion.

Freud very much intended for his theory of psychoanalysis to be consistent with, and indeed an extension of, the biological and physical sciences. One of Bowlby's primary motives for developing attachment theory was that those sciences had changed since Freud's day and that these changes necessitated an updating of psychoanalytic theory. This is particularly true with respect to evolutionary biology and ethology (the latter being quite a recent development). Freud's psychic energy model of motivation no longer is consistent with the conceptualizations of ethology and other sciences regarding the organization of animal or human behavior. The control-systems approach favored by Bowlby, in which behavioral systems or mental "mechanisms" or "organs" are activated and deactivated under various conditions, is now the norm. The conceptualization of motivation as pressurized steam seeking to escape a boiling pot is no longer consistent with theorizing in the biological and social sciences. The popular idea of Freud's time that "ontogeny recapitulates phylogeny," which influenced much of Freud's theorizing (Shafranske, this volume), is no longer taken seriously by evolutionary scientists.

Moreover, the Lamarckian model of inheritance of acquired characteristics fell into disfavor with evolutionists long ago. In light of current understandings of the evolutionary process, the idea that the memory of an experienced event (e.g., the murder of the father by the primal horde) can be handed down genetically across generations makes no more biological sense than the idea that your own future children or grandchildren will someday "remember," without being told, what you had for breakfast this morning. Bowlby's theory was developed specifically with the goal of reflecting these contemporary developments in evolutionary thinking; it represents an attempt to update psychoanalytic theorizing in this regard.

With respect to the primacy of the sex instinct in particular, Bowlby's crucial insight was to identify the attachment system as a motivational system distinct from that concerned with sex and reproduction. This distinction is particularly important with respect to the psychology of religion, as the path from "instinct" to a comforting, protective God can be conceptualized quite directly. In contrast, Freud's approach involves a rather circuitous route from maternal bonding to a protective God by way of the Oedipal complex. As noted in a previous section, other psychologists of religion have similarly failed to acknowledge attachment and sexual mating as distinct systems and looked to the latter as a psychological basis for religious beliefs (e.g., Coe, 1916, Thouless, 1923).

As I have tried to argue in the preceding pages, it is the attachment system rather than the sexual mating system that provides the biological/motivational basis for a variety of religious beliefs and experiences. Human beings are built to seek the secure base and haven of an attachment figure across the lifespan, and religious experience may result from the functioning of this system for many people in many contexts. (See Hazan and Zeifman, 1994, for a discussion of the interaction of sex and attachment in adult relationships.)

Bowlby's emphasis on attachment as a distinct behavioral system also represents a critical divergence from early psychoanalytic thinking which traced the mother-infant bond to the mother's role as a provider of food. Influenced particularly by Harlow's (1958) classic studies of surrogate mothers with nonhuman primates, Bowlby showed that the motivational basis for this bond was independent of her role as a supplier of food. As a result, the pivotal role of mother's breast in much psychoanalytic thinking—for example, that of Melanie Klein—disappears almost entirely from attachment theory. (See Ainsworth, 1969, and Maccoby and Masters, 1970, for discussions.)

Thus, although the attachment approach to religion in some ways resembles the Freudian tradition from which it evolved, crucial differences are apparent that have important implications for the psychology of religion. Perhaps the most important of these concerns Freud's critique of religion. Although some aspects of Freud's disdain for religion fall clearly outside the purview of science, his theory certainly points in the direction of a disdainful view of religion as infantile, regressive, and immature. This impression, however, hinges entirely on the (mistaken) assumption that attachment relationships in the Bowlbian sense are a product of childhood that should be outgrown by mature adults.

Bowlby's view of the entire process is fundamentally different. The need for a stronger, wiser other upon which one can depend for support and comfort when needed is simply a part of what it means to be human. Such attachments may take different forms at different ages and in different circumstances, but in the end attachment is an entirely natural process across the lifespan. Individual differences emerge over time and, indeed, some of these patterns are pathological. However, there is nothing inherently pathological, infantile, or regressive about religious belief from an attachment perspective. Rather, it is an empirical question as to which varieties of religious belief and experience prove to be efficacious, and which detrimental, to healthy psychological functioning (see Batson et al., 1993, for a review of the multifarious relationships between religion and mental health).

Although Bowlby intended for attachment theory to replace Freudian theory, the psychoanalytic community has so far shown little inclination to follow his lead. However, some theorists have begun to look for ways to integrate the two perspectives. Whether such compromise positions will prove influential remains to be seen. Silverman's (1991) attempt to integrate the two models, for example, seems to simply tack an attachment dynamic onto an otherwise intact Freudian drive model. Given the fundamental differences between Bowlby's control-systems model and Freud's drive model of motivation, however, such a scheme seems internally inconsistent and misses the main thrust of Bowlby's contribution.

Attachment and Other Psychoanalytic Traditions

It would be impossible within a brief section of a brief chapter to draw comparisons and contrasts between attachment theory and the many variants of psychoanalytic thought that have evolved over recent decades. Many of these schools have rejected or sidestepped some of the same aspects of Freudian theory as did Bowlby, and some overlap substantially with attachment theory. For example, object relations approaches generally downplay or reject outright Freud's drive theory, instead placing close relationships at the center of psychological landscape. Applications of these ideas to religion generally focus on the dynamics by which early parental relationships serve as a basis for mental representations of God. Nevertheless, many differences between the approaches exist, and in important ways the chasm between these approaches and attachment is deep indeed. Below I outline a few of these.

First, psychoanalytic thinking is based largely on observation of clinical cases. Much of the empirical literature on object relations, for example, involves attempts to discriminate normal from pathological populations (Fishler, Sperling, and Carr, 1990). This is clearly appropriate when, for example, the focus of theorizing is the etiology of pathology, but seems potentially misleading as a basis for generalizing to the "normal" range of human experience and relationships—including religious belief and experience. Attachment theory, in contrast, has always been as much a theory of normative development as one of developmental psychopathology.

Second, psychoanalytic approaches generally have focused on adult experience, and tend to approach childhood experience and behavior by generalizing backwards from adulthood (Fishler et al., 1990). Attachment theory, in contrast, works prospectively by focusing on the dynamics of childhood relationships and projecting developmental trajectories forward in time (Bowlby, 1969). Much empirical research on infant attachment is longitudinal in nature, predicting subsequent personality development from individual differences in infancy (see Bretherton, 1987, for a review). Similarly, research on adult attachment relationships has begun to adopt prospective methodologies designed to predict subsequent relationship functioning from individual differences in attachment style (e.g., Kirkpatrick and Davis, 1994; Kirkpatrick and Hazan, 1994).

This difference between psychoanalytic and behavioral perspectives on infancy and childhood is captured neatly by Stern's (1985) distinction between the "observed infant" of developmental psychology and the "clinical" infant reconstructed from a psychoanalytic point of view. As summarized by Fishler et al. (1990:500), attachment researchers "are less interested [than object relations researchers] in the presumed intrapsychic origins of attachment behavior than in the individual differences and cognitive/organizations properties of that behavior." This focus is clearly more in tune with the nomothetic research orientation of contemporary developmental and social psychology, and is probably the primary reason that attachment theory has been far more successful than psychoanalysis in generating empirical research in these areas.

Third, in contrast to the preoccupation with fantasy and imagination of many object relations theories, Bowlby believed that mental models were tolerably accurate representations of real experience. Considerable research evidence now exists to support the claim that individual differences in childhood attachment patterns are related to parental behavior and attitudes (e.g., Ainsworth et al., 1978; Sroufe and Waters, 1977a). This emphasis on actual experience and deemphasis of the role of fantasy distinguishes Bowlby from some object relations theorists such as Klein, Winnicott, and Rizzuto. Other object relations theorists, however—notably Fairbairn and Guntrip—share Bowlby's concerns on this point.

Fourth, in certain respects attachment theory is more precisely and narrowly defined than object relations theories. It is a theory about one specific kind of relationship, in which one person derives comfort and security from the secure base and haven provisions offered by the other, rather than close relationships in general (cf., e.g., Sullivan and Fairbairn). Rather than speaking of "good" and "bad" objects, for example, or of generic human needs for "connectedness" or "relatedness" (e.g., Mahler), Bowlby focused on one specific, crucial dimension of attachment figures' behavior (i.e., sensitive responsiveness to infant attachment behaviors) and laid the groundwork for a descriptive typology of individual differences resulting from experience related to this dimension. This is not to say, of course, that mental representations of close relationships are built exclusively on this basis. However, it does focus attention on one crucial dimension that can be (and has been) operationalized in ways that readily lend the theory to empirical testing—as evidenced by the burgeoning attachment literatures in developmental and social psychology.

In my view, the most important difference between Bowlby's approach and that of most contemporary psychoanalytic approaches is his emphasis on the evolutionary origins of the attachment system. It is one thing to agree that close relationships—and particularly early parental relationships—represent a cornerstone of personality development; it is another thing entirely to explain why. Bowlby's clearly specified answer to the question "why?" leads directly to a variety of operationalizable and empirically testable hypotheses and fits well with other sciences (e.g., evolutionary biology) and other research fields within psychology (e.g., social and developmental psychology).

For the reader interested in exploring the similarities and differences between attachment theory and psychoanalytic theories, several good sources are available. Bowlby (1969) himself explicitly contrasted many of his ideas with Freudian and other psychoanalytic approaches. Early articles by Ainsworth (1969) and Maccoby and Masters (1970) offer in-depth discussions of attachment theory vis-à-vis dependency theories and object relations. Bretherton (1987) includes in her review of the attachment literature sections contrasting attachment theory with the theories of Fairbairn, Sullivan, Mahler, and Stern.

Conclusions

Freud's genius, in my view, was his recognition of the importance of unconscious, innate motivational forces driving much of human behavior. Bowlby's genius was his ability to recognize, in the context of a greatly changed scientific landscape, which insights of Freud's held up and which should be discarded. Bowlby's efforts to update psychoanalysis in light of modern developments in evolutionary biology, ethology, and the other social sciences were intended to supplant the theory of psychoanalysis with a new and improved psychodynamic theory. Although clearly he was pleased with the enormous impact of his theory on research in developmental psychology, Bowlby was somewhat disappointed in the failure of the clinical psychoanalytic community to come aboard (see, for example, the preface to Bowlby, 1988).

As long as psychoanalytic theories continue to thrive, psychoanalytic theories of religion will do likewise. I have no expectation that in this brief chapter I will have convinced adherents of these traditions to "convert" to attachment theory. However, I do hope I have succeeded in providing a glimpse of what attachment theory has to offer the psychology of religion. In particular, attachment theory has the potential to help bridge the apparently enormous gulf that has evolved between psychoanalytic and "empirical" or "correlational" approaches to religion, just as it has begun to bridge the chasm between these approaches in other areas of psychology. As summarized by one leading developmental psychologist:

> No longer does one need to choose between a vital but untestable theory and sterile, operationalized part theories which have dominated behavioral psychology. By pointing again to the centrality of vital relationships as the bedrock of human experience, and by reconceptualizing these within the evolutionary framework, Bowlby has led the way to a fully satisfactory theory of human behavior. This evolved psychoanalytic theory not only is testable but has received ample validation from empirical research. At the same time it remains a clinically rich theory, which does justice to the complexity and subtlety of the human animal. Bowlby's theory is certain to be a major part of the science of human behavior for years to come (Sroufe, 1986:848).

This is the kind of theory on which an adequate psychology of religion ultimately must be based. As the richness and scope of attachment theory continues to be increasingly recognized and tested in other areas of psychology, so too I hope it will be recognized as an equally powerful tool for researchers and practitioners in the psychology of religion.

NOTES AND REFERENCES

1. Preparation of this chapter was facilitated by a summer research grant from the College of William and Mary.

2. The author is grateful to Bradley Hawkins for sharing his insights on Eastern religious traditions and for his comments on a previous draft of this chapter.

Ainsworth, M. D. S.
1969 Object relations, dependency, and attachment: A theoretical review of the infant-mother relationship. *Child Development* 40:969-1025.
1985 Attachments across the life span. *Bulletin of the New York Academy of Medicine* 61:792-812.

Ainsworth, M., M. C. Blehar, E. Waters, and S. Wall
1978 *Patterns of attachment*. Hillsdale, NJ: Erlbaum.

Allport, G. W.
1950 *The individual and his religion*. New York: Macmillan.

Argyle, M., and B. Beit-Hallahmi
1975 *The social psychology of religion*. London: Routledge & Kegan Paul.

Baker, M., and R. Gorsuch
1982 Trait anxiety and intrinsic-extrinsic religiousness. *Journal for the Scientific Study of Religion* 21:119-122.

Batson, C. D., P. A. Schoenrade, and W. L. Ventis
1993 *Religion and the individual*. New York: Oxford University Press.

Benson, P., and B. Spilka
1973 God image as a function of self-esteem and locus of control. *Journal for the Scientific Study of Religion* 12:297-310.

Bowlby, J.
1969 *Attachment and loss. Vol. 1: Attachment*. New York: Basic Books.
1973 *Attachment and loss. Vol. 2: Separation, anxiety, and anger*. New York: Basic Books.
1979 *The making and breaking of affectional bonds*. London: Tavistock Publications.
1980 *Attachment and loss. Vol. 3: Loss*. New York: Basic Books.
1988 *A secure base: Parent-child attachment and healthy human development*. New York: Basic Books.

Bretherton, I.
1985 Attachment theory: Retrospect and prospect. In *Growing points in attachment theory and research*, edited by I. Bretherton and E. Waters, Vol. 50 of *Monographs of the Society for Research in Child Development* (1-2, Serial No. 209).
1987 New perspectives on attachment relations: Security, communication, and internal working models. In *Handbook of infant development*, 2nd ed., edited by J. D. Osofsky. New York: Wiley.

Broen Jr., W. E.
1957 A factor-analytic study of religious attitudes. *Journal of Abnormal and Social Psychology* 54:176-179.

Campos, J. J., and C. Stenberg
1981 Perception, appraisal, and emotional: The onset of social referencing. In *Infant social cognition: Empirical and theoretical considerations*, edited by M. E. Lamb and L. R.

Sherrod. Hillsdale, NJ: Erlbaum.
Caspi, A., and D. J. Bem
1990 Personality continuity and change across the life course. In *Handbook of personality: Theory and research,* edited by L. A. Pervin. New York: Guilford.
Collins, N. L., and S. J. Read
1990 Adult attachment, working models, and relationship quality in dating couples. *Journal of Personality and Social Psychology* 58:644-663.
Coe, G. A.
1916 *Psychology of religion*. Chicago: University of Chicago Press.
Cutrona, C. E., and D. Russell
1987 The provisions of social relationships and adaptation to stress. In *Advances in Personal Relationships*, Vol. 1, edited by W. H. Jones and D. Perlman. Greenwich, CT: JAI.
Deutsch, A.
1975 Observations on a sidewalk ashram. *Archives of General Psychiatry* 32:166-175.
Egeland, B., and L. A. Sroufe
1981 Attachment and early maltreatment. *Child Development* 52:44-52.
Feeney, B. C., and L. A. Kirkpatrick
1993 *Attachment security and presence of romantic partners as moderators of autonomic responses to stress in college women*. Unpublished manuscript, College of William and Mary, Williamsburg, VA.
Feeney, J. A., and P. Noller
1990 Attachment style as a predictor of adult romantic relationships. *Journal of Personality and Social Psychology* 58:281-291.
Fishler, P. H., M. B. Sperling, and A. C. Carr
1990 Assessment of adult relatedness: A review of empirical findings from object relations and attachment theories. *Journal of Personality Assessment* 55:499-520.
Flakoll, D. A.
1974 *Self esteem, psychological adjustment and images of God*. Paper presented at the Meeting of the Society for the Scientific Study of Religion, Washington, DC, October.
Galanter, M.
1979 The "Moonies": A psychological study of conversion and membership in a contemporary religious sect. *American Journal of Psychiatry* 136:165-170.
George, C., N. Kaplan, and M. Main
1985 *The Berkeley Adult Attachment Interview*. Unpublished manuscript, University of California, Berkeley.
Gorsuch, R. L.
1968 The conceptualization of God as seen in adjective ratings. *Journal for the Scientific Study of Religion* 7:56:64.
Greeley, A.
1977 *The Mary Myth: On thefemininity of God*. New York: Seabury.
1981 *The religious imagination*. New York: Sadlier.
1990 *The Catholic myth: The behavior and beliefs of American Catholics*. New York: Scribner's.
Hazan, C., and P. R. Shaver
1987 Romantic love conceptualized as an attachment process. *Journal of Personality and Social Psychology* 52:511-524.
1994 Attachment as an organizational framework for research on close relationships. *Psychological Inquiry* 5:1-22.
Hazan, C., and D. Zeifman, D.
1994 Sex and the psychological tether. In *Advances in personal relationships*, Vol. 5, edited by D. Perlman and K. Bartholomew. London: Jessica Kingsley.
Heiler, F.
1932 *Prayer*. New York: Oxford University Press.
Hiebert, P. G.
1992 Conversion in Hinduism and Buddhism. In *Handbook of religious conversion*, edited by H. N. Malony and S. Southard. Birmingham, AL: Religious Education Press.

Hine, V. H.
1969 Pentecostal glossolalia: Toward a functional interpretation. *Journal for the Scientific Study of Religion* 8:211-226.
James, W.
1902 *Varieties of religious experience*. New York: Longmans, Green.
Jolley, J. C.
1983 *Self-regarding attitudes and conceptions of deity: A comparative study*. Paper presented at the Meeting of the Rocky Mountain Psychological Association, Snowbird, UT, April.
Kahoe, R. D.
1974 Personality and achievement correlates of intrinsic and extrinsic religious orientations. *Journal of Personality and Social Psychology* 29:812-818.
Kahoe, R. D., and R. F. Dunn
1975 The fear of death and religious attitudes and behavior. *Journal for the Scientific Study of Religion* 14:379-382.
Kakar, S.
1978 *The inner world: A psycho-analytic study of childhood and society in India*, 2nd Ed. Delhi, India: Oxford University Press.
Kaufman, G. D.
1981 *The theological imagination: Constructing the concept of God*. Philadelphia: Westminster.
Kildahl, J. P.
1972 *The psychology of speaking in tongues*. New York: Harper & Row.
Kirkpatrick, L. A.
1992a An attachment-theoretical approach to the psychology of religion. *International Journal for the Psychology of Religion* 2:3-28.
1992b *A longitudinal study of changes in religious belief and behavior as a function of individual differences in adult attachment style*. Paper presented at the annual meeting of the Society for the Scientific Study of Religion, Washington, DC, November.
1993 *A(nother) longitudinal study of changes in religious belief as a function of individual differences in adult attachment style*. Paper presented at the annual meeting of the Society for the Scientific Study of Religion, Raleigh, NC, October.
1994 The role of attachment in religious belief and behavior. In *Advances in personal relationships*, Vol. 5, edited by D. Perlman and K. Bartholomew. London: Jessica Kingsley.
Kirkpatrick, L. A., and K. E. Davis
1994 Attachment style, gender, and relationship stability: A longitudinal analysis. *Journal of Personality and Social Psychology*.
Kirkpatrick, L. A. and C. Hazan
1994 Attachment and close relationships: A four-year prospective study. *Personal Relationships* 1:123-142.
Kirkpatrick, L. A., and R. W. Hood Jr.
1990 Intrinsic-extrinsic religious orientation: The "boon" or "bane" of contemporary psychology of religion? *Journal for the Scientific Study of Religion* 29:442-462.
Kirkpatrick, L. A., and P. R. Shaver
1990 Attachment theory and religion: Childhood attachments, religious beliefs, and conversion. *Journal for the Scientific Study of Religion* 29:315-334.
1992 An attachment-theoretical approach to romantic love and religious belief. *Personality and Social Psychology Bulletin* 18:266-275.
Kirkpatrick, L. A., S. Kellas, and D. Shillito
1993 *Loneliness and perceptions of social support from God*. Paper presented at the Convention of the American Psychological Association, Toronto (August).
Lambert, W. W., L. M. Triandis, and M. Wolf
1959 Some correlates of beliefs in the malevolence and benevolence of supernatural beings: A cross-societal study. *Journal of Abnormal and Social Psychology* 58:162-169.
Levy, M. B., and K. E. Davis
1988 Lovestyles and attachment styles compared: Their relations to each other and to various relationship characteristics. *Journal of Social and Personal Relationships* 5:439-471.

Loveland, G. G.
1968 The effects of bereavement on certain religious attitudes. *Sociological Symposium* 1:17-27.
Maccoby, E. E., and J. C. Masters
1970 Attachment and dependency. In *Carmichael's manual of child psychology*, Vol. 2, 3rd ed., edited by P. H. Mussen. New York: Wiley.
Main, M., and R. Goldwyn
1984 Predicting rejection of her infant from mother's representation of her own experience: Implications for the abused-abusing intergenerational cycle. *Child Abuse and Neglect* 8:203-217.
Main, M., N. Kaplan, and J. Cassidy
1985 Security in infancy, childhood, and adulthood: A move to the level of representation. In *Growing points in attachment theory and research*, edited by I. Bretherton and E. Waters. Vol. 50 of *Monographs of the Society for Research in Child Development* (1-2, Serial No. 209).
McClain, E. W.
1978 Personality differences between intrinsically religious and nonreligious students: A factor analytic study. *Journal of Personality Assessment* 42:159-166.
Oates, W. E.
1967 A socio-psychological study of glossolalia. In *Glossolalia: Tongue speaking in biblical, historical, and psychological perspective*, edited by F. Stagg, E. G. Hinson, and W. E. Oates. New York: Abingdon.
Pargament, K. I., and J. Hahn
1986 God and the just world: Causal and coping attributions to God in health situations. *Journal for the Scientific Study of Religion* 25:193-207.
Plog, S.
1965 UCLA conducts research on glossolalia. *Trinity* 3:38-39.
Pratt, J. B.
1920 *The religious consciousness*. New York: Macmillan.
Reed, B.
1978 *The dynamics of religion: Process and movement in Christian churches*. London: Darton, Longman & Todd.
Richardson, J. T.
1973 Psychological interpretations of glossolalia. A reexamination of research. *Journal for the Scientific Study of Religion* 12:199-207.
Rizzuto, A.-M.
1979 *The birth of the living God: A psychoanalytic study*. Chicago: University of Chicago Press.
Rohner, R. P.
1975 *They love me, they love me not*. New Haven, CT: HRAF Press.
Shaver, P. R. and C. Hazan
1993 Adult romantic attachment: Theory and evidence. In *Advances in personal relationships*, Vol. 4, edited by D. Perlman & W. Jones, 29-70. London: Jessica Kingsley.
Shaver, P. R., C. Hazan, and D. Bradshaw
1988 Love as attachment: The integration of three behavioral systems. In *The psychology of love*, edited by R. J. Sternberg and M. L. Barnes. New Haven, CT: Yale University Press.
Silverman, D. K.
1991 Attachment patterns and Freudian theory: An integrative proposal. *Psychoanalytic Psychology*. 8:169-193.
Simpson, J. A.
1990 Influence of attachment styles on romantic relationships. *Journal of Personality and Social Psychology* 59:971-980.
Simpson, J. A., and W. S. Rholes
1994 Stress and secure base relationships in adulthood. In *Advances in Personal Relationships*, Vol. 5, edited by D. Perlman and K. Bartholomew. London: Jessica Kingsley.

Simpson, J. A., W. S. Rholes, and J. S. Nelligan
1992 Support seeking and support giving within couples in an anxiety-provoking situation: The role of attachment styles. *Journal of Personality and Social Psychology* 62:434-446.
Spilka, B., J. Addison, and M. Rosensohn
1975 Parents, self, and God: A test of competing individual-religion relationships. *Review of Religious Research* 16:154-165.
Spilka, B., P. Armatas, and J. Nussbaum
1964 The concept of God: A factor-analytic approach. *Review of Religious Research* 6:28-36.
Spilka, B., R. W. Hood, Jr., and R. L. Gorsuch
1985 *The psychology of religion: An empirical approach*. Englewood Cliffs, NJ: Prentice-Hall.
Sroufe, L. A.
1986 Appraisal: Bowlby's contribution to psychoanalytic theory and developmental psychology; Attachment: Separation: Loss. *Journal of Child Psychology and Psychiatry and Allied Disciplines* 27:841-849.
Sroufe, L. A. and J. Fleeson
1986 Attachment and the construction of relationships. In *Relationships and development*, edited by W. W. Hartup and Z. Rubin, pp. 51-71. Hillsdale, NJ: Erlbaum.
Sroufe, L. A. and E. Waters
1977a Attachment as an organizational construct. *Child Development* 48:1184-1199.
1977b Heartrate as a convergent measure in clinical and developmental research. *Merrill-Palmer Quarterly* 23:3-28.
Stern, D. N.
1985 *The interpersonal world of the infant: A view from psychoanalysis and developmental psychology*. New York: Basic.
Stouffer, S. A., et al.
1949 *The American soldier. II. Combat and its aftermath*. Princeton, NJ: Princeton University Press.
Strickland, B. R., and S. Shaffer
1971 I-E, I-E, and F. *Journal for the Scientific Study of Religion* 10:366-369.
Tamayo, A., and L. Desjardins
1976 Belief systems and conceptual images of parents and God. *Journal of Psychology* 92:131-140.
Thouless, R. H.
1923 *An introduction to the psychology of religion*. New York: Macmillan.
Ullman, C.
1989 *The transformed self: The psychology of religious conversion*. New York: Plenum.
Vivier, L.
1960 *Glossolalia*. Doctoral dissertation, University of Witwatersrand, Department of Psychiatry and Mental Hygiene.
Weiss, R. S.
1973 *Loneliness: The experience of emotional and social isolation*. Cambridge, MA: MIT Press.
1982 Attachment in adult life. In *The place of attachment in human behavior*, edited by C. M. Parkes and J. S. Hinde. New York: Basic Books.
Wenegrat, B.
1989 *The divine archetype: The sociobiology and psychology of religion*. Lexington, MA: Lexington Books.
Wood, W. W.
1965 *Culture and personality aspects of the Pentecostal Holiness religion*. The Hague: Mouton.
Woodberry, J. D.
1992 Conversion in Islam. In *Handbook of religious conversion*, edited by H. N. Malony and S. Southard. Birmingham, AL: Religious Education Press.
Wulff, D. M.
1991 *Psychology of religion: Classic and contemporary views*. New York: Wiley.

20

The Body in Religious Experience

CAROLE A. RAYBURN

McGuire (1990) has urged that social scientists of religion take seriously the fact that human beings are embodied. Conceiving the mindful body—subjects who experience a material world through and in their bodies—would bring about a true transformation of the social sciences of religion. She has called for deeper awareness of the social and political uses of human bodies, seeing this as a better guide to research and theory. Humans relate to society through their bodies: Primarily, consciousness involves "I can" rather than "I think that." Loss of a part of the body that had enabled direct acting with the world is viewed by individuals as an assault upon their whole being.

Second, bodies are matter and perceive and interpret the real world: Bodies experience pain, pleasure, disabilities, birth, and death. In the most intimate and meaningful way, we are our bodies. Loss of a part of our bodies or loss or disruption of bodily functions is taken as a loss of integrity and of a sense of wholeness of the individual. Further, interpretations that society places upon the body, its parts, and attributes, give the body social meanings beyond the mere physical aspects: Political power given by society as to the color of the skin, the gender of the body, and body size will determine what is considered negative or positive about bodies. It is in the context of certain economic, ecological, social, and political conditions rather than through mere variation in abstract symbols that body rituals have meaning: Social meanings of the body are closely linked with the political body. The body is also important in power relations, since religion often serves to legitimize political bodies to exercise privilege and power over other bodies: Proscribing more limitations of the body (social mobility, economic freedom, reproductive choice, marital freedom of choice, etc.) for women than for men.

The present chapter will look at the ways in which the body is involved in religious experience. The analysis will be limited to the Judeo-Christian uses of the body in religious experience.[1] Only the body as a whole will be discussed.

THE BODY AS A WHOLE

Eilberg-Schwartz (1992a) wisely points out that the human body in many respects is a misleading abstraction, since all cultures have many ideas and teachings about specific parts, organs, or processes of the body. "The body" is actually constructed in piecemeal fashion, organ by organ, with little coherent theory of the body and usually only a multiplicity of competing assumptions about various body parts, organs, and processes. These assumptions are imperfectly incorporated, for the most part. Fragmentation of the body necessitates turning toward cultural influences on specific organs. The present chapter has taken the direction that both Eilberg-Schwartz and Wasserfall (1992) recommend: Away from focusing on the body through an analysis of texts but rather through ethnography, an embodied practice of interpretation in which the writer begins with the biological, then the psychological and/or social, and finally the theological in light of the biological and psychological/social.

The Embodied God

Postulating that the human body was caught between two conflicting impulses, Eilberg-Schwartz (1992b) speaks of humans being created in the image of God, but God has no-body (no one with whom to relate nor a completely conceptualized body to interact with others), and procreation is given as a mandate from God, but semen is thought to be polluting (even when discharged during sexual intercourse). Judaism is especially concerned with what passes in and out of the orifices, particularly the mouth and genitals. Genital emissions such as menstrual blood, semen, and other irregular discharges cause pollution (Leviticus 15). These restrictions stem from a concern with wholeness and with threats to the integrity of the body. This, however, is only part of the explanation. Tension between being made in the image of God and being obliged to reproduce pull people in opposite directions. How does a God who may have no body as we know bodies and no organs of reproduction (or elimination and digestion, for that matter) create us in the image of God?

Whether God has form or is bodiless, the biblical imagery about God's body is rich. In David's song of praise (2 Samuel 22:7-16; Psalm 18:7-9), God is metaphorically described in very poetic and graphic terms: "From his temple he heard my voice; my cry came to his ears. The earth trembled and quaked, the foundations of the heavens shook; they trembled because he was angry. Smoke rose from his nostrils; consuming fire from his mouth, burning coals blazed out of it. He parted the heavens and came down; dark clouds were under his feet. He mounted the cherubim and flew; he soared on the wings of the wind. He made the darkness his canopy around him—the dark rain clouds of the sky. Out of the brightness of his presence bolts of lightning blazed forth. The Lord thundered from heaven; the voice of the Most High resounded . . . the foundations of the earth laid bare at the rebuke of the Lord, at the blast of breath from his nostrils."

So, we have the image of a hearing and listening God, an angry God with nostrils raging with smoke, fire from his mouth, clouds at his feet, thundering and resounding voice, and darkness covering him (perhaps to hide gender, as has been suggested by Eilberg-Schwartz), and a bright presence. The Jews, who have a God without a body nonetheless have a need to metaphorize God with form to better understand and relate to God. Only when form is superimposed on the omnipotent, omnipresent, and omniscient God can humans even begin to be able to deal with divinity. Otherwise, even the idea of God is overwhelming to the mind of humans. Further, isolating body parts rather than attempting to deal with the whole form of God makes the problem of understanding and communicating with God an easier matter.

God and Sexuality

The priests who wrote in the times of the Old Testament were the most concerned of all Israelite communities with human reproduction, since procreation is central to life and responsibility. Circumcision is the physical sign of God's promise of genealogical increase of the number of Abraham's male descendants, and the priests inherited the priesthood from their fathers (the priests were primarily responsible for the "begats" of Genesis). If God has no sex, reproductive organs of males and females becomes a problem; if God does have a sex, male or female, God's reproductive organs are useless. To envision God as having reproductive organs on a body of a monotheistic God, the no-body and no-sex God who is monotheistic plus that prohibition on representing God in material form and thus hiding the problem of God's sex presents multiple problems. A monotheistic God cannot have both sexual experience and a body. Attempts to embody God would jeopardize God's sexuality. Only metaphoric copulation is possible for a monotheistic God. It is not possible to hold at the same time the idea that God has a body with a sex and is a sexual being. For God to have sex, God must not have a body; to have a body, God can have no sex. This is because there are no other gods with whom God could have sex. Priestly absorption in legal restrictions turned attention of the religious community from basic conflicts about the body, a rich source of symbols (Eilberg-Schwartz, 1992b).

The Body of God and the Virgin Mary: There is another serious problem with a monotheistic God who is held to have no body but to be engendered with male attributes: How to explain the Virgin Mary's mating with what would seem a male Holy Spirit. Though Holy Spirit in Greek is *pneuma*, a feminine noun, this divine being of the godhead has been given male attributes by the patriarchal ecclesiastical system too. Given the times in which Jesus was to be born, a male child would have been dictated without question; society was certainly anything but kind and fair to women and girls. For Mary, who had never had sexual intercourse with a man at the time of her marriage to Joseph, to conceive a male child, she would have had to have semen with the male Y chromosome. Women have the XX chromosomes, while men have the XY chromosomes: The woman's X and the man's X would need to combine for the conception of a female child, and her X and his Y for a male child. Matthew 1:18-25 and Luke 1:26-2:7 speak of Jesus being "conceived by the Holy Spirit and born of the Virgin Mary." Bryant (1967) points out that "virgin birth" means that Christ was conceived without the mediation of an earthly father and not as a result of sexual intercourse but from the supernatural "overshadowing" of the Holy Spirit. Simultaneous connection with and discontinuity with humankind through Mary and her conception through the Holy Spirit for the spiritually and physically miraculous birth of the divine Second Adam was achieved through the virgin birth. If God does not have sex or semen or a penis, why are theologians referring to God in the male nouns and pronouns? It would be just as appropriate to refer to God as Mother, or at least as Mother/Father God. It is not inconceivable that, at least symbolically, God has both sexual organs or neither.

God and an Engendered Body: Judaism denies that God has any physical form or body, so being made in God's image would refer to human minds, individuality, and unique self. Eilberg-Schwartz (1992a) argues that the whole debate over whether God has a human-like body or form is really a cover-up for a more serious and problematic matter, the problem of questioning whether God has gender. Alpert (1992), looking at complementarity as an overly confining notion that to be whole women must be partners with men because men and women anatomically "fit" together, holds that God has been considered to be male but relatively genderless. Maleness and sexlessness of God devaluate women and sexuality to a very high degree. Thinking of God in female pronouns and attributes of female body parts to reclaim elements of ancient Near Eastern worship have met with strong negative reaction from the Jewish community. The maleness postulated for God is held to be asexual. Because women are traditionally thought not to exist without men, thinking of God as female threatens both the maleness of God and the asexuality at the same time. Association between women and worshiping images of women and women loving women has been suggested: This is the association between Goddess worship and fears of lesbianism.

It is possible that God has attributes of both genders, both physically and spiritually. Only then could females as well as males feel included as being made in the image of God and as being a decided part of the covenant. After all, within women grows the new life that becomes the child of the family. Women are very much involved, not just physically, but psychologically and spiritually too. This would also give special affirmation to Galatians 3:28, "There is neither . . . male nor female, for you are all one in Christ Jesus."

Haddon (1988) proposes a pluralistic approach to worship instead of neutering ecclesiastical language. She developed gender metaphors, drawn from the Bible, from words of familiar Protestant hymns, and from popular theology. Four ways of worship emerged: *Phallic* (Rising, Penetrating, Assertive Style)—God as mighty conqueror, commander-in-chief; victorious over sin and death, fighting the good fight and winning the race; meeting God in the mountaintop experience; bowing down before God and stressing God's majesty and our lowliness; and vertical emphasis in hierarchical polity and church architecture. *Gestative* (Receiving, Nurturing, Serving Style)—God as suffering servant, loving parent, good shepherd, mother hen, compassionate healer, caring friend; bread of life, living water; shadow of a great rock in which to hide, comforter. *Testicular* (Steadfast, Unchanging, Conserving Style)—God is faithful, steadfast, everlasting, Rock of Ages; trustworthy and dependable. *Exertive* (Pushing, Birthing, Transforming Style)—God as Destroyer and Recreator; whom God loves, God chastens; experienced in the "dark night of the soul," being cast into outer darkness; resurrection, always as a complete surprise; Good Friday through Easter morning.

Haddon maintains that the sacrament of Holy Communion is replete with nonphallic meaning, with the cup and its shape recalling images of the Divine womb and in the exertive gender mode using destruction to create new life. The womb theme, she suggests, is like the cup that worshipers view in and down, unlike the phallic imagery that is observed in the upward direction. She mentions that during prayers, the hands may be placed so that palms are brought together with fingers extended. This forms a dark opening where the thumb joints leave a gap, creating a visual pattern resembling female genitals. This brings the service more in balance genderwise.

Analyzing imagery in hymns used over a two-month period in the worship services of three denominations, Haddon (1988:59) found that 63 percent of the imagery was phallic, 17 percent gestative, 15 percent testicular, and 5 percent exertive. She suggests that the appropriate gender pronouns be used with each gender metaphor to highlight the imagery of each. The problem, though, is that the gender metaphors do not avoid the patriarchal phallic stereotypes or those that place females in the passive mode. Seeing the well-like depths of the spirit is all right for gestative imagery, but holding the mountaintop experience as phallic is less than gender-fair or inclusive. For instance, Biale (1982) has argued that "El Shaddai," rendered "Almighty God" in the KJV was actually an Akkadian derivative "shadu," meaning "mountain," and that the original meaning was "breast" (pp. 240-241).

Similarly, Haddon's creating the feminine imagery of "being at rest in God" and "God as suffering servant," while imaging the masculine as "aggressively working for the kingdom," "fight the good fight, win victories for Christ," "all-seeing, powerful," and "commander-in-chief" (the latter image that many women have of Deborah of Judges 4 and 5) places females in a passive mode that would be certain to displease many females. This is an instance of what McGuire (1990) was alluding to in the body as power relations and as social meaning. In some imagery of worship involving the body in religious experience, an androgenous mode—with both genders sharing the same traits—would be the preferable solution. Otherwise at least one gender is very likely to sense rejection or disenfranchisement in the process.

The Body and Prayer, Tefillin, and the Rosary

Prayer: Let us look at the body in prayerful posture. The head is bowed (in some cases, even touching the floor) in supplication, awe, and respect. The hands are folded, perhaps palms brought together with fingers pointing spire-like toward heaven. The shoulders may slope downward in humility, the knees may be bent in kneeling posture, placing the person's entire body at a lower level than one would be in the standing position, with recognition of human frailty and smallness before the almighty God of vast being (omnipotence, omniscience, omnipresence). Often the eyes are closed, perhaps so that no other vision could be seen before the person who should be mindful only of God. Such is the body prayerful, with the use of the entire body in prayer to God. This might also be the position assumed before royalty (at least the bowing) and by beggars beseeching others for alms (the believer coming before the Lord to beg for forgiveness, mercy, and special needs).

Tefillin: The *Tefillin* is a small box containing verses such as Deuteronomy 6:6, "These commandments . . . are to be upon your hearts"; Deuteronomy 6:8, "Tie them as symbols on your hands and bind them on your forehead" or "Bind them as a sign upon your arm, and as symbols before your eyes." These boxes are bound by straps on the forehead and arm for Jews when they recite prayers in the morning.

Tefillah or "prayer" is considered the origin of *tefillin*. The Sh'ma (Deuteronomy 6:4, "Hear, O Israel; The Lord our God, the Lord is one") is recited. The Midrash has pictured God wearing *tefillin*, connoting that there is oneness of the people of Israel. This is the complement of the Sh'ma's oneness of God (Raphael, 1985; Portnoy, 1993; Oler, 1993). Binding to the limb of responsibility and strength and to the eyes and forehead or site of control, thought, and responsibility is symbolic of assuring that the prayers are fixed in the whole body of the believer. The involvement of so many body parts keeps the prayers as an integral part of the person's being. Jews also touch and kiss the *mezuzuh* ("door-post"), a small case with two passages from the Torah (Deuteronomy 6:4-9; 11:13-21) and attached to the entrance doorpost of the home. The kissing and touching are done to show love and respect for God's word and laws. The *tallit* or prayer shawl is a four-cornered garment with fringes that serves as a mnemonic aid and injunction of Torah to keep all of the other laws of God. Jews wrap the fringes of the prayer shawl around their fingers, and they kiss the fringes when they say the word "fringes" (Oler, 1993).

***The Rosary*:** Reciting prayers while wrapping fringes of the *tallit* around the fingers is reminiscent of Roman Catholics reciting the rosary prayers reflecting on Christ or the Virgin Mary while counting rosary beads. On the regular rosary of five decades, a loop and the cross, the believer recites "Our Father," "Hail, Mary," and "Glory be to the Father, to the Son, and to the Holy Spirit." They reflect on the mysteries of the life of Christ and Mary and pray and praise Mary, petitioning her intercession. As their fingers run over the rosary beads, the touch becomes a memory cue for the mind and heart to think and feel meaningfully about the prayers, the whole being then getting in a worshipful posture for prayer (Jordan, 1993).

The Body and Touch

Kelsey (1988) points out the importance of human touch to healing, commenting on the quieting effect of touch. Jesus often healed by touching a part of the body of others that was affected with disease or sin. Physically and psychologically, touch signifies acceptance of our bodies/ourselves by others: the touch involved in healing, anointing, ordaining, greeting a brother or a sister in the faith are examples of such acceptance.

Circumcision

In Judaism, circumcision is done by a mohel on a male infant on the eighth day after birth. According to the Torah law, the priestly blessings are given over the body of the infant during the ceremony in which the foreskin is removed from the infant's penis. The bris or brit is a sign of keeping of the covenant with God and a promise of fertility (increase in numbers) for the Israelites. Wine may be placed on the lips of the infant to lessen the pain, and loving hands placed on the baby's body as a sign of comfort and community. There has been a covenant for female infants in North America, called brit banot ("blessing for girls"). This is a baby-naming ceremony, but nothing physical is done. However, American Jews have also practiced at times simchat bat ("joy of a girl"): The rabbi places his hand on the baby's head and says a blessing for the infant eight days after her birth. The physical act of covenant is footwashing or ear piercing for remembrance of the revelation at Mt. Sinai (Portnoy, 1993).

Footwashing

Footwashing, a practice of some Christian churches today, is referred to in Luke 7:38, John 11:2, 12:1-11, and 13:5-10. Here Mary, sister of Martha, anointed Jesus by wetting his feet with her tears, wiping his feet with her hair, and pouring perfume on them. She was anointing Jesus, in humility and great love, for burial before his crucifixion. Jesus washed his disciples' feet just before the Passover feast and before the time of his death on the cross. Taking off his outer clothing and wrapping a towel around his waist, Jesus poured water into a basin, washed his disciples' feet, and dried them with the towel. Peter did not want Jesus to humble himself by washing his feet, but Jesus told him that unless he washed Peter's feet, Peter could not be identified (have a part) with him. When Peter then wanted Jesus to wash his hands and head, wanting even greater identification with his Lord, Jesus said that a person who has had a bath needs only to wash his feet because his or her whole body is clean. In other words, this was not a physical cleansing but a spiritual one.

As practiced in the Seventh-day Adventist Church today, footwashing or the Service of Humility involves saying a prayer for the footwashing partner before washing the partner's feet. This is done after each person has forgiven others' errors and has asked others to forgive her or his errors. After the footwashing, the Eucharist follows with the symbolic taking in of the bread/body and grape juice/blood of Christ in celebrating the new spiritual body of the resurrected Christ. This is then sometimes followed by anointing of the congregants by the minister. Thus, there is humbling, forgiveness, praying for each other, and spiritual cleansing, identifying with the resurrected Christ in spiritual triumph and renewed spirit of mission, and anointing to go forth in love and invigorated spirit of spreading the word of the gospel of the Lord (Meyers, 1993).

In the Old Testament footwashing was a rite of hospitality, with hosts washing the dusty feet of their guests when the guests arrived at their homes. In the New Testament, footwashing is an ordinance. White (1898) thought that this ordinance of humility was to make our hearts tender toward one another. As currently practiced in the Seventh-day Adventist Church, however, women and men, girls and boys are segregated for the footwashing ordinance. The excuse proffered for such segregation is that it would be "immodest" for women to take off their stockings in front of men or for men to have to deal with kneeling before a woman's skirt or perhaps undergarments. Even married couples do not wash each other's feet. Such an explanation does not answer the question of why girls and boys do not wash each others' feet, since the children usually wear socks and the girls are generally careful to keep their skirts close to their bodies. Too, most women do not remove their pantyhose or stockings for this ordinance but place their feet in the washbowl or pail with stockings on, and their partners easily towel-dry their feet in seconds (Rayburn, 1993).

The Eucharist

The Eucharist, with its allusions to body and blood, which might be rendered flesh and blood, has much involvement with the body in religious experience. Bishop (1992) prefers *soma* or "body" being reserved for the whole composed by the flesh and blood combined. The whole person is expressed as flesh and blood, as two extremes such as body and soul or flesh and bones. When Jesus invited the disciples to partake of the bread and wine representing his body and blood, or of his entire identity or being, he was focusing on the spirit of the Lord. Bishop points out that the blood would need to reproduce the spirit for it to be appropriate to consume it. The blood of a sacrifice should only be poured out at the base of the altar, so drinking that would be an abomination. Psychologically, Jesus is asking the Christian community to feed on his body and blood until he returns in the second coming. Such body and blood would become the actual life and personality of the risen Lord (at least, from the Roman Catholic perspective), through identification of the community with Christ. So it is the nurturing Christ who transforms the being of his followers by feeding them with his spiritual being. The resurrected rather than the mortal body of Christ is the focus of the sacramental rite of the Eucharist. The faithful emulate the one whom they love: the Lord, their Savior. By repeating this act, they become like Christ, identifying with his sacrifice, suffering, death, and resurrection and victory over death. Christ experienced death, but not destruction of the body forever nor death for all time—nor will his believers die for all time. Great hope of salvation and comfort of life everafter is promised to Christ's followers.

Laying-on-of-Hands and Anointing

The laying-on-of-hands involves the gifts and rights of an office. Deuteronomy 34:9 says: "Joshua the son of Nun was full of the spirit of wisdom, for Moses had laid his hands upon him." Acts 6:6, speaking of Stephen, Philip, and others set aside for holy service, says: "These they set before the apostles, and they prayed and laid their hands upon them." When Barnabas and Saul were being set aside for God's work, Acts 13:3 relates: "Then after fasting and praying, they laid their hands on them and sent them off." 1 Timothy 4:14 commands: "Do not neglect the gift you have, which was given you by prophetic utterance when the elders laid their hands upon you." In 2 Timothy 1:6 we read: "I remind you to rekindle the gift of God that is within you through the laying on of my hands." Thus, laying-on-of-hands connotes being set aside, consecrated as in the act of ordination of holy office, and being sent on a holy mission or quest.

Closely related to laying-on-of-hands is anointing. Anointing is usually done by putting a drop of oil on the finger of the minister or elder and then that person touches the forehead of the one to be anointed with that oil, verbalizing a blessing and prayer for the person. The women came to Jesus' sepulcher on Easter morning to anoint his body but they found that he was no longer in the grave, Thus Christ, the Messiah or "anointed one," was only anointed before death and by the woman Mary, who then represented the incarnate faithful church at the time of Christ's abandonment by all others on earth (de Dietrich, 1961; Argyle, 1963).

Platt (1977) commented that a primary function of Israel's prophets, such as Nathan and Samuel, was to anoint the king's head with holy oil, in much the same way as they would conduct a royal coronation. Exodus 28:41 says of Aaron's sons at their priestly anointing: "Anoint them and ordain them and consecrate them, that they may serve me as priests." Mary of Bethany represented woman standing in the prophetic office for Israel when she anointed Christ as Messiah of the House of David, anointing the King of kings with precious, royal ointment.

Baptism

In baptism, all who believe in Christ as the savior, are invited to go down to a watery grave and arise in resurrection symbolically with Christ. This is also a spiritual cleansing, as well as a rite of Christian invitation, involving the whole body. Originally, the entire body was immersed in water at a river or in a baptistry, and some denominations of Christianity still practice total immersion. Other churches do symbolic immersion by pouring or sprinkling water on the one professing belief in Christ as Savior. Baptism took place in the time of Moses, when it was connected to laws of purification (Exodus 30:17-21; Leviticus 11:25), indicating washing or cleansing (Bryant, 1967). Jews were also baptized as an act of repentance and as remission of sins, readying the body for the coming of the Messiah (Bryant, 1967).

The Mikvah

Related to baptism is the *mikvah*. The *mikvah* is the ritual bath into which the convert to Judaism must immerse her or his body to be spiritually cleansed. Jews clean their bodies well before coming to the *mikvah*, not a physical but a spiritual cleansing, a rebirth and a recleaning.

Niddah, Hebrew for "a menstruating woman," "Menstruation," "separation," "seclusion," and "a woman who has been separated while she is menstruating and for a time after her menstrual flow has ended" (Wasserfall, 1992), must follow specific legal codes concerning the *mikvah*. Sexual relations are prohibited for the wife and husband while she is menstruating and seven days after the end of the period. Women count five days for menstruation and add seven days of purity (she must verify daily that no emission of menstrual blood occurs during this time). After the period of purity, women immerse their bodies in the *mikvah* before they resume sexual relations.

At childbirth, similar restrictions apply (Leviticus 12:1-8). For the birth of a boy, women are in severe impurity for seven days and lesser impurity for an additional thirty-three days. For the birth of a girl, both of these periods are doubled. Thus, the gender of the body once again gives the disadvantage to females. Further, a man who had many relations with a menstruating woman was threatened with *karet* (being cut off from the community). Focused on preserving the purity of the temple cult, these biblical codes remained in force even after the second temple was destroyed in 70 C.E. (Wasserfall, 1992).

To take part in the *mikvah*, there must be no barrier between the body and the cleansing water: No nail polish, contact lenses, jewelry, or clothing must be on that would act as an impediment (Oler, 1993; Portnoy, 1993).

Wasserfall (1992) studied the meaning of *niddah* for Moroccan women immigrants to Israel. The ritual bath or *mikvah* ends the period of separation that follows menstruation. Older women in this study sometimes neglected the physical appearance of their bodies during their menstruation, a time when they must avoid being near or touching their husbands. Perhaps they are making it easier for their husbands to abstain from desiring sexual intercourse with them during this time. Practicing *niddah*, like all *mitzvot* (religious obligations) offers the possibility of nonperformance. Choosing to practice it, however, establishes a connection between identity and religion. While menstruation is very important to female identity in making a woman out of a girl, the *mikvah* is a sign of this developmental change and makes a Jewish woman out of a menstruating woman. Thus, through the physiological event, there is a link between personal and collective identities. Menstrual blood becomes the symbol of feminine essence, potential conception, construction of the Jewish household, the coming of age for females, and the continuity of the Jewish people. In regard to personal health, menstruation cleanses the woman and is thought to be healthy for her. To women, menstruation is a sign of virility and fertility (St. Hoyme, 1993).

As to why menstrual blood is seen as both a "sickness" and as a cleansing and gaining possible longer life is suggested by Wasserfall (1992) to be the connection between the prohibition against Jews eating blood and the restrictions on menstrual blood. Since blood is held to be the essence of life, swallowing blood would be mixing life and blood because blood from a dead animal would be used for nourishment. Since menstrual blood indicates that opportunity for conception has been missed, the possibility for a new birth has been lost. Both situations concerning blood, then, involve a repugnant mixing of life and death. Too, sexual intercourse is seen as dangerous to a potential infant, since menstrual blood, linked with death, could mingle with the potential blood of the infant. This connection is held despite women knowing that conception at the time of menstrual flow is extremely unlikely to occur. Nonetheless, women become those who bear simultaneously the signs of life and death within themselves. Besides *niddah* involving renewal of the sexual intimacy once the woman returns from the *mikvah*, it is symbolically where division of power between wife and husband is carried out: the husband sends his wife to the *mikvah*, but the bargaining power of the man and woman over sexual relations and going to the *mikvah* becomes a power game in which the spouse who is labeled as having more sexual need is perceived as the loser. This is the use of the body as power and social meaning, here as the symbolic manipulation of sexuality. Denial of desire hides a desire for symbolic and social power. Men are forbidden to masturbate, and women can emerge as winners in power relations games by postponing the *mikvah* and increasing their husbands' desires for sex.

The Sexual Body

Commenting on sexuality and religious experience, Kelsey and Kelsey (1986) speak of Song of Songs as pure erotic and graphic love poetry that celebrates and glorifies passionate physical love, physical beauty, and attractiveness. Symbolic of continuous and never failing love of God, the deepest and most intimate love and sexual intimacy with lover and beloved symbolized, by contrast, the even greater love of God for the people of God. This use of the body also is significant because it is the one place in scripture in which humanness is stressed in appreciation for the sexual and for loving intimate relations. That which is often held to be secular is now put in the context of the sacred and totally acceptable. This is a true instance of recapturing embodiment in the mindful body, reality of being in the world, and having to relate with others in a socially meaningful way.

Ruth and the Relative-Redeemer

In Ruth 3, Ruth performs a series of body rituals in announcing to her late husband's relative that he is next in line to carry on her husband's family name and to give him heirs by marrying her. Instructed in the procedure by her mother-in-law, Ruth washed and perfumed her body and dressed in her best clothes. After Boaz, the relative, was done with his dinner, he lay down to sleep. Ruth then went and uncovered Boaz's feet and lay down at them. Later that night, when Boaz discovered Ruth at his feet, she told him that she was his servant and asked him to spread the corner of his garment over her because he was her relative-redeemer. That this was not an act of seduction by either person is shown by Boaz' sending Ruth away before it could be discovered that she came to him. He was to act as her redeemer, her rescuer, at once an act of respect and loving kindness on the parts of both people. Her humbling act encouraged his respect and love toward her, and he followed the religious prescription of the times for a widow who was a kin.

Dancing, Singing, and Clapping: Making a Joyful Noise

We have the image of religious celebration by dancing, singing, clapping, and in general making a joyful noise (Psalm 100; 149:3; 150:4). In 2 Samuel 6:14-16, we are told that, when King David moved the ark of God from Obed-Edom to the City of David with rejoicing, he wore a linen *ephod*, "danced before the Lord with all his might, while he and the entire house of Israel brought up the ark of the Lord with shouts and the sound of trumpets . . . King David leaping and dancing before the Lord." This seems to be the equivalent of "jumping for joy," in a spiritual sense. Perhaps related to dancing spiritually for joy and making a joyful noise is the glossalalia or speaking in tongues and interpreting the message (1 Corinthians 14), in its ecstatic and joyful experience, primitive frenzy, deep religious emotion, fulfillment, and release. Both give a sense of nearness to God. Kelsey (1964) speaks of glossalalia as "a spontaneous utterance of uncomprehended and seemingly random speech sounds, usually accompanied by a sense of joy and deep religious emotion" (p.12). Speaking in tongues (and here "tongues" refers to the experience and to the expression of "language") is also mentioned in Acts 2:4 and Mark 16:17.

Mourning Rituals

The Jewish mourning rituals involve the body to a great extent in religious experience. After the burial of a loved one, Jews sit *shiva*, a three to five day period of mourning ritual. They may "rend" or cut/tear a corner of their clothing, or in the more modern version they pin a small black ribbon that the rabbi gives them at the graveside onto their clothing. The ribbon has a small cut in it to show disruption or a tearing asunder of their lives by the loss of a loved one. At the *shiva* house of the deceased's family or relatives, the family sits on the floor or on a small and often hard chair to experience physical discomfort to represent the emotional and spiritual pain and suffering that the loss has brought about. All mirrors and other glass surfaces may be covered during the time of mourning so as not to reflect their sorrow. While they go through a specific period of mourning, they are not to feel excess sorrow for themselves but are to get back to living as soon as possible and not "die with the dead." Prayers are offered at the *shiva* and at the synagogue by the rabbi and nine other people, forming the *minyan* (in many synagogues, women now share in this experience). Jews *davan* in prayer, swaying back and forth with their bodies while chanting the Torah and other religious texts. This is a whole body experience, with the making of a joyful noise in celebration before God in prayer and adoration. To *davan* and form a *minyan* are not limited to mourning rituals.

Greeting of Peace

In some Christian churches, there is a ceremony called "passing of the peace" or "greeting of peace." In the Roman Catholic Church, this is done at high mass. The kiss of peace is passed from one congregant to another, with a kiss on the cheek and hands on the shoulders to embrace or to give a hug. The recipient of the embrace usually put her or his hands under the elbow of the passer of peace. Each would then say, "The peace of the Lord Jesus Christ be with you." The kiss and embrace are signs of loving kindness of one believer toward another believer in the community of Christians. It is a bodily symbol of fellowship (Jordan, 1993).

Gendered Bodies

Concerning gendered bodies, Queen Vashti (Esther 1) suffered humiliation when her drunken husband, King Xerxes, determined to bring her before his male guest to be put on display as his beautiful property. When she refused to be so maltreated, her husband became furious and consulted his legal experts (of course, all males!). These experts advised the king to depose the queen, "for the queen's conduct will become known to all the women, and so they will despise their husbands and say, 'King Xerxes commanded Queen Vashti to be brought before him, but she would not come.' This very day the Persian and Median women of the nobility who have heard about the queen's conduct will respond to all the king's nobles in the same way. There will be no end of disrespect and discord." The king was advised to depose the queen. "Then when the king's edict is proclaimed throughout all his vast realm, all the women will respect their husbands, from the least to the greatest." So, what began with a drunken attempt to insult and deeply humiliate the queen became a justification by an egoistic and loutish ruler to replace his wife and for the men of his palace to keep all women in submission, no matter what treatment they suffered from their husbands. Such is the social meaning of the gendered body, and in some parts of the world still is.

Judges 19 tells the story of a Levite and his concubine, who is called "a girl" throughout the account until Judges 19:26. At that point in the narrative, after she and a Benjamite's virgin daughter were offered to rapists to be ravaged in place of the Levite, she was finally called "woman." The concubine, who alone was sacrificed in the end to save the Levite, died after being raped and otherwise abused all night, and then her body was cut in twelve parts by the Levite and sent to all areas of Israel. Thus was the difference in value placed upon the female and the male body. While the man is called "husband" (Judges 19:3) and he has a "father-in-law" (the "concubine's" father), she is never accorded the status of "wife" but is treated more like a slave or chattel. So the Judges 19 incident is also an example of the political use of the body, with males coming out the undisputed winner over females through societal brutality toward the female body/being.

As mentioned, Haddon (1988) discusses God and the engendered body by body metaphors and their use in experiencing God images in worship. Hood and Hall (1980) studied gender differences in the description of erotic and mystical experiences. In mystical experiences, there have been reports of ego loss in the sense of the ego turning inward and being transformed. The Western approach to mysticism is often seen as "masculine," in that entering and more active orientation is implied, or agentive orientation. Eastern mysticism is more receptive (at least, as seen by Hood and Hall), or "feminine" in that the individual is entered by that with which it is to be united or unified with. Thus, there could be some relationship between eroticism and mysticism, with descriptive terms bearing a relationship to typical experiences of males and females when they are being sexually intimate. However, "erotic" did not necessarily mean "sexual intercourse" in the descriptions written about erotic experience. For the mystical experiences, the subjects were asked about times when they felt an "undifferentiated state of awareness or a consciousness of simply being," "to be a part of or united with reality" (Hood and Hall, 1980:199). Words were also selected to represent mainly agentive orientations (entering or penetrating), mainly receptive (absorbing or flooding), and neutral (fascinating or satisfying). They concluded that males described erotic experiences in agentive terms but mystical experiences in receptive as frequently as agentive terms. Females were found to have descriptions of experience in eroticism and mysticism that paralleled their actual experiences. Further, both females and males cited sexuality as a catalyst of mystical experience, but they do not necessarily see sexual experiences as the same thing as mystical experiences.

In the study of Hood and Hall (1980), females tended to receptively experience both eroticism and mysticism. Males, however, did not describe their mystical experiences in agentive terms. The explanation given for this was that a male God with male methaphors for God and male figures for incarnate God (Christ, Buddha, etc.) do not lend themselves easily to males describing erotic and mystical union with a male God.

Carmelite nuns, who consider themselves as the "brides of Christ" can easily relate to the male image of God for mystical and erotic bodily experiences. It was concluded that females might have more religious sensitivity because of the ease with which their experiences can be conceptualized due to a more socially acceptable masculine God-image.

This study is also a reflection of the political use of the body in religious experience: Females are the products and the victims of an extremely gender-biased society in which to be more agentive (acting upon, doing, causing, initiating) would be construed by some as "playing the whore," being immoral, being promiscuous. Females cannot be seen as mere passive receptacles into which other things go, are accepted, or are received or allowed to enter.

Too often and too unfairly, females have been seen as having a passive, receptive-only role in erotic experiences with males, more fitting to a description of a static, passive receptacle like a key hole to a key or a socket to a plug than to a female to a male. Females have been socialized to fear ownership of their assertive actions, particularly as these actions involve sexuality.

Females have been conditioned from early childhood to be the "nice little girl, to behave like a lady," and to assume a passive role, whether that meets their needs or is truly their personality or, for that fact, their biology. It would be more productive and more accurate to conceive of females being agentive as well—when societal taboos are stripped away from expectations of females—with females as latching onto, grabbing, and surrounding in an active, agentive way just as males do in a penetrating and entering way. Then both males and females could be allowed to be both agentive and receptive with each other, both taking and giving in a reciprocal and alternating relationship. Too, the male metaphors of God, without female images to balance them, prohibit healthy identity of females with their Creator in whose image they too were created. What Hood and Hall may be documenting, then, are the effects of socialization in expressing descriptive terms for eroticism and mysticism, which is an important part of the story but not the last chapter.

Male biases in interpreting scripture can be noted in the account of woman being created from the rib of man. A rib is one of the paired curved bony or partly cartilaginous rods stiffening the body walls and protecting the viscera. The Genesis 2:22-23 account of woman being made from the rib of man is "So the Lord God caused the man to fall into a deep sleep; and while he was sleeping, he took one of the man's ribs and closed up the place with flesh. The Lord God made a woman from the rib he had taken out of the man." Noteworthy is the symbolic nature of the rib: It is not by itself a vital part of the body, since there are many pairs of ribs going down the back. The important aspect about the rib, however, is that physically a rib is part of a *pair*, thus symbolizing that this made man and woman equals and each were part of a pair. Then both can say, "This is now bone of my bones, and flesh of my flesh" (Genesis 2:23), for both together as one complete whole, "they will become one flesh" (Genesis 2:24).

The Body and Political Power

In addition to the political uses of the body as seen in Vashti (Esther 1), the concubine in Judges 19, and the females and males in the Hood and Hall (1980) study, there is the political power shown in Samuel being instructed by God to pick Saul for king of Israel. In 1 Samuel 9:1, we are told that Saul was "an impressive young man without equal among the Israelites . . . a head taller than any of the others." The KJV expresses Saul's height in this way: "From his shoulders and upward he was higher than any of the people." So, body size in the sense of height meant power relations and political strength. The account of David and Goliath (1 Samuel 17) shows another instance of body size and power relations, with a nine-foot-tall giant who fought for the dreaded enemy of Israel, the Philistines. When the young and far smaller David asked in deep religious faith how anyone dared to defy the army of the living God, he decided to fight the giant with stones and a sling. Not by his size, but through his faith and through God's might, David won for Israel over Goliath and the Philistines. Here the usual power and political strength of humans were not allowed to triumph over God's chosen leader. David's smaller size served to highlight that not David's but God's might was that which vanquished the enemy of God's people.

In the account of Ruth being told by Naomi in Ruth 2:20 that Boaz "is our close relative; he is one of our kinsman-redeemers," Ruth is saved from the vulnerability and socially undesirable and lowly esteemed position of widow by, in effect, being bought as part of a package deal with a piece of land that belonged to her husband. She had laid down at Boaz' feet, in recognition of her male relative's political power and position to redeem her from her position of little political power.

Rayburn (1993) pointed out that the rituals of footwashing, of laying-on-of-hands in ordination, and the Lord's Supper have usually included officiating males but not females. This has led to acceptance and empowerment for males and rejection and disenfranchisement for females. In the case of footwashing, women are usually not permitted to wash the feet of men, even their fathers, brothers, or husbands. Men wash each other's feet, and women wash other women's feet. Girls and boys, even siblings, do not wash each other's feet. In denominations in which there are clergywomen, these women can ordain other pastors and elders. However, not all denominations have clergywomen. Women are often not allowed to hand out the bread and wine in the eucharist, especially in denominations without female clergy. In such instances, women may only be involved in bringing in the bread and wine and in uncovering the platters on which these elements are placed. If women from girlhood have been treated as inferior and lacking in power in ritual in their denominational settings, they will transfer this poor self-image to other settings—home, workplace, and community. They will strive for little because they have been taught to see themselves as less worthy than males and less important in the eyes of God because they are not males.

Jews as an Embodied People

Jews themselves are both People of the Book and People of the Body, since the human body was the field on which conflicting cultural impulses came together in battle. Eilberg-Schwartz (1992a) looks at the Jews themselves and their body image or stereotypes. Defending themselves against the image of having a primitive religion, unacceptable to Christian and rationalist tastes, Jews wanted to spiritualize Judaism and to rid it of lower practices and texts that involved bodily functions and the body. Jews were stereotyped in European minds as having long noses, big feet, menstruating men, sexually alluring women, and more primal and animalistic natures and thus being more embodied than white, Protestant European males.

Jews were doubly cursed. They were thought to be inferior because of bodily defects (weak feet and bodies, often resulting from lack of adequate physical exercise). Thus, Jews were seen as inadequately embodied. They were also held to be too embodied, too near to nature and gross bodily senses, and as having concrete ways of thinking embodied in rituals and aimed at matters of the flesh. They chose to escape embodiment through spiritualization of their tradition and, by extension, themselves as Jews. Suppressing concern with the body, they sought an identity as a "People of the Book." Orthodox Jews maintained more embodiment, though. Pursuit of embodiment also took place, especially among Zionist thinkers who wanted to strengthen anemic, pale, weakened Jewish bodies frail from underdevelopment, too little physical work-out and over-emphasis on spirituality and learning (disembodiment). Thus, the Jews seek to create a balance in their image as both People of the Book and People of the Body.

CONCLUSION

We have looked at the body as a whole, albeit a possible abstraction of wholeness as Eilberg-Schwartz would argue. Scripture is rich in body allusions in religious experience. Thus, if there has been a disembodiment in religious experience, it has occurred to satisfy a dualism of mind/body, sacred/secular, and spirit/flesh in which splitting of body and mind have come about. To reconcile the parts into a meaningful whole and reconstruct the complete picture in the light of scripture and traditions built around scripture not only enriches our imagery and understanding but also brings back to religious experience the fullness that was intended from the beginning. Such reconciliation also promises the possibility of more meaningful ways to study religious experiences of the embodied, as McGuire so cogently recommended.

Looking at embodiment once again, and with more open eyes and minds, breathes new life into scripture and into biblical metaphors, bringing new vitality for all who would study and refer to scripture in teaching, preaching, and in the comparative study of religion. Once we make the conscientious effort to include embodiment in what we read, we will no longer gloss over the compelling descriptions to bodily allusions which give us the complete picture and more accurate understanding: We will be learning the whole rather than just the various parts of the words and experiences of religion. We will also have a more comprehensive picture of how the parts fit together in working as a whole. Only then will we truly gain an appreciation for the complexity of the human being in religious experiences, a totality of the biological/physiological, psychological/sociological, and spiritual/religious.

NOTES AND REFERENCES

1. For biblical references, except where otherwise noted, the New International Version (NIV) is used. Otherwise, the King James Version (KJV) is the reference.

Alpert, R.
1992 Challenging male/female complementarity: Jewish lesbians and the Jewish tradition. In *People of the Body: Jews and Judaism from an embodied perspective*, edited by H. Eilberg-Schwartz. Albany, NY: State University of New York Press.

Argyle, A. W.
1963 *Cambridge bible commentary: The gospel according to Matthew*. Cambridge: Cambridge University Press.

Biale, D.
1982 The God with breasts: El Shaddai in the bible. *History of Religions*. 20:240-256.
Bishop, J.
1992 *Some bodies: The Eucharist and its implications*. Macon, GA: Mercer University Press.
Bryant, T. A.
1967 *New compact bible dictionary*. Grand Rapids, MI: Zondervan.
de Dietrich, S.
1961 *The layman's bible commentary: Matthew*. Richmond, VA: John Knox.
Eilberg-Schwartz, H.
1992a Introduction: People of the body. In *People of the body: Jews and Judaism from an embodied perspective*, edited by H. Eilberg-Schwartz. Albany, NY: State University of New York.
1992b The problem of the body for the people of the book. In *People of the body: Jews and Judaism from an embodied perspective*, edited by H. Eilberg-Schwartz. Albany, NY: State University of New York.
Haddon, G. P.
1988 *Body metaphors: Releasing God-feminine in us all*. New York: Crossroad.
Hood Jr., R. W., and J. R. Hall
1980 Gender differences in the description of erotic and mystical experiences. *Review of Religious Research*. 21:195-207.
Jordan, M. E.
1993 Personal communication with the Reverend Milton E. Jordan, Ph.D., Mother Seton Parish, Germantown, MD, November 4, 1993.
Kelsey, M. T.
1964 *Tongue speaking: An experiment in spiritual experience*. Garden City, NY: Doubleday.
1988 *Psychology, medicine and Christian healing*: San Francisco: Harper & Row.
Kelsey, M. T. and B. Kelsey
1986 *Sexuality and the sacred*. Rockport, MA: Shaftesbury Dorset.
McGuire, M. B.
1990 Religion and the body: Rematerializing the human body in the social sciences of religion. *Journal for the Scientific Study of Religion*. 29:293-296.
Meyers, M. R.
1993 Personal communication with Pastor Michael R. Meyers, I, Alpha Seventh-day Adventist Church, Austin, TX, September 26, 1993.
Oler, I. D.
1993 Personal communication with Rabbi Dr. I. David Oler, Washington Pastoral Counseling Service, Silver Spring, MD, November 3, 1993.
Platt, E. E.
1977 The ministry of Mary of Bethany. *Theology Today*. 34:29-39.
Portnoy, M. A.
1993 Personal communication with Rabbi Mindy A. Portnoy, Temple Sinai, Washington, DC, November 4, 1993.
Raphael, C.
1985 *The Sabbath evening service*. New York: Behrman House.
Rayburn, C. A.
1993 Ritual as acceptance/empowerment and rejection/disenfranchisement. In *Women and religious ritual*, edited by A. Northup. Washington, DC: Pastoral Press.
St. Hoyme, L. E.
1993 Personal communication with Dr. Lucile E. St. Hoyme, Physical Anthropologist Emeritus and Curator Emeritus, Smithsonian Institution, Washington, DC, October 16-17.
Wasserfall, R.
1992 Menstruation and identity: The meaning of niddah for Morrocan women immigrants to Israel. In *People of the body: Jews and Judaism from an embodied perspective*, edited by H. Eilberg-Schwartz. Albany, NY: State University of New York Press.
White, E. G.
1898 *Review and Herald*. 75:22, May 31, 1898.

21

Transpersonal Theory and Religious Experience

SUSAN F. GREENWOOD

What Is Transpersonal Theory?

Some immediate questions probably occur to those not familiar with the term "transpersonal": What *is* it? Doesn't the term sound suspiciously unacademic? Why does the topic appear in a scholarly handbook? In addressing these questions, this chapter first examines the theory as well as the explicit history of the term "transpersonal," summarizes different viewpoints, and ends with criticisms of transpersonal work. The second half of the chapter uses criticisms to construct theory that relies on an implicit history grounded in the work of the sociologist Émile Durkheim and the psychiatrist C. G. Jung, a pioneer in transpersonal psychology. Definitions of religious experience and transpersonal theory follow this history. The chapter concludes by citing relevant work in the natural as well as the social sciences.

"Transpersonal," literally meaning "across or beyond the individual person or psyche," has been the designation given from about 1967 to the study of religious or spiritual experiences that involve assumptions not part of traditional scientific methodology (Sundberg and Keutzer, 1984:441). These assumptions include not only the possibility of altered, paranormal, and mystical states of consciousness, higher entities, and ultimate purposes, but also the meaningfulness and validity of these phenomena.

Transpersonal research, the latest major movement within psychology, is characterized as the discipline's fourth force. It succeeds behaviorism (the first force), psychoanalytic theory (the second force), and humanistic psychology (the third force) (Sundberg and Keutzer, 1984:441). It is consciousness research with particular interest in nonordinary states described as religious experiences. The terms "transpersonal psychology" and "transpersonal psychotherapy" are often used interchangeably and deal with theory and practice in varying degrees (e.g., Vaughan, 1986; 1991). Comprehensive bibliographies on transpersonal psychotherapy and psychology may be found in Boorstein (1980:387-398) and Tart (1992:451-471). Within the last few years the more inclusive term "transpersonal theory" has been introduced.

Transpersonal theory and religious experience are inextricably linked, as researchers struggle to clarify the theory which enhances understanding of the experience. Religious experience as addressed by transpersonal theory encompasses 1) the varieties named by James ([1902] 1961); 2) the kinds outlined in other chapters of this book; 3) transcendent experiences that seem to lift people outside of themselves or that engender a feeling of connectedness or cosmic unity (e.g., Underhill, [1911] 1990); 4) reported paranormal experiences including "channeling," or receiving information from a nonphysical intelligence (e.g., Hastings, 1991); near-death and out-of-body experiences (e.g., Moody, 1988); 5) religious dreams (e.g., Hood and Morris, 1992); and 6) a diversity of topics on recent consciousness research—meditation, healing, dying, for example (McNeill and Guion, 1991). In other words, the kinds of religious experiences addressed by transpersonal theory are not limited. Often, though, these experiences, as Walsh (1992:20) laments, are seen to be "insignificant at best or pathological at worst." Scientific research into these experiences based on transpersonal theory provides a different starting point.

Yet beneath the seeming objectivity of a theory which may shed light on subjective experience lies a paradox: Religious experience may in fact be the object from which the subjectivity of transpersonal theory is derived. Is it possible that what seems objective in our everyday world could actually be subjective?

Like the Hindu veil of *maya*—the illusion of the everyday world—to which the philosopher Schopenhauer was so fond of referring, layers of what seem to be objective reality may obscure a deeper perception attested to by scores of time-honored religious figures and mystics, as noted by Granfield (1991). This higher awareness has been characterized by Stace (1960) as common to mystical experiences, studied by Maslow (1970) as peak experiences, argued by Greeley (1974) as a capacity built into the structure of human personality, and outlined by various authors in Tart (1992) as integral to seven great spiritual traditions. Studying and attaining this level of perception may well be a significant outcome as research expands the meaning of human consciousness (e.g., Ornstein, 1973, Hood, 1975; Grof, 1975; Grof and Bennett, 1993).

Growing interest in transpersonal work is revealed by the fact that I found several hundred articles listed since 1980 in a multijournal database under the heading of "transpersonal." Also from 1989 to 1992 sixty master's and doctoral theses cited in *Dissertation Abstracts* were classified under the heading "transpersonal." Thirty-five of these theses were written under the aegis of APA-certified graduate programs.

Many academicians might wonder whether the designation of "theory" is accurate and whether this kind of investigation can gain legitimacy. Again questions arise: Can scientific method be used to evaluate that which is beyond the ken of the five senses? Is this kind of research so near the fringe of faddish New Age beliefs and practices that it will be given no credence in academia?

Indeed, some psychologists have been scathing in their assessment of transpersonal research; these criticisms are reviewed later. On the other hand, impeccably credentialed researchers are increasingly dissatisfied with statistical analysis as an explanatory tool. They believe new approaches are needed to answer aeons-old religious and spiritual questions. For them the Holy Grail of positivism has lost some of its earlier luster. Polkinghorne (1983), for example, reviews systems of inquiry, offers new research strategies for studying human behavior, and provides an extensive bibliography.

To understand the reasoning behind these new approaches, we now turn to the history of the word "transpersonal."

Origins of "Transpersonal"

The Oxford English Dictionary (Simpson and Weiner, 1989:Vol. XVIII:420) offers a summary of usage dating from William James's 1905-6 invocation of the term in a lecture series. James, a founder of American psychology, was from the beginning critical of a purely naturalistic study of psychology and especially of religious experience (Hood, 1992). Vich (1988:109) cites James's first documented use of "transpersonal": "Phenomenalism or idealism is usually accused . . . of denying the 'objective' import of experience. It is important in discussion to disentangle certain ambiguities in the word 'objective' as used here. That an idea represents an 'object' may mean that it represents something . . . trans-personal—as when my object is also your object." James's words reverberate with nineteenth-century philosophy of representationalism in which the sensing mind is presumed to apprehend objects through ideas which stand for—represent—the object (Flew, 1984:305). Representationalism transcended the Cartesian subject-object split and pervaded the intellectual climate in which Durkheim and Jung wrote, as discussed later.

Vich (1988:108) notes that Jung's 1917 word "*überpersonlich*" was first translated as superpersonal and then as transpersonal. Another entry in *The Oxford English Dictionary* (Simpson and Weiner, 1989:Vol. XVIII:420) for "transpersonal," dated 1968, draws from the *Journal for Humanistic Psychology*: "Transpersonal (or Fourth Force) Psychology is the title given to an emerging force in the psychology field by a group of psychologists and professional men and women . . . who are interested in . . . *ultimate* human capacities and potentialities." Specifically, this research included exceptional levels of psychological health, meditation, and altered states of consciousness, including the effects of psychedelic drugs (Sundberg and Keutzer, 1984:441).

At about this time interest peaked in the possibility that psychedelic drugs provided therapeutically helpful religious or mystical experiences. Researchers studied the effects of these drugs before legal, psychological, and physiological problems emerged. See Clark (1969), Grof (1975), and Wulff's (1991:184-188) summary of an experiment in drug-induced mysticism. Interestingly, Chaudhuri (in Tart, 1992:270) states that most religious gurus warn against drugs, though one has called drug use the "back door method to God." Grof and Bennett (1993) eventually turned their attention to developing therapeutic techniques—hyperventilation, music, and bodywork—to duplicate heightened awareness without the use of drugs.

The fourth force stemmed directly from Abraham Maslow's third force humanistic psychology and Roberto Assagioli's work on psychosynthesis (Washburn, 1988:2). Humanistic psychology was a plea to escape from the narrow confines of behaviorism and to establish the importance of human values in research. Yet according to Walsh and Vaughan (1984:442), Maslow eventually found humanistic psychology inadequate to account for extraordinary states of consciousness. He first began using the term "transpersonal" around 1967 in correspondence with Stanislav Grof (Vich, 1988:107).

Maslow understood "transpersonal" as "beyond individuality, beyond the development of the individual person into something which is more inclusive than the individual person" (Vich, 1988:107). Maslow (1970) believed his studies of peak experiences revealed essential religious experiences. These studies provided the impetus for the formal launching in 1969 of *The Journal for Transpersonal Psychology* with Anthony Sutich as the first editor. Sutich (in Boorstein, 1980), therefore, became a key figure in establishing both the humanistic and transpersonal schools.

Words describing kinds of religious experience have appeared year after year in *The Journal of Transpersonal Psychology*. Lajoie, Shapiro, and Roberts (1991:177) note these terms: peak experiences, ecstasy, mystical experience, essence, bliss, awe, wonder, unitive consciousness, oneness, cosmic awareness, cosmic play, spirit sacralization of everyday life, and individual and species-wide synergy.

The next section summarizes what "transpersonal" means for different writers and researchers.

Transpersonal Perspectives

As the following excerpts illustrate, transpersonal psychology provided new ways to study and analyze religious experience. Vaughan (1982:39) writes that transpersonal psychology "acknowledges the importance of bringing about a balance of inner and outer experience and awareness, recognizing that these are two sides of a mutually interdependent reality."

Wilber acknowledges this overall bipolar and transpersonal nature of experience through a comprehensive approach to human evolution (1981), through a detailed treatment of physical, mental, and spiritual ways of knowing (1983a), and through a sociological method for identifying authentic religions (1983b). He (1983b:106) calls attention to the multidisciplinary nature of transpersonal theory by stating that "'transpersonal sociology' is a discipline desperately awaiting birth."

In discussing Leibniz's and Huxley's use of the term "perennial philosophy," which refers to the transcendental essence of the great religions, Wilber (1983a:155) notes that the notion of "nonduality" lies at its core. This means that "reality is neither one nor many, neither permanent nor dynamic, neither separate nor unified, neither pluralistic nor holistic."

For Mann (1984:119) transpersonal psychology "is defined by the primary place it gives to the concept of the absolute in its analysis of human life . . . [but it] . . . should not be confused with a commitment to any specific imagery, formulation, or spiritual practice." He (p.142) also states that "we are the primary case of our own research."

A "transpersonal-spiritual" approach is one of four ways of understanding the unconscious, according to Caputi (1984). In summarizing a number of theorists' views, Caputi (pp. 136-137) notes that most share a belief that the unconscious links people to a world which includes "God, gods, angels, ancestors, and other transpersonal entities, beings, or powers." Caputi also provides further links of the unconscious to Schopenhauer and the Romantic heritage which influenced Durkheim and Jung.

Echoing the specific definition in *The Oxford English Dictionary*, Sundberg and Keutzer (1984:441) write that transpersonal psychologists see the emerging discipline as an "integration of ancient wisdom and modern science and a rapprochement between Eastern mysticism and Western rationalism." Connecting the two approaches, Rothberg (1986) addresses a key philosophical issue in transpersonal psychology: the centrality of a hierarchical ontology—a developmental structure of the self and the world in which each level incorporates yet transcends the previous level.

Washburn (1988:1) declares that transpersonal psychology is a synthesis of several disciplines, including religion and philosophy. In view of its multidisciplinary nature, Washburn believes the designation "transpersonal theory" is more accurate. It is also "the study of human nature and development that proceeds on the assumption that human beings possess potentialities that surpass the limits of the normally developed ego." More explicitly, Tart (1989) develops a transpersonal creed in opposition to an industrialized society's creed—the latter describes a material universe; the former, a spiritual as well as a material one.

Harman (1990:86) notes that the term "transpersonal," while ambiguous, invites consideration of dimensions currently "unacceptable to the orthodox scientific community." Certainly, the following statement by Nelson (1990:9) would fall into that category: "At the root of the transpersonal perspective is the idea that there is a deep level subjectivity, or pure spirit, that infuses all matter and every event—the spiritual ground . . . [which] manifests itself in the world as energy."

Finally, trying to counter scientific orthodoxy, Lajoie et al. (1991:180) write of the transpersonal movement, "Criticism persists [but] . . . one reason for creating [the movement] was apparently to study the phenomenon of 'religious experiences' independently of institutionalized religions and theological frameworks . . . " (For examples of the latter kinds of study, which may be enhanced by transpersonal theory, see Beit-Hallahmi [1989], Wulff [1991], and McGuire [1992]. Their texts also offer comprehensive bibliographies in the psychology and sociology of religion.)

Lajoie and Shapiro (1992:91) propose the following definition: "Transpersonal psychology is concerned with the study of humanity's highest potential and with the recognition, understanding, and realization of unitive, spiritual, and transcendent states of consciousness." Vich (1992), in commenting on this definition, calls attention to the evolving nature of transpersonal psychology.

Grof and Bennett (1993:83) ask that for us to understand "the transpersonal realm, we must begin thinking of consciousness . . . as infinite . . . beyond the limits of time and space." In exploring this realm they (p.87) delineate three experiential regions: 1) an expansion or extension of consciousness *within* the everyday concept of time and space; 2) an expansion or extension of consciousness *beyond* the everyday concept of time and space; and 3) "psychoid" experiences (archetypal experiences which mediate the previous two realms but belong to neither).

We turn now to two writers who have grappled with defining transpersonal theory, Ken Wilber and Michael Washburn.

Recent Work in Transpersonal Theory

***Wilber's model: Developmental structuralism*:** In Wilber's (1983b) theory, the mind and society are compound structures containing two dimensions: horizontal—surface structures—and vertical—deep structures. The tension between these dimensions provides the motive power for evolution of consciousness both for the individual and for society. This evolution is hierarchical as it incorporates and transcends previous, lower structures; it moves from prepersonal to personal to transpersonal. (The word "rational" may be substituted for "personal" to provide an added dimension to the concept.) Evolution, however, is only one half of the process; it implies matter ascending into spirit. The other half, involution, is a reverse process with spirit descending into matter. Noting the recent pejorative meaning attached to "hierarchy," Wilber (1993:57) substitutes the word "holoarchy," which means increasing orders of wholeness.

Wilber uses the terms "translation" and "transformation" to describe the work of the horizontal and vertical structures, respectively. Translation refers to uncovering distortions—Freud's theory of sexuality, for example—at a particular level of human consciousness. Once enough distortions have been cleared up, transformation takes place. An example of this evolutionary transformation would be the mass movement from reason and reductionism to a level that included both but that transcended them through an integrative consciousness.

Wilber identifies a major problem: Many transpersonalists in confusing lower states of consciousness with higher states are unable to see the difference between pre- and transrational. He (1983a:201-246) labels this juxtaposition a "pre-trans fallacy." A common and often disastrous consequence of this confusion occurs when a prepersonal state—a return to magical thinking with undue reliance on a charismatic religious leader—is mistaken for a transpersonal state. In Wilber's opinion, Jonestown is a notorious example of a pre-trans fallacy.

***Washburn: The dynamic-dialectical model*:** While acknowledging Wilber's significant contributions to transpersonal theory, Washburn (1988) challenges his model by proposing a dialectic between the dynamic ground and the ego. Rejecting what he terms Wilber's "ladder to oneness," Washburn (p.50) suggests that rather than moving inevitably to ever higher levels of consciousness we are constantly in the dialectical tension created by the opposition of the ego, which is essentially material, but which can strive toward the spiritual, and the dynamic ground, which is essentially spiritual but which contains a material or negative potential.

In Washburn's (1990a:85) "spiral-to-integration" model, transcendence occurs as the ego separates from the ground, represses the knowledge of the union, develops mentally, and then from time to time reaches back beyond the original repression to get in touch with the ground. This so-called "U-turn" is regression in service of transcendence. Washburn refers to this process as bipolar; it involves the egoic pole of the personality and the nonegoic pole of the ground. He (1990a:104) concludes that Wilber's model and the spiral model, in reflecting Western and Eastern religious approaches to transcendence, are not likely to be unified; both are logically consistent and should maintain their distinctions.

We now review criticisms of transpersonal approaches.

Criticisms of Transpersonal Work

Rollo May, an existential, humanistic psychologist, was the first major figure to campaign actively against transpersonal psychology (Simpkinson, 1990:31). In questioning the field's legitimacy, he was later joined by the developer of rational-emotive therapy Albert Ellis (1986:149), who asserted that transpersonal psychology dangerously promoted fanaticism and antiscientific thinking. See also Rubin's (1990:31-33) summary of this controversy.

Reflecting such criticisms, the American Psychological Association (APA) has to date refused to grant licensing status to alternative psychology programs. A major reason for the refusal is the APA's belief that the established licensing standards assure the public of well-qualified psychologists. Assurance of quality is also necessary for reimbursement through federal health programs (Simpkinson, 1990:22-25).

Criticism also comes from other researchers in the field. Chinen (1988:96) reviews Washburn's 1988 book positively but notes that his arguments lack "adequate argumentation, documentation, or application." Wilber (1990:134) too is critical of Washburn's (and Jung's) "spiral-to-integration" thesis. Wilber objects to the placement of the so-called U-turn toward origins as "profoundly incorrect" and in disagreement not only with the perennial philosophy but also with modern developmental theory. Washburn (1990b:7), on the other hand, believes that Wilber's criticism is based on an "unproved and questionable assumption," that pre-egoic and trans-egoic have only surface similarities. Washburn's position is that these seemingly different poles "reflect the very same potentials at two different levels of expression" and that (1990a:94) "full self-realization . . . is a unity that contains duality rather than a unity pure and simple." He (pp.103-104) draws on Jung's use of *enantiodromia*, the process involving the reversal of opposites and the ideal, but never fully realized outcome, the *coincidentia oppositorum*, "the complete functional unity of opposite psychic poles, and selves."

While these arguments may seem abstract and hard to measure, Thomas et al. (1993) have undertaken an empirical examination of the two theories. The team investigated whether spiritually mature people had undergone a regression in service of transcendence or whether they had reached transpersonal levels without regression. Their data indicate support for Wilber's theory.

Walsh (1992:39) notes that in transpersonal endeavors "some thinking is sloppy and intellectually unsophisticated." Advocating rigorous thinking, integrative and wide-ranging scholarship, and research to overcome the isolationism of transpersonal psychology, he observes that "few attempts have been made to link transpersonal concepts to mainstream work."

A major difficulty for the acceptance of transpersonal psychology or theory to date may be that it is perceived to be more concerned with the content of sensational phenomena rather than with the development of rigorous theory. Ellis (1986:149) derisively lists this content as including "astrology, fortune telling, sorcery, psychic healing, witchcraft, shamanism, exorcism, clairvoyance, telepathy, miracles, spiritualism, past lives therapy, out-of-the body experiences, reincarnation therapy, magic, and cosmic consciousness." His perception is borne out by Tart's (1992:ix) observation that the New Age movement is a mix of "genuinely useful transpersonal knowledge and techniques" and "nonsense and immature fantasy."

Using Criticisms to Promote Theory Construction

Surveys in the United States (e.g., Gallup and Castelli, 1989; Greeley, 1989; Donahue, 1991) testify to widespread belief in the mystical and paranormal. Certainly this prevalence indicates the need for reports of these experiences to be studied and explained through the enhanced perspective of transpersonal research.

Such studies could counter Ellis's charge of fanaticism and could initiate a return to a more rigorous use of the term "theory." In its classical sense "theory" means more than just an explanation for known facts and findings. Rather it contains formal expressions that characterize a "well-articulated domain of investigation with explanations for all attendant facts and empirical data" complete with propositions to be tested for their truth value (Reber, 1985).

Social-science studies of religious experience have generally been marked either by objectivity, the need to remain outside the experience itself, or at the opposite pole, by subjectivity, the need for researchers to place themselves within the experience. Meštrović (1988:15-18) addresses this split between objective and subjective data as a "contemporary crisis," and warns that sociology, as the "grand experiment born from the synthesis of objectivism and subjectivism . . . is in real danger of dying out if this synthesis is not achieved and maintained." The same admonition is applicable to psychology which is still dominated by an overemphasis on behaviorism.

Moving from a standard methodology to a transpersonal one demands coming to grips with this dichotomy. Mann (1984) has previously stated that in transpersonal psychology humans are simultaneously both the researcher and the research. Parallel findings in theoretical physics make murky the distinction between objectivity and subjectivity with the realization that the most infinitesimal bits of solid matter-subatomic particles— eventually become "tendencies to exist" or "tendencies to occur" (Capra, 1983:80).

The origins of the debate between objective and subjective modes of knowing can be traced back centuries to the philosophical argument between apriorism and empiricism to which both Durkheim and Jung offered reconciling ideas. In developing transpersonal theory, I review these arguments which stem from ancient Greek philosophy and the problem of opposites, discuss relevant ideas of Durkheim and Jung, and suggest a Durkheimian-Jungian synthesis addresses Walsh's concern that transpersonal research be linked to more mainstream efforts.

Using a Durkheimian-Jungian Foundation for Transpersonal Theory

***The long history of reconciliation of opposites*:** Reconciliation of opposites is integral to ancient and modern spiritual traditions. In the earliest times creation myths explained the existence of sky and earth, day and night, male and female. These myths provided the grounding for ancient Greek philosophy as it grappled with whether diverse substances were actually part of one substance, known as the problem of the One and the Many (Khursheed, 1987:8).

In medieval times this search continued through secret Gnostic and Hermetic societies and the practice of alchemy. Briggs (1990:4) suggests that the ultimate objective of the alchemist, far more than providing a feckless foray into modern chemistry, may have been "to transform *himself* into the philosopher's stone." At present we have both implicit as well as explicit multidisciplinary spiritual approaches to reconciling opposites. Among the possibilities suggested at the end of this chapter are the Myers-Briggs Type Indicator (Myers, 1980) and chaos theory (Gleick, 1987; Briggs and Peat, 1990).

This general pattern of reconciliation of opposites undergirds the transpersonal theory developed in this chapter. Reconciliation here means a conscious awareness that opposites are polarities unified by virtue of being part of a single system. Reconciliation does not imply a perfect balance or an indistinguishable blending but rather highlights the dialectical process in which opposites are identified and seen in relationship.

The tension between opposites informed the work of Durkheim and Jung as they sought, in different areas, to reconcile the dispute between apriorism and empiricism. Apriorism held that such categories as time and space were innate—of the mind—and preceded sense perception or empiricism. Empiricism, on the other hand, held that sense perception was responsible for creating the categories.

Meštrović (1988:15) contends that Durkheim sought to find the "social origins of what has come to be known as the object-subject debate." Similarly, Jung sought the psychic origins of the same debate through his depiction of archetypes which mediated conscious and unconscious realms. His concepts of psychological type—the categories of perception and judgment on which the Myers-Briggs Type Indicator is based—are in actuality archetypal processes for how people gather information and then make decisions. In fact, apriorism and empiricism were refractions of the psychic perceptive functions that Jung ([1921] 1974) identified as intuition and sensation. Thus Durkheim's and Jung's work was characterized by a search for a middle ground.

In a previous paper I synthesized Durkheim's sociology and Jung's psychology to propose a transpersonal sociology of religion (Greenwood, 1990). This approach used simultaneously Durkheim's collective consciousness with its psychological implications to understand social religious experience and Jung's collective unconscious with its social implications to understand private religious experience. This dialectical process reconciled opposites—individual and collective religious experience—in the organization of both society and the self.

This chapter builds on this framework by extending the comparison of Durkheim's collective consciousness comprised of collective representations, including social facts, and of Jung's collective unconscious comprised archetypes. Jung's theory of archetypes, in designating enduring patterns of human behavior, signify *form*, while Durkheim's collective representations, socially and historically specific patterns, signify *content*.

Jung ([1921] 1974:par.427), in dealing empirically with the collective unconscious, believed that raising unconscious material or functions to conscious awareness provided a higher awareness through the "transcendent function" which was a "transition to a new attitude." Similarly, Durkheim ([1950] 1992:92) postulated a higher consciousness embodied by the state whose duty it was "to superimpose on this [the mass of people's] unreflective thought a more considered thought, which [is] . . . different."

This middle ground, however, was not a static position but was comprised of the energy or tension existing between opposites. The cultural manifestation of this conflict was found in the philosophy of representationalism which was carried into the turn of the century by Schopenhauer (Meštrović, 1988). Schopenhauer ([1818] 1969) postulated that humans suffer through the tension between the will—a blind, instinctual force, Kant's thing-in-itself—and representation, whose essential form combines object and subject. This suffering, he thought, could very infrequently be transcended through a pure, will-less perception, akin to a religious experience or meditative practice, a not unlikely surmise, given Schopenhauer's fascination with Eastern religious thought.

Durkheim and Jung, as well as other writers of the times—Freud, Levy-Bruhl, Bergson, Hesse, and Hardy—drew upon the vastly influential philosophy of Schopenhauer (Magee, 1983), though his ideas are seldom observed in social or psychological theory. Meštrović (1988) demonstrates that these ideas involved a fundamental dualism of human nature, a *homo duplex*, stemming from a Platonic intellectual heritage and permeating the culture at the turn of the twentieth century.

The turn of the century has been characterized by the term *fin de siècle*, which connotes the spirit of an intellectual and cultural milieu. This spirit as identified by Ellenberger (1970:278) contains four distinct currents: pessimism, aestheticism, eroticism, and mysticism. It was *not* a time marked by one-sided rationality, a fact borne out by Durkheim's ([1893] 1984; [1912] 1965; [1914] 1960) and Jung's ([1938] 1969) researches which revealed that unconscious influences affected society as well as the self, particularly where religion and religious experience were concerned.

We examine now some of the specific features of their work that enhance transpersonal theory.

***Émile Durkheim, 1858-1917*:** Durkheim ([1912] 1965:31-32) proposed to renovate rationalism as a reconciliation to the aforementioned debate between apriorism and empiricism. This term reflected Durkheim's conclusion that the categories were the result of aeons of social experience. Because the categories were social in origin, they confirmed the partial truth of both apriorism and empiricism.

Using renovated rationalism, then, one could study both conscious and unconscious processes through the effects of the collective representations, which subsumed Durkheim's better-known designation of social facts and which comprised the collective consciousness (Durkheim [1898] 1974:1-34). Durkheim ([1897] 1951:43) believed that even so-called obvious causes were obscured by the unconscious. Unconscious as well as conscious factors for Durkheim existed in the most compelling of collective representations—those of a religious nature, the sacred and the profane. When social action distinguished the sacred and profane, then religion occurred.

Religion manifested itself consciously, for example, by a totem which represented the totality of the group. The totem energized people into a "single moral community," the church, which "makes it clear that religion should be an eminently collective thing" (Durkheim [1912] 1965: 62-63). Yet religion also manifested itself unconsciously by a spark—for Durkheim this implied the soul—of social solidarity within each individual. He (p.282) concluded that the soul is "the totemic principle incarnate in each individual." For Durkheim, the essence of religion was bipolar—the sacred and the profane, the conscious and unconscious, as reflected in the tension between self and society. Religion, in binding social groups together through both conscious and unconscious forces of sacred collective representations and thereby incorporating but transcending the object-subject distinction, demonstrates the implicitly transpersonal nature of Durkheim's work.

The sacred and profane realms were circumscribed by collective representations. Durkheim ([1912] 1965:29) defined collective representations as "the result of an immense cooperation, which stretches out not only into space but into time as well; to make them, a multitude of minds have associated, united and combined their ideas and sentiments; for them, long generations have accumulated their experience and their knowledge." Their variations, however, "prove that, far from being engraven through all eternity upon the mental constitution of men, they depend . . . upon factors that are historical and consequently social." These characterizations closely resemble Jung's description of archetypes (Greenwood, 1990).

***C.G. Jung, 1875-1961*:** Since a comprehensive treatment of Jung's work appears earlier in this volume, I select only his concepts which contribute to an understanding of transpersonal theory developed in this chapter.

Jung ([1934] 1980:par.5) described archetypes as "primordial types . . . universal images that have existed since the remotest times. The term 'représéntations collectives,' used by Levy-Bruhl . . . could easily be applied to unconscious contents." Archetypes as identified by Jung consist of opposites, or more precisely, polar unities. The mother archetype, for example, consists of representations of both the benevolent, as well as malevolent, goddess (par.189). All archetypes comprise a dynamic system with the tension producing a tendency for one pole to slide continually into its opposite—an endless but potentially reconciling flow of energy.

To describe this archetypal flow of energy, Jung ([1921] 1974: par.708) borrowed the term *enantiodromia* from Heraclitus, a fourth-century B.C.E. Greek philosopher. The tension or continual flux generated by oppositions is reflected in his familiar statement, "The way up and the way down are the same." Jung linked this ancient philosophy to Hermeticism, whose doctrines are typically revealed in the statement, "Spirit and Matter are but two poles of the same thing, the intermediate planes being merely degrees of vibration" (Three Initiates [1912] 1940:150).

A similar philosophical flow connected Hermeticism with gnosticism and alchemy. Reconciliation of opposites was not only the *theory* but also the *methodology* for alchemy, which Jung ([1945] 1967) spent a number of years researching, not as protochemistry but as a metaphor for evolution of spiritual consciousness. For Jung, mythology also reflected the dialectical tension between opposites: The creation myths were to be used metaphorically in understanding the unconscious.

Using the insights of ancient philosophies with their connections to Platonism and Neoplatonism, Jung described a process of psychic development. Though archetypes exerted an unrecognized force over human behavior, it was an individual's responsibility to attempt a reconciliation of conscious and unconscious psychic contents. This act of reconciliation was, Jung believed, primarily a religious experience, and he used Christian religious terms to make his meaning clear: The ego must be crucified and resurrected through a transcendent function, the transcendent function activated by the energy or tension of raising unconscious material to conscious awareness (Jung [1955] 1984:par.1664).

The importance of the numinous, or holy, is reflected in Jung's ([1952] 1973) work on synchronicity, which demonstrated the often unseen and unacknowledged relationship between inner mental states and outer physical happenings, a relationship implicit in Durkheim's discussion of the totemic principle.

Jung ([1934] 1980: par 99.) made specific his meaning: "There are as many archetypes as there are typical situations in life. Endless repetition has engraved these experiences into our psychic constitution, not in the form of images filled with content, but at first only as *forms without content*, representing merely the possibility of a certain type of perception and action." The major opposition—for Jung archetypes were engraved on the human psyche; for Durkheim collective representations were *not* engraved—signifies a distinction between form and content.

This opposition, in reviving the nature-nurture debate, raises the relevance of sociobiological (or biosociological) considerations.

Some Suggestions from Sociobiology (A Modern Heresy)

The distinction between form and content in regard to "engraving" does indeed invoke sociobiological considerations. (Since neither many sociologists nor biologists are wild with enthusiasm about the merger of the two fields, could this be yet another manifestation of the problem of opposites engendered by disciplinary patriotism?) Let us briefly examine the somewhat differing views of three researchers who have dealt with the relationship of Jung's theory of archetypes to biology.

Stevens (1983) calls attention to Jung's feeling that psychiatry was the empirical field common to biological and spiritual facts. Referring to the human genome as the "archetype of archetypes," Stevens (284-285) believes that "religious belief is planned for in the genome . . . Both Self [meaning the biological reality akin to a God-image] and society need religion; without it both suffer and both ultimately perish." However, he (p.227) warns that the "liberal, egalitarian consensus of the present time" will object mightily to sociobiological endeavors.

Wenegrat (1990:31-71) offers another sociobiological approach to the psychology of religion. He discusses the "divine archetype"—religious beliefs—as linked to four "innately probable social strategies." These include proximity maintenance (attachment to God), sexual competition, mutualism, and altruism, all of which provide the grounding for religious belief. Believing that Jung "treated the archetype as the knowledge inherent in species-typical behavior," Wenegrat (p.110) develops his thesis on the assumption that "knowledge structure" and "archetype" are equivalent terms.

A third sociobiological alternative comes from the work of Henry (1992) completed over thirty years ago but only recently published. In combining brain research—left-right, reason-emotion—with Jung's work on archetypes and their bridging mechanism between inner and outer worlds, Henry concludes that the balancing of opposites has a possible physiological basis. This would indicate that religious experience is partially determined by a particular brain region. (Compare this last theory with yoga psychology's body chakras or energy centers, as outlined by Chaudhuri [in Tart 1992:265-269].)

For a summary of the biological foundations of religion, including the work of G. Stanley Hall and Julian Jaynes, see Wulff (1991:41-110).

Other Possibilities

Meštrović (1993:5) draws upon Tocqueville's and Veblen's cultural analyses in collapsing the essence of Durkheim's collective representations and Jung's archetypes into "habits" in order to analyze humans' barbaric tendencies. He notes that habits are "something semi-permanent that is able to transmit social traits across generations without recourse to heredity or even the mind, but through the medium of culture." These habits can be clearly seen in social patterns, although people are often unable to give a rational explanation for them.

Grof (1993) emphasizes that birth experiences, which he calls "basic perinatal matrices," may affect adult behavior. He believes that his psychotherapeutic practice and other studies have revealed, for example, that difficult or even violent births may be implicated in problems later in life ranging from addictions to suicide. Healing, however, may occur through a therapist trained to recognize the connections between physical and mental states or through the individual's own realizations.

Both Meštrović (1993:272) and Grof (1993:204) acknowledge the power of "habits" and of "basic perinatal matrices" upon religious experience, albeit on different forms.

Combining psychological, sociological, and other scientific endeavors through a Durkheimian-Jungian synthesis may provide insight into transpersonal research questions asked by Tart (1992:ix):

- "Does the experience of so-called higher consciousness actually deal with a reality, or is it just a kind of delusion?"
- "How can we make the mystic experience the common property of humans, instead of the almost accidental experience of a few?"
- "How can we guide the aftereffects of transcendental experience so they result in greater psychological maturity, rather than religious fanaticism?"

Answers to these questions necessitate the bridging of traditional psychological and sociological concerns with the natural sciences and with the phenomena mentioned earlier—altered states of consciousness, higher entities, and ultimate purposes. If they can be answered, even partially, then we may have a more complete idea of the nature of the relationship between conscious and unconscious aspects of the self, between self and society, and among societies.

Defining Religious Experience

The preceding discussions lead to a key hypothesis: *that reconciliation of opposites is the fundamental religious experience*. The following definition of religious experience draws upon a Durkheimian-Jungian synthesis. In preceding a definition of transpersonal theory, it is essential to constructing the latter:

> While religious experience has varieties of content—collective representations—which are social and historical, its essential nature has an underlying dialectical form—archetype—comprised of polar unities and the tension—the endlessly reconciling flow of energy—between them.

To illustrate the archetypal form underlying collective representations of religious experience, consider the following examples: the role of the rational mind with the intuitive mind in Zen Buddhism (Owens in Tart, 1992:156); the union of human's will with God's will in Christianity (McNamara in Tart, 1992:379; the transcendence of the subject-object dichotomy in yoga psychology (Chaudhuri in Tart, 1992-234); the real and the imaginary in the Gurdjieff tradition (Riordan in Tart, 1992:320); and the simple and complex in sufism (Ornstein in Tart, 1992:364). The content of religious experience then is specific to social, historic settings, whereas the form of religious experience remains constant.

A refraction of this idea appears in Meštrović (1992:110), who deconstructs the postmodern idea that cultural life is nonreferential. He writes, "Religion always refers to *homo duplex*, the opposition between the sacred and the profane. The formula is constant, but the representations that attach themselves to the sacred and profane vary with societies." Referring to Durkheim's "dynamic sociology," Meštrović thus validates a comparison with Jung's dynamic psychology.

This method of understanding religious experience addresses the debate over whether all religions have a common core or not. The common core is assumed by Huxley's (1944) perennial philosophy and Smith's primordial tradition (1976), whereas Katz (1978) argues for the opposite view that mystical revelation is tempered by a cultural consciousness. A Durkheimian-Jungian synthesis would reveal that both views are partially correct.

Toward a Working Definition of Transpersonal Theory

Let us return briefly to the ideas of Wilber and Washburn in order to develop a definition of transpersonal theory. I suggest that Wilber's transpersonal theory could be extended to include the recognition that horizontal structures, which promote translation, can be analyzed using Durkheim's collective representations, and that vertical structures, which promote transformation, can similarly be analyzed by Jung's archetypes.

Wilber states, however, that some bipoles or polarities contain a pre-trans fallacy (e.g., ego-nonego) and some do not (e.g., yin-yang). But both Jung and Washburn suggest that it is in the very nature of bipoles to contain their opposite: A transpersonal pole, for example, could contain the seed of its opposite, a prepersonal pole. Is not yin-yang capable of producing a pre-trans fallacy? Consider, for example, the current biological and social controversies over what is male and what is female, and is there not a literal twilight zone that is neither day nor night? One could even cite plant physiology: Since both root and shoot possess the potential to develop into their opposite, the lower form is in the higher as well as the higher being in the lower.

The very symbol of yin-yang does *not* emphasize so much clear-cut distinctions between such opposites as male-female and day-night as it does a holistic system that integrates both and that sees both in relationship. Wilber thinks Jung creates a pre-trans fallacy by confusing archetypes (e.g., Platonic ideas) with archetypal manifestations (e.g., mythology). This point raises the question of whether or not Wilber recognizes the spiritually significant, dialectical nature of Jung's archetypes (Jung [1934] 1980:par.85).

Washburn has earlier stated that he believes Wilber has overlooked this nature. Yet Washburn does not believe that his and Wilber's approaches can be unified. Perhaps this argument actually hinders development of theory by not recognizing that his approach and Wilber's are actually polar unities. Washburn's conclusion, therefore, embodies a contemporary aspect of the ancient problem of opposites. The "problem" he sees can be overcome when opposites are recognized as polar unities and therefore in relationship.

Applying this logic to Washburn's and Wilber's theories, we see that *together* the theories complement each other. Wilber reconciles horizontal and vertical (surface and deep) social structures; Washburn reconciles psychic structures—spirit (dynamic ground) and matter (ego). The *process* orientation of Washburn's individually oriented dialectic between the ego and the dynamic ground provides an essential counterpart for the *product* orientation of Wilber's collectively oriented dialectic between horizontal and vertical structures.

In Washburn's theory, it is necessary and inevitable for the ego to undergo the reversals between "pre-trans" in order to develop. In Wilber's theory, such reversals are dangerous for individuals or groups and impossible once the great mass of human consciousness has moved on to another level. But both actions may be appropriate for the theorized levels on which they are occurring.

Also seeing complementarity between Wilber and Washburn is Chinen (1988:95), who analogizes Wilber to a geographer "outlining the terrain of transpersonal experience" and Washburn to a geologist "looking for the underlying volcanic activity which presumably shapes the topography." Overall, Washburn's theory is more psychological, whereas Wilber's is more sociological, though each contains elements of the other. The resulting synthesis is, in effect, a legitimate social psychology that informs several levels of transpersonal theory.

To these levels is added yet another—the Durkheimian-Jungian interplay of content and form. A definition of transpersonal theory based on the previous definition of religious experience follows:

> Transpersonal theory is a multilevel methodology of nonduality employing simultaneous subjective and objective awareness of polar unities within an identified system. These polar unities have many forms: They can be immanent and transcendent, material and spiritual, individual and collective, psychological and sociological. Transpersonal theory is a collective representation, a current manifestation of the archetypal form of religious experience.

Further elaboration follows:

Earlier I proposed that religious experience is an archetype because it is a primal human experience born of the dialectic produced by the tension between polar unities. Grounded in that assumption and observing the connections between Durkheim and Jung, I have, therefore, suggested that transpersonal theory is a collective representation of the archetype of religious experience. As a collective representation, transpersonal theory, as now formulated by different writers, is socially and historically specific to the late twentieth century: It fulfills Durkheim's ([1912] 1965:29) description because it is comprised of ideas that have "associated, united, and combined" over long generations. It has evolved as a "new" way for understanding and evaluating religious experience. Thus it exemplifies its definition: It is simultaneously theory and practice.

Ongoing Related Work

Many of the authors cited herein draw upon a multidisciplinary cornucopia of implicitly transpersonal work. In the social sciences the following authors present perspectives that transcend traditional scientific approaches: John-Raphael Staude (1976), and Kyriacos Markides (1990).

In the natural sciences Capra (1983:370), a physicist, links Wilber's and Grof's work in making connections between ancient mystical traditions and modern discoveries in theoretical physics. He states, "Transpersonal experiences involve an expansion of consciousness beyond the conventional boundaries of the organism and, correspondingly, a larger sense of identity. . . .This mode of consciousness often transcends logical reasoning and intellectual analysis, approaching the direct mystical experience of reality."

Other representative work in the natural sciences follows: in physics—Bohm (1980) and Margenau (1987); in plant physiology—Sheldrake (1981); in medicine and related fields—Dossey (1989) and Chopra (1993); in efforts that combine science with other areas—Weber (1986). These authors provide reconciliatory measures between science and religion.

Implications and Applications

The preceding definition of transpersonal theory raises questions: If transpersonal theory is a form of religious experience, does this mean that transpersonal theory is both scientific as well as spiritual? Does it mean that its theory and methodology or practice are inseparable? If so, does this mean a transcendence of the subject-object distinction which Schopenhauer long ago implied through his concept of pure, will-less knowing? If we can answer "yes" to these questions, and I submit that we can, one implication then is that human consciousness collectively is entering a less positivistically oriented epoch.

This implication leads us to Wilber's (1983b) characterization of the coming epoch as one in which we will realize an increasingly integrative consciousness. An integrative consciousness allows us to reconcile opposites by seeing them as polar unities and to identify the archetypal or deep structures below the surface of collective representations. Specifically, we can begin to understand that a transpersonal theory is both scientific and spiritual because the theory incorporates a methodology that itself is a religious experience. Cause and effect then become the same thing through *enantiodromia*, the endlessly flowing tension between opposites.

We come to some startling realizations: Transpersonal theory diminishes many perceived separations: for example, those between religion and science, rationality and irrationality, objectivity and subjectivity, and psychology and sociology. Closing the gap in this way allows us to make some very specific observations for use of theory.

Using the theoretical base of reconciliation of opposites, we can identify current methodologies not ostensibly labeled as "transpersonal." The Myers-Briggs Type Indicator (MBTI) reconciles opposing Jungian functions of perception and judgment. Chaos theory reconciles forces of order and disorder in nature as well as in social theory. I make brief application below.

Durkheim ([1912] 1965:14) urged that "one must know how to go underneath the symbol to the reality which it represents and which gives it its meaning." An example of this kind of reality would be the *sui generis* nature of society which Durkheim likened to the concepts of totality and divinity (p.490). The *sui generis* nature may be understood through chaos theory which provides an example of a self-organizing principle—a strange attractor—through the enantiodromia of order and disorder. Strange attractors present a pattern appearing in the midst of seeming randomness. If chaos theory is a Durkheimian collective representation—an historically specific way of explaining the ancient question of order and disorder—then Jung's theory of archetypes may provide an explanation for chaos theory's strange attractors (Greenwood, 1991).

This argument raises the following question which is crucial to the definitions of religious experience and transpersonal theory: *Is it possible that the ground, earlier referred to by Nelson and Washburn, may be located in the tension—energy or vivifying spirit—between opposites*? It is from this question that we can see the importance of simultaneous consideration of temporal and timeless processes with its resultant multilevel dialectic. Social order is born out of this dialectic, for as Durkheim ([1895] 1982:99) implied, it is the disorder—his specific example is crime—in society that gives order its meaning. Almost one hundred years later Young (1991) analyzes crime through chaos theory.

The psyche also contains an self-organizing principle. Jung ([1921] 1974: par. 709) believed that when an "extreme, one-sided tendency dominates conscious life in time an equally powerful counterposition is built up, which first inhibits the conscious performance and subsequently breaks through the conscious control." Barbarism, he thought, is often the result of a overly rational consciousness that discounts the power of irrationality. Through use of the Myers-Briggs Type Indicator, based on what Jung described as the core of the psyche—the functions of perception (sensation and intuition) and judgment (thinking and feeling)—one can ameliorate destructive one-sidedness or ego-domination. A sense of the totality of the Self, an archetype analogous to a God-image, is thus regained.

Finally moving to more general considerations, we could say that an immediate and important implication of transpersonal theory is that out-of-balance situations in the world whether they involve religious, economic, or social collective representations, are in an inexorable archetypal process, a process in which opposites endlessly move toward each other. Currently we could focus on countries whose populations are overeating themselves into disease and death and countries whose populations are starving themselves into similar conditions. Human intervention may alleviate misery caused by these kinds of tensions, but only if the action, which will obviously be based on collective representations, is realized as part of an inevitable, archetypal process and is therefore balanced. The process is *sui generis*, a power unto itself.

To reiterate, for Durkheim this self-organizing power was embodied in collective representations comprising the collective consciousness. For Jung this power was embodied in archetypes comprising the collective unconscious. A Durkheimian-Jungian synthesis offers a methodology that is both psycho-social and socio-psychological, that enhances traditional scientific analyses of religious experience by incorporating unconscious with conscious factors, and that provides validity to the transpersonal enterprise through reconciliation of what appear to be opposites.

The polar unities of temporal content and timeless form and the energy created through the dialectical process are the life force of the transpersonal theory herein developed. Will future research, using an ever-evolving transpersonal theory, be able to determine more precisely the nature of that energy?

REFERENCES

Beit-Hallahmi, B.
1989 *Prolegomena to the psychological study of religion*. Cranbury, NJ: Bucknell University Press.

Bohm, D.
1980 *Wholeness and the implicate order*. London: Routledge & Kegan Paul.

Boorstein, S. (Ed.)
1980 *Transpersonal psychotherapy*. Palo Alto, CA: Science and Behavior Books.

Briggs, J.
1990 *Fire in the crucible: The self-creation of creativity and genius*. Los Angeles: Jeremy P. Tarcher.

Briggs, J. and F. Peat
1989 *Turbulent mirror*. New York: Harper & Row.

Capra, F.
1983 *The turning point.* New York: Bantam.
Caputi, N.
1984 *Guide to the unconscious.* Birmingham, AL: Religious Education Press.
Chinen, A.B.
1988 Review of Michael Washburn's *The ego and the dynamic ground: a transpersonal theory of human development. Journal of Transpersonal Psychology* 20:93-96.
Chopra, D.
1993 *Ageless body, timeless mind.* New York: Harmony Books.
Clark, W.
1969 *Chemical ecstasy.* New York: Sheed and Ward.
Donahue, M.
1991 Prevalence of New Age beliefs in six Protestant denominations. Paper presented at the annual meeting of the Society for the Scientific Study of Religion, Pittsburgh, PA, November.
Dossey, L.
1989 *Recovering the soul: A scientific and spiritual search.* New York: Bantam.
Durkheim, E.
[1893]
1984 *The division of labor in society*, translated by W. D. Halls. New York: Free Press.
[1895]
1982 *The rules of sociological method*, translated by W. D. Halls. New York: Free Press.
[1897]
1951 *Suicide*, translated by J. A. Spaulding and G. Simpson. New York: Free Press.
[1898]
1974 Individual and collective representations. In *Sociology and philosophy*. New York: Free Press.
[1912]
1965 *The elementary forms of the religious life*, translated by J. W. Swain. New York: Free Press.
[1914]
1960 The dualism of human nature and its social conditions, translated by C. Blend. In *Emile Durkheim*, edited by K. Wolff. Columbus, OH: State University Press.
[1950]
1992 *Professional ethics and civic morals*, translated by C. Brookfield. London: Routledge.
Ellenberger, H. F.
1970 *The discovery of the unconscious: The history and evolution of dynamic psychiatry.* New York: Basic Books.
Ellis, A.
1986 Fanaticism that may lead to a nuclear holocaust: The contributions of scientific counseling and psychotherapy. *Journal of Counseling and Development* 65:146-151.
Flew, A.
1984 *A dictionary of philosophy*, 2nd ed. New York: St. Martin's Press.
Gallup, G. and J. Castelli
1989 *The people's religion*. New York: Macmillan.
Gleick, J.
1987 *Chaos: Making a new science*. New York: Penguin.
Granfield, D.
1991 *Heightened consciousness: The mystical difference*. New York: Paulist Press.
Greeley, A.
1974 *Ecstasy: A way of knowing*. Englewood Cliffs, NJ: Prentice-Hall.
1989 *Religious change in America.* Cambridge, MA: Harvard University Press.
Greenwood, S.
1990 Emile Durkheim and C. G. Jung: Structuring a transpersonal sociology of religion. *Journal for the Scientific Study of Religion* 29:482-495.
1991 At the margin: Interfacing religion and science with chaos theory. Paper presented at the

November, 1991, annual meeting of the Society for the Scientific Study of Religion, Pittsburgh, PA.

Grof, S.
1975 *Realms of the human unconscious: Observations from LSD research*. New York: Viking Press.

Grof, S., with H. Z. Bennett
1993 *The holotropic mind*. San Francisco: Harper San-Francisco.

Harman, W., and J. Hormann
1990 *Creative work: The constructive role of business in a transforming society*. Indianapolis, IN: Knowledge Systems.

Hastings, A.
1991 *With the tongues of men and angels: A study of channeling*. Fort Worth: Holt, Rinehart and Winston.

Henry, J. P.
1992 *Instincts, archetypes, and symbols: An approach to the physiology of religious experience*. Dayton, OH: College Press.

Hood Jr., R. W.
1975 The construction and preliminary validation of a measure of reported mystical experience. *Journal for the Scientific Study of Religion* 14:29-41.
1992 A Jamesean look at self and self loss in mystical experience. *The Journal of the Psychology of Religion* 1:1-24.

Hood Jr., R. W. and R. J. Morris
1992 Religious dream experiences: A preliminary investigation. Paper presented at the annual meeting of the Society for the Scientific Study of Religion, Washington, DC, November.

Huxley, A.
[1944]
1970 *The perennial philosophy*. New York: Harper Colophon.

James, W.
[1902]
1961 *The varieties of religious experience*. New York: Collier Books.

Jung, C. G.
[1921]
1974 *Psychological types*. Collected Works, Vol. 6, trans. by R. F. C. Hull. Princeton, NJ: Princeton University Press.
[1934]
1980 *The archetypes and the collective unconscious*. Collected Works, Vol. 9, Part I, translated by R.F.C. Hull. Princeton, NJ: Princeton University Press.
[1938]
1969 *Psychology and religion: West and east*. Collected Works, Vol. 11, translated by R. F. C. Hull. Princeton, NJ: Princeton University Press.
[1945]
1967 *Alchemical studies*. Collected Works, Vol. 13, translated by R. F. C. Hull, Princeton, NJ: Princeton University Press.
[1952]
1973 Synchronicity: An acausal connecting principle. In *The structure and dynamics of the psyche*. Collected Works, Vol. 8, translated by R.F.C. Hull. Princeton, NJ: Princeton University Press.
[1955]
1984 *The symbolic life*. Collected Works, Vol. 18, translated by R. F. C. Hull. In *Psychology and western religion*. Princeton, NJ: Princeton University Press.

Katz, S. T.
1978 Language, epistemology, and mysticism. In *Mysticism and philosophical analysis*, edited by S. T. Katz. New York: Oxford University Press.

Khursheed, A.
1987 *Science and religion: Toward the restoration of an ancient harmony*. London: Oneworld Publications.

Lajoie, D., S. I. Shapiro, and T. B. Roberts
1991 A historical analysis of the statement of purpose. *The Journal of Transpersonal Psychology* 23:175-182.
1992 Definitions of transpersonal psychology: The first twenty-three years. *The Journal of Transpersonal Psychology* 24:79-98.
Magee, B.
1983 *The philosophy of Schopenhauer*. New York: Oxford University Press.
Mann, R. D.
1984 *The light of consciousness*. Albany, NY: State University of New York Press.
Margenau, H.
1987 *The miracle of existence*. Boston: New Science Library.
Markides, K. C.
1990 *Fire in the heart: Healers, sages, and mystics*. New York: Paragon House.
Maslow, A. H.
1970 *Religion, values, and peak experiences*. New York: Penguin.
McGuire, M. B.
1992 *Religion: The social context*. Belmont, CA: Wadsworth.
McNeill, B. and C. Guion (Eds.)
1991 *Noetic Sciences Collection, 1980-1990: Ten years of consciousness research*. Sausalito, CA: Institute of Noetic Sciences.
Meštrović, S. G.
1988 *Émile Durkheim and the reformation of sociology*. Totowa, NJ: Rowman and Littlefield.
1992 *Durkheim and Postmodern Culture*. New York: Aldine de Gruyter.
1993 *The barbarian temperament: Toward a postmodern critical theory*. London: Routledge.
Moody, R. A., with P. Perry
1988 *The light beyond*. New York: Bantam.
Myers, I. B., with P. Myers
1980 *Gifts differing*. Palo Alto: Consulting Psychologists Press.
Nelson, J. E.
1990 *Healing the split: A new understanding of the crisis and treatment of the mentally ill*. Los Angeles: Jeremy P. Tarcher.
Ornstein, R.
1973 *Psychology of consciousness*. San Francisco: W. H. Freeman.
Polkinghorne, D.
1983 *Methodology for the human sciences*. Albany, NY: State University of New York Press.
Reber, A. S.
1985 *The Penguin dictionary of psychology*. New York: Viking Penguin.
Rothberg, D.
1986 Philosophical foundations of transpersonal psychology: An introduction to some basic issues. *Journal of Transpersonal Psychology* 18:1-34.
Rubin, J.
1990 Is transpersonal psychology dangerous? *Common Boundary* 8:31-33.
Schopenhauer, A.
[1818]
1969 *The world as will and representation*, Vols. I and II, translated by E. F. J. Payne. New York: Dover.
Sheldrake, R.
1981 *A new science of life*. Los Angeles: J.P. Tarcher.
Simpkinson, C. H.
1990 Alternative psychology programs: Fight for licensing. *Common Boundary* 8:22-25.
Simpson, J.A. and E. S. C. Weiner, preparers
1989 *The Oxford English Dictionary, Vol. XVIII*, 2nd ed. Oxford: Clarendon Press.
Smith, H.
1976 *Forgotten truth: The primordial tradition*. New York: Harper & Row.
Stace, W. T.
1960 *Mysticism and philosophy*. Philadelphia: Lippincott.

Staude, J. R.
1976 From depth psychology to depth sociology. *Theory and Society* 3:303-38.
Stevens, A.
1983 *Archetypes: A natural history of the self.* Quill: New York.
Sundberg, N. and C. Keutzer
1984 Transpersonal psychology I. In *Encyclopedia of psychology* Vol. 3, edited by Raymond J. Corsini. New York: Wiley.
Tart, C. T.
1989 *Open mind, discriminating mind: Reflections on human possibilities*. New York: Harper & Row.
1992 *Transpersonal psychologies: Perspectives on the mind from seven great spiritual traditions*. New York: HarperCollins.
Thomas, L. Eugene, S. Brewer, P. Kraus, and B. Rosen
1993 Two patterns of transcendence: An empirical examination of Wilber's and Washburn's theories. *Journal of Humanistic Psychology* 33:66-81.
Three Initiates
[1912]
1940 *The Kyballion: A study of the Hermetic philosophy of ancient Egypt and Greece*. Chicago: The Yogi Publication Society.
Underhill, E.
[1911]
1990 *Mysticism*. New York: Image Books.
Vaughan, F. E.
1982 The transpersonal perspective: A personal overview. *Journal of Transpersonal Psychology* 14:37-45.
1986 *The inward arc*. Boston: Shambhala.
1991 Spiritual issues in psychotherapy. *The Journal of Transpersonal Psychology* 23:105-119.
Vich, M. A.
1988 Some historical sources of the term 'transpersonal.' *Journal of Transpersonal Psychology* 20:107-110.
1992 Changing definitions of transpersonal psychology. *The Journal of Transpersonal Psychology* 24:99-100.
Walsh, R.
1992 The search for synthesis: transpersonal psychology and the meeting of East and West, psychology and religion, personal and transpersonal. *Journal of Humanistic Psychology* 32:19-45.
Walsh, R. and F. Vaughan
1984 Transpersonal psychology II. In *Encyclopedia of psychology*, Vol. 3, edited by R. J. Corsini. New York: Wiley.
Washburn, M.
1988 *The ego and the dynamic ground.* Albany, NY: State University of New York Press.
1990a Two patterns of transcendence. *Journal of Humanistic Psychology* 30:84-112.
1990b Two patterns of transcendence. *ReVision* 13:3-15.
Weber, R.
1986 *Dialogues with scientists and sages*. London: Routledge & Kegan Paul.
Wenegrat, B.
1990 *The divine archetype: The sociobiology and psychology of religion.* Lexington, MA: Lexington Books.
Wilber, K.
1981 *Up from Eden: A transpersonal view of human evolution*. Boulder, CO: Shambhala.
1983a *Eye to eye: The quest for the new paradigm.* Garden City, NY: Anchor Books.
1983b *A sociable God: Toward a new understanding of religion*. Boulder, CO: New Science Library.
1990 Two patterns of transcendence: A reply to Washburn. *Journal of Humanistic Psychology* 30:113-136.

1993 The great chain of being. *Journal of Humanistic Psychology* 33:52-65.

Wulff, D. M.

1991 *Psychology of religion: Classic and contemporary views*. New York: Wiley.

Young, T. R.

1991 Chaos and crime: Nonlinear and fractal forms of crime. Part I. *The Society for the Study of Social Problems Newsletter* 22:17-21.

22

Feminist Theory and Religious Experience

MARY JO NEITZ

The intersection of the topics of feminist theory and religious experience elicits a relatively small literature. This is especially true if we confine ourselves to the social sciences and to contemporary society. Relatively few feminist researchers in the social sciences have considered the topic of religious experience, and among the social scientists who study religious experience few have given much consideration to gender. This chapter begins with a very brief overview of current feminist perspectives and asks what those perspectives might contribute to the study of religious experience. The chapter examines the dominant narrative of religious experience and then suggests how that narrative reflects the dominant male culture. Next, the chapter shows how the narrative excludes women and can be linked to ways that religious culture condones exploitation and even violence against women. The chapter then examines an alternative model of religious experience.

Feminist Perspectives

What constitutes feminist research in the sociology of religion? One definition of feminism would have it refer to a political stance in favor of equality for men and women. Feminist social scientists since the late 1960s have debated about whether specific theoretical perspectives or methodological approaches are necessary to feminist research. These debates have enormously enlarged the conceptual tools available for understanding the experience of women and the gendered nature of social relations in our society. They have not provided a single consensually defined "feminist theory" or "feminist method."

Early feminist work tried to explain the causes of inequality. Out of this came various feminist theories and feminist revisions of existing theories including marxism, liberalism, and psychoanalysis. The question of the day was "Where are the women?" which fueled critiques of existing bodies of sociological literature (e.g., Millman and Kantor, 1975). Much of this work emphasized differences between women and men. One response of the discipline was to "add women and stir": introduce gender as a variable without altering the conceptual frames of the study.

Another response came out of methodological and epistemological debates among feminist researchers. Feminist methodological critiques argued that feminist research should be done "for women"—from the perspective of women and in the interests of women (Smith, 1977). These feminist researchers carried on the critique of positivism insofar as feminists contended that models of research as objective and disinterested both failed to capture women's realities and been used to support structures of oppression. This position, however, soon came under criticism itself because it seemed to assume that "women" constituted a unitary group with a single set of interests (Dill, 1983; Collins, 1991). Clearly feminist research needs to explore differences among women, including differences in power.

The development of the concept of a sex/gender system also supported the move toward looking at "difference" among women. Rubin (1975) and Kelly-Gadol (1976) argued that the explanation for the oppression of women could be found by studying the social structures and cultural practices through which biological sexuality is transformed into *gender*, meaning the relations between the sexes. This perspective challenges the taken-for-grantedness of heterosexuality. Developed among anthropologists and historians, it encourages the analysis of specific sex/gender systems in particular contexts.

The following assumptions then are central to feminist research today: first, understanding that experience is gendered, and second, that any analysis must consider the specific context of women's experience, including race and class position. Current "feminist" work may "give voice" to women who do not express particularly feminist views, but such work can show both how women are constrained by the structures of gender and how they resist those constraints. Putting women at the center of analysis produces more than a critique of oppressive social systems; it also can transform our concepts and theories for thinking about the social order. Following this practice, in this chapter I begin by asking how conceptions of religious experience in the dominant culture are gendered.

Reflecting space considerations this chapter does not attempt to review all the literature that addresses religion and gender issues. (For a review of the feminist social-science literature on women and religion see Neitz, 1993.) In addition, there is a large body of feminist work on religion that is not sociological. This includes theological critiques, anthropological discussions of religion and culture outside the United States, and work by historians on women and religion (see O'Connor, 1989).

Religious Experience

The idea of religious experience encompasses a wide variety of possibilities, but it has received relatively little attention from sociologists of religion. Despite the fact that the inspirational writings of mystics and seekers of all sorts witness to the centrality of religious experiences expressed variously as individual experiences of the "sacred" or "supernatural," feelings of transcendence of the self, feelings of unity with all being or with the void, sociologists have tended to give their attention to other aspects of religion. Even those who acknowledged such experiences as critical for the formation of religions tended to see those experiences as rare, or even nonexistent in the modern world. On the other hand, participants in modern religious movements claim that such transcendent experiences are crucial for them.

In the literature of religious experience most attention to such experiences of otherness is given to those which can be described as life-changing experiences. In some of my earlier work, however, I have shown how even everyday experiences of "talking with god" motivate the religious person to continue in pursuit of her or his transformed/transforming path (Neitz, 1987). Women as well as men obviously seek and find these experiences of otherness. Yet the meaning of religious experience has been different for men and women reflecting both differences in personality structure and the constraints of gendered life opportunities. It is these differences which are the subject of this chapter.

In their book, *Religions and the Individual: A Social-Psychological Perspective*, Batson, Schoenrade, and Ventis present a model of religious experience. Stripped to its essentials, they describe a four-stage sequence: first there is the existential crisis, followed by self-surrender, then the formulation of a new vision, and finally, a new life (1993:115). This sequence of events can be elaborated through examining the histories of saints and mystics, and Batson, Schoenrade, and Ventis present many examples from the famous to the not so famous.

In the dominant narrative of religious transformation, we hear of an attractive young man, one who possesses considerable resources—wealth, intelligence, charm, good looks. This young man lives a life of little care; often, in the story, he dissipates these resources living a self-indulgent life. Then, at some point, he has a profound religious experience. This leads to a crisis in his life; he wrestles with whether to accept the call to a new life or to continue in his old ways. He surrenders to the new vision and builds a new life.

This story is familiar to us from the lives of the great saints, including St. Augustine and St. Francis of Assisi. Critical to the story is the idea of the surrender of the (old) self; the content of the new vision includes submission to some form of discipline, reigning in the impulsive expressions of the former life. While we find stories of women as well as men who have the visions, the crises, who surrender and submit, a feminist reading suggests that this sequence of events is likely to have a profoundly different meaning for women than for men.

The preexisting condition for the men in the narrative is autonomy. It can be argued that it was through renunciation that female religious virtuosi exercised a kind of autonomy within their own cultural contexts (see Flinders, 1993; Bynum, 1987). Still, St. Clare's refusal to eat for days at a time hardly represents the kind of wholeness that we would want for our sisters or daughters. Although it is inappropriate to read our lives back into the actions of medieval mystics and saints, it is not inappropriate to ask about the implications of this still dominant narrative of religious experience for women today. A feminist perspective forces us to ask whether a story that assumes autonomy as the starting point and then suggests that the outcome of religious experience is a wholeness that comes from pursuing a kind of disciplining of the will is equally appropriate for males and females in our culture.

If we assume that women enter into religious experiences without having had the experience of willfulness that is the expression of the autonomy of the males in the narrative, then we need to ask what will be the consequences of further discipline and submission? It seems possible that, rather than the cultivation of the neglected side of the self and movement toward fuller humanity, for women embracing demands for discipline and submission can impede spiritual development.

Feminists have written about how women have found ways of exercising autonomy in religious contexts within the constraints of demands for submission (Davidman, 1991; Gilkes, 1985; Kaufman, 1991; Rose, 1987). Feminists might also explore the implications of surrender and discipline as modeled in the narrative for women who start from different preconditions.

The strand of contemporary feminist theory coming out of the work of Nancy Chodorow and Carol Gilligan suggests that the processes of gender identification in early childhood produces a self that is autonomous for boys, but that for girls the self is experienced as connected to others. Chodorow (1978) argued that this connected or relational self develops out of the universal experience of women's mothering. Males develop gender identity in households where "women mother" and fathers are largely absent. Boys therefore establish their gender identity by becoming "not female." Girls identify with their mothers, who are present and with whom they remain in relation. They never separate in the extreme ways that boys must. Gilligan's (1982) work on moral development showed girls with "connected selves" working through moral choices in ways that are markedly different from the prevailing models developed with male subjects. Subsequent work (e.g., Tronto, 1987) has emphasized that the observed differences in behavior are not due to some essential characteristic of women (even one that is based in nearly universal early childhood experiences) but rather comes out of a particular context. This model of the self in relation to others has many ramifications for the sociology of religion.

The second part of this chapter reviews several recent studies by feminist researchers which suggest several ways that the dominant narrative of religious experience does not fit with women's experience. However, if we assume that women are more likely to start out from relationality, rather than autonomy, and that women have experienced more constraint than their male counterpoints, we might expect that women would find different kinds of spiritual paths appropriate to the development of whole selves than those paths which men have traditionally walked. Indeed feminist theologian Carol Christ has suggested that religious experiences for women might entail exercising the will rather than disciplinary measures calling for submission. The third section of the chapter examines women's religious rituals which move away from the surrender/submission model.

Surrender and Submission

To this point I have referred to autonomy in two different ways, both explored in feminist literature. First there are the social structural constraints that have limited women's autonomy in terms of what women could do in public spheres and defined their responsibilities in the private spheres. While only a part of women's experience, these constraints—and the degree to which religion has been instrumental in defining and enforcing them—have been extensively documented across many societies.

Some feminists, as discussed above, have also suggested that the role of women as mothers in the nuclear family facilitates the development of autonomy as the central characteristic of adult males and relationality as the central characteristic of adult females. Autonomy here is contrasted with a quality of relatedness, rather than with constraint that is imposed from outside. However, Chodorow's initial interest in this developmental process was its usefulness for explaining the existence of gender inequality. She argued that social structures that discriminate against women are the result of male's desires for autonomy and their need to differentiate themselves from women. These social psychological and social structural processes interact in women's religious experiences. The notions of surrender and submission for women have meanings that are both social psychological and social structural.

The work of Janet Jacobs on defectors from religious cults of the 1970s brings together both of these strands. Jacobs uses psychoanalytic object relations theory to better understand the charismatic relationship between the leader and his followers. In the relatively small sects and cults to which her respondents had belonged transcendent religious experiences were tied to the relationship with the spiritual leader. Jacobs argues that "the charismatic authority attributed to the leader is identified with three representations in the unconscious: the symbol of the divine; the idealized parental image; and the idealized self" (1989:73). The goal—the religious experience of mystical union—occurs through a process of internalization and merging of the charismatic leader as both a paternalistic god figure and a masculine ego ideal. Jacobs found that the experience of mystical union was far more common among males than females in her study.

Followers define their relationship to the charismatic leader in terms of their love for him. Jacobs notes, "As love becomes the defining emotion experienced during conversion, the notions of surrender and submission become dominant themes in the charismatic relationship" (1989:73). Respondents described their spirituality in terms of submission, obedience, and subservience (1989:75). Jacobs describes the first stage of devotional love as one in which "merging with the leader is experienced as a primary connection to an omnipotent parent on whom the devotee relies for love, protection and external control" (1989:76). With each succeeding stage the boundaries between the leader and devotee become more blurred. The second stage involves the projection of the ego ideal onto the leader, with the final stage the mystical union of self and other.

Jacobs postulates the first two stages of identification with the male leader are facilitated both by representation of god primarily in male terms in Western religious traditions, and by the predominance of family structures in Western society in which fathers are relatively distant. Jacobs argues:

> Further, the absence of the father figure in the patriarchal family also contributes to the need for religious movements that can provide a means through which the ideal father may be realized in the person of the charismatic leader who represents a transcendental father with the qualities of spirituality as well as familial paternalism. . . .The spiritual father offers the male devotee an affirmation of the self and at the same time provides a role model on which to project the ego ideal. This view of male bonding helps to explain the gender differences . . . wherein male devotees were found to experience religious phenomena in far greater numbers than female devotees. . . . Male devotees are much more likely to merge completely, experience the mystical revelation of the undifferentiated self in connection to the all powerful spiritual father. Female devotees, on the other hand, have more difficulty projecting the ego ideal onto a masculine love object, as the nature of their relationship is not only defined by gender differences but by gender roles which are hierarchical (1989:87).

Not only did the women in Jacobs' study encounter considerable barriers to the identification/merger religious experience enjoyed by most of the males, but the women also experienced forms of submission that involved physical, psychological, and sexual abuse (see also 1984:159). In cases of the latter the women reported feeling abused and exploited rather than enlightened.

Sexual surrender could exist with spiritual transcendence, and the women in Jacobs' study reported that their erotic relations did provide a form of intimacy with the leader. However, their experience was one of submissiveness, not merger or transcendence. In attributing this to the "context of subordination that is characteristic of heterosexual norms in a male-dominant culture" (1989:87) Jacobs points to the importance of context for understanding religious experience: both the gendered psychological development process and the hierarchical gender structures within the cults contribute to the religious experience of the female devotees differing from those of males in the same group.

While Jacobs focuses on conversion and religious experience, feminists are beginning to explore other ways that the themes of surrender and submission are articulated in women's religious socialization. In a case study of the relationship between a young woman and her spiritual advisor Stange (1991) examines the story of Jessica Hahn, the young woman whose rape by Jim Bakker became a part of the PTL scandal. Hahn was asked to "minister" to Bakker by John Fletcher, who also raped her. Hahn had been introduced to Fletcher, a traveling evangelist whom she had met through her own pastor for whom Hahn worked as a church secretary and babysitter. After the rapes Hahn became her pastor's mistress as well as secretary. Hahn appears to have accepted Fletcher and Bakker's view that God wanted her to offer her sexual services, that by ministering to Bakker and Fletcher she was serving the church, and that she should keep what happened to her secret among the "family" of the church leaders.

Stange presents Hahn's case as paradigmatic of women's "saintly masochism" (1991:110). Stange notes that

> in conservative Christian churches women's culpability (sexuality defined) and subordination are established in Genesis 2 and 3, with the reinforcement of an androcentric reading of Paul. In traditional Roman Catholicism, women are encouraged to "offer up" to God their suffering (and prime among the forms of female suffering is sexual abuse), this offering being in imitation of Christ (1991:110).

In Stange's account Hahn's rape occurs because Hahn identifies her spiritual leaders with God the father. Hahn's surrender and submission coexist with exploitation and abuse that are legitimated within the religious traditions themselves.

In another example, Young's (1989) analysis of the twentieth-century Italian saint, Maria Goretti shows how what Jacobs calls the "context of subordination" is in fact perpetuated in the virgin martyr myths, myths that condone sexual violence against women. Canonized by the Roman Catholic church in 1950, Maria Goretti was a twelve-year-old virgin in 1902. She was threatened with murder if she refused to have sex with her assailant. She refused, he stabbed her repeatedly, and she died. In the official story before she dies she asks her mother to forgive her for causing her distress, and she appears (in a vision) to her attacker in prison and forgives him.

Her sexuality is not her own; in the account sexual defilement is portrayed as worse than death. According to Young, "In the Western cultural tradition women's sexuality makes them physically and spiritually vulnerable. Their vulnerability is a necessary cultural production. A sexually autonomous woman undermines patrilineality and the legitimacy of children" (1989:480). Goretti is described as offering up her suffering, accepting responsibility for what happens (she asks her mother for forgiveness and forgives her attacker). It is through her ultimate surrender and submission—her virgin martyrdom—that transcendence is possible. (Stange points out that when Hahn rejects the role she in which she has been cast and becomes a "survivor" rather than a victim, going public with her story including pictures in *Playboy* magazine, it is she that is criticized.)

The tradition of "saintly masochism" has served to legitimate the sexual abuse of women and children in religious settings. Within a context of subordination it is one of the cultural accounts available for giving meaning to life events which otherwise are not interpretable. Yet this process of interpretation cannot be seen as the experiences of surrender and submission, freely chosen, described in the dominant religious experience narrative. The established meaning of that narrative rests on the precondition of autonomy.

Feminist Alternatives

Many feminist alternative models of religious experience emphasize processes that affirm the self rather than deny the self. While there are examples in many different religious practices, the position is most clearly articulated within the Goddess movement. In her essay, "Why Women Need the Goddess," Christ suggests several ways that Goddess symbolism has the potential for responding to particular needs of contemporary American women and for providing new models.

Most significant, she states, is that "the symbolism of the goddess is the acknowledgement of the legitimacy of female power as a beneficent and independent power" (Christ, 1987: 121). This symbol contrasts with the characteristic depictions of women—as passive, often as dependent, even as victims—in Western religious traditions.

The second reason Goddess symbolism is important is that it affirms the female body. The denigration of women in many cultures has been tied to women's bodies. Women have been seen as "closer to nature" and, like nature, in need of subjugation by male-culture (see Ortner, 1974; Griffin, 1978). The Goddess symbols carry a vision of life that is cyclic rather than linear; cycles of birth and death, cycles of ovulation and menstruation are invested with a renewed sanctity.

Third, in witchcraft circles the symbol of the Goddess offers a "positive evaluation of the will":

> The basic notion behind ritual magic and spellcasting is energy as power. Here the Goddess is a center or focus of power and energy: she is the personification of the energy the flows between beings in the natural and human worlds (Christ, 1987:127).

In this practice the exercise of will occurs within a context that emphasizes balance and harmony: the primary ethical tenet succinctly states "and ye harm none, do what ye will."

Finally, the Goddess symbolism prepares the way for a reevaluation of women's bonds and heritage, including but not limited to the bond between mothers and daughters (Christ, 1987:129). At the end of her essay Carol Christ envisions a future where the Goddess symbols will strengthen not only individual women, but also women's bonds with each other.

Implicit in Christ's essay is a model of religious experience very different from surrender-submission model described above. It suggests that religious ritual for women might affirm the self rather than demanding the surrender of the self, and it sees the body as integral to spiritual growth, a tool for the spiritual path, rather than something which stands in the way of spiritual development and must be spurned.

The Body as an Instrument of Religious Experience

While much of the religious literature has described the body as an impediment to religious experience, with women's bodies in particular the site of temptation and sin, we can also find places where the body is the route to the religious experience. Nonwestern tantric traditions, for example, use sexuality to bring about states of enlightenment. Both survey research and personal accounts of childbirth suggest that for some women this is a religious experience (McCreedy and Greeley, 1976; Rich, 1976). Also, the newly created rituals of women's spirituality present examples of religious experience using the body as an instrument.

A feminist study of a traditional religion where the body is used as an instrument is Brown's (1991) study of Haitian vodou in New York. Brown suggests that in the transfer from Dahomean religion to slavery vodou lost its institutional base. The body became its main ritual tool with extemporaneous and expressive possession performances as the central ritual practice. In New York, however, Haitians practice vodou adapted to an urban locale, removed from land and often from family. Gender differences are also reflected in the symbols. Brown argues that while vodou is misogynous, it is also extremely flexible. With movement from rural to urban residence in Haiti and the migration to the United States, roles of men and women have changed. Women engage in market activities and piece together the means of survival for themselves and their children. Priestesses like Mama Lola reflect these changes. When they become possessed by the female spirits in the pantheon they act out the forces that define the lives of female congregants, and, in the process, clarify the choices the women face. Brown argues that religious experience is enacted through the body of the priestess as she engages in possession-performance: unlike more familiar Western traditions her body becomes united with the spirit force in the religious experience. The very flexibility of vodou offers a way for women to seek autonomy within the significant constraints of their race and class context.

The women in the goddess movement which I have been studying are creating rituals which use the body as an instrument. Many of these rituals use biological processes as metaphors for natural forces and cycles. New rituals celebrate birthing, menarche, and menopause. Life cycle rituals provide ways of both affirming the body, symbolically expressing and sometimes achieving transcendence.

Life cycle rituals are dramatic, and they borrow most clearly from other traditions. As an example here I want to focus on menstrual rituals I have collected. When I spoke with women in the field who were engaged in menstrual rituals they knew little about menstrual rituals of other peoples. They had not done research on myths and prehistory in order to tie their rituals into ancient women's religion. They mostly were doing small rituals which seemed right to them and which they felt connected them in some vague way they could not articulate to other women and to women's power.

The menstrual rituals that I have collected so far are of three types: divining, fertility magic, and artistic.

Divining was done primarily in a circle and with reference to a particular question that was important to the group. A menstruating woman takes a piece of clean white paper and places it between her legs. She then either wipes her vulva producing a smear of blood, or she lets the blood drip onto the paper until there is a pattern. She then passes the paper around the circle. The women present say what they see in the pattern.

Fertility magic with menstrual blood makes a direct connection to the life sustaining properties of the endometrium. A woman, usually by herself, collects her menstrual blood, either by using cloth pads or a menstrual sponges. She then rinses the pad or sponge in a special bowl reserved for this purpose. The blood and water is then used for watering plants, in the garden, or in transplanting plants. One woman told me about doing a similar kind of fertility magic in the spring with her menstrual blood: after dark she would go outside and squat, bleeding directly onto garden soil.

The third type of menstrual rituals are those which produce a product which is artistic. One example was to simply bleed on pieces of paper, and then see the resulting patterns as works of art. Several women mounted public exhibitions of their "blood prints." Others displayed them in their homes. One woman made blood prints on 5 x 7 cards and used them as stationery. (The process is similar to the one used in divining, but outcome is different.) A more elaborate project was to bleed on squares of material then to piece the squares together in a quilt. Some mothers give such a quilt to her daughter as her "power quilt" as part of a coming of age ritual.

This last type of ritual may at first seem less "magical" than the other two. But it does accomplish two important effects. First, its symbolization broadens the referent beyond fertility to creativity in general. Second, it says that menstrual blood is not something dirty to be hidden, but rather a part of something beautiful, something shared among women. I also observed other ways that women affirmed their bodies during menstruation, through taking some time for themselves to withdraw, most commonly to drink a special herbal tea invested with ritual significance.

On one level any ritual that celebrates menstruation represents an inversion of the common Western understanding of menstruation as the curse visited upon women with the ejection of Eve from the garden of paradise. Inversion of traditional symbols is common among witches and among some of the more radical practitioners of women's religion. Much of Daly's (1978) work represents an effort to re-name, to take traditional meanings, especially where those meanings have placed a negative value on women, and invert that meaning (e.g., pp. 1-34).

Daly also argues that the renaming is also a reclaiming of women's power. Women who can do menstrual rituals are claiming their power. For some it is the traditional power of fertility, the power of women to give birth. But in the rituals I have described we can see in the beginnings of naming other power as well: the power to create, as demonstrated in the ritual use of menstrual blood to create art objects, the power to "tell forth" as in the use of menstrual blood for divination.

The broader understanding of power is especially important for feminist and lesbian witches. For them the narrow definition of women's power in terms of fertility is particularity unacceptable, and they have taken the lead in developing a broader symbolism. With individual acts of willfulness—choosing to recognize and invest with meaning their monthly bleeding—these women find religious meaning in their bodies. They see their own cycles as demonstrating connection to the cycles of nature.

CONCLUSION: AUTONOMY AND RELIGIOUS EXPERIENCE

Starhawk, a feminist wiccan thealogian, distinguishes between what she calls "power over" and "power within" (1982). I posit that part of what is occurring for women in current religious movements is the attempt to gain legitimacy for power defined as A's ability for A to do what A wants.

Sociologists usually discuss legitimacy in the context of what Starhawk (1982) calls "power over." In these analyses we learn why it is that women accept the right of men to make decisions and request/demand that women comply. For members of the dominant group there is no need to generate legitimacy for acting autonomously: that power can be taken for granted. This is not necessarily the case for women or members of other subordinate groups.

A workshop I attended as part of my fieldwork on the goddess movement was revealing to me. The conference brochure described the workshop in the following way: "Exploring our own personal places of power through meditative visualization, and learning how to return to that power to be nourished and sustained in our struggles for justice and peace." I expected some reference to those struggles, either at the beginning or the end of the workshop, especially since the meditation itself was quite short, and the workshop was finished about a half hour early. But no. The women there talked about their meditation experiences, talked about going some place far away, isolated, sometimes in nature but sometimes just to a space or a color.

Although I initially felt frustrated with what I felt was the individualistic and apolitical nature of most responses, it struck me that there was a parallel between these women and readers of romance novels as described by Radway (1985). Radway reports that the women viewed themselves as radical just because they took time out for themselves to read (rather than watching television with their husbands). In an interesting application of Chodorow (1978), Radway suggests that the act of reading is an act of nurturing the self by women whose daily life is mostly filled with acts of nurturing others.

I began to understand a little more why the women in the workshop might visualize a quiet, calm place away from everything and everybody as "their place of power." Yet, clearly they are using the term power in a nontraditional way; they mean freedom from constraint not the ability to control or influence others. What they, and Starhawk, are referring to as "power" is closer to what I have been discussing here as autonomy. The visualization exercise then becomes a spiritual practice which is intended to foster autonomy: when the leader told people to find their "places of power" she was helping them to have an experience of autonomy. The intention of the exercise is that the experience of autonomy in context of meditation will nurture the practitioner's ability to exercise autonomy in a nonmeditative situation as well.

We need to use both definitions of power and to examine how religion provides legitimacy for control over others (especially women) as well as how religion provides legitimacy for acting autonomously (again, especially for women). Feminist research on women's religious experiences illustrates both how women feel constrained by religious institutions and how women have been able to exercise agency through religious institutions. This explication of religion and power may help us better understand the participation of women and other socially marginal individuals in effervescent or ecstatic religious practices. One traditional explanation has seen these behaviors as compensatory (Glock, 1964, Lewis, 1971), a release from life's difficulties. But the analysis proposed here suggests the possibility that these women are not only victims of oppression, but also as engaging in negotiating and constructing their social reality. Autonomy grows out of the process of nurturing the self and feeling that that is a legitimate activity.

But does autonomy look the same when it is sought from the vantage point of the relational self rather than a self constructed out of rejection of the (m)other? Feminist political theorists find a model of nurturing power in mothering. Nedelsky (1989) points out that not only does mothering suggest a model of power that is directed toward nurturance, but that it also provides a way to reconceptualize autonomy. Rather than seeing the autonomous individual as unrealistically isolated from others, in the actions of a mother and child we see a form of autonomy that develops through relationship. This model of autonomy is particularly interesting in the context of thinking about a religious practice. It is in marked contrast to a model which assumes that an individual already exercises power in his life and must enter a religious practice which will provide discipline through submission—the model for the traditional male saint in many religions. For women, who have not been able to take for granted the legitimacy of acting autonomously, the appropriate religious practice might be that which nurtures autonomy rather than surrender and submission.

REFERENCES

Batson, C. D., P. Schoenrade, and L. Ventis

1993 *Religion and the individual: A social-psychological perspective.* New York: Oxford.

Brown, K. M.

1991 *Mama Lola: a vodou priestess in Brooklyn.* Berkeley, CA: University of California Press.

Bynum, C. W.

1987 *Holy feast and holy fast: The religious significance of food to medieval women.* Berkeley, CA: University of California Press.

Chodorow, N.

1978 *The reproduction of mothering,* Berkeley, CA: The University of California Press.

Christ, C.

1982 Why women need the goddess: Phenomenological, psychological, and political reflections. In *The politics of women's spirituality,* edited by C. Spretnak. Garden City, NY: Anchor.

1987 *The laughter of aphrodite.* San Francisco: Harper & Row.

Collins, P. H.

1991 *Black feminist thought.* New York: Routledge.

Daly, M.

1978 *Gyn/ecology: The metaethics of radical feminism.* Boston: Beacon.

Davidman, L.

1991 *Tradition in a rootless world: women turn to orthodox Judaism.* Berkeley, CA: University of California Press.

Davidman, L., and J. Jacobs

in press Feminist perspectives on new religious movements. In *A handbook of sects and cults in America: Assessing twenty years of research,* edited by D. Bromley and J. Hadden. Norwich, CT: JAI Press.

Dill, B. T.

1983 Race, class and gender: Prospects for an all inclusive sisterhood. *Feminist Studies* 9:131-150.

Flinders, C. L.

1993 *Enduring grace: Living portraits of seven women mystics*. San Francisco: Harper San Francisco.

Gilkes, C.

1985 Together and in harness: Women's traditions in the sanctified church. *Signs* 10:678-99.

Gilligan, C.

1982 *In a different voice*. Cambridge, MA: Harvard University Press.

Glock, C.

1964 The role of deprivation in the origin and evolution of religious groups. In *Religion and Social Conflict*, edited by R. Lee and M. E. Marty. New York: Oxford University Press.

Griffin, S.

1978 *Woman and nature*. New York: Harper & Row.

Hood Jr., R. W., and J. R. Hall

1980 Gender differences in the description of erotic and mystical experiences. *Review of Religious Research* 21:195-207.

Jacobs, J.

1984 The economy of love in religious commitment." *Journal for the Scientific Study of Religion* 23:155-171.

1989 The effects of ritual healing on female victims of abuse: A study of empowerment and transformation." *Sociological Analysis* 50:265-279.

1990 Women-centered healing rites: A study of alienation and reintegration. In *In gods we trust: New patterns of religious pluralism in America*, rev. ed., edited by T. Robbins and R. Anthony. New Brunswick, NJ: Transaction.

1991 *Divine disenchantment*. Bloomington, IN: Indiana University Press.

Kaufman, D.

1991 *Rachel's daughters: Newly orthodox Jewish women*. New Brunswick, NJ: Rutgers University Press.

Kelly-Gadol, J.

1976 The social relations of the sexes: Methodological implications of women's history. *Signs* 1:809-824.

Lewis, I. M.

1971 *Ecstatic religion: An anthropological study of spirit possession and shamanism*. London: Penguin.

McCready W., and A. Greeley

1976 *The ultimate values of the American population*. Beverly Hills, CA: Sage.

Millman, M., and R. Kantor

1975 *Another voice: Feminist perspectives on life and social science*. Garden City, NY: Doubleday.

Nedelsky, J.

1989 Reconceiving autonomy: Sources, thoughts, and possibilities." *Yale Journal of Law and Feminism* 1:7-56.

Neitz, M. J.

1987 *Charisma and community: A study of religion and commitment among the Catholic charismatic renewal*. New Brunswick, NJ: Transaction.

1990 In goddess we trust. In *In gods we trust: New patterns of religious pluralism in America*, rev. ed., edited by T. Robbins and R. Anthony, New Brunswick, NJ: Transaction.

1993 Inequality and difference: Feminist perspectives in the sociology of religion. In *Future for religion: New paradigms for social analysis*, edited by W. Swatos Jr. Newbury Park, CA: Sage.

Neitz, M. J., and J. V. Spickard

1990 Steps toward a sociology of religious experience: The theories of Mihaly Czsikszentmihalyi and Alfred Schutz. *Sociological Analysis* 51:15-34.

O'Connor, J.

1989 Rereading, conceiving and reconstructing traditions: Feminist research in religion. *Women's Studies* 17:101-120.

Ortner, S.
1974 Is female to male as male is to culture? In *Woman, culture and society*, edited by M. Rosaldo and L. Lamphere, Stanford, CA: Stanford University Press.

Radway, J.
1985 *Reading the romance*, Chapel Hill, NC: University of North Carolina Press.

Rich, A.
1976 *Of woman born: Motherhood as experience and institution*. New York: Norton.

Rose, S.
1987 Woman warriors: The negotiation of gender in a charismatic community. *Sociological Analysis* 48:245-58.

Rubin, G.
1975 The traffic in women. In *Toward an anthropology of women*, edited by R. Reiter. New York: Monthly Review Press.

Smith, D.
1977 A sociology for women. In *prism of sex: Essays in the sociology of Knowledge*, edited by J. Sherman and E. Beck. Madison: University of Wisconsin Press.

Stange, M. Z.
1991 Jessica Hahn's strange odyssey from PTL to Playboy. *Journal of Feminist Studies in Religion* 7:105-116.

Starhawk
1982 *Dreaming the dark*, Boston: Beacon Press.

Tronto, J.
1987 Beyond gender difference to a theory of care. *Signs* 12:644-63.

Williams, D.
1985 Women's oppression and lifeline politics in women's religious narratives. *Journal of Feminist Studies in Religion* 1:59-72.

Young, K. Z.
1989 The imperishable virginity of Maria Goretti. *Gender and Society* 3:474-482.

23

Religious Instruction and Religious Experience

JAMES MICHAEL LEE

"The glory of Him who moves all things rays forth
through all the universe, and is reflected
from each thing in proportion to its worth."
***   ***   ***   ***
"For throughout all the universe God's ray
enters all things according to their merit
and nothing has the power to block its way."
—Dante (1970:1, 11.1-3, 31, 11.22-24)

INTRODUCTION

Twenty-two of the twenty-four chapters in this handbook examine in depth and in breadth the nature and manifestations of religious experience. The final two chapters, including this one, deal with how religious experience can be intentionally and effectively facilitated in persons. In this connection it is well to recall the view of many scholars (Aquinas 1272:II-II, q.188, a.6, c.) and spiritual writers (Merton, 1949:182-189) throughout the ages who maintain that while research and study are necessary and important, nonetheless it is even better to share with others the knowledge gained by this research and study. The axis of this chapter revolves around what I regard as a yet more excellent way, namely, to teach others to fully partake in those forms and levels of religious experience which scholars have both researched and shared intellectually.

In the task of making a better world there are, therefore, three ascending levels of research on religious experience: the research activity itself, the sharing of the fruits of this research with scholars and laypersons, and the facilitation in others of those kinds of religious experience which scholarship has explored and identified.

The first one-third of this chapter will be devoted to providing the necessary background of the nature, operations, and underlying theory of religious instruction. This relatively extended treatment is required in order to properly appreciate the place and the possibilities of religious experience in religious instruction—especially for theologians, social scientists of religion, pastoral counselors, and those other readers who are understandably unfamiliar with the field of religious instruction.

DEFINITIONS

Religious Instruction

Religious instruction is defined as that kind of deliberative activity in which desired learning outcomes are intentionally and effectively facilitated in others. Religious instruction, therefore, consists in any and all kinds of facilitation activities which are designed to produce and do indeed produce desired learning outcomes. Thus religious instruction cannot be equated with any one specific mode of facilitation such as didactics, lecture, group discussion, role playing, simulation, or the like. Nor can religious instruction be confined to any particular kind of setting, be that setting a formal one such as a classroom or an informal one such as a playground. The term "instruction," then, is a synonym for teaching in its totality with no restriction as to environment, subject-matter, structure, or product. Though there are occasional demurrers (Westerhoff, 1976:76; Eisner, 1979:158-159), nonetheless in educational science the term "instruction" is generally preferred to the term "teaching" because instruction underscores the fact that teaching is an art/science (Lee, 1973:215-221), namely, a well-honed skill deployed intentionally from a scientific base (Gage, 1978:17-20, 41).

Religious instruction is not equivalent to religious education. Rather, religious instruction is a form of religious education. The other two forms are religious guidance/counseling and the administration of religious education activities.

Religious Experience

In this chapter religious experience is defined as the engagement of the self with the transcendent in any form in which the transcendent might manifest itself.

In this chapter, furthermore, religious experience is conceptualized as taking place at any and every level ranging from the delicate intimation of the transcendent awared upon seeing the sunlight glint off a wildflower in a May Alpine meadow to the most profound and intense of mystical experiences such as mystical marriage (Raymond of Capua, 1960:164-196; Batson and Ventis, 1982:56-96; Lee, 1982:100).

In this chapter, moreover, religious experience is viewed as independent of specific theological commitments or entanglements. This principle means that the existence and level of religious experience does not flow from this or that particular theology on the one hand nor is restricted only to persons holding this or that particular theology on the other hand. History gives ample evidence that persons with little or no theology, as well as individuals with differing and often basically conflicting theologies have had religious experience at virtually all levels of intensity. Indeed, it would appear that theology is fundamentally shaped by, flows from, and derives its content from religious experience rather than the other way around. The Bible, for example, is basically a record of a people's religious experience over the centuries (Lee, 1983:8-11).

In this chapter, finally, religious experience is regarded as a form of general experience or, perhaps more accurately, a way of experiencing. Thus religious experience is not apart from human experience but an integral part of it. The basic characteristics of all experience as identified by Lee (1985a:651-652) are used in this chapter to characterize religious experience. These four characteristics are holism, process, interaction, and certitude. Like experience in general, religious experience is holistic in that it is the all-inclusive life of the self and thus is wider than any one particular human function such as cognition or affect. Like experience in general, religious experience is processive in that it is the ongoing, dynamic living out of one's existence. Like experience in general, religious experience is interactional in that it is the living encounter of self with the environment. Like experience in general, religious experience is certain because it takes place in the life of the self and hence is both immediate and subjectively sure.

THE PLACE OF RELIGIOUS INSTRUCTION IN THE LIFE OF THE CHURCH

In the religious dimensions of virtually every society of which we have knowledge, the two central, core, and indispensable activities have always been worship and religious instruction.

In primitive societies, the care of worship was typically given over to recognized religious leaders who took great pains to conduct various kinds of worship services in such a way as to provide an optimally focused set of religious experience to the tribesperson (Hargrove, 1971:65-80). Religious instruction activity in primitive societies, by contrast, was usually the function of the whole community in varying degrees: the nuclear and extended family members who, in a variety of ways, taught their children the religious experiences and affects and doctrines of the tribe, the elders who provided more intense religious instruction to persons at key times in their lives such as at the onset of puberty, shamans and medicine men who interwove a great deal of religious instruction in their attempts to cure persons with physical or spiritual maladies, significant others, and the like (Radin, 1957:78-104). Religious instruction in primitive societies was not exclusively for the young but rather was conducted in such a pervasive manner that persons of every age level could broaden and deepen their religious experiences, religious conduct, religious feelings, and religious knowledge (Durkheim, 1947:299-414).

This double centrality of worship and religious instruction is also characteristic of all Christian churches today—to say nothing of Judaism where the principal religious leader bears the official title of Teacher (Rabbi). This dual centrality can easily be appreciated by examining three fundamental facts, namely The Great Commission, the ceremony in which Christian clergy are ordained, and the weekly activities of the clergy.

In his final and summary commission to his church immediately prior to his ascension into heaven, Jesus (Matthew 28:19-20) only commanded his church to perform two tasks which he obviously regarded as central and indispensable, namely to teach religion and to baptize. It is well worth noting that in his Great Commission to the church, Jesus mentioned teaching first. (Parenthetically it is helpful to observe that Paul the Apostle, whom Thomas Aquinas labeled *the* Apostle, baptized only on rare occasions, consciously directing virtually all of his activities toward religious instruction).

It is the firm contention of most if not all Christian religions that the ordination ceremony not only bestows special powers upon the ordinand but also represents a sacred commission given by the church to that individual. This sacred commission, among other things, summarizes the essential and most important functions which the particular church expects the ordinand to perform as a member of the clergy. Almost invariably, the ordination ceremonies of the various churches expressly mention religious instruction as a core, indispensable, and pervasive function of the clergy.

If one were to make a daily log of the activities of the typical member of the parish clergy, one would find that most of their day is devoted to activities which in one way or another involve heavy doses of religious instruction. The basic axis and context of such regular clergy activities as home and hospital and community visitation, sermon preparation, meetings with church groups and committees, professional reading, and the like are primarily religious instruction in nature. Even the celebration of worship services is essentially (though not exclusively) religious instruction in character. This fact holds true both in the nonsacramental as well as in the sacramental churches. In the nonsacramental churches the worship service is manifestly religious instructional (sermon, Bible reading, hymns, prayer content). In the sacramental churches the worship service is at once manifestly religious instructional (sermon, Bible reading, hymns, prayer content) and latently but no less genuinely religious instructional (the consecration of the Eucharist and its subsequent distribution to the faithful are shot through with fundamental religious instruction content).

Because religious instruction is so central to the essential nature and life of the church, and because religious instruction necessarily includes the intentional facilitation of all manner of religious outcomes (including religious experience), social scientists, theologians, litterateurs, and others conducting various kinds of research on religious experience can ill afford to exclude, marginalize, or otherwise minimize the place of religious instruction in their scholarly investigations. To do so would be to bar a priori and frivolously a central and pervasive zone in which religious experience both occurs and is facilitated.

Despite the essential importance of religious instruction in the life of the church, serious research into the nature and operation of religious instruction activity usually has been disvalued both by theologians and by social scientists of religion.

By and large, theologians have regarded religious instruction as flowing directly and uniquely from theology in one way or another—though they usually affirm that they do not know how the religious instruction act works in the concrete. For the great bulk of theologians, religious instruction is nothing more than transmitting theological knowledge, understandings, and values to learners in as undiluted a form as possible. Nothing more than this is needed, and anything more is superfluous. All that is required for effective religious instruction activity in its totality is a good grasp of "solid" theology (Miller, 1963:5; Warren, 1970:31). Consequently theologians tend to look down in bewilderment and sometimes with disdain at religious instruction as a separate field of scholarly research. Though Richard McBrien (1976:170) is primarily a theological popularizer rather than a top-level scholar, his indictment of the current state of religious instruction research is probably shared by the overwhelming number of theologians both scholars and popularizers: "Let it be said candidly and openly: religious education has a less than elevated reputation within the academic community at large and within the theological community in particular."

The disdain which most theologians have for religious instruction as a serious realm of scholarship and as a research-based distinct area of facilitational endeavor is equaled and possibly exceeded by the level of low regard in which religious instruction is held by social scientists of religion (Hood, 1993).

It is not surprising, therefore, that for the most part social scientists of religion have neglected to make a concerted effort to actively, directly, and continuously interject their scholarship into religious instruction activity—

and, curiously, into the bloodstream of church life in general. Major exceptions to this statement include: 1) a few specific and quite practical fields such as pastoral counseling; 2) certain acute areas which are potentially or currently embarrassing to the churches, such as devising psychological inventories to identify personality disorders in candidates for the clergy or in proposing strategies for dealing with inservice dysfunctional clerics; 3) some arenas which have direct or indirect financial consequences for the denomination such as identifying causes for declining church membership or proposing methods for increasing the amount of money donated to the church by parishioners or by wealthy community leaders.

It is probably accurate to assert that the social-scientific study of religion has begun only faintly to achieve its potential global impact on religion in all its phases from basic theory to practical activities such as religious instruction. Social scientists of religion have to ask themselves whether they wish to help ensure that their theories, research findings, and scholarly based practical procedures to become operative and yeasting in the life of the churches and in other concrete religious activities, or whether they wish to continue to function in a realm which is usually detached from the life of the churches and sometimes is even esoteric. The danger in the current situation is that the social-scientific study of religion will continue to be trivialized, marginalized, and distrusted by the very group (churches) which should value it the most, and that as one result both the discipline and its scholars will face extinction.

Lee (1971:246-251; 1977:120-122; 1982:154) has suggested that religious activity (and therefore church life) is not governed by theological theory alone but rather is governed by a mixture of theories including social-science theory. In other words, theology is not *the* theory of religion but only *one* theory of religion. Other theories ranging from biological theory to literature theory to most notably social-science theory constitute legitimate theories of religion. The overall, comprehensive, inclusive theory of religion is religionology.

The theology of religious activity desperately needs social science as a coequal partner (Berger, 1967:179) in order to expand, correct, and give new and essential data from the outside, not only for the development of an adequate comprehensive theory of religious activity, but also for the viability, vitality, and adequacy of theology itself. Conversely, the social-scientific theory of religious activity urgently needs theology as a coequal partner to offer new fundamental data, values, and horizons which are not available to social science through its own procedures.

More specifically, religious instruction urgently needs social-scientific theory, procedures, and data if it is to achieve adequate grounding and effectiveness. It would be an enormous boon to the study and practice of religious instruction if social scientists of religion would include on a more or less regular basis the field of religious instruction as one of the areas to build theories, conduct research, and work toward extensions of this theory and research.

MACROTHEORY IN RELIGIOUS INSTRUCTION

There are currently two major competing macrotheories of religious instruction, namely, the theological macrotheory and the social-science macrotheory.

The term "macrotheory" is used in this chapter to mean a grand, overall, global form of theory into which are inserted theories and subtheories of lesser scope. These theories and subtheories of lesser scope may be complementary or conflicting. The atomic theory is a major macrotheory in chemical science. Macrotheory is of an essentially different order than metatheory. The term "metatheory" usually denotes a theory of theories, a critical theoretical examination of the nature and structure of theory in general (Lee, 1982:122).

The theological macrotheory of religious instruction is not the same as theology in itself, nor is the social-science macrotheory of religious instruction the same as social science in itself. The theological macrotheory of religious instruction is the fundamental approach which religious educationists and educators have toward religious instruction activity in order to ultimately explain, predict, and verify their teaching work. The same holds true with respect to the social-science macrotheory.

The theological macrotheory of religious instruction has been the dominant approach for millennia and remained fundamentally unchallenged until 1971. This macrotheory conceptualizes religious instruction as a formal branch of practical theology (Osmer, 1990:216-238). Thus, to teach religion consists first and foremost of the educator and the learners theologizing together or separately. The theological macrotheory holds that theology and theology alone possesses the power to adequately explain, predict, and verify all religious instruction activity. The basic reason undergirding this statement is that in one way or another theology is the queen of the sciences, especially of the religious sciences, and hence governs the work of all the sciences and scientifically-based arts including that of teaching religion (Westerhoff, 1982:218-220; Lamport, 1992:85-86). All religion and all religious activity, including that of religious instruction, is basically and most authentically expressed in theological form (McBrien, 1974:135; Marthaler, 1975:13). For the theological macrotheory, theology and theology alone is capable of devising and testing teaching procedures, of explaining the conditions under which religious learning can or cannot be facilitated, and of predicting both who will or will not be an effective religious educator and which instructional procedure will or will not be successful. In this view, only theology possesses the competence to devise, implement, and substantiate the entire range of religious education phenomena (Miller, 1980:153-164). And only theology is capable of deciding if a particular instructional practice is genuinely Christian and truly meets the criteria of what one or another denomination asserts is theologically correct (Darcy Bérubé, 1978:118-119). Religious learning is not only ultimately but in a key sense also immediately the unfathomable act of the Holy Spirit who is the only true religious educator—and it is theology which is solely and uniquely competent to explore and pronounce on the nature and workings of the Holy Spirit (Little, 1961:168; Smallbones, 1990:109-112).

Though there were some glimmerings of a social-science macrotheory of religious instruction in the writings of George Albert Coe (1917; 1929) and C. Ellis Nelson (1967), the development of a full-blown, comprehensive, and systematic social-science macrotheory did not come until 1971 with the publication of *The Shape of Religious Instruction* by James Michael Lee. This macrotheory conceptualizes religious instruction as an instance of general instruction. In the term "religious instruction," the word "instruction" is the noun not only grammatically but ontically, and hence properly situates the word "religious" as its qualifying adjective. Since the instructional process is by definition, comprehension, and observation a branch of social science, religious instruction is social scientific in nature and activity—social science being the generic term for the collection of those disciplines which are focused on the detailed, systematic, and empirical study of human beings and their interrelations with individuals, groups, and institutions. To teach religion consists first and foremost in the effective facilitation of desired learning outcomes in learners of all kinds. The social-science macrotheory holds that social science forms the basic ecology, essential structure, foundational processes, and immediate procedures of all forms of religious instruction. Consequently social science possesses the power to adequately explain, predict, and verify the whole range of religious instruction phenomena. Only social science is capable of devising and testing teaching procedures, of explaining the conditions under which religious learning can or cannot be facilitated, and of predicting both who will or will not be an effective religious educator and which instructional procedure will or will not be successful. The social-science macrotheory of religious instruction in itself is value-free in the sense that it not only accommodates all sorts of diverse theological views as a dimension of the subject matter of religion teaching, but is admirably capable of explaining, predicting, and verifying the effective selection and implementation of the entire spectrum of complementary or conflicting religious content (Lee, 1982:132-133).

Of the many adverse criticisms leveled at the theological approach to religious instruction (Lee 1988a:99-117) six are worthy of mention here. (The first four deal with negative critiques at the theoretical level while the last two consist of unfavorable judgments at the practical level.) First, the theology of practice is fundamentally different from practice itself, in this case from the practice of religious instruction. If theology of practice were the same as practice itself then all reality would be essentially theology and the crassest form of reductionism would ensue. Second, theology provides only a theological description of the nature and workings of any particular reality, including the reality of religious instruction. Theology does not provide a description of the intrinsic nature and workings of the particular reality itself. Thus the theology of a given reality is always a description external to a description of the reality in and of itself. Third, theological science does not possess the methodological tools capable of adequately explaining how the teaching-learning act takes place, of predicting which teaching procedures will fail and which will succeed, and of verifying the degree to which teaching-learning has taken place. Fourth, every version of the theological approach necessarily rests upon one particular brand of theology and necessarily excludes all other theological positions. This lack of incorporation of the entire range of theological positions (value freedom) makes it impossible for the theological approach to serve as an adequate macrotheory for teaching all varieties of religious content. Fifth, throughout history theology has never devised as much as a single instructional procedure, nor has it ever shown directly how the effectiveness of the teaching-learning act in itself can be improved. Sixth, when they do write or lecture on teaching procedures or on learning events, advocates of the theological approach typically begin by briefly stating that theology constitutes the central axis for explaining, predicting, and verifying the process of religious instruction. Having done this, the advocates spend the overwhelming bulk of their presentation in proposing various instructional procedures devised totally and exclusively by social science with no serious attempt made to show how their particular theology generated these instructional procedures, how their particular theology uniquely enfleshes these procedures, or how their particular theology explains/predicts/verifies these procedures. It is as if these persons sprinkle a little theological holy water on their topic and after this perfunctory sprinkling go about using social-science material on instructional procedure with absolutely no relation to the sprinkling or to the theological holy water.

Very few in-depth or specific negative critiques have been directed toward the social-science approach to religious instruction, probably because advocates of the theological approach assume a priori that theological science provides the basic macrotheory and thus it is neither necessary nor important to examine seriously the fundamental approach to religious instruction. Two adverse criticisms of the social-science approach have nevertheless surfaced. First, the social-science approach, qua approach, is value free. Thus in its generalized form it is not wedded to any particular brand of "solid and correct" theology, and consequently is unsuitable as a basis for teaching this or that specific religion or doctrine (Warren, 1970:31; Gangel, 1976:32-33; McBrien, 1976:174). Second, the social-science approach uses educational and other forms of social-scientific language, rather than theological language, and thus is not suitable for the task of religious instruction (McIntyre, 1976:6; Darcy Bérubé 1978:119).

The foundational issue of whether theological science or social science forms the fundamental and pervasive macrotheory of religious instruction has many and grave consequences for the topic of this chapter, namely, religious instruction for religious experience. Some of these practical consequences include the possibility and advisability of teaching for religious experience outcomes, the specific instructional procedures to be selected and used in teaching for religious education outcomes, the ways of validly and reliably evaluating the results of teaching for religious experience outcomes, and the allowable range of interpretation both of religious experience and the teaching of it.

In concluding this section, it is illuminative to note that of the three basic forms of religious education (instruction, guidance/counseling, and administration), only religious instruction has not deserted completely the theological approach and embraced wholeheartedly the social-science macrotheory.

ON THE TEACHING OF RELIGIOUS EXPERIENCE

The History of Religious Experience in Religious Instruction

Religious instruction as a distinct area of specialized study by and large did not exist prior to the twentieth century. When pre-twentieth-century writers dealt with religious instruction, they did so in a much broader and far less focused fashion than is the case today.

As a general rule, it is safe to assert that those scholars, church leaders, and other writers who have written or ruled on religious instruction from the first century right down to the present day by and large have not included religious experience as a content to be taught. Two major reasons can be adduced for this phenomenon.

First, with only rare exceptions such as the ancient catechumenate (Justin, 152:61; Dujarier, 1962:50; Lee, 1985a:633-637) cognitive content, especially in its ratiocinative nonintuitive form, has almost always occupied center stage in the history of religious instruction in the churches. This statement holds true not only for ancient and medieval Catholic writers and church leaders such as Augustine (389; 399) and Thomas Aquinas (1259:q.11), but also for the Protestant Reformers as Martin Luther (1935:xi-xv) and John Calvin (1971:246-248) as well as for the Counterreformers including Charles Borromeo and Robert Bellarmine, both of whom wrote important and influential Catholic catechisms. The supremacy of ratiocinative nonintuitive cognition in Christian religious education has continued from the Reformation era down through the present. Some writers such as Wrenn (1991:75-137) see cognitive content in terms of teaching doctrinal tenets. Other writers such as Hofinger (1962) view cognitive content in terms of "heralding the Good News of salvation." Others such as Herbart (1908) regard cognitive content as providing the sure footing for the goal of a good moral life. Others such as Marthaler (1978:77) look on cognitive content as an especially potent means of molding and otherwise formatively socializing learners into faithfully obeying the mandates of ecclesiastical officials. Still others, notably those of a neo-Marxian bent such as Groome (1980), view cognition as the most effective pathway to political power in both the ecclesiastical and secular arenas.

The very strong and pervasive emphasis on cognition throughout the history of Christian religious instruction has had as its natural consequence the virtual exclusion of religious experience from the task of teaching religion. This is only natural since ratiocinative cognition and religious education do not mix; indeed they are antipodes, a fact recognized by almost all masters of the Christian spiritual life before and after a splendid formulation of this principle by the Pseudo-Dionysius (1987:135-141). History has shown that where ratiocination is present, there religious experience is absent, or at the very least seriously diminished.

The second major reason for the historical exclusion of religious experience from the content of religion teaching has been the generally accepted a priori assumption that religious experience has never and can never be taught by a human teacher. In this view, religious experience occurs by direct divine infusion or by some other kind of unfathomable zap of God's grace and never because of the work of a religious educator (Moran, 1966:116-117; Rood, 1968:74). Hence all human efforts to teach religious experience are folly.

Since it relies on empirical evidence and excludes virtually nothing on a priori grounds, the social-science approach to religious instruction, in marked contrast to the theological macrotheory, keeps open the possibility of teaching religious experience. Indeed, Lee (1985a:42-49, 649-672) and one of his former students Bickimer (1983:44-62) contend that religious experience can be taught and has been taught, and that religious experience should constitute the most important terminal goal of religious instruction.

Can Religious Experience Be Taught?

Like faith, religious experience is a construct and thus cannot be taught except as a construct (Lee, 1990:271-273). The issue for this chapter, then, is not whether religious experience can be taught but whether the specific experiences out of which the construct is created can be taught. In order to keep the semantics and linguistics of this chapter parallel with the rest of the present volume, this chapter in general and this section in particular uses the term religious experience in two ways, namely as a construct and as one or another specific religious experience.

There is general agreement among theologians, social scientists of religion, and religious educationists that it is possible to teach *about* religious experience. The disagreement occurs over the issue of whether it is possible to teach religious experience *directly.*

In order to address this question adequately, it is necessary to define instruction (teaching). Instruction is typically defined by general educationists as the broad process by and through which learning is intentionally caused in an individual in one way or another. This definition suggests that all teaching, including religious instruction, is varied in 1) procedure, 2) substance, 3) context. First, teaching is varied in procedure in that there exist numerous instructional methods and techniques. Teaching, then, is procedurally far wider than talking. Second, teaching is varied in substance in that there are at least nine principal substantive contents in any instructional act (Lee, 1985a). Cognitive content constitutes only one of these nine principal substantive contents. Affective content and lifestyle content are two other molar contents, and in religious instruction for overall religious outcomes constitute far more important substantive contents than intellection. Third, teaching is varied in context in that it is enacted in a wide variety of environments ranging from formal settings such as a classroom or church building to informal settings such as a playground or in the home over dinner. There is no such thing as formal and informal teaching; there is only teaching in formal and informal settings.

Teaching, therefore, is not restricted to standing in front of a group of people and verbally pumping out cognitive content. Religious instruction is not a messenger boy for theology whose sole task is to transfer theological content as safely and as purely as possible to the ears of waiting students in a school setting (Lee, 1971:246-248). Rather, teaching consists essentially in structuring the molar variables present in any teaching-learning situation in such a manner that the desired learning outcome ensues (Lee, 1973:230-268): The four molar structural variables present in each and every teaching act in all settings are the teacher, the learner, the subject-matter, and the environment.

The foregoing proper and adequate definition of teaching indicates that at the theoretical level it is indeed possible to teach religious experience directly.

At the empirical level, there is a great dearth of empirical, and most notably of experimental or even quasi-experimental studies on actually teaching religious experience in formal or informal settings. This fact holds true worldwide, even in England where a great deal of the empirical research on religious experience is conducted with a school-based population (Hyde, 1990:177-185). The extreme paucity of empirical research on the act of teaching religious experience is probably due to the lack of familiarity, to the anestheticization, and even to the fear of empirical research on the part of many (most?) religious educationists. However, as Hood's chapter in the present volume amply demonstrates, there does exist a corpus of empirical research conducted by social scientists of religion to suggest that religious experience has indeed been facilitated using various procedures. Most of these facilitation procedures can be legitimately classified as teaching when the teaching process is properly understood.

Should Religious Experience Be Taught?

From the strictly humanistic perspective, religious experience should be taught because this kind of experience, however widely or narrowly it is defined, is part of the human condition (Maslow, 1964; Greeley, 1974:139-142; Thomas and Cooper, 1978:433-437; Gallup and Jones, 1989:159-173). From any perspective, authentic humanistic education is always well-rounded (Maritain, 1936:17-36; Lamont, 1957:1-19). By definition, well-rounded education requires that every important kind of experience which forms a fundamental positive dimension of human existence should be taught if at all possible.

From the religious standpoint, religious experience should be taught because it is central and foundational to religious living. Virtually every major religion, and a host of minor ones, assert that religious experience constitutes not only the basis but also the validation of everything which the particular religion stands for existentially and asserts cognitively. In the final analysis, God in his many manifestations is primarily to be experienced, rather than to be defined (Kempis, 1940:1-2; Armstrong, 1993). Indeed, all major religions ranging from Hinduism to Catholicism regard the mystic as the pinnacle of religious achievement—and the mystic is the one who has the most frequent and most intense religious experiences.

Throughout its two millennia history, Catholicism has consistently exalted two prime realities, namely the Eucharist and mystical experience. Catholicism unreservedly asserts that the Eucharist constitutes its energizing center because the Eucharist is above all a personal encounter, an immediate existential experience not only between the person receiving Communion and the here-and-now actually present Jesus but also between the here-and-now actually present Jesus and anyone who gazes upon him in the tabernacle. Catholicism also exalts mystical experience as the highest level of the spiritual life here on earth (Tanquerey, 1930:682-696; Fischer, 1969:136-142), a level which every person should strive to attain. It is therefore ironic that institutional Catholicism (Sacra Congregatio pro Clericis 1971; National Conference of Catholic Bishops 1979), almost all of Catholicism's best-known religious educationists (Groome, 1980; Moran, 1989), and all of Catholicism's school-based curricular textbook series eschew religious experience in the instruction proposals they offer or support, opting instead for the primacy of one or another form of cognitive content.

At the center of Evangelical Protestantism lies the conviction that a personal born-again experience with Jesus is necessary for present and future salvation. It is therefore ironic that most institutional Evangelical Protestant denominations, most of its best-known religious educationists (Gangel, 1985) and virtually all of its officially accepted school-based curricular textbook series eschew religious experience in the religious instruction they propose or incorporate, opting instead for doctrinal content or other kinds of theology.

Though mainline Protestantism typically does not accept the real presence of Jesus in the Eucharist and the concomitant religious experience attendant upon this presence, and does not place nearly as much emphasis as do their Evangelical counterparts on the centrality of a born-again experience, nonetheless like Catholics and Evangelicals, mainline Protestant religious educationists (Miller, 1980; Nelson, 1967) and officially church-sanctioned curricula eschew religious experience as a content to be taught or learned.

In addition to the reasons already adduced, it is evident that religious experience constitutes a major place in the repertoire of religious instruction content because religious instruction is precisely that, namely *religious* instruction and not theological instruction. Without its experiential dimension, religious instruction is no longer truly and authentically religious (Glock, 1962:s-98—s-100; Lee, 1971:10-19; Gillespie, 1988).

In deciding whether religious experience should be taught, it is essential to underscore that this chapter deals with religious instruction and not with theological instruction. The function of theological instruction is essentially and exclusively cognitive, that is to teach learners to come to requisite knowledge of God and of his infinite manifestations, as well as to engage in cognitive reflection on these truths both in themselves and in terms of the theological consequences of these truths for other phenomena. Thus theological instruction cannot and therefore ought not include teaching for religious outcomes. For its part, the task of religious instruction is holistic, that is to teach learners not only that kind of theological knowledge and reflection which may be relevant to the instructional task at hand, but also to directly facilitate all appropriate kinds of affective, lifestyle, and existential realities including religious experiences. This crucial distinction between theological instruction and religious instruction shows unmistakably that while facilitating religious experience falls outside the purview and competence of theological instruction, such facilitation constitutes a necessary dimension of overall religious instruction activity.

As a scholium to this section, the foregoing paragraph suggests that religious instruction is inherently more valuable to the church and to persons than is theological instruction.

THE SHAPE OF TEACHING FOR RELIGIOUS EXPERIENCE

The complete and proper content of religious instruction is the religious instruction act itself, nothing more and nothing less. This global content is composed of a fused compound of two fundamental contents, namely substantive content and structural content (Lee, 1985a:2-3, 8). Substantive content is subject matter. Structural content is the way in which subject matter is taught; it is the whole interactive set of instructional procedures. Substantive content and structural content become comprehensive constituent contents of the religious instruction act only when they are conjoined in the deployment of the act itself. It is in this existential deployment that substantive content and structural content become fused into an ontically new mediated reality, namely the religious instruction act (Lee, 1973:17-19, 29-31; Lee, 1982:165-174). Because of this mediated fusion of substantive content and structural content, it follows that the more that these two fundamental contents are in harmony with each other, the greater will be the probability that the desired learning outcome will be achieved.

Structural content is an authentic and powerful content in its own right because the way in which a person teaches is also what that individual teaches. The "that which" a person teaches is not only substantive content but also the instructional process with which this substantive content is thoroughly fused. Indeed, structural content is often a more potent content than substantive content in the instructional dynamic in the sense that it alters to a greater or lesser extent the coloration of substantive content and in the sense that it comprises a fundamental co-constituent content. Religion changes in the act of teaching it (Coe, 1929:23). In short, the way in which an educator teaches often has greater effects on the learner and on learning than the substantive content which the educator teaches.

In terms of teaching for religious experience, the analysis given in the foregoing paragraphs suggests that in teaching for religious experience outcomes, the substantive content is religious experience and the structural content consists of teaching in a religiously experiential fashion. In order to teach religious experience effectively, the educator must first of all select as the substantive content holistic existential religious experience itself and not some single dimension of religious experience such as religious affect or some content external to religious experience such as theological reflection on religious experience. Second, in order to teach religious experience successfully, the religious educator must employ instructional procedures which are in harmony with religious experience and hence productive of religious experience outcomes. For example, the religious educator endeavoring to teach religious experience will refrain from large doses of cognitive teaching procedures such as the lecture (Broadwell, 1980; Miller, 1991:340 319) or higher-order questioning (Rousseau and Redfield, 1981:237-245; Dantonio, 1990) or even exclusive reliance on affective procedures such as role playing (Pearlman, 1990:27-36), but instead will rely heavily on experiential lifestyle procedures such as simulation (Cairns, Woodward, and Savery, 1989:245-271) or environmental teaching (Habermas and Issler, 1992:145-146).

The confluence of substantive content and structural content which occurs in the enactment of the instructional event takes place in a fluid but still circumscribed configuration. The basic elements of this configuration, and to a certain extent its circumference, are constantly changing. The basic elements or molar variables of this configuration are four: the teacher, the learner, the subject matter, and the environment. From the processive and architectural point of view, all teaching, including religious instruction, essentially consists in the continual structuring and restructuring of the four molar variables in such a manner that the desired learning outcome is thereby produced. This foundational concept of teaching as structuring the pedagogical situation is illustrated in a model of teaching proposed by Lee (1973: 234):

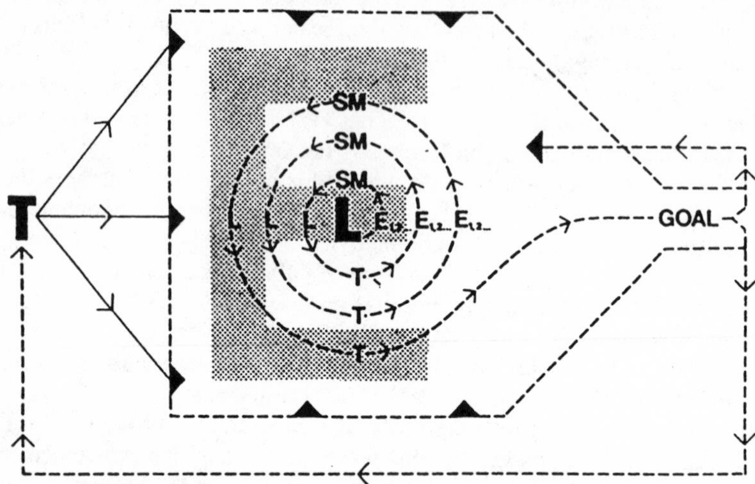

In this model T stands for the teacher, L for the learner, E for the environment, and SM for the subject matter. The large square circumscribed by dotted lines represents the instructional situation. It is immediately apparent that there is a large shaded-in E which covers the entire instructional situation; this indicates that the instructional situation is an environment and therefore all four molar variables in the teaching situation have their locus in an environment. Learning necessarily takes place within an environmental context and therefore is constantly being modified by all the relevant variables inside and outside it (Lines, 1987:48-54).

This dynamic interactive modification, plus the fact that two of the four molar variables are human beings, underscores the fact that the instructional process is not mechanistic. Consequently, even the most carefully designed structured teaching situation does not automatically yield the desired learning outcome; it only enhances the probability that the desired learning outcome will ensue. The religious educator can never be sure ahead of time that his scientifically based and artfully enacted efforts to teach religious experience will be successful.

Social-scientific and theological evidence suggests that God does not come on demand to persons through religious experience, whether this demand is the religious educator's or anyone else's. All that the religious educator can say is that history has generally but by no means invariably shown that God tends to come to persons in religious experience when certain kinds of conditions coexist in one way or another (and the person is one of these conditions). Theologians might have their own conflicting theories, whether immanentist or transcendist, to explain this phenomenon with or without applications to religious instruction (Knox, 1976). For their part, religious educators have to proceed on the available historical and other social-scientific evidence and deliberatively structure the four molar variables in such a way that their interaction enhances the probability that the desired religious experience outcomes result.

Parenthetically, it might be illuminative to note that church leaders holding a transcendist view of God's action in the world are not infrequently the very persons who exercise the greatest care, and indeed the tightest controls, on constantly structuring religious instruction situations in such a way that the desired learning outcomes are thereby produced—the rhetoric of these church leaders to the contrary notwithstanding. One only has to look at a Billy Graham rally—to say nothing of an Ernest Angley crusade—to appreciate this fact. Of interest in this connection is a study conducted by Hoge and Smith (1982:69-81) which concluded, among other things, that the salvation-inspired religious experiences in Protestant youth occurring disproportionately at eleven or twelve was possibly due to the churches programming for it. This statement is reminiscent of Argyle's (1958:2) empirically grounded observation that many religionists who maintain that conversions are brought about by God unaided and with no human assistance whatever make sure to so structure the situation that "potential converts shall be exposed to the utmost social pressure, persuasion, and emotional arousal." Moberg (1962:421) likewise notes from an empirical perspective that while conservative, theologically transcendist Christian church leaders "usually deny the social aspects of conversion, claiming it to be supernatural. Their efforts to make converts and their expected results of conversion indicate that their working definition is social as well as theological."

The Lee model shows that it is very helpful, and in some ways almost essential, to think of the nature and flow of teaching in terms of structuring the pedagogical situation. Teaching, basically, is structuring.

Because this model has a great deal to say about the teaching act *in se*, it therefore has a great deal to say about teaching for religious experience. The remainder of this chapter is devoted to illustrating how each of the four molar variables in every instructional situation can work singly and in concert to yield religious experience outcomes.

Teacher

The diagram of the Lee model illustrated on a previous page indicates two functions of the teacher. The T outside the instructional situation puts emphasis on the religious educator as the initial and constant structurer of the pedagogical situation. It is the teacher who sets up the instructional situation and continually adjusts it to promote the attainment of the desired learning outcomes. The T inside the dotted lines indicates that the teacher is also one aspect of the learning environment itself, a variable which dynamically interacts with the other variables in the ongoing instructional act.

Among the many consequences of this view of the teacher, several can be briefly highlighted in terms of teaching for religious experience outcomes.

The teaching model clearly shows that the entire instructional act, from the educator's initial structuring right on through the continuing rearrangement of the molar variables during the instructional event itself, is directed toward the accomplishment of a goal. Teaching for religious experience, like teaching for any other kind of learning outcome, means that the religious educator must of necessity formulate both general goals and specific objectives with great care (Lee, 1991:226).

Teaching is a matter of intentionality; it is not a random event. Nor is teaching the high-sounding, amorphous, and free-for-all "happening" as was proposed in many Catholic catechetical circles in the 1960s (Lee, 1973:190). Teaching is grounded in and permeated with intentionality, the conscious and deliberative intention to facilitate desired outcomes in learners. Before setting out to teach religious experience, then, the educator should consciously make religious experience the goal of the instructional event—and not just religious experience in general but some particular kind and level of religious experience. After this has been done, the educator should carefully construct performance objectives (Mager, 1962; Kibler, Barker, and Miles, 1970; Bickimer, 1980:78-83) which will guide every phase of instructional activity, and which will indicate whether and to what degree the desired religious experiences have indeed been actually facilitated. Depending on the kind of religious experience to be facilitated, these objectives will be open or specific. To set goals and objectives, and to make these the gyrocompass of the ongoing religious instruction dynamic, does not in any way rule out, marginalize, or minimize God's pervasiveness in religious experience. Indeed, it may be legitimately argued that when religious educators set goals and objectives for all of religious instruction, including instruction for religious experience, they are following the lead of (and therefore the way in which) God usually works in his own religious instruction endeavors (Lee, 1983:1-11).

Quite clearly the teaching model reveals that religious instruction for religious experience is not a set of cookbook procedures. On the contrary, effective religious instruction of every sort is a complex multifaceted affair involving constant adjustment and readjustment of the interacting molar variables (Lee, 1973:35-38). In order to help ensure that this dynamic adjustment and subsequent readjustments proceed in a goal-directed fashion, the religious educator must have continuous awareness of what is actually happening in the instructional event (Lee, 1991:231-233). One important way of engaging in continuing awareness is that of reflective teaching, which Cruikshank and Applegate (1981:553) define as the cognitive process by which an educator thinks about what has happened in the instructional event, why it happened, and what else could have been done to attain the desired learning outcomes. Reflective teaching and other kinds of awareness activities can happen during the religious instruction event itself, as well as after the event, the latter taking place by analyzing videotapes of the event through relevant interaction analysis systems or other instruments designed to give the religious educator a true rather than a perceived picture of what actually happened in the teaching event (Lee, 1973:251-268; Cruikshank and Metcalf, 1990:477-479). Let us say, for example, that the religious educator structures a flexibly arranged simulation situation whose objective it is to teach learners to have a particular kind of experience of awe for God. During the enactment of the instructional event, the educator notices that some learners do not seem to be responding as the educator had predicted (Lee, 1972:43-54). Depending on what the religious educator knows are the characteristics and response patterns of these learners, she adjusts and readjusts both the environment and selected subject-matter aspects in the simulation so as to enhance the possibility that the learners will acquire the desired religious experience.

An intriguing aspect of the Lee model is that it puts into bold relief the often overlooked fact that the educator is systemically (Lines, 1987) a molar variable that changes during the enactment of the religious instruction event. Thus the religious educator is not a catalyst, namely an element which remains unchanged during the course of the religious instruction act (Lee, 1973:221-225). The systemically interactive noncatalytic character of the religious educator means that the substantive and structural texture of the instructional event in which religious experience is taught directly affects the teacher as well as the learners. Thus the educator's spiritual life in general and his religious experiencing in particular grow in direct proportion to the religious experience features of the instructional event (Lee, 1985b:7-42). Virtue—in this case the virtue of teaching deeply and well—is more often than not its own reward for the religious educator. And the converse also tends to hold true.

Another fruitful way of looking at the religious educator as a changing variable in the instructional act is to reflect on the fact that teaching is not simply an art/science but more accurately a cooperative art/science (Lee, 1963:229, 270; Lee, 1973:218-221). An operative art is one which is exercised on passive matter, such as sculpting. A cooperative art is one which is exercised together with an interactive agent, as in the case of religious instruction. In this interactive cooperative endeavor, all variables change, including the religious educator. Thus the subject matter—in our case religious experience—becomes not only the learner's subject matter, but the religious educator's subject matter as well. Religious experience not only changes in the act of teaching it, but also changes the teacher with whom it interacts during the instructional event.

As an artist/scientist, the religious educator is both a procedurologist and a procedurist (Lee, 1988a:185-187). As a procedurologist, the religious educator possesses a working knowledge of the scientific theory and research on teaching and learning. Wagner's study (1973:229-305) concludes that practicing a particular teaching skill in the absence of the scientific basis of this skill does not of itself lead to the mastery of that teaching skill. As a procedurist, the religious educator fashions the subject-matter content (in our case religious experience) interactively with the other molar variables in such a way as to lead to the acquisition of the desired learning outcome.

The scientific basis of religious instruction suggests which specific teaching procedures are likely to be effective or ineffective in the light of the religious educator's personality (Pajak and Blase, 1989:283-310) and teaching style (Lines, 1992), the learner's personality and learning style (Keefe, 1987), the nature and characteristics of the subject matter, the texture and valence of the psychophysical environment, and the desired learning outcomes to be achieved. If the particular religious experience (subject matter) to be facilitated is of this or that affective cast, then the religious educator as artist selects and deploys that affectively-oriented teaching procedure (Case, 1975; Miller, 1976; Cohler, 1989:41-45) which is most likely to yield the desired religious experience outcome with these learners in this psychophysical environment with this teacher.

Learner

The diagram of the Lee model of teaching given a few pages earlier places the learner at the center of the instructional dynamic. This is where the cycle of learning—not teaching—begins. (The cycle of teaching already began prior to this time when the religious educator selected and structured a particular pedagogical situation). In terms of learning, the model indicates that it is the learner—his existential maturational and learned self, her perceptions and needs and goals—that forms the starting point. The circular lines indicate the path by which the learner modifies her behavior; this is the path which the teaching act will therefore follow.

The teaching model expands and operationalizes the age-old philosophical principle (Aquinas, 1261: II, 4. C. Pera) and modern psychological truism (Caprara et al., 1993:281-283) that all learning occurs according to the mode of the learner.

In teaching for religious experience, it is imperative to remember that during the planning and enactment phases, the educator radicates a considerable portion of his or her efforts in the general and specific characteristics of the learners for whom the instruction is intended. These characteristics have important consequences for how and why and what each learner learns, and therefore for the way in which the religious educator teaches. Some of the more salient learner characteristics which the research has shown to significantly impact learning include age (Zanden, 1985), early family life (Fowlkes, 1988:121-151), socioeconomic status (Gamoran, 1992:1222-1229), self-concept and self-esteem (Wicklund and Gollwitzer, 1982; Markus and Wurf, 1987:229-310; Aldridge, 1993), dominant patterns of unconscious activity (Caputi, 1984), general affective tone (Kelsey, 1977), attitudes (Tesser and Shaffer, 1990:479-523), overall perceptual field (Lee and Pallone, 1966:275-277; Combs, 1982:57-73) and in the case of religious experiencing, the level and valence of one's own religiosity (Allport, 1960:257-267). In the last-mentioned connection, the empirical data suggest that persons whose general religious orientation can be characterized as intrinsic tend to be more prone to have religious experience than persons whose religiosity is extrinsic (Hood, 1971:370-374; Hood, 1972:192-196). Breed and Fagan (1972:866) found that persons whose religiosity was less conformist and less rigid reported a greater number of intense religious experiences than their more religiously conformist and more rigid counterparts. Suggestibility level has been found to correlate positively with reports of religious experience (Dittes, 1969:645-648; Hood, 1973:549-550). Overall (1982:47-54) contends that intense religious experience requires the possession and exercise of a special talent or skill, like art, and that different people have differing degrees of ability and proficiency in the art of intense religious experience.

Educators who seek to broaden and deepen the religiosity of learners of every age and circumstance should not only be acutely aware of findings such as those adduced in the previous paragraph but also capitalize on these findings in planning and enacting religious instruction.

It is a veritable truism that other things being equal persons tend to learn to the degree to which the subject matter is meaningful for them. Meaning is typically a function of an individual's personality and interests (Dewey, 1916:124-131). Empirical research, as well as conclusions from this research, suggest that religious experience, including intense religious experience, might well be a basic part of the human condition (Maslow, 1971:313-317; Hardy, 1976:13-23, 140-153) thus indicating that religious experience in one way or another is meaningful for a significant number, and possibly even all, of the population.

Whether the capacity and the tendency toward religious experience which seems to be characteristic of a significant segment of humanity is inbuilt, learned, or a combination of both has not been sufficiently determined by the empirical research to date. As previously mentioned in this chapter, the research is slowly but increasingly showing that quite a few persons of all ages are having religious experiences of varying kinds and intensity (Greeley, 1974:139-142; Thomas and Cooper, 1978:433-437; Glock and Wuthnow, 1979:56; Hay, 1982; Gallup and Jones, 1989:159-173; Tamminen, 1991:38-39). Bearing in mind the empirical research on the causative role played by expectation (Rosenthal and Jacobson, 1968; Baker and Crist, 1971:48-64; Saracho, 1991:27-41), religious educators should deal with each learner as a person who might well be capable of having religious experience in some degree. In this connection, Morse (1992:viii) contends that his research group's empirical investigations of near-death experience, plus those conducted at the University of Florida and the University of Utrecht, show convincingly that persons are spiritual beings and not just biological machines—and, it may be added, not as primarily cognitive entities either. Religious educators would also do well to view the learner's religious experiences not just in and of themselves but additionally as an especially enriched pathway toward the further deepening and widening of the learner's growth in spiritual awareness and in overall religious living.

Subject Matter

The diagram of the teaching model shows that subject matter (in our case, religious experience) is not something outside of the instructional dynamic which is brought in externally by the religious educator, but rather is a molar variable intrinsically within the instructional dynamic itself. This suggests that religious experience as subject-matter content interacts with the other three molar variables and therefore changes significantly in the act of teaching it. Hence to teach religious experience is not to treat it as if this subject matter were somehow in a box ready to be delivered unopened to the learner, or as if it were an interior compartment within the learner waiting to be released intact. Instead, religious experience, insofar as it is taught, interacts and changes in texture and form and shape and extension during the instructional dynamic as it interacts with each and all of the other three molar variables. Each of the molar variables, then, significantly affects the quality and hue of the learner's religious experience. Recognition, appreciation, and implementation of the interactive nature of subject-matter content will do much to help change and make more effective the way in which the religious educator teaches religious experience.

Since the present book is devoted to religious experience, it would be superfluous to deal with this subject-matter content at any length in this chapter. However, in terms of teaching religious experience, some very brief observations might be helpful.

First, religious educators should avoid any attempts to "spookify" either religious experience or the teaching of it. By "spookification" is meant the transmogrification of a humanly-experienced reality into a sham pseudomystery permeated by amorphousness and wrapped in a veil of vagueness (Lee, 1973:202-204). Spookification is typically couched in high-sounding, ethereal, overly-pious, but essentially meaningless language. Historically, spookification has been and still remains a major source of the ruination of successful religious instruction. In the ultimate sense, of course, all reality, including religious experience, is essentially a profound mystery. But in the penultimate and immediate level where human beings live and where religious educators work, reality must be dealt with as it is encountered in its immediacy as well as in its fullness if persons are to live effective, human, and religious lives.

Second, religious educators should treat religious experience as embracing and permeating all of life rather than being a compartmentalized entity reserved solely for certain kinds of reality and for certain kinds of people. Thus all kinds of instructional situations hold potential to a greater or lesser degree for teaching religious experience. The words over Carl Jung's villa are pertinent here: "Called or not, God is present."

Third, religious educators, as appropriate, should incorporate into their teaching the entire range of religious experience from simple affective experiences of the numinous to a fullblown mystical encounter. Different states of the learner, different times, different interactive environments, and the like all work together in such a way as to result in different kinds of personal receptivity to the many forms and levels of religious experience.

Fourth, religious educators should be inclusively holistic when teaching for religious experience. Because religious experience is a human experience, it is necessarily a holistic blend of cognitive, affective, and lifestyle elements. And since religious experience is religious, the lifestyle element is the most important of the three, followed by the affective element and then last, but still essential, the cognitive element.

Fifth, religious educators should treat the subject matter of religious experience not simply as a substantive product content but also, and in many ways more importantly, as a substantive process content. (Substantive process content is distinguished from structural content which is also processive in nature. Structural content is the teaching dynamic in action, in process. By contrast substantive process content is the processive element inherent in all subject matter, in all reality. A knowledge of the Ten Commandments, for example, is a substantive product content. The process of acquiring this knowledge and also the process of cognitively doing this knowledge is a substantive process content) (Lee, 1985a:35-128). As they teach for religious education outcomes, religious educators should not only center in on the acquisition of one or another specific kind of substantive religious experience, but also put even greater store on the present and ongoing process of religious experiencing.

Sixth, religious educators should prize religious experience as an important content and a major outcome in its own right and not simply as an entry vehicle for theological reflection. Virtually all major world religions, and even Christian theology itself, have historically accorded far greater primacy to religious experience than to theology. Religious experience needs no external justification; it is its own justification. By stark contrast, theology requires external justification. Religious experience is capable of overturning or at least seriously revising many prevailing theological views and systems, and can force conventional "accepted" theology to take a serious look into other tentative theological explanations of religion and reality such as those offered by Bergson's (1911; 1946) *élan vital*, by Schleiermacher's (1928:131-256) primordial feeling, by Native American spiritual perspectives (Reichard, 1950; Black Elk, 1953), and by panentheism (Macquarrie 1984:51-251), to name just a few.

The Environment

The diagram of the teaching model depicted some pages earlier highlights the crucial importance of the learning environment in the religious instruction act (Lee, 1973:240-248). It shows graphically that the learning situation consists of all persons, objects, and symbols in the learner's environment. Therefore everything the learner encounters is in one sense an environmental variable which can be adjusted or structured to enhance the attainment of the desired learning outcome. All learning takes place in one or another kind of environmental context. In instructional circles the term environment means that aggregate of external physical, biological, cultural, and social conditions or stimuli to which an individual consciously or unconsciously responds (Lee, 1973:65).

The conclusion of Burgess's (1975:83-84, 119-120, 154-158) research investigation remains true today, namely that advocates of the theological macrotheory of religious instruction almost completely neglect the environment whereas advocates of the social-science macrotheory of religious instruction place great store in the powerful and pervasive role of environmental variables in the teaching act.

One empirical research study (Swanson, O'Connon, and Cooney, 1990:533-556) comparing expert seasoned educators with novice unseasoned educators found that the expert educators were more likely to rely on environment interventions than were the novices.

While the environment in and of itself is facilitative (Lee,1991:230) the environment does not automatically produce learning outcomes (Mazzuca,1990:473-488), including religious experiences. The environment and the other three molar variables are interactive. The other three molar variables must play an active role if the environment is to enrich the learning event with its particular potential. Hood and Morris (1981:261-273) found that in a controlled extreme-degree solitude environment (isolation tanks) persons of intrinsic religiosity reported religious imagery more often than did their extrinsic counterparts (learner variable interacting with the environment variable). Elkind and Elkind's (1963:102-112) study discovered that the most intelligent, the least conformist, and the subjects who conceived of God in broader terms were more likely to feel close to God in a solitude environment (again learner variable interacting with the environment variable). Some persons like Lee (1985a:42-49, 62-64, 670-672), and some groups like the Cursillo, contend that when focused, pervasive, affective, and appropriately intense religious subject matter is placed into a structured environment having corresponding characteristics, the probability of increasing religious experience outcomes in learners is enhanced. However there does not yet seem to be a body of empirical evidence to support (or disprove) these otherwise plausible claims, probably because no researcher has investigated them in a serious and sophisticated experimental manner.

Of the various kinds of environment mentioned in the definition given in the first paragraph of this section, two are especially characteristic of both formal and informal instructional environments and thus fall under the general pedagogical control of the religious educator. These two settings are the physical environment and the psychosocial environment. The empirical research on physical environment such as isolation tanks, nature settings, and the like directly adduced in Hood's chapter in this present volume and less directly mentioned in other chapters suggests that physical environments, if used skillfully by the religious educator, can help facilitate religious experience outcomes. Furthermore, the empirical research on psychosocial environments such as solitude, nonstress, and affective valence cited by Hood in the present volume and also by Hyde (1990:170-186) show the potency of this kind of environment in enhancing the probability of the successful facilitation of religious experience outcomes. Maslow's (1971:170) research found that peak experiences were reported in environments in which persons listened to classical music or were dancing but not in environments in which persons listened to abstract music (John Cage) or looked at popular nonclassical paintings (Andy Warhol). While not dealing expressly with religious experience, nonetheless the empirical data indicating the potency of socioemotional climate in facilitating desired learning outcomes (Lee, 1970:90-92; Khan and Weiss, 1973:774-777) can be legitimately extrapolated in large degree to the facilitation of any kind of learning outcome including religious experience.

One of the most effective things religious educators can do to heighten and widen the potency of their efforts to teach religious experience is to utilize the environment more pervasively. One especially enriched and focused environment for facilitating religious experience outcomes is, at least for sacramental churches, the liturgy (Lee, 1985a:645-648). With its many nonverbal and directly experiential elements, with its deliberate engagement of all five senses, with its frequently intergenerational participation (White, 1988:46-53), with its conscious twin central purpose of religious instruction and worship, and with its inbuilt thrust toward religious experience on the part of all its participants, the liturgy offers an especially enriched environment for facilitating a whole array of religious experiences of every intensity level (White, 1980:44-109; Dix, 1982:397-526; Jones et al., 1992:485-547).

The liturgy is rooted in human experience and cuts across both ecclesial and nonecclesial environments. Thus there are major liturgies for pivotal events in a person's life such as birth, coming to physical manhood or womanhood, marriage, and death. There are also minor liturgies for less important though still significant personal and societal events such as planting and harvesting. Like all human experience, liturgy is radicated in those two essential and pervasive qualities of space and time. It is radicated in space in that liturgy usually takes place in a formal or informal environment which is designed or utilized to enhance religious experience. Liturgy is radicated in time in that it brings into play a temporal environment which celebrates through its liturgical seasons such past events as the episodes in the life of Jesus, such present events as a liturgy for a sick person, and such future events as the parousia.

CONCLUSION

There are two major zones of inquiry into the issue of the actual teaching of religious experience. The first of these is the empirically based instructional theory and set of pedagogical principles upon which rests the here-and-now teaching for religious experience outcomes. The second is the review and discussion of the pertinent empirical studies on various instructional procedures for teaching religious experience. This chapter has concentrated exclusively on the first while sidestepping the second. With the exception of adducing studies which can be legitimately extrapolated to or conjoined with the teaching of religious experience, this chapter has avoided the issue of reviewing instructional procedures for teaching religious experience because religious educationists and educators have not yet conducted legitimate empirical investigations directly on this area. What Godin (1962:s-166) wrote many years ago remains true today, namely that religious educationists and educators typically discuss the theological pertinence of religious instruction without any reference at all to the empirically demonstrated effectiveness of a specific form of teaching or of a particular instructional procedure. Tamminen (1991:328-329) who, like Oser (1991), began his career in the field of religious instruction and still remains very closely associated with this area, points out that there is a growing body of empirical research on human development (including religious development) but an insufficient knowledge on the relationship between this development and religious instruction. Thus in terms of specific empirically demonstrated research on particular procedures for teaching religious experience, we are more or less in the dark except for overall illumination from general instructional theory and principles as well as from legitimate extrapolation and application from other relevant studies on the facilitation of religious experience. Such lack of empirical research is especially unfortunate because of the centrality of religion in general and of religious experience in particular in the life of religious persons.

I would like to conclude this chapter by offering two general comments. The first deals with structural content of teaching for religious experience while the second treats substantive content. While neither conclusion is verified empirically through specific studies, both are empirical in the sense that they represent empirically derived general observations made by a wide variety of persons over various time frames.

First, an especially potent general instructional strategy (Lee, 1973:34) is to structure the pedagogical situation so that it is a laboratory for religious living (Lee, 1971:81-86). Extending this point, effective teaching for religious experience can be brought into existence by structuring the pedagogical situation so that it becomes a living laboratory for religious experiencing.

Second, spiritual masters in a wide variety of religious traditions from Christian (Merton, 1955:xv-13) to classical Buddhist (Hopkins, 1980:85; Oh and Park, 1988:249-270) have consistently asserted that the degree to which persons enter into the deepest center of themselves and pass through that center into God is directly proportional to the degree to which these individuals pass out of themselves and give themselves to other persons in the purity of selfless love. Thus effective teaching for religious experience outcomes should include that kind of substantive and structural content which places learners in situations in which they can engage in selfless love.

REFERENCES

Aldridge, J.
1993 *Self-Esteem; loving yourself at every age.* Birmingham, AL: Doxa.
Allport, G. W.
1960 *Personality and social encounter.* Boston: Beacon.
Aquinas, T.
1259 *De veritate.*
1261 *Expositio in librum beati Dionysii divinis nominibus.*
1272 *Summa theologica.*
Argyle, M.
1958 *Religious behavior.* London: Routledge & Kegan Paul.
Armstrong, K.
1993 *A history of God.* New York: Knopf.
Augustine
389 *De magistro.*
399 *De catechandis rudibus.*
Baker, J. P., and J. L. Crist
1971 Teacher expectancies: a review of the literature. In *Pygmalion reconsidered,* edited by J. D. Elashoff and R. E. Snow. Worthington, OH: Jones.
Batson, C. D., and W. L. Ventis
1982 *The religious experience.* New York: Oxford University Press.
Berger, P. L.
1967 *The sacred canopy.* Garden City, NY: Doubleday.
Bergson, H.
1911 *Creative evolution,* translated by A. Mitchell. Lanham, MD: University Press of America.
1946 *The creative mind,* translated by M. L. Andison. New York: Greenwood.
Bickimer, D. A.
1983 *Christ the placenta.* Birmingham, Al: Religious Education Press.

Black Elk
1953 *The sacred pipe: seven rites of the Ogala Sioux,* edited and recorded by J. E. Brown. Norman, OK: University of Oklahoma Press.

Breed, G., and J. Fagan
1972 Religious dogmatism and peak experiences. *Psychological Reports* 31:866.

Broadwell, M. M.
1980 *The lecture method of instruction.* Englewood Cliffs, NJ: Educational Technology Publications.

Burgess, H. W.
1975 *An invitation to religious education.* Birmingham, AL: Religious Education Press.

Cairns, K. V., J. B. Woodward, and J. Savery
1989 The life choices simulation. *Simulation and Games* 20:245-271.

Calvin, J.
1971 Catechism of the Church of Geneva, translated by H. Beveridge. In *Early Protestant educators,* edited by F. Eby. New York: AMS.

Caprara, G. V., et al.
1993 The "big five" questionnaire: a new questionnaire to assess the five factor model. *Personality and Individual Differences* 15:281-288.

Caputi, N.
1984 *Guide to the unconscious.* Birmingham, AL: Religious Education Press.

Case, L.
1975 *The other side of the report card: a how-to-do-it program for affective education.* Pacific Palisades, CA: Goodyear.

Coe, G. A.
1917 *A social theory of religious education.* New York: Scribner's.
1929 *What is Christian education?* New York: Scribner's.

Cohler, B. J.
1989 Psychoanalysis and education: motive, meaning, self. In *Learning and education: psychoanalytic perspectives,* edited by K. Field, B. J. Cohler, and G. Wool. Madison, CT: International Universities Press.

Combs, A. W.
1982 *A personal approach to teaching.* Boston: Allyn and Bacon.

Cruikshank, D. R., and J. Applegate
1981 Reflective teaching as a strategy for educational growth. *Educational Leadership* 38:553-554.

Cruikshank, D. R., and K. K. Metcalf
1990 Training within teacher preparation. In *Handbook of research on teacher education,* edited by W. R. Houston. New York: Macmillan.

Dante
1970 *Divine comedy,* translated by J. Ciardi. New York: Norton.

Dantonio, M.
1990 *How can we create thinkers? Questioning strategies that work for teachers.* Bloomington, IN: National Educational Service.

Darcy Bérubé, F.
1978 The challenge ahead of us. In *Foundations of religious education,* edited by P. O'Hare. New York: Paulist.

Dewey, J.
1916 *Democracy and education.* New York: Macmillan.

Dittes, J. E.
1969 Psychology of Religion. In *Handbook of social psychology,* Vol. 5, 2nd ed., edited by G. Lindzey and E. Aronson. Reading, MA: Addison-Wesley.

Dix, G.
1982 *The shape of the liturgy.* New York: Seabury.

Dujarier, M.
1962 L'évolution de la pastorale catéchuménale aux six premiers siècles de l'eglise. *Maison Dieu* 70 (2ième trimestre).

Durkheim, E.
1947 *The elementary forms of the religious life,* translated by J. W. Swain. Glencoe, IL: Free Press.
Eisner, E. W.
1979 *The educational imagination.* New York: Macmillan.
Elkind, D., and S. Elkind
1963 Varieties of religious experience in young adolescence. *Journal for the Scientific Study of Religion* 2:102-112.
Fischer, H.
1969 Mysticism. In *Sacramentum mundi,* Vol. 4, edited by K. Rahner et al. New York: Herder and Herder.
Fowlkes, M. A.
1988 Religion and socialization. In *Handbook of preschool religious education,* edited by D. Ratcliff. Birmingham, AL: Religious Education Press.
Gage, N. L.
1978 *The scientific base of the art of teaching.* New York: Teachers College Press.
Gallup Jr., G., and S. Jones
1989 *One hundred questions and answers: religion in America.* Princeton, NJ: Princeton Religion Research Center.
Gamoran, A.
1992 Social factors in education. In *Encyclopedia of Educational Research,* sixth ed., vol. 4, edited by M. Alkin. New York:Macmillan.
Gangel, K. O.
1976 Review. *Christianity Today* 20 (May 21):32-33.
1985 *Church education handbook.* Wheaton, IL: Victor.
Gillespie, V. B.
1988 *The experience of faith.* Birmingham, AL: Religious Education Press.
Glock, C. Y.
1962 On the study of religious commitment. *Religious Education* 57, (res. supp.):98-110.
Glock, C. Y., and R. Wuthnow
1979 Departures from conventional religion: The nominally religious, the non-religious, and the alternatively religious. In *The Religious Dimension,* edited by R. Wuthnow. New York: Academic Press.
Godin, A.
1962 Importance and difficulty of scientific research in religious education: The problem of the "criterion". *Religious Education* 57, (res. supp.) :163-171.
1985 *The psychological dynamics of religious experience,* translated by M. Turton. Birmingham, AL: Religious Education Press.
Greeley, A. M.
1974 *Ecstasy; a way of knowing.* Englewood Cliffs, NJ: Prentice-Hall.
Groome, T. H.
1980 *Christian religious education.* San Francisco: Harper San Francisco.
Habermas, R., and K. Issler
1992 *Teaching for reconciliation.* Grand Rapids, MI: Baker.
Hardy, A.
1976 *The biology of God.* New York: Taplinger.
Hargrove, B. W.
1971 *Reformation of the holy.* Philadelphia: Davis.
Hay, D.
1982 *Exploring inner space: scientists and religious experience.* New York: Penguin.
Herbart, J.
1908 *The science of education,* translated by H. M. and E. Felkin. Boston: Heath.
Hofinger, J.
1962 *The art of teaching Christian doctrine.* Notre Dame, IN: University of Notre Dame Press.
Hoge, D. R., and E. I. Smith

1982 Normative and non-normative religious experience among high-school youth. *Sociological Analysis* 43:69-81.

Hood Jr., R. W.
1971 A comparison of the Allport and Feagin scoring procedure for intrinsic/extrinsic religious orientation. *Journal for the Scientific Study of Religion* 10:370-374.
1972 Normative and motivational determinants of reported religious experience in two Baptist samples. *Review of Religious Research* 13:192-196.
1973 Hypnotic susceptability and reported religious experience. *Psychological Reports* 33:549-550.
1993 Conversation with James Michael Lee (October).

Hood Jr., R. W., and R. J. Morris
1981 Sensory isolation and the differential elicitation of religious imagery in intrinsic and extrinsic persons. *Journal for the Scientific Study of Religion* 20:261-273.

Hopkins, J.
1980 Preface: in praise of compassion. In *Compassion in Tibetan Buddhism,* edited and translated by J. Hopkins. London: Rider.

Hyde, K. E.
1990 *Religion in childhood and adolescence.* Birmingham, AL: Religious Education Press.

Jones, C., et al.
1992 *The study of the liturgy,* rev. ed. New York: Oxford University Press.

Justin
152 *I Apologia.*

Keefe, J. W.
1987 *Learning style: theory and practice.* Reston, VA: NASSP.

Kelsey, M.
1977 *Can Christians be educated?* Birmingham, AL: Religious Education Press.

Kempis, Thomas à
1940 *Imitation of Christ.* Milwaukee, WI: Bruce.

Khan, S. B., and J. Weiss
1973 The teaching of affective responses. In *Second handbook of research on teaching,* edited by R. M. W. Travers. Chicago: Rand McNally.

Kibler, R. J., L. L. Barker, and D. T. Miles
1970 *Behavioral objectives and instruction.* Boston: Allyn and Bacon.

Knox, I. P.
1976 *Above or within?* Birmingham, AL: Religious Education Press.

Lamont, C.
1957 *The philosophy of humanism.* New York: Philosophical Library.

Lamport, M. A.
1992 The state of the profession of youth ministry. *Christian Education Journal* 13:85-100.

Lee, J. M.
1963 *Principles and methods of secondary education.* New York: McGraw-Hill.
1970 The *teaching* of religion. In *Toward a future for religious education,* edited by J. M. Lee and P. C. Rooney. Dayton, OH: Pflaum.
1971 *The shape of religious instruction.* Birmingham, AL: Religious Education Press.
1972 Prediction in religious instruction. *The Living Light* 9:43-54.
1973 *The flow of religious instruction.* Birmingham, AL: Religious Education Press.
1977 Toward a new era: A blueprint for positive action. In *The religious education we need,* edited by J. M. Lee. Birmingham, AL: Religious Education Press.
1982 The authentic source of religious instruction. In *Religious education and theology,* edited by N. H. Thompson. Birmingham, AL: Religious Education Press.
1983 Religious education and the bible. In *Biblical themes in religious education,* edited by J. S. Marino. Birmingham, AL: Religious Education Press.
1985a *The content of religious instruction.* Birmingham, AL: Religious Education Press.
1985b Lifework spirituality and the religious educator. In *The spirituality of the religious educator,* edited by J. M.. Lee. Birmingham, AL: Religious Education Press.
1988a How to teach: foundations, processes, procedures. In *Handbook of preschool religious*

education, edited by D. Ratcliff. Birmingham, AL: Religious Education Press.
1988b The blessings of religious pluralism. In *Religious pluralism and religious education,* edited by N. H. Thompson. Birmingham, AL: Religious Education Press.
1990 Facilitating growth in faith through religious instruction. In *Handbook of Faith,* edited by J. M. Lee. Birmingham, AL: Religious Education Press.
1991 Procedures in the religious education of adolescents. In *Handbook of youth ministry,* edited by D. Ratcliff and J. A. Davies. Birmingham, AL: Religious Education Press.

Lee, J. M., and N. J. Pallone
1966 *Guidance and counseling in schools: foundations and processes.* New York: McGraw-Hill.

Lines, T. A.
1987 *Systemic religious education.* Birmingham, AL: Religious Education Press.
1992 *Functional images of the religious educator.* Birmingham, AL: Religious Education Press.

Little, S.
1961 *The role of the bible in contemporary Christian education.* Richmond, VA: Knox.

Luther, M.
1935 Preface. In *Small catechism,* rev. ed., translated by J. Stump, xi-xv. Philadelphia: United Lutheran Publication House.

Macquarrie, J.
1984 *In search of deity: An essay in dialectical theology.* New York: Crossroad.

Mager, R.
1962 *Preparing instructional objectives.* Palo Alto, CA: Fearon.

Maritain, J.
1936 *Humanisme intégral.* Paris: Aubier.

Markus, H., and E. Wurf
1987 The dynamic self-concept: A social psychological perspective. In *Annual review of psychology,* vol. 38, edited by M. R. Rosenzweig and L. W. Porter. Palo Alto, CA: Annual Reviews.

Marthaler, B. L.
1975 Review. *National Catholic Reporter* 11 (9/11) :13.
1978 Socialization as a model for catechetics. In *Foundations of religious education,* edited by P. O'Hare. New York: Paulist.

Maslow, A. H.
1964 *Religion, values and peak-experiences.* New York: Penguin.
1971 *The farther reaches of human nature.* New York: Penguin.

Mazzuca, S. A., F. Vinicor, R. M. Einterz, W. M. Tierney, J. A. Norton, and L. A. Kalasinski
1990 Effects of the clinical environment of physicians' response to postgraduate medical education. *American Educational Research Journal* 27:473-488.

McBrien, R. P.
1974 Faith, theology and belief. *Commonweal* 101 (11/15) :134-137.
1976 Toward an American catechesis. *The Living Light* 13:167-181.

McIntyre, M.
1976 Review. *Review of Books and Religion* 5:6.

Merton, T.
1949 *Seeds of contemplation.* New York: New Directions.
1955 *No man is an island.* New York: Harcourt, Brace.

Miller, J. P.
1976 *Humanizing the classroom: Models of teaching in affective education.* New York: Praeger.

Miller, M. T.
1991 Understanding basic teaching methods: profile of discussion, lecture, and personalized systems of instruction. In *ERIC:*340 319.

Miller, R. C.
1963 *Education for Christian living,* 2nd ed. Englewood Cliffs, NJ: Prentice-Hall.
1980 *The theory of Christian education practice: How theology affects Christian education.*

Birmingham, AL: Religious Education Press.
Moberg, D. O.
1962 *The church as a social organization.* Englewood Cliffs, NJ: Prentice-Hall.
Moran, G.
1966 *Catechesis of revelation.* New York: Herder and Herder.
1989 *Religious education as a second language.* Birmingham, AL: Religious Education Press.
Morse, M.
1992 Foreword. In *Embraced by the light,* by B. J. Eadie. Placerville, CA: Old Leaf Press.
National Conference of Catholic Bishops
1979 *Sharing the light of faith.* Washington, DC: The Conference.
Nelson, C. E.
1967 *Where faith begins.* Louisville, KY: Westminster/Knox.
Oh, Y. B., and S. Y. Park
1988 Buddhist education and religious pluralism. In *Religious pluralism and religious education,* edited by N. H. Thompson. Birmingham, AL: Religious Education Press.
Oser, F., and P. Gmünder
1991 Religious judgement, translated by N. Hahn. Birmingham, AL: Religious Education Press.
Osmer, R. P.
1990 Teaching as practical theology. In *Theological approaches to religious education,* edited by J. L. Seymour and D. E. Miller. Nashville, TN: Abingdon.
Overall, C.
1982 The nature of mystical experience. *Religious Studies* 18:47-54.
Pajak, E., and J. J. Blase
1989 The impact of teachers' personal lives for professional role enactment. *American Educational Research Journal* 26:283-310.
Pearlman, W. D.
1990 Psychodrama: Discovering new meaning in personal drama. *New Directions for Adult and Continuing Education* 45:27-36.
Pseudo-Dionysius
1987 *The mystical theology* in *Complete works,* translated by C. Luidheid. New York: Paulist.
Radin, P.
1957 *Primitive religion.* New York: Dover.
Raymond of Capua
1960 *The life of Catherine of Siena,* translated by G. Lamb. New York: Kenedy.
Reichard, G. A.
1950 *Navaho religion,* 2nd ed. New York: Bollingen.
Rood, W. R.
1968 *The art of teaching Christianity.* Nashville, TN: Abingdon.
Rosenthal, R., and L. Jacobson
1968 *Pygmalion in the classroom.* New York: Holt, Rinehart and Winston.
Rousseau, E. W., and D. L. Redfield
1981 A meta-analysis of experimental research on teacher questioning behavior. *Review of Educational Research* 51:237-245.
Sacra Congregatio pro Clericis
1971 *Directorium catechisticum generale.* Città del Vaticano: Libreria Editrice Vaticana.
Saracho, O. N.
1991 Teacher expectations of student performance: a review of the research. *Early Childhood Development and Care* 76:27-41.
Schleiermacher, F.
1928 *The Christian faith,* edited by H. R. Mackintosh and J. S. Stewart. Edinburgh: Clark.
Smallbones, J. L.
1990 What's wrong with Christian education in evangelical churches today. *Christian Education Journal* 11:105-112.
Swanson, H. L., J. E. O'Connor, and J. B. Cooney
1990 An information processing analysis of expert and novice teachers' problem solving.

American Educational Research Journal 27:533-556.

Tamminen, K.
1991 *Religious development in childhood and youth.* Helsinki: Suomalainen Tiedeakatemia.

Tanquerey, A.
1930 *The spiritual life,* 2nd ed., translated by H. Branderis. Westminster, MD: Newman.

Tesser, A., and D. R. Shaffer
1990 Attitudes and attitude change. In *Annual review of psychology,* vol. 40, edited by M. R. Rosenzweig and L. W. Porter. Palo Alto, CA: Annual Reviews.

Thomas, L. E., and P. E. Cooper
1978 Measurement and incidence of mystical experiences: An exploratory study. *Journal for the Scientific Study of Religion* 17:433-437.

Wagner, A. C.
1973 Changing teaching behavior: A comparison of microteaching and cognitive discrimination training. *Journal of Educational Psychology* 64:299-305.

Warren, M.
1970 All contributions cheerfully accepted. *The Living Light* 7:20-39.

Westerhoff III, J. H.
1976 *Will our children have faith?* New York: Seabury.
1982 A catechetical way of doing theology. In *Religious education and theology,* edited by N. H. Thompson. Birmingham, AL: Religious Education Press.

Wicklund, R. A., and P. M. Gollwitzer
1982 *Symbolic self-concept.* Hillsdale, NJ: Erlbaum.

White, J. F.
1980 *Introduction to Christian worship.* Nashville, TN: Abingdon.

White, J. W.
1988 *Intergenerational religious education.* Birmingham, AL: Religious Education Press.

Wrenn, M.
1991 *Catechisms and controversies.* San Francisco: Ignatius.

Zanden, James W. V.
1985 *Human development,* 3rd ed. New York: Knopf.

24

The Facilitation of Religious Experience

RALPH W. HOOD JR.

The major faith traditions are not without their own internal histories and debates concerning conditions that facilitate religious experience. Only recently has the psychology of religion attempted quasi-experimental studies on the facilitation of religious experience. Some of these studies have generated controversy not unrelated to issues in religious history associated with the "provoking of God." As with many issues in the psychology of religion, conceptual issues are as important as empirical studies. Accordingly this chapter is divided in two distinct parts. In the first part we focus upon a reconsideration of Schleiermacher's views of religious experience to integrate much of the conceptual literature. In the second part we look at quasi-experimental studies that have attempted to facilitate religious experience under conditions of alteration of the body, enhanced solitude, and set stress/setting stress incongruities. Our consideration of the conceptual issues in religious experience in the first part should serve to make the purely empirical studies discussed in the second part of interest not only to social scientists but to philosophers, theologians, and religious educators as well.

RELIGIOUS EXPERIENCE: CONCEPTUAL ISSUES

Various theoretical perspectives within psychology offer unique definitions as to what constitutes religious experience and thus, by implication, what factors might facilitate such experiences. Depending upon the author's perspectives, whether one ought to foster the facilitation of religious experience is itself problematic. Even within the great faith traditions the precise role of experience has been and remains problematic. For instance, Kirk (1966) has traced the long history of the Christian doctrine of the *summum bonum* in Western thought. He notes how civilizations eager to anticipate a worldly encounter with God were gradually shaped by social forces to relegate the desire for such experiences to secondary consideration. Primary consideration was given to corporate discipline and to institutionalized articulation of dogma. No direct "this worldly" experiential encounter with God was necessary to comfort the faithful. Believers were assured that such experiences would come in their own proper time. Yet the acceptance of encounters with God upon those whom it is bestowed have always been an option in Western (and most other) faith traditions. It is worth emphasizing that both mystical and dogmatic theologies parallel one another in their early formative years. A strong case can be made that many Christian beliefs are mystical doctrines formulated dogmatically (Louth, 1981:xi). Likewise, in Eastern traditions, direct encounters with foundational reality, conceived in God language or not, have been accepted, if not mandated, for the adept. While neither in the West nor in the East have the great faith traditions rooted their entire traditions upon the experience of the faithful, it is fair to state that all traditions defend both the reality of what is experienced in ultimate states and the possibility that at least some of the faithful in fact have such experiences within the span of their temporal lives. For these reasons a psychology that is at least not incompatible with such claims seems to offer the greatest chance for meaningful dialogue among social scientists, philosophers, theologians, and religious educators.

Religious Experience: Numinous and Mystical

The immense diversity of that which has been included under the umbrella "religion" is perhaps less puzzling than need be if one accepts that religions are human products and hence as varied as cultures. Yet to make religion a human phenomenon is neither to deny the transcendent nor to imply that the nature of the transcendent can be ignored by psychologists. What is human about religion is the response, individual and collectively, to the transcendent (Hick, 1989). Between transcendent and response; between Creator and creature; between the ultimately real and the individual person lies all the diversity that is religion. While theologians and philosophers grapple with the nature of the transcendent, psychologists and religious educators grapple with the nature of the response. Yet the human response to the transcendent is most effectively analyzed in light of the possibility that the response is not merely human, but is at least potentially a real sense of the transcendent (Bowker, 1973). We shall shortly accept Berger's (1980) plea for a reconsideration of Schleiermacher, as a theorist of contemporary relevance to the study of religious experience. We hasten to add that we have not picked a

Protestant theologian, although at least nominally a Protestant he was. Schleiermacher was often criticized as a pantheist, continually refusing to emphasize the personal nature of God and chiding readers who found phrases such as "world spirit" incompatible with Christianity (Crouter, 1988:71). In addition, by the time of the final revision of *On Religion,* Schleiermacher's friend, Schlegel, who had instigated and encouraged the first edition, converted to Catholicism as did Schleiermacher's own wife. Schleiermacher's influence can be identified in phenomenological studies of religious experience. In particular, both Otto and Stace whose categories of the numinous and the mystical will define the domain of religious experience for us are best understood within the shadow cast by Schleiermacher.

Foundational Reality: Contemporary scholars suggest that the numinous and the mystical are the great roots from which the diversity of the transcendent is revealed to human consciousness. Natural factors that may facilitate religious experience, either of the numinous or the mystical, are not themselves exhaustively explanatory of the transcendent. The most fruitful hypothesis that guides this review is to ask, What are the factors that facilitate the experience of foundational reality? We shall use the term foundational reality to imply that religious traditions can in some meaningful sense articulate reality, individually and collectively. This reality is foundational in two senses. First, such realities are foundational to a way of life. They are normative for both belief and practice. Second, such realities are genuine encounters and not simply constructions. Part of the experience of any religious form of life is the possibility of experiencing its foundational reality. Furthermore, even if the foundational reality is not actually experienced, other forms of religious experience entail the proper attitude to the foundational reality which itself is formative of what we might call a religious tradition's "religious-experiencing-of-life." Thus, for purposes of this review we shall focus upon religious experiences that are either numinous or mystical. The reason for this is that in Schleiermacher's thought both experiences are properly religious, and in fact poles of a single experience that defines religion in its essence. Our return to Schleiermacher will permit a discussion of religious experience that neither reduces such experiences to the social psychological factors that may facilitate them, nor denies the reality of the variations with which such experiences are acknowledged as foundational for the forms of life from which they ultimately derive. As with more balanced contemporary philosophies of science we assume that neither a naive realism, in which facts are presumed to dictate theory, nor a radical constructionism in which theories are presumed to create facts, are adequate to the reality of religious experiencing (Toulmin, 1962; Toulmin and Leary, 1985).

Back to Schleiermacher

Berger appropriately argues for a reconsideration of the work of Schleiermacher in discussing the inductive possibility as one of the "heretical" options available for contemporary religious affirmation (Berger, 1980:114-142). By inductive possibility Berger refers to the empirical task of historically reconstructing the experiences at the root of the great faith traditions. Berger perceptively selects Schleiermacher as the relevant theologian. This selection cannot be attributed to a liberal Protestant preference (for Schleiermacher is undoubtedly, to use Barth's words, the paradigmatic figure of Protestant liberalism) nor simply to Berger's own assessment of portions of Schleiermacher's *On Religion* as a "precocious treatise in the sociology of knowledge" (Berger, 1980:119). Rather, like Berger, we see Schleiermacher as providing the theoretical model within which the empirical possibilities of religions foundational reality can be inductively acknowledged. Thus, our own discussion of Schleiermacher is not a detour into theology and our findings do not depend upon Schleiermacher's theology for their validity. Rather we use Schleiermacher to provide an exemplar of exploration of but one model relevant to a contemporary social psychology in which the "troublesome transcendence" can be directly acknowledged (Garrett, 1974). Schleiermacher and Feuerbach are often cited as compatible theologians who introduced psychological reductionism into theology. Feuerbach's reduction of theology to anthropology provided both Freud and Marx with a theological basis for their respective scientific reductionistic views of religion. Likewise, a common misinterpretation of Schleiermacher is that in locating religion in feeling he provided the possibility of a permanent reductionistic explanation of religious experience. Yet one need no more interpret a feeling as indicative of God than of a variety of other possibilities. As we shall see, the Schacter and Singer (1962) study which has become the exemplar in quasi-experimental studies of the facilitation of religious experience, has been seen as relevant to discussion of religious experience precisely in this sense (Proudfoot, 1985). Yet this is to missunderstand what Schleiermacher meant by feeling as well as to distort the role of cognition or of language in the mediation of feelings. The issue must first be conceptually clarified before the empirical data can be properly confronted.

Schleiermacher and Religious Feeling

Scholarship abounds documenting the many changes Schleiermacher struggled with in two of his major works, *On Religion* first published in 1799, and *The Christian Faith,* first published in 1820-1821. *On Religion* went through several editions, the final one published in 1821, the same year in which *The Christian Faith* was first published. In both works, Schleiermacher defends religion as a feeling. He struggles through editions of each work to clarify this central concept. Ultimately, this feeling is *sui generis* and cannot be described, but only elicited in the reader. Thus for Schleiermacher the task of description is less to explicate religious experience than to elicit the experience such that the inadequacies of language are no hindrance to its recognition. Since at least the time of Hegel, the basic philosophical argument against Schleiermacher is that he attempts the impossible: to talk of an unmediated experience identified by language, inevitably involves mediation in the description of what is purported to be an unmediated relationship. (See Almond, 1982; Crouter, 1988; Katz, 1978, 1992; Proudfoot, 1985.) However, such arguments miss the point. The criticism is already explicit in Schleiermacher and others who follow in his tradition. To unpack their responses to such anticipated criticism will help us clarify the research findings on the facilitation of religious experience discussed below.

Contemporary appreciation of Schleiermacher is hindered by a too narrow interpretation of what Schleiermacher meant by feeling in general, and by the feeling of absolute dependence in particular. As Bettis (1969) has emphasized Schleiermacher neither intended to identify religion with an emotional response nor did he ground religion in subjective experience. Bettis (1969:144) suggests with good grounding in Schleiermacher's own writing (e.g., Schleiermacher,1830-31/1963:6-7), that the term "feeling" be replaced with the phrase "immediate self-consciousness." This consciousness is not representational, although feeling may sometimes rest in thinking which "fixes it" or result in action which "expresses it" (Schleiermacher, 1963: 10-11). Furthermore, this consciousness is identified with the infinity of God consciousness which can be elicited by finite objects (Schleiermacher, 1799/1988:109).

Schleiermacher's concept of religious feeling has both mystical and numinous characteristics as we shall note shortly. Furthermore, any finite object may serve to facilitate this sense of infinity, a point relevant to empirical studies to be discussed below. Thus Berger (1988:116-117) is correct in noting that the common linking of Feuerbach and Schleiermacher as if both were psychological reductionists is fallacious. Feuerbach reduced the infinite (God) to the finite by the mechanism of projection; Schleiermacher elevated the finite to the infinite via the primary unity of intuition and feeling. To emphasize that religious feeling is a mode of elicited awareness and no mere emotion is crucial. It assures radical variations in conceptual explications of this feeling. "Divine abundance" is the rule over "barren uniformity" (Schleiermacher, 1988:108; 136-137). Yet concepts, necessary as articulation of feeling and intuition, are to be judged solely by the extent to which such religion feeling is elicited. The particular concepts are then seen to be superfluous. Rather than recommend Bettis's replacement of the term "feeling" with "immediate self-consciousness" we recommend a more appreciative understanding of Schleiermacher's unspeakable unity of intuition and feeling that rests in immediate self-consciousness. In Schleiermacher's (1988:112) words:

> Intuition without feeling is nothing and can be neither the proper origin nor the proper force; feeling without intuition is also nothing; both are therefore something only when and because they are originally one and unseparated.

That Schleiermacher has come to be identified with merely articulating the feeling of absolute dependency as the essence of religion is a poor, one-sided reading of his work. The force of emphasis does not undermine his focus on a complex intuition/feeling essence of religion that allows for noetic claims independent of their expression in concepts. This is the truly authoritative basis of religious experience but it applies to only to those in whom it is elicited.

> In spiritual things the original cannot be brought forth in you except when you beget it through an original creation in yourselves, and even then only in the moment you beget it (Schleiermacher, 1988:100).

Schleiermacher's analysis is central to contemporary considerations of religious experience. His model permits a critical analysis of what would otherwise be puzzling empirical findings as we shall note in our discussions of the research that follows. We will clarify Schleiermacher's analysis in direct discussion of the mystical and the numinous below. For now we need but emphasize the following conclusions from our brief discussion of Schleiermacher:

1) To experience religiously is to become aware of God or foundational reality by sense, intuition, and feeling. Factors that facilitate religious experience do not totally create that which is experienced.
2) Diverse factors may facilitate religious experience. The issue is the extent to which any factor, perhaps trivial in and of itself, elicits religious feeling.
3) The fixing of awareness in concepts is "religion" in the sense of myth. Part of the adequacy of myth is the extent to which it facilitates the elicitation of religious experience. Language and concepts are central to religious experience but are not constitutive of the experience. Religious experience is a prereflective encounter with foundational reality.
4) Religious (mythical) language and symbols are not privileged. Various descriptions of religious experience are always possible but do not in and of themselves define different religious realities. "One religion without God may be better than another with God" (Schleiermacher, 1988:136-137).
5) Religious feeling has both numinous and mystical aspects. These have been assessed in empirical studies.

Thus, the return to Schleiermacher is not to randomly pick a theologian to organize current empirical literature. Schleiermacher's conceptualization of religious feeling is central to both the conceptual and empirical literature. In his day, Schleiermacher argued against Enlightenment theories that would reduce most religious belief to mere superstition as much as he opposed religious dogma that would salvage religious belief by means of institutional tyranny. Yet in the preface the final edition of *On Religion* Schleiermacher argued equally against the "new pietism" which would make religion merely feeling in the contemporary sense of emotion that is without noetic merit (Crouter, 1988:70). That religious experience is not merely belief, not merely emotion; not merely the interaction of belief and emotion is the organizing theme that will clarify the empirical literature on the facilitation of religious experience.

The Numinous

Otto (1917/1958) remains the classic theorist whose illumination of the experience of the holy provides clarification of the foundational object of religions. Otto was careful to insist that the transrational element in religion be confronted only after immersion in the rational elements of any tradition. While rational articulations of faith in the form of theologies are appreciated by Otto, such formulations cannot capture the essence of the transrational. For Otto this essence is in the experience of the holy, characterized by the Janus-faced nature of religious mystery: *tremendum and fascinans.* The experience of this mystery is psychologically characterized by the numinous consciousness. Numinous consciousness is both compelled to seek out and explore the range and nature of the transcendent object *(mysterium fascinans)* and to be repelled in the face of the majesty and awfulness of this foundational object in whose presence one's creatureness is revealed *(mysterium tremendum).* Here is the psychological basis that articulates and comprehends the experience of the real as the limiting case of the personal. The *tremendum,* explicated in rational concepts such as the wrath of God, provides a reflexive location of one's feeling of creatureness for which Otto credits Schleiermacher's feeling of absolute dependency being if not primary, at least what might be called its phenomenological derivative (Otto, 1958:136-142). The *fascinans,* explicated in such rational concepts as grace, is the mystical pole of religion in which the inadequacy of reality as merely an analog to human personality is revealed. Otto explicates the personal dimension rooted in Schleiermacher's notion of religious feeling. For now, it is sufficient to emphasize that religious experiences of the personal, however inarticulate and distorted have a possible linkage to the foundational reality that many of the great faith traditions have articulated in names such as Krishna, Yahweh, Allah, or God.

The Mystical

If Otto provides the classic formulation of the numinous consciousness, Stace (1960) provides the classic formulation of the mystical consciousness. In numinous consciousness the personal nature of foundational reality is emphasized; in mystical consciousness the impersonal nature of foundational reality is emphasized. In mysticism, *fascinans* triumphs over *tremendum.* However the attempt at articulation, the experience of unity beyond subject/object dichotomies remains so well documented both within and out of faith traditions that its existence as a human experience of a foundational reality cannot be doubted. Stace's (1960) own phenomenological analysis distinguished between an introvertive mysticism of undifferentiated unity and an extrovertive mysticism of unity in diversity. These terms are derived from Otto's (1932:47-72) mysticisms of introspection and unifying vision. Thus both Otto and Stace have rather direct linkages to Schleiermacher. In extrovertive mysticism discrete objects of consciousness are revealed as constituting a totality. "To have religion means to intuit the universe" (Schleiermacher, 1988:132). However, perhaps most strongly revelatory of the impersonal nature of foundational reality is the mysticism of introversion in which the self's unity with foundational reality is complete. That Schleiermacher's feeling of absolute dependency has its mystical pole in both introvertive and extrovertive mysticism is revealed in Schleiermacher's claim that, "to accept everything individual as a part of the whole and everything limited as a representation of the infinite is religion (Schleiermacher, 1988:105). Likewise, introvertive mysticism is revealed in Schleiermacher's insistence on the prereflective awareness of a unity to life that is a component of the feeling of absolute dependency, a point often overlooked in discussions of Schleiermacher (Crouter, 1988). Here we will not explore the theological and philosophical issues involved in efforts to articulate mystical experience except to note, in support of our thesis, that as with the numinous, religious experiences of an impersonal foundational reality, even if distorted or misidentified, have a possible linkage to what the great faith traditions have articulated in such terms as Brahman, nirvana, sunyata, emptiness, or Godhead.

Religious Experience: Personal and Impersonal

By focusing upon a model that assumes a foundational reality which religious traditions struggle to articulate in their theologies we do not thereby propose a psychological theory attempting to verify of falsify any theological claims. Instead, we propose to look at the factors that facilitate religious experience. This experience is both numinous and mystical, both personal and impersonal. Part of the context in which such experiences are possible is itself the belief that foundational reality is being encountered. That experiences of the numinous and the mystical, of the personal and the impersonal occur is an issue of no small contemporary theological and philosophical concern. Yet the conditions under which these experiences occur is largely an empirical question to which we can now turn. Our approach relieves us of the inevitable constructionist position that a priori rules out of consideration, to paraphrase Bowker (1973), that some of the sense of God just might come from God. Religious traditions have been rightfully disdainful of psychologies that would deny even the possibility of their foundational objects; psychologies have been rightfully disdainful of religions that would deny the psychologies of their believers. In religious experience, religion and psychology meet in the exploration of reality that neither can rightfully dominate or claim to be exhaustively their own. That modern scholars have identified the mystical and the numinous, the impersonal and the personal, as fundamental modes of religious experiencing is but to emphasize the relevance of Schleiermacher, in which both the numinous and the mystical are intertwined in what scholars tend to one-sidedly define as the feeling of absolute dependency. That such experiences may be common and elicited under a variety of conditions should come as no surprise for those to whom the legacy of Schleiermacher strikes a sympathetic cord.

The Radical Constructionist Thesis

The conceptual literature on religious experience has been dominated in recent years by what we shall refer to as the radical constructionist thesis. Its roots lie in the well-documented influence of cultural factors that obviously shape human experience. However, in its extreme form, this hypothesis argues that all experience is constituted by cultural or social factors. Language is typically cited as the example par excellence for consideration. The debates have largely centered around two claims. First, that religious experience is or can be foundational for faith claims. Second, that at least some experiences are ineffable and hence beyond the pale of constructionist claims. In much of the literature these two theses are interrelated in debates surrounding mystical experience. We need to clarify the nature of these debates to help shed light upon the empirical studies that are relevant to the role of language as a facilitator of religious experience.

The extreme form of the constructionist thesis has gained popularity with the work of Proudfoot (1985), on religious experience in general, and Katz (1978, 1992) on mysticism in particular. Both these authorities argue that no unmediated experience is possible. Furthermore, since experience of any sort must be described to be recognized, the language used is itself constitutive of the experience. Proudfoot has argued this persuasively with respect to Schleiermacher's claim that a particular feeling, one of dependency, is foundational for religion. Proudfoot argues that the contextual matrix of Schleiermacher provided the context within which this supposedly unique feeling is socially constructed as foundational for religion. In a similar vein, Katz (1992:4) argues that mystical experience is largely available to be studied in its reports, typically maintained in written texts. The language of such texts does not simply describe the experience, but in fact constitutes the experience. Thus, a difference in language is indicative of a difference in experience. The roots of these debates can be found in William James who focused upon the distinction between experience and interpretation to sensitize readers of the *Varieties* to contextual and linguistic factors to be ignored in favor of the experience to which they refer (see Hood, 1992). Thus, the Jamesean thesis is opposed to an extreme constructionist position, arguing instead that variations in description may mask similar, if not identical, experiences. In the conceptual literature this Jamesean thesis has been typically referred to as the common core thesis. This thesis does not deny that language is relevant to experience. It does deny that language is constitutive of experience.

Language Effects on Religious Experience

We reject the view that language is sufficient to be constitutive of experience. Yet that language affects the report of religious experience is well established. It does so in four major ways: 1) it can facilitate awareness of foundational realities, including being a factor in the phenomenological description of the experience; 2) it can provide the necessary mediation by which experience becomes reflexively conscious; 3) it can facilitate the report of experiences within what Wittgenstein would call a particular language game; 4) it can lead one to reject experiences as legitimate religious ones. In each of these ways language plays a crucial role in religious experience, but not one that can carry the weight of constituting the experience. This will become apparent in our discussion of the relevant empirical literature dealing with the quasi-experimental facilitation of religious experience.

QUASI-EXPERIMENTAL STUDIES ON FACILITATION OF RELIGIOUS EXPERIENCE

Recent studies in psychology of religion have been influenced by research on the elicitation of emotion in quasi-experimental conditions. The prototypical study has been that of Schacter and his colleagues.

The Schacter and Singer Experiment

Within the conceptual literature on religious experience, Proudfoot (1985:98-102) has introduced an empirical study by Schacter and Singer (1962) as a psychological critique of classical views of emotion. He does this in a text that rightly starts with a sophisticated critique of Schleiermacher's view of religious feeling. As such, Proudfoot has provided the conceptual frame within which constructionist critiques of religious experience operate. He has found the experimental study by Schacter and Singer to be relevant to the basic logic of constructionist critiques. In this Proudfoot has done a great service, as the empirical and conceptual literatures have too long been separated in discussion of religious experience. However, despite the Schacter and Singer study being the prototypical study in the facilitation of emotion (and by implication in Proudfoot's treatment, religious feeling) it cannot establish what Proudfoot suggests.

Schacter and Singer (1962) have developed a well-known two factor theory of emotion. It essentially argues that emotion is an interaction between a state of physiological arousal and a cognitive framework within which the person evaluates this arousal. Neither alone is sufficient to produce emotion. In a now classic experiment participants were given injections of adrenaline under conditions of truthful or false expectations of physiological effects. A control group received a placebo injection. In addition, participants were exposed to situations where confederates of the experimenters expressed either anger or joy associated with relevant tasks that all participants undertook. Both observation and self report measures were taken of the participants to determine which ones experienced what emotion. Generally, as predicted, physiological arousal alone for both experimental groups was appropriately identified (for instance, variations in heart rate). The placebo group did not experience physiological changes. Under conditions of arousal, emotions of joy or anger were observed and reported for participants in the relevant confederate context. Thus, overall this study is interpreted by Proudfoot to support the two-factor theory of emotion. Identical physiological arousal is differentially interpreted based upon context to constitute a particular emotion. Despite excellent methodological critiques of this study (Marlasch, 1979; Plutchik and Ax, 1967; Schacter and Singer, 1962: 393-399), the conceptual point is strongly insisted by Proudfoot that language and context determine the particularity of emotions. Yet the relevance to Schleiermacher's view is either missed by Proudfoot's critique or Proudfoot's critique is actually unwittingly supportive of the common core thesis.

On the one hand, Schleiermacher, as well as Otto and Stace, insist that no clear conception of foundational reality is possible. Awareness is sensed prereflexively and pushes to find expression. It cannot be conceptually articulated as foundational reality transcends rationality. Rational expression merely suggests an adequacy for the moment and the possibility of awakening more fully this identical awareness in another. Proudfoot erroneously interprets the meaningfulness of the Schacter and Singer study as if injections had created an experience based upon physiological arousal. Whatever role physiological arousal might play in the restricted sense of emotion, it is not germane to Schleiermacher's rich sense of feeling.

On the one hand, Schleiermacher also noted that the moment of arousal is crucial, but such arousal is other than to report a physiological state. It is the elicitation of an intuition and a feeling. Schleiermacher (1988:113) is appropriately humble, "If I could create it in you, I would be a god; may holy fate only forgive me that I have had to disclose more than the Eleusinian mysteries."

On the other hand, Proudfoot has merely pushed the common core thesis back one step. His constructionist critique actually supports the view he wishes to criticize. He postulates that identical physiological arousal is variously labeled based upon linguistic and contextual factors. It is to this identical feeling, so easily explicated when we merely equate it with diffuse physiological arousal, that the common core theorists argue is the basis of religious feeling. That the mystical or numinous might be identical in a prereflexive sense is denied by Proudfoot but is exactly what Proudfoot holds to be true of physiological arousal, in a very explicit measured sense. As Spickard (1993:114-115) has also argued, Proudfoot merely replaces one common core for another and his constructionist critique fails.

With these criticisms we are ready to confront quasi-experimental studies of the facilitation of religious experience. We shall confront deliberate facilitation of religious experience in terms of both psychedelics and solitude. We shall confront spontaneous occurrences in terms of set and setting contrasts. The focus on a limited number of areas is dual in nature. First, it exhaust what little quasi-experimental literature there is. Second, it nevertheless allows for the range of conceptual issues involved in the facilitation of religious experience. The conceptual issues in this area of research are no less crucial than the collection of more empirical data.

Psychedelics: Body Alterations and the Facilitation of Religious Experience

If the Schacter and Singer study has become the exemplar for the elicitation of emotion in laboratory contexts, the dissertation by Pahnke (1963) is the more appropriate exemplar for the elicitation of religious experience. The literature on psychedelics is massive and balanced methodological critiques of psychedelic research readily available (Spilka, Hood, and Gorsuch, 1985:161-164). Yet what stands out is that virtually every major text in the psychology of religion discusses the Pahnke dissertation (for instance, Batson, Schoenrade, and Ventis, 1993:128-131; Spilka et al, 1985:163; Wulff, 1991:184-188). Why this experiment has caught the imagination of researchers is itself interesting. It does have the virtue of being more relevant than the Schacter and Singer study to an assessment of Schleiermacher's assessment of religious feeling. Furthermore, psychedelic studies are prototypical for any claim that religious experience is facilitated by alteration of bodily states, however induced.

The "Miracle" of Marsh Chapel

What makes the Pahnke study so interesting is that it represents within the scientific community a thin slice of a larger countercultural movement in which drugs of a wide variety were utilized for their common experiential effects in humans. For our purposes, such drugs were used to facilitate religious experience and the Pahnke study is simply an effort to see if within the context of a scientific laboratory such effects could be demonstrated. It parallels the Schacter and Singer study in that a religious context is provided within which participants given a drug or a placebo would be asked to label their responses. However, unlike the Schacter and Singer study, Pahnke's study employed psilocybin, a psychedelic drug whose drug specific effects are not as easily identified as are those of adrenaline. Thus, Panhke's participants cannot simply identify physiological arousal but must respond to more complex experiences.

Pahnke's study utilized twenty volunteers, none of whom admitted taking psychedelic drugs prior to this study. All were graduate students at Andover-Newton Theological Seminary. The participants meet to hear a broadcast of a Good Friday service after having had been given either psilocybin or nicotinic acid (as a placebo). The service was over two hours long and included prayers, personal meditation, and religious music. Participants meet in groups of four each, two experimental and two controls matched for compatibility. Each group had two leaders assigned, only one of which had been given psilocybin.

Various assessments were made, but most importantly for our purposes are explicit assessments according to specific criteria derived from Stace's (1960) phenomenological study of mysticism. His common core criteria of mystical experience, including both extrovertive and introvertive mysticisms were found to remarkably characterize the experimental but not the control group. Variations within the common core criteria were noted but with one exception the experimental group reliably reported over 50 percent of the maximum mystical common core while none of the control group reported more than 50 percent of the common core criteria. The one exception is on extrovertive mysticism which was only 38 percent in the experimental group. This is reasonable given the high introvertive percentage (62 percent) indicating

Table 1: Evaluation of Experience in Terms of Stace's Criteria

Common Core Criteria of Stace	Percent of Maximum Score on Each Criteria Distinguishing Between Groups Psilocybin	Placebo
Qualitatively Complete Experience of:		
Introvertive Unity	62	7
Transcendence of Space/time	84	6
Paradoxicality	61	13
Qualitatively Intermediate Experience of:		
Extrovertive Unity	38	2
Joy, Blessedness, Peace	51	13
Ineffability	66	18
Qualitatively Minimal Experience of:		
Sacredness	53	28

(Modified from Pahnke, 1970, Tables 1 & 2, pp. 155-177).

that a sense of unity more compatible with prayer and mediation was elicited in this study. If we note only Stace's common core criteria of mysticism, Pahnke's results can be summarized as follows:

The results of this study were found to hold in a follow up assessment six months later.

In a second study discussed only in Wulff's (1991:187-188) text, Pahnke (1967) utilized forty professionals as a participants in a modification of the original study. The setting was distinctively aesthetic and not religious. Classical music was played and there were flowers, and landscape art distinctively visible. While the experimental group received psilocybin the control group received a more complex placebo to better mimic some psychedelic effects. Preliminary results suggest 35 percent of the experimental group but only 5 percent of the control group would have been identified as having a mystical experience by use of Stace's common core criteria. Complete results are unavailable due to the untimely death of Pahnke.

A simple interpretation of the Pahnke studies is that given an appropriate context, physiological modifications of the body are interpreted as religious experiences. Thus, in both studies psilocybin produced more reports of mystical experience than placebos. Furthermore, comparing the Marsh chapel study to its sequel, even with psilocybin, a religious setting produces more mystical experience than a nonreligious one. Thus, similar to the naive reading of the Schacter and Singer study, arousal is interpreted as religious given the appropriate context. Context and physiology interact to produce religious experience.

This type of interpretation is supported by earlier research with psychedelic drugs. Leary (1964) had earlier reported research in which LSD therapy between two psychiatrists was compared. One psychiatrist conducted his therapy in a religious context (including showing religious articles during therapy sessions) while the other did not. Dramatic differences in religious experience resulted as noted in the following table:

Table 2: Theraputic Context and Differential Report of Experience

	THERAPIST A (N=74) (No Religious Context)	THERAPIST (N=96) (Religious Context)
Felt LSD was greatest personal experience	49	85
Felt this was a religious experience	32	83
Felt a greater awareness of God, a Higher Power, or Ultimate reality	40	90

(Adapted from Leary, 1964: 327).

Two points are worth emphasizing here. First, rather than the explicit criteria of Stace's common core criteria of mysticism, more numinous qualities of religious experience are indicated since the reference is to an awareness of God, a Higher Power, or Ultimate Reality and not one of unity. Second, fewer people within therapist groups report religious as opposed to what we have referred to as numinous experiences. As we shall see, some persons are unwilling to label numinous experiences as religious, given that religion can have a specific meaning within a particular context. Furthermore, one study suggests that reports of experiences relevant to God or Higher Powers can be variously subclassified. Thomas and Cooper (1978) obtained 302 questionnaires, largely from women, who had responded to the question, "Have you ever had the feeling of being close to a powerful spiritual force that seemed to lift you out of yourself?" (Thomas and Cooper, 1978:434). This is the same question used in several national surveys of reported religious experience (Spilka et al., 1985:183-185). Consistent with survey research, Thomas and Cooper found that approximately one-third of the participants answered this question affirmatively. However, upon content analyzing descriptions of these responses they found the following:

Table 3: Content Analysis of Positive Claims to Mystical Experience

Affirmative response to "Have you ever had the feeling of being close to a powerful spiritual force that seemed to lift you out of yourself?" (34% of 302 young adults (44 males/258 females)

Type of Experience	Frequency	Key Concepts Identifying Code Category
Not further codeable	8%	Insufficient information or irrelevant experience
Mystical	2%	Unity with God/nature; noetic' ineffability; time perception; reordering of life priorities
Faith/Consolation	12%	Religious experiences of traditional church-nature; no indication of extraordinary or supernatural
Psychic	12%	Other worldly experiences" in which spiritual element present. Includes paranormal experience.

(Modified from Thomas and Cooper, 1978, Table 1, pp. 434-435).

Thomas and Cooper document the relevant point that any affirmative response to a question can be further articulated in a first person account such that it may be other than the investigator thought. Yet whether a further analysis of the code categories of Thomas and Cooper might reveal some of these experiences to be numinous or mystical is an open question. Who is to say that traditional religious language might not indicate the numinous? Similarly, psychic experience can also be mystical experiences; these two categories need not be mutually exclusive (Hood, 1989). Likewise, of the nearly two hundred negative responses to the question, who is to say if these were explicated how many of them might not have reported religious experiences of a truly religious nature if probed more deeply? In all research on religious experience one must work with language to seek an expression of something other than what language expresses. Neither the words nor their use alone suffice. The key would appear to be to seek the phenomenological nature of what experience might have been evoked such that any particular language seems most relevant to experience.

As with Schleiermacher, the issue is a contextual-based definition of authenticity linked to whether or not any finite experience elicits a sense of the infinite. "To a pious mind religion makes everything holy and valuable, even unholiness and commonness itself" (Schleiermacher, 1799/1988: 109). Further analysis of the Thomas and Cooper data would be necessary to see whether or not any given paranormal or church related experience might also be elicitative of the numinous or mystical, indeed, of genuine religious feeling.

With LSD spontaneous reports of religious experience are quite common. (Masters and Houston, 1966:265) argue that almost all their participants report religious imagery as part of their psychedelic experience. If we focus only upon explicitly traditional religious imagery from Masters and Houston summary of 206 participants we obtain the following percentages of reported imagery:

Table 4: Religious Imagery During Psychedelic Experience

Traditional Religious Imagery	Percent Reporting Imagery During Psychedelic Experience
Religious architecture	91
Religious art	43
Religious symbols	34
Religious persons	58
Devil, demons	49
Angels	7

(Modified from Masters and Houston, 1966:265)

However, Masters and Houston (1966:260) argue that a common practice of psychedelic participants is to describe their experiences in terms of sacramental or religious metaphors, whether or not their experiences are authentically religious. Their own more rigorous assessment as to what constitutes a genuine religious experience is relevant in terms of language issues noted above. For now it is important to emphasize that all evaluation of experience is contextual. To use religious language to describe an experience is not necessarily to make that experience religious in the sense of eliciting either numinous or mystical feelings of absolute dependency. However, in another context religious traditions have long struggled with novices and the maturity of their faith, often in terms of how they report and understand their experiences. Within traditions or theories religious experiences can be misidentified or only partly realized. Yet it remains of interest why it is that even nonreligious participants struggle to use religious language to describe their psychedelic experiences. Part of the reason may be that such experiences facilitate numinous and mystical awareness at whatever level.

The type of studies reported here suggest the dilemma of trying to assess experience. How religious experience is assessed requires a clear conceptualization of its nature. Influenced by the Schleiermacher tradition, mystical and numinous states are difficult to ultimately confirm. Reports of their occurrence must contrast first and third person judgments. Even assessments by measurement criteria such as questionnaires indicated only self reports. Ultimately, a judgment must be made for which no single criterion will suffice. Yet it seems safest to affirm that in religious contexts the language utilized to describe drug elicited experiences suggests that numinous and mystical experiences are reported, and in fact are present probably in approximately a third of all participants. The power of psychedelic drugs to elicit religious awareness is surely not a drug specific effect. As Deikman (1966) has argued, perhaps there is a deautomatization in which habitual ways of sensing or perceiving are shifted for biochemical reason. This permits one to become aware of other aspects of reality. However, only when the alteration of awareness is directed to a sense of the transcendent, whether numinous or mystical, can it be properly spoken of as a religious experience. The weight of evidence on drug elicited states is to the effect that alterations of awareness permit but do not necessitate religious awareness. To respond merely to altered body states or to see the world in varieties of aesthetic alteration is neither necessarily numinous nor mystical. Yet to have a religious feeling, numinous or mystical, elicited by psychedelics is something that is not uncommon. If one surmises from the available empirical literature it would appear that somewhere between 35 and 50 percent of psychedelic participants report religious experiences of a mystical or numinous nature, even without religious contexts. The figure may rise to as high as 90 percent, but only if one counts as religious experience any imagery of a religious nature, or any religious language used to describe the experience. Yet the curious fact is that the percentage of reported religious experience elicited by psychedelics under unprompted conditions is no more than that reported for subjects in the general population (see Greeley, 1974, 1975; Spilka et al., 1985:183-185). Thus, the surprising fact is that researchers have focused so heavily upon drug elicited states that are on par with self reported experiences in the general population. Another way to express this finding is that among persons who use psychedelic drugs their report of religious experiences are no more common than among persons who do not use such drugs. In our studies we have shown that among persons identified for equally common reports of mystical experience based upon a scale derived from Stace's common core criteria of mysticism, one-third of the recreational (illegal) psychedelic drug users reported mystical experiences facilitated by drug use, matching exactly the proportion of the traditionally religious who had their mystical experience facilitated by traditional religious activities such as prayer (Hood, 1977a).

However, it has also been shown that for identically described experiences, those identified as facilitated by drugs are less positively evaluated than those identified as facilitated by prayer, especially among more dogmatic persons (Hood, 1980). This probably partly accounts for the fact that in national surveys psychedelic drugs seldom show up as a facilitator of mystical experience, while phenomena such as prayer and moments of quiet reflection are often cited as facilitators (see Greeley, 1975:64).

The implication of drug facilitated religious awareness are paradoxical. In a culture largely hostile to the use of drugs to facilitate religious awareness the lasting importance of religious experience may be lost. Troeltsch (1931) long ago noted the emergence in Western culture of two mysticisms, one nourished within religious traditions and another, devoid of social form and importance insofar as it was free of an institutional or collective form of expression. This latter mysticism perhaps accounts for the similar rates of reported mystical experience among those who define themselves as not religious and those who define themselves as religious. In terms of psychedelics, one need but remember that many of the participants as guides, researchers, or subjects in the Miracle of Marsh chapel now read like a "who's who" of the psychedelic movement. In an excellent history of the psychedelic movement in America (Stevens, 1988) has traced the various roles of such figures as Timothy Leary, Richard Alpert (Ram Dass), Alan Watts, and Aldous Huxley in terms of what amounts to a genuine cult movement fostered by drugs. For those who argue the Jamesean position that drugs facilitate religious experience, but that such experiences must be judged by their fruits, it is curious that we have few studies of the actual effort to use psychedelics in a sacramental sense. Perhaps the parallel case is in the Native American use of peyote, the successful institutionalization of which is well documented in the anthropological literature.

Isolation Tanks: Enhanced Solitude and the Facilitation of Religious Experience

The study of solitude as a deliberate method to invoke religious experience has a checkered history. In contemporary research both prayer (Brown, 1994) and meditation (Naranjo and Ornstein, 1971) have been the most common vehicles for studying solitude and the facilitation of religious experience. Not surprisingly, it has been shown that participants in prayer and mediation studies who are religious tend to report religious imagery during various prayer and meditative practices. To define such experiences as religious is to equate religious language and imagery with religious experience in the sense of the mystical and numinous, something that may not be true. However, if religious imagery occurs, its elicitation during periods of solitude may have numinous or mystical qualities.

What is common to a wide variety of prayer and meditative practices is the deliberate effort to focus upon a particular object, devotional or not, or to turn within and to maintain a state of direct, nonreflexive awareness. Techniques to achieve this vary widely and serve to define various approaches. While largely restricted to religious traditions, such practices have a curious overlap with studies of sensory isolation. The early studies of sensory isolation have parallels to the psychedelic movement, in which extreme claims for the power of isolation to elicit experience ranging from the pathological to the religious have been made. Perhaps Lilly (1977) more than anyone else fostered the study of isolation with his isolation tank. Lilly's tank permits the immersion of a person into a environment in which external sources of auditory and visual stimulation are eliminated as the person is floated slightly submerged in a hydrated magnesium sulfate solution maintained at external skin temperature (see Lilly, 1977:137-169). Such conditions maximize sensory isolation. We have explored the use of isolation tanks to experimentally maximized solitude and to explore the effect of such solitude on the production of religious experience. In two studies we have attempted to provoke religious imagery and to assess the possibility that such imagery may for some be an experience that is either mystical or numinous in nature.

In the first study we selected persons for their extreme scores on either the intrinsic or extrinsic scales (Hood and Morris, 1981b). The domination of Allport's religious orientation measures is well documented (Kirkpatrick and Hood, 1991). For purposes of this study, extremely intrinsic participants were selected to be contrasted to extrinsics for who reasons; 1) they are well practiced in prayer; 2) they have been repeatedly shown to have higher rates of religious experiences (see Hood, 1985). It was assumed that the isolation tank would produce conditions that would facilitate maximum solitude, a condition that should facilitate religious experiences in persons prone to seek such states in prayer or mediation. Furthermore, the well known elicitation of imagery in isolation conditions led us to produce two set conditions, one in which participants were instructed to try to imagine cartoon figures, the other in which participants were instructed to try to imagine religious figures. Thus, since ethically we were mandated to inform persons that imagery was a common occurrence in the isolation tank, we simply tried to facilitate the content of imagery based upon explicit set and the nature of religious orientation (intrinsic/extrinsic) of the participants.

Using a four point scale from "never experienced" (1) to "frequently experienced" (4) the relevant means and standard deviations for this study were as follows:

Table 5: Isolation Tank Imagery by Religious Type and Set

Reported Imagery	Set Conditions	Religious Type Intrinsic Mean	SD	Extrinsic Mean	SD
	Cartoon	2.10	.86	1.10	.32
Religious Figures	Religious	3.10	.74	1.90	.74
	Cartoon	2.30	.95	2.50	1.27
Cartoon Figures	Religious	1.30	.68	1.50	.71

Adapted from Hood and Morris, 1981b: Table 1, p. 267).

Thus, intrinsic participants reported religious imagery more frequently than did extrinsic participants under the appropriate set conditions. They did not differ from extrinsic when told to think of cartoon figures indicating that capacity to imagine is not relevant.

These study did not directly assess religious experience of a numinous or mystical type that persons might have under isolation tank conditions. However, this study does suggest that religious imagery occurs in isolation tank settings and that this imagery may have numinous characteristics. Among intrinsics, probably well versed in prayer, religious imagery is most facilitated by isolation tank conditions perhaps because the enhanced solitude parallels the state and experience intrinsics achieve in private prayer (Hood, Morris, and Watson, 1989). Thus, religious imagery elicited in isolation tank studies is unlikely to be simply spurious.

A control for the possibility that religious imagery is simply differentially reported by intrinsics and extrinsics under any conditions was run. An independent sample of similarly selected extrinsic and intrinsic participants were asked under religious set, cartoon set, and no set conditions to give religious imagery responses to Rorschach cards (Hood and Morris, 1981b: 269-272). Of relevance to our present discussion is the fact that under no condition did intrinsic participants report more religious imagery than extrinsics, even when specifically instructed to give religious responses. Thus, the suggestion is enhanced that religious imagery in the isolation tank is genuine and part of a genuine religious experience and not just a tendency to report religious imagery when instructed to do so.

Still, the issue remains regarding the facilitation of mystical or numinous experiences under conditions of solitude. Certainly the conceptual literatures on prayer and meditation are replete with reports both of how particular techniques might facilitate religious awareness. The question of whether or not quasi-experimental studies could support such claims was an unresolved one until recently.

In a second isolation tank study (Hood, Morris, and Watson, 1990) we specifically selected religiously committed participants who were naive to the isolation tank experience. Participants were then placed in the isolation tank with an intercom utilized to present a simple set condition found to be useful in studies of mystical prayer (de Mello, 1984:13). The specific instructions were identical for experimental and control conditions with the exception of a single word (below in boldface for the experimental an italics for the control conditions):

> I am now going to invite you to keep silent for a period of ten minutes. First, you will try to attain silence, as total silence as possible of heart and mind. Having attained it, you will expose yourself to whatever (*religious revelation/insight)* it brings. (Adapted from de Mello, 1984:13)

When relaxed in the tank, participants were read this simple instruction. While still in the tank participants were assessed on Stace's common core criteria of mysticism using a shortened version of Hood's (1975) Mysticism scale. This shortened version allowed participants to respond to their specific experiences in the isolation tank by answering "yes" or "no" to questions indicative of both components of the mysticism scale, a common experiential core (factor I) and a religious interpretation (factor II). Examples of questions are: "Did you have an experience in which everything seemed to disappear from your mind until you were conscious only of a void?" (factor I) or "Did you experience awe?" (factor II). Scores could range from 0 to 6 on both factors. Participants were selected not only for religious commitment but also for the nature of that commitment. For purposes of our discussion we will focus only upon comparisons between extrinsic and intrinsic participants. Relevant results for these two groups are presented below:

Table 6: Mystical Experience as a Function of Isolation Tank Set

	Religious Set					No Religious Set			
	Factor I		Factor II			Factor I		Factor II	
Type	Mean	SD	Mean	SD	Type	Mean	SD	Mean	SD
Intrinsic (n = 11)	4.09	1.30	4.63	1.36	Intrinsic (n = 9)	3.78	1.38	=5.00	1.11
Extrinsic (n = 15)	4.20	1.74	2.27	1.44	Extrinsic (n = 13)	4.38	.61	2.30	1.89

(Adapted from Hood, Morris, and Watson, 1990: Table 1, p. 169)

As anticipated, intrinsic participants when presented with a prayer set in the isolation tank setting reported more religiously interpreted mystical experiences on an objective scale (factor II) than did extrinsics. Interestingly, neither group differed in the report of the more phenomenologically derived common core criteria of mysticism, especially unity items. Thus, we can safely conclude that under these powerful conditions both extrinsic and intrinsic participants found a meaningful prayer set to facilitate a religious experience. The veridicality of the experience is attested to by the fact that both groups, regardless of set conditions report the minimal factor I experience while only the intrinsics, (again regardless of set) interpreted this experience religiously. (Part of this study was directed to altering the religious interpretation of experiences as a function of set for other groups, a prediction not germane to our discussion of extrinsics and intrinsics.) Once again, the question of the validity of such reports must be addressed (if only for the skeptical despairs of our day). The refusal to accept that mystical experiences can be facilitated and reported in such quasi-experimental conditions is largely due to two common biases.

The first bias is that mystical experience is rare, a fact continually refuted by survey studies. As noted above, at least one-third of the populations of Western cultures report mystical and/or numinous experiences. Thus, that persons in laboratory contexts report mystical experience is itself to be expected (Hood, 1985). The empirical issue is how to facilitate such experiences and certainly enhanced solitude is one such way.

The second bias is that participants merely claim to have mystical experiences. Usually critiques come from two concerns. First, that in using scales such as mystical inventories, any intense experience out of the ordinary will be expressed on the scale if no other measures are provided. This has been a persistent criticism of the Pahnke study since he only used Stace's common core criteria to assess the experience at Marsh chapel. However, in our studies this criticism is tempered by the focus on differences between groups of participants on the same measure and differences within groups of participants on different measures . Thus, participants are not merely using the mysticism scale to indicate an experience "out of the ordinary." In addition, Hood and Morris (1981a) have shown that persons reporting mystical experiences, and those who either are uncertain or deny having such experiences, do not differ in knowledge about what constitutes mysticism but only on whether or not they have had mystical experiences. Thus, we can reasonably conclude that participants report experiences, even mystical experiences, based upon a meaningful self report of what in fact is their own experience.

Third, in an independent study we assessed by means of a voice stress analyzer tensions involved when persons either affirmed or denied having had mystical experiences (Hood, 1978). In the portion of this study relevant to our present concerns it was found that purely intrinsic persons both 1) report mystical experience and 2) indicate little or no stress when they do so.

Likewise, purely extrinsic persons both 1) deny having mystical experiences and 2) indicate little or no stress when they do so. These results can be interpreted to support the truthfulness of intrinsics and extrinsics when reporting experiences they might or might not have had. Extrapolating to the isolation tank study, there is no a priori reason to doubt the validity of the self report of the experience of religious imagery among intrinsics (or lack of it among extrinsics) and even less reason given the documented truthfulness of intrinsics in their report of religious experiences.

Quasi-experimental studies suggest the powerful effects of enhanced solitude tempered with appropriate religious set to facilitate religious experiencing. That the great faith traditions all demand some form of private prayer is suggestive of the facilitating effect of such solitude in the enhancement of awareness their foundational realities. In a sense, however such activities are studied, the ultimate criterion is always a sympathetic assessment and evaluation of whether or not such reality has in fact been appropriately apprehended. That extrinsics and intrinsics differ in their religious evaluation of experiences as noted in this study is suggestive of the relevant role religious education can play in the broader contextual interpretation on experience in and of itself. Part of the low rate of reported religious experience among extrinsics may be due to their failure to understand the meaningfulness of religious language in articulating experience, perhaps due to their extremely functional orientation to religion, whether personal or social.

Spontaneous Religious Experience: Stress Set and Setting Stress Incongruities

It is ironic to talk of the facilitation of spontaneous religious experiences until one considers that the distinction between deliberately facilitated religious experience and spontaneous religious experience is never absolute. At best, deliberately facilitated experience is a conscious effort to engage in some activity such that a religious experience is made more likely. A spontaneous experience is one in which there is no deliberate or conscious effort to facilitate a religious experience, but nevertheless such an experience occurs. To attempt to list or categorize such situations were religious experiences spontaneously occur is fruitless although several list have been compiled (see Spilka et al., 1985:193-194). Efforts at higher order conceptualizations seem more fruitful. One effort that has been studied in quasi-experimental studies is that of set and setting incongruities.

Several studies have suggested that incongruities between set and setting stress serve to elicit spontaneous religious experiences. Rosegrant (1976) studied Outward Bound participants in North Carolina. His intent was to study participants three day solo experiences using a variety of set and setting variables on an objective measure of religious experience modified after one developed by Hood (1970). Rosegrant's study is noteworthy as perhaps the first to study spontaneous religious experience in a natural setting.

However, he found that only a measure subjective stress was correlated (negatively) with the religious experience measure.

We attempted to replicate aspects of Rosegrant's initial work with specific attention to assessing religious experience as a function of set and setting incongruities (Hood, 1977). Like Rosegrant's study, we used participants in a nature field experience. These were graduating seniors at an all male preparatory school. Part of their graduating semester they spent a week in the outdoors engaged in a variety of activities ranging from such relatively nonstressful activities as backpacking and canoeing a calm river to more stressful activities such as rock climbing, white water rafting, and an all night solo experience. Thus, we could easily classify activities according to setting stress. Paralleling Rosegrant's study, we used an objective measure of felt stress that participant took just before a specified activity to assess his anticipatory stress. In addition, immediately after each activity participants completed Hood's Mysticism Scale.

As anticipated, different activities produced differing degrees of anticipatory stress. Our goal was to compare religious experience scores for all possibilities of set and setting stress. However, it turned out that the low setting stress conditions were not anticipated by any participants as stressful and hence only one incongruity could be assessed—high stress events anticipated to be low stress. The following table shows the relevant means and standard deviations:

Table 7: Mysticism as a Function of Anticipated Stress

High Stress Activity	Anticipatory Stress			
	Mean	SD	Mean	SD
White Water Rafting	Low	(n=10)	High	(n=13)
I	76.0	12.2	63.2	8.4
II	46.0	10.3	40.1	7.3
Rock Climbing	Low	(n=12)	High	(n=11)
I	70.1	10.2	60.0	10.6
II	43.3	6.0	37.9	4.4
Night Solo	Low	(n=11)	High	(n=12)
I	74.7	9.7	59.8	14.2
II	47.7	5.2	37.7	7.0

(Hood, 1977: Table 1, p. 160)

Appropriate statistical tests on differences between means indicated that with one exception (factor II white water rafting) the low stress participant had higher mysticism scores than the high stress participants. Hence, it is not the stressful situation per se that facilitates mystical experience, but rather the incongruity between anticipatory stress and setting stress. Furthermore, with the exception noted above, this holds for both factors indicating that not only are the minimal phenomenological properties of mysticism experienced (such as unity, factor I), but these are seen as religiously relevant in the broadest sense of the term (such as experiences of awe, factor II). Thus we not only extended Rosegrant's specific study of solitary nature experiences (the evening solo) but also studied other stressful nature conditions such as rafting and rock climbing). Furthermore, while Rosegrant used a measure of religious experience (discussed below) that mixes numinous and mystical descriptions, this study use only an explicit measure of mystical experience derived from Stace. Based upon these two studies, stress incongruities in nature can facilitate either numinous or mystical awareness.

In the following year, a second study was undertaken to more explicitly test the set/setting incongruity hypothesis (Hood, 1978a). In this study the nature experience for students from the same preparatory school was designed such that all students were to have a night solo experience consisting of being led into the mountains in the early evening with only minimal equipment and food. They were individually separated and were to stay alone all night and find their way back to camp at daybreak. Various participants soloed on different evening over a five-day period. As in the previous study, anticipatory stress was measured. This time all participants were assessed on the evening just before being left for their solo. Immediately upon return at daybreak. Immediately following each activity all participants completed Rosegrant's modification of Hood's Religious Experience Episodes Measure (REEM). This measure is derived from descriptions of religious experiences that are mixtures of numinous and mystical experiences. Each experience is briefly described in a paragraph and persons can indicate the extent to which their experience was like the ones described (see Hood, 1970; Rosegrant, 1977).

Initially, we had intended to manipulate setting stress by location. However, fortuitous circumstances occurred such that on three of the nights there were tremendous thunder storms. Thus, participants soloing on those nights were defined as soloing under a relatively stressful setting; those on the calm nights as soloing under a relatively less stressful setting. REEM scores for the 64 participants who completed their solos by classification of set and setting were as follows:

Appropriate statistical analyses indicated that both incongruous conditions differed from both congruous conditions, but neither of the congruous or incongruous conditions differed between themselves. As anticipated, incongruity is what facilities religious experience and not simply low anticipatory stress/high setting stress incongruity which we documented previously (Hood, 1977b).

It is important to emphasize that our measurement of religious experi-

Table 8: Religious Experiences as a Function of Stress Incongruities

	Setting Stress			
	(High-Thunderstorm)		(Low-No Thunderstorm)	
	Mean	SD	Mean	SD
High Anticipatory Stress	32.44	12.75	52.83	14.72
	(n=16)		(n=12)	
Low Anticipatory Stress	51.43	9.37	42.07	14.95
	(n=21)		(n=15)	

Adapted from Hood, 1978a, Table 1, p. 283)

ence in both these studies was not anticipated by the participants. Most quasi-experimental studies of eliciting religious experience are "artificial" in that deliberate efforts are made to either alter body states or produce maximum solitude in a context that might also manipulate the specific religious nature of the setting. However, in these studies only outdoor activities in the context of a senior culminating experience in the wilderness are utilized to assess spontaneously occurring religious experiences. The fact that being in nature often facilitates religious experiences is supported by correlational studies in which nature experiences are among the most commonly cited triggers of religious experiences, and especially of those that appear to occur spontaneously (Greeley, 1975; Hood, 1977a). The criticism that only religious indices are used to report whatever experiences occur is minimal given a variety of measures utilized in Rosegrant's research in which, without manipulating set and setting incongruities, he found overall that participants in his study did not differentially report religious experience. However they did not differ in reports of the meaningfulness of their solo experiences.

Why spontaneously occurring religious experiences are facilitated by set and setting incongruities in nature settings is worthy of future study. Our own thinking has been to place these studies in the context of the sudden transcendence of limits such that a figure/ground reversal occurs. Paralleling Deikman's (1966) deautomatization hypothesis, old limited ways of seeing are suddenly transcended and new or other aspects of reality are perceived. However, the conceptual literature on religious experience has focused upon the notion of "see-as" rooted in Wittgenstein (1958). Wittgenstein's examples are psychological in that they refer to such things as Kohler's vases/profiles. These examples, common in introductory psychology textbooks, demonstrate that individuals can perceive either a single vase or two profiles depending upon figure/ground reversals. The conceptual importance of these still puzzling examples is that whether one sees two profiles or a single vase cannot be a function of sensation since the same stimulus material is presented to the person who perceives a vase as to the one who perceives two profiles. Thus, those influenced by Wittgenstein have argued that religious experience is an instance of "seeing as" with the dispute between those who see religiously and those who do not being analogous to those who see two profiles vs. those who see a vase (Almond, 1982:157-180).

While the concept of a figure/ground reversal is an intriguing one and does appear to permit a resolution of otherwise incompatible claims it actually sneaks in the solution to the problem it claims to resolve. The psychologist can stand aside and note the lack of problem between disputants who claim to see profiles while others see only one vase only because he or she knows that a broader context, that of reversible figures, is in fact presented. The reversible figure must be what it is for others to see profiles, a vase, or with a little reflection both. The reversible figure, however remains constantly what it is.

Religious experiencing is less seeing a vase where others see profiles, than noting the reversible figure itself. In Schleiermacher's sense, the intuiting of the reversible figure is analogous to religious feeling, while experiencing the vase and the profiles is akin to religious myth. We suggest that spontaneous religious experiences are not analogous to suddenly seeing the vase where previously two profiles were seen, nor to seeing both alternatively. Rather it is more analogous to moving beyond the phenomena of such reversals to intuit the context of reversible figures where such alterations are possible.

CONCLUSION

Despite a wide variation in the conditions used to facilitate religious experience in quasi-experimental studies a fairly consistent picture emerges. Whether by alteration of body states, enhanced solitude, or set/setting stress incongruities in nature settings, religious experience is consistently reported. This holds for measurements of religious experience on indices that assess either mystical or numinous experiences or a mixture of both. That such experiences can be facilitated is not surprising given the fact that such experiences are documented to be common in Western cultures.

The prejudice that would make sensitivity to the numinous or the mystical a privilege of a few is empirically unwarranted. However, as with our efforts to articulate the conceptual fruitfulness of a return to Schleiermacher, how to judge such experiences is no simple task. To argue that under quasi-experimental conditions a sensitivity to numinous or mystical realities is facilitated is not to understand how it is that such experiences are contextualized and incorporated into lives—both personal and collective. If we assume that religious experience is foundational to faith, its facilitation ought not to be simply assessed in quasi-experimental studies, but followed through in its contextualization. In the tradition of Schleiermacher, a social psychology of religious experience ought to provide empirical possibilities for understanding religious beliefs and rituals in the contexts that both codify and elicit religious feeling. Thus to return to Schleiermacher makes tradition itself the context for the recovery of experience. In anticipation of the post-modern condition, Schleiermacher's insistence of a core religious experience mandates diversity in communities of the faithful. Berger (1980:120) perceptively notes: "Schleiermacher proposes a method of inquiry by which every religion, even if it has degenerated into empty rituals and abstract theories, is traced back to its experiential source." A social psychology that studies this must be historically based, longitudinal in nature, and phenomenologically sensitive. At best, quasi-experimental studies are analogies to conditions that facilitate religious feelings in real life contexts. That persons might find their sensitivity to religious intuitions and feelings facilitated under the conditions we have reviewed is no more surprising than the diverse conditions reported within the continuing histories of the great faith traditions. In neither case can the origin alone bear the burden of the tradition. This is but the historical side of the relationship between experience and interpretation for which a sensitivity to Schleiermacher corrects the extremes of the naive realists and the radical constructionists.

REFERENCES

Almond, P. C.
1982 *Mystical experience and religious doctrine.* Berlin: Mouton Publishers.
Batson, C. D., P. Schoenrade, and W. L. Ventis
1993 *Religion and the individual.* Oxford: Oxford University Press.
Berger, P. L.
1980 *The heretical imperative.* New York: Anchor.
Bettis, J. D. (Ed.)
1969 *Phenomenology of religion.* New York: Harper & Row.
Bowker, J.
1973 *The sense of God.* London: Oxford University Press.
Brown, L. B.
1994 *The human side of prayer.* Birmingham, AL: Religious Education Press.
Crouter, R.
1988 Introduction. In F. Schleiermacher, *On religion.* Cambridge: Cambridge University Press.
Deikman, A.
1966 Implications of experimentally produced contemplative mediation. *Journal of Nervous and Mental Disease* 142:101-116.
de Mello, A.
1984 *Sadhana: A way to God.* New York: Image Books.
Garrett, W. R.
1974 Troublesome transcendence: The supernatural in the scientific study of religion. *Sociological Analysis* 35, 167-180.
Greeley, A.
1974 *Ecstasy: A way of knowing.* Englewood Cliffs, NJ: Prentice-Hall.
1975 *The sociology of the paranormal: A reconnaissance.* Beverly Hills, CA: Sage.

Hardy, A.
1979 *The spiritual nature of man.* Oxford: Clarendon.
Hick, J.
1989 *An interpretation of religion.* New Haven, CT: Yale University Press.
Hood Jr., R. W.
1970 Religious orientation and the report of religious experience. *Journal for the Scientific Study of Religion* 9:285-291.
1975 The construction and preliminary validation of a measure of reported religious experience. *Journal for the Scientific Study of Religion* 14:29-41.
1977a Differential triggering of mystical experience as a function of self-actualization. *Review of Religious Research* 16:155-163.
1977b Eliciting mystical states of consciousness with semistructured nature experiences. *Journal for the Scientific Study Of Religion.* 16:155-163.
1978a The usefulness of the indiscriminately pro and anti categories of religious orientation. *Journal for the Scientific Study of Religion* 17:419-431.
1978b Anticipatory set and setting: Stress incongruities as elicitors of mystical experience in solitary nature situations. *Journal for the Scientific Study of Religion* 17:279-287.
1980 Social legitimacy, dogmatism, and the evaluation of intense experience. *Review of Religious Research* 21: 184-194.
1985 Mysticism. In *The sacred in a secular age,* edited by P. H. Hammond. Berkeley, CA: University of California Press.
1989 Mysticism, the unity thesis, and the paranormal. In *Exploring the paranormal,* edited by G. K. Zollschan, J. F. Schumaker, and G. F. Walsh. New York: Avery.
1992 A Jamesean look at self and self loss in mysticism. *The Journal of the Psychology of Religion* 1: 1-24.
Hood Jr., R. W., and R. J. Morris
1981a Knowledge and experience criteria in the report of mystical experience. *Review of Religious Research* 23:76-84.
1981b Sensory isolation and the differential elicitation of religious imagery in intrinsic and extrinsic persons. *Journal for the Scientific Study of Religion* 20:261-273.
Hood Jr., R. W., R. J. Morris, and P. J. Watson
1989 Prayer experience and religious orientation. *Review of Religious Research* 31:39-45.
1990 Quasi-experimental elicitation of the differential report of religious experience among intrinsic and indiscriminately pro religious types. *Journal for the Scientific Study of Religion,* 29:164-172.
Katz, S. T. (Ed.)
1978 *Mysticism and philosophical analysis.* New York: Oxford.
1992 *Mysticism and language.* New York: Oxford.
Kirk, K. E.
[1931]
1966 *The vision of God.* New York: Harper & Row.
Kirkpatrick, L. A., and R. W. Hood Jr.
1990 Intrinsic-extrinsic religious orientation: The boon or bane of the contemporary psychology of religion? *Journal for Scientific Study of Religion* 29:315-334.
Leary, T.
1964 Religious experience: Its production and interpretation. *Psychedelic Review* 1:324-346.
Lilly, J. C.
1977 *The deep self.* New York: Simon & Schuster.
Louth, A.
1981 *The origins of the Christian mystical tradition.* Oxford: Clarendon.
Marlasch, C.
1979 The emotional consequences of arousal without reason. In *Emotions in personality and psychophysiology,* edited by C. E. Izard. New York: Plenum.
Masters, R.E.L., and J. Houston
1966 *The varieties of psychedelic experience.* New York: Delta.
Naranjo, C., and R. E. Ornstein

1971 *On the psychology of meditation.* New York: Viking.

Otto, R

1932 *Mysticism East and West,* translated by B. L. Bracey and R. C. Payne, New York: Macmillan.

[1917] 1958 *The idea of the holy,* translated by J. W. Harvey. London: Oxford University Press.

Pahnke, W. N.

1963 *Drugs and mysticism: An analysis of the relationship between psychedelic drugs and mystical consciousness.* Doctoral dissertation, Harvard University.

1970 Drugs and mysticism. In *Psychedelics,* edited by B. Aarson and H. Osmond. New York: Anchor.

Pahnke, W. N., and W. A. Richards.

1966 Implication of LSD and experimental mysticism. *Journal of Religion and Health* 5: 175-208.

Plutchik, R., and A. F. Ax.

1967 A critique of 'Determinants of emotional state' by Schacter and Singer. *Psychophysiology* 4:79-82.

Proudfoot, W.

1985 *Religious experience.* Berkeley, CA: University of California Press

Rosegrant, J.

1976 The impact of set and setting on religious experience in nature. *Journal for the Scientific Study of Religion* 15:301-310.

Schacter, S., and J. E. Singer

1962 Cognitive, social, and physiological determinants of emotional state, *Psychological Review* 69:379-399.

Schleiermacher, F.

[1830-31;1920-21] 1963 *The Christian faith,* 2 vols., translated by H. R. Mackintosh and J. S. Stewart. New York: Harper & Row.

[1799; 1806; 1821] 1988 *On religion: Speeches to its cultured despisers,* translated by R. Crouter. Cambridge: Cambridge University Press.

Spickard, J. V.

1993 For a sociology of religious experience. In *A future for religion? New paradigms for social analysis,* W. H. Swatos Jr. Newbury Park, CA: Sage.

Spilka, B., R. W. Hood Jr., and R. Gorsuch

1985 *The psychology of religion: An empirical approach.* Englewood Cliffs, NJ: Prentice-Hall.

Stace, W. T.

1960 *Mysticism and philosophy.* Philadelphia: Lippincott.

Stevens, J.

1988 *Storming heaven.* New York: Harper & Row.

Thomas, L. E., and R. E. Cooper

1978 Measurement and incidence of mystical experience: An exploratory study. *Journal for the Scientific Study of Religion* 17:433-437.

Toulmin, S.

1962 *Foresight and understanding.* San Francisco: Harper & Row.

Toulmin, S., and D. Leary

1985 The cult of empiricism in psychology and beyond. In *A century of psychology as science,* edited by S. Koch and D. Leary. New York: McGraw-Hill.

Troeltsch, E.

1931 *The social teachings of the Christian church.,* 2 vols., translated by O. Wyon. New York: Macmillan.

Wittgenstein, L.

1958 *Philosophical investigations,* 2nd ed., translated by G. E. M. Anscombe. New York: Macmillan.

Wulff, D. M.

1991 *Psychology of religion: Classic and contemporary views.* New York: Wiley.

Contributors

Benjamin Beit-Hallahmi teaches in the Department of Psychology at the University of Haifa. Among his many books are *Prolegomena to the psychological study of religion, Dictionary of modern religious movements,* and *The psychoanalytic study of religion.* He is a recipient of the William James award given by the division of Psychology of Religion of the American Psychological Association.

Herbert Burhenn is Professor and Head of the Department of Philosophy and Religion at the University of Tennessee at Chattanooga. He is also Executive Director of the Southeastern Commission for the Study of Religion. His recent publications include studies of religion and liberal arts education.

Michael J. Donahue is a Research Scientist at Search Institute, Minneapolis, Minnesota. He is a Catholic layman. His most recent research concerns religious giving among mainline Protestants and positive youth development in religiously-based institutions.

Susan F. Greenwood is an instructor in the Department of Sociology at the University of Maine. Her published research has focused upon theoretical issues in the sociology of religion.

Fredrica R. Halligan is Associate Director in the Counseling Center at Fordham University. She co-hosts the Psychotherapy and Spirit Seminars at Cafh Foundation, New York City. She is co-editor of *The fires of desire; Erotic energies and the spiritual quest,* and author of *The art of coping.*

Peter Hill is Professor in the Psychology Department of Grove City College, Pennsylvania. He is the editor of *Journal of Psychology and Christianity.* He is co-editing a volume of assessment instruments in the psychology of religion.

Nils G. Holm is Professor of Comparative Religion and former First Vice Rector at the Åbo Akademi University in Turku/Åbo (Swedish University in Finland). He is author of *Scandinavian psychology of religion* and has edited *Religious ecstasy.* He is active as a Nordic representative to many international organizations.

Gui-Young Hong is Assistant Professor of Psychology at the University of Tennessee at Chattanooga. Her research includes investigations of the social construction of gender as well as cross cultural studies of distributive justice.

Ralph W. Hood Jr. is Professor of Psychology at the University of Tennessee at Chattanooga. He is co-author of *The psychology of religion: An empirical approach.* He is a co-editor of *The International Journal for the Psychology of Religion.* He is a past president of the division of Psychology of Religion of the American Psychological Association and a recipient of its William James award.

Ronald E. Hopson is Assistant Professor of Psychology at the University of Tennessee at Knoxville. His research focuses upon the interface between therapeutic psychology and religion. He is a licensed clinical psychologist and an ordained minister.

Janet L. Jacobs is Associate Professor of Women's Studies at the University of Colorado at Boulder. She is author of *Divine disenchantment: Deconverting from new religious movements* and of *Victimized daughters: Incest and the development of the female self.*

Lee A. Kirkpatrick is Assistant Professor of Psychology at the College of William and Mary. His research interests include intrinsic/extrinsic religious orientation and attachment. He is currently coediting a special issue of the *Journal of Social Issues* regarding religion and well-being. Twice he has been a finalist for the distinguished article award of the Society for the Scientific Study of Religion.

James Michael Lee is Professor of Education at the University of Alabama at Birmingham. His research interests center on the fundamental social-scientific basis and pervasive context of religious education. Among his many works is the massive trilogy: *The shape of religious instruction, The flow of religious instruction,* and *The content of religious instruction.* He has lectured widely in America and abroad. He is listed *Who's who in America, Who's who in the world,* and *Who's who in religion.* He is also the publisher of Religious Education Press.

Beverly J. (Macy) McCallister has taught at the University of Toronto and at McMaster University. She specializes in cognitive psychology. She is currently treasurer of the division of Psychology of Religion of the American Psychological Association. She is editor of *A guide for graduate programs in the psychology of religion.*

Daniel N. McIntosh is Assistant Professor of Psychology at the University of Denver. He specializes in the social psychology of emotion. His published research includes papers on religion and physical health and the role of religion in coping behavior.

H. Newton Malony is Senior Professor in the Graduate School of Psychology at Fuller Theological Seminary, Pasadena, California. He is a Fellow of the American Psychological Association and a Diplomate in Clinical Psychology of the American Academy of Clinical Psychology.

Among his many works are *Glossolalia: A behavioral science understanding of speaking in tongues.* He is editor of *The psychology of religion: Personalities, problems, possibilities* and *Handbook of religious conversion.*

Fouad Moughrabi is Professor of Political Science at the University of Tennessee at Chattanooga. He has served as a member of study groups on the Middle East for the Brookings Institute and the American Academy. He is a former editor of *Arab Studies Quarterly*. He is co-author of *Public opinion and the Palestine question.*

Mary Jo Neitz is Associate Professor of Sociology and Woman Studies at the University of Missouri at Columbia. Her research interests include gender and religion, and the contemporary Goddess movement. She is co-author of *Culture: sociological perspectives* and author of *Charisma and community.*

Kari E. Nurmi is Head of the Department of Education in the University of Helsinki, Finland, docent in adult education and lecturer in higher education. His research interests focus upon church education and the education of theology students.

Kurt Openlander graduated *summa cum laude* in English. He is currently pursuing a doctorate in clinical psychology at the University of Tennessee at Knoxville.

Margaret M. Poloma is Professor of Sociology at the University of Akron, Ohio. She is also a resident chaplain at Akron General Medical Center. Among her many works are *The Assemblies of God at the crossroads* and the co-authored works, *Varieties of prayer* and *Exploring neglected dimensions of religion in quality of life research.*

Kaisa Puhakka teaches at West Georgia College. Her research interests include Eastern philosophies and transpersonal psychology. She is editor of *The Humanistic Psychologist* and coeditor of *The Journal of The Psychology of Religion.* She is also author of *Knowledge and reality.*

Carole A. Rayburn is a clinical, consulting, and research psychologist in Silver Spring, Maryland. She is a past president of the Maryland Psychological Association and the Section on the Psychology of Women in the Division of Clinical Psychology of the American Psychological Association. She is a fellow of the American Psychological Association, the Maryland Psychological Association, the American Orthopsychiatric Association, and the American Association of Applied and Preventive Psychology.

Edward P. Shafranske is Professor of Psychology in the Graduate School of Education and Psychology at Pepperdine University. He is a Clinical Associate of the Southern California Psychoanalytic Institute and maintains a private practice in psychoanalytic treatment. He is a former president of the division of Psychology of Religion of the American Psychological Association.

Bernard Spilka is Professor of Psychology at the University of Denver. He is a former president of the division of Psychology of Religion of the

American Psychological Association and a recipient of its William James award. He is co-author of *The psychology of religion: An empirical approach* and *Religion in psychodynamic perspective: The contributions of Paul W. Pruyser.*

Kalevi Tamminen is Emeritus Professor of Religious Education at the University of Helsinki. He is a member of the Finnish Academy of Science and Letters. His research interests include the history of religious education, education in the churches, and the religious development. He is author of *Religious development in childhood and youth.*

David M. Wulff is Professor of Psychology at Wheaton College, Norton, Massachusetts. He received an honorary doctorate of Theology from the University of Lund, Sweden. He received the Quinquennial Prize awarded by the International Commission for the Scientific Psychology of Religion for his text, *Psychology of religion: Classic and contemporary views.* He also is a recipient of the William C. Bier award given by the division of the Psychology of Religion of the American Psychological Association.

Index of Names

Aanstoos, C.M., 191-192, 198
Aarson, B., 597
Abbott, W.M., 33, 46
Abelson, R.P., 291, 302, 329-330, 351, 366-367, 372
Abou-Allam, A., 302
Abrahamian, E., 82, 86
Abrams, R.D., 440, 443
Abramson, L.Y., 433, 443
Ackerman, B., 344
Adams, J., 71, 226
Addison, J., 309, 373, 454, 475
Adler, A.. 279
Adler, G., 348, 204
Adler, R., 15, 17, 28
Agosin, R.T., 233, 250-251
Ahmad, E., 75, 82, 86
Ainsworth, D., 302
Ainsworth, M., 471
Ainsworth, M.D.S., 471
Ajzen, I., 291-292, 294, 304, 371, 373
Alba, J.W., 344, 364, 373
Albrecht, C., 198
Albrecht, S. L., 46
Aldridge, J., 561
Aleshire, D., 63, 69
Allen, D., 198
Allen, R.O., 302
Allinsmith, W., 69
Allison, J., 59, 68, 262, 265
Allport, G.W., 5, 60-62, 63, 68-69, 302-303, 371, 372, 436, 456, 471, 561
Almond, P.C., 167, 177, 179, 595
Alpert, R., 137-138, 140-141, 493
Alston, W.P., 159
Altemeyer, B., 63, 68
Ames, E.S., 274, 379, 394
Anderson, J., 330, 344
Anderson, J.M., 142
Anderson, J.R., 376, 377
Anderson, N., 327, 344
Anderson, R., 329, 344, 377
Anthony, R., 47
Appleby, S., 76, 86
Appleton, 69, 305, 394
Aquinas, T., 561
Aranya, H., 127, 129-132, 140-141
Archer, T., 346
Argyle, A.W., 493
Argyle, M., 303, 471, 561
Armatas, P., 453, 475
Armstrong, J.R., 394
Armstrong, K., 561
Aronson, E., 267, 440
Ashcraft, M., 315, 344
Ashton, D., 28-29
Atkinson, J., 50, 68
Attig, M.S., 364, 373
Atwood, G.E., 263, 266, 268
Augustine, 144, 407, 410, 419, 522, 544, 561
Avalon, A., 133, 141
Averill, J.L., 369, 372
Ayer, A.J., 151, 159-160

Babin, P., 279, 303
Back, K.W., 60, 68, 422, 433, 440
Badia, P., 339, 344
Bahr, H.M., 36, 46
Baither, R.C., 369, 372
Baken, D., 226, 266
Baker, J.P., 396, 418, 456, 471, 561

Bakker, J., 526
Balka, C., 28-29
Balmer, R., 68
Bandura, A., 387, 392-394
Banton, M., 118, 120
Barbanel, L., 267
Bargh, J.A., 368, 372, 374
Barnard, G.W., 159
Barnes, M. L., 374
Barnes, N.S., 29, 91, 117
Bartholomew, K., 375, 472-474
Bartlett, R., 337, 342, 344
Basham, A.L., 122, 141
Batson, C.D., 62, 68, 324-325, 337, 344, 378, 394, 456-457, 467, 471, 532, 561, 595
Beardsworth, T., 432, 435, 438, 440
Beckley, R.E., 180
Bedeutung, 311
Beechick, R.A., 285-286, 303
Begg, I., 344
Beit-Hallahmi, B., 7, 57, 68, 254, 259, 261, 266, 293, 303, 366, 372, 456-457, 471
Bell, M.D., 256, 268, 381, 388
Bellah, R.N., 55, 68, 180, 431, 440
Bellicki, K., 339, 344
Belzikoff, B., 413, 417
Bem, D.J., 455, 472
Benson, P.L., 46, 303, 440
Berenstein, B., 440
Berger, P.L., 161-162, 164-166, 179, 400, 402-404, 417, 561, 595
Bergmann, M.S., 210, 226
Bergson, H., 405, 561
Berhowitz, L., 376
Berkerian, D., 329, 344
Berkow, D.M., 89, 120
Bernstein, S., 349, 433
Besner, D., 345
Bettis, J.D., 595
Biale, D., 494
Bickimer, D.A., 561
Biddle, J., 398, 417
Bijur, P.E., 361, 372
Bishop, J., 494
Björkhem, Ö, 413, 417
Black, D., 226
Blackburn, T.C., 429, 445
Blackmore, S.J., 173, 180
Blaney, D., 344
Blase, J.J., 23
Blehar, M.C., 449, 471
Bloom, H., 55, 66, 68, 341
Blum, H.P., 267
Boehlich, W., 201-202, 226
Bohm, D., 514
Bonami, M., 311
Bonaventure, St., 251
Bond, R.N., 215-216, 372
Boorstein, S., 514
Bootzin, R., 344-346, 348
Borke, H., 320, 344
Borstein, M.H., 266
Bosnak, R., 238, 251
Bouchard, T.J., 377
Bourque, L.B., 60, 68, 422, 433, 440
Bovet, P., 296, 303
Bower, G., 314, 327, 344, 384
Bowers, J., 329, 344
Bowers, P., 339, 344
Bowker, J., 3, 11, 595
Bowlby, J., 9, 365, 373, 447-451, 453-454, 461, 464-471, 475
Bradshaw, D., 451, 460, 474
Brainerd, C.J., 320, 345
Bransford, J., 345
Breckler, S.J., 350, 371, 373
Breed, G., 562
Breger, L., 202, 226
Bretherton, I., 448, 450, 463, 468, 470-471, 474
Brickman, P., 338, 345
Briggs, J., 514
Briggs, K.A., 46
Broadwell, M.M., 562
Brock, K.F., 360, 375, 428, 443
Brockington, J.L., 122, 141
Broen Jr., W.E., 471
Brooks, L., 327, 345
Brown, A., 345, 377, 444
Brown, D., 138, 141
Brown, G.A., 377, 444
Brown, H.I., 151, 159
Brown, J., 345
Brown, K.M., 532
Brown, L.B., 303, 310, 352, 374, 394-395, 441, 595
Brown, P., 345
Brown, R.D., 440
Bryant, T.A., 494
Buber, M., 22, 28, 264

Buchbinder, J.T., 263, 266
Bucher, A.A., 301-303, 307, 309
Bufford, R.K., 391, 394
Bulan, H.F., 176, 180
Bullman, I., 360, 373, 430-431, 440
Bulman, R.J., 113, 117, 440
Bunnag, J., 109, 115, 118
Burgess, H.W., 562
Burns, H., 329, 349
Butler, N.M., 305
Butterfield, E., 314, 348
Butters, N., 346
Bychowski, G., 260, 266
Bynum, C.W., 532
Byrnes, J.F., 40, 46

Cabezon, J.I., 91, 118
Cacioppo, J., 345
Cairns, F., 252
Cairns, K.V., 562
Calhoun, L.G., 366, 373
Calvin, J., 51-52, 144, 562
Campos, J.J., 457, 471
Cantor, A., 18, 28
Cantor, N., 345, 349, 352, 374, 377
Capps, D., 66, 69, 262, 266, 413, 417
Capra, F., 515
Caprara, G.V., 562
Caputi, N., 515, 562
Carman, J.B., 124, 142
Carnap, R., 151, 159
Carr, A.C., 468, 472
Carroll, J.B., 440,433
Carroll, J.W., 63, 69
Carroll, M.P., 35, 42, 46, 260, 266
Cartwright, R., 338-339, 345, 351
Carver, C., 334, 351, 360, 376
Case, L., 213, 217, 220, 225, 562
Casey, E.S., 198
Casler, L., 394
Caspi, A., 472
Cassidy, J., 474, 450
Cassidy, S.A., 377, 363
Cassidy, S.E., 424, 430, 432, 434-435, 438, 444
Cassirer, E., 66, 69
Cermak, L., 345, 349
Cernovsky, Z., 89, 118
Chalfant, H.P., 179-180
Chapman, L., 345
Chase, W., 324, 345
Chasseguet-Smirgel, J., 224, 226
Chave, E.J., 310
Cheesman, J., 345
Chelland, D., 71
Ch'en, K.S., 91, 94, 105, 115, 118
Chodorow, N., 532
Chopra, D., 515
Christ, C., 532
Christianson, S., 345
Cirlot, J.E., 250-251
Clark, E.T., 295, 303, 430, 432, 435, 440, 458
Clark, M.S., 373
Clark, T.E., 252, 248
Clark, W., 303, 440, 515
Clark, W.H., 303, 440, 443
Clason, G., 180
Clayton, R.R., 62, 69
Clift, J.D., 241, 243, 251
Clift, W.B., 241, 243, 251
Clore, G.L., 357, 376
Coates, D., 338, 345, 357, 376
Coe, G.A., 458-459, 466, 472, 562
Cohen, C., 345
Cohen, D., 342, 345
Cohen, L.H., 361, 376
Cohen, N., 314, 345-346
Cohler, B.J., 562
Cohler, J., 554
Cohn, N., 261, 266
Collins, A., 376
Collins, J.E., 180
Collins, N.L., 472
Collins, P.H., 532
Collins, R., 180
Combs, A.W., 562
Conway, F., 440
Conway, M., 440
Conze, E., 87, 91-92, 94, 116, 118
Cooney, J.B., 558, 566
Cooper, J.C., 250-251
Cooper, P.E., 421, 424, 445, 547, 555, 567, 582, 583, 596
Cornwall, N., 428, 443
Corsini, J., 518
Costanzo, P.R., 398, 419
Coupez, A., 276, 305
Cousins, E.H., 234, 251
Coward, H., 125, 142, 248, 251

Cowell, A., 251
Craik, F., 323, 327, 345-346, 349
Crandall, V.C., 62, 69
Crane, M., 349
Crist, J.L., 555, 561
Crocker, J., 313, 352, 359, 377, 431, 445
Crosby, F., 111, 118
Crothers, V., 372
Crouter, R., 595
Crowe, K., 376
Cruikshank, D.R., 562
Custers, A., 311
Cutrona, C.E., 472

Daane, J., 440, 443
Dahrendorf, R., 398-399, 417
Daly, M., 532
Dante, 535, 562
D'Antonio, W., 31, 46
Dantonio, M., 562
Darcy Bérubé, F., 562
Darley, J.M., 378, 394
David, J., 6, 40-41, 183, 278, 429, 434, 444
Davidman, L., 17, 23, 28, 532
Davidson, J., 31, 46, 349
Davidson, R., 349
Davidson, R.M., 91, 112, 118
Davies, J.A., 46
Davis, C.F., 160, 350
Davis, J.A., 40, 46
Davis, K.E., 451, 468, 473, 563
De Jong, G.E., 179-180
De Mello, A., 593
Dean, Jr., O.C., 229
Deconchy, J.P., 279, 281, 303
de Dietrich, S., 484, 494
Deforces, C., 345
Deikman, A.J., 167, 180
Deleuze, G., 3, 11
DeLuca, A.J., 219, 226
DeMartino, R., 87, 118
De Mello, A., 595
Dennett, D., 317, 343, 346
DePaola, S.J., 360, 375, 428, 443
DeRosa, D., 333, 350
Derry, P., 348
Deutsch, A., 472
Deutsch, E., 142
Dewey, J., 562
Diamond, G.A., 372, 374
Dicker, S., 16-17, 28
Dienstbier, R.A., 426, 440
Dill, B.T., 532
Dillenberger, J., 52, 69
Diller, J., 205, 226
Dittes, J.E., 383, 394, 422, 440, 562
Dix, G., 562
Dobbs, A.R., 369, 375
Dolan, J.P., 34-35, 38-39, 45-46
Dollard, J., 388-389, 394
Donahue, M.J., 4, 30, 33, 47, 295, 303, 436, 440, 453
Donaldson, M., 346
Donaldson, W.J., 442
Donn, L., 234, 251
Dornbusch, S.M., 368, 373
Dorsey, L., 443
Dourley, J.P., 248, 251
Dreitzel, H.P., 399, 417
Driver, M., 324, 351
Duchler, D., 252
Duffy, R.A., 33, 46
Dujarier, M., 562
Dumais, S.T., 372, 377
Dunn, J., 226
Dunn, R.F., 456, 473
Durkheim, E., 6, 38, 47, 88, 117-118, 120, 148, 161, 163-164, 178, 180, 264, 398, 417
Durkin, M.G., 32, 38, 41, 46-47
Duval, S., 334, 346-347, 352
Dykstra, C., 303, 347

Eby, F., 562
Edie, J.M., 59, 69, 188, 190, 198
Edinger, E.F., 239, 243, 248, 251
Edwards, J., 160
Edwards, M., 118
Egeland, B., 461, 472
Eich, E., 339, 346
Eilberg-Schwartz, H., 494
Einterz, R.M., 565
Eisenstadt, S.N., 163-164, 180
Eisner, E.W., 563
Ekman, P., 357, 373
Eliach, Y., 429, 441
Eliade, M., 138, 140, 142, 198
Eliot, C., 91, 118
Elk, B., 558, 562
Elkind, D., 303-304, 306, 349, 563

Elkind, S.L., 558, 563
Ellenberger, H.F., 234, 251, 515
Ellis, A., 515
Ellison, C.G., 361, 373
Ellwood Jr., R.S., 441
Enelow, A., 445
Engler, J., 138, 141
Englesman, J.C., 250
Enquist, G., 333, 350
Epstein, M., 89, 118
Erickson, E., 304
Erikson, J.A., 295, 303-304
Everett, H.C., 59, 69
Eysenck, M., 332, 335, 346
Ezer, M., 62, 69

Faber, M.D., 89, 118
Fagan, J., 255, 562
Falk, G., 400, 417
Fanon, F., 81, 86
Farrar, M., 118, 329-330, 346
Faulkner, J.E., 179-180
Fauteux, A., 260, 266
Fauteux, K., 89, 118
Fazio, R.H., 368, 372-373
Feather, N.T., 369, 373
Fecher, V.J., 431, 441
Fee, J.L., 42-43, 47
Feeney, B.C., 451, 472
Feinstein, D., 288, 304
Feinstein, M.H., 377
Feldman, M., 223, 226
Felkin, E., 563
Feltey, K.M., 178, 180
Fenichel, O., 266
Fenigstein, A., 334, 346
Fenner, P., 89, 118
Festinger, L., 295, 304, 35, 366, 373, 411
Feuerbach, L., 201, 217, 223, 226, 229
Feuerstein, G., 127-128, 142
Fichter, J.H., 432, 441
Field, K., 562
Fine, L., 20-21, 28
Finesinger, J.E., 433, 440
Finn, M., 259, 266, 350
Fischer-Barnicol, H.A., 189, 198
Fish, D., 423, 440
Fishbein, M., 291-292, 294, 302, 304, 309, 371, 373
Fisher, D.J., 213, 226
Fisher, L.E., 421, 423, 445
Fishler, P.H., 468, 472
Fiske, D.W., 118
Fiske, S.T., 373, 441
Fivush, R., 330, 346-347
Flakoll, D.A., 454, 472
Flavell, J.H., 304, 323, 346
Fleeson, J., 454, 475
Flew, A., 515
Flinders, C.L., 533
Folkman, S., 356, 360-361, 373
Fontana, D., 89, 98, 118, 346
Fordham, M., 234, 252, 348
Forgie, J., 157, 160, 180
Forman, R.K., 157, 160
Fowler, J.W., 270, 272, 275, 298-299, 301-304, 307, 310, 322, 346, 388, 394
Fowlkes, M.A., 563
Fraisse, P., 324, 351
Francis, L.J., 293-294, 304
Franks, J., 350
Freedman, S., 344
Freud, S., 6, 7, 59, 88, 118, 148, 200-207, 209, 211-215, 217-218, 220-226, 228-230, 233-235, 246, 251-254, 257-259, 265-266, 272, 281, 287-288, 304, 313, 315-316, 329-330, 346, 350, 372, 384, 394, 406, 447, 449, 465-468, 470, 501
Friedel, L., 376
Friedman, R., 181
Friedman, S.B., 181, 372
Fromm, E., 87, 118
Fukuyama, Y., 179-180
Fuller, E.Q., 56, 58, 69, 186, 395

Gaertner, S.L., 426, 445
Gage, N.L., 563
Galanter, M., 458, 472
Gallagher, J., 33, 46
Gallup, G., 515
Gallup, J.G., 69
Gallup Jr., G.H., 181
Gamoran, A., 563
Gangel, K.O., 563
Gannoushi, R., 78-80, 82, 84, 86
Gardiner, A., 338, 346
Garfield, J.L., 377
Garrett, W.R., 595
Garrod, A., 117, 119
Gartner, J., 259, 266

Gautama, S., 90
Gay, P., 203-205, 214, 220-221, 226, 228
Geels, A., 404, 418
Geertz, C., 89, 91, 109, 117-118
Geller, L., 24-25, 28
Gelman, R., 320, 346
George, C.N., 118-119, 472
George, L.K., 360, 375, 386, 451, 472
Gershon, Y., 23
Geyer, K., 413, 418
Gibson, H.M., 293, 305
Giddens, A., 82, 86, 177, 180
Gielen, U.P., 119
Gilkes, C., 533
Gillespie, V.B., 563
Gilligan, C., 533
Gilligan, S., 344, 523
Giorgi, A., 190-193, 196, 198
Gladden, J.W., 62, 69
Gleick, J., 515
Glock, C.Y., 162, 168-170, 179-180, 296, 305, 436, 441, 563
Gnostic, 248, 262, 504
Goffman, E., 398, 400, 418
Goldman, R., 269, 272, 274, 277-283, 305, 315-316, 319-322, 328, 346-347
Goldwyn, R., 460, 474
Gollwitzer, P.M., 555, 567
Gombrich, R., 91, 115, 118
Goodman, F.D., 441
Goodman, G., 346
Goodman, S.D., 118
Gorer, G., 359, 373
Gorsuch, R.L., 40, 48, 59, 61, 63, 69, 71, 321, 351, 360-362, 368, 373, 376-377, 379, 396, 453, 456, 459, 471-472, 475
Goslin, O., 348
Govinda, L.A., 87, 118
Gozali, J., 62, 69
Graebner, O.E., 280, 305
Granfield, D., 515
Grant, W.H., 154, 248, 252, 355, 471
Greeley, A.M., 30-32, 34, 38, 40-47, 60, 69, 170-171, 178, 180-181, 421, 428, 430, 437-439, 441, 452-453, 472
Green, A., 16, 20, 22, 28-29, 73, 119, 248, 305, 442, 473
Greenberg, D.E., 266
Greenberg, J., 228
Greene, R., 346
Greene, T.A., 252
Greenleaf, E.A., 43, 47
Greenwald, A.G., 373
Greenwood, S., 10, 266, 515
Greer, J.E., 278, 293-296, 305, 322, 347
Greil, A.L., 17
Gresser, M., 14-15, 28
Greven, P., 66, 69
Grevengoed, N., 376, 444
Griffin, S., 533
Grof, S., 235, 238, 252, 512, 516
Grönblom, G., 169, 180
Groome, T.H., 563
Grubrich-Simitis, I., 202, 228
Gruehn, D.W., 280, 284, 305
Grunbaum, A., 217, 228
Grusec, J., 320, 347
Guenther, H.V., 87, 119
Guitarri, F., 3
Guntrip, H., 256, 258-259, 263-264, 266, 469
Gupta, A.S., 142
Gupta, S.R.S., 142
Guthrie, E.R., 394
Gyatso, T., 115, 119

Haas, D.D., 368, 374
Habermas, J., 398, 400, 418
Hadaway, C.K., 175, 180
Haddon, G.P., 494
Hahn, J., 456, 474
Hall, G.S., 305
Hall, J.A., 252
Hall, J.R., 252
Hallez, M., 281, 305
Halligan, F.R., 7, 231, 234, 238, 240, 246, 251-253
Halperin, D.A., 267
Hammond, N., 346
Hammond, P.E., 440
Hanna, F., 130-131, 142
Happold, F.C., 167, 180
Hardy, A., 380, 421, 423-424, 430, 437-439, 441, 563, 596
Hargrove, B.W., 563
Harlow, J., 18, 28, 467
Harman, W., 516
Harms, E., 279, 305
Harris, L., 16-17, 23, 28
Harrison, I., 265-266

Hart, C., 372
Hartman, S.G., 290, 305
Hartorf, A., 347
Hartup, W.W., 347, 475
Hartz, G., 59, 69
Harvey, J.H., 374, 442
Harvey, J.W., 160, 198
Hasher, L., 344, 364, 373
Hastings, A., 516
Hastorf, A.H., 313, 347, 373
Hathaway, W., 376, 444
Hay, D., 305, 394, 441, 563
Hay, M., 71
Hazan, C., 448, 450-451, 455, 460, 467-468, 472-474
Heidegger, M., 129, 142
Heider, F., 429, 441
Heiler, F., 457, 472
Helve, H., 277, 05
Hempel, C.G., 151, 160
Hemrick, E., 347
Henderson, J., 260, 266
Henley, T., 349
Henry, J.P., 50, 52, 413, 417, 516
Herb, L., 361, 376
Herbart, J., 563
Herbrechtsmeier, W., 117, 119
Herdt, G., 120
Hewstone, M., 422, 441
Heywood, D., 306
Hick, J., 314, 347, 596
Hiebert, P.G., 464, 472
Higgins, E.T., 322, 347, 368, 374, 377, 445
Hilgard, E.R., 356, 374, 384
Hill, P.C., 8, 181, 349, 353, 368, 370, 372, 374
Hilliard, F.H., 279-280, 306
Hillman, J., 238, 246, 252-253, 342, 347
Himmelfarb, M., 431, 441
Hinde, J.S., 475
Hine, V.H., 459, 473
Hinshaw, R., 252
Hinson, E.G., 474
Hirsch, I., 267
Hjelmquist, E., 311
Hoffer, P., 210, 228
Hoffman, M.S., 67, 69
Hofinger, J., 563
Hoge, D., 31, 46, 63, 280, 295, 306, 308, 322, 326, 328, 336, 397, 563
Holden, P., 29
Hollander, V., 25-26, 28
Hollingworth, H.L., 394
Holm, N.G., 9, 348, 385-386, 394, 397-398, 404, 407, 412, 418
Holmberg, D., 327, 351
Holt, R., 201, 228, 351, 396, 418
Homans, P., 209, 228
Hong, G.Y., 5, 87, 110, 117, 119
Honko, L., 398, 413-415, 418
Hood Jr., R.W., 48, 69, 71, 160, 396, 441, 443, 445, 473, 475
Hood, D.R., 69
Hood, T.C., 71
Hopkins, J., 561, 564
Hopkins, T.J., 142
Horton, P.C., 261, 266
Houston, W.R., 235
Hovland, C., 325, 351
Howard, R., 62, 71
Howes, D.H., 433, 442
Htin Aung, V., 89, 119
Hudson, J., 251, 329-330, 336, 346-347
Huebner, A., 117, 119
Hughes, R., 372
Hull, J., 347
Hull, R.F.C., 70, 253, 348
Hume, D., 146, 153, 155, 160
Hunsberger, B., 325, 347, 351, 364, 374, 435, 442
Hunt, R.A., 61-62, 70, 169, 181, 436, 442
Huntington, S., 76, 86
Husserl, E., 185
Hutch, R.A., 265-266
Hutsebaut, D., 280, 306
Huxley, A., 516
Hyde, K., 306, 347, 564
Hyde, K.E., 306, 564
Hymes, D., 440

Iben, T.D., 279-306
Ickes, W., 374, 433, 442
Inglehart, M., 312, 332, 352
Inhelder, B., 306
Isen, A., 347, 374
Isen, A.M., 374
Isherwood, C., 125, 132-133, 136, 143
Ishler, K., 376
Issler, K., 549, 563
Izard, G.E., 357, 374

Jaakkola, M., 290, 306
Jackson, L., 347
Jackson, N.J., 442
Jacobs, J.L., 13, 28
Jacobs, L., 28
Jacobson, L., 555, 566
Jacobson, N.P., 119
Jacoby, L., 346
Jacoby, M., 252
Jaffee, A., 244, 252
Jahoda, G., 89, 119
Janoff-Bulman, R., 338, 345
Jarvin, D., 299, 307
Järvinen, P., 413, 418
Jaspard, J.M., 310
Jaspers, K., 185, 188, 198
Jay, M., 34, 219, 228
Jenkins, R., 360, 374
Jennings, M.A., 368, 374
Johansson, R.E.A., 87, 105, 119
Johnson, A.L., 46
Johnson, M., 345, 349
Johnson, N., 349
Johnson, P., 70
Johnson, S., 442
Johnston, C., 142
Johnstone, R.L., 163, 181
Jolley, J.C., 454, 473
Jones, C., 564
Jones, E.E., 374, 442
Jones, J., 228
Jones, K., 226
Jones, S., 225
Jones, W.H., 472
Jones, W.I., 442
Jordan, M.E., 494
Jordan, W., 70
Joseph, R., 86
Jubis, R., 374
Jung, C.G., 7, 38, 58, 65-67, 70, 203-204, 228-229, 231-248, 250-253, 272, 287-288, 306, 313, 315, 317, 319, 338-342, 348, 406, 495, 497, 499, 502-514, 516
Justin, 544, 564

Kagan, J., 369, 374
Kahn, Y.H., 25, 28
Kahneman, D., 366, 377
Kahoe, R.D., 40, 47, 292, 295-296, 307, 436, 442, 456, 473
Kakar, S., 262, 267, 463-464, 473
Kalasinski, L.A., 565
Kallstad, T., 348, 395
Källstad, T., 418
Kalupahana, D.J., 87, 91, 99-101, 108, 119
Kantor, R., 521, 533
Kaplan, L.V., 267
Kaplan, N., 472, 474
Kardes, F.C., 373
Kass, J.D., 181
Katz, J., 14, 29, 157-160, 510, 516, 572, 576, 596
Kaufman, D., 456, 473, 523, 533
Kawai, G., 249, 253
Kawamura, W.I., 379, 395
Kay, W., 278, 294, 306
Keefe, J.W., 554, 564
Keenan, J., 327, 345
Kegan, R., 70, 86, 118, 142, 226, 299, 303, 305-306, 345-346, 418, 443, 471, 514, 518, 561
Kellas, S., 457, 473
Kellerman, H., 372
Kelley, H.H., 119, 427, 429, 432
Kellner, H., 400, 418
Kelly, F.D., 47
Kelly-Gadol, J., 521, 533
Kelly, G.A., 374
Kelsey, B., 494
Kelsey, M., 442, 494, 564
Kelsey, M.T., 442, 494
Kempis, T., 411, 547, 564
Kennedy, E.C., 395
Kepel, G., 83-84, 86
Kernberg, O., 256, 258, 267
Kessler, R.C., 361, 375
Keutzer, C., 495-496, 498-499, 518
Khan, S.B., 559, 564
Khursheed, A., 504, 516
Kibler, R.J., 552, 564
Kidd, R., 374, 442
Kihlstrom, J., 344-346, 348-349, 352, 374
Kildahl, J.P., 381, 395, 425, 432, 442, 460, 473
Kim, J.Y., 119
King, G., 374
King, M.B., 70, 181
King, S.B., 160
King, W.P., 395
Kirk, K.E., 596

Kirk, R.E., 70
Kirker, W., 313, 334, 351
Kirkpatrick, L.A., 9, 356, 361, 365, 368, 371, 374-375, 377, 422, 429, 442, 444, 446-447, 451-452, 454-455, 457-461, 468, 472-473, 586, 596, 599
Klein, M., 258-260, 267, 287, 306, 467, 469
Klen, G.S., 267
Klingberg, G., 280, 296-297, 306
Knipe, D.M., 122, 134, 142
Knox, I.P., 494, 551, 564, 566
Koch, S., 394, 597
Koenig, H.G., 360, 375
Kohlberg, L., 270, 272, 298-300, 321, 348
Kohut, H., 224, 228, 258, 262, 267
Kojetin, B.A., 377, 435, 443
Kolers, P., 324, 348
Koller, J.M., 142
Koppe, W.A., 277, 306
Kopplin, D., 434-435, 442
Kotarba, J.A., 360, 375
Kovel, J., 215, 228
Kozin, M., 338, 351
Kraft, D., 377
Kramer, Y., 267
Kraus, P., 396, 518
Krause, N., 429, 442
Kriegman, D., 222, 229
Krippner, S., 288, 304
Krishnamacharya, V., 142
Krosnick, JA., 367, 375
Kruglanski, A.W., 377
Kuhn, T., 151, 160, 201, 228
Kuiper, N., 313, 334, 348, 351
Kulik, J,A., 432, 442
Küng, H., 42, 47

La Barre, W., 2, 11
Laabs, C.W., 278, 308, 322, 350
LaBerge, S., 339, 348
Lacan, J., 66, 70
Lachman, R., 314, 348
Ladd, K., 429, 434, 442, 444
Lajoie, D., 498, 500, 517
Lamb, G., 566
Lamb, M.E., 471
Lambert, W.W., 419, 463, 473
Lamont, C., 547, 564
Lamphere, L., 534
Lamport, M.A., 541, 564
Langman, L., 258, 267
LaPointe, N., 351
Larsen, G., 142
Larsen, S., 306, 348
Laski, M., 433, 439, 443
Lasky, J., 267
Latourette, K.S., 50-52, 54-55, 70
Layden, M.A., 433, 442
Lazarus, R.S., 375
Lea, J., 347
Leary, D., 349, 597
Leary, T., 570, 581, 585, 596
Lee, J.M., 564-565
Lee, R., 372, 441, 533
Leserman, J., 181
Leuba, J.H., 57, 395, 443
Leung, K., 111, 119
Levenson, H., 443
Leventhal, H., 375
Levin, J.S., 181
Levin, S., 178, 445
Levine, D., 442
Levinson, H., 349
Levitt, L., 27, 29
Levonian, E., 349
Levy, A., 347
Levy, J., 142
Levy, M.B., 473
Lewin, B.D., 267
Lewis, B., 86
Lewis, H., 47
Lewis, I.M., 159, 160, 533
Lifrak, S., 372
Lilly, J.C., 586, 596
Lincoln, C., 66, 70
Lincourt, A., 366, 373
Lind, E.A., 111, 119
Lindbeck, G.A., 386,-387, 389, 395
Lindskoog, D., 63, 70
Lindzey, G., 398, 418-419, 440
Lines, T.A., 550, 553-554, 565
Linton, M., 349
Linton, R., 418
Linville, P.W., 359, 373, 431, 441
Lisle, D.J., 337
Little, S., 542, 565
Lockhart, R., 320, 327, 346-347
Loewald, H., 224, 228
Loewenthal, K.M., 428, 443
Lofland, J., 381, 395, 435, 443

Loftus, E., 329, 345, 349
Lombardi, W.J., 372
Long, D., 306, 349
Louth, A., 569, 596
Loveland, C.G., 457, 474
Luckmann, T., 400, 403-404, 417
Ludwig, D.J., 185, 279, 306-307
Luidheid, C., 566
Luoma, M., 413, 418
Lupfer, M.B., 360, 375, 428, 431, 443
Luria, A., 324, 349
Luther, M., 50, 58, 60, 68, 271, 304, 410, 419, 544, 565
Lutzky, H., 264, 267
Lykken, D.T., 377
Lynn, M.L., 369, 374-377
Lysak, H., 369, 375

Maccoby, E.E., 467, 470, 474
Machalek, R., 434, 444
MacKinnon, G., 345
Mackintosh, H.R., 566, 597
MacPhillamy, D.J., 119
Macquarrie, J., 558, 565
Madhavananda, S., 142
Madigan, S., 324, 350
Madison, 267, 534, 562
Madsen, R., 68
Magee, B., 505, 517
Mager, R., 522, 565
Mahler, M.S., 258-259, 267, 469-470
Main, M., 450-451, 458, 470, 472, 474, 528
Malinowski, B., 119, 223, 228
Malony, H.N., 198, 332, 352, 395-396, 418, 422, 435, 440, 443, 472, 475, 599
Mamiya, L.H., 66, 70
Manchester, F., 302, 440
Mandell, A., 340, 349
Mandler, G., 323, 349
Mandler, J., 349
Mann, R.D., 499, 503, 517
Mannheim, K., 403, 418
Margenau, H., 512, 517
Maritain, J., 142, 547, 565
Markides, K.C., 512, 517
Markman, E.M., 369, 375
Markus, H., 312, 325-326, 334, 349, 555, 565
Marlasch, C., 596
Marthaler, B.L., 541, 545, 565
Martin, C.B., 150, 152, 160
Martindale, C., 421, 443
Martinsson, E., 285, 307
Martos, J., 37, 47
Marty, M., 70, 76, 86, 533, 441
Marx, K., 571
Masci, J., 372
Maslow, A.H., 443, 496, 498, 421, 517, 565
Masson, W.W., 263, 267, 547, 555, 559
Master, J.W., 497
Masters, J.C., 474
Masters, R.E.L., 596
Mathewson, K., 372
Maton, K.I., 360, 375
Mattlin, J.A., 361, 375
Maududi, A.A'LA, 86
Mavin, G.H., 368, 374
Mayeda, S., 142
Mayer, J., 314, 344
Mazzuca, S.A., 558, 565
McBrien, R.P., 36-37, 298, 535, 539, 541, 543, 565
McCallister, B., 312, 327, 336, 349, 359, 599
McClain, E.W., 474, 456
McCourt, K., 31, 47
McCready, W.C., 47, 181
McCreedy, W., 528
McDargh, J., 70, 272, 307
McGillis, D., 366, 374
McGrady, A.G., 278, 285-287, 307, 322, 349
McGuire, M.B., 494, 517
McGuire, M.J., 89
McGuire, W., 119, 253
McIntosh, D.N., 9, 359-360, 372, 375, 421, 431-432, 435-436, 443
McIntyre, M., 544, 565
McKay, D., 392, 395
McKenzie, B., 347
McNeill, B., 496, 517
McSpadden, M., 349
Mead, G.H., 418
Mead, R.K., 418
Meadow, M.J., 40, 47, 297, 295-296, 307, 431, 443, 537
Meier, S., 327, 357
Meissner, W.W., 201, 205, 214, 216-217, 225-226, 228, 263, 267

Meng, H., 204, 220, 229
Merikle, P., 345
Merton, R.K., 418
Merton, T., 565
Meštrović, S.G., 503-505, 508-510, 517
Metalsky, G.I., 433, 443
Metcalf, K.K., 553, 562
Meyers, M.R., 483, 494
Miles, D.T., 73, 431, 552, 564
Mill, J.S., 101
Miller, A.S., 116, 119
Miller, D., 349
Miller, D.E., 566
Miller, G.R., 63, 71
Miller, J.P., 554, 565
Miller, M.T., 549, 565
Miller, N., 377, 394
Miller, R.C., 539, 541, 548, 565
Miller, W.A., 253
Millman, M., 259, 533
Milner, M., 259, 267
Minton, B., 436, 443
Mitchell, T., 83, 86, 561
Mlshra, R.S., 142
Moberg, D.O., 374, 376-377, 551, 566
Moeser, S., 350
Monteiro, K., 344
Montgomery, H., 311
Moody, R.A., 496, 517
Moore, R.L., 122, 248, 251-253
Moran, G., 545, 547, 566
Morisy, A., 296, 305, 421, 441
Morlan, K., 350
Morris, C., 350
Morris, R.J., 47, 71, 411, 443, 445, 516, 564, 596
Morrison, S.E., 54,70
Morse, M., 556, 566
Moseley, R.M., 299, 307
Muecke, M.A., 117, 119
Mueller, J.H., 180
Mullin, M., 436, 444
Mullins, N., 161, 181
Murphy, R.J.L., 307
Murphy, S., 285-286, 307, 312, 332, 352
Murty, K.S., 124, 142
Muzzy, R.E., 373
Myers, I.B., 504, 517

Nagera, H., 257, 267
Naranjo, C., 586, 596
Nasby, W., 334, 350
Nedelsky, J., 532-533
Neisser, U., 312, 326, 331, 337, 346, 348-351, 350
Neitz, M.J., 10, 173-174, 181, 520-522, 533, 600
Nelligan, J.S., 451, 475
Nelsen, C.E., 542, 548
Nelsen, H.M., 307, 308
Nelson, G.K., 67, 70
Nelson, J.E., 500, 513, 517
Nelson, K., 350
Nelson, M.O., 307
Nelson, T., 350
Nembach, U., 294, 307
Neumann, E., 251, 253
Neusner, J., 28-29
Newcomb, T.M., 398, 400, 402, 405, 408, 418
Newman, J., 230, 376, 413, 417, 444, 567
Newston, D., 333, 350
Newton, T.B., 8, 308, 378, 599
Nicholson, S., 28, 71
Niebuhr, R.R., 159-160, 228, 432, 443
Nielsen, H., 372
Nikhilananda, S., 134, 142
Nipkow, K.E., 208, 302, 304, 307
Nisbett, R.E., 422, 442, 444
Niwano, N., 92, 96, 106-108, 120
Noam, G., 320, 350
Noller, P., 451, 472
Northup. A., 494
Norton, J.A., 86, 228, 266, 304, 374, 534, 562, 565, 601
Nussbaum, J., 453, 475

O'Conner, J., 522, 533, 566
O'Hare, P., 562, 565
O'Neil, H., 327, 345
Oates, W.E., 460, 474
Obeyesekere, G., 91, 115, 118
Occhiogrosso, P., 32, 47
Ochs, V.L., 19, 29
Oden, T.A., 383, 395
Oerter, R., 292, 307
Oh, Y.B., 515-516, 561, 564, 566
Oler, I.D., 481-482, 486, 494
Olson, J., 307, 351, 376, 443
Olson, J.M., 307, 376, 443-444

Olsson, P.A., 262, 267
Ornstein, R.E., 262, 496, 510, 517, 596
Ortner, S., 527, 534
Ortony, A., 357-358, 376
Oser, F., 270-272, 274, 276, 298-301, 304, 307, 310, 560, 566
Osmer, R.P., 541, 566
Osmond, H., 597
Osofsky, J.D., 471
Ostow, M., 262, 267, 395
Otto, R., 147, 149, 160, 167, 181, 186, 198, 405, 419, 423, 443, 499, 511, 540-541, 546, 548, 555-556, 560, 578, 593, 597
Overall, C., 566
Overmyer, D.C., 91, 120
Ozorak, E.W., 350, 363-364, 376

Paffard, M., 295-297, 308
Page, R.C., 73, 89, 120
Pahnke,W.N., 70, 579-581, 589, 597
Paivio, A., 324, 337, 344, 348, 350
Pajak, E., 544, 566
Pallone, N.J., 555, 565
Palmer, C.E., 180
Paloutzian, R., 59, 71
Pancer, S., 325, 347, 351
Pahnke, W.N., 60, 70, 580
Pargament, K.I., 333, 350, 356, 360-362, 374, 376, 434-435, 444, 456, 474
Park, C., 361, 376
Park, S.Y., 533, 561, 566, 597
Parker, I., 3, 11
Parks, S., 46, 303, 308, 346
Parrinder, G., 166-167, 181
Parsons, A., 306
Parsons, J., 347
Parsons, T., 419
Pasquali, L., 311
Pattyn, M.R., 311
Payne, R.C., 597
Peat, F., 504, 514
Peatling, J.H., 278, 283, 308, 321-322, 350
Pendleton, B.F., 170-172, 175-176, 178, 181
Perlman, D., 375, 472-474
Perriello, L., 284, 309
Perry, K., 372
Perry, P., 517
Pervin, L.A., 472
Peters, B., 372
Peterson, R., 317-318, 351
Petrillo, G.. 322, 326, 328, 347
Pettersson, S., 285, 290, 305, 308, 413, 419
Petty, R., 208, 345
Pfister, O., 203, 229
Philibert, P., 347
Piaget, J., 269-270, 272, 277, 281, 285, 298-300, 303, 306, 315, 319-323, 326, 328, 344-345, 350, 384, 395
Pichert, J., 326, 344
Pillemer, D., 330, 352
Pirinen, H., 282, 289-290, 308
Pittman, N.L., 444
Pittman, T.S., 444
Plantinga, A., 160
Platt, E.E., 485, 494
Plog, S., 459, 474
Plunkett, K., 348
Plutchik, R., 372, 578, 597
Pogel, M.C., 372
Pollner, M., 181
Pollock, G.H., 261, 267
Polls, 171, 376
Poloma, M.M., 6, 161, 170-172, 175-176, 178, 180-181, 600
Pomerans, A., 226
Porter, L.W., 565, 567
Possage, J., 376
Potts, G., 327, 345
Potvin, R.H., 280, 307-308
Powell, M.C., 373
Prabhavananda, S., 123, 125, 132-133, 136, 139, 143
Pratkanis, A.R., 373
Pratt, J.B., 395, 474
Pratt, M., 351
Preston, D., 181
Preus, J.S., 11
Proudfoot, W., 160, 181, 376, 444, 597
Pruyser, P., 267, 444

Radhakrishnan, S., 181
Radin, P., 566
Radway, J., 534
Raghavendrachar, H.N., 143
Ramanan, K.V., 120
Rambo, L.R., 198, 395
Randall Jr., J.H., 396
Rao, P.N., 143
Rapaport, D., 267

Raphael, C., 494
Ratcliff, D., 308
Rausch, D., 71
Ray, J.J., 71
Rayburn, C.A., 494
Reber, A.S., 517
Rector, L., 198
Reed, B., 474
Reich, K.H., 308
Reichard, G.A., 566
Reid, T., 444
Rice, E, 229
Ricerche, 311
Rich, A., 534
Richards, A.D., 267
Richards, A.K., 267
Richards, L., 36, 47
Richards, W.A., 597
Richardson, J.T., 474
Richmond, R.C., 292-293, 308-309
Ricoeur, P., 206-207, 210-211, 217, 219, 229
Ridley, P., 372
Rieber, R.W., 120
Riecken, H.W., 295, 304
Rieff, P., 201, 203, 211, 219, 229
Rissland, E.L., 377
Ritvo, L., 202, 210, 222, 229
Ritzer, G., 161-162, 181
Roazen, P., 219, 229
Robbins, T., 533
Roberts, T.B., 498, 517
Robinson, M.P., 276, 309
Robson, R., 372
Rocheblave-Spenlé, A.M., 398, 408, 419
Rogers, T., 184, 313, 334, 351
Roheim, G., 259, 264, 268
Rohner, R.P., 463, 474
Rohr, R., 47
Rokeach, M., 62-63, 71, 292, 309
Rood, W.R., 566
Roof, W.C., 365, 376
Rooney, P.C., 564
Rosaldo, M., 534
Rose, A., 29, 419
Rose, S., 534
Rosegrant, J., 597
Rosen, B., 518
Rosenau, P., 3, 11, 76, 86
Rosenbaum, D.A., 377
Rosenberg, M.J., 284, 291, 302, 309
Rosenblith, J.F., 69
Rosensohn, M., 281, 309, 454, 475
Rosenthal, R., 566
Rosik, C.H., 360, 376
Rosko, J., 372
Ross, J.M., 292, 303, 371-372
Ross, L., 422, 444
Ross, M., 303, 327, 351, 360, 376, 426, 434, 440, 443-444
Ross, N., 264, 268
Roth, D., 351
Roth, P.A., 11
Rothbaum, F.M., 429, 445
Rothberg, D., 117, 120, 517
Rousseau, E.W., 566
Rowe, R., 370, 374
Rowiller, R., 376
Roy, S.S., 124, 143
Rubin, D., 350-351
Rubin, G., 534
Rubin, J., 517
Rule, B.G., 80, 159, 369, 375
Russell, D., 472
Russell, J.A., 376
Ryan, E.R., 268
Ryan, M.. 312, 268

Sage, J., 21, 46, 69, 90, 180-182, 251, 533, 595, 597
Said, E., 4, 19, 21, 26, 35, 75, 83, 86, 100, 129, 132, 134-135, 164, 167, 184, 186, 187, 190, 539
Sales, S.M., 436, 444
Salih, T., 86
Saltzberg, L., 369, 372
Samarin, W.J., 385-386, 396
Sanford, J.A., 232, 253
Saracho, O. N., 555, 566
Saranson, R.S., 14-15, 17, 19, 29
Sarbin, T.R., 398, 400-402, 405, 415, 419
Sargent, W., 71
Sasson, R.S., 324, 351
Saunders, E.D., 115, 120
Savage, C., 261, 267
Savage, D., 229
Savery, J., 549, 562
Scarlett, W.G., 284, 304, 307, 309
Schacter, D., 344-346, 348, 351
Schacter, S., 376, 597

Schaefer, C.A., 360-361, 376
Schank, R., 329-330, 351
Scharfenberg, J.,205, 229
Scheier, M.F., 334, 351, 360, 376
Scheler, M., 403, 419
Scherer, K.R., 373
Schleiermacher, F., 6, 11, 144-147, 149, 154-155, 158, 160, 172-173, 181, 558, 566, 568, 570-579, 583-584, 594-595, 597
Schmeck, R., 316, 327, 351
Schmidt, G., 428, 431, 435, 444
Schoenrade, P.A., 456, 471, 522, 532, 579, 595
Schooler, J., 349
Schopenhauer, A., 496, 499, 505, 512, 517
Schreck, A., 48
Schroder, H., 324, 351
Schumaker, J.F., 28, 596
Schur, M., 205, 221, 229
Schutz, A., 174, 182, 533
Schütze, F., 275
Schwartz, G., 345
Schwartz, S., 351
Schweitzer, F., 275, 301-302, 304, 309
Seligman, M.E.P., 362, 376
Selman, R.L., 299, 309
Sethi, S., 362, 376
Sexton, V.S., 383, 396
Seybold, K.S., 368, 374
Seymour, J.L., 566
Shaffer, D.R., 555, 567
Shaffer, S., 436, 445, 456, 475
Shafranske, E., 6, 200, 229, 465-466
Shapiro, D., 345
Shapiro, S.I., 517
Sharma, A., 117
Sharpe, E.J., 185-186, 198
Shaver, P.R., 356, 361, 363, 375-377, 422, 427, 429, 444, 448, 450-452, 454-455, 458, 460, 472-474
Shaw, B.W., 71
Shaw, M.E., 419
Shea, J.J., 234, 246, 251-253
Sheldrake, R., 512, 517
Sherif, C.W., 351, 394, 419
Sherif, M., 325, 351, 419, 394
Sherman, J., 534
Sherrod, L.R., 472
Sherry, P., 3, 12
Shields, J., 307
Shiffrin, R.M., 372, 377
Shillito, D., 457, 473
Shotter, J., 3, 11
Shrivastava, S.N.L., 125, 143
Shweder, R.A., 89, 117-118, 120
Sidera, J., 345
Siegel, 267, 360, 375
Siegelman, J., 432, 440
Siegler, I.C., 360, 375
Siikala, A.L., 414-415, 419
Siladi, M., 349
Sills, D.L., 394
Silverman, D.K., 474
Silverman, S., 467
Simmel, G., 163-164, 182
Simon, B., 229
Simon, H., 345
Simpkinson, C.H., 501-502, 517
Simpson, J.A., 451, 460, 474-475, 497, 515, 517
Simutis, Z., 327, 345
Singer, J.E., 238, 253, 355, 359, 370, 376, 426, 444, 571, 577-579, 581, 597
Singh, L.P., 133, 143
Skinner, B.F., 378, 387, 389-392, 396
Sklar, D., 23, 29
Skonovd, N., 435, 443
Slavin, O., 222, 229
Slee, N., 285, 286, 309
Smallbones, J.L., 542, 566
Smart, N., 143, 167, 182
Smith, A., 372
Smith, C.D., 253
Smith, C.S., 373, 377
Smith, D., 534
Smith, E.I., 306
Smith, H., 143, 517
Smith, J., 12, 349
Smith, J.E., 3, 12, 160
Smith, S., 2-3, 351, 372-373, 510
Smith, W.C., 2, 4, 12, 160
Smith, W.P., 119
Sneck, W.J., 193-195, 198
Snow, D.A., 434, 444
Snow, R.E., 561
Snyder, M., 332, 351, 364, 377
Solomon, R. L., 41, 433, 442
Solovay, S.A., 180
Southard, S., 198, 329, 395-396, 472, 475

Spaulding, J.A., 47, 515
Sperling, M.B., 468, 472
Spero, M.H., 262, 268
Spickard, J.V., 162, 172-175, 177-179, 181-182, 533, 579, 597
Spilka, B., 9, 40, 48, 59-60, 64, 66, 71, 278, 281, 283, 292, 302, 306, 309, 321, 328, 351, 363, 377, 379, 396, 421-422, 424, 428-430, 432-436, 438, 440, 442-444, 453-454, 456-457, 459, 461, 471, 475, 579, 582, 584, 590, 597
Spiro, M.E., 120, 223, 229
Spiro, R., 87-89, 91, 93, 107-114, 117, 351
Spradlin, W., 332, 352
Squire, L., 342, 346
Sroufe, L.A., 448, 450, 454, 461, 469-470, 472, 475
Srull, T., 347
St. Hoyme, L.E., 486, 494
Staal, J.F., 143
Stace, W.T., 71, 182, 342, 352, 422, 424, 431, 437, 445, 496, 517, 570, 574-575, 578, 580-582, 585, 588-589, 592, 597
Stagg, F., 60, 140, 143, 167, 474
Stambaugh, J., 97, 99, 102, 108, 120
Stanford, R., 42, 48, 86, 373, 534
Stange, M.Z., 526-527, 534
Stanik, P., 376
Starbuck, E.D., 57, 71, 295, 309, 379, 396, 430, 432, 438-439, 445, 459
Starhawk, 530-531, 534
Stark, R.A., 141, 162, 166, 168-171, 179-180, 182, 295, 309, 381, 395, 422-425, 438, 445, 557
Staude, J.R., 512, 518
Steele, R.E., 435, 444
Stein, M., , 238, 246, 251-253
Stenberg, C., 457, 471
Stepansky, P., 201, 228-229
Sterling, B., 426, 445
Stern, D.N., 468, 470, 475
Stern, J., 226
Sternberg, R.J., 474
Stern, T., 226
Stevens, A., 518
Stevens, J., 597
Stewart, J.S., 566, 597
Stiefler, C., 372
Stigler, J.W., 120
Stillings, N.A., 372, 377
Stolorow, R., 263, 268
Stouffer, B.R., 457, 475
Strachey, J., 227, 306, 346
Strange, M.Z., 80, 146, 513, 534
Streufert, S., 324, 351
Strickland, B.R., 436, 445, 456, 475
Strommen, M.P., 289, 303, 310
Strothmann, F.W., 226
Strunk, O., 281, 310
Stump, J., 565
Sukthankar, Vishnu S.S., 143
Suler, J., 89, 120
Sullivan, M.S., 435, 444, 469, 470
Sullivan, W., 68
Sulloway, F., 202-203, 229
Sundberg, N., 495-496, 4980499, 518
Sundén, H., 9, 336, 352, 381, 383, 386, 391, 395-396, 398-399, 405-414, 417-420
Sutcliff, J., 253
Suzuki, D.T., 87, 94, 98, 103-104, 108, 115, 118, 120
Swami, P., 142-143
Swan, P., 372
Swanson, H.L., 558, 566
Swatos Jr., W., 533, 597
Swearer, D.K., 98-99, 107-108, 120
Swidler, A., 68
Swinburne, R., 151-154, 159-160

Taimni, I.K., 136, 143
Takieddine-Amyuni, M., 81, 86
Tamayo, A., 311, 453, 475
Tamminen, K., 7, 269, 276-284, 286, 289-290, 293-298, 301, 310-311, 322, 352, 555, 560, 567, 601
Tanquerey, A., 547, 567
Tarsk, W.R., 142
Tart, C.T., 496, 498-499, 502, 508-510, 518
Tate, E.D., 63, 71
Taylor, S.E., 359, 361, 377, 427-431, 433, 437, 441, 445
Taylor, T., 340, 348
Tedeschi, R.G., 366, 373
Tesser, A., 364, 375, 555, 567
Thibaut, J.W., 120
Thomas, E.J., 398, 417, 419
Thomas, L.E., 547, 555, 567, 582, 583, 597
Thomas, S.E., 377, 424, 428, 445

Thompson, A., 347
Thompson, G., 47
Thompson, H.M.
Thompson, N.H., 252, 564-567
Thomson, D., 314, 317, 327, 341, 350, 352
Thouless, R.H., 284, 310, 452, 458-459, 466, 475
Thun, T., 284, 310
Thurstone, L.L., 272, 310
Tierney, W.M., 565
Tillich, P., 64-67, 71, 298, 301
Tipton, S., 68
Tomarken, A.J., 355, 375
Tota, M.E., 372
Toulmin, S., 352, 570, 597
Tracy, D., 40-41, 48
Travers, R.M.W., 564
Triandis, L.M., 463, 473
Trilling, L., 219, 230
Troeltsch, E., 178-179, 182, 585, 597
Tronto, J., 534
Trout, D.M., 396
Tulving, E., 312, 314, 317, 326-327, 336-337, 341, 352
Turabi, H., 85-86
Turner, E.B., 310
Turner, J.E., 199
Turner, R.H., 419
Turton, M., 563
Tversky, A., 366, 377
Tyler, F.B., 435, 444

Ulanov, A.B., 237, 253
Ullman, C., 268, 352, 445, 475
Ullman, M., 253
Umansky, E.M., 24-25, 28-29
Underhill, E., 140, 143, 182, 496, 518
Unger, J., 412, 419
Uren, A.R., 379, 396

Valsiner, J., 113, 120
Van Buitenen, J.A.B., 124, 142-143
Van de Kemp, H., 396
van der Lans, J., 333, 336, 348, 352, 412, 419
van der Leeuw, G., 185-186, 199
Van Herik, J., 230
Van Tranh, T., 429, 442
Vanman, E.J., 357-358, 377
Vaughan, F.E., 496, 498, 518
Venkatesananda, S., 131, 143
Ventis, L., 68, 344, 471, 532, 561, 595
Ventis, W.L., 561, 595
Vergote, A., 225, 230, 281, 311
Verhoeven, D., 280, 306
Vetter, G.B., 389, 391, 396
Vianello, R., 279, 281, 310-311
Vich, M.A., 497-498, 500, 518
Vinicor, F., 565
Virkkunen, T.P., 284, 291, 311
Vitz, P., 230
Vivier, L., 459, 475
Von Franz, M.L., 232, 253
Voss, C.H., 60, 71
Vreeland, R.S., 373
Vygotsky, L.V., 110, 120

Wach, J., 179, 400, 419
Wagner, A.C., 554, 567
Walker, L., 111, 120
Wall, S., 449, 471
Wallace, B., 421, 423, 445
Wallace, P.J., 46
Waller, M., 419
Waller, N.G., 377
Waller, T., 345
Wallston, K.A., 372
Walsh, G.F., 596
Walsh, R., 518
Walters, G., 320, 347
Walther, G., 189, 199
Wang, A., 117, 120, 340, 348
Ward, M., 46-47, 376
Warning, E.G., 226
Warren, M., 539, 543, 567
Warshaw, S., 267
Wasburn, M., 10
Wasserfall, R., 477, 485-486, 494
Wasserman, S.A., 26-27, 29
Waters, E., 17, 27, 73, 448-450, 469, 471, 474-475
Watkins, M., 142, 247, 253
Watson, B., 435, 442
Watson, J.B., 396
Watson, P.J., 47, 436, 445, 587-589, 596
Watts, F., 314, 352, 585
Webber, J, 29
Weber, M., 120, 182
Weber, R., 518
Weber, T., 306

Weekley, E., 3, 12
Wehr, G., 248, 253
Weigert-Vowinkel, E., 259, 268
Weinborn, M., 376
Weiner, B., 377
Weiner, E.S.C., 517
Weisberg, D., 19, 29
Weisler, S.E., 377
Weiss, J., 564
Weiss, R.S., 475
Weisz, J.R., 429, 445
Welch, C., 69
Welch, H., 120
Welwood, J., 89, 121
Wenegrat, B., 453-454, 475, 508, 518
Westerhoff III, J.H., 567
Westling, G., 290, 305
Wethington, E., 361, 375
Wetzel, C.G., 377
White, E.G., 494
White, J.F., 559, 567
White, J.W., 567
White, P., 332, 351
White, S., 330, 352
Whitmont, E.C., 236, 238, 240, 243, 246, 253
Wicklund, R.A., 346-347, 555, 567
Wiggins, E.C., 371, 373
Wikstrom, O., 348, 407, 412
Wilber, K., 10, 141, 499-502, 510-512, 518
Williams, D., 121, 534
Williams, D.L., 46
Williams, M., 314, 352
Williams, P., 121
Williams, R.N., 369, 375
Wilson, B., 71
Wilson, T.D., 363, 366, 372
Wimberly, R.C., 71
Winnicott, D.W., 65, 71, 258-259, 261, 268, 469
Winograd, E., 346, 348, 350
Wisdom, J., 223, 230, 484, 499
Wittgenstein, L., 3, 151, 577, 593, 597
Witztum, D.E., 263, 266
Wolf, M., 201, 204, 220, 463, 473
Wood, F.G., 71
Wood, W.W., 475
Woodberry, J.D., 462, 475
Woods, J.H., 143
Woods, R., 142, 143
Woodward, J.B., 549, 562
Wool, G., 562
Wortman, C.B., 113, 117, 360, 373, 430-431, 440
Wren, T., 350
Wrenn, M., 544, 567
Wrightsman, JR. L.S., 395
Wulff, D.M., 2, 6, 12, 40, 48, 57-58, 71, 183, 186, 189-190, 199, 259, 268-269, 311, 314, 352, 384-387, 389, 393, 396, 413, 420, 463, 475, 498, 500, 508, 519, 579, 581, 597, 601
Wurf, E., 555, 565
Wuthnow, R., 296, 305, 555, 563
Wyer, R., 347

Yandell, K.E., 159-160
Yeatts, J., 324, 352
Yerushalmi, Y., 230
Yoon, S.H., 95, 101, 103, 121
Young, K.Z., 534
Young, T.R., 519
Yuille, J., 324, 350

Zachry, W., 319, 322-323, 352
Zaehner, R.C., 143, 167, 182
Zahn, J.C., 180
Zajonc, R.B., 312, 332, 352, 356-357, 377
Zanden, J.W.V., 555, 567
Zanna, M., 351, 377
Zanna, M.P., 307, 377, 445
Zanni, G., 329, 349
Zeifman, D., 467, 472
Zeininger, K., 284, 311
Zimdars-Swartz, S.L., 48
Zimmer, H., 143
Zimmerman, N., 246, 253
Zollschan, G.K., 596
Zuttermeister, P.C., 181
Zysk, K.R., 141

Index of Subjects

Abhava (emptiness), 93; *see also* Emptiness; Negation
Abortion, 31, 44, 359
Absolute, The; *see* Allah; Atman; Brahman; *Ein Sof*; God; Nirvana; Purusha; Shiva; *Tathata*
Abuse; *see also* Crime; Rape; Trauma
  physical, 525
  sexual, 26, 27; *see also* Submission; Surrender
Acayagamghaga (method of agreement), 101; *see also* Method of Agreement, Mill's
Accommodation, cultural, 91, 110
Act/Action, 8, 105, 147; *see also* Behavior; Affect
  affective, 163
  evaluation of, 358; *see also* Religious experience, evaluation of
  obsessive; *see* Personality, neurotic; Personality, obsessive
  of human will, 133, 189; *see also* God, will of
  rational, 163; *see also* Rationality; Reason
  ritual; *see* Rituals
  rooted in consciousness, 101, 102, 189
Actor/Agent; *see also*Agent-Structure theory; Individual, social status of; Society, structure of
  religious, 110, 111, 358, 422-423, 438
  social, 177-178
Adolescent, 262-263, 269, 270, 279, 380; *see also* Child; Human development; Personality, development of; Psychospiritual development, age-related: Religious experience, age differences in
Adonai , 21; *see also* God, names for
Adultery, 44, 77
Affect, 3, 4, 8, 163; *see also* Attitudes; Emotion; Feelings
  attitude, compared to, 356
  cognitive influence on, 358-359
  definition of, 356, 371n1
  emotion, contrasted with, 356
  prominence of, 354-355
  storage of, 363-364; *see also* Memory, systems of
  theories,
    affect conceptualization in, 356-357
    cognitive-arousal theory, 359-360
    need for, 369
    prototype theory, 369-371
Afflictions, Hindu principle of, 129, 130-131, 141
African-Americans, 56, 61, 66; *see also* Bigotry; Prejudice; Slavery
Age; *see* Life, cycles of; Conversion, age differences in; Dreams, mid-life; Psychospiritual development, age-related; Religious experiences, age differences in
Agent; *see* Actor/Agent
Agent-Structure theory, 162, 177-178; *see also* Society, structure of
Aggression, 204, 218, 240; *see also* Anger; Behavior, barbaric; War
Agreement; *see Acayagamghaga*; Method of Agreement, Mill's
AIDS, 26, 44
Akron Area Survey, 170-171
Alienation, 20-21, 106
Allah, 76; *see also* God, names for; Islam
Allport, Gordon, 5, 60-62, 63, 371
Altered states of consciousness, 8, 138-140, 235, 338-343, 383, 423; *see also* Consciousness; Psychedelics; Religious experience, facilitation of
Ambivalence, 209, 212, 449-450, 454; *see*

Ambivalence continued
also Aversion; Avoidance; Withdrawal
American Psychological Association (APA), 502
Amnesia; *see also* Memory, systems of; Repression
adult, 329, 330
childhood, 316, 330
ritual, 329-334
Anal stage; *see* Freudianism, stages of growth; Personality, development of
Analogical imagination; *see* Analogy; Imagination
Analogy; *see also* Analogical imagination; Language, metaphorical
everyday, 186
Freud's use of; *see* Freudianism, analogy use in
Anatman (non-Self), 96, 97-99; *see also* Atman
Angels, 187, 422
Anger, 155, 194; *see also* Aggression; Emotion; Feelings
study of, 370-371
Anglican Church, 49, 63
Anima; see Archetypes, Jungian
Animals, 126, 209; *see also* Taboo; Totem
Animism, 62, 211; *see also* Religion, origins of; Religion, primitive
Animus; see Archetypes, Jungian
Anitya, 96; *see also* Impermanence
Annanathata (invariability), 100
Annihilationist theory, 100; *see also* Nihilism
Anointing; *see* Body, anointing of
Anthropology, 5, 115, 201
Anthropomorphism; *see* God, images of, anthropomorphized
Anti-Semitism, 205; *see also* Attitudes; Bigotry; Jews, stereotypes of
Anxiety, 9, 50, 222; *see also* Depression; Neurosis
separation anxiety, 262, 449-450, 454; *see also* Attachment
Apologetics, 4-5, 146, 147, 149; *see also* Piety; Protestantism
Arabs, 74, 75, 79, 80, 81
Aranya (biographer of Buddha), 127, 130; *see also* Buddha; Buddhism
Archetypes, 233-235, 237, 239; *see also* Jungianism
as mediator of conscious-unconscious, 504, 508
as habits, 508
dialectical nature of, 510
examples of,
divine, 508
God-Man, 244
Great Mother/Mother, 251n7, 506-507
Jungian,
anima, 239, 240, 250-251n6
animus, 239, 240, 250-251n6
libido, 234
persona, 239, 242
Self, 239, 514
shadow, 239, 240
symbol, 235, 237, 243, 246-247, 317, 340, 341; *see also* Symbol
trickster, 246
psychic accessibility and, 248; *see also* Psyche
Asana (posture), 129; *see also* Yoga
Assemblies of God, 172, 175
Assimilation, cultural, 91, 110
Association theory, 8, 384, 387-388; *see also* Behavioral psychology
Astitva , 92; *see also* Being
Atheists, 245, 456; *compare* Non-religious persons
Atman (individual Self), 90, 99, 100, 123, 133, 135, 245; *see also* Anatman
Atonement, 212, 214; *see also* Forgiveness; Sin
Attachment; *see also* Attachment theory; Clinging; Non-attachment; Personality, development of; Symbiosis
activated by punishment, 461
adolescent, 459
adult, 451, 460
affect and, 364-365
behaviors, 447-450
cross-cultural differences in, 462-465
dangers of, 136, 139
Eastern religions and, 131, 136, 139, 464-465
false, 98, 103, 104
father-child, 263, 264, 265; *see also* Oedipus Complex
illusion of, 92
individual differences in, 453-455, 461
loneliness and, 454, 457
male-male, 525
measurements of, 9
mother-child, 262, 265, 365, 448-450, 528
narcissism and, 463-464
object relations, contrasted with, 468-470; *see also* Object relations; Object relations theory

patterns of, 9, 449-450
phenomenology of, 450-451
religious experience and, 451-452
schema and, 365-366
systems of, 448
to God, 452-457
universal, 462-463
worldly, 132, 133
Attachment theory,
ethological, 447-450
Freud and, 465-468
psychoanalytic traditions and, 468-470
psychology of religion and, 446-447
implications for, 467
Attitudes, 9, 43, 44, 63; *see also* Affect; Bias; Bigotry; Prejudice
accessibility of, 367
central, 367
coping and, 361-363
definition of, 371n1
development of, 291-295
heredity and, 290, 291
motivational, 270, 290-291
religious experience and, 270, 291-295, 433-436
social, 63, 67
statements of, 275-276
theories of, 270
toward African-Americans, 53, 61
toward homosexuals, 24, 355
toward Native Americans, 53
toward women, 489; *see also* Body, political uses of; Women
Attribution; *see also* Attribution theory; Misattribution
basic human needs and, 428-430
collaborative, 435
control and, 429, 434-436
coping and, 361-363
dispositional, 437
divine/diabolical, 424-425, 431, 438
emotions, 426-427
expectations and, 437-438
errors in, 437
general, 427-428
group influences on, 430-431
illness and, 429, 433-434
motivational influences on, 428, 429, 430
pre- and post-experience, 434
schema and, 313, 359, 431-433
self-esteem and, 433
Attribution theory, 8, 9; *see also* Attribution theory; Misattribution
cognitive-arousal, 359-360
unqualified, 437
Augsburg Confessions, The, 66
Augustine, Saint, 50, 144, 262, 522; *see also* Sin, Augustinian; Saints/Saintliness
Authoritarianism, 61, 63, 66
Authority; *see also* Autonomy; Power
apostate, 36
charismatic, 164, 524-527; *see also* Religious experience, charismatic
divine; *see* God
ecclesiastical, 34, 36, 45, 50, 52, 60
historical, 203
moral, 111, 112
of consciousness, 149
paternal, 204, 218; *see also* Father; Father-God
pluralistic undermining of, 164; *see also* Pluralism
political, 50
sacred, 265
totemic, 209
transcendental, 168
Autobiography, 148, 204; *see also* Narrative; Tradition, biographical
Autonomy, 10, 522, 524; *see also* Authority; Power
Aversion, 132, 136, 265; *see also* Ambivalence; Avoidance; Withdrawal
Avitatha (necessity), 100
Avoidance, 9, 449, 454, 462; *see also* Ambivalence; Aversion; Withdrawal
Awareness, 94, 139, 193; *see also* Consciousness; God, awareness of
bodily, 183, 255
introspective, 183
mutual, 425
Awe, 186, 424, 439; *see also* Mystical experience, emotional core of; Sacred, The

Baptism, 65, 485, 538; *see also* Bath; Purification
Baptists, 54, 55, 56, 61, 62, 169
Bath; *see also* Footwashing; *Mikvah*; Purification
healing, 25, 26
Jesus' instructions for, 482-483
ritual, 15-17, 77
Behavior, 4, 8, 9, 43, 63, 109, 115, 157, 174, 179n6; *see also* Behavioral psychology; Consequences
barbaric, 508, 513
birth experience and, 509

Behavior continued
definition of, 378-379
determinants of, 254; *see also* Drives/Drive theory; Personality, as drive-based system
feminine- masculine, 240
God's, *see* God, behaviors attributed to
instinctive, 384; *see also* Instincts
learned, 172, 173-174, 206, 384-387; *see also* Religious instruction; Socialization; Social learning
linked to religion, 202, 206, 207; *see also* Religion
observable, 378-379; *compare* Experience, nonobservable
obsessive, 204; *see also* Neurosis; Personality, obsessive
private, 204
psychic energy and, 254
ritual; *see* Obsession; Rituals
self-reporting of, 183-184, 584; *see also* Interviews; Narrative; Religious experience, descriptions of; Self-report
sexual, 17, 225n2, 451, 477, 489; *see also* God, sexuality and; Mating; Sexuality
premarital 31, 44
symbolic, 400-401
systems of, 451
totemic; *see* Totemism
Behavioral psychology, 8, 183, 272-273
assumptions in, 384
behavioral models in,
Bowlby's ethological, 447-450, 470; *see also* Attachment theory
learning paradigms, 384-387
operant conditioning, 389-392
S-O-R, 380-383
behaviorist overemphasis in, 503
biocentric basis of, 383
theories in,
associationist, 384, 387-388, 392, 393
social learning, 392-393; *see also* Social learning theory
state/trait, 379-380
Being; *see also* Existence
primitive, 239; *see also* Archetypes
psychophysical, 101, 102
Ultimate, 241, 300
non-being, contrasted with, 92
Belief; *see also* Religious belief
folk, 32, 35, 92, 176; *see also* Folklore; Folk religion
formation of, 159
motivated, 110
suspension of, 193, 194, 195
systems of, 233, 260
Beyond the Pleasure Principle, 210
Bhagavad-Gita, 126, 132, 133, 137; *see also* Scripture; Text; Word of God
Bhakti marga (path of devotion), 464; *see also* Yoga, devotional
Bhava (desire for existence), 101
Bias; *see also* Bigotry; Prejudice
Christian, 316
gender, 229, 489, 490, 491; *see also* Women, gender constraints and; Body, political uses of
in reasoning, 369; *see also* Intellect; Rationality; Reason
scientific, 43, 162, 175, 192, 195, 196, 343, 589
Bible, 52, 66, 67, 204; *see also* Bible stories; Religious concepts, development of; Religious instruction; Scripture; Word of God
decoding of metaphor in; *see* Language, metaphorical
literal readings of; *see* Language, literal
BIBLE Scale, 322
Bible stories, 277-278, 281, 282; *see also* Parables
Bigotry, 61, 64; *see also* Anti-Semitism; Prejudice
Biology; *see* Embryology; Evolutionary biology
Bird from the East, 80
Birth, 65, 101, 125, 241, 509
Birth control, 31, 44, 46
Birth of the Living God, 224
Blacks; *see* African-Americans
Blood, 15, 28
menstrual, 15, 485-487; *see also* Menstruation; *Mikvah*
Bodhi, 90, 94, 96, 101; *see also* Buddhism; Enlightenment
Bodhisattva (ideal person), 93, 94, 95, 102; *see also* Buddhism; Ideal Person
Body, 10; *see also* Religious experience, physical displays of
abstraction of, 477, 493
abuse of; *see* Abuse
anointing of, 195, 484-485
as religious instrument, 528-530
"bodymind" concept and, 174
cleansing of; *see* Bath; Mikvah; Purification
Eucharist and, 483-484

experience of material world and, 476
female, affirmation of, 527, 528; *see also* Menstruation
flesh-and-blood, 483-484
gendered, 488-491
healing of, 26 27, 482
holistic view of, 477
impermanence of, 98, 99; *see also* Impermanence
impurity of, 15-17; *see also* Mikvah; Purification
interpretations of, 477
laying of hands on, 484-485
modesty and, 483
mourning and, 488
orifices of, 477
political uses of, 476, 489, 491-492
prayer postures and, 481-482
psychedelic alteration of, 579; *see also* Altered states of consciousness
rituals; *see* Rituals
Rosary and, 481-482
sexual, 487; *see also* Behavior, sexual; God, sexuality and; Sexuality
social meaning of, 476; *see also* Role; Social "me"
submission of; *see* Submission
surrender of; *see* Surrender
Tefillin and, 481-482; *see also* Judaism; Prayer
touch and, 482
unity with mind, 102, 493
Body of Christ, 245, 261; *see also* Eucharist
Bonaventure, Saint, 249
Bonding; *see* Attachment
Bondage, spiritual, 123-124; *see also* Hinduism
Born-again person, 176; *see also* Conversion; Religious experience, once-born/twice-born
Bracketing; *see* Epoché; Phenomenology, bracketing of suppositions in
Brahadaranyaka Upanishad, 126; *see also* Philosophy, Upanisadic; Upanishads
Brahma (universal Self), 90; *see also* Hinduism
Brahman (ultimate reality), 90, 124, 125, 126, 132,135, 248; *see also* Hinduism
Brahman caste, 90, 108, 126; *see also* Caste system
Brain research, left-right, 508
Brotherhood, monastic, 84; *see also* Monks
Buddha, The, 94, 100, 101; *see also* Buddhism
biographer of, 127
birth/death of, 90
disciples of, 90
enlightenment of, 90
teachings of, 92, 95, 105
Buddhi (I-sense), 128, 130, 136, 137
Buddhism; *see also* Buddha, The
apolitical nature of, 116
apotropaic, 93
as religion of people vs. religion of texts, 88, 95, 109, 113, 114
attachment behaviors in, 464-465
belief communities in, 92, 105, 109, 117
belief diversity in, 5, 87-89, 115
belief motivation in, 110-111
bodhisattvas in, 93
Buddha-role in, 412; *see also* Role; Role Theory
Burmese, 88, 109-115
caste system in, 90
Chinese, 92, 115, 116
conflict resolution in, 103, 106, 113, 114; *see also* Dualism; Opposites
core of, 117
Dharma, 92, 99
doctrines of, 91, 92, 105-108
egalitarianism in, 90, 91
Eightfold Path in, 95, 102, 105
Emptiness principle in, 103, 106; *see also* Negation; Nirvana
founder of, 90
four major branches of
Ch'an , 91-95
Hinayana, 91-95
Mahayana, 91-95, 96, 98, 102, 103, 465
Theravada/Old, 91, 103, 464
Four Noble Truths of, 90, 95-105
Freudian analysis of, 110
historical context of, 90-95
Japanese, 94, 116
kammatic; *see* Buddhism, non-normative
karma in, 90, 91, 93, 96, 100, 102, 107, 108, 110, 111-113
Korean, 116
lack of central authority in, 87
Law of, 92
Lesser; *see* Buddhism, Theravada
Middle Path in, 103-104, 105, 106
mystic experiences in, 107-108
nibbanic; *see* Buddhism, normative
Nirvana; *see* Nirvana
non-normative, 87, 88, 93, 94, 110
normative, 88, 93, 110-113, 114

Buddhism continued
of the Elders, 93
ontological issues in, 88, 92, 107
practicality in, 105-108
regional changes in, 90-95, 102, 103, 110-115
right living in, 105, 106
role of mediation in, 109, 1171
role of meditation in, 90, 105-108
salvation as ultimate goal, 88, 104, 109
Self vs. Non-Self in, 96-100
Six Gateways in, 101
Six Perfections in, 95, 102
social responsibility in, 93, 111-113
sociocultural contexts of, 88, 89, 94, 109-117
soteriological, 91, 93, 94; *see also* Salvation
spread of, 91, 94, 105
study of, 87, 88, 115, 117
suffering and, 95
three Jewels (Treasures) of, 92
Twelve Causes of Existence in, 101, 104; *see also* Causality; Existence
unity principle in, 5, 87-88, 90-91
universality-uniformity in, 89
Western interpretations of, 97, 98, 99, 116
worldview in, 88, 109, 110
Zen, 94, 98, 105, 108, 116, 173-174, 412, 465, 509-510

Calvinism, 51, 52, 54, 144
Capitalism, 63, 75, 82; *see also* Economy; Wealth
Caregiver, 9, 447-450; *see also* Attachment; Child; Parents/Parenting
divine vs. human, 456
Caste system, 90, 126; *see also* Hinduism
Castration complex, 213; *see also* Oedipus complex
Cataleptic state, 139; *see also* Altered states of consciousness; *see also* Trance
Catechumenate, ancient, 544; *see also* Religious instruction
Catholicity, 37, 45; *see also* Catholicism
Catholic Myth, The, 40, 45
Catholicism, 4, 63, 67, 261
belief diversity in, 32
"cafeteria-style," 32, 38, 39
characteristics of, 33-37, 45
deep structure of, 33
defection rate in, 31, 34
divisions within, 31, 32, 37
ethnicity in, 32
hierarchy in, 31, 34, 45, 46, 50; *see also* Papacy; Popes; Second Vatican Council
mystical experience and, 60, 178
pre-Vatican, 34, 35; *see also* Second Vatican Council
progressive, 36
Protestantism, contrasted with, 41, 44, 453
religious instruction in; *see* Religious instruction
Roman, 49, 194
sacraments in, 33-34; *see also* Sacraments
self-identity in, 31, 32
Spanish, 53
theological foci in, 37
values in, 62
Caucasians; *see* Whites
Causality, 98, 100-102, 106, 107, 117; *see also* Buddhism, Twelve Causes of Existence in
Celibacy, 31
Centering-down, 189; *see also* Phenomenology
Ceremonials; *see also* Rituals
analogous, 209, 210, 221, 225n2
neurotic vs. religious, 207, 208
Ch'an Buddhism; *see* Buddhism
Change, institutional, 163, 167, 172, 175
Channeling, 496; *see also* Transpersonal theory, definitions/explanations of
Chaos theory, 504, 513
Characteristics, human; *see also* Instincts; Ontogeny; Phylogeny
acquired, 203, 210, 466
inherited, 203, 210, 211
Charismatic Experience Index, 175
Charismatic leaders, 524-527; *see also* Charismatic religion
Charismatic religion, 22, 67, 74, 163, 164, 172, 173, 175-176, 232; *see also* Charismatic leaders; Religious experience, charismatic
Charity, 33, 106, 175
Chassidism; *see* Judaism, Hassidic
Child, 9, 215, 254, 448, 449, 450; *see also* Adolescent; Human development; Infant; Parents/Parenting; Personality, development of
behaviors of,
attachment; *see* Attachment; Significant other
neurotic, 213
social referencing, 457
development of,

critical periods in, 255-258; *see also* Personality, development of
nature-nurture debate, *see* Freudianism; Ontogeny; Phylogeny
equated with savage, 209
infantile helplessness of, 215, 216
mental processes of, 207; *see also* Cognition; Religious thinking
object relations of; *see* Object relations; Object relations theory
pre-verbal, 257-258
sacrifice of, 210
China, 92, 115, 116
Christ; 210, 211; *see also* Christianity; Jesus Christ; Judeo-Christian Religion
archetype, 243
as Self, 243
divinity of, 32
fish symbol and, 244
incarnation of God, 243
son of God, 212
sacrifice of, 212
Christianity, 50, 57, 72, 93, 94, 212, 213, 249; *see also* Judeo-Christian religion
as relationship, 452
Christian Mystical Perceptual Doxastic Practice (CMP), 159n4
Church; *see also* names of individual denominations; Church life
attendance, 31, 52, 62, 67, 178, 179n6, 315
evangelism and growth of, 175; *see also* Change, institutional
Church Dogmatics, 324
Church life, 537-541; *see also* Church; Religious instruction
Church of Christ, 55, 63
Church of God, 53
Church of Jesus Christ of Latter-day Saints; *see* Mormons
Circumcision, 478, 482; *see also* Body, as religious instrument; Rites of Passage
Civilization, 90, 200-202, 208-209; *see also* Culture; History; Progress; Society
Aryan, 90, 204
contribution of religion to, 219
Dravidian, 133
emergence of Judaic monotheism in, 212; *see also* Judaism
guiding principles of, 270
Indus, 90
Oedipus complex, linked to, 109, 217-221
pre-Aryan, 133
primitive, 209
Vedas, 90
Civilization and Its Discontents; 208
Civil liberties, 74, 85
Clairvoyance, 170, 171, 178, 179n2; *see also* ESP; Precognition; Telepathy
Clans, 90; *see also* Caste system; Sects
Cleansing; *see also* Bath; Body; *Mikvah*; Purification
Clergy, 45, 54, 61
Clinging behavior, 101, 104; *see also* Attachment; Afflictions, Hindu principle of
CMP (Christian Mystical Perceptual Doxastic Practice), 159n4
Code, moral, 52; *see also* Morality; Mores; Values
Cognition, 3, 4, 62, 110, 123, 124, 131, 169; *see also* Cognitive dissonance; Cognitive psychology; Developmental psychology
accommodation/assimilation in, 320
affective influence on, 363-369
attributional process in, 363
confusion in, 258-259
development of, 269-270, 277-278
logical, 319-320
Cognitive dissonance, 193, 295, 411; *see also* Cognition; Cognitive psychology
Cognitive Psychology, 8; *see also* Cognition; Cognitive dissonance; Developmental psychology
basic assumptions of, 315
contribution to study of religion, 343
models in,
contextual, 317
hierarchical, 324-325
theories in
cognitive consistency theory, 270
limitations and ambitions of, 312-319
Piaget's theories, 277-278; *see also* Piagetian paradigm
linguistic point of view in, 285-287
Collective experience; *see* Community, sense of; Religious experience, collective
Collective unconscious, the, 235, 237; *see also* Unconscious, The
Colonialism, 79, 82
Commandments; *see also* Law; Moses; Ten Commandments
female-male, 15, 25
in Torah, 14, 24, 25
Commemoration; *see* Ceremonials
Communion, 35, 45; *see also* Holy Communion; God, union with
Community, sense of, 59, 67; *see also* Re-

Community continued
ligious experience, collective
Buddhist, 92, 105, 109, 116
Catholic, 32, 33, 34, 37, 38, 39
Protestant, 50
spiritual, 17-19
Concentration, 129, 136, 139; *see also* Meditation; Religious experience facilitation of; Trance; Yoga
Concepts; *see* Religious belief; Religious concepts
Confirmation, 33, 65
Conflict; *see also* Dualism; Opposites
psychic, 220, 223
sexual-aggressive, 218; *see also* Oedipus Complex
Congregationalists, 54, 55
Conjunctio, The, 240, 248
Conscience, 163, 384; *see also* Guilt
Consciousness, 7; *see also* Awareness; Mind; Unconscious, The
actions and, 101, 102; *see also* Behavior
altered states of; *see* Altered states of consciousness
as cause of reality, 100, 101
authority of, 149
bridged with Self, 239, 240; *see also* Individuation
constitution of phenomena in, 193
continuity of, 149
cosmic, 496, 502
ego as center of, 239
emptying of, 189; *see also* Emptiness; Negation
epiphenomenal, 385
evolution of, 500
extraordinary, 498
immediate, 145, 154
impure-pure forms of, 145, 157
intentional structure of, 186
learning paradigm for, 384
male, 251n8
models of, 7; *see also* Depth psychology; Freudianism; Jungianism
modern, 165; *see also* Modernism; Pluralism
mystical, 238
narratized Self and, 338-343; *see also* Narrative; Self-report
numinous, 186; *see also* Mystical experience, numinous
objectless, 140
objects of, 574, 575
ordinary vs. non-ordinary, 139, 189
overrational, 513
phenomenology of, 188-189
psychic states of, 188-189
rationalistic, 149
shared, 18
societal tension and, 500
transformation of, 117, 124, 127-132, 137-141; *see also* Altered states
Consequences; *see also* Behavior
institutional, 175-176
personal, 176-177
social, 175, 177
Conservatives, religious, 165, 178; *see also* Fundamentalism
Constructs, 367-368, 372n2, 576-577, 578; *see also* Schema; Reality, social construction of
Contexts, social, 161-179; *see also* Buddhism, sociocultural contexts of; Reality, social construction of; Socialization; Society
Contraception; *see* Birth control
Control, as basic human need, 428-430; *see also* Needs, human
Conversion, 8, 9, 28, 64, 67, 68
age differences in; *see also* Religious experience, age differences in; Psychospiritual development, age-related
adolescent, 262-263, 458, 459
child, 295-296, 297
peak age, 295
analysis of, 411-413
as destroyer of schema, 316
as public performance, 59; *see also* Experience, private
dramatic, 334-338, 457-459
psychological interpretations of, 334-338
falling in love, compared to, 458
interpersonal components of, 59
instruction in, 33; *see also* Religious instruction
Islamic, 84
James's categories of, 59; *see also* James, William
narratives of, 316-317, 434; *see also* Consciousness, narratized Self and; Narrative; Religious experience, articulation of; Tradition, biographical
personality dynamics and, 262-263
phenomenology of, 196
Protestant emphasis on, 54, 57, 58, 59, 60
psychoanalytic explanations for, 262-263
study of, 457-458
sudden, *see* Conversion, dramatic

Coping, 356
collaborative, 361
gender differences in, 361-362
ineffective, 362-363
religious, 360-363
strategies for, 360-363
Corruption, 35
in church hierarchy, 45, 46, 50, 51
Countertransference, 246; *see also* Transference neurosis
Covenant, 187
Credulity, principle of, 152, 159n4; *see also* Rationality
Crime, 177; *see also* Abuse; Aggression; Violence
primal, 211; *see also* Parricide
Cult, 42, 524, 585; *see also* Clan; Sect
Culture; *see also* Civilization; Society
authority of religion in, 200-201
dreams and, 206
defined, 109
fixated, 219
Freud's exegesis of, 207; *see also* Oedipus Complex
progression of, 219
transmission of, 177, 211
wish-fulfillment, 219, 220
Cultural neurosis, 202; *see also* Oedipus Complex

Dancing, 487-488; *see also* Religious experience, physical displays of
Darwin, 201, 202; *see also* Social Darwinism
Davan, 17, 23, 488; *see also* Judaism; Prayer
Da'wah (missionary activity), 80
Day of Atonement, 18; *see also* Judaism; Atonement
Death, 65, 101, 125; *see also* Nirvana
fear of, 61
inevitability of, 134
integration of, 140; *see also* Individuation; Personality, integration of
preparation for, 288, 289
Deep sleep; *see* Dreams; Sleep; Trance
Defense mechanisms, 207
denial; *see* Religious belief, denial-doubt
displacement, 224, 329
projection, 201, 223, 224, 263-265, 535
repression, 78, 128, 209, 210, 211
sublimation, 225n1
Dehumanization, 83; *see also* Oppression; Persecution
Deity, 123, 148, 221, 248, 263; *see also* God; Goddess
Dejá-vu, 170, 171, 178
Delusion, 6, 133, 236; *see also* Insanity
Demons, 187, 192; *see also* Devil; Evil
Dependence,
absolute, 146, 575
self-identical, 146
Depression, 58, 61, 439; *see also* Anxiety; Mental health
in infants, 261
Depth psychology, 5-6, 183, 184, 197, 206, 270, 271, 313; *see also* Freudianism; Jungianism; Object relations; Psychoanalysis; Psychotherapy
and denigration of human experience, 183
and dreams, 206
Desire, 101, 114, 126, 131, 132, 139, 189; *see also* Libido; Wish-fulfillment
infantile, 261, 265
libido, contrasted with, 234
linked to religion, 206, 207, 216-218
ritual denial of, 486-487
uncivilized, 239
Determinism, 6; *see also* Psychic determinism
Deva (heavenly existence), 94, 114
Development, human; *see* Child, development of; Developmental psychology; Embryology; Evolutionary biology; Infant; Personality, development of
Developmental psychology; *see also* Cognitive Psychology
analytical tradition in, 287-290
change as central phenomenon in, 271
depth psychology and, 270, 273
models,
behaviorist, 272
biographical, 271-273, 275, 276; *see also* Narrative; Tradition, biographical
psychometric trait, 272-273, 275-276
theories,
attitude, 270
cognitive-stage, 272-273
linguistic point of view and, 270
operational thinking, 269
Piagetian, 270, 274, 276; *see also* Piagetian paradigm
psycho-social, 270
structural, 270, 274
Devil, 53, 76, 260, 424, 425; *see also* Demons; Evil; Object, bad-good
Devotion, *see* God, individual's relationship to, devotion to; Love, devotional; Religious practices, devotional; Yoga, devotional

Dharana (fixation), 129, 131
Dharma, 92, 99; *see also* Right living
Dhyana, 107, 131
Dialogue, therapeutic, 233
Dichotomies; *see also* Dualism; Opposites
body-mind; *see* Consciousness, "body mind" concept in; Mind
external-internal, 246; *see also* Object relations
sacred-profane, 264, 510
Disciples of Christ church, 55
Displacement, 224, 329; *see also* Defense mechanisms
Disposition, Buddhist principle of, 97, 99
Divine election, doctrine of 52, 57; *see also* Calvinism; Doctrines
Divine Mother, 134, 135; *see also* Archetype; Goddess; Great Mother
Divine, The, 4, 36, 126, 135, 136, 524
dreams of, 233
experiencing of, 4, 14, 41, 168, 169; *see also* Experience, divine-diabolical God, encounter with; Mystical experience
female-male unity in, 20-21, 25, 27
moon rituals and , 25
touch of, 169
Divorce, 44, 52
Dogma, 61, 65, 72, 569; *see also* Theology
Doctrines; *see also* names of individual denomination or faith tradition
functionality of, 110
of divine election, 52, 57
of emanation, 20
of justification, 58
of Manifest Destiny, 55
of separation of church and state, 54
traditional, 146
Domestic culture, 23, 25; *see also* Home
Doubt; *see* Religious belief, denial-doubt
Dreams, *see also* Freudianism; Jungianism
archetypal, 233, 23, 236, 250n3, 340, 341
as gift from Self, 249
continuous with personality, 339
development of wholeness and, 240
empowerment and, 246
female-male, 240
image-meaning link in, 246
individual impact of, 232, 233
manifest content of, 233, 246, 247, 338-341
mid-life, 241, 245; *see also* Psychospiritual development, age-related; Religious experience, age differences in
numinous, 231, 237, 243; *see also* Mystical experience, numinous
Oedipal, 250n3
personal history and, 235, 236
sacred elements of, 233
studies of,
cognitive, 338, 339
Freudian, 206
Jungian,
examples of dreams, 231-233, 235-237, 242, 245, 246, 248, 250
synchronicity in, 232
interpretive techniques in, 233, 246-248, 256
free-association, 246, 247
objective-subjective, 246
implications
for psychology of religious experience, 233, 248-250
for cognitive psychology, 248
symbolism in, 236, 246, 317; *see also* Symbol
Dreamwork; *see* Dreams, studies of, Jungian; Jungianism
Drives/Drive theory, 254, 256, 467, 468; *see also* Motivation; Personality, as drive-based system
Drugs; *see also* Altered states of consciousness; LSD; Psychedelics; Religious experience, facilitation of
hallucinogenic, 60
psychedelic, 11, 235, 579, 580, 583-585
Dualism/Duality, 12, 124, 126, 137, 177; *see also* Opposites
fundamental human, 505
transcendence of, 133, 134, 137
Dukkha (suffering), 96, 111
Durkheim, Emile, 6, 59, 161, 163, 164, 177, 178
transpersonal theory and, 503-508

Eastern religions, 9; *see also* Buddhism; Hinduism; Islam
Economy; *see also* Capitalism; Socioeconomic classes; Wealth
and Islam, 78
and Protestant ethic, 55, 56, 67
Ecstasy, 135, 169, 215, 265; *see also* Eroticism; Mystical experience, ineffable; Religious experience, ecstatic
raw, 178
religiousness trait and, 379
Education; *see* Religious instruction
Egalitarianism, 90, 91, 124; *compare* Elitism;

see also Body, political uses of; Power, distribution of
Ego, 124, 128, 189, 203, 210, 215, 226n3, 249, 341; *see also* Freudianism; Id; Superego
  centrality of, in Freudianism, 239, 256
Egocentricity, 101
Ego-defensive function, 113; *see also* Defense mechanisms
Ego-feeling, 215
Ego-ideal, 218, 525; *see also* Superego
Ego-involved persons, 325
Egoless state, 134; *see also* Samadhi
Ego psychology, 226n7
Ego-Self axis, 239
Ego-strength, 241
Ein Sof, 20; *see also* Godhead
Elementary Forms of Religious Life, The, 163
Elitism, 83, 92, 116; *compare* Egalitarianism
Emanation, doctrine of, 20; *see also* Doctrines
Embodiment, 10; *see also* God, embodiment of; Jews, as embodied people
Embryology, 210-211; *see also* Evolutionary biology; Child, development of
Emotion; *see also* Affect; Feelings
  attachment behavior and, 450-451
  attribution, 426-427
  as core of religious belief, 195; *see also* Feelings, as core of religion
  as a given in religious experience, 123
  bodily changes and, 370, 578-579
  cognitive effects on, 359-360
  conceptualization of, 355, 369
  evaluation of,
    models/theories,
      ACE, 370-371
      biosocial, 357
      cognitive appraisal, 155, 355, 357-358
      feasibility of, 370
      prototype scripts for, 369
      two-factor, 578-579
  feelings, contrasted with, 155
  feminine-masculine, 240
  interruption of mental operations and, 355
  memories of, 364-365
  plausible descriptions of, 156; *see also* Feelings, descriptions of; Language, inadequacy of
  pure, 173
  psychology of, 155, 577-579
  social-religious, 163
Empiricism, 149-151, 154, 158, 159n3, 504
Emptiness, 103, 106; *see also* Negation; Nirvana; Nothingness
Enantiodromia, 507, 513; *see also* Opposites
Encounter,
  cooperative, 197
  mystical, 261-262; *see also* God, encounter with
Energy, 127
  Kundalini, 238; *see also* Buddhism, Tantric
  psychic, 254
  religious, 215, 237, 238
Enlightenment, spiritual, 90, 94, 102-105, 165; *see also* Buddha; Buddhism
Episcopal church, 49, 54, 55, 62
  renewal movement in, 172, 175-176
  religious experience as factor in growth of, 163, 167, 172
Epistemology, 148, 151-154, 254; *see also* Knowledge
Epistles of Saint Paul, 41; *see also* Paul; Saints/Saintliness
Epoché, 185, 187, 195; *see also* Phenomenology, bracketing of suppositions in
Equality; *see* Egalitarianism
Eroticism, 489-491; *see also* Mystical experience, gender differences in; Religious experience,
  ecstatic
ESP, 170, 171, 178; *see also* Clairvoyance; Phenomena; paranormal
Esteem, 428-430; *see also* Self-esteem
Eternalist theory, 100
Ethnography, 477; *see also* Narrative; Self-report
Ethology, 447, 448; *see also* Attachment theory
Eucharist, 33, 34, 39, 237, 483-484, 547, 548; *see also* Body of Christ
Evangelism, 50, 59, 63, 66, 547
  as factor in church growth, 175-176
Event, 8, 378; *see also* Religious experience, as event
Evidential experience; *see* Religious experience, evidential
Evil, 58, 179n5; *see also* Devil; Religious experience, evil
  attribution of, 424-425, 438
  bodily, 105, 106; *see also* Body
  root of, 77
Evolution, 202, 239; *see also* Evolutionary biology; Social Darwinism
Evolutionary biology, 201, 205, 222; *see also* Ontogeny; Phylogeny
Existence, 64, 79, 92, 93; *see also* Being;

Existence continued
Reality
affirmation of, 103
causes of; *see* Buddhism, Twelve Causes of Existence in
desire for, 101
dimensions of, 96, 97, 125
experiential, 101
heavenly, 93
illusory, 125
individual finite, 146
non-existence; *see* Self, vs. Non-Self
phenomenal, 96, 103, 104, 125
study of, 101
truth of, 104; *see also* Buddhism, Four Noble Truths of
social, 161
Existential psychology, 197; *see also* Phenomenological psychology
Experience; *see also* Mystical experience; Religious experience
archaic, 203, 222; *see also* Heredity, archaic
behavior and, 8, 378-396
bipolar nature of, 499
charismatic; *see* Charismatic religion; Religious experience, charismatic
comprehension of, 188
cognitive, 193
credulity of, 152, 153
definitions of, 2-3, 275, 318-319, 378-379
direct-indirect, 187-189; *see also* Phenomenology
ecstatic, 135, 169, 179n6
denigration of, 183, 184
dualism in, 133; *see also* Dualism/Duality; Opposites
identification of, 155-157
indescribable; *see* Mystical experience, ineffable
intentionality of, 218, 409-410
interpretations of, 152, 155, 188
knowledge and, 158; *see also* Epistemology
labeling of, 173
linked to religion, 3
meaningful, 147
mediation of, *see* Imitation; Religious experience, mediation of; Religious instruction
metaphysical, 100, 145
modification of, 185, 193
near-death, 496
neutral, 151
nonobservable, 378; *compare* Behavior, observable
rational, 179, 186
numinous; *see* Mystical experience, numinous
Oedipal/pre-Oedipal, 224, 257-259
ontogenetic, 201; *see also* Ontogeny; Phylogeny
ordinary, 124, 125, 147, 179n2
out-of-body, 496
paranormal, 170; *see also* Channeling; Religious experiences, psychic occurrences
peak, 170-171
personal, 179, 184
raw, 155
religious, defined, 162
sensory; *see* sensation/senses
sexual, 207; *see also* Behavior, sexual; Sexuality
shaped by concepts and beliefs, 155
shaped by psychic processes, 254; *see also* Psyche
shaped by sociocultural influences, 576
spiritual,
empirical/phenomenological analysis of, 190
essential steps in, 190-191
meaning units in, 190-191
subjective, 184, 319
supranormal, 413-415, 417
total, 410
unitary, 179n2
unverifiable, 100
vicarious; *see* Experience, direct-indirect; Religious experience, second-hand
Extinction; *see* Buddhism, Four Noble Truths of
Extrasensory perception; *see* ESP

Fairy-tales, 236; *see also* Folklore; Wish-fulfillment
Faith; *see also* Religious belief; Religious concepts
as protest, 64
as way to salvation, 51, 465
autonomous, 292
Buddhist, 92, 106
fantasy and, 65
feeling of growth in, 169
Hindu, 136
inimical to reason, 220
Islamic, 75, 77, 78, 462
mature-naive, 284, 584
personal, 201, 436

philosophical justification of, 354
seat of, 239
self-esteem and, 289, 290; *see also* Identity, crisis of
stages in development, 299
"stepping out" in, 195
transcendence and, 298-299
Faith traditions, major, listed; 1
Fallacy, genetic, 217; *see also* Ontogeny; Phylogeny
Family, 57; *see also* Home; Parents/Parenting
nuclear, 524, 538
patriarchal, 525
purity laws for, 15
Fanaticism, 81; *see also* Politics, activism and
Fantasy; *see also* Desire; Libido; Wish-fulfillment
autism and, 259-260
dreams and, 206, 236, 247
faith and, 65
models of, 259-260
Fascination, 186; *see also* Mysterium fascinans
Fasting, 18, 77; *see also* Religious practices
Fate, 215; *see also* Karma
Father; *see also* Father-God; God; Parents/Parenting
and son rivalry, 204, 206, 209, 210, 212; *see also* Oedipus Complex
death of, 209, 263; *see also* Parricide
figures, 209, 211, 216, 236
primal, 216
omnipotent, 214
protector, 215, 216
spiritual, 525
Father-God, 210, 216, 222; *see also* Father; God
Fatima, 35, 42; *see also* Miracles
Feelings, 8, 99, 129, 141, 146, 168 ; *see also* Emotion; Intuition
as core of religion, 123, 147, 195
descriptions of, 214, 215; *see also* Emotion, plausible descriptions of; Religious experience, descriptions of
dream exploration and, 236
elements of, 99, 571-574
emotion, contrasted with, 155
feminine–masculine, 240
infantile, 215
mythical, 573, 594
numinous, 232, 243; *see also* Mystical experience, numinous
sui generis, 571; *see also* Religious experience, *sui generis* quality of
Female; *see* Body, political uses of; Gender; Menstruation; *Mikvah*; Women; Religious experience, gender differences in
Feminist theology, Judaic, 25, 29, 524; *see also* Feminist theory; Goddess; Liturgy, feminist innovation in; Witchcraft
Feminist theory, 10, 24, 42, 273; *see also* Feminist theology
definition of, 520-521
methodology in, 521
Fetishism, 269
Feuerbach's Thesis, 201, 217
Folklore, analysis of, 398, 405, 413-415; *see also* Belief, folk; Folk religion; Legend; Myth
Folk religion, 32, 35
philosophy and, 92
Footwashing, 482-483; *see also* Religious experience, physical displays of; Rituals
Formal Operational Reasoning Test (FORT), 322
Forgiveness, 18, 173 ,194; *see also* Atonement
Foundationalism, 154, 158; *see also* Empiricism; Reality, foundational
Four, as mystical number, 243; *see also* Numbers
Four Noble Truths of Buddhism, 90, 95-105
Free-association, 183, 235, 246, 313; *see also* Freudianism; History, personal
Freedom of worship, 251n8; *see also* Oppression; Worship
Freud, Anna, 222
Freud, Jacob, 204
Freud, Sigmund, 59; *see also* Freudianism; Religion, Freudian critique of career,
as cryptobiologist, 203
Jung and, 203-204; 234; *see also* Jung; Jungianism
Darwin's influence on, 202, 203
Lamarck's influence on, 210, 466
ontogenetic contribution of, 214; *see also* Ontogeny; Phylogeny
preliminary works of, 207-209
religious ideas of, 216-218
seminal contributions, 384, 470
childhood/youth,
ambition of, 202
anti-Semitic experiences, 204, 205
father-son conflict during, 205, 213-214, 216
personal suffering of, 221
religious experiences of, 204-205, 214-216

Freudianism, 6, 7, 110; *see also* Freud, Sigmund; Religion, Freudian critique of
analogy use in, 206, 207, 220
attachment theory and, 465-468
authority of the past and, 203
civilization theory, 200-202, 208-209
complementary postulates, 205-207
defense mechanisms, 207; *see also* Defense mechanisms
dream theory, 205-207
ego; *see* Ego
father-son conflict; *see* Oedipus Complex
free-association, 183, 235, 246
Jungianism, contrasted to, 203, 204, 234, 235
id; *see* Id
libido, centrality of, 203, 204, 234
Oedipus Complex, *see* Oedipus Complex
parricide theory, 209, 210, 212-213; *see also* Oedipus complex
political aspects of, 204-205
regression, 139
renunciation of instincts, 218-221
stages of growth,
anal stage, 257
oral stage, 257
phallic stage, 257
super-ego; *see* Superego
wish-fulfillment theory; *see* Wish-fulfillment
Friday sermons, 73, 74; *see also* Islam
Friends, 45, 169; *see also* Relationships; Significant other
Fundamentalism/Fundamentalists, 49, 52, 62, 63, 66; *see also* Conservatives, religious
cognitive narrowness of, 324-325
Future of an Illusion, 203, 208

Gautama, Siddhartha (Buddha), 90; *see also* Buddha, The
Gays; *see* Lesbians/Gays; *see also* Attitudes, toward Homosexuality; Gender; Homosexuality; Sexuality
Gender, 10, 28, 91; *see also* Female; Men; Religious experience, gender differences in; Women
differences, 521
absent father and, 523, 524
mothering and, 523
identity, 239, 240
inequality, 520-521, 524; *see also* Body, political uses of; Power, distribution of
sociocultural effects on, 489-491, 521
General Psychopathology, 188
General Social Survey (GSS), 40
Genetic fallacy, 217; *see also* Heredity; Ontogeny; Phylogeny
Gestalt, 337
Gita; see *Bhagavad-Gita*
Glaubenslehre, 146
Glossolalia, 9, 172, 175, 487-488; *see also* Speech
as attachment behavior, 459-461
as learned behavior, 385-386, 425, 432
anxiety crises and, 460
baby-talk aspect of, 46-461
God, 3, 10, 11, 12, 13, 37, 65, 165; *see also* Allah; Buddha; Christ; Father-God; Godhead
appreciation of, 136
awareness of,
through mystical encounters, 261-262, 547, 548, 569
through God-consciousness, 147
through perceived presence/revelation of, 16, 22, 24, 41, 150-152, 169, 170, 191, 192, 550-551
spoken revelation, 166, 169, 179n2
visionary revelation, 21, 37, 145, 150, 167, 169, 179n2
behaviors attributed to; *see also* Religious experience, misattributions of
activity, 153
actual, 455
bestowing of blessings, 24
causality, 361
healing, 429
punishment, 280
response to prayer, 232, 233
belief in, 222; *see also* Religious belief
conceptualization of,
archetypal, 201, 212, 223-225
asexual, 477, 478-481; *compare* God, images of, anthropomorphized; God, sexuality and
as object, 137, 153, 281
as real, 384
cognitive, 280
feminine principle of, 20, 42; *see also* Goddess; Mary
finite-infinite, 572
Godhead and, 20-21, 126, 232
Holy Ghost/Spirit, 232
monotheistic, 478
omnipotent, 153, 280
omniscient, 153

projected essence of man, 201, 217, 384
Self of, 137
contemplation of, 132-133; *see also* Meditation; Prayer; Religious experience, facilitation of; Yoga
existence of,
evidence for,
mystical experience, 159n4
religious experience, 154
probable, 154
images of, 25, 40-44, 212, 216, 237, 238, 251n8, 260, 454; *see also* Icon
anthropomorphized, 62, 279, 280
embodied, 126, 477-478; *compare* God, conceptualizations of, asexual
child-parent dynamics and, 281, 468
cross-cultural differences in, 462-465
gender differences in, 489-491
human images, contrasted with, 477
internalized, 279
dreams and, 236, 237, 238
positive-negative images,
angry, 461, 478, 574
dark, 238
forgiving, 279, 280, 436
jealous, 461
just, 279-280
merciful, 238
roles attributed to,
divine partner, 410-411
father-mother, 43, 210, 216, 222, 223, 465
friend, 223
lover, 43; *see also* God, sexuality and
meaning giver, 433-435
significant other, 176
sovereign, 77
surrogate parent
Truth holder, 125
Wholly Other, 186; *see also* Mysterium
individual's relationship to, 15, 50, 144, 452-455
adoption of God role, 409, 410-411, 416-417; *see also* Role/RoleTheory
attachment behavior and, 297, 365-366, 453-457
awareness of; *see* God, awareness of
belief in, 222
devotion to, 132, 136
faith in, 136, 239
fear of,
abandonment by, 26
punishment by, 280
love for, 452-453
schema and, 365
self-esteem correlated with, 454
self-realization through, 37, 124, 136, 137
surrender to, 133-135; *see also* Salvation; Submission; Surrender
union with, 132-137, 140, 167, 173, 212, 261-262; *see also* Unity
knowledge of, 133,
personal; *see* God, awareness of
scriptural,
codified in Torah, 14
names of, 21; *see also* Absolute, The Old Testament, 461
paths to, 22, 135; *see also* Path
sexuality and, 4, 478-481
son of, 212; *see also* Jesus Christ; Son-religion
Virgin Mary and, 479
will of, 19, 39, 169; *compare* Will, human
names of, 21, 126; *see also* Absolute, The; Names and forms
Goddess, 134, 251n8, 479, 527-528; *see also* Divine Mother; Feminist theology; Feminist theory; God, feminine principle of; Great Mother
GRACE scale, 43, 44
Great Awakenings, *see* Revivals
Great Mother, 251n7; *see also* Archetypes; Divine Mother; Goddess
Grief, 263; *see also* Mourning; Object, loss of
Group dynamics, 399-400; *see also* Community, sense of; Interaction, social; Religious experience, collective; Religious experience, group dynamics in
Guilt, 50, 51, 63, 297, 209, 222; *see also* Conscience

Habit; *see also* Behavior, learned; Personality, obsessive; Rituals
dull, 148
reinforcement of, 388, 389-392; *see also* Operant conditioning
religious observance and, 58, 67, 388
Hajj (pilgrimage), 77
Halacha (spiritual path), 14-19; *see also* Judaism; Path
Hallucinations/Hallucinogens, 60, 189, 340; *see also* Altered states of consciousness; Psychedelics; Religious experience, facilitation of

Happiness, 116, 171, 176, 221; *see also* Life, quality of
context of, 426
individual, 208
worldly, 132
Hasidic movement; *see* Judaism
Hedonism; 208; *see also* Desire; Pleasure Principle
Healing,
ritual, 26, 27
miraculous, 194
Pentecostal belief in, 172, 175
spiritual, 21
Heaven, 44, 132; *see also* Nirvana; Paradise
Hegemony, Western, 73, 74, 75
Hell, 81
Heredity, 201, 203; *see also* Characteristics, human; Genetic fallacy; Instincts
archaic, 210
biological, 222; *see also* Evolutionary biology
phylogenetic, 201; *see also* Ontogeny; Phylogeny
Hermeneutics, 147
Heterosexuality, 521; *see also* Behavior, sexual; Mating; Sexuality
Hijra (migration), 80, 84
Hinduism, 5, 90, 91, 248; *see also* Mystical experience; Transcendence; Yoga
as religion of transcendence, 122-123
attachment behavior in, 464
belief diversity in, 122-123, 124
branches of,
Tantric, 127, 132, 133, 134
Vedantic, 125, 127
Vedic, 133
concepts in,
afflictions principle, 128, 130-131, 132, 136, 138, 139, 140
bondage of spirit principle, 123-124, 127-128, 132
dualism, reconciliation of, 124, 133, 134, 137; *see also* Opposites
enlightenment paths, 464
liberation as goal of, 123-124, 128
surrender principle, 132, 133-135
theism vs. non-theism, 123
stories in, 126, 127; *see also* Folklore; Religious instruction, story forms in
transcendent practices in, 123, 124-127, 135, 464
mysticism, 140
Yoga, 127-141; *see also* Yoga; *Yoga Sutras*
Hispanics, 32
History, 85, 90, 91; *see also* Prehistory
authority of, 203
bridging gaps in, 213
criticism of, 146
narratives in; *see* Narrative
of religion, 219
of science, 151
personal, 233, 235, 333
primeval, 221
reformative, 76
restorative, 76
transmission of, 210, 211; *see also* Culture, transmission of
Holism, 499, 501, 523, 537
Holy, The, 237; *see also* Numinous, The
Holy Eucharist; *see* Eucharist
Holy war; *see* Jihad
Home,
as spiritual path, 23
fundamentalist, 63; *see also* Fundamentalism
religious atmosphere of, 294, 301; *see also* Religious instruction
Homo duplex, 505, 510
Homosexuality, 24, 31, 44, 61, 355; *see also* Attitudes; Heterosexuality; Lesbians/Gays
Human development, 201, 202, 203, 214; *see also* Child, development of; Personality, development of
Human nature,
growth-oriented, 184
intrinsically good, 184
self-determined, 184
Human rights, 74, 85; *see also* Oppression
Hypnosis; *see* Self-hypnosis; Trance

Icon, 236, 237; *see also* God, images of; Idols/Idolatry; Symbol
Id, 203, 206, 210, 211, 226n3; *see also* Ego; Freudianism; Superego
Idappaccayata (conditionality), 100
Ideal,
cultural, 220
masculine, 220
person, 92, 93, 94
psychological, 220
Ideas; *see also* Imagination; Phenomenology
abstract, 212, 319
as illusions, 216-218
desire and, 216-218
development of, 216-218
innate, 384

meaningless, 173
religious, 200
shared, 174
undermining of, 335
value of, 200-201
Identification; *see also* Identity; Object relations
God-representations and, 201, 212, 223, 224
personal, religious, 204
Identity; *see also* Identification; Personality; Role; Self
Arabs and, 81
collective, 59, 486; *see also* Religious experience, collective
consolidation of, 65
crisis, 270, 288, 289, 290
female-male, 491
gendered, 239, 240
group, 59
Hindus and, 124
Muslims and, 83
of Self, 137
true, 124
Ideograms, 186
Ideology, 62, 76, 83, 85, 111, 403; *see also* Worldview
Idols/Idolatry, 41, 64, 225n1; *see also* Icon
Ignorance, 79, 100, 101, 102, 105, 130, 133, 237;*compare* Enlightenment; Knowledge
Ijtihad (individual interpretation), 78
Illusions, 6, 189, 221
epistemological theory of, 125
extinction of, 105
of attachment, 92t
of civilization, 200-201
of immortal Self, 98
of pleasure, 108
wish-fulfillment and, 206t
world as, 125, 496
Image; *see also* God, images of; Icon; Idols; Self-image
concrete, 41
effects of, on attitudes/behavior, 43
hypnotic-guided, 235
matrimonial, 41
mnemonic, 210
mystical, 237
self-effacing, 238
Imagination; *see also* Ideas; Image
active, 247, 249
analogical, 4, 40, 41; *see also* Analogy
Casey's study of, 188
Catholic, 41, 42, 65
comic, 4; *see also* Jokes
dialectical, 41, 44; *see also* Dualism; Opposites
Muslim, 83; *see also* Islam
Protestant, 65
sacramental, 41, 45
Imago; *see* Image; Ideal person
Imitation, 148, 386, 393; *see also* Experience, mediation of; Role-playing; Role-taking
Imitation of Christ, The, 393, 411
Immortality, 215; *see also* Self, immortal
Impermanence, principle of, 95, 96, 97, 100, 102, 134
Impurity, bodily, 15-17; *see also* Bath; Body; Purification
Incest, 209; *see also* Oedipus Complex; Taboo
Individual; *see also* Actor/Agent; Self
authority of, 67; *see also* Autonomy
salvation, 92, 93
self-consciousness and, 146
social status of, 399; *see also* Actor/Agent
Individualism, 35, 38
Individuation, 240, 241, 242, 243, 244; *see also* Integration, psychological; Personality, Psychospiritual development
Industrialization, 55, 57, 82
Infant, 9, 215, 254; *see also* Caregiver; Child; Wish, infantile
Inheritance; *see* Heredity
Insanity, 206, 236; *see also* Delusion; *see also* Mental health
Instincts, human
renunciation of, 79, 208, 210, 212, 218-221; *see also* Freudianism; Renunciation
Institution-building practices, 163, 172; *see also* Change, institutional
Institutions, religious, 167; *see also* Change, institutional; Church
Integration,
psychological, 139, 240; *see also* Individuation
psychospiritual, 248; *see also* Psychospiritual development; Unity
Intellect, 133, 212, 220, 221, 285; *see also* Ratiocination; Rationality; Reason
Interaction, social, 163, 177, 193, 537; *see also* Group dynamics; Relationships
International Journal for the Psychology of Religion, 31
Interpretation of Dreams, 206, 234
International Social Survey Project, 40
International Study of Values, 40, 44;

Interpersonal relationships; *see* Relationships
Interviews, 187, 192 194, 263; *see also* History, personal; Self-report; Tradition, biographical
Intrapsychic dynamics, 221, 255-256
Introjection, 256
Introspection, 183, 184, 186
Intuition, 166, 572, 573
Irreality, 192; *see also* Illusion; Phenomenology; Reality
I-Sense, 128, 136, 139; *see also* Buddhism
ISKON, 263
Islam, 5; *see also* Mecca; Muslims
  Allah/God in, 72, 76
  emancipatory politics and, 82-85
  existential questions in, 82
  historical vs. real, 85
  individual's role in, 75, 80, 84
  modernity and, 72, 73, 78, 81, 82, 83
  official vs. reform, 73, 74, 75
  principles of, 77, 78
  sacred vs. temporal in, 5, 72, 75, 79
  sects,
    Hanafite,78
    Hanbalite, 78
    Shi'a, 73
    Sufism, 84, 510
    Sunni, 74
  worldview in, 75, 76
Israel, 14, 79, 225n1

Jahiliya (ignorance/darkness), 79, 84
James, William, 3-7, 50, 57-60, 108, 144-149, 164, 166, 172-175; *see also* Religion, definitions of; Religious experience, evaluation of
Jesus Christ, 35, 53, 453, 479, 482, 483; *see also* Christ; Messiah; Son-religion real presence of, 547, 548; *see also* God, awareness of
Jews, 13, 16, 22, 23, 157, 429; *see also* Judaism; Judeo-Christian religion
  as embodied people, 492-493
  body image and, 15-17; 492; *see also* Mikvah
  dreams of, 237
  religious values and, 62
Jihad, 75, 77, 79
Jivatman (Self), 124; see also *Anatman; Atman*;
Janana marga (path of wisdom), 464
Jokes, 206; *see also* Imagination, comic
Joseph, 479
Journey, religious, 78-82, 84; *see also* Migration
Joyful noise, 487-488
Judaism, 72, 211; *see also* Jews; Judeo-Christian religion
  as a living religion, 25
  body's role in, 481-482
  branches of,
    Conservative, 13
    Hasidic, 13, 16, 20, 21
    Lubavitcher, 16, 23
    Orthodox, 13, 492
    New Age, 23
    Reform, 13, 431
  communal worship in, 18; *see also* Community, sense of
  halachic, 14, 17, 28
  Mikvah, 15-17
  mystical tradition in, 205
  Passover, 18
  rabbis, 13, 538
  reconstructions of, 13
  relational aspects of, 18
  Talmud and, 18, 19; *see also* Law; Scripture; Text
  Torah and; *see also* Law; Scripture; Text
    cognitive element of, 19
    laws codified in, 14
  normative element of, 19
  study of, 18, 19, 22, 23, 29
Judeo-Christian religion, 101, 125, 179n4, 221; *see also* Judaism; Christianity
  body's role in, 477; *see also* Body, as religious instrument
Jung, Carl G., 38, 58, 65, 67; *see also* Jungianism; Freudianism
  Ancient Greeks' influence on, 248
  feminist critique of, 250n1
  Freud and, 203-204, 234
  religious heritage of, 233
  transpersonal theory and, 508-509
  youth of, 233-234
Jungianism, 6, 7, 90
  archetypes, 240; *see also* Archetypes, Jungian
  Freudianism contrasted with, 203-204, 234-235
  dreamwork; *see* Dreams, studies of, Jungian
  psychological theory and, 238
  rejection of Freud's libido theory, 204
Jung's Quest for Wholeness, 244
Justice, 73, 77, 85, 111; *see also* Jihad; Law
Justification, doctrine of, 58; *see also* Doctrines

Kaivalya (freedom), 128, 129, 138, 141
Kala (devourer of time), 134
Kali, Goddess, 134, 135; *See also* God, feminine principle of; Goddess
Kama (sensual pleasure), 101
Karma (destiny); *see* Buddhism, *karma* in
Karma marga (path of duty), 464
Klesas (afflictions); *see* Afflictions, Hindu principle of
Knowledge, 3, 8, 167; *see also* Cognition; Epistemology
  as merit, 94
  authoritative, 3
  Buddhists and, 91, 93, 94, 108
  complete, 129
  empirical theory of, 150
  experience as basis of, 68, 150, 156; *see also* Experience; Phenomenology; Reality
  Hindus and, 124
  Muslims and, 76, 77
  of God, 133; *see also* God, awareness of
Koran, *see* Quran, the
Krishna, 126, 133, 134, 135

Laity; *see also* names of individual religious denominations
  Buddhist, 105, 117
  Catholic, 39, 45, 46
Lamp of Umm Hashim, 80
Language, 3, 66, 73, 99, 106, 158; *see also* Narrative; "Semantics of desire"; Religious experience, descriptions of; Text
  "abracadabra," 412
  as shaper of thinking, 433
  attributions and, 433
  communal, 178
  dialogue, 403
  double meanings in, 206-207
  effects on religious experience, 577
  foundational reality and, 577
  French, 73
  God language, 569
  inadequacy of; *see* Mystical experience, ineffable; Religious experience, indescribable
  Latin, 35, 50
  literal, 283, 299, 323
  metaphorical, 259, 279, 285, 286, 287, 321, 583-584
    gender metaphors, 480-481, 489-491
  metaphysical, 99
  mythical, 573
  natural expression of, in religion, 155
  of probability, 159n4
  sexual, 425
  social interaction and, 178, 400-401
  unequal to experience, 576, 577, 584
Last Supper, 209
Law,
  religious, 14, 15; *see also* Commandments; Moses; Ten Commandments
  Law of the Twelve Causes of Existence; *see* Buddhism
  Law, The, 92
Laying on of hands, 484-485; *see also* Religious experience, physical displays of; Religious practices
Leadership Training Institute, 176
Learning; *see also* Behavior, learned
  conceptualization of, 387-393
  paradigms for, 384-387
  social, theories of, 8, 172, 173-174, 392-393
Legends; *see* Bible stories; Fairy-tales; Folklore; Myths
Lesbians/Gays, 4, 13, 24-29, 31; *see also* Gender; Homosexuality
  goddess worship and, 479; *see also* Feminist theology; Goddess; Worship
  witchcraft and; *see* Witchcraft
Lesser Buddhism; *see* Buddhism, Old
Levant, The, 80, 84
Libido, 204,
  desire, contrasted with, 234
  dreams and, 233
  Freudian centrality of, 204
  Jungian rejection of, 204
  transcendence of, 248
Life; *see also* Birth; Church life; Experience; Right living
  cycles of, 241, 298-302
  eternal; *see* Heaven; Nirvana
  mental, 186, 202
  mystery of, 2, 15
  phases of, 65, 241, 242
  politics of, 82
  previous, 111-112; *see also* Karma; Samsara
  quality of, 148, 176
    test for, 154
  temporalization of, 209
  unity inherent in, 575; *see also* Union; Unity
Lifestyles, 355
Literature, as source of religious experience, 148

Liturgy,
Catholic, 35, 46
feminist innovation in, 25, 27; *See also* Feminist theology
Logos, 220; *see also* Word, The
Lord, The, 195, 206, 233; *see also* God; Christ; Jesus Christ
Lotus Sutra, 95, 116
Love, 41, 132, 134, 167, 269
adult, 451, 451
devotional, 525; *see also* God, individual's relationship to, devotion to; Religious practices, devotional; Yoga, devotional
of God, 452-453
perfect, 186
physical, 487
selfless, 561
LSD, 138; *see also* Psychedelics; Religious experience, facilitation of
Luther, Martin, 5, 50, 51, 58, 60, 64, 149
Lutherans, 50, 54, 63

Madhyamakasastra, 103
Mahabhrarata, 122, 126, 138
Mandala, 243, 412; *se also* Archetypes; Symbol
Mandukya Upanishad, see Philosophy, Upanisadic; Upanishads
Marian cult, 42; *see also* Mary
Marriage, 33, 44, 65; *see also* Family; Home; Parents/Parenting
inner, 240; *see also* Individuation
mystical, 248
Mary, Mother of Jesus, 35, 42, 46
as feminine side of God, 42
Mary Myth, The, 453
Mass, Catholic, 34, 35, 210; *see also* Worship
Mating, 451; *see also* Behavior, sexual; Marriage
Matter, physical; 202, 250
Meal, sacrificial, 209; *see also* Sacrifice; Totemism
Meaning,
as basic human need, 428-430
cross-cultural, 237
reframing of, 361-362
search for, 429
subjective, 161
units, 190
Mecca, 73, 77, 84; *see also* Islam
Mediation, 37, 45, 109, 117, 577; *see also* Experience, mediation of; Reality, mediation of; Medium, spiritual; Religious experience, facilitation of
Meditation, 21, 75, 90, 93, 104, 105, 129, 173, 188, 245; *see also* God, contemplation of; Yoga;
autonomy through, 531-532
role-taking and, 412, 416
Medium, spiritual, 137, 170; *see also* Mystical experience; Mystics
Memorat, 413-415; *see also* Folklore; Narrative
Memory, 105, 106, 128, 165
affective, 364-366
autobiographical, 338
childhood, 216
collective, 165
dreams and, 338-342
emotional effects on, 335
healing of, 194
implicit, 340
learning styles and, 327
mood congruence and, 332, 333
recall patterns in, 336, 337
repressed; *see* Repression
schematic, 325-326, 363, 364-366; *see also* Schema
systems, 314, 315, 326, 327, 330, 363-366
episodic, 326-329, 343
semantic, 326-329, 343
traces, 210, 213, 216
unconscious, 209, 210, 211
Menstruation, 15-17, 477, 527, 530; *see also* Mikvah; Purification
Mental health, 28, 63, 233, 264, 421
Mental modifications, 128, 129; *see also* Yoga
Messiah, The, 211
Men; *see also* Family, patriarchal; Father; Misogyny; Power, distribution of; Religious experience, gender differences in
archetypal man, 90
self-conscious, 148
feeling-oriented, 240
Metaphor; *see* Language, metaphorical
Metaphysical experience; *see* Experience
Metaphysics, 145
Metapsychology, 201, 202
Methodist Episcopal Church, 56
Methodists, 55, 56, 63, 192
Method of Agreement, Mill's, 101
Methodology; *see also* Model; Paradigm; Religious experience, evaluation of
context-independent, 89
empirical; *see* Empiricism
phenomenological, 187-189, 193

positivistic, 162, 185; *see also* Positivism
Migration, 80, 84; *see also* Journey, religious
Mikvah (ritual bath), 15, 16, 28, 29, 485-487; *see also* Menstruation
Military activity, 79, 82, 84; *see also* Jihad; War
Mind, 92, 128, 129, 131, 132, 135; *see also* Body; Consciousness; Unconscious, the
Hilgard's trilogy of, 356
intuitive vs. rational, 509-510
pious, 582
Mind-cure, 148; *see also* Psychoanalysis; Psychotherapy
Minyan (quorum), 28n1, 488
Miracles/Miraculous, the, 34, 35, 36, 45, 172, 175, 425
Misattribution, 359-360, 363, 427; *see also* Attribution
Misogyny, 528
Mission/Missionaries,34, 41, 46, 55, 80
Mitzvet (good deeds),14, 15, 16
Mitzvot (religious obligations), 486
Model; *see also* Methodology; Paradigm; Religious experience, evaluation of, models for; Theory
biological, 255
developmental structure (Wilber's), 500-501, 510-512
Duquesne, 196
dynamic-dialectical (Washburn's), 10, 501, 510-512
ethological (Bowlby's), 447-450, 470; *see also* Attachment theory
interactionist, 9, 400-405
interdisciplinary, 162, 177
learning models, 384-387
Lee's, 548-554; *see also* Religious instruction
operant conditioning, 389-392
perceptual, 9, 405-413
Pruyser's, 259-260
sociological, 161, 177-179
S-O-R, 8, 380-383
structural-analytical, 9, 399-400
Modes of Appearing, 193, 194, 195; *see also* Observation; Phenomena
Modernism, influence on religion, 73, 78, 80, 81, 82, 83; *see also* Postmodernism
Monks, 92, 103, 105, 117
Monotheism, 72, 211, 212; *see also* Theism
Moral code, 52; *see also* Mores; Morality; Values
Morality, 31, 44, 58, 61, 68, 73, 80, 87, 93, 109, 145, 208, 219
conventional, 261
experiential basis of, 384-385
Moral Philosophy, 56
Mores, 61; *see also* Norms; Taboo
Mormons, 35, 46, 55
attracted to Catholicism, 36
Moses, 19, 25, 211, 225n1, 226n4
Moses and Monotheism, 206, 211, 213, 221, 225n5, 226n6
Mother, 10, 215, 216, 258, 259, 262, 265; *see also* Divine Mother; Great Mother; Mary
bad-good, 260-261, 265
mother figure, 236
mother structure, 300
rejection of, 532
worship of, 259
Motivation, 110; *see also* Attitudes, motivational; Behavior, learned; Attribution
drive model for, 467-468; *see also* Drives/Drive theory; Personality, as drive-based system
religious, 225, 428
sexual-aggressive, 204, 211; *see also* Oedipus Complex
Mourning, 263, 463, 488; *see also* Grief; Object, loss of
Multivariate analysis, 176, 274; *see also* Religious experience, evaluation of
Mundaka Upanishad, 124; *see also* Philosophy, Upanisadic; Upanishads
Murder, 209, 211; *see also* Parricide; Violence
Music, religious,
hymns, 90
social aspects of, 174
Muslims, 72-75; *see also* Islam
activism and, 76, 77, 79
during World War II, 79, 82, 83
religious duties of, 77
Mutuality, 425, 508
Myers-Briggs Type Indicator (MBTI), 504, 513
Mysterium, 186, 235; *see also* Psyche
fascinans, 186, 574, 575
tremendum, 186, 574, 575
Mystical experience, 11, 13, 30, 166-170; *see also* Ecstasy; Mystics; Religious experience, facilitation of
anticipated stress and, 591-594
as third form of religious expression, 178
attributed to external forces, 423, 424
belief in God and, 159n4
benefits of, 342

Mystical experience continued
childhood trauma and, 263
communion and, 261-262
conceptualization of,
context-dependency of, 177
divine-diabolical, 424, 425
extroversive-introversive, 60, 140, 167, 342, 575
feminine-masculine, 489-491
inward-outward, 167
James's perspective on, 60
one vs. many forms of, 167
Otto's perspective on, 147, 149, 167, 186, 423
theistic-monistic, 167, 170, 179
diverse shaping of, 157
ego loss in, 489
emotional core of, 424
eroticism and, 489-491
evaluation of,
by voice stress, 589, 590
common-core criteria for, 582, 585
comparative study of, 166-167
content analysis of, 582
frequency of, 165, 166, 168, 171
gender differences in, 489-491
Greeley's measurement of, 170-172
models of, 167-168
substantive approach to, 167-168
typology of church-sect mysticism in, 179n1
verbal ability and, 342-343
visualization ability and, 342-343
Eastern, 107-108, 158
encounters in, 261-262
"eyes-closed" type, 167
facilitation of; *see* Religious experience, facilitation of
higher type of, 261
holistic views of, 167, 170, 189
ineffable, 60, 171, 190, 342-343
individualistic nature of, 60
Jewish, 20-24
mainstreaming of, 170
mental health, 189, 421
mutuality in, 424-425
mystical union and, 167
mystics' disagreement about, 140
noetic quality of, 60, 190
nonreligious type, 424, 436
numinous, 147, 149, 167, 171, 178, 179n2, 232, 243, 249, 569-570, 574
origins of, 263-265
paranormal aspects of, 170
personality dynamics and, 262-263
Protestant, 60
psychic experience, contrasted with, 424; *see also* Religious experience, psychic occurrences and
religious experience, contrasted with, 149, 157, 166-168, 423, 424
schizophrenia, compared to, 262
second-hand, 147, 189; *see also* Experience, direct-indirect
shamanic, 414, 415
sociology and, 177-179
supernatural power and, 423, 424
transiency of, 60, 190
unanimity of, 167
unmediated, 157; *see also* Mediation; Religious experience, facilitation of
Mysticism; *see* Mystical experience
Mystics, 20, 21, 28, 166, 140 148, 157, 158, 178, 179, 235, 249, 342-343, 522, 547; *see also* Mystical experience; Spiritualists
Myth, 201, 209, 236, 507; *see also* Folklore; Parables

Nafs (self), 77
Nagarjuna, 98, 103, 106; *see also* Buddhism
Names and forms, in Hinduism, 123, 126, 136; *see also* God, names of
Narcissism; *see* Personality, narcissistic
Narrative, 271-272, 338-343; *see also* Consciousness, narratized Self and; Ethnography; Folklore;*Memorat*; Tradition, biographical
development of, 329-330, 335
male-dominated, 520
Nastitva (non-being), 92, 93; *see also* Being; Existence
National Opinion Research Center, 40
Nature, 65, 215, 216, 217, 218
Nature-Nurture debate; *see* Ontogeny; Phylogeny
Needs, human, 100, 106, 255, 290, 380, 428-430
Negation, 96, 97, 103, 104, 139; *see also* Emptiness; Nirvana; Nothingness
Neurosis; *see also* Freudianism; Oedipus Complex; Personality, obsessive
cultural neurosis, 202, 211
private vs. universal, 211, 219
psychodynamics of, 220
religion, relationship to, 202, 206, 211
transference neurosis, 202; *see also* Coun-

tertransference
Niddah (impurity), 17, 485, 486; *see also* Bath; Mikvah; Purification
Nihilism, 99, 103; *see also* Annihilationist theory
Nirvana, 91, 92, 93, 107, 108, 110, 111, 113-115, 173; *see also* Emptiness; Karma; Samsara
Nirvija (objectless *Samadhi*), 130, 140; *see also* Samadhi
Niyama (devotionals), 129; *see also* Yoga, devotional; Religious practices, devotional
Non-attachment, 136; *see also* Afflictions; Attachment; Clinging
Non-dualism, 137; *see also* Dualism; Opposites
Non-religious persons, 63, 301; *compare* Atheists
Non-Self , 97-98, 99, 100; *see also* Negation; Nirvana; Self
Norms, 109, 241; *see also* Mores; Taboo
  heterosexual, 526; *see also* Heterosexuality
NORC Survey, 171, 178
Nothingness, 166, 167; *see also* Emptiness; Negation; Nirvana
Noumena, 175; *see* Mystical experience, numinous; Supernatural, The
Numbers,
  mystical, 20
  significance of ten, 17
Numinous, The; *see* Mystical experience, numinous; Holy, The; Sacred, The
Nuns, 31, 105, 148, 238, 249, 490
Nurturing, 10, 531-532; *see also* Child; Parents/Parenting; Significant other

Object; *see also* Object relations; Object relations psychology; Phenomenology
  apprehension of, 291, 497
  bad-good, 260-261, 469
  concrete, 319
  internalized, 224
  loss of, 263, 264; *see also* Grief; Mourning
  Oedipal, 260; *see also* Oedipus Complex
  pre-genital, 260, 262; *see also* Freudianism, stages of growth
  projected, 260; *see also* Projection
  recognition of, 153
  reified, 2
  religious, 153, 481-482
  sacred, 263-265
  satisfying, 261
  supernatural, 262
  transitional, 261
Object relations; *see also* Object; Object relations psychology
  attachment, contrasted with, 468-470
  charismatic relationships and, 524-525
  Buddhism and, 100
  formation of, 254-259
    object-splitting mechanism in, 260-261
  mystical encounter and, 261-262
  maturity of, 256
  primitive, 255
  psychological integration and, 263-265; *see also* Individuation
Object relations psychology, 5, 7, 9, 254-268
  British school of, 258
  theories in,
    approach to religion and, 259-260
  definition of, 254
  psychoanalysis, contrasted with, 254, 255, 256, 257
Objectivity, 100, 202; *compare* Bias, scientific
Observation, 151; *see also* Behavior, observable; Experience, nonobservable
  accessible, 183
  theory-laden, 155
Obsession, 131, 132, 204, 207, 214; *see also* Neurosis; Personality, obsessive; Rituals
Obsessive Actions and Religious Practices, 207
Occult, The, 170-171; *see also* Primitive religion; Supernatural, The
Oedipus Complex, 6, 7, 11; *see also* Freudianism; Parricide
  amplification of, 217-218
  attachment systems and, 465-466
  crossroads of civilization and, 209
  Freud's limited view of, 223
  latent, 233
  personality development and; *see* Personality, development of
  resolution of, 214, 216, 220
  rooted in ontogeny and phylogeny; *see* Ontogeny; Phylogeny
  universality of, 210, 215, 221, 222, 223
Oneness, 5, 132; *see also* Being, ultimate; God, union with; Unity
"On Miracles," 153
On Religion, 145, 571
"On Schoolboy Psychology," 216
Ontogeny, 64, 201, 206, 210, 214, 216, 222, 466; *see also* Phylogeny
Operant conditioning, 389-392; *see also* Behavior, learned

Operational thinking, 269-270; *see also* Piaget; Piagetian paradigm
Opposites, reconciliation of, 10, 241, 248; *see also* Dualism
  as key to religious experience, 503-504, 505, 506, 507
Oppression, 20, 21, 23, 27, 83, 219, 489, 521, 531
Oral stage; *see* Freudianism, stages of growth; Personality, development of
Ordination, 538
Organization, social, 163, 164; *see also* Group dynamics; Society, structure of
Original Sin, 102, 210, 211; *see also* Sin
Orthodoxy, 6, 7, 37, 63, 170
Otto, Rudolf, 147, 149, 167, 186
Overbelief, 149, 172; *see also* God, belief in; Religious belief
"Overview of the Transference Neuroses," 202

Pain, 150, 191, 192, 194; *see also* Suffering
Pancakkhandha (aggregate of existence), 97
Panenhenic mysticism, 167; *see also* Mystical experience; Mystics
Pantheon, Olympian, 248
Papacy, 50, 52; *see also* Catholicism; Popes; Second Vatican Council
Parables, 6, 7, 285-287; *see also* Bible stories; Folklore; Legend; Myth; Narrative
Paradigm, 6, 7; *see also* Model; Theory
  Durkheim's social facts paradigm, 161, 167, 178
  Piagetian, 270, 274, 276
    Goldman's formulation of, 277-278, 279
  psychometric trait paradigm, 272
    shifts, in, 201
  Weber's social definition paradigm, 161
Paradise, 44, 80, 116, 261; *see also* Heaven; Nirvana
Paradox of existence, 162; *see also* Existence
Paramita (perfection); 106, 107; *see also* Perfection; Buddhism
Paranormal experience; 170-171, 176, 238; *see also* Clairvoyance; ESP; Religious experience, psychic occurrences in
Parapraxes, 206; *see also* Imagination, comic; Jokes
Paravairagya (supreme non-attachment), 136; *see also* Emptiness; Negation
Parents/Parenting, 209, 258, 265, 462-464, 455, 469; *see also* Child; Adolescent; Father; Mother
  cross-cultural differences in, 462-465
Parricide, 209, 210, 212-213; *see also* Murder; Oedipus complex
Particularism, 154-157; *see also* Reductionism
Parvati, Goddess, 134; *see also* God, feminine principle of; Goddess
Patanjali's yoga; *see* Yoga, classical
Pathogenesis, human, 204, 211; *see also* Evolutionary biology
Path, The, 76, 90, 93, 95, 102, 134; *see also* Buddhism, Paths in; God, path to; Halacha
  psychospiritual, 249
  spiritual, 23, 237, 522
  yogic, 130, 137; *see also* Yoga
Paul, Saint, 41, 51, 194, 360, 538; *see also* Saints/Saintliness
  androcentric reading of, 526
Peace,
  greetings of, 488
  sense of, 170, 189, 195, 245
Pentecostal church, 172, 176
Perceiving God, 159n4
Perception, 8; *see also* Consciousness; God, awareness of; Observation; Phenomena
  Buddhist,, 99
  casual theory of, 152
  extrasensory (ESP), 170
  functions of, 513-514
  ordinary, 152, 153
  reliability check for, 152, 153
  sense, 159
  subjective, 171
  subordinated to ideas, 212
Perfection, human capacity for, 124-125; *see also* Transcendence, human capacity for
Persecution, 21, 23; *see also* Oppression
Persona, 239, 242; *see also* Archetypes, Jungian
Personal Religious Experience Scale, 169
Personality, 10, 61; *see also* Self; Social "me"
  androgenous aspects of, 250n1
  as drive-based system, 256; *see also* Drives/Drive theory; Motivation
  as information-processing system
  behavior stability in, 257
  borderline, 258
  contrasexual elements of, 240
  development of, 256-259; *see also* Freudianism, growth stages in
    arrest in, 288
    childhood experience and, 255,256
    critical period of, 255-258
    epistemological ordering in, 254, 255

irreversibility of, 255, 257
parental influence on, 258, 260
dreams and, 246, 339
dynamics of, 262-263
exhibitionist, 240
female- male, 35, 240
inherited, 240
instincts and, 257, 258
integration of, 240, 262-263; *see also* Individuation; Jungianism
introverted, 233
maturation of, 256, 288
narcissistic, 61, 215, 240, 463-464
neurotic, 220
obsessive, 131, 132, 204, 207, 214
prototypes of, 240; *see also* Archetypes
unique, 242
Peyote, 585; *see also* Psychedelics; Religious experience, facilitation of
Phänomenologie der Religion, 185, 199
Phenomena; *see also* Phenomenological psychology; Phenomenology
analogy and, 186
change as, 271
concealed, 194
conscious constitution of, 193, 195
everyday analogies and, 186
interpretation of, 162
investigation of, 193
metaphysical handling of, 285, 286
multifaceted, 168
objective, 162
occult, 179n2
of existence, 96, 125
paranormal, 170-171, 176; *see also* Clairvoyance; ESP; Telepathy
psychological descriptions of, 186
religious, 57, 162, 174; *see also* Religious experience
reduction of, 202
social, 162
transitory, 163
Phenomenological psychology; *see also* Phenomena; Phenomenology
American vs. European, 185
as response to behaviorism, 183-184
Husserl's founding of, 185
personal interviews and, 187; *see also* Interviews; History, personal
phenomenology of religion, contrasted with, 187
reclamation of experience and, 183-184
Phenomenology; *see also* Phenomena; Phenomenological psychology
as descriptive approach to experience, 184
attention to distortions in, 184
bracketing of suppositions in, 185, 195; *see also* Epoché
connotations of, 184-185
direct-indirect, 187-199
hermeneutic, 194
methodology in, 193-194
of conversion, 196
of mystical consciousness, 188-189; *see also* Mystical experience
centering down analysis of, 189
mystical absorption in, 189
of religion, 6, 174, 182-197
investigator's experiences and, 187-188, 195, 196; *see also* Bias
philosophical vs. psychological, 188, 189
propaeudeutic, 187, 197
psychology of religion and, 187
sociology and, 165
Spiegelberg's contribution to, 188, 193
spiritual gifts and, 193-197
Philosophy, 5, 6, 115, 117n1
Chinese, 116
religious experience and, 144-160
Upanisadic, 90, 91; *see also* Upanishads
twentieth-century, 158
Western, 72, 78, 81, 248
Phylogenetic fantasy, 202, 214; *see also* Phylogeny
Phylogeny, 201, 203, 206, 211; *see also* Ontogeny
origin of religion and, 209-214, 222
Piaget, Jean, 269, 270; *see also* Cognition; Cognitive psychology; Developmental psychology; Piagetian paradigm
Piagetian paradigm, 270, 274, 276
Goldman's formulation of, 277-278, 279
Piety, 54, 80, 144, 173, 190, 411; *see also* Apologetics; Puritans
characteristics of, 145
neurosis and, 206, 208
sexuality and, 225n2
Pleasure, 101, 107; *see also* Desire; Pleasure Principle
addiction to, 136
Pluralism, 2, 55, 480; *see also* Modernism
Politics; *see also* Body, political uses of; Freudianism, political aspects of; Ideology
activism and, 81, 173
emancipatory, 82-85
Polytheism, 72; *see also* Monotheism; Theism

Popes, 38, 45, 51, 251n8; *see also* Papacy; Second Vatican Council
Positivism, 162, 497, 521
Possession, spiritual, 179n5, 425; *see also* Evil; Religious experience, evil
Postmodernism, 3, 6; *see also* Modernism; Pluralism
Power, distribution of, 111-113, 530-532; *see also* Authority
Prajna (wisdom), 103, 139; *see also* Knowledge; "Wise Old One"
Prakrti (energy), 127; *see also* Bondage of spirit; Purusha
Pranayama (breathing method), 129; *see also* Yoga
Pravrajana (banishment), 90, 101; *see also* Buddha, The
Pravrtti-dharma, 132; *see also* Dharma
Pratyahara (restraint), 129
Prayer, 4, 9, 13, 14, 24, 25, 169, 179n6, 194; *see also* God, contemplation of; Meditation; Religious instruction; Religious practices; Tefillin; Worship
  answered, 232, 232
  as proof of relationship with God, 457
  attire for, 481-482
  development of, 278, 283-284
  experienced, 171, 176, 178, 457
  Catholic, 38
  Islamic, 75, 77, 78
  lesbians/gays, 25
  mature, 284
  memorization of, 329
  postures for, 481-482
  study of, 328-329
Precognition, 179n2; *see also* Prophecy
"Preface to the Psalms," 51
Prehistory, 203, 214, 218-219, 222; *see also* Civilization; History
Prejudice, 61, 62; *see also* Bias; Bigotry
Prepersonal state, 138-141
Presbyterians, 54, 55, 56
Priests, 37, 46, 50, 147, 178, 195, 237
Primal father, 216; *see also* Archetypes; Jungianism
Primitive forms, 202, 206; *see also* Archetype; Jungianism
Primordial power, 135; *see also* Religion, primitive
Principles of Psychology, 312, 398
Printing press, 50, 51; *see also* Language; Text
Project for a Scientific Psychology, 202
Projection, 201, 223, 224, 525; *see also* Identification
  theories of, 263-265
Prophecy, 172, 175, 194; *see also* Precognition; Prophets
Prophets, 23, 72, 77, 165, 166, 178; *see also* Mystics; Prophecy
Protestant Ethic, 55, 57; *see also* Protestantism
Protestant Ethic Scale, 63
Protestantism/Protestants, 5, 32, 34, 38, 41, 42, 67, 172, 178; *see also* Christianity; Piety; Prostestant Ethic; Judeo-Christian Religion
  academic values and, 55
  American, 53-57
  anti-Catholic camp in, 61
  anti-immigrant camp in, 61
  as Apologetics, 4-5, 146, 147, 149
  attributions and, 431
  Bible and, 66
  Calvinist, 51-52; *see also* Calvinism
  Catholicism, contrasted with, 41, 44, 453, 547, 548
  developmental nature of, 62
  evangelical, 50, 59, 60, 63, 66, 547, 548
  individualistic, 52, 60, 61
  institutional, 52, 67
  political values and, 53
  rise of, 51-53
  slavery and, 55-56
  social content of, 56, 57, 431
  Social Darwinism and, 57
Protestant Reformation, 49, 51, 54, 58, 59, 60, 65
Proximity maintenance; *see* Attachment; Attachment theory
Psilocybin, 580, 581
Psyche, 7, 231, 234-238; *see also* Mind; Unconscious, the
  access to, 248
  archetypes in; *see* Archetypes; Jungianism
  drug effects on; *see* Altered states of consciousness
  levels of, 234-238
    mysterium, 235, 237; *see also Mysterium*
    ontogenetic, 235-236
    phylogenetic, 235, 236
    sensorium, 235; *see also* Sensation/Senses
  limitlessness of, 241
  Self as centering force of, 241
  self-organizing power of, 513-514
  teleological pull of, 231

total, 241
ultimate model of, 235
wisdom of, 250
Psychedelics, 11, 235, 579, 580, 583-585; *see also* Altered states of consciousness; LSD; Peyote; Psilocybin; Religious experience, facilitation of
Psychiatrists, 234
Psychic determinism, 6, 200, 221, 254
Psychic powers, 139
Psychical, the, 187; *see also* Religious experience, psychic occurrences in
Psychics, 233; *see also* Mystics; Spiritualists
Psychoanalysis; *see also* Depth psychology; Freudianism; Jungianism
biological foundation of, 255
clinical, 213
Freudian, 202, 204, 205, 211, 221
Freud-Jung bifurcation in, 234
interpretation of the unconscious in, 206
of religion; *see* Religion, Freudian critique of
Psychoanalytic theory, classical, 254, 255, 257
Psychodynamics, 9, 202, 206, 217; *see also* Personality, psychodynamics of
Psychology, 5, 162, 177
as substitute for science of nature, 217
behaviorist, 272-273; *see also* Behavioral psychology
denigration of mystical consciousness and, 189
existential, 197
individual, contrasted with group, 213
interpretive, 185
objectivity in, 385; *see also* Bias, scientific
of form and structure, 186
of personality, 184
of Protestant religious experience, 57-62
of religion, 5, 6, 186-188, 197
Otto's analysis of, 186; *see also* Otto, Rudolf
proper object of, 187
religious ideas and, 200
revolutionary shifts in, 183
rise of Behaviorism in, 183
Psychology of religion, 56, 186-188, 197, 314, 405-411, 446-447
Psychology of Religion, 57
Psychopathology, 238, 258
Psychospiritual development, 235, 240-242, 249-250; *see also* Religious instruction age-related, 273-274; *see also* Religious experience, age differences in
development of,
individuation as path of, 242;
Self as aim of , 242
unidimensional, 273-274
Psychotherapy, 188, 189, 240, 255; *see also* Psychoanalysis
depth, 183, 184
self-revelatory techniques in, 183, 184; *see also* Hypnosis; Interviews
spirituality and, 234, 235
Puberty; *see* Adolescent
Purification, 15-17; *see also* Bath; Mikvah
psychological, 131, 132, 133, 140
Puritans, 52, 53, 146; *see also* Protestantism
Purusha (pure spirit), 90, 127, 134, 136, 140; *see also* Prakrti; *see also* Shiva

Quakers, 54
Quest,
feminist spiritual, 251n7
Jungian, 239
transcendent, 123; *see also* Transcendence
yogic, 123, 131-134, 138, 140-141; *see also* Yoga
Question of Values, A, 31
Quran, 72, 77, 78

Rabbi (teacher), 538; *see also* Judaism; Religious instruction
Ramakrishna, Sri, 134
Ramadan, 77
Ramayana , 122, 126
Rape, 26, 27; *see also* Abuse, sexual
Ratiocination, 545; *see also* Rationality; Religious instruction; Religious thinking
Rationalism, 147, 505, 506
Rationality, 152, 153, 222, 578; *see also* Ratiocination; Reason; Intellect
Rat Man, 204; *see also* Wolf Man
Reality; *see also* Experience; Modes of Appearing; Phenomena Buddhism and, 96, 97, 98, 100-102, 105
causality of, 100-102
dimensions of, 100
distorted, 256
existential, 98
experiential understanding of, 101
externalized, 175, 215, 259, 403
foundational, 569, 570, 573, 574-575, 578
Freud's view of, 217
maintenance of, 404
mediation of, 165; *see also* Mediation
micro- macro approaches to, 177

Reality continued
models of, 173
nihilation of, 404
ordinary, 165
phenomenal, 96, 125
principle of, 219, 220
private, 175
religious, 402, 403, 404, 531
social construction of, 161, 162, 164-166; *see also* Construct
transcendent, 37, 122, 123, 140
true, 93
ultimate, 90, 108, 167
unseen, 155
Zen and, 173; *see also* Buddhism
Reason/Reasoning, 219-220; *see also* Intellect; Rationality
intellectual, 103
primacy of, 202
syllogistic, 369
transcendental, 104
Rebirth, 90, 94; *see also* Karma; Samsara
Recapitulation; *see* Ontogeny; Phylogeny
Redeemer, 244, 487; *see also* Christ; Messiah
Reductionism, 155, 156, 175, 384; *see also* Particularism
Reformed church, 51, 54; *see also* Judaism, Reformed; Protestant Reformation
Regression, 138-140, 261
Relationships; *see also* Attachment; Object relations; Interaction, social; Significant other
affective, 169
Ego-object, 264
internalization of, 255-256
interpersonal, 44, 45, 193, 236, 255
mother-child, 258, 265
quasi-interpersonal, 195
psychoanalysis of, 255
Religion; *see also* Religiosity; Religious belief; Religious experience; Religious instruction
academic discipline of, 5
affective base of, 353
animistic origins of, 211, 219; *see also* Religion, primitive
approaches to,
animistic, 211, 219
attachment theory, 446-447, 465
Berger's social-construction, 164; *see also* Reality, social construction of
cultural-linguistic, 148, 155, 386, 389
empirical, 446
experiential-expressive, 3, 145-146, 386, 389
extrinsic-intrinsic, 60, 62, 383, 436
Freudian, 201-208, 211, 465-468
Kantian, 17, 145, 146, 157, 175
object relations, 259-260
Oedipal, 208, 222
operant conditioning, 389-392
oscillation theory, 457
phenomenological, 162, 185-197
phylogenetic, 210, 269
psychoanalytic, 446, 468-470
psychological, 185; *see also* Psychology of religion
sexual primacy, 458, 459, 465, 466
social learning, 392-393
social scientific, 3, 31
sui generis, 172, 173, 174
as basic need, 145, 388, 508
as cultural neurosis, 202, 211, 222
as delusion, 217
as language game, 3; *see also* Language
as piety, 144-145
as quest for meaning, 62
as relationship between humans and God, 144
as repentance and remembrance, 210
as schema, 359
as system of beliefs and practices, 145, 147
authority of, 164, 201
bipolar nature of, 506
ceremonials in, 207, 208; *see also* Ceremonials; Rituals; Worship
connotations of, 2, 144, 145; *see also* Religion, definitions of
consequences of, 175-177
core activities of, 537
definitions of, 2-3, 117, 147, 163, 259; *see also* Religion, connotations of
Calvin's, 144;*see also* Calvinism
Durkheim's, 163, 177; *see also* Durkheim, Emile
error in, 177
James's, 57-58, 380; *see also* James, William
Simmel's, 163
deistic, 210
devotional, 132-137
development of, 6, 211; *see also* Religious instruction
monotheistic stage, 211
prophetic stage, 211
deviant, 263; *see also* Cult

dialectical relationships in, 165; *see also* Dualism; Opposites
dimensions of, 162, 168-170, 176
diversity of, 146; *see also* Pluralism
dream interpretation and, 206
egotistic, 175
emotion and, 155; *see also* Religious experience, emotion as a given in
essence of, 185, 201, 221
Far Eastern; *see* Buddhism; Hinduism; Islam
feminine aspects of, 39; *see also* Feminist theology; Feminist theory
Freud's critique of, 201-208; *see also* Religion, Oedipal nucleus of
gender bias in, 220; *see also* Religious experience, gender differences in
human side of, 569
Judeo-Christian; *see* Judeo-Christian religion
infantile helplessness and, 215, 216
living, 163, 238
magical, 204
meaning of life and, 301
mental health and, 63
modernity and, 164; *see also* Pluralism
morality, contrasted with, 145
neo-pagan, 251n8
neuroses and, 202, 206, 211
Oedipal nucleus of, 208, 222
phenomenology of, 162, 185-197
phylogenetic context of, 210
popular, 124, 145
primitive, 109, 115, 148, 157, 174, 179n6, 178, 202, 206, 537-538; *see also* Animism; Superstition; Voudou
psychology's contribution to study of, 185; *see also* Psychology of religion
public, 54
reason and, 220
retroactive reform in, 208, 212
revelations in, 146
science and, 220
social basis of, 63, 163, 506
sociology of, 3, 31
true, 51, 144
truth-claims in, 148, 149, 157, 217
universality of, 301
value of, 222-225
voudou, 528-529
Western notion of, 144
wish-fulfillment and, 215
Religion and Roles, 398
Religion and the Individual, 522
Religion in America, 31
Religion in Essence and Manifestation, 185
Religiosity; *compare* Spirituality
as most common form of religious experience, 379
best predictor of, 176
components of, 62, 63, 179n3
dimensions of
phenomenological, 168-170, 176
religious experiential, 168-170
ecstasy and, 379
extrinsic-intrinsic, 60, 61, 62, 63, 66, 292, 371, 383, 436, 558
ideology and, 62
interiorized-institutionalized, 61
neurosis and, 208
Religious Belief, 150
Religious belief; *see also* Belief; Religious concepts; Religious instruction
age and; *see* Psychospiritual development, age-related; Religious experience, age differences in
attitudes and, 367-369
biased reasoning and, 369
dark side of, 461-462; *see also* God, dark side of; Experience, dark side of
denial-doubt, 192-193, 293; *see also* Cognitive dissonance
faith and, 220
linked to puberty, 458-459; *see also* Conversion, adolescent
magical, 204
maladaptive, 461
motivated by desire, 215, 216-218
neuroses and, 202, 206, 211
superstitious; *see* Primitive religion; Superstition
validity of, 217, 225
Religious concepts,
as construct system, 367-368; *see also* Construct; Reality, social construction of development of, 269-270, 278-285, 298-302
attitudes and, 290-291
Bible stories and, 281-283, 320
cognitive dissonance in, 295
gender differences in, 294
judgment and, 300-302
magical phase in, 238-284
Piagetian stages in, 277-278, 283
prayer and, 283-284
linguistic approach to, 285-287
measurement of, 321-323

Religious concepts continued
theological interpretations of, 278-279
Religious experience; *see also* Experience; Mystical experience; Religiosity
absence of theology and, 537
age differences in, 178, 270, 271-274, 277-278, 290, 295-302, 551
altered states of consciousness and; *see* Altered states of consciousness
as archetype, 511
as control, 428-430, 434-435
as event, 8, 380, 382, 437-439
as object, 496; *see also* Object relations; Object relations psychology
as one dimension of religiosity, 168-170
as immediate consciousness, 145, 155
as incorrigible sense experience, 155
as possible cause of cultural change, 159n6; *see also* Culture, transmission of
as private perception, 152
as problematic concept, 144-160, 166, 270-277
as social phenomenon, 164, 165
as state vs. trait, 379-380
as superstitious behavior, 389-390
as a teachable construct, 545
attachment behavior and, 451-452
attitudes in, 433-436
attributed to external forces, 423
beliefs vs. experience in, 156-158, 168-170, 173
Bible, as record of, 537; *see also* Bible stories; Parables
body as instrument in, 528-530; *see also* Religious experience, physical displays of
born-again, 176, 547; *see also* Religious experience, once-born vs. twice-born
catalytic nature of, 166
characteristics of, 537
charismatic, 163, 164, 172, 175-176, 383, 460; *see also* Religious experience, physical displays of
childbirth as, 528
codification of, 57
cognitive dimension of, 179n3, 314-315, 343
collective, 17, 59, 60, 61, 163, 165, 174, 178
complexity of, 156, 168-170, 314, 556, 557
conceptualization of, 144-160, 162, 166, 270-277, 288-290, 353, 537
ambiguities in, 162
Schleiermacher's, 573
transpersonal, 496, 497-500
consistent reporting of, 594; *see also* Religious experience, descriptions of contexts of,
context-specific, 426-427, 510
cultural, 430-431
social, 174-177; *see also* Construct; Reality, social construction of
theological; *see* Theology
theoretical, 163-166
counterculture and, 579; *see also* Cult
credulity of, 152, 153
creeds and, 179n3, 231
cultic dimension of, 179n3; *see also* Cult; Sect
definitions of, 2, 144, 152, 166, 168, 399, 422, 509-510, 536-537
Durkheim's, 163, 177
Glock and Stark's, 168
psychological, 162
Swinburne's, 151-154
denigration of, 183, 184
denominational differences in, 169, 172, 178
descriptions of, 152, 153, 154, 155, 167-169, 171, 172, 195, 354, 498, 520, 522, 524; *see also* Religious experience, facilitation of, descriptions of;
development of, 269-270, 273-274, 405-511
cognition and, 277-278
states in, 274
devotional, 179n3
discontent as factor in, 63, 64
divine-diabolic, 424-425; *see also* Religious experience, evil
duality and, 177-179; *see also* Dualism; Opposites
domestication of, 165
dream interpretation and, 206
early childhood, 295-298
ecstatic, 179n6, 425
effects on individuals, 54, 152, 172, 174, 175, 177, 430
elements of, 8, 9, 163
emotional readiness and, 363-364, 426-427, 435
emotions as a given in, 173
religious vs. social emotions in, 163
epistemological value of, 151-154
ethnic differences in, 178
evaluation of, 57, 61, 144, 147, 148, 150,

156, 168-170, 171
absence of theory in, 302, 355-356
Akron Area Survey of, 170-171
assessment-explanation of, 155, 156
by participants, 580-583; *see also* Religious experience, descriptions of
cognitive scale for, 169
conservative, 165
constructivist, 172, 173, 174, 178
danger of reductionism in, 155, 156, 164, 165, 571
deductive, 164, 165
Durkheimian error in, 177
empirical, 162, 168-179, 179n3
Freudian; *see* Religion, Freud's critique of
Greeley's measurement of, 170-172
Hood's Religious Experience Episodes Measure, 592
idiographic, 157
inductive, 164, 165
introspective study of, 183
James's approach to, 3, 58, 59, 172-173
longitudinal, 276-277, 302
models for,
attitude process, 368
cognitive, 272, 273, 274
feminist, 273, 527-528
interactionist, 400-405
interdisciplinary model, 162
learned behavior, 384-387
Lee's, 550-554
linguistic, 270
multivariate, 274
narrative, 271-272, 276-277, 302
object relations, 259-265
perceptual, 405-413
Piagetian, 269, 270, 276, 277-278
psychometric trait, 272, 379
sociological, 170-179
social construction, 164-166
social definitionist 162, 163
social learning, 172, 173-174
S-O-R, 8, 380-383
structural analytical, 399-400
submission/surrender, 524-527
paradigms for, 271-273;
personal scale for, 169
research methods for, 270, 271-273
reductive, 164, 165
scientific bias in, 175, 343
social scientific, 157
taxonomy of, 168-170, 171, 179n5
typology of, 168-170
evidential, 4, 5, 10, 151-154
evil, 179n5, 425; *see also* Religious experience, divine-diabolic
expectations of, 437-438
experience, linked to, 3
facilitation of, 2, 10-11
biases in, 589
by religious instruction, 535, 536
rationale for, 547-548
by role-taking, 406-407
conceptual issues in, 568-569
debates about, 568, 569
enhanced solitude for, 558, 568, 585-590
facilitated vs. spontaneous experience in, 590-591
foundational reality in, 570
intrinsic-extrinsic participants in, 586, 587, 588, 589
intrinsic religiosity and, 558
isolation tank for, 585-590
liturgies and, 559-560
participants' descriptions of, 579-590 passim; *see also* Religious experience, descriptions of
placebo effect in, 579, 580, 581
psychedelics for, 11, 23, 498, 579, 583-585
quasi-experimental studies of, 577-594
Marsh Chapel Miracle study, 579-585
Pahnke's, 579-581
Schaefer/Singer, 577-579
Stace's criteria for, 580-582
religious vs. non-religious settings in, 539, 581, 590-593
radical constructionist thesis in, 576-577
Schleiermacher's influence on, 570-574
spontaneous religious experience, 590-594
stimuli in, 380-383
stress factors in, 590-594
feminist alternatives/perspectives, 522-52 527-528; *see also* Feminist theology; Feminist theory;
goddess worship movement, 531; *see also* Goddess
figure-ground reversal in, 593-594
forgiveness and, 173, 176
forms of, 2, 3, 177, 178, 423-426
most common, 379
frequency of, 165, 166, 171
gender differences in, 10, 178, 294, 295-297, 521, 528, 529
personality-based, 522

Religious experience continued
glossolalia in; *see* Glossolalia
group dynamics in, 178, 430-431; *see also* Group dynamics
heightened awareness during, 581; *see also* Awareness; God, awareness of
historical deduction of, 144
human side of, 7
impersonal, 575-576
indescribable; *see* Mystical experience, ineffable; Transcendent, The, ineffability of
institutional effects of, 163, 167, 172, 175-176; *see also* Change, institutional
intellectual dimension of, 179n3
intentionality of, 409-410
interactional, 537
intuition and, 572, 573
knowledge and, 150, 179n3
language and, 159n4, 577; *see also* Language; Religion, as language game
meaningful, 147, 179
mediated; *see* Mediation; Religious experience, facilitation of
meditative vs. non-meditative, 173-174; *see also* Meditation
medical settings and, 429-430; *see also* Healing
mental health and, 189, 421
miraculous, 169
misattributions of, 359-360, 363, 427; *see also* God, behaviors attributed to
monistic, 167, 170
mutuality in, 424-425
mystical experience, contrasted with, 149, 157, 166-168, 170
mystical union in, 525
mysticism as essence of, 423-424
nature of, 422-423
need-based, 381
numinous, *see* Mystical experience, numinous
occult and, 170-171, 178
odd-brain state in, 173
of healthy mind vs. sick soul, 58, 59; *see also* James
once-born vs. twice-born, 59; *see also* Religious experience, born-again
ordinary experience, contrasted with, 57, 147, 163, 354, 380-381
original, 147
origins of, 177
overbelief in, 149, 172
paranormal, 170, 238
peak experience in, 170-171, 178
Pentecostal; *see* Religious experience, charismatic
personal-impersonal, 575-576
personality dynamics and, 262-263, 433-436
phenomenology of, 175, 577
philosophic ironies in, 158-159
physical displays of; *see also* Religious experience, body as instrument in; Religious experience, charismatic
dancing, 487-488
greetings, 488
hand-clapping, 487-488
joyful noises, 487-488
singing hymns, 90
speaking in tongues; *see* Glossolalia
physiological basis of, 508
political activism and, 173, 176
postmodern society and, 6, 162
prayer and; *see* Prayer
primacy of, 557; *see also* Religious experience, sexual primacy of
Protestant; *see* Protestantism
psychic occurrences and, 170-171, 178, 424; *see also* Mystical experience, psychic experience
psychology and, 7, 575, 576
psychopathology and, 238
quality of life and, 148, 159n4, 175, 176
reconstruction of, 169; *see also* Reality, social construction of
sacred feeling and, 169, 424, 425; *see also* Sacred, The
schema and, 431-433; *see also* Schema
second-hand, 147, 189; *see also* Experience, direct-indirect
self-esteem and, 289, 433-434; *see also* Self
sexual primacy of, 204, 211; *see also* Religious experience, primary of
shamanic, 414-415
shared-time approach to, 172, 174, 178
normative vs. non-nonormative, 379-380, 383
spontaneous, 239, 590-594
sui generis quality of, 172, 173, 174; *see also* Feelings, *sui generis*
supernatural power and, 423, 424-425
taxonomy of, 168-170, 171, 179n5,
teaching of; *see* Religious experience, facilitation of; Religious instruction
theistic, 167, 170
totality of, 410
transcendental deduction of, 144
transforming influence of, 354

triggers for, 422, 430, 439
truth of, 424, 425
typologies of, 168-170
varieties of, 3, 178; *see also* James, William
undermining of, 164-166
well-being and, 171, 173, 176
wish-fulfillment and, 216-218
worship and, *see* Worship
Religious Experience, 154
Religious freedom, 54
Religious Imagination, The, 43
Religious instruction, 57, 84, 319-329, *see also* Religious concepts; Religious experience, facilitation of
as experience, 319
Catholic, 547
Christian, 538
communal, 537-538
complexity of, 552, 553
content of,
affective, 546
cognitive, 544-545, 549
subject matter, 556-558
context of, 546, 550
environmental, 558-560
substantive-structural, 548-549, 553, 560-561
creation of gaps during, 315
definitions of, 536
denigration of, 539, 540
emotions and, 357
empathic, 391
future of, 556-558
historical perspectives,
dogmatic, 391
James's view of, 316
Jesus' command for, 538
Jung's view of, 317
religious experience omitted in, 544-548
holistic nature of, 557
intentionality in, 552
learner, 554-556
lifestyles and, 546, 549
theoretical perspectives,
Goldman's view of, 315-316, 319-323
Lee's model, 550-554
macrotheory, 541-544
criticisms of, 542-544
Peatling's view of, 321-323
psychological interpretations of, 319-329
social science, 539-541
measurement of,
Peatling's, 321-322
social scientific, 541-544
theological, 541-544
ordination and, 538
place of, in church life, 537-541, 548; *see also* Church life
prayer in; *see* Prayer
religious education, contrasted with, 536
religious thinking and, 277-278; 320-323
ratiocination, 545
rituals and, 316, 317
role-playing in, 391
schools and,
parochial, 62
seminaries, theological, 55
story forms in, 335-336, 544; *see also* Bible stories; Parables
teacher, 551-554
teaching, shape of, 548-551
theology and, 537, 539, 541
transmission of values in, 357; *see also* Culture, transmission of; Values
value of, 547-548
variables in, 549-550, 552, 553, 558
Religious practices, 5; *see also* Fasting; Mikvah; Meditation; Prayer; Rituals; Worship
belief-forming, 159
devotional, 5, 107, 129, 132-137, 148, 179n3
doxastic, 159
gender disparity in, 492
obsessive actions and, 202, 204, 206-208
Religious thinking, 277-278, 320-323, 545
Religious Thinking Total Abstract Scale, 322
Religious Thinking Very Abstract Scale, 322
Renunciates, The, 132
Renunciation, 208
of instincts, 210, 212, 218-221
Repression, 78, 128; *see also* Defense mechanisms
Judeo-Christian, 248
of desire, 206, 219, 239
of memory, 209-211
Reproduction, human, 478-481; *see also* Mating; Sexual intercourse
Revelations, 52, 60, 146, 149; *see also* God, awareness of
Review of Religious Research, 31
Revivals
Cane Ridge, 55
Islamic, 73, 78
Protestant, 34, 54, 55

Right living, 105, 106; *see also* Buddhism; Dharma
Rig-Veda, 90, 122
Rites of passage, 244; *see also* Circumcision
Rituals, 15, 34, 35, 36, 59, 65, 68, 178, 179n6, 187; *see also* Bath; Blood; Purification; Sacrifice; Totemism
footwashing, 482-483
linked to religion, 202, 206, 207
mnemonic, 329-334
mourning, 463, 488
neo-pagan, 251n8; *see also* Religious experience, feminist alternatives to
new moon, 25
obsessive, 204, 329
private, 204
psychological interpretations of, 329-334
Freud's repression model, 329-331
Role; *see also* Role model; Role playing; Role taking; Role theory
definition of, 401
expectations, 401
group existence and, 399
Self and, 401
social, 241, 398, 399
Role model, 196, 336, 393, 408; *see also* Role; Role playing; Role taking
Buddha, 412
God, 409-410, 411, 416-417
latent, 409
mythical, 408-409
shamanic, 414-415
supranormal, 414-415, 417
Role playing, 239, 400-405; *see also* Role; Role model; Role taking
Role taking, 393, 400-405; *see also* Role; Role model; Role playing
Role theory, 8, 9, 397-420
interactionist model in, 398, 400-405, 415
perceptual model in, 399, 405-413, 415
structural-analytical model in, 399-400, 415
Rosary, 481-482
Rosh Hodash (new moon ritual), 25
Rules for living, 67; *see also* Commandments; Norms; Taboo
Rupa (material form), 97

Sacrament/Sacramentalism, 4, 33, 37, 39, 50, 64, 65
Sacred Canopy, The, 164
Sacred, The, 157, 164, 179n5, 187, 192, 237, 263-265, 425
Sacrifice, 145, 210; *see also* Saints/Saintliness
of children, 210, 259
of Christ, 210, 212
Sadhus (God-intoxicated devotees), 134; *see also* Yoga, devotional
Saints/Saintliness, 35, 38, 46, 134, 175, 226n7, 522-523, 532; *see also* Augustine; Bonaventure; Paul
Salah (daily prayer), 77; *see also* Prayer
Salvation, 5, 21, 50, 62, 115, 169, 186; *see also* Conversion; Unity collective, 93; *see also* Religious experience, collective
degrees of, 93
fantasy and, 263
messianic, 263
through faith, 51; *see also* Faith
through Nirvana, 87, 90, 92, 93, 108; *see also* Nirvana
Samadhi (tranquillity), 104, 128-141
Samapatti (concentration), 106
Samgha (community of believers), 92; *see also* Community, sense of
Samsara (cycle of rebirth), 90, 91, 93, 94, 96, 100, 107; *see also* Rebirth
Samskaras (residue of experience), 130, 131, 140
Samkhya yoga, 127
Sangha (monastic orders), 105
Sankhara (disposition), 97
Sanna (perception), 97
Sanskrit, 105, 109, 128
Satan; *see* Devil
Satanic Verses, 76
Satipatchana (mindfulness), 108
Satori (awareness), 94, 98
Schema, 325, 326, 331, 359, 364, 372n2; *see also* Construct
affective memories of, 364-365
destruction of, 316
religious, 359, 431-432
sociocultural shaping of, 433
Science, 145, 151, 175, 221
civilization and, 202
of religions, 149
tradition of, 144-149
Schizophrenia, 262
Schleiermacher, F.E.D., 6, 11, 173, 571-574
Scriptures, 50, 52, 491; *see also* Bible; Judaism, Talmud/Torah; Quran; Text; Word of God
Season of Migration to the North, 81
Second Vatican Council, 30, 33, 34, 35
Second World War; *see* War

Secrets, ancestral, 211; *see also* Heredity, archaic
Sects, religious, 73, 91, 95, 178, 524-525; *see also* Cults
Secularists, 75
Seder (feast), 18
Sefirot (mystical numbers), 20
Self; *see also* Ego; Identity; Personality
  aggregates of, 97, 98, 99, 100
  archetype of, 239, 514
  as action agent, 358
  as center of personality, 239, 241, 242
  as social product, 334, 401
  attachment to, 103, 104
  autonomous, 523
  bridged with consciousness, 239, 240; *see also* Archetypes, as mediators
  divinization of, 246
  during sleep, 138-140
  empirical, 132
  enhanced, 334-338
  God's, 137
  illusory, 98, 99
  immortal, 98, 99, 100
  liberated, 141
  manifestations of, 100-102, 124, 127-128
  narratized, 334-343; *see also* Narrative
  Non-Self , contrasted with, 96-100
  nurturing of, 531, 532
  relational, 523, 524, 532
  sacred messages in, 237
  totality of, 514
  true, 98, 341
  universal, 139
  wise, 246
  yogic, 136; *see also* Yoga
Self-absorption, 138
Self-actualization, 63
Self-affirmation, 104
Self-awareness, 94, 98
Self-centeredness, 104, 105
Self-confidence, 289
Self-consciousness, 146, 147
Self-construct; *see* Construct; Schema
Self-control, 92; *see also* Control
Self-criticism, 38, 104, 434; *see also* Attribution
Self-denial, 97; *see also* Sacrifice
Self-discovery, 77, 79, 80
Self-esteem, 289, 433-434
Self-examination, 51, 239
Self-focus, 332, 333, 334
Self-fulfillment, 287
Self-hypnosis, 138-139
Self-identification, 31, 137, 523
Self-image, 113
Self-in-Itself, 138
Self-knowledge, 239
Self-observation, 187
Self-perception, 99
Self-realization, 128, 130, 136, 342, 342, 459
Self-renewal, 38
Self-report, 183, 584; *see also* Religious experience, descriptions of; Interviews; Narrative
Self-revelation, 183
Self-schema, 325, 332, 343, 372n2; *see also* Construct; Schema
Self-surrender, 132, 134, 135, 136; *see also* Submission; Surrender
Self-transformation, 90, 140; *see also* Altered states of consciousness; Transcendence
Self-transposal, 196
Self-understanding, 36, 270
"Semantics of desire," 206, 207, 217; *see also* Desire; Language
Sensations/Senses, 101, 102, 123, 133, 149, 150, 151, 168, 235, 243, 384, 504; *see also* Emotion; Feelings
Sensory deprivation, 235; *see also* Religious experience, facilitation of, isolation tank for
Sensuality, 212; *see also* Eroticism; Sexuality
Sensus fidelium (believer as sacrament), 39
Seventh-day Adventists, 483
Sexual abuse, 26, 27; *see also* Abuse
Sexuality, 25, 38, 79, 80, 81; *see also* Behavior, sexual; God, sexuality and; Heterosexuality; Homosexuality; Gender; Lesbians/Gays; Religion, Oedipal
  masochistic, 225n2
  piety and, 225n2
  primacy of, in religious experience, 204, 211
  sacramental, 41
  sadistic, 225n2
Shadow, 239, 240; *see also Archetypes*
Shamanism, 23, 24, 28, 414-415
Shekinah (mystical numbers), 20; *see also* Numbers
Shintoism, 94, 116
Shiva (pure consciousness), 126; *see also* Shiva-Shakti
Shiva (mourning ritual), 463, 488
Shiva-Shakti, 134; *see also* Divine Mother
Siddha (ideal person), 94; *see also* Ideal Person

Sign, 66, 67, 68; *see also* Language; Symbol
Significant other, 7, 176; *see also* Attachment; Love; Object relations; Relationships
    internal representations of, 255, 257, 258
Sin, 17, 18, 36, 51, 54, 65, 140; *see also* Guilt; Suffering
  atonement for, 212
  attribution and, 435; *see also* Temptation
  Augustinian, 34
  Oedipal, 210; *see also* Oedipus Complex
  Original, 102, 210, 211
  poverty, as cause of, 55, 528
  Protestant, 54
  poverty as cause of, 55
  slavery and, 56
Slavery, 53, 555-56
Sleep, 125, 139-140, 232, 338-339; *see also* Dreams
Social construct, 367-368, 403; *see also* Construct; Reality, social construction of
Social Darwinism, 57
Social Definition paradigm, 6, 161, 162
Social Facts paradigm, 6, 161, 162
Social interaction; *see* Interaction
Socialization, 270-271, 403, 433
Social learning theory, 8, 172, 173-174, 392-393; *see also* Behavioral psychology, theories in
Social "me," 398; *see also* Individual; Self; Role
Social psychology, 9, 397, 398
Society, 161; *see also* Civilization; Construct; Culture; Socialization
  aggregate aspect of 399
  consciousness and, 500-501, 505
  cultured, 239
  deification of, 163
  human body and, 476; *see also* Body; Self-image
  interaction within, 399-400
  progression of, 220
  structure of, 398-399;
    actor/agent in, 177, 178
    religious challenge to, 165
  sui generis nature of, 513
Sociobiology, 508
Socioeconomic classes, 50, 51
Sociological Analysis, 30
Sociology, 5, 115
  dualism in, 177; *see also* Dualism; Opposites
  Durkheimian, 161, 162; *see also* Durkheim, Emile
  founders of, 161-164
  origins of, 177
  phenomenological, 165
  religion and, 174, 179
  Weberian, 161, 162
Sociology of Religion, 30
Solitude, 11, 585-590; *see also* Meditation; Religious experience, facilitation of
Son-Religion, 212; *see also* Christ
Soteriological system, 91, 93; *see also* Salvation
Soul, 41, 124
  "dark night of", 131
  female-male, 249
  Jungian approach to, 231
  sick, 50, 58, 59, 190; *see also* James, William
Speaking in tongues; *see* Glossolalia
Speech, 106; *see also* Glossolalia; Language
Speeches to Its Cultural Despisers, 145, 146
Spirit, 127-128, 175, 236; *see also* Godhead; Spirituality
Spiritual gifts, belief in, 190, 191, 192, 193-197
Spiritualists, 55, 148, 170; *see also* Mystics; Spirit
Spirituality; *compare* Religiosity
  apaphatic, 249
  approaches to, 37
  feminine, 13, 26-27, 39; *see also* Religious experience, feminist alternatives to
  image-based, 249
  kataphatic, 249
  nature spirituality, 251n8
  relationship to psychotherapy, 234, 235
Splitting of object; *see* Object Relations, splitting mechanism in
Stereotypes, 207,
  Jewish, 492
  patriarchal, 480; *see also* God, images of
Stimuli,
  cognitive, 258
  external, 99, 101
Stories, *see* Bible stories; Folklore; Parables
Stress,
  antecedent to religious experience, 435
  mysticism as function of, 590-594
Subject-Object relations, 146; *see also* Object Relations
Sublimation, 225n1; *see also* Defense mechanisms
Submission, 523, 524-527; *see also* Surrender
Sudras caste (the untouchables), 90
Suffering, 20, 21, 58
  aggregates of, 97
  causes of, 102, 128

inevitability of, 93
interpretations of, 95, 96, 97, 107, 111, 113
reality of, 97
transient, 93
Suicide, 44, 509
Sukkavati (paradise), 116
Sunnah (sayings and deeds), 77
Sunyata (emptiness), 103, 104; *see also* Emptiness; *see also* Negation
Superego, 210, 218, 226n3; *see also* Ego; Freudianism; Id
Supernatural, The, 44, 65, 152, 165
Superstition, 214, 389, 574; *see also* Religion, primitive; Voudou
Surrender, 58, 132, 133-135, 523, 524-527; *see also* Submission
Sutra, 95, 116, 127; *see also* Yoga; Yoga-Sutras
Svabhava (Self -nature), 93, 98
Symbiosis, 258, 261, 262, 265; *see also* Attachment
Symbol; *see also* Rituals; *see also* Sacraments
archetypal, 235, 237; *see also* Archetypes, symbol
Buddhist, 109, 117
Catholic, 33-34
cultural, 155
decoding of, 155
finite
fish, 244
mandala, 243
meaning of, 400-401
mystical, 157
Muslim, 74, 78, 81, 83
of feminine essence, 486; *see also* Mikvah
phallic, 250n4, 464, 480
pine-cone, 250n4
tree, 250
Symbolism, 38, 41, 65, 66, 67, 68, 203, 250; *see also* Dreams; *see also* Symbol
in dreams, 233, 236
totemic, 209
Synchronicity, 232; *see also* Dreams, Jungian analysis of

Taboo, 209, 490; *see also* Incest; Mores; Norms; Totem
Talmud, The; *see* Judaism, Talmud; *see also* Judaism; Torah
Taoism, 116, 245
Tathata (objectivity), 100
Taxonomy of religious experience, 162, 168-169, 170; *see also* Typology of religious experience
Teaching; *see* Religious instruction
Tefillin, 481-482; *see also* Judaism; Prayer
Telepathy, 179n2; *see also* Clairvoyance; ESP; Phenomena, paranormal; Precognition
Temenos, 243; *see also* Sacred space
Temperament, 58, 59, 190; *see also* Personality
Temptation, 34, 50, 66, 179n5
attributions of, 425, 435; *see also* Attribution
Ten Commandments, 25; *see also* Commandments; Law; Moses
Testimony, religious, 153, 154; *see also* Credulity; Religious experience, articulation of
Tevilah (immersion), 16; *see also* Bath
Text, religious; *see also* Bhagavad-Gita; Bible; Judaism, Talmud/Torah; Quran; Yoga-Sutras
as experience, 147
decoding of, 155
primitive, 147
sacred, 416
Theism, 123, 149, 153, 154, 462; *see also* Monotheism
Theology, 115, 185, 194
basis of, 537
dogmatic, 61, 65, 72, 569
mystical, 569
of Luther, 50
rational, 146
religious instruction and; *see* Religious instruction
Theory; *see also* individual chapter headings; Model; Paradigm; Religious experience, evaluation of
agency-structure in, 162, 177-178
appraisal theory, 357-358
Aristotelian, 285
biosocial, 357
classical psychoanalytic, 254
cultural-linguistic, 179n6
empirical, 150
eternalist, 100
micro-macro, 162, 177, 541-544
of knowledge, 150; *see also* Epistemology
proximate-causal, 202
psychosocial, 270
radical constructionist, 576-577
recapitulation, 269, 284; *see also* Ontogeny; Phylogeny
religious coping, 356, 360-363
social learning; *see* Social learning theory
structural, 224, 225n3

Theology continued
ultimate-causal, 202
value-free, 542
Thinking/Thought, 8
archetypal, 243; *see also* Archetypes; Psyche
blasphemous, 225n2
epiphenomenal, 386
primitive, 211; *see also* Religion, primitive
ratiocination, 545
religious; *see* Religious concepts, development of; Religious thinking
shaped by language, 433
Thinking About the Bible test, 321
Third World, 76, 80, 248, 260
Thomas Theorem, 162
"Three Essays on Sexuality," 222
Threefold Lotus Sutra, 116; *see also* Buddhism
Time-Space, 60, 337, 500
Tolerance, 44, 74
Torah, the; *see* Judaism, Torah
Totem, 90, 126, 209; *see also* Animals; Taboo; Totemism
Totem and Taboo, 204, 206, 208, 209, 211, 212, 221
Totemism, 109, 115, 157, 174, 179, 209, 210, 211, 214; *see also* Totem
Tradition; *see also* Institutions; Religion
analytical, 287-290
attachment and, 462-465
behaviorist, 272-273
biographical, 271-272; *see also* Developmental psychology, models; Narrative
cognitive-arousal, 355
collective memory and, 165
halachic, 14-17
hermeneutic, 155
Judeo-Christian, 10
rabbinic, 4, 13, 18; *see also* Judaism; Religious instruction
mystic, 4, 20, 158, 205
phenomenological, 162
Piagetian, 269-270, 274; *see also* Cognition; Cognitive Psychology
pragmatic, 155
psychoanalytic, 468-470
religious, 185
Vedic, 90
Training, religious; *see* Religious instruction
Trance, 107, 138, 139; *see also* Meditation; Self-hypnosis
Tranquillity, 104; *see also* Nirvana
Transcendence, 5, 37; *see also* Mystical experience; Nirvana; Unity
Brahman, 123
faith and, 298-299
human capacity for, 133, 136; *see also* Perfection, human capacity for
signals of, 164
study of, 137-138, 140
yogic quest for, 123, 131-134, 138, 140-141, 508, 509-510
Transcendent, The, 2, 4, 66, 67, 536, 569
ineffability of, 60, 123, 190; *see also* Mystical experience, ineffable
Transference neurosis, 202, 246; *see also* Attachment; Countertransference; Neurosis
Transformation, religious; *see* Religious experience, transforming influence of; Consciousness, transformation of; Self-transformation; Transcendence
Transpersonal psychology,
aims of, 498, 499-500
applications of, 512-514
as fourth force of psychology, 496-497
consciousness expansion and, 512
criticisms of, 501-502
theory construction and, 503
definitions/explanations of, 495-498, 510-512
Durkheimian-Jungian foundation for, 503-508
implications of, 512-514
methodology in, 512-514
models,
Washburn's dynamic-dialectical, 501, 510-512
Wilber's developmental structure, 500-501, 510-512
object-subject in, 496-497, 498, 503
ontological centrality of, 499
perspectives in, 498-500
recent work in, 500-501
religious experience, encompassed by, 496
reconciliation of opposites in, 503-504; *see also* Opposites
sociobiology and, 508
synthetic nature of, 599, 511, 514
Trauma, 213, 265; *see also* Abuse; Mystical experience, childhood trauma and
Tree of Life, 250, 250n4; *see also* Archetype
Truth; *see also* Enlightenment; Knowledge; Truth-Claims
eternal, 231
Four Noble Truths, in Buddhism, 90, 95-105
historical, 213, 217, 221

of cause, 90, 100-102
of extinction, 90, 102
of the Path, 90, 95, 102
of suffering, 90, 96, 97, 102
orders of, 149
power of, 217
revealed, 122; *see also* Revelations
ultimate, 125
Truth-Claims, 148, 149, 157, 217
Twelve Causes of Existence, 101, 104; *see also* Buddhism; Existence
Typology of religious experience, 168-170
of church-sect mysticism, 179n1

Ultimate being; *see* Being
Unconscious, The, 6, 65, 237; *see also* Consciousness; Mind; Psyche
accessibility of, 200, 205, 239
archetypal nature of, 244; *see also* Archetypes; Jungianism
distinguished from God, 239
collective, 235, 249, 250n3, 505; *see also* Memory, collective
dynamics of, in religious practices, 221
exploration of, 236
learning paradigm for, 384-385
linked to neurosis, 206
linked to prehistory, 206
memory and, 209; *see also* Memory, collective
personal, 236
Understanding, 16; *see also* Enlightenment; Self-knowledge; Self-understanding
Dilthey's notion of, 185
Union; *see* God, communion with; Unity
of opposites, 241, 250n1; *see also* Opposites
Jung's emphasis on, 248
Unity, 20, 60, 77, 79, 90, 91, 98, 117; *see also* Negation; Transcendence; Union
attributions of, 438, 439
of body and mind, 102, 174
cosmic, 496
Unitarians, 49
Universe, 100, 215, 232, 251n8
special, 403-404
spiritual, 499
symbolic, 404-405
Untouchables, the, 90; *see also* Caste system
Upanishads, 122, 123, 139; *see also* Philosophy, Upanisadic

Vairagya (non-attachment), 130, 131, 136
Vaisyas caste, 90; *see also* Caste system
Value-judgment, 147
Values, 62, 298
balancing of, 208, 212
Catholic, 31, 35, 44
Protestant, 44
transmission of, 357; *see also* Culture, transmission of; Religious instruction
Western, 72, 78, 81
Varieties of Religious Experience, 57, 147, 148, 155, 159n2, 189, 190, 193, 197, 313, 354, 355
Vasanas (subconscious desire), 130, 131, 140
Vatican, The, 30; *see also* Papacy; Popes; Second Vatican Council
Vedana (feeling), 97
Vedanta, 90, 122, 124
Vedas (sacred scriptures), 122
Verstehen, 185; *see also* Understanding
Verstehende, 185; *see also* Psychology, interpretive
Via negativa, 138; *see also* Negation
Vibhava (desire for nonexistence), 101
Victimization, 27; *see also* Abuse; Submission; Surrender
Vijhana (consciousness), 103
Vinnana (consciousness), 97
Violence, 26; *see also* Abuse; Parricide; Trauma
Virgin Mary; *see* Mary, Mother of Jesus
Virtues, Buddhist, 106-108; *see also* Values
Vishnu, 126
Visions, 4, 236, 262; *see also* Dreams; God, awareness of; Prophecy; Trance
religious, 21, 145, 167, 169, 179n2
Voices; *see also* Glossolalia; God; awareness of; Speech
revelatory, 166, 169, 179n2
Voudou, 528-529

Waking Dreams, 247
War, 177; *see also* Military activity; Politics, activism and
holy, 75, 77, 79; *see also* Jihad; Islam
World War II, 79, 82, 84, 85, 275
Water; *see* Baptism; Bath; Mikvah; Purification
Wealth, 66, 77, 85, 132; *see also* Capitalism; Economy
Weber, Max, 6, 161, 163, 164, 178; *see also* Protestant Ethic
Well-being, 171, 358
Weltanschauung, 205, 220; *see also* Worldview
Wesley, John, 58, 411; *see also* Methodists
Wheel of Life, 109; *see also* Buddhism

Whites, 56
Wholeness, 240, 248; *see also* Holism; Integration, psychological; Union; Unity
Wilber's Hierarchy, 10; *see also* Transpersonal Psychology
Will, human, 133; *see also* God, will of
Wisdom, 103, 106; *see also* Enlightenment; Knowledge
Wise Old One, 243; *see also* Self, archetype of
Wish; *see also* Desire; Wish-fulfillment
  aggressive, 219; *see also* Oedipus complex
  disguised, 207, 221
  for favor, 219
  for protection, 215, 216, 217
  fulfillment of, *see* Wish-fulfillment
  infantile, 215, 216, 217, 220
  instinctual, 208; *see also* Instincts
  personal responsibility and, 218
  repressed, 206, 207, 219
  sexual, 219
Wish-fulfillment; *see also* Desire; Freudianism
  a priori nature of, 206, 207
  as basis of religion, 215, 216-218
  God and, 212
  psychoanalytic appreciation of, 217
Witchcraft, 251n8, 527-528, 530; *see also* Lesbians/Gays, goddess worship; Religious experience, neo-pagan
Withdrawal, 84, 136, 139; *see also* Aversion; Avoidance
Wolf Man, 201, 204, 220; *see also* Rat Man
Women; *see also* Feminist theology; Feminist theory; Goddess; Gender; Lesbians/Gays; Mary; Mother
  anima of, 240
  assertiveness in, 240
  Buddhist, 90, 91
  Catholic, 35, 46
  dreams of, 240
  frequency of religious experience among, 178; *see also* Relgious experience, gender differences in
  gender constraints and, 477, 483, 485, 486; *see also* Body, political uses of
  God's image and; *see* God, images of; God, feminine principle of; God, gender pronouns for; God, sexuality and
  Lubavitcher, 22
  menstruation and; *see* Menstruation; Mikvah
  Muslim, 83, 85; *see also* Islam, emancipatory politics
  oppression of, 489, 521; *see also* Oppression; Power, distribution of
  ordination of, 31
  purification of, 15-17, 485-487; *see also* Mikvah
  societal expectations and, 490, 491; *see also* Role; Society
  spirituality of, 13, 26, 27, 29, 251n8
  Torah scholarship and, 19, 23; *see also* Judaism; Religious instruction
Word of God, 14, 18, 52, 66, 72; *see also* Logos; Scripture; Text, religious
  carved in stone, 25
Word, The, 52, 66; *see also* Logos; Word of God
World,
  empirical, 123, 132; *see also* Empiricism
  external, 215, 259; *see also* Object Relations
  illusory, 125, 496
  internal, 264
  representational, 7; *see also* Object relations
  revelatory, 41, 44
Worldview, scientific, 205; *see also* Weltanschauung
Worship, 17, 41, 388, 487-488; *see also* Liturgy; Mass; Ritual; Sacrament
  body's role in, 481, 484; *see also* Body, anointing of; Footwashing
  communal, 17; *see also* Religious experience, collective
  gestative, 480
  instructional, 538-539; *see also* Religious instruction
  phallic-nonphallic, 480
  primitive, 41, 537-538; *see also* Religion, primitive
  styles of, 480
Wu (comprehension), 94
Wudu-ablution (cleansing of body), 77; *see also* Bath; Purification

Yama (restraint), 129
Yoga; 5, 108, 127-141; *see also* Hinduism; Transcendence; Yoga-Sutras
  aphorisms in, 127
  classical (Patanjali's), 123, 127-128, 131, 132, 135-137
  devotional, 132-137
  goals of,
    liberation, 123-125, 127-129, 136, 137-140
    union, 128, 137, 139-140; *see also* Union; Unity
  healing power of, 188
  mysticism and, 140; *see also* Mystical

experience; Mystics
Patanjali's; *see* Yoga, classical
popular meaning of, 129
psychological-spiritual aspects of, 131, 140
theological neutrality of, 140
transcendence in,
of spiritual bondage, 123-124, 132
of dualism/opposites, 124, 126, 127, 133, 134, 137; *see also* Dualism; Opposites
techniques for, 129, 136, 137, 140; *see also* Meditation
transformative, 127-132
Yoga-Sutras , 123, 127-131, 136, 138, 139
Yogin, 5, 127, 129

Zakat (purity), 77
Zen; *see* Buddhism, Zen